9th edition

California Workers' Comp

How to Take Charge When You're Injured on the Job

Attorney Christopher A. Ball

NINTH EDITION	MAY 2012
Editor	BETH LAURENCE
Book Design	TERRI HEARSH
Proofreading	ROBERT WELLS
Index	THÉRÈSE SHERE
Printing	BANG PRINTING

Ball, Christopher A.

California workers' comp : how to take charge when you're injured on the job / attorney Christopher A. Ball. -- 9th ed.

p. cm.

ISBN 978-1-4133-1711-4 (pbk.) -- ISBN 978-1-4133-1724-4 (epub e-book)

1. Workers' compensation--Law and legislation--California--Popular works. I. Title.

KFC592.B35 2012

344.79402'1--dc23

2011048777

Please note

We believe accurate, plain-English legal information should help you solve many of your own legal problems. But this text is not a substitute for personalized advice from a knowledgeable lawyer. If you want the help of a trained professional—and we'll always point out situations in which we think that's a good idea—consult an attorney licensed to practice in your state.

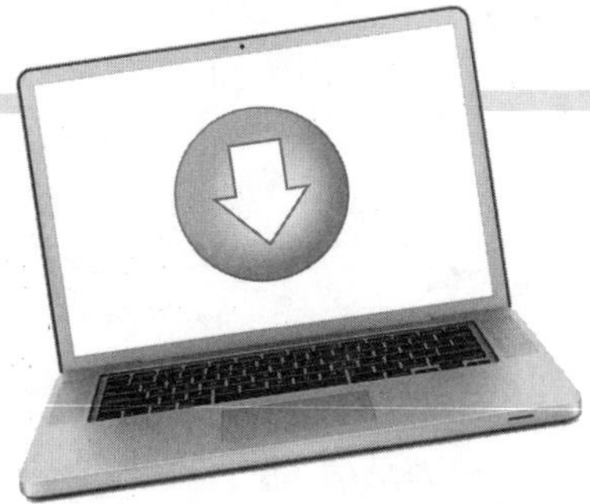

This Book Comes With a Website

Nolo's award-winning website has a page dedicated just to this book, where you can:

DOWNLOAD FORMS – All the forms and worksheets in the book are accessible online

KEEP UP TO DATE – When there are important changes to the information in this book, we'll post updates

READ BLOGS – Get the latest info from Nolo authors' blogs

LISTEN TO PODCASTS – Listen to authors discuss timely issues on topics that interest you

WATCH VIDEOS – Get a quick introduction to a legal topic with our short videos

You'll find the link in the appendix.

And that's not all. Nolo.com contains thousands of articles on everyday legal and business issues, plus a plain-English law dictionary, all written by Nolo experts and available for free. You'll also find more useful **books, software, online services,** and **downloadable forms.**

Get forms and more at **www.nolo.com**

Acknowledgments

Linda Foley and Kathryn Phillips, two extremely competent paralegals, whose expertise in the area of vocational rehabilitation was greatly utilized by this author, and whose review of the vocational rehabilitation chapter is gratefully acknowledged and appreciated.

Ralph "Jake" Warner, founder and owner of Nolo, who took an unwieldy and seemingly unmanageable subject matter and somehow managed to put it in a format that makes sense.

Lisa Goldoftas, former editor extraordinaire at Nolo, whose expert guidance and suggestions were always right on target and appreciated.

Beth Laurence, who has edited new editions of this book since 1998, for her help in translating the many legislative updates to the law that have occurred in recent years.

Judge Kenneth Peterson and Judge David Hettick (Oakland Workers' Compensation Appeals Board), for their exemplary reading of the manuscript and excellent suggestions for improvement.

Applicants' attorney Jeffrey E. Friedman (Jones, Clifford, McDevitt, Naekel & Johnson law firm, San Francisco), whose expertise greatly enhanced the book.

Attorney Moiece Palladino (State Compensation Insurance Fund), for her careful reading of the manuscript and outstanding suggestions.

John Hopper, Information & Assistance Officer (Van Nuys), for his review and excellent comments.

Robert S. Lichtenstein, M.D. (Mountain View, California), Board Certified Neurosurgeon, for his fine and compassionate reading of the medical chapters; Mike Mansel (insurance broker), for his excellent critique of the book; and Bill Nickoloff, for his helpful suggestions.

Stephanie Harolde, for her careful and patient treatment of so many drafts of the manuscript; and Terri Hearsh, for her beautiful design and artful handling of a complicated manuscript.

Dedications

To Mom—You gave me what money can't buy, and I'm forever indebted.

To my children, Jennifer and Christopher—I'm certain I neglected you while writing this book, but you understood and accepted my commitment. You are both responsible and caring young adults and I'm very proud of you. Thank you both for your help.

To my loving wife, Marian—Without your support and understanding, this book would never have been completed. Thanks for putting up with me when the long hours made me irritable, and for the encouragement you gave when it seemed as though this book would never be finished. You are truly my inspiration.

About the Author

Christopher A. Ball received his bachelor's degree in Business Administration from Long Beach State in 1972 and graduated from Western State School of Law in 1975. Since 1991, Mr. Ball has practiced workers' compensation law exclusively. He is certified as a Worker's Compensation Specialist with the State Bar of California.

MAKING A FALSE OR FRAUDULENT WORKERS' COMPENSATION CLAIM IS A FELONY SUBJECT TO UP TO FIVE YEARS IN PRISON, OR A FINE OF UP TO $50,000 OR DOUBLE THE VALUE OF THE FRAUD, WHICHEVER IS GREATER, OR BY BOTH IMPRISONMENT AND FINE.

Table of Contents

Part I: All About Worker's Compensation

Part II: Protecting Your Rights

Part IV: Settling Your Case

Part V: The Workers' Compensation Appeals Board

Appendixes

FIND IT ONLINE

Appendixes online. All appendixes can be found on the companion page for this book on Nolo's website at **www.nolo.com/back-of-book/WORK9.html.**

Part I

All About Workers' Compensation

CHAPTER

1

Introduction to Workers' Comp

Over the years, I have advised many injured workers about how the law applies to their particular workers' compensation claim. I have yet to talk to an injured worker who felt that the workers' compensation laws were fair or adequate. There is good reason for this. Legal limitations and restrictions as to how much an injured worker may recover result in many workers receiving inadequate benefits. Unfortunately, the workers' compensation system was not designed primarily to benefit the injured worker. Instead, it was created to protect employers and workers' compensation insurance companies by limiting their legal liability and obligations.

Despite these negatives, workers' compensation has evolved over the years to include some decent worker protections. Although many of these are buried in hard-to-understand rules and procedures, informed workers who understand how the system works and are willing to assert their rights have a good chance of being treated fairly. Sadly, most workers have little, if any, knowledge about their workers' compensation rights. This book aims to change that.

Legal Citations

Throughout this book, you'll see references to laws that govern the California workers' compensation system. If you want more information, you can look up these legal citations, as explained in Chapter 27.

Labor Code (LC). The vast majority of workers' compensation laws are contained in the California Labor Code, the basic state laws that regulate employment matters.

California Code of Regulations (CCR). These rules and regulations expand upon, interpret, and explain procedures for implementing and enforcing the California Labor Code.

United States Code (USC). Many laws that apply to people not covered by California workers' compensation laws can be found in the United States Code.

This book can help you if you're handling your own workers' compensation case or filing a claim on someone else's behalf, such as a minor. (In legal terms, this is referred to as acting in the capacity of a guardian ad litem, where you file a workers' compensation claim on behalf of a minor or someone who is incompetent.) If you're represented by an attorney, being well informed about workers' compensation procedures and the important decisions you'll need to make will help your lawyer guide you through the process.

A. What Is Workers' Compensation?

Workers' compensation is a system of benefits set up to help employees who are injured on the job. (And, if a worker dies as a result of work injuries, the employee's dependents are entitled to receive workers' compensation death benefits.)

Work-related injuries (and occupational illnesses and diseases) are also referred to as "industrial injuries." For workers' compensation purposes, an industrial injury is any injury—in any occupation—that occurs as a result of your employment. Put another way, "industrial" is synonymous with "work." You may also hear the term "compensable injury," another term that refers to an injury that's covered by workers' compensation.

Workers' Compensation Jargon

In few places on earth will you find a system that uses as much confusing, contradictory, and just plain batty terminology as workers' compensation. Unfortunately, you will simply have to master a number of confusing terms and acronyms used in the workers' compensation system, or you won't understand how to handle your claim. Whenever you hit a mind-boggling term, take a moment to learn what it means. In no time at all, you'll be talking with ease about your TTD, VRMA, QME, MMI, and QRR.

Workers' Compensation Fraud

Over the last several years, alleged workers' compensation fraud (the filing of false claims) has been a major concern of employers and workers' compensation insurance companies alike. In response to these concerns, California passed major revisions to its workers' compensation laws, which are incorporated in this book. *It is now a felony for anyone to knowingly file a false or fraudulent workers' compensation claim.* The maximum fine for workers' compensation fraud is $150,000, or twice the amount of the fraud, whichever is greater. (Insurance Code § 1871.4.)

The laws that make it harder to commit fraud unfortunately also make it much more complicated for injured workers to file and receive compensation for legitimate claims.

The workers' compensation system is sometimes described as a "no-fault" system of give and take. The injured employee gives up the right to sue an employer in court. In return, the employee receives compensation without having to prove that the employer caused the injury—the only thing that matters is that the injury occurred at work. In exchange for providing compensation regardless of fault, the amount the employer must pay is limited to benefits specified in the California Labor Code. Not surprisingly, these amounts are almost always significantly less than what might be available if employees could sue in court. For the vast majority of cases, the rule that work-related injuries must go through the workers' compensation system is a fact of life. (There are a few situations where an injured employee is not covered by workers' compensation and may sue an employer in the regular court system; see Chapter 17 for a discussion.)

At first glance, a no-fault system sounds like a fair deal—workers who are hurt are taken care of without having to go through a costly process of assigning blame. Unfortunately, the existing system is complicated and hard to understand. It has evolved into what too often becomes a bureaucratic nightmare that intimidates and hinders people with valid claims. But perhaps the worst aspect of the California workers' compensation system is that it doesn't deliver on its fundamental promise to cover all injured workers on a no-fault basis. The employer and its workers' compensation insurance company will often fight an employee's perfectly legitimate claim every step of the way.

B. What an Injured Worker Is Entitled To

Enough about the problems with workers' compensation laws. If you've been injured on the job, you probably want to know how you'll be compensated. California workers' compensation laws provide a limited number of benefits (mostly money payments). Workers' compensation benefits are tax exempt; in other words, they are not considered income for income tax purposes.

1. Workers' Compensation Benefits

This summary discusses what is available and refers you to the chapters that explain how to obtain and make the best use of available benefits:

- **Medical treatment and related costs.** You are entitled to medical treatment, at no cost to you, to cure and relieve the effects of your industrial injury. You are also entitled to be reimbursed for mileage costs going to and from your medical appointments. You are not, however, entitled to mileage reimbursement for attending court hearings or traveling to the insurance company's office. (Chapters 9, 10, and 11 cover all aspects of medical benefits.)
- **Temporary disability.** You are entitled to receive monetary payments while you are off work and temporarily disabled due to your injury. The amount of temporary disability is based upon two-thirds of your average weekly wage, with established maximums, depending upon the date of your injury. In short, don't expect

to receive as much money as when you were on the job. (See Chapter 12.)

- **Permanent disability.** If your injury affects your ability to participate in the job market in the future, you may receive a set dollar amount as compensation. How much you'll receive is determined by the part of your body that is injured, your age, your occupation, and any work restrictions as determined by various doctors. These factors are plugged into a standard rating schedule to determine how much you can recover. If you're 70% to 99.75% disabled, you may additionally receive a small pension for the rest of your life. If you're 100% (totally) disabled, the amount you are entitled to receive increases substantially. (See Chapter 13.)
- **Supplemental job displacement.** The supplemental job displacement benefit is available to workers injured in 2004 or later. This benefit, available only to workers whose employers did not offer them modified or alternative work, provides a trimmed-down version of vocational rehabilitation: a $4,000 to $10,000 voucher for education-related retraining and skill enhancement at state-approved or accredited schools. (See Chapter 14.)

CAUTION

If you were injured years ago. If you have a claim for an old injury that occurred prior to 1/1/04, you are not entitled to Supplemental Job Displacement Benefits. You used to be able to get a benefit called Vocational Rehabilitation Benefits, but that benefit was revoked, effective 1/1/04, and nothing was created to replace it for injuries before 1/1/04.

- **Death benefits.** If you were a total or partial dependent (someone who relied upon another person for support) of an employee who died as a result of an industrial injury, you may have the right to recover certain benefits, including burial expenses and a sum of money. (See Chapter 15.)

Other Workers' Compensation Benefits

In unusual circumstances, you may be entitled to benefits that are not available in a typical workers' compensation claim. Turn to Chapter 16 if any of the following remedies may apply to your situation:

- **Subsequent Injuries Benefits Trust Fund.** You may be eligible if you had a prior injury or illness before your present workers' compensation injury, regardless of whether the prior injury happened at work.
- **Uninsured Employers Benefits Trust Fund.** This fund is available if your employer does not have workers' compensation insurance and is not self-insured.
- **Discrimination benefits under LC § 132a.** You may be eligible to file a separate claim if your employer discriminated against you because you asserted your right to file a workers' compensation claim.
- **Employer's serious and willful misconduct.** You may qualify for increased benefits if your employer's seriously improper action or inaction—such as the failure to remedy an obvious safety violation—contributed to or caused your work injury.

2. Take an Active Role in Obtaining Benefits

It's a fact of life that you're the one who must see to it that the insurance company provides you with benefits. If you (or your attorney, if you have one) don't go after all the benefits to which you are entitled, you will likely be shortchanged. In the workers' compensation system of limited benefits, you cannot afford to be complacent.

Lest you let your pride get in the way, clearly understand that workers' compensation benefits should not be considered charity or welfare. Whether you like it or not, the existence of the workers' compensation system means that you have given up valuable legal rights. For example, you cannot sue your employer, you are not entitled to payments to cover lost wages (past, present, or future), and you cannot receive compensation for your pain and suffering.

Accept workers' compensation benefits for what they are: part of a system set up to get you medical treatment for your injury, provide minimum income while you are off work, and help you get back to work in some capacity as soon as possible.

3. Other Benefits and Remedies

You may qualify for benefits and remedies outside the workers' compensation system, including:

- **State disability (SDI).** Most workers have a small amount deducted from each check for "SDI," or State Disability Insurance. In the event of disability for any reason (work or otherwise), you may be entitled to disability payments. SDI is usually paid where workers' compensation temporary disability is not being paid. (See Chapter 17, Section A.)
- **Social Security benefits.** If your injury is severe enough, you may qualify for Social Security disability, which is paid by the federal government. (See Chapter 17, Section B.)
- **Claims or lawsuits for personal injuries.** If your work injury was caused, entirely or in part, by an outside third party (someone not working for your employer), you may be able to sue that person or entity in civil court for damages. (See Chapter 17, Section C.)
- **Claims or lawsuits based on discrimination.** In some instances where you have experienced discrimination, you may be able to file a claim under the Americans with Disabilities Act, the California Fair Employment and Housing Act, or other laws. (See Chapter 17, Section D.)

C. Where to Get Additional Information and Help

While this book may answer many of your questions, it's quite possible that you'll need further assistance. You may contact any of the agencies listed below for help. In addition, Chapter 27 provides information on how to make use of the law library and the Internet to do legal research. If you decide that you want to be represented by an attorney, you may also find Chapter 26, on working with lawyers, helpful. Be aware, however, that it may be difficult to find a workers' compensation attorney willing to take your case, as lawyer fees are relatively low and most workers' compensation attorneys have many more cases than they can handle.

1. Information and Assistance Officers

The Workers' Compensation Appeals Board is the place where documents in your case are filed and where your matter is heard by a workers' compensation judge. Despite its name, all workers' compensation matters (not just appeals) are handled by the Workers' Compensation Appeals Board, also known as the appeals board or the WCAB. There are approximately 18 appeals boards in the state of California.

Each Workers' Compensation Appeals Board has at least one information and assistance officer (also called an I&A officer), whose job is to give you free help in pursuing your workers' compensation claim. The information and assistance officer's role is to assist injured workers in navigating their way through the workers' compensation system. Some I&A officers can be your best source of information and help in resolving problems you encounter.

The number of your local workers' compensation office is available on Nolo's website. See Chapter 29, "Online Appendixes" for the link to Appendix 1: Workers' Compensation Office Addresses and Code Lists.) You may also get helpful general information from the automated Workers' Compensation Information and Assistance Unit line at 800-736-7401, which provides prerecorded information about workers' compensation.

In addition, "Injured Worker Workshops" are held every month at every district office. These free one-hour workshops consist of a presentation by an information and assistance officer followed by a question and answer session. Call your district office for dates and times.

2. Workers' Compensation Insurance Rating Bureau (WCIRB)

The Workers' Compensation Insurance Rating Bureau (WCIRB) is helpful in finding out who your employer's workers' compensation company was at the time of your injury. Here's where to reach the WCIRB:

Workers' Compensation Insurance
Rating Bureau
525 Market Street
Suite 800
San Francisco, CA 94105
415-777-0777

3. Division of Workers' Compensation Website

The Workers' Compensation Division has developed a helpful website at www.dir.ca.gov/DWC/dwc_home_page.htm. Here you can find an overview of workers' comp laws and rules, a FAQ (frequently asked questions) area, and guides for injured workers on topics such as how to object to a summary rating, how to file an appeal, and how to fire your attorney. This site also provides workers' compensation forms and the manual for rating permanent disabilities, in PDF format.

D. How to Use This Book

FIND IT ONLINE

Forms online. All of the forms, tables, and lists of district workers' comp offices contained in this book can be found on Nolo's website. (See Chapter 29, "Online Appendixes" for the link to these pages.) In addition, if workers' comp laws or forms change before the next edition of this book, you'll find updates to the book on this Web page.

No two injuries are alike, and no two injuries are ever handled the same way by the same insurance company, let alone by different companies. How much of this book you'll choose to read will depend on your individual circumstances.

I suggest that you read Chapter 2 (Overview of a Workers' Compensation Claim) to get a good understanding of the workers' compensation system, and to determine where your claim is in the system. Read Chapter 21 (Preparing Your Case) in conjunction with Chapter 2, as trial preparation should begin on day one of your claim and continue until the day of the trial.

If you have a cumulative trauma or a repetitive stress injury, read Chapter 4 (Cumulative Trauma Disorders).

A thorough reading of Chapter 6 (Keep Good Records to Protect Your Claim) will ensure that you properly prepare and maintain the information you will need for trial.

At least glance at Chapter 5 (What to Do If You're Injured) to make certain that you have done everything you should following your injury. Feel free to turn to relevant chapters as the need arises and to skip any chapters that do not apply to your situation. For example, if the employer's workers' compensation insurance company has already accepted your case and begun providing benefits, you may want to skip Chapter 3 (Is Your Injury Covered by Workers' Compensation?). Likewise, if the insurance company has proposed a settlement, you'll want to turn to Chapter 19 (Figure Out a Starting Settlement Amount).

While great care has been taken to provide you with a comprehensive and informative book on your workers' compensation benefits, this book cannot cover each and every aspect of workers' compensation law in detail. Particularly if your claim has been denied or delayed, you'll need to go beyond this book. (See Chapters 26 and 27 on hiring a lawyer and doing your own legal research.)

E. What This Book Does Not Cover

Workers' compensation laws have changed tremendously over the last ten years. This has inevitably resulted in uncertainty, as different laws will apply to you depending on when you were injured (primarily, whether your injury took place before 2004, or in 2004 or later). Many of the new or revised laws are subject to interpretation and will continue to be interpreted for many years to come as workers' compensation cases are brought to trial and legal decisions are appealed.

While I have given my best effort to provide you with accurate explanations of the law, this book is not a legal opinion on any issue or law and should not be relied on as such. If you have questions or concerns regarding a workers' compensation issue or law, you should attempt to consult with a workers' compensation attorney, get help from an information and assistance officer. A list of offices is provided on Nolo's website (see Chapter 29, "Online Appendixes" for the link to Appendix 1: Workers' Compensation Office Addresses and Code Lists) or do your own research.

If you face any of the following issues, you should seek help beyond the book:

- **You were injured before January 1, 1994.** For assistance, see an information and assistance officer or a workers' compensation attorney.
- **Your employer was not insured.** By law, your employer must carry workers' compensation insurance or be permissibly self-insured. If, however, your employer does not have workers' compensation insurance, you'll probably need to seek compensation from the Uninsured Employers Benefits Trust Fund, discussed in Chapter 16, Section B.
- **An injured worker died.** If an employee's death was due to a work injury, at least in part, the worker's dependents may file a claim for death benefits. The worker's estate may be entitled to any accrued workers' compensation benefits as of the date of death. (See Chapter 15 for more information.) If you feel the death was due to the work injury and the insurance company denies coverage, seek help from an information and assistance officer or see a lawyer.
- **You have a stress-related (psychological) injury.** Insurance companies almost always deny these claims and will fight you every step of the way. If at all possible, find a workers' compensation attorney to represent you or seek help from an information and assistance officer. (See Chapter 3, Section B7, for more information.)
- **If the statute of limitations has run.** If the insurance company has denied your claim because it asserts that you failed to file your claim in a timely manner, you'll need help beyond the book. Contact an information and assistance officer or see a lawyer. (See Chapter 5, Section C1, for more information.)
- **Posttermination claim.** Sometimes an insurance company will deny a claim if you were terminated or laid off. If this happens, seek help from an information and assistance officer or see a lawyer.

CHAPTER

2

Overview of a Workers' Compensation Claim

If you've been injured on the job, your workers' compensation claim will stumble and saunter its way through the workers' compensation system. It will seem that all you do is wait for something to happen. When you request medical treatment, you may wait weeks for a response. You may wait for a doctor's appointment, then wait for the medical report. And if you file for a hearing before the Workers' Compensation Appeals Board, you may wait months for your hearing date.

And so it will go. At every turn, it is likely to take months before anything is accomplished. It probably won't make you feel much better to realize you are not alone. An average workers' compensation case takes two to three years to be resolved. And many cases take much, much longer.

It probably won't come as a surprise that the workers' compensation system is bureaucratic: Lots of forms, reports, and other documents are shuffled through what sometimes seems like an endless maze. Above all, the workers' compensation system is confusing. It's fraught with rules and regulations—and it sorely lacks understandable information for the injured worker.

This chapter helps take the mystery out of the workers' compensation system by clearly outlining the steps involved in a "typical" workers' compensation case. Inevitably, there will be some variations depending on your particular situation and whether or not you're represented by an attorney. But the basic steps are usually similar in all workers' compensation cases.

SKIP AHEAD

Death claims. If you were totally or partially dependent upon someone who died due to an industrial injury, you may have a workers' compensation claim for death benefits. Skip ahead to Chapter 15.

Step 1. Notify Your Employer of the Injury

If you are injured at work, notify your supervisor or boss at your first opportunity. If your injury developed over a period of time, as with a repetitive stress or cumulative trauma injury, notify your employer as soon as you have symptoms and realize you've been injured as a result of your job.

Although you may initially tell your supervisor of the injury in a face-to-face meeting, it is important that you also give your employer written notice within 30 days of the injury. This will prevent any misunderstanding about whether or not you reported the injury and will protect your right to workers' compensation benefits.

If you have a union representative, contact that person right away; you may need help obtaining additional benefits that are secured by a union contract. (Your union representative may be instrumental in protecting your legal rights should your employer attempt to terminate you because you can't return to work for a while. Also, some employers may have salary continuation agreements for union members injured at work.)

Make certain that you complete any required in-house accident reports. Also, review any accident reports prepared by your supervisor or employer for accuracy, and obtain a copy for your records. If you disagree with the report, write your employer a letter explaining your position. (Chapter 5 takes you through all the rules and procedures involved with reporting your injury and filing a claim.)

Step 2. Get Medical Treatment If Needed

It is important to promptly seek medical treatment if needed. Not only will prompt medical treatment protect your health, but it will establish a medical record of your work injury.

If you gave your employer the name of your own doctor before your injury ("predesignated your treating physician," in workers' compensation jargon), you may go to that doctor under certain conditions (see Chapter 9, Section B1).

If not, the employer usually has the right to send you to a doctor the employer chooses, which often turns out to be the "company doctor" or "medical provider network"—a doctor or medical clinic that the employer sends its injured workers to on a regular basis.

If you have a medical emergency that requires immediate medical attention, you may go to the nearest emergency room for treatment. But after your emergency medical condition has been stabilized, you must continue follow-up medical treatment with the physician selected by your employer, unless you designated a doctor in advance. (See Chapter 9 for a detailed discussion of medical care.)

Step 3. Paying for Medical Treatment If Your Employer Denies Your Claim

If you report what you believe to be a work-related injury to your supervisor, your employer will most likely agree to accept responsibility. Authorization for medical treatment may be given orally or in writing to the doctor by your employer or its workers' compensation insurance company.

Within one day of your filing the DWC-1 claim form (see Step 6), your employer or its insurance company is required to authorize and agree to pay for your medical treatment until your employer or the insurance company either accepts or denies your claim. The insurance company is liable only for $10,000 in medical treatment until it accepts or denies your claim. (LC § 5402(c).)

If your claim is eventually accepted, the employer or insurance company will continue to pay for your treatment. If your claim is denied, the employer or insurance company will not authorize further medical treatment. This may work to your advantage (assuming that you have a valid claim): By denying your claim, your employer gives up its right to control your medical treatment. If your claim is denied, you are not bound to go to the company doctor for treatment and may be treated by a doctor of your choice. (See Chapter 9, Section B, for details.)

If your employer denies your claim right away, seek prompt treatment by relying on private health insurance, if you have it. If you do not have medical insurance and your employer refuses to pay, you have three choices.

1. You may pay for treatment yourself and seek reimbursement later.
2. You may find a doctor to treat you on a "lien basis," where the doctor waits for payment until your workers' compensation case is settled. (See Chapter 9, Section B2b, for more on liens.)
3. Or you may get a judge to order your employer's insurance company to pay for treatment. An information and assistance officer can help with this procedure. (See Step 10, below.)

CAUTION

Always apply for state disability insurance (SDI). Whenever you have an injury that results in your inability to work, always—and immediately—apply for SDI from the State Employment Development Department (EDD). That way, you'll receive income from this source in case of a delay or denial of your claim. When your workers' compensation benefits begin, it's important that you promptly inform the EDD, so it will discontinue SDI payments. (You may also be entitled to retroactive temporary disability benefits from the insurance company if you received less in SDI payments than you would have from the workers' compensation insurance company.) We cover SDI in Chapter 17, Section A.

Step 4. Tell the Doctor About Your Injuries

The insurance company will often rely on the doctor's first report to determine the extent of your injuries and whether they resulted from your employment. Tell the doctor that you injured yourself at work (if that's true) and how the injury occurred (if you know). In addition to giving the doctor a complete history of your medical problems (if asked), be sure to cover all your symptoms and sources of pain. For instance, even if most of your pain is in your back, if your arm hurts even a little, tell the doctor! You'll find detailed information on dealing with doctors in Chapter 9.

Injured Workers Who Are Fired

Employees often ask if they can be fired while off work because of an industrial injury. The answer is "not usually," unless the employer can prove that the termination is due to "business necessity," such as the company's going out of business or closing a factory or store. Otherwise, an employer cannot terminate a worker until the worker's condition stabilizes (called a "permanent and stationary" designation in workers' compensation jargon) and doctors determine that permanent disabilities prevent the worker from returning to work at the same job. Even then, an employer may be prohibited from discriminating against an injured worker. Under the Americans with Disabilities Act, an employer must make a reasonable effort to accommodate a worker's disability.

If you have an employment contract with your employer or a union bargaining agreement, review the contract or check with your union representative to determine whether your employer may terminate you after a specified time off work. For example, members of the Retail Clerks Union (grocery clerks and checkers) arguably have one year from the last date worked to return to work before an employer may terminate them—and even after that, they may be able to get their job back.

Step 5. The Doctor Decides Whether You Need Time Off

The first doctor you see will probably determine whether or not you need some time off from work to recover from the effects of your injury. Depending on the doctor's findings, you will receive one of the following:

- off-work order
- limited duties work order (also called a light duty work order or modified work order), or
- return to work order—that is, you can return to work with no restrictions.

Especially if you are given an off-work order, it's essential that you keep your employer advised of your medical status. If you neglect to do so, you may be fired for failing to report to work without a valid excuse. If, however, you keep your employer informed, you cannot legally be fired for injuring yourself, filing a workers' compensation claim, and obeying doctor's orders.

Step 6. Complete Workers' Compensation Claim Form and Application for Adjudication of Claim Form

Your next step is to protect your rights as an injured worker under the workers' compensation system by completing two forms promptly:

- **Workers' Compensation Claim Form (DWC-1).** Your employer is required by law to give you this form within one working day of learning that you had an injury that resulted in medical treatment beyond first aid or in your taking time off work (beyond the shift during which the injury took place). (LC § 5401(a).) You must fill in the DWC-1 form and give it to your employer. A downloadable copy of DWC-1 is available on Nolo's website. (See Chapter 29, "Online Appendixes" for the link to this and other forms in this book.)

- **Application for Adjudication of Claim.** You must also complete an Application for Adjudication of Claim form and file it with the Workers' Compensation Appeals Board. An Application for Adjudication of Claim form is included in Appendix 5, online at Nolo's website on this book's "companion page". (See Chapter 29, "Online Appendixes" for the link to this and other forms in this book.)

CAUTION

Time limits to file a claim. Your workers' compensation claim form (DWC-1) and the Application for Adjudication of Claim must by law be filed within one year from the date of injury. But, as a matter of common sense, you should complete and file these within 30 days of your injury, or at your first opportunity. (We provide sample forms and detailed instructions in Chapter 5, Section C.)

Step 7. Secure Control of Your Medical Care

As emphasized throughout this book, your treating doctor makes many important decisions that affect your workers' compensation case. Among other things, this doctor decides whether you are seriously injured, what type of treatment you need, and when and if you can return to work.

If you gave your employer a written designation of your treating physician prior to your injury, you may receive medical care from that doctor if you meet certain requirements (see Chapter 9, Section B1).

If you did not designate a treating physician in advance, you cannot pick your own doctor until a certain period of time has passed after your injury. For most workers, this time period is 30 days. Pay attention to this time period, and choose your own doctor as soon as you legally can. (See Chapter 9, Section B, for details.)

If your employer has established a medical provider network, you cannot go to a doctor outside the network (unless you predesignated your doctor). You can request a second and third opinion within the network and, if you're still not satisfied, submit an "independent medical review application" to the administrative director asking to be sent to another doctor, outside of the network. For more information, see Chapter 9, Section A3d.

Step 8. You May Receive Temporary Disability Benefits

When an injury limits you from working, you are entitled to receive temporary disability benefits. These payments are designed to help support you while you are not receiving full pay and are recovering from the effects of the injury or illness.

If the treating doctor has determined that you are temporarily disabled but the insurance company has not automatically begun temporary disability payments, you'll need to take charge. Contact the insurance company and request payment of "temporary disability indemnity" (also referred to as TD). It's okay to make your request by telephone, but it is always wise to follow up with a confirming letter, such as the one in Chapter 12, Section C2.

If you have an off-work order and your claim is accepted, the insurance carrier should promptly begin making temporary disability payments for all but the first three days you were off work. (If you are temporarily disabled for more than 14 days or your injury requires an overnight stay in the hospital, you will be paid for these three days.) (LC § 4652.) See Chapter 12, Section B, to determine the amount you are entitled to receive.

Within 14 days of your request, the workers' compensation insurance company should begin making temporary disability payments or advise you by mail why payments cannot be made within the 14-day period (known as a "delay letter").

If you receive a delay letter, you may be asked to provide additional information to the insurance company so that it can decide whether temporary disability payments are owed. The delay letter will also state when the insurance company expects to have the information required to make the decision.

(LC § 4650, CCR § 9812.) The insurance company has 90 days from knowledge of your claim in which to make a decision as to whether you are eligible for temporary disability payments.

If you do not receive either a check or a delay letter within 14 days of your request for benefits, the insurance company is liable for a 10% penalty on any temporary disability payments that you should have received by the 14th day. But don't sit around waiting for your check to appear. This is just one more instance where the old adage "the squeaky wheel gets the grease" holds true.

Step 9. Handling a Denial of Your Claim or Benefits

If you're unable to work because of your injury, the last thing you want to face is a battle with the insurance company. Unfortunately, this isn't in your control. Some insurance companies deny many claims as a matter of course or routinely reject requests for temporary disability payments, medical treatment, or other benefits.

If your workers' compensation claim or any request for benefits is denied, the insurer should notify you of the reason in writing. The reason could be any of the following:

- The insurer does not believe you sustained an industrial injury.
- The insurer does not believe that you are temporarily totally disabled.
- The insurer does not believe you need medical treatment.
- Your case involves two or more employers or insurance companies, each of whom refuses to pay benefits, claiming that the payment of benefits is the other's responsibility.

In any of these situations, you may need to take immediate steps to secure benefits. If a letter or phone call proves fruitless, you'll probably need to request a hearing before the Workers' Compensation Appeals Board, as discussed in Step 10, below. Consider seeing a lawyer, if you haven't already. (See Chapter 26 for information on hiring a lawyer.)

Step 10. Taking Problems to the Appeals Board

The Workers' Compensation Appeals Board oversees the California workers' compensation system. You may request a hearing (either expedited or regular) before the appeals board to resolve virtually any disputed issue. Examples of problems that may necessitate a hearing include:

- **Refusal to authorize medical treatment.** Your employer or its insurance company refuses to pay for your medical treatment.
- **Refusal to authorize surgery or tests.** Your treating doctor requests authorization to do surgery or perform tests, such as an MRI, and the insurance company refuses to authorize it.
- **Refusal to provide benefits.** The treating doctor says that you are entitled to benefits and the insurance company refuses to provide them.
- **Insufficient benefits.** The insurance company pays temporary disability benefits at a lower rate than your earnings justify.
- **Inadequate medical care.** You believe the quality of medical treatment you are receiving is inadequate, and the insurance company refuses to send you to another doctor.

Information on requesting and preparing for a hearing before a workers' compensation judge is contained in Chapters 22 and 24.

Step 11. After It Is Determined That You Are Permanent and Stationary (P&S) or Have Reached Maximal Medical Improvement (MMI)

You may continue to receive temporary disability payments until your doctor says that your medical condition is "permanent and stationary" or that you can return to work. Permanent and stationary (also referred to as "P&S") is workers' compensation jargon meaning that your doctor believes your medical condition has plateaued and medical treatment at this time won't improve your condition.

A new definition of permanent and stationary was put into effect in 2005. It is similar to the old definition, but legalistically different. It is defined as the point in time that you have reached "maximal medical improvement" (MMI), meaning that your condition is well stabilized and unlikely to change substantially in the next year, with or without medical treatment. This new definition of permanent and stationary, or MMI, will apply whenever the new (2005) rating schedule applies. (The new schedule applies if you were injured in 2005 or later and in a few other circumstances—for more information, see Chapter 18, Section B1.)

Exactly when this determination is made depends upon the severity of the injury, the length of your treatment, and your prospects for further recovery. It could be weeks, months, or even several years before your doctor concludes that your condition has reached a plateau.

Once you are determined to be permanent and stationary, you are no longer entitled to temporary disability payments, even if you cannot return to work or have not been released to return to work. You may, however, still be entitled to further medical treatment on an as-needed basis.

After your doctor's permanent and stationary diagnosis, you can expect to receive a letter from the insurance company advising you of the company's position on several critical issues in your workers' compensation case, including:

- whether you have a permanent disability (if so, the insurance company will begin making payments)
- whether you qualify for vocational rehabilitation or a "supplemental job displacement benefit," and
- whether you are entitled to future medical care.

If you or the insurance company disagrees with the treating doctor's opinion on any issues in the doctor's permanent and stationary report, the disputing party has 30 days to request that the issue be determined by going to a qualified medical evaluator (QME). (See Chapter 10 for a detailed explanation of medical-legal evaluations.)

Step 12. You May Recover Completely and Return to Work

Many work injuries result in a minimum amount of time off from work—at least a few days or weeks. After recovering, the injured worker often returns to the job without any work restrictions or long-term disability. In such situations, your main concern is to make certain that you were fairly paid by the insurance company for the days you were off, and that all medical treatment was paid by the insurance company or, if you paid your own medical bills, that you were reimbursed.

Be aware that even if you go back to work, you may still be entitled to a monetary permanent disability award. (See Step 14, below.)

Step 13. You May Be Entitled to Supplemental Job Displacement Benefits

For injuries that occurred in 2004 and later, you may be entitled to a "supplemental job displacement benefit" if you have sustained some permanent disability and if you do not return to work for your employer (the employer you were working for when you were injured) within 60 days of your last temporary disability payment. This benefit consists of vouchers for education-related costs.

Specifically, you will be eligible for this benefit only if your employer did not offer you:

- modified work that lasts at least 12 months, or
- alternative work that you are able to perform and that lasts at least 12 months, pays within 15% of preinjury earnings, and is within a reasonable distance of where you lived at the time of injury.

See Chapter 14 for more on the supplemental job displacement benefit.

Step 14. You May Be Partially Permanently Disabled

If you can't go back to your former job, or you can return but only with work restrictions or limited duties, you may be entitled to permanent partial disability payments. After your condition becomes permanent and stationary, or reaches maximal medical improvement, you should try to negotiate a settlement with the insurance company.

The factors you should consider when negotiating a settlement are covered in detail in Chapters 19 and 20, and should include the amount and value of your permanent disability, any past-due benefits (such as retroactive temporary disability benefits), and either the right to future medical treatment or its dollar value.

By negotiating your settlement, you eliminate the hazards of litigation. For example, if the case goes to trial, you're likely to wait many months or more to finally get to trial. You may even end up with less than you'd have received if you had settled the case.

Step 15. Go to Trial If There Is No Settlement

If you and the insurance company cannot agree to a settlement, either side may file appropriate documents with the Workers' Compensation Appeals Board to set the case for trial. (See Chapter 22, Section A.)

First, you'll attend a preliminary hearing, called a pre-trial conference or mandatory settlement conference. There, you will have a final opportunity to settle the case.

If you and the insurance company still cannot reach a settlement, you will be assigned a trial date to have your case heard before an appeals board judge. The trial date will probably be set anywhere from two to eight months later, depending upon how crowded the trial calendar is.

Step 16. Judgment Is Paid or the Matter Is Appealed

If the judge rules in your favor, the insurance company must either pay the judgment to you within 25 days or file a Petition for Reconsideration, which is the first of three steps in the appeal process. If you don't agree with the judge's ruling, you may also file a Petition for Reconsideration. If a petition is denied, the appealing party may file a Writ of Review with the Court of Appeal and, finally, with the California Supreme Court. (Appeals are covered in Chapter 25.)

CHAPTER

3

Is Your Injury Covered by Workers' Compensation?

SKIP AHEAD

If your claim was accepted. If you filed a claim that has already been accepted by the workers' compensation insurance company, you can safely skip this chapter. Your claim is "accepted" if the insurer considers yours a work-related injury and agrees to cover it. Acceptance by the insurance company may come in the form of a letter or may be inferred if the insurer provides benefits, such as temporary disability payments and medical treatment. However, if at a later date the insurance company denies your claim because of a claimed coverage problem, you may need to review this chapter.

If you are in doubt as to whether your job or injury is covered by workers' compensation, this chapter will help you decide. You need only read the sections of this chapter that address your situation, as follows:

- If you don't know whether your job is covered by workers' compensation, read Section A.
- If you aren't sure whether your injury is work-related (compensable), turn to Section B.
- If you significantly contributed to or purposefully caused the injury, see Section C.
- If your injury didn't occur while you were working on the job, see Section C8.
- If you didn't file a workers' compensation claim within one year of the injury, see Section C9.

A. Is Your Job Covered by Workers' Compensation?

If you work for almost any employer, whether it's a large multinational corporation, a small business, or a mom and pop store, you are almost surely covered by workers' compensation. If you were hired in California or are regularly employed in California and you suffer a work-related injury (either inside or outside of the state), that injury is covered under California workers' compensation laws. The fact is, most injured workers are covered by workers' compensation and must seek benefits exclusively through that system. But a few categories of workers—notably independent contractors and some federal workers—must pursue other avenues for compensation.

1. Employees Covered by Workers' Compensation

To be eligible for benefits, you must be an employee—not an independent contractor. (See Section 2a, below.) If you receive a salary, you are probably an employee, even if that term is not used. (See Section 2, below.)

Employees include legal and illegal aliens, minors (even if they are too young to be legally employed), and prisoners. You might even be covered by workers' compensation through a homeowners' policy if you were hired by a homeowner to perform gardening, maintenance, housecleaning, child care, or the like. (LC § 3351.)

To qualify as an employee, you do not have to be employed full time, employed by only one employer, or employed for any particular number of days or months. An exception to this rule applies to industrial injuries involving emotional stress or injury to the psyche. For emotional injuries, you probably must be employed for at least six months prior to the date of injury to qualify for workers' compensation. (See Section B7, below.) Another exception pertains to part-time workers, such as gardeners or housekeepers.

CAUTION

Special procedures for minors. Although minors (people under age 18) who are injured are entitled to workers' compensation benefits, they cannot legally file a claim for benefits, because they are not of legal age to do so. Therefore, a minor must have an adult "guardian ad litem" (someone who is legally responsible for pursuing a claim) appointed to file a claim on the minor's behalf. (We discuss this requirement in Chapter 5, Section C4b.)

You are covered by workers' compensation from the moment you start work, and sometimes even before you're hired. For example, if you are "trying out" for employment and are injured in some required activity—say an agility test—you are eligible for workers' compensation benefits.

In short, never assume that because yours is an unusual employment situation, you are not covered by workers' compensation. For workers' compensation law purposes, the definition of an employee is extremely broad. With the few exceptions described, if your injury had any connection with any sort of employment, you are presumed to be an employee covered by workers' compensation. (LC § 3357.)

2. Workers Not Covered by Workers' Compensation

Certain categories of workers are not covered by workers' compensation. If injured on the job, these workers may not use the workers' compensation system—although other ways of seeking compensation may be available.

SEE AN EXPERT

If you are excluded from filing a claim. If you're not entitled to file a workers' compensation claim, you may have the right to file a claim in a federal or California civil court. To do this, you'll probably need the help of a lawyer. Don't delay in finding a lawyer, because you will be barred from filing your claim unless you do it within a specified period of time.

a. Independent Contractors

Independent contractors are not employees—and therefore aren't covered under the workers' compensation system. People who often work as independent contractors include freelancers, plumbers, electricians, building contractors, auctioneers, and doctors.

If the person who hired you has no right to control how you get the job done, you may be an independent contractor. Here are some other indicators that you may be an independent contractor rather than an employee:

- Independent contractors do not get paid vacation, holidays, medical insurance, or other benefits. They pay their own Social Security and self-employment taxes.
- Independent contractors generally offer services to the public at large, and do not work for just one person or business.
- Independent contractors generally provide their own equipment and supplies and have a separate business location or work out of their home.

SEE AN EXPERT

Employees misclassified as independent contractors. Some employers or insurance companies may try to claim that you are an independent contractor when you are really an employee. Even if you have a contract stating that you are an independent contractor, it doesn't necessarily mean you are. You'll probably need the help of a workers' compensation lawyer if the insurer denies your claim on the premise that you're an independent contractor.

b. Certain Business Owners

If you work for yourself or own a business, you may not be covered by workers' compensation. Sole proprietors, partners, LLC members, and officers of closely held corporations are generally not considered employees unless specifically listed under the business's workers' compensation insurance policy.

Of course, if a small business hires employees, they are covered under workers' compensation, even if the owner is not.

c. Certain Part-Time Workers

Certain part-time workers are excluded from workers' compensation coverage. The most common of these are household employees, such as gardeners or housekeepers, who were employed fewer than 52 hours during the 90 calendar days immediately preceding the date of the injury or who earned less than $100 in wages from the employer during the 90 days preceding the date of injury. (LC § 3352(h).)

d. Most Federal Employees and Transportation Workers

Most federal employees and certain types of workers in the transportation industries who are injured on the job must file a lawsuit in federal court to receive compensation, rather than using the workers' compensation system. Under the Federal Employers Compensation Act (FECA), injured federal employees must file in federal or state court (5 USC §§ 8101–8193), but they cannot use the workers' compensation system.

Transportation workers excluded from workers' compensation include:

- **Seamen.** Under the Jones Act, a seaman (someone who works in or around the oceans or seas) who is injured because of an employer's failure to provide a seaworthy vessel may recover damages only in federal court. (46 USC §§ 688 and following.)
- **Railroad employees.** Under the Federal Employers Liability Act (FELA), all railroad employees have to file in federal or state court for injuries sustained at work. FELA applies to any injury sustained due to an accident, but does not apply to injuries due to continuous traumas or occupational diseases. (45 USC §§ 51–60.)

e. Longshoremen, Harbor Workers, and Defense Workers

People whose injuries occur at a few specified locations—most commonly on the ocean or other navigable waters or on defense bases—are excluded from filing under California workers' compensation. Here are the rules:

- The Longshore and Harbor Workers' Compensation Act covers injuries occurring upon the navigable waters of the United States, including any adjoining pier, wharf, dry dock, or terminal or other adjoining area customarily used by an employee in loading, unloading, repairing, or building a vessel. The majority of these types of injuries involve longshoremen, whose job involves loading and unloading seagoing vessels. Anyone so injured has to file a lawsuit in state or federal court. (Someone who actually works full-time upon a vessel would probably be considered a seaman, and thus be subject to the Jones Act. See Section 2d, just above.)
- The Outer Continental Shelf Lands Act covers all persons injured on the ocean beyond three miles from shore. (43 USC §§ 1331–1356.) Anyone so injured may have a choice between being compensated under the California workers' compensation laws or the Longshore and Harbor Workers' Compensation Act. (If in doubt, see an attorney.)
- All deaths at sea beyond the three-mile limit are covered by the Death on the High Seas Act. (46 USC §§ 761 and following.)
- Employees doing work on defense bases or public works outside the continental United States are covered by the Defense Base Act.

f. Employees Hired Outside of California

If you were hired in another state and are only temporarily working in California, you are not covered under California law. Fortunately, you are probably covered under the workers' compensation laws of your home state or the state where you were hired. (LC § 3600.5(b).)

TIP

If you live and work in different states. If you live in another state but work permanently in California, you are probably covered under both states' workers' compensation laws. File your claim in the state with the better benefits.

g. Volunteers

Persons who volunteer for a public agency or private nonprofit organization and receive no payment other than meals, transportation, lodging, or incidental expenses generally are not covered by workers' compensation. (But volunteers who work for a for-profit business may be considered employees, especially if they receive something of value, such as food or lodging.)

Usually excluded from workers' compensation coverage are:

- unpaid volunteers who provide services to charitable institutions
- volunteer ski patrol workers, and
- volunteer disaster service workers.

However, certain types of volunteers are covered by workers' comp. Under workers' compensation laws, the following people are considered to be employees, rather than volunteers:

- sheriff's reserve deputies while on duty
- any volunteer who assists a police officer at the officer's request
- volunteer police officers or firefighters while on active duty
- state fish and game reserve officers while on active duty, and
- anyone who performs hazardous work at the request of a fire or law enforcement officer.

In addition, it is possible for organizations to elect to cover volunteers under workers' compensation. For example, a church may specifically cover a person who does repairs for the church on a volunteer basis.

h. Nonworking Students

A student injured at school while participating in normal school activities is not covered by workers' compensation. Even student athletes who participate in amateur sporting events sponsored by the school are excluded from coverage.

There is one exception to the rule that students aren't covered by workers' compensation: A student injured while participating in a school work experience or community occupational training program is covered. And, of course, a student employed at a regular job, such as at a hamburger joint or a campus store, is an employee and is fully covered under workers' compensation.

B. Do You Have a Compensable Injury?

To qualify as having a compensable injury (one covered under workers' compensation), you need to have suffered some form of work-related physical or emotional harm. Because some industrial injuries are not easy to spot, many people are working today with industrial injuries and don't even know it. Let's look at some of the major categories of compensable injuries.

1. Specific or Traumatic Injuries

The most straightforward injury can be traced back to a single incident that happened to you while working, even if you didn't realize you sustained an injury until later. Following are a few examples of specific or traumatic injuries:

- You are hit by a falling object at work.
- You slip on something while at work and fall, dislocating your knee.
- You cut your hand with a knife or tool at work.
- You are involved in a car accident while delivering packages at work. You think you're fine, but several days later you trace the pain in your neck to a whiplash sustained in the car accident.

2. Cumulative Trauma or Continuous Trauma Injuries

An injury caused by work activities that extend over a period of time may not be easily identified. In the workers' compensation world, this is called a continuous trauma or cumulative trauma injury. This type of injury may also be referred to as a repetitive motion or repetitive strain injury. The common denominator in these types of injuries is the repetitive nature of the activities that caused the injury.

> **EXAMPLE 1:** A computer user does eight hours of programming and design work every day. She gets tingling and numbness in her fingers after one year of work.

> **EXAMPLE 2:** A laborer who does heavy lifting often has a sore lower back after work. Over a period of time, the symptoms get worse. Eventually, his back hurts so much he can't go to work.

> **EXAMPLE 3:** A grocery store checker pulls thousands of groceries across her check stand every day. One day, she realizes that her hands are going numb. Her doctor tells her she has carpal tunnel syndrome, brought on by the repetitive motions used in scanning groceries.

> **EXAMPLE 4:** A factory worker is constantly exposed to toxic chemical fumes on the job. Over a period of several years, she develops respiratory problems due to this exposure.

There is no required time period for an injury to qualify as a cumulative trauma injury. Some injuries occur over years, while others can develop over a relatively short time. The final determination of whether you have a cumulative trauma injury will be made by your doctors. (See Chapter 4 for more information on cumulative trauma injuries.)

A continuous trauma does not have to occur all at one job. You may have done similarly repetitive work for several different employers over many years. If so, the employers (and their respective insurance companies) for which you worked during the last year of the continuous trauma are responsible for paying workers' compensation benefits. See Section 6, below. (Also, in Chapter 5, Section C, we discuss how to file a claim form that lists all employers who may be responsible for your workers' compensation coverage.)

3. Sickness Due to Harmful Exposure

An illness or disease may qualify as an industrial injury if it was caused or made worse by conditions at work. You probably would have a claim for workers' compensation in situations such as these:

- A construction worker is exposed to asbestos while working and many years later develops a condition called asbestosis.
- A maid is required to use a cleaning solution at work and breaks out in a rash, develops a migraine headache, and suffers severe stomach problems.
- A doctor is pricked by a needle at work and later tests HIV-positive.

If you are thinking that some of these injuries are also cumulative injuries, you are correct. For example, sickness that results from long-term exposure to a toxic substance is also a cumulative injury.

CAUTION

If you have asbestosis. Do not attempt to represent yourself in this very specialized field, as you'll probably miss out on important rights. Find a workers' compensation attorney who deals with asbestos claims.

4. Injuries That Are Automatically Work-Related

Certain injuries are assumed to be work-related unless the employer or its insurance company successfully offers sufficient evidence to dispute it. If an employer disputes whether one of the following kinds of injuries is job-related, the employee still has an excellent chance of winning, because all laws and facts must be liberally construed in the employee's favor. (LC § 3202.)

- **Injuries in high-risk law enforcement professions.** This applies to police officers, firefighters, and other law enforcement personnel who develop heart trouble, cancer (including leukemia), or hernias. (If you are employed in any occupation that involves protecting the public, please refer to Labor Code §§ 3212–3213 for a complete list of the types of injuries that are presumed to be work-related.)

- **Injuries where there was no other reasonable explanation for the injury.** In certain situations, no one knows how the injury occurred and there's no evidence to contradict that it was work-related. For example, an employee was welding a pipe at work one day. The next thing she remembers is waking up in the hospital with a gash to her head. Unless there is evidence to the contrary, it will be presumed that the injury occurred as a result of her employment.
- **Injuries that resulted in the employee's dying or becoming incompetent or otherwise mentally incapacitated.** Since, for obvious reasons, the injured employee cannot explain how the injury occurred, it is presumed that the injury occurred as a result of her employment.

5. Injuries Resulting From a Prior Condition

If you're injured at work as a result of a preexisting or underlying condition, you may still have a workers' compensation claim. (LC § 4663.) But to be covered, there must be something new about the injury. It can't just be a recurrence or one-time flare-up of the old injury. To qualify for workers' compensation, the injury must be either:

- an aggravation (worsening) of an underlying condition, whether work-related or not, or
- a new injury that developed as a result of a prior industrial injury.

EXAMPLE 1: Marci suffered a mild carpal tunnel injury in her right wrist as a result of repetitive data entry work. She filed a workers' compensation claim and eventually settled her case. Marci returned to work and, after several months, began feeling pain in her right wrist again. Her doctor determined that Marci had exacerbated (suffered a recurrence) of her original injury, but that she did not have a new or additional injury, and therefore did not have a new workers' compensation claim.

EXAMPLE 2: Farhad breaks his leg at work and files a workers' compensation claim. The bone heals, but because of the break, Farhad develops an altered gait (he begins to walk differently). Over time, this eventually causes pain and disability to his back. Farhad has a subsequent injury to his back as a result of the original industrial injury to his leg.

An important concept to remember is that an employer "takes each employee as is." This means the employer cannot deny workers' compensation coverage simply because a person in perfect health would not have been injured. Nor does it matter that the employer did not know about the employee's previous underlying condition, even if the employee withheld information about the condition prior to employment.

However, if an employee had a preexisting injury, an employer may not be responsible for paying the full amount of any permanent disability. (See the discussion on apportionment that follows.)

EXAMPLE: Dan injured his back playing football in college and had back surgery. Twenty years later, Dan lifts a 15-pound weight on the job and ruptures a disc in his back. Dan is entitled to workers' compensation coverage, despite the fact that someone without Dan's back condition probably would not have been hurt lifting 15 pounds. (But it's possible that if Dan has a permanent disability, his employer will not be responsible for the full amount.)

6. Apportionment

Even if you are legitimately injured on the job and suffer a permanent disability, the insurance company may claim that it is responsible for only a portion—not all—of your permanent disability. This issue is likely to arise if you had a preexisting injury to the same body part that you injured at work.

It is often difficult to medically determine how much disability is due to the injury on the job and how much is due to a preexisting condition or other factors. However, your doctor must address all of the factors that contributed to your injury when writing a report concerning permanent disability.

If a portion of your present permanent disability is not due to your current job, the insurance company may be able to apportion part of it to outside factors. This allows the insurance company to reduce its payments to you and escape liability, to some extent.

> **EXAMPLE:** Cathy was involved a car accident that resulted in an injury to her back. She received medical treatment and then recovered. Two years later, she moves a heavy filing cabinet and injures her back at work. The workers' compensation insurance company claims that part of Cathy's present permanent disability is due to the earlier automobile accident, and Cathy's doctor agrees. As a result, the insurance company is not responsible for paying Cathy the total amount of permanent disability that she otherwise would be entitled to receive, unless Cathy can prove that she completely recovered from the automobile accident and had no problems working until she was injured on the job.

Apportionment based on a claim of a preexisting injury or for another reason can be a difficult and confusing issue for many people, including insurance adjusters. You will need to get medical reports to back your claim. Look into getting an attorney if apportionment is raised as an issue in your case, or seek help from an information and assistance officer.

Apportionment is discussed in greater detail in Chapter 18, Section D1.

7. Stress-Related Injuries

To qualify for workers' compensation benefits for a stress-related injury, you must be able to show by competent medical evidence that you have a psychiatric or perhaps a physical injury as a result of stress on the job.

CAUTION

Beware of stress claim scams. Be leery of television or radio commercials that ask you to call a toll-free number if you were subjected to stress on the job. For the most part, doctors who solicit business from workers with stress-related injuries are interested in fattening their own wallets, not in workers' health or legal rights. You may get medical or psychiatric treatment (whether you need it or not), but you probably won't get any monetary benefits from the workers' compensation insurance company.

a. Psychiatric Injuries

RELEVANT CASE LAW

See *California Youth Authority v. WCAB (Walker)*, *Rodriguez v. WCAB*, and *Cristobal v. WCAB*, in Chapter 28.

A stress claim generally involves injury to the psyche (one's emotional well-being) due to stressful conditions at work. In other words, this is an emotional injury that limits one's ability to perform certain job functions, such as following instructions or communicating with others.

Although workers' compensation is supposed to be a "no-fault" system that covers employees pretty much across the board, this is no longer true for psychiatric injuries. For starters, you must have been employed by your employer for at least six months (not necessarily continuous employment) prior to the date of injury. You may lose your eligibility for workers' compensation if you were terminated or laid off prior to filing a stress claim. See "Special Rules If a Job Was Terminated," below.

In addition, you must demonstrate by a preponderance (51%) of the evidence that the actual events of your employment predominantly caused the psychiatric injury. In other words, if you are disabled due to a variety of factors—such as stress at work, personal financial problems, and a recent divorce—you may qualify for workers' compensation benefits only if the work stress contributed at least 51% of the cause of your overall psychiatric disability.

EXAMPLE: Manuel works on a production line in a factory. His supervisor constantly pressures Manuel to work faster and frequently threatens to terminate him. His supervisor humiliates Manuel in front of his coworkers on a daily basis, calling him a "stupid wetback" who can't follow instructions or saying he's too fat to do factory work. As a result of the constant harassment, Manuel becomes too nervous to continue working and files a workers' compensation claim. Manuel has few stresses other than his work life, so he is sure he can prove that at least 51% of his disability was caused by his work environment.

There is an important exception to the 51% requirement: If you were the victim of a work-related violent act or were directly exposed to a significant violent act, you qualify for workers' compensation benefits if your employment caused at least 35% of your overall psychiatric disability.

You may need medical treatment and temporary disability payments as a result of your psychiatric injuries. But bear in mind that if you qualify for permanent disability, you will have proven to the world that you have a permanent psychiatric disability. Be sure that this is something you are willing to live with. Although future employers may not legally discriminate against you because you have a psychiatric disability, realistically you may face that possibility.

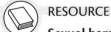

RESOURCE

Sexual harassment on the job. Sexual harassment by coworkers or superiors at work may also result in physical or emotional injury. In addition to workers' compensation benefits, you may be entitled to pursue other remedies in civil court. To do this, you must take action within one year from the date of the alleged harassment, or your case may be forever barred. If you are interested in learning more about your rights in this area, refer to *Your Rights in the Workplace*, by Barbara Kate Repa (Nolo).

Problems Finding Attorneys to Handle Psychiatric Stress Claims

Most psychiatric stress cases result in few or no permanent disability benefits, because leaving the stressful environment (the job), will generally result in the employee's full recovery. This means you will probably have difficulty finding a lawyer to represent you, because attorney fees are based on a percentage of permanent disability recovery. In short, if you have a psychiatric stress claim, you're likely to end up representing yourself. But because this type of claim is often contested and can be particularly complicated, I recommend you make a concerted effort to find competent counsel to represent you.

b. Physical Stress-Related Injuries

Sometimes stress at work not only causes emotional injury but also manifests itself in physical injury to the body.

EXAMPLE 1: Ted works for a convenience store. While at work one evening, he is held up at gunpoint. After the incident, Ted finds that he is fearful of every customer who comes into the store. He has difficulty sleeping and has frequent nightmares about the incident. Before long, Ted develops an ulcer and suffers a nervous breakdown.

EXAMPLE 2: Larry is a sales representative for a large pharmaceutical company. He has been under a great deal of pressure from his supervisor to meet monthly sales quotas and has been told that he will be terminated if he fails to do so. Larry's wife is expecting their third child, and he can't afford to lose his job. Larry begins working 18-hour shifts, constantly worrying about failing to meet quotas and being fired. Larry suffers a heart attack, which he alleges is due to the stress at work.

It's even possible to have a legitimate stress claim for an injury that results from the stress experienced because of a workers' compensation injury and claim.

EXAMPLE: Denny slips a disc in his back at work. The insurance company denies him benefits, causing him severe financial hardship. This results in further physical and emotional injury from the stress placed upon Denny due to the lack of money.

C. Injuries Not Covered by Workers' Compensation

When an employer carries workers' compensation insurance, the usual rule is that any work injury falls under that coverage. For example, an injured employee is not excluded from coverage just because the act resulting in the injury was careless, negligent, or even just plain dumb. However, as you'll see, a few types of injuries can legally be excluded from workers' compensation coverage.

1. Injuries Caused by Intoxication or Drugs

If you were intoxicated at the time of the industrial injury, you may not be entitled to workers' compensation benefits. (LC § 3600.) But be careful not to jump to conclusions. Mere intoxication or illegal drug use or misuse of legal drugs is not an absolute bar to recovery. It must be proven that your intoxication caused the injury.

Special Rules If a Job Was Terminated

Additional rules apply for stress injuries if you were fired, laid off, or voluntarily quit prior to filing a claim for workers' compensation benefits. In addition to other requirements, you must show that at least one of following applies:

- **Sudden and extraordinary events during your employment caused the injury.** This means that your psychiatric injury was due to something one would normally not experience in the workplace; for example, witnessing a violent act.
- **Your employer had notice of the psychiatric injury prior to the notice of termination or layoff.** Sufficient notice might be a memo to your supervisor saying that you were planning to file a stress claim. Certainly, an actual filing of a claim would qualify.
- **Medical records prior to the notice of termination or layoff contain evidence of treatment of the psychiatric injury.** For example, you may have seen a doctor or therapist about your problems before receiving notice of a layoff.
- **Your date of injury is after the date of notice of the termination or layoff, but prior to its effective date.** If you receive notice of termination that is to take place in a week or a month, you could file a stress claim without being subject to the termination rules above.
- **You were sexually or racially harassed at work.**

2. Self-Inflicted Injuries

An injury that is intentionally self-inflicted is not covered by workers' compensation. (LC § 3600.)

> **EXAMPLE:** Jorge gets angry at Cathy, his supervisor. Because Jorge knows that Cathy is criticized by her superiors whenever an employee files a workers' compensation claim, he intentionally slams his fist into a wall, injuring his hand. He is not entitled to benefits under workers' compensation.

However, self-inflicted injuries can be covered where the employee's action is deemed to be an "irresistible impulse," meaning that the action could not be helped.

> **EXAMPLE:** Jorge slams his fist into the wall in an immediate and direct reaction to learning that he has been denied a promotion. Court cases seem to indicate that Jorge will be allowed recovery under the theory that his was an irresistible impulse. But, in this situation, Jorge must prove that his actions were really the result of an irresistible impulse—in other words, he slammed his fist into the wall in a fit of rage, without thinking.

Claims filed by dependents of employees who died as a result of a work injury will be denied if it is proven that the employee committed suicide. However, it's up to the employer to prove that such a death was intentional, not an accident.

An exception to this rule involves a situation where an employee commits suicide because of an industrial injury. (This area usually requires the help of an attorney.)

> **EXAMPLE:** Martin is paralyzed in an accident at work. He experiences continuous pain. In addition, Martin becomes deeply depressed by the injury and the resulting financial hardships and commits suicide. Even assuming the employer can prove that Martin's death was a suicide, his surviving dependents can still recover if they can show that the suicide was directly caused by the industrial injury.

3. Injuries From Fight Started by Employee

If employees begin an argument at work and a fight ensues, the initial physical aggressor will be barred from workers' compensation benefits. (LC § 3600.) It's possible that the argument need not even be related to the workplace; courts have held that an argument about anything will do, as long as it started at work.

Who the initial physical aggressor is may be difficult to prove. It is not necessarily the person who threw the first punch. The initial physical aggressor is the one who first engaged in physical conduct that a reasonable person would believe presented a real threat of bodily harm.

> **EXAMPLE:** Joe stands 6'3" tall and weighs 250 pounds. Tom, a coemployee, stands 5'2" and weighs 105 pounds. Joe and Tom begin arguing about the quality of work each is doing. Joe calls Tom's mother a name Tom doesn't care for, and Tom pushes Joe. Joe breaks Tom's hand, then grabs his throat and starts choking him, yelling all the while that he's going to kill Tom for touching him. Fearing for his life, Tom grabs a pipe and strikes Joe over the head, sending him to the hospital. Since Joe could not have reasonably believed that Tom's push presented a threat of bodily harm, Joe will probably be considered the initial aggressor. Joe will not be allowed to collect workers' compensation benefits, but Tom will.

In certain situations, the initial aggression may be forgiven as reasonably necessary. This might occur, for example, where an employee initiates force to protect herself from a sexual advance or to retrieve stolen property from another employee.

4. Horseplay-Related Injuries or Injuries in Violation of Company Policy

Simply put, horseplay is equivalent to "goofing off" or acting in a careless and immature manner. If an injury is caused by horseplay that is clearly discouraged by the employer, it probably will not be covered by workers' compensation. (LC § 3600.) On the other hand, if the employer condoned the horseplay, the injury should be covered.

EXAMPLE 1: Gina's boss, Tony, installs a basketball hoop in the back of the shop. During breaks, he shoots baskets with his employees. One day, while shooting baskets, Gina sprains her ankle. Because this activity was condoned by the employer, Gina should receive workers' compensation coverage.

EXAMPLE 2: During work, Sam sneaks outside and shows off his double loop flip on his skateboard. In the process, Sam breaks his leg. Sam's employer had reprimanded him several times for skateboarding on company premises. Sam's injury is not covered under workers' compensation laws.

SEE AN EXPERT

If horseplay was a factor. The issue of horseplay is often a gray area. If this concerns you, it would be wise to do some legal research or see a lawyer.

5. Felony-Related Injuries

An employee who is injured as the result of committing a felony (a serious crime, such as murder or burglary), or a crime that could have been prosecuted as a felony, even if it was prosecuted as a less-serious misdemeanor, is not covered by workers' compensation if the employee is convicted. (LC § 3600.)

EXAMPLE: Audrey works as a nurse at a hospital where several patients die under suspicious circumstances. Audrey is investigated by her employer because she's suspected of murder. As a result of the investigation, she suffers a mental breakdown. If Audrey is later convicted for murder, she would not be entitled to workers' compensation benefits for the breakdown.

6. Off-Duty Recreational Activity Injuries

An injury that arises out of voluntary participation in any off-duty recreational, social, or athletic activity generally is not covered by workers' compensation. (LC § 3600.) If, however, the activities are a requirement of the employment, or are perceived as such by the employee, the injury is covered. It doesn't matter if the employee was mistaken, as long as the belief is reasonable.

EXAMPLE 1: Lanny is invited by his boss to dinner. His host accidentally drops a heavy platter on Lanny's foot, breaking several bones. Lanny would be entitled to workers' compensation benefits if he thought it would be "suicidal to one's career" to refuse an invitation by the boss.

EXAMPLE 2: Jerry and a few of his coworkers get together after work to play racquetball at the request of their supervisor. Jerry fractures his ankle during the game. Whether or not Jerry is entitled to workers' compensation benefits depends upon whether Jerry felt he was obligated to play because his supervisor made the request.

Other common nonworkplace situations where workers' compensation coverage may be granted might include playing on a company-sponsored softball team or attending a company picnic.

7. Injuries Claimed After Employee Was Terminated or Laid Off

You generally must have filed a claim for workers' compensation benefits before you were fired, were laid off, or voluntarily quit. You may, however, be entitled to workers' compensation benefits if you can show at least one of the following:

- **Your employer had notice of the injury prior to the notice of termination or layoff.** For example, if you told your supervisor that you were planning to file a workers' compensation claim and received a layoff notice the following week, you would qualify under this exception.
- **The date of injury is after the date of notice of termination or layoff, but prior to its effective date.** If, for example, you receive notice that you'll be laid off at the end of the month, you could file a workers' compensation claim before then.
- **You received medical treatment for the injury.** This applies if you receive treatment before receiving notice of the termination or layoff and your medical records contain evidence of the injury prior to the notice of termination or layoff.

8. Injuries Outside Work or Job-Related Activities (AOE/COE)

Most industrial injuries happen at the job site, during regular work assignments. But, to qualify, an industrial injury need not be so cut-and-dried.

To be covered by workers' compensation, your injury or illness must meet two important criteria:

- The injury must have happened as a result of your work activities or environment. In legal jargon, this is known as "arising out of the employment," or "AOE."
- The injury must have occurred while you were performing activities required by your job. In legal jargon, this is known as "in the course of employment," or "COE."

SEE AN EXPERT

If possible, see a lawyer for AOE/COE issues. If your employer or the insurance company raises these issues, it is highly recommended that you consult with a workers' compensation attorney or discuss your case with an information and assistance officer. These issues are critical to your entitlement to workers' compensation benefits and involve complex legal arguments.

The Difference Between AOE and COE

To the uninitiated, AOE and COE can seem like pretty much the same thing. Here's how they differ.

AOE (arising out of the employment) refers to whether the injury happened as a result of your work activities or environment. AOE addresses whether or not the type of injury you have is consistent with the type of work you did. For instance, did the exposure to heavy smoke while burning trash at work *cause* the lung cancer?

COE (in the course of employment), on the other hand, refers to whether the injury was caused while you were performing job-related activities. It addresses whether or not the *activity* that caused the injury was a work-related activity—for example, was burning trash part of the employee's job? Taking an on-premises break, using the restroom, and even changing a tire in the company parking lot are all covered in the course of employment.

9. Injuries Where Claim Not Filed on Time

You must make your claim for workers' compensation benefits within certain time limits—usually within one year from the date of injury. If you missed this deadline, see the discussion in Chapter 5, Section C.

CHAPTER

4

Cumulative Trauma Disorders

A cumulative trauma disorder (CTD) is an injury that occurs over a period of months or years. Cumulative trauma disorders are commonly known by many other names, such as repetitive stress injuries, continuous trauma injuries, repetitive trauma injuries, repetitive microtrauma injuries, repetitive strain injuries, repetitive motion injuries, repetitive motion syndrome, occupational overuse injuries, or overuse syndrome.

Cumulative trauma disorders now account for almost two-thirds of all job-related injuries, and one in eight American workers has been diagnosed with a CTD. Is it any wonder that employers and workers' compensation insurance companies look at these claims with increasing scrutiny?

Although many insurance companies now realize that these injuries are legitimate, if you have suffered a cumulative trauma injury it is not unlikely that your claim will initially be denied by the insurance company. It is therefore very important that you know as much as possible about the nature of your injury so that you can effectively prove the injury is work related.

In Section A of this chapter, we review the different kinds of cumulative trauma disorders, as well as their respective treatments. We also explore the various factors, including improper ergonomics, that lead to the development of a CTD. In Sections B through F, we introduce you to the practical aspects of properly handling a CTD claim: reporting your injury, getting a diagnosis, and getting appropriate medical treatment, which might include taking time off, returning to work, and being compensated for a permanent disability. These issues are then discussed in more detail in the remaining chapters of this book.

A. What Is a CTD?

There is no one accepted definition of a cumulative trauma disorder, but here is a general definition that combines the more common theories: A cumulative trauma disorder is a disorder of the muscles, ligaments, bones, nerves, tendons, or vascular system, alone or in combination with each other, that is caused by repeated exertions or movements. A cumulative trauma disorder develops over a prolonged period, usually months or years.

Other CTD definitions concentrate on soft tissue as the focal cause of the injury: CTDs are painful and limiting soft tissue disorders that result from repeated or continual application of physical stress to a particular body part over extended periods of time. This physical stress causes microtrauma and overwhelms the tissue's normal adaptive ability to repair itself, and the result is often damage to muscles, tendons, tendon sheaths, bursas, cartilage, bone, joint surfaces, nerves, or other soft tissues.

1. Common CTDs

Some of the more common upper-extremity CTDs include nerve entrapment syndromes (for example, carpal tunnel syndrome and ulnar nerve compression), bursitis, tendinitis, de Quervain's tenosynovitis, epicondylitis, and others. To better understand these injuries, let's consider the various body parts that can be affected by cumulative trauma.

a. Muscles

Muscle problems can include muscle strain or muscle spasm. A few muscle fibers may be injured at first, which can lead to spasm and eventual pain in the whole muscle. The cause of this type of injury includes awkward positions or sustained static positions. The most commonly affected muscles include those along the neck and lower spine, the shoulders, and the arms.

b. Tendons

The most common injury to the tendons is tendinitis, or inflammation of the tendon. Tendons attach the muscle to the bones, and repetitive movements that decrease the lubrication of tendons can lead to inflammation, swelling, and scarring. Tendinitis can cause great discomfort that can either be a dull ache or a sharp pain. The most common locations for tendinitis are the front and back of the wrists, the elbows, and the shoulders.

Epicondylitis is a form of tendinitis involving the tendons attaching to the elbow (outside elbow in "tennis elbow," and inside elbow in "golfer's elbow"). This injury is not just limited to tennis players and golfers, however. Overuse of a computer mouse and keyboard as well as playing musical instruments can lead to this form of tendinitis.

Another form of tendinitis common today is de Quervain's tenosynovitis, a painful inflammation of the thumb side of the wrist, which can be caused by repetitive activities requiring sideways motion of the wrist while gripping with the thumb, as in hammering, filing, and joystick or mouse use.

c. Nerves

An increasingly common CTD is nerve entrapment syndrome. Repetitive motion can sometimes squash or pinch the nerves that run through the shoulders, inside the arm muscles, along the bones, through the wrist to the hands.

Carpal tunnel syndrome, which results from repetitive or awkward positioning of the wrist, can increase pressure and cause tendons in the wrist to swell up and compress the median nerve in the carpal tunnel at the wrist. Symptoms include numbness in the hand; tingling in the thumb and the index, third, and fourth fingers; pain; weakness; and clumsiness. The causes of carpal tunnel syndrome include working with the wrist bent in any nonneutral (flexed) position, forceful pinching or gripping, and exposure to constant vibration.

Ulnar nerve compression involves your "funny bone" nerve, which runs down the upper arm alongside the triceps, through the bones of the elbow (called the "cubital tunnel") and down the outside of the wrist. The ulnar nerve feeds the fourth and fifth finger, and symptoms can include numbness and tingling in those fingers plus elbow and wrist pain. It is not yet known exactly what causes ulnar nerve compression, although it can occur as a result of repetitive or awkward positioning of the wrists and hands and frequent bending of the elbows at angles of more than 90 degrees.

Both of these nerve entrapment syndromes can be exacerbated by poor posture. Allowing the shoulders to slump and roll forward can trap the nerves and vessels as they travel to and from the arm, worsening the pain and numbness.

This can cause another nerve entrapment syndrome, called thoracic outlet syndrome. This problem occurs when the blood vessels or nerves that pass into the arms from the neck are squashed, and can be due to weak shoulder and back muscles or enlarged chest muscles. Thoracic outlet syndrome can also be caused by repetitive activities that require the arms to be held overhead or extended forward or by poor posture, especially when the shoulders are dropped and slouched forward. Symptoms include pain in the shoulder, arm, or fourth and fifth fingers.

Other less common nerve entrapment syndromes include pronator teres syndrome, which involves entrapment of the median nerve at the elbow, and radial tunnel syndrome, which involves entrapment of the radial nerve in the forearm.

d. Bones, Joints, and Discs

Repetitive bending, reaching, or twisting is a primary cause of injuries such as degenerative arthritis and degenerative disc disease. The most common locations for this type of problem are the lower back (lumbosacral spine), neck (cervical), shoulder, and elbow.

e. Bursas

Bursas are fluid-filled sacs located near the body's joints that reduce friction between the body's bones and muscles. Bursitis occurs when bursas become inflamed from injury or overuse. The most common areas affected are the shoulders, elbows, hips, and knees.

f. Associated Problems

Depression and reflex sympathetic dystrophy syndrome (a constant, burning pain at the site of an injury) can develop following any of the above CTDs.

2. Activities That Cause CTDs

There are probably as many factors that cause cumulative trauma injuries as there are types of jobs. Virtually any repetitive, sustained, or forceful exertion over a long enough period of time can lead to a cumulative trauma injury. Other causes include vibration, repetitive impact, and working in a fixed position for a long period of time.

The most common CTDs today involve injury to the upper extremities (wrists, elbows, and hands) due to repetitive keyboard activities. Employees often spend hours at a time inputting or manipulating computer data, and if this is done without regard to proper ergonomics or for too many hours without sufficient breaks, a nerve entrapment syndrome such as carpal tunnel syndrome may develop.

An occupation that has a higher-than-normal incidence of CTDs is that of the grocery checker. With the advent of scanners that read bar codes on grocery products, grocery checkers are required to pull or slide the product across the scanner. This repetitive activity often leads to the development of cumulative trauma injury to the upper extremities. The repetitive turning of the neck from side to side may also cause a CTD to the neck or shoulders. In addition, constant lifting activities may cause injury to the back.

Occupations that require working in a fixed position for a prolonged period of time, called static posturing, can also lead to CTDs. Some examples of static posturing include prolonged sitting or standing, prolonged gripping or grasping, and holding a particular position for long periods. For example, an operator or front desk clerk who holds a telephone receiver between the head and shoulder, or an airline mechanic who has to crawl and work in a twisted position may develop cumulative trauma disorders.

Other work-related activities that lend themselves to repetitive stress injuries include:

- playing musical instruments
- assembly line work
- polishing, sanding, and painting
- pipesetting
- jackhammering
- any overhead work
- butchering/meat packing
- sawing and cutting
- writing
- driving
- stocking shelves and packing
- massaging clients, and
- working as a mechanic.

Improper ergonomics, such as poor workstation setup or posture, is a primary cause of CTDs, regardless of the type of activity someone performs. Ergonomics is the study of how people interact with their physical environment, and how to modify the environment to prevent or reduce injuries such as musculoskeletal disorders. Ergonomics uses scientific knowledge about objects, systems, and environments (like a workstation) to maximize productivity and minimize injuries.

Ergonomics is starting to play an important role in our understanding of the cause and prevention of work-related cumulative trauma injuries. Some employers are working with ergonomic experts to improve their employees' workstations. For example, the proper ergonomic model for the prevention of carpal tunnel syndrome (a CTD injury to the wrist) would include keeping the wrists in a neutral position (straight), the elbows down by the sides and the shoulders back, and would aim for reducing the frequency of repetitive activity.

Remember, however, that workers' compensation is a no-fault system. Even if you wouldn't have been injured at work if you hadn't typed while slumped in your chair or with your feet on your desk, your injury still falls under the workers' comp system because it happened at work.

B. Becoming Aware of Your Injury

Because it can be months after a CTD starts to develop that you realize that your work is causing you pain, identifying a CTD is more complicated than discovering you've sprained an ankle.

1. Warning Signs

There are no clear early warning signs to alert you that you are headed for a cumulative trauma injury. Often, by the time you realize that something is wrong, damage has already been done. For this reason, don't ignore the following signs; report them to a physician knowledgeable in cumulative trauma injuries as soon as possible:

- **Pain.** You may feel sharp or dull and aching pain in your limbs that increases in intensity over time. Some feel this pain after working on the computer or cash register for a few hours, while others start to notice it only when they make certain movements outside of work, such as twisting a doorknob to open a door or washing their hair.
- **Tingling or numbness.** Sometimes your hand or arm may have a tingling sensation or you may experience numbness or tingling in certain fingers. This is a sign that damage to your nerves may have already occurred and should be taken seriously.
- **Fatigue.** You may notice that you tire easily and can no longer do the same amount of work you used to be able to do.
- **Weakness or clumsiness.** You may notice a loss of strength or find that you are dropping items or have difficulty in picking things up.

CTDs often go unreported in their early stages, prior to the development of real impairment, because the individual considers the signs and symptoms of the disorder as necessary characteristics of aging or as normal "aches and pains" that do not represent a potentially disabling process.

If you have a physical problem (for example, pain or limitation of movement) but you don't know its cause, you should make an appointment with your family doctor or primary care physician. Discuss with the doctor your symptoms and all of your activities during the past six months, both on and off the job. The doctor will probably be able to identify the cause of your problem, and chances are it will be your job activities. If your family doctor does tell you that your injury is work-related, you should immediately report the injury to your employer.

2. Reporting Your Injury

Reporting your injury to your employer is discussed in detail in Chapter 5. However, because it can be difficult to identify a work-related cumulative trauma injury, reporting a CTD is more complicated than reporting specific, traumatic injuries. There are a few things you can do to protect your rights if you suspect that you may be suffering from a CTD.

a. Designate a Treating Physician

First, if you suspect that you have any injury (for example, you have pain in your wrist that's getting worse with time), before reporting the injury to your employer, advise your employer that you wish to designate your personal physician to treat you in the event you have an injury at work. A sample of such a letter can be found in Chapter 9, Section B1.

Designating your doctor in advance may allow you to be treated by this doctor right after you report the injury, rather than having to see the company doctor for the first 30 days or longer. This prevents the possibility that the company doctor will send you back to your job before you are medically able to work or, worse yet, write a report after only one or two visits saying that you have fully recovered and have no disability whatsoever.

b. Report the Injury Within 30 Days

Second, once you have designated a physician, don't delay in reporting the injury to your employer. The Labor Code requires you to report a work injury to your employer within 30 days of the date of the injury. If you fail to report the injury on time, your employer might try to argue that your workers' compensation claim is barred by the statute of limitations.

How do you determine the date of your injury when the damage may have occurred over a long period of time? Good question. The law says that the date of a continuous trauma disorder is the date that the employee first suffered disability and knew or "should have known" that the disability was caused by work.

Let's break this down one part at a time. You first suffer disability when you take time off of work because of the problem (even one sick day) or go to a doctor for the problem. When you knew or should have known that the disability was caused by your job is when you have reason to believe your pain or other symptoms are caused by activities you do at work. This can be:

- when you go to a doctor and tell the doctor you believe you injured yourself doing your job, or
- when you go to a doctor and the doctor tells you your injury is probably work-related.

What this means for practical purposes is that once you have taken time off work or seen a doctor for the problem, you should report the injury to your employer within 30 days. If you haven't seen a doctor or taken time off work for the problem, you should report your injury when it becomes clear to you that your symptoms are being caused by your job.

There is one exception to the rule that you must report your injury to your employer within 30 days of the date of injury: If you failed to officially report the injury to your employer within 30 days, you may still file a workers' compensation claim if your employer had knowledge of the injury from some other source. Perhaps you mentioned to a supervisor that you were having pains during work, or a coemployee told a manager that you were complaining of pain.

Follow the instructions in Chapter 5 to report your injury and file a workers' compensation claim.

CAUTION

Be careful what you say! Once you file a CTD claim, you may be interviewed by an investigator or the insurance company adjuster. You will be asked when you first believed your symptoms were caused by your work. Make sure your answer is within the 30 days prior to the date you reported the injury to your employer. If you say that you knew six months before you finally reported the injury that your disability was caused by your work, you may have a problem.

3. The Insurance Company's Response

Within 14 days of your filing a claim, your employer's insurance company will send you written notice that it has received the claim. This initial letter will advise you whether the insurance company accepts, denies, or needs more time to investigate before accepting or denying your claim. If the insurance company states it needs more time, it then has 90 days to accept or deny your claim. If this happens to you, see Section C3, below, for information on getting medical treatment.

If the insurance company notifies you that it is investigating your claim (or even that it accepts your claim), it will probably ask you for a statement about how your injury occurred. You're best off sending in a written statement rather than giving your statement over the phone. An example of a written statement is shown below; see Chapter 7, Section E, for further guidance.

If the insurance company denies your claim, it won't pay for medical treatment or temporary disability benefits so that you can take time off work to recover from your injury. You'll need to get what's called a "medical-legal evaluation" to establish that your injury should be covered by workers' compensation.

Medical-legal evaluations are medical assessments to prove your case, not to provide medical treatment, and are performed by doctors approved by the workers' compensation system, called qualified medical evaluators (QMEs). See Chapter 10, Section C, for more information on medical-legal evaluations.

Sample Statement

1. Date of injury: 6/26/xx.
2. How injury happened: Repetitive keyboard activities on the computer.
3. Parts of body injured: Bilateral upper extremities.
4. Reporting the injury: I told my supervisor, Mary Akins, I was having pain in both wrists when I worked on my computer. She had me fill out a company injury report.
5. Medical treatment: Mary Akins sent me to the Industrial Medical Clinic at 1444 W. Main St. in Los Angeles. I was examined and told to take time off work for two weeks. I was also given a prescription for ibuprofen, 800 mg.

If a QME files a medical-legal report that says the insurance company should compensate you for your injury, the insurance company should begin providing you benefits. If it doesn't, you have one year from the date of injury to file an Application for Adjudication of Claim with the Workers' Compensation Appeal Board. See Chapter 5, Section C, for instructions on how to file this application.

SEE AN EXPERT

If your claim is denied, see a lawyer. A claim that has been denied by the insurance company, whether it is about a specific injury or a CTD, usually requires legal assistance.

C. Diagnosis and Treatment

When you have a CTD, you may be treated by a doctor for six months to a year or longer. As with any work-related injury, the fate of your case will be in the hands of your treating doctor, so it's important to find one who understands your problem and has experience in dealing with your specific CTD.

1. Diagnosis of Your Injury

The diagnosis of cumulative trauma injuries can be difficult because by definition the injury usually involves soft tissue, not broken bones, and because most doctors have become familiar with these injuries only in recent years, if at all.

The types of injuries caused by cumulative trauma usually can't be validated by objective testing such as X-rays. This can make it both harder for the doctor to diagnose your injury and easier for a company doctor to report that you did not sustain a true injury.

Sometimes the primary—and oftentimes only—evidence of injury is the pain and other symptoms that you feel. This is particularly true with injuries such as back strain from prolonged sitting or standing, a stiff or painful neck from staring at a computer monitor, or pain in one or both wrists from using a computer keyboard for extended periods of time. This lack of objective evidence can make it difficult to convince some doctors and insurance companies that you really are injured.

The laws passed in 2004 require the diagnosis and treatment of your injury to be based upon the Occupational Medicine Practice Guidelines, published by the American College of Occupational and Environmental Medicine (ACOEM). These guidelines may make it more difficult to prove a continuous trauma injury because the guidelines require scientific, verifiable tests to establish your injury.

2. Objective and Subjective Evidence of Your Injury

There are a few ways a doctor can try to document an injury objectively, but they are far from perfect. Currently, the best source of objective testing for soft tissue injuries are magnetic resonance imaging (MRI) and nerve conduction studies (NCS), but these tests often come out negative even in patients with valid injuries. Again, many cases involve injuries that can't be verified by any type of objective test, even though the pain is no less debilitating.

As a result, it is extremely important that you tell each and every doctor exactly what you are experiencing. Here is a short list of the things you should discuss with any doctor you see for your injury.

- For each part of your body that hurts, tell the doctor exactly where the pain is.
- Tell the doctor about the type of pain you have. Is it a dull or sharp pain? Is it a shooting type of pain or an aching type of pain?
- Tell the doctor the frequency of the pain. Is it constant, frequent, intermittent, or just occasional?
- Tell the doctor about the severity of the pain. On a scale of 1 to 10, with 1 being minimal and 10 being unbearable, give the doctor your best estimate of each type of pain you are experiencing. Most doctors are familiar with this pain scale.
- Maintain a pain diary. A few sample diary entries are shown below; see Chapter 6, Section C10, for more information on how to keep a pain diary.

Sample Pain Diary

Saturday, 6/26/xx. Doctor Jones took me off work yesterday for two weeks. He prescribed ibuprofen, 800 mg, twice a day. Pain seems a little less today with medication. My left wrist is a 4 on a scale of 10, but is a constant dull ache. Right wrist is a little worse—maybe 6 on a scale of 10. Pain in right wrist seems to shoot up into elbow area.

Tuesday, 7/1/xx. Doctor returned me to work today on a trial basis with a limitation of no repetitive keyboard activity. My employer had me on the computer for an hour straight today. My wrists started hurting again after typing. Tonight I notice a definite increase in pain. Before work today, my pain was probably 3 on scale of 10. Tonight it's a 6 on scale of 10. I am calling the doctor tomorrow a.m. to advise and will also tell my supervisor.

Again, because CTDs often can't be documented by objective tests, the doctor may rely heavily on your subjective complaints to make a diagnosis and treatment recommendations. This can affect whether your claim is accepted by the insurance company and whether you are provided with temporary disability payments for time off work. And later on, the amount of your permanent disability may be rated according to how the doctor records your symptoms, which will dictate the amount of monetary benefits you'll receive. Therefore, it's critical that the doctor believes what you say.

You should never exaggerate your symptoms, and, at all times, you should be truthful and cooperative with the doctor. Doctors have furtive methods of determining whether you are actually experiencing pain or loss of mobility. For instance, a doctor may do several tests that test the same thing. If you have different results in two tests that should have the same result, the doctor may decide that you are not being truthful. Company doctors and qualified medical examiners in particular are constantly observing your movements and actions, looking for inconsistencies in your story. They are also trained to notice your attire and your attitude and will note it for the record. But as long as you are truthful and do not exaggerate, you shouldn't have any problems.

3. Seeking Medical Treatment If Your Claim Is Denied or Delayed

Early and aggressive treatment of cumulative trauma injuries is critical to stopping the injury from getting worse. Unfortunately, treatment can be delayed if a CTD claim is denied by the insurance company.

If the insurance company denies your claims, you won't be allowed to see a doctor through workers' compensation. But you should immediately seek treatment through your group medical insurance carrier if you have one.

If the insurance company puts off a decision on your claim for 90 days (discussed in Section B3, above), you should be able to see a doctor through workers' compensation during this time. The insurance company (or your employer) is required to authorize and agree to pay for your medical treatment until the insurance company (or your employer) either accepts or denies your claim. The insurance company must authorize the treatment within one day of your filing the DWC-1 claim form, but it is liable only for $10,000 in medical treatment until it accepts or denies your claim. (LC § 5402(c).)

4. Treatment of Your Injury

Early treatment of CTDs focuses on diminishing your pain, controlling any inflammation, and reducing activity levels. Actual treatment may include taking time off work, taking prescribed anti-inflammatory medications, and participating in physical therapy, which can include applying superficial heat or cold, ultrasound, splinting, bracing, and massage. As a last resort, surgery may be indicated for certain CTDs, such as carpal tunnel syndrome. For other CTDs, such as ulnar nerve compression, surgery is rarely helpful or recommended.

Obtaining a good treating physician is important in all cases of CTDs because early, aggressive treatment can oftentimes prevent further injury. Treatment of CTDs requires specialized knowledge and understanding of the underlying causes of the problem. Almost all doctors will say that they can treat the problem, but only a few really have the specific training and patience to treat these injuries (CTDs often take longer to treat than specific injuries).

You should seek out a doctor who specializes in the diagnosis and treatment of continuous trauma disorders, and in your type of injury in particular. For example, a particular doctor may have developed a reputation for successfully treating pianists with repetitive strain injuries.

In my opinion, you don't want to start off with a surgeon—surgery should be a last resort. A surgeon may often offer you a surgical alternative right off the bat, and, if you decline, many surgeons won't be able (or willing) to offer much in the way of alternative treatment.

For information on choosing or changing doctors, see Chapter 9, Sections B and D.

a. Physiatrists

I would recommend finding a doctor who specializes in "physical medicine and rehabilitation," otherwise known as a physiatrist. Physiatrists are often sports medicine doctors, but increasingly they are being called upon to treat work-related repetitive stress injuries. These doctors treat acute and chronic pain and musculoskeletal disorders, and they focus on restoring as much function to the patient as possible, similar to what occupational and physical therapists do.

Physiatrists are accustomed to injuries that can take a long time to heal and they are not averse to referring patients out for nontraditional treatments, such as acupuncture. If your physiatrist can't "cure" you, he or she can always recommend you for a surgical consultation, but will do so only after all possible conservative avenues have been explored.

The American Academy of Physical Medicine and Rehabilitation is the best place to start in finding a good physiatrist (go to www.e-aapmr.org/imis/imisonline/findphys/find.cfm).

b. Support Groups

You might also consider contacting other people who have gone through what you are going through now. There are many groups of people that get together either in person or on the Internet to discuss their injuries and treatment. To find a website or online group that focuses on your type of injury, use a search engine such as Google or try Yahoo Groups at http://groups.yahoo.com.

5. Temporary Disability

When or for how long a doctor takes you off work (puts you on "temporary total disability") for a CTD is not as clear-cut as for a specific injury like a fractured ankle or a hernia. Most doctors will rely heavily on what you tell them in deciding whether or not you need some time off work.

If your doctor has not taken you off work and you believe that your symptoms are not getting any better or are getting worse, tell your doctor. Do not be afraid to ask whether some time off work might help you recover faster. Your doctor may take you off work for a week or two initially and extend that to a month or more depending on your progress. In Chapter 12, we discuss temporary disability in detail.

D. Recovery and Permanent Injuries

It's not unlikely that you'll be left with some degree of permanent disability after you recover, even if your injury was not severe. Having a permanent partial disability for workers' compensation purposes doesn't mean you'd qualify for a disabled parking permit (though you might). It simply means that, once you have recovered (become "permanent and stationary" in workers' comp lingo), you may be left with a physical restriction, such as no heavy lifting, that prevents you from taking certain types of jobs.

1. Permanent and Stationary Status

Once your treating doctor has determined that your medical condition will not improve substantially with further medical treatment, he or she will declare you to be "permanent and stationary" (P&S), or state that you have reached "maximal medical improvement" (MMI), meaning that your condition is unlikely to improve or worsen in the next year. At this point, you will be released from further treatment and your temporary disability payments will stop, even if you have not yet returned to work.

The doctor will write a final report (often called the permanent and stationary report, or P&S report). The report will list what restrictions you should follow to avoid worsening your condition, the type of future medical treatment you might need for flare-ups or if your condition disintegrates, and your factors of permanent disability, if any.

If you have suffered permanent disability as a result of your injury, the doctor's P&S report will then be used to determine the percentage of disability you have suffered (called "rating" your disability, which is discussed in Section 2, below).

Oftentimes, a treating doctor may release you from medical treatment (declare you to be P&S) before you think you are ready. Especially if you have been recovering for a long period of time, the doctor may feel pressured by the insurance company to declare you P&S even if he or she thinks you may get better with more therapy and even more time off work. If this happens to you, and you don't think you can handle returning to work, don't be afraid to tell the doctor that you don't think you are ready to go back to work. Be prepared to be specific as to why you don't think you can resume working (for example, you still can't do any lifting or you still have significant pain when typing) and why you think further medical treatment could help.

Do not be discouraged if you disagree with the doctor and the doctor releases you from treatment anyway. Remember that a declaration that you are P&S or MMI does not mean that you have no permanent disabilities or that you should necessarily go back to work. It just means that the doctor does not think your condition will change substantially over the next year; it also means that your temporary disability payments will stop. For a complete discussion of permanent and stationary status, please refer to Chapter 9, Section E.

If your condition gets worse after the doctor has declared you P&S or MMI, you can always return to your doctor for a reevaluation. However, if you follow your doctor's orders, it is likely that your condition may continue to get better over time, even after you are released from treatment.

If the doctor doesn't think you can go back to doing your former work activities, you may be returned to work with restrictions such as no heavy lifting or no working on the computer for more than three hours per day. Alternatively, if the doctor decides you can't return to your former job at all, you may be entitled to vocational rehabilitation benefits or a job displacement benefit, which will help you retrain for other employment. See Section E, below, for a discussion of returning to the workforce.

2. Permanent Disability

Unless you have recovered 100%, your treating doctor's final (P&S) report will probably indicate that you have some permanent disability from your injury. In that case, the insurance company may ask the workers' compensation Disability Evaluation Unit (DEU) to rate your disability. This means that the DEU will review the doctor's report and assign a percentage, such as 25%, to your permanent disability. The insurance company will send you a letter stating the amount of permanent disability benefits it believes is payable, and it may even propose a settlement at that time.

If you disagree with your disability rating, you may request an "advisory rating" from the administrative director of the workers' compensation system. See Chapter 18, Section A2, for how to do this. In this case, it helps to understand how the rating system works.

If you were injured in 2005 or later, your permanent disability will be determined by using the "new" rating schedule, and must be based on doctors' reports that rely solely on objective medical conditions to rate disabilities rather than on work restrictions and subjective complaints. The new rating schedule may make it more difficult for workers with repetitive stress injuries to prove their inability to do certain kinds of work. (The new schedule may also apply in a few situations even if you were injured earlier than 2005—for more information, see Chapter 18, Section B1.)

For injuries that occurred in 2004 and earlier, ratings for CTDs are largely based on the work restrictions the doctor sets out in the P&S report, as well as your subjective complaints, rather than on objective tests. Rating a continuous trauma disability follows the same rules as a specific injury, such as a ruptured spinal disc from falling off a ladder. This is because the rating manual uses the same percentages for work restrictions and subjective complaints, regardless of whether the injury was specific or cumulative.

Common work restrictions for an upper extremity disability, such as carpal tunnel syndrome, might include no repetitive gripping and grasping, no heavy lifting, and no forceful pushing and pulling—very similar to restrictions for a rotator cuff injury or ruptured disc, for example. As a result, if your injury was in 2004 or earlier, you can use the same general information in Chapter 18, Section E, to estimate your permanent disability, and the information in Chapters 19 and 20 to negotiate a settlement in your case.

3. Following Through

Even if you receive a low permanent disability percentage, say 3%, because your physical restriction is not that limiting, for example "no repetitive squatting or kneeling," make sure you follow through on your permanent disability benefits to get the compensation you deserve.

Especially if your doctor gives you onerous physical restrictions, such as "no computer use," make sure you either understand enough about rating permanent disabilities to negotiate a fair settlement or hire a lawyer. Any disability percentage over 25% could bring you a significant amount of money.

E. Returning to the Workforce

After you have finished with your medical treatment (your doctor has said you are permanent and stationary, or that you have reached maximal medical improvement), you should receive a letter from the insurance company telling you:

- whether you should go back to work
- whether you may have a permanent disability, and

- whether you qualify for supplemental job displacement benefits.

If the doctor's report states that you are well enough to return to your old job, the insurance company may direct you to go back to work. In this case, the doctor's report may contain restrictions on the type of work you can do—permanent limitations that you should observe that are the result of your cumulative trauma disorder.

Of course, your doctor may not want you to return to your previous job once your condition becomes permanent and stationary, or reached maximum medical improvement. Because CTDs result from doing a particular job activity over and over, it is common sense that returning to a job doing the exact same thing is likely to result in further injury. In that case, the insurance company will work with your employer to determine whether modified or alternative work is available.

If you were injured in 2005 or later (or if your permanent disability will be determined by using the new rating schedule for another reason—see Chapter 18, Section B1), note that whether the company offers modified and alternative work, and whether you accept it, may affect your permanent disability award. A refusal to accept an offer of modified work could result in a 15% decrease in your permanent disability award! (For more information, see Chapter 13, Section E3.)

Considering whether to take a modified or alternative job is also your first step in getting job displacement benefits.

1. Supplemental Job Displacement Benefit

For injuries that occurred in the year 2004 and later, you may be entitled to a "supplemental job displacement benefit" if you have sustained some permanent disability and if you do not return to work for your employer (the employer you were working for when you were injured) within 60 days of your last temporary disability payment. This benefit consists of vouchers for education-related costs.

Specifically, you will be eligible for this benefit only if your employer did not offer you:

- modified work that lasts at least 12 months, or
- alternative work that you are able to perform and that lasts at least 12 months, pays within 15% of preinjury earnings, and is within a reasonable distance of where you lived at the time of injury.

Please refer to Chapter 14 for a complete discussion on the supplemental job displacement benefit.

2. Preventing Reinjury

Again, when you return to work, it should be to a job that fits within your new physical limitations. Your doctor's P&S report should list all of the preventive restrictions (probably called "prophylactic" restrictions in the report) that the doctor recommends. For example, restrictions for bilateral (both arms) carpal tunnel syndrome might prohibit you from doing work that requires repetitive gripping and grasping. In other words, the doctor is saying that if you return to any type of work that requires repetitive gripping and grasping activities, you are likely to cause further injury to your wrists.

Other work restrictions for someone who suffers a computer-related injury might include:

- no prolonged sitting
- no prolonged fixed positioning of the neck
- a time limitation on computer use
- a weight limitation on lifting and carrying, and
- a weight limitation on overhead reaching.

If you return to your previous job, make certain that your employer receives a copy of the doctor's restrictions before you go back to work and make sure the employer abides by them. Don't feel bad about declining to do certain work that your doctor has recommended against. If your employer has provided you with modified or alternative work, you can't legally be fired for refusing to do work that your doctor says you can't do.

In addition, you should provide your treating physician with a detailed and accurate description of your job duties so the doctor can make appropriate recommendations for changes to be made to your work environment to prevent further injury.

If your injury is caused by repetitive use or overuse of a computer, an ergonomic evaluation of your workstation is critical in preventing injury reoccurrence upon your return to work. Necessary and appropriate modifications to your workstation, taking into consideration your height, weight, and body build, are mandatory if you are to return to the same type of work.

If you go to work for a new employer, make sure that your employer is aware of your work restrictions. Employers are required to make a reasonable accommodation for your disability under the federal Americans with Disabilities Act (ADA) and California's Fair Employment Housing Act (FEHA). Generally speaking, if you have a disability, a new or former employer must make a reasonable effort to change the duties of your job so that you can do the "essential functions of the job."

> **EXAMPLE:** Your doctor has given you a permanent work restriction of "no lifting objects weighing more than 50 lbs." You find a new job as a receptionist at a doctor's office. The "essential functions" of the job are greeting patients, answering the telephone, and scheduling appointments with the doctor. However, every Friday the doctor's office gets a delivery of supplies, which you would normally be required to unload from the truck and carry into the office. Some of the boxes of supplies weigh more than 50 lbs. If it's reasonable for the employer to accommodate you so that you can avoid having to lift the supplies (for example, by having someone else help you or providing for a dolly to roll the supplies), then you can't be refused employment or terminated because of your work restriction.

SEE AN EXPERT

Disability discrimination is a complicated area. If you suspect that an employer is not being fair with you, failed to hire you, or terminated you because of your disability, you should contact an attorney who specializes in this area.

3. Reinjuring Yourself

If you return to work, whether with the same employer or a new one, and you reinjure yourself, your options regarding medical treatment and compensation depend on whether you have suffered a new injury or simply an exacerbation of your original injury. This determination is up to your doctor.

a. New Injury

If your doctor concludes your new pain is a new injury, you should file a new workers' compensation claim against your current employer so that you will receive medical treatment and time off work if you need it.

> **EXAMPLE:** In the year 2010, Mary Sater is diagnosed and treated for bilateral carpal tunnel syndrome due to computer activities that required her to enter data by way of a keyboard. After Mary is released by her treating doctor, she returns to work in 2011 in an alternative job as a receptionist. Her new job duties require her to answer the telephone and take messages. Her employer does not provide a headset, and she must cradle the phone between her neck and ear as she writes down messages. After six months, Mary again begins to experience pain in her wrists. She thinks that she has exacerbated her original carpal tunnel syndrome from writing, so she returns to her doctor. However, after doing an MRI of her neck, the doctor determines that Mary is experiencing pain in her wrists due to an injury to her neck resulting from constantly holding

her neck in a crooked position while taking messages on the phone. This is a new injury, and she should file a new claim against her current employer.

b. Exacerbation of a Previous Injury

If your doctor concludes your new pain is a worsening of your original injury, and you have not yet settled your case, you're in luck. You can simply continue to be treated by your doctor until you are once again declared to be permanent and stationary and the doctor writes a final report setting forth your increased factors of disability.

If your doctor concludes your pain is a worsening of your original injury and you have settled your case, by stipulations with request for award (see Chapter 19, Section B1), the insurance company will pay for the medical treatment you need. In addition, you may be entitled to receive more permanent disability payments. If your case is not more than five years old from the date of injury, you may file a petition to reopen your case for new and further disability (see Chapter 19, Section B1c) so that your disability may be rerated. However, if it has been more than five years from the date of your injury, you can't reopen your case for new and further disability. (Again, however, you can at least go to a doctor for treatment of the original injury, and the insurance company will pay for it.)

If your doctor concludes your pain is a worsening of your original injury and you have settled your claim by compromise and release (see Chapter 19, Section B), you may be out of luck. The only way you can get workers' compensation benefits in this case is to file a new workers' compensation claim, and you can do this only if you can show that at least 1% of your current disability is due to your current employment (see the discussion of apportionment in Section 4, below), and not to your prior injury.

If you try this route and your employer denies your claim because a doctor says your problems are due 100% to a prior injury that was settled by compromise and release, you should get an attorney. You will have to treat this like any other denied claim and proceed to develop medical evidence that your injury is at least partly due to your current employment. (See Chapter 10 on medical-legal evaluations.)

4. Apportionment

Apportionment—when an employer says another company is wholly or partly responsible for paying for your disability—is often an issue in continuous trauma disabilities. That is because if you have a subsequent reinjury at a new job, it is very likely that at least part of your current medical disability is due to your prior injury.

> **EXAMPLE:** While working for a software company as a computer programmer, Sherri experiences pain in her elbows, wrists, and trapezius muscles. Her doctor diagnoses her with ulnar nerve neuropathy and takes her off work for several months. A year later, Sherri is hired by a different employer. While the employer is aware of her past disability, Sherri and the employer do not anticipate a problem because Sherri will be doing light computer and office work rather than computer programming. Unfortunately, Sherri does develop repetitive strain problems; this time her injury presents itself as carpal tunnel syndrome in her wrists. Her doctor concludes that 20% of her disability is due to her new employment, and 80% is due to her previous injury.

If you have a subsequent injury that is apportioned, you may receive fewer permanent disability benefits from your current employer because you were presumably compensated for your previous injury by your previous employer. To avoid having a new injury apportioned, you must have rehabilitated yourself completely so that you have no remaining disability at the time of the reinjury.

Note that if you have received a prior award of permanent disability from the workers' comp system, the doctor must find that your prior permanent disability still exists at the time of your current work injury, whether or not you have actually recovered. (LC § 4664(b).) Please refer to Chapter 18, Section D1, for a complete discussion of apportionment.

RELATED TOPIC

If you are returning to work, please read Chapter 8, Section D, for more information on communicating well with your employer and keeping your job.

F. Further Medical Treatment

After your doctor has released you from medical treatment and you have settled your claim and returned to work, you may need to seek medical treatment from time to time to treat flare-ups of your cumulative trauma disorder. Whether you can be treated by a doctor authorized by the workers' compensation insurance company or go to your own group medical insurance for treatment depends on several factors.

If you settled your case by stipulations with request for award or were awarded future medical treatment in a findings and award (see Chapter 19), you have the right to be treated by a doctor of your choice and have the workers' compensation insurance company pay for it.

If you settled your case by compromise and release (see Chapter 19), you gave up your right to have your future medical treatment paid for by the workers' compensation insurance company. You will therefore have no choice but to go to your group insurance carrier for treatment. Whether or not your group insurance carrier will agree to pay for this treatment depends upon the insurance company's policy regarding preexisting medical conditions. Many group insurance carriers will treat preexisting conditions; some will cover treatment only if you have gone treatment-free for a period of time (usually six months).

Oftentimes what you tell (or don't tell) your group insurance carrier will determine whether or not it will authorize treatment for your cumulative trauma injury. If you point out to the doctor that you are seeking treatment for a prior work injury, you will cause "red flags" to appear and you may have problems getting authorization for treatment. If you simply go in for treatment "because my wrists have been hurting lately," you'll be less likely to experience problems in getting treatment. Of course, if you are specifically asked whether you injured your wrists at work, you must be truthful and say so. But if there is some activity that you recently did that you believe "lit up" your work injury (such as gardening), be sure to tell the doctor. That may be reason enough to allow the doctor to treat you through your group insurance.

Part II

Protecting Your Rights

CHAPTER

5

What to Do If You're Injured

This chapter explains the four most important things you need to do if you are injured on the job:

- Request medical treatment. (See Section A.)
- Promptly report your injury. (See Section B.)
- File a workers' compensation claim, which means filling in and filing two documents: a DWC-1 form and an Application for Adjudication Claim. (See Section C.)
- Take appropriate steps to protect your workers' compensation rights. (See Section E.)

Right at the beginning, one important point cannot be overemphasized: *From the moment you file your claim, you should begin preparing your case as if it were going to result in a contested trial.* This is true even though most cases settle and never actually go to trial—despite the likelihood of settlement, if you wait until you know whether settlement is actually possible, you won't have time to gather and organize your evidence in time for a trial. So be organized and thorough right from the beginning—it could save you a lot of work at the back end.

A. Request Medical Treatment

If you're injured in the course of your employment, it's important to seek prompt and appropriate medical treatment. Whether you get first aid on the job, are rushed to the emergency room, see your family doctor after work, or report to a company doctor, you should always see that you get the treatment you need as soon as you can. You won't gain a thing by being stoic and delaying treatment.

1. Which Doctor Will Treat You

A fundamental principle of this book is that it is always best to get treatment by a doctor of your own choice. For starters, you are likely to get better medical care from someone you know and trust. In addition, the doctor who provides your medical treatment may be influential in determining whether you're entitled to workers' compensation benefits and how much you'll receive. It's even fair to say that whoever has control of your medical treatment (called the "treating doctor") has control of your case.

Because being treated by a doctor who is picked by your employer may affect your treatment, I recommend that you designate your doctor *now*, whether you have already been injured or not. Once your written notification is on file, it will allow you to see that doctor should you ever suffer any work injury in the future. (See Chapter 9, Section B1, for a step-by-step explanation of how to designate your doctor.)

With the exception of treatment you receive on an emergency basis, if you fail to "predesignate" your doctor (and your claim has been accepted by the insurance company), your employer has the legal right to decide what doctor you see for the first 30, 90, 180, or 365 days after you are injured. (The number of days depends upon the facts of your case; refer to Chapter 9, Section D.) Although not all employers will insist on exercising this right, if yours does, you must see your employer's chosen doctor.

For injuries that occur in 2005 or later, your employer is allowed to set up a "medical provider network" from which you must choose a doctor when you need treatment for a work-related injury. (LC § 4616.) If your employer has set up a provider network, you cannot see a doctor of your own choosing unless you have predesignated your primary physician as your doctor. You must go to a doctor within the medical provider network. For information on switching doctors when your employer has set up a medical provider network, see Chapter 9, Section D2.

2. How to Get Medical Care

These are the steps to take if you are injured on the job:

- **Emergencies.** If your injury is life-threatening or requires immediate emergency attention, call an ambulance or get to the nearest emergency room. Under these circumstances, your employer has no immediate control over what doctor you see for treatment, even if you have not filed a written request asking for a specific doctor in advance. Your employer (or its workers' compensation insurance company) is required to pay for emergency medical treatment.

- **Nonemergency injuries.** If your injury does not require immediate medical attention, notify your supervisor or employer and request medical treatment. It's a good idea to ask someone to accompany you when you make this request. It may be necessary later to have a witness who can verify that you notified your employer of your injury and requested medical attention.

    If you previously designated your personal physician, simply tell your employer that you will see this doctor. Otherwise, your employer may choose which doctor you'll see for treatment. If your employer does not specify a doctor or is unavailable to authorize medical treatment, you may arrange for it yourself.

Medical Care Is Covered in Chapter 9

This chapter gives only a brief overview of how to handle your medical care. Please refer to Chapter 9 for an in-depth discussion of your medical treatment, including:

- the role of the treating doctor
- when and how you may change treating doctors
- what to do if your employer or its insurance company won't authorize medical treatment, and
- what to say to the doctor to best preserve your legal rights.

B. Report the Injury Within 30 Days

An employer is not responsible for providing any workers' compensation benefits until it has notice of your job-related injury. It's up to you to provide this notice in writing within 30 days from the date of the injury. (LC § 5400.) Filing the workers' compensation DWC-1 form gives the proper notice to your employer. (See Section C, below.)

1. When to Report Slow-Developing Injuries

It may be months or even years after an injury first starts developing—or after you first feel mild discomfort—before you realize the link between your pain and your job. Injuries that occur over a period of weeks, months, or even years are usually known as continuous trauma or cumulative trauma injuries. These injuries are usually the result of:

- continuously doing an activity that causes wear and tear on your body over a period of time—such as constant bending and stooping activities or repetitive hand movements, or
- being subjected to working conditions that cause you to gradually become ill—for example, when you have an allergic reaction to workplace toxins.

Many of these types of injuries occur in occupations requiring continuous heavy lifting activities, data entry, computer use, or being present in an atmosphere containing dust, smoke, chemical fumes, or other airborne or waterborne hazards.

As a practical matter, you should report the injury as soon as you feel your symptoms are job-related or are told the injury is job-related. By law, you must report the injury within 30 days from the date you first suffered disability (lost time from work or got medical treatment) and knew, or reasonably should have known, that the disability was caused by your job. (LC § 5412.) See Chapter 4, Section B2, for more information.

2. How to Report Your Injury

At your first opportunity, report your injury to someone in a position of authority. This may be your foreman or forewoman, your supervisor, or perhaps the owner of your company. If you have a union, you should also report the injury to your union steward or business agent. If yours is a medical emergency, get treatment first and report the injury promptly when things calm down.

If your company has a standard form for reporting injuries, make certain that you either personally fill out the form or at least check it very carefully for accuracy. You may also use the workers' compensation DWC-1 form as your formal written notice of injury. (Instructions for completing this form are in Section C2, below.)

If you'll be out of work for a while, call your boss or send a note and keep a copy. As a practical matter, you should give written notice, even if your employer was told about the injury. Should your employer later deny that you gave notice, it is much easier to produce a copy of a written notice than to call witnesses to testify that you called the employer. You may give a note to your employer or send it by certified mail, return-receipt requested. The note should be dated and specify:

- the date of injury
- the parts of the body injured
- where the injury occurred, and
- how the injury occurred.

Once your injury has been reported, your employer will likely want to document and review what happened. It's your responsibility to see that you get copies of any documents your employer fills out.

Sample

To: G & H Technologies

I, Jamie Gordon, wish to inform you that I injured my right leg on 3/3/xx at 9:30 a.m. I was hit from behind by a forklift driven by David Letz. The injury occurred in the main warehouse at G & H Technologies.

________ ________________

Date Signature of employee

I, (supervisor's name), acknowledge report of such injury.

________ ________________

Date Signature of supervisor

3. If You Don't Report the Injury on Time

RELEVANT CASE LAW

See *Reynolds v. WCAB*, in Chapter 28.

If you fail to give your employer written notice within 30 days of an injury, you may be barred from receiving workers' compensation benefits unless either of the following applies:

- You can show that your failure to give notice didn't "mislead or otherwise prejudice your employer." Stated differently, the employer must not be able to show that your delay harmed your employer's ability to dispute your claim of injury (LC § 5403).
- You can show that the employer knew about the injury. If the employer found out about the injury from any source, it is equivalent to written notice by the employee. (LC § 5402.) For instance, if you strain your back working for a small retail store and another employee tells the owner, that's adequate notice. Similarly, if you are a secretary for a law firm and occasionally complain to your supervisor that your wrists and lower arms hurt all the time, that's notice.

EXAMPLE 1: Mary is working alone and slips on some oil, causing her to twist her knee. Mary doesn't mention the injury to her employer. After more than 30 days, Mary's knee is still bothering her, and she tells her employer of the injury. Because the employer had no other way of knowing about the injury and more than 30 days have elapsed since the date of injury, Mary may be barred from receiving workers' compensation benefits.

EXAMPLE 2: While working on a forklift in the yard of his employer, Mark falls off and is knocked unconscious. Several employees witness the accident. One employee tells Mark's supervisor what happened, and the supervisor calls an ambulance. Mark is not required to give his employer written notice of the injury, because the employer has already been put on notice of the injury.

C. File Your Workers' Compensation Claim

Reporting an injury to your supervisor or boss simply informs your employer that you have been injured; it is not the same thing as filing a workers' compensation claim. You must also take care of the paperwork necessary to initiate a claim.

You must file two forms:

- a DWC-1 claim form, which you give to your employer, and
- an Application for Adjudication of Claim, which you file with the Workers' Compensation Appeals Board.

We cover how to complete these important forms later in this section. For now, let's look at the rules governing when you need to file them.

CAUTION

All forms are online. All forms can be found on the DWC website at www.dir.ca.gov/dwc. Once there, go to "Find a form," and then "EAMS OCR FORMS" and you will be given a complete list of forms. (All forms now must be from the EAMS (Electronic Adjudication Management System, so older versions of forms won't work.) You can either fill in the form you need online and print it, or you can use the forms we provide you in this book. Also, each form you file must be submitted with a "separator sheet" on top of the form and a "cover sheet." Downloadable copies of the cover sheet and separator sheet are available on Nolo's website. (See Chapter 29, "Online Appendixes" for the link to these and other forms in this book.)

1. When to File Your Claim

Your best bet is to file the DWC-1 form as soon as possible so that you can qualify for all benefits that you may be entitled to.

By law, you must file your workers' compensation claim within certain time limits or you won't be entitled to any benefits. The time limit within which to file a claim is known in legal language as the "statute of limitations." You must file a workers' compensation claim:

- **within one year from the date of injury** if the insurance company denied responsibility for your injury (for instance, sent you a letter denying your claim) or did not acknowledge your injury (neither responded nor provided any benefits)
- **within five years from the date of injury** if the insurance company provided benefits—for example, paid temporary disability or medical treatment, or
- **for death benefit claims, within one year from the date of death.** In addition, the death must have occurred within 240 weeks of the date of the injury. (See Chapter 15 for more on death benefits.)

To protect your rights, you should always file a claim for an injury requiring anything beyond minor first aid, even if you do not think the injury is serious. If there is any possibility that future complications could develop, file your claim! If you don't, you may lose your right to compensation. You'd be wise to file your workers' compensation claim within 30 days of your injury, if possible.

EXAMPLE: Julie slips at work and injures her back. She reports the injury to her supervisor, who gives Julie a DWC-1 form. Julie takes the day off, puts the form in the glove compartment of her car and returns to work the next day. Although Julie gets a letter from her employer stating that she may have a workers' compensation claim, she continues to work with the pain in her back, thinking that it will eventually go away. More than a year later, Julie sees her family doctor for a checkup. The doctor discovers that she has two slipped discs in her back that were likely caused by her injury at work the previous year. Julie digs out the DWC-1 claim form from her car and files it. She gets a letter from the workers' compensation insurance company denying her claim. Because Julie failed to file a claim within one year from the date of her injury, her claim is barred forever by the statute of limitations.

SEE AN EXPERT

If you didn't file a claim on time. If the insurance carrier denies your claim on the basis that the statute of limitations has run, get help from an information and assistance officer or an attorney. You may have another chance. For example, if your employer didn't give you written information that you may have a workers' compensation claim (a blank DWC-1 form would be sufficient), the statute of limitations does not begin to run until you learn of that right.

a. Statute of Limitations for Specific Injuries

If you were involved in an accident at work, the statute of limitations begins to run from the date of the injury or accident.

EXAMPLE: Fred falls at work on December 11, 2011 and breaks a leg. He has until December 11, 2012 to file his claim.

b. Statute of Limitations for Continuous Trauma Injuries

For continuous trauma injuries, including occupational diseases, the date of the injury is calculated from the date on which two conditions are met: First, the employee takes time off from work due to the injury or sees a doctor for the injury; and second, the employee knows (or should have known, as a reasonable person) that the disability was caused by work.

EXAMPLE 1: Stan misses work on and off for several months because of ill health. After a series of tests and doctor's visits, Stan's doctor tells him that he has toxins in his system due to exposure to cleaning chemicals at work. Stan's date of injury is the date the doctor told him that his injuries were work-related. Stan has one year from that date within which to file a claim.

EXAMPLE 2: Laura does data entry at a computer terminal all day long. She notices pain in her right wrist and sees her family doctor, who does some testing. Laura's doctor tells her that she has carpal tunnel syndrome, an injury involving the nerves in her wrist, which is caused by her constant typing at the computer terminal at work. Laura continues to work for another five months before finally telling her supervisor that she can't work anymore because of carpal tunnel syndrome and goes home. Laura's date of injury is the date that Laura first took off work. She has one year from that date within which to file a claim.

2. Complete and File a DWC-1 Form

The DWC-1 form (Workers' Compensation Claim Form) documents the date you were injured and provides details about the injury.

By law, your employer must give you the form and written information within one working day of finding out about an injury (from any source) if the injury results in:

- lost work time beyond the date of injury, or
- medical treatment beyond first aid—one-time treatment of minor injuries such as scratches, cuts, burns, or splinters. (CCR § 10119, LC § 5401.)

If your supervisor does not give you the form within 24 hours of your request, make a written request to higher management. If you still cannot get the form, a downloadable copy of DWC-1 is available on Nolo's website. (See Chapter 29, "Online Appendixes" for the link to this and other forms in this book.)

a. How to Fill In a DWC-1 Form

You must complete and file a separate DWC-1 form for each incident resulting in injury. If yours is a continuous trauma injury involving more than one employer, you'll have to prepare one form for each employer.

> **EXAMPLE 1:** Tom slips and falls on a greasy spot in the warehouse and injures his wrist and his knee. He need file only one DWC-1 form listing both injuries, since they both arose from the same incident.

> **EXAMPLE 2:** Martha injures her right shoulder lifting a heavy box off an overhead shelf at work on July 4. She goes to a doctor who says that while she did injure her shoulder lifting the box on July 4, her shoulder also has a cumulative trauma injury stemming from the warehouse work she is currently doing for two different employers. Martha files three DWC-1 forms: one for the specific injury of July 4 at Job A, one for a continuous trauma injury (for the previous one-year period) at Job A, and one for a continuous trauma injury (for the previous one-year period) at Job B.

The DWC-1 claim form has two parts to it: an upper part, which you complete as the employee, and a lower part, which your employer fills in. If you get the DWC-1 form from your employer, it will probably be a carbon form in quadruplicate; however, you may use a single form and make copies. Either fill in the form using a typewriter or neatly handwrite the information with a pen. Here's how to fill it in; see the sample below.

1. Name and today's date. Provide your full name. If you go by a nickname or use another name at work (some women use a premarriage name, for example), provide that as well—for example, "Richard (Skip) Whitmore" or "Susan Davis, AKA Susan Smith." ("AKA" stands for "also known as.") Also fill in today's date.

2-3. Home address. Fill in your home address, including the city, state, and zip code.

4. Date and time of injury. The date you were injured controls important rules about your case, such as how long you have to file a workers' compensation claim and what benefits you may receive.

If your injury resulted from a specific incident, such as an accident at work, simply fill in the date and time it happened and proceed to the instructions for Item 5 on the form.

If yours is a cumulative injury, the date of injury can be a little less obvious, and you'll need to carefully read the rest of this discussion. The date of injury for these types of injuries should be set out as a period of time, rather than one specific date—for example, September 20, 2011 to September 20, 2012. To determine the continuous trauma period, you first need to determine the ending date of the continuous trauma and then go back up to a *maximum of one year.* The ending date is the date you first suffered disability as a result of your injury—meaning you took off work due to your injury—*and* knew, or should have known, that your disability was caused by your present or prior employment. (LC § 5412.)

The one-year limit for a continuous trauma period is purely a legal technicality to determine which insurance companies are responsible for your claim. Only the companies that insured your employer during the last year of your cumulative injury are responsible for paying benefits. Of course, the actual injury may have occurred over many years. When discussing your injury with doctors, the insurance company, or the workers' compensation judge, you should point out all periods that you believe contributed to your injury, not just the last year.

> **EXAMPLE 1:** Shawn works as a carpenter, building cabinets for new homes. He works with wood and spends a great deal of time sanding. He has worked in this capacity for the same employer for the past five years. On December 3, 2011, Shawn leaves work because he has difficulty breathing. After about ten days he returns to work but is scheduled for some tests the following month. On January 6, 2012, Shawn's doctor tells him that his lungs have been damaged from breathing sawdust particles at work. The ending date for the continuous trauma would be January 6, 2012, the date

Shawn lost time off from work *and* knew that his illness was due to his work. While it's likely that Shawn's exposure to dust over the five years of employment caused the injury, the continuous trauma period he lists in the DWC-1 form is for only one year: January 6, 2011 to January 6, 2012. Only insurance companies that insured Shawn's employer from January 6, 2008 to January 6, 2012 would be responsible for his claim.

EXAMPLE 2: Let's use the same fact situation as in Example 1, but let's assume that Shawn began working for his current employer on July 1, 2011 and, prior to that, worked for three years for another employer doing the same type of work. Shawn would have to file separate claims against each employer. The insurance carriers that insured Shawn's present employer from July 1, 2011 to January 6, 2012 would be responsible, as would be the insurance carrier or carriers that insured Shawn's prior employer from January 6, 2011 to July 1, 2011.

5. Address/place where injury happened. If the injury happened at work, list the work address. Otherwise, fill in the address or location of the injury. For example, if you were involved in an accident while driving a truck on company business, the location of the injury would be where the accident occurred, not your employer's address.

6. Describe the injury and part of body affected. Give a brief and clear statement about how the injury occurred. For example: "fell from platform," "repetitive lifting of heavy objects," or "repetitive keyboard and mouse use."

Make sure you list *all* of the body parts injured. Be as thorough as possible, even listing body parts that may not be seriously injured. If you even suspect you might have injured a certain part of your body, list it. If you fail to list a certain part of your body, the employer or its workers' compensation insurance company may later deny that an injury occurred to that body part.

For example, if you have pain in your right hand, wrist, elbow, and shoulder from typing, list all of them: "entire right arm and shoulder, including hand, wrist, and elbow." It doesn't matter if you use technical medical terms or not; "collar bone" is just as acceptable as "clavicle," for example. It is, however, better to use general terms rather than specific terms. For instance, if you injured your lower back, use the term "back" or "spine" instead of "lumbar region of back." If you limit yourself to "lumbar region of back" now, and later find out you really injured other parts of your back, the insurance company may try to deny your claim.

7. Social Security number. Insert your Social Security number here.

8. Signature of employee. Sign the form, using the name you listed in Item 1, above. Leave the rest of the form blank; your employer will complete it.

b. How to File a DWC-1 Form

To file a DWC-1 form, promptly give it to the employer you worked for when the injury happened. You may file the DWC-1 form by personally handing it to your employer, having someone else deliver it, or mailing it by certified mail with a return-receipt requested. Although you can send the form by regular mail, you could run into problems if the employer claims it didn't receive it or got it after the one-year filing deadline.

Within one working day of receipt of the claim form, your employer must complete the lower part of the DWC-1 form and send or give a dated copy both to you and its workers' compensation insurance company. (CCR § 10121.) The completed bottom part will contain the name and address of your employer's workers' compensation insurance carrier.

TIP

If you're running out of time to file. If the one-year (or five-year) statute of limitations is about to run out, you'll need to act quickly. Fill out and sign your half of the DWC-1 and keep a copy for your records. Give the original to your employer, or mail it certified mail,

State of California
Department of Industrial Relations
DIVISION OF WORKERS' COMPENSATION

Estado de California
Departamento de Relaciones Industriales
DIVISION DE COMPENSACIÓN AL TRABAJADOR

WORKERS' COMPENSATION CLAIM FORM (DWC 1)

PETITION DEL EMPLEADO PARA DE COMPENSACIÓN DEL TRABAJADOR (DWC 1)

Employee: Complete the **"Employee"** section and give the form to your employer. Keep a copy and mark it **"Employee's Temporary Receipt"** until you receive the signed and dated copy from your employer. You may call the Division of Workers' Compensation and hear recorded information at **(800) 736-7401**. An explanation of workers' compensation benefits is included as the cover sheet of this form.

You should also have received a pamphlet from your employer describing workers' compensation benefits and the procedures to obtain them.

Any person who makes or causes to be made any knowingly false or fraudulent material statement or material representation for the purpose of obtaining or denying workers' compensation benefits or payments is guilty of a felony.

Empleado: *Complete la sección **"Empleado"** y entregue la forma a su empleador. Quédese con la copia designada **"Recibo Temporal del Empleado"** hasta que Ud. reciba la copia firmada y fechada de su empleador. Ud. puede llamar a la Division de Compensación al Trabajador al **(800) 736-7401** para oir información gravada. En la hoja cubierta de esta forma esta la explicatión de los beneficios de compensación al trabajador.*

Ud. también debería haber recibido de su empleador un folleto describiendo los benficios de compensación al trabajador lesionado y los procedimientos para obtenerlos.

Toda aquella persona que a propósito haga o cause que se produzca cualquier declaración o representación material falsa o fraudulenta con el fin de obtener o negar beneficios o pagos de compensación a trabajadores lesionados es culpable de un crimen mayor "felonia".

Employee—complete this section and see note above ***Empleado—complete esta sección y note la notación arriba.***

1. Name. *Nombre.* Penelope Watson Today's Date. *Fecha de Hoy.* 4/4/xxxx
2. Home Address. *Dirección Residencial.* 720 Ninth Street
3. City. *Ciudad.* Sacramento State. *Estado.* CA Zip. *Código Postal.* 95814
4. Date of Injury. *Fecha de la lesión (accidente).* 3/2/xxxx Time of Injury. *Hora en que ocurrió.* 9:30 a.m. ______ p.m.
5. Address and description of where injury happened. *Dirección/lugar dónde occurió el accidente.* Andrews Construction, 8978 Elk Grove Road, Elk Grove, CA
6. Describe injury and part of body affected. *Describa la lesión y parte del cuerpo afectada.* Fell from elevated platform and injured my back, neck, and right leg.
7. Social Security Number. *Número de Seguro Social del Empleado.* 000-00-0000
8. Signature of employee. *Firma del empleado.* Penelope Watson

Employer—complete this section and see note below. ***Empleador—complete esta sección y note la notación abajo.***

9. Name of employer. *Nombre del empleador.* ______
10. Address. *Dirección.* ______
11. Date employer first knew of injury. *Fecha en que el empleador supo por primera vez de la lesión o accidente.* ______
12. Date claim form was provided to employee. *Fecha en que se le entregó al empleado la petición.* ______
13. Date employer received claim form. *Fecha en que el empleado devolvió la petición al empleador.* ______
14. Name and address of insurance carrier or adjusting agency. *Nombre y dirección de la compañía de seguros o agencia adminstradora de seguros.* ______
15. Insurance Policy Number. *El número de la póliza de Seguro.* ______
16. Signature of employer representative. *Firma del representante del empleador.* ______
17. Title. *Título.* ______ 18. Telephone. *Teléfono.* ______

Employer: You are required to date this form and provide copies to your insurer or claims administrator and to the employee, dependent or representative who filed the claim within **one working day** of receipt of the form from the employee.

SIGNING THIS FORM IS NOT AN ADMISSION OF LIABILITY

Empleador: *Se requiere que Ud. feche esta forma y que provéa copias a su compañía de seguros, administrador de reclamos, o dependiente/representante de reclamos y al empleado que hayan presentado esta petición dentro del plazo de **un día hábil** desde el momento de haber sido recibida la forma del empleado.*

EL FIRMAR ESTA FORMA NO SIGNIFICA ADMISION DE RESPONSABILIDAD

❑ Employer copy/*Copia del Empleador* ❑ Employee copy/ *Copia del Empleado* ❑ Claims Administrator/*Administrador de Reclamos* ❑ Temporary Receipt/*Recibo del Empleado*

6/10 Rev.

return-receipt requested. If your employer doesn't return a completed copy of the form prior to the end of the one- or five-year time period, the fact that you filed your part will protect your claim.

Uninsured Subcontractors: Who to File Against

If you were employed by a subcontractor (usually in the construction business) who does not have workers' compensation insurance, and there was a general contractor on the job, you automatically become the general contractor's employee for workers' compensation purposes. There is no point in filing a claim against a subcontractor who doesn't have workers' compensation coverage. Instead, file the claim with the general contractor and consider the general contractor your employer. If you aren't sure whether the subcontractor is covered, file against both.

c. If Your Employer Won't Complete a DWC-1 Form

Sometimes employers refuse to complete their part of a DWC-1 form because they don't want to tell their insurance company that a workers' compensation claim was filed. If this happens, you'll need to contact your employer's workers' compensation insurance company directly.

Employers are required to post the name of their insurance carrier or claims administrator on the premises. But if you can't readily find this information, check with an information and assistance officer. Or contact the Workers' Compensation Insurance Rating Bureau (WCIRB), which keeps current records of all employers' workers' compensation insurance companies. You need to send a written request, including the name of your employer, your date(s) of injury, and your return address. Include a check for $8 for each year you want to know about. (The telephone number and address for the WCIRB is provided in Chapter 1, Section C2.)

Sample

May 24, 20xx

Workers' Compensation Insurance Rating Bureau
525 Market Street
Suite 800
San Francisco, CA 94105

To Whom It May Concern:

Please provide me with the name and address of the workers' compensation insurance company for ACME Tools, 3333 West 4th Street, Anytown, CA 99999. The date of coverage needed is April 5, 20xx. Enclosed please find my check for $8.

Thank you,
Darlene Chan
Darlene Chan
555 North 7th Street
Anytown, CA 99999

Once you have the name and address of your employer's workers' compensation insurance company, send the original signed DWC-1 form to the insurance company. Remember to keep a copy for your records and send the form certified mail, return-receipt requested.

If you discover that your employer did not carry workers' compensation insurance, see Chapter 8, Section C1, for your options.

d. Amending a DWC-1 Form

If, after filing your DWC-1 form, you learn of new body parts you injured that you did not know of when you completed the form, you should change (amend) the DWC-1 form. Photocopy your original and mark the changes directly on the copy. (This way, you will have the original without the amendments, should you ever need it.)

Draw a line through any parts you want to change and write in the changes above the lined-through parts. Because you want to be able to see what changes you made on the form, do not "white out" anything. On the top of the form, in front of the word DWC-1, write "amended" (or, if you go through this process more than once, "2nd or 3rd amended," such as the case may be). Finally, deliver the amended DWC-1 to your employer as if it were the original.

If you amend the DWC-1 form, make sure you also amend your Application for Adjudication of Claim, if it also needs to be modified. We cover this below.

3. Complete an Application for Adjudication of Claim

You must also complete and file an Application for Adjudication of Claim form with the Workers' Compensation Appeals Board within the one-year or five-year deadline discussed in Section C1, above. You must file a separate application for each date of injury you are claiming. Let's take a step-by-step look at how to fill in the application, which is provided below and as a downloadable copy on Nolo's website. (See Chapter 29, "Online Appendixes" for the link to this and other forms in this book.)

FIND IT ONLINE

Forms are available online. After downloading them, you can either print them out and fill them out manually or complete them on your computer. The forms are located at www.dir.ca.gov/dwc/Forms.html. Click on the link for the Application for Adjudication form. You cannot save the form to your computer, so you must be prepared to complete it and print it in one sitting. It's a good idea to print a blank form and handwrite in the responses, then use that draft to prepare your final form. (They are also available on Nolo's website. See Chapter 29, "Online Appendixes" for the link to the forms in this book.)

TIP

Make sure that you fill out the form properly. The WCAB may reject your application if it can't read it. If you handwrite, print legibly in all capitals. If you type, use all capitals. The WCAB has gone to a paperless system, and will electronically scan your application—and any other documents you file—and then destroy it. Make sure everything you submit is legible, and keep copies of absolutely everything you submit.

The application consists of five pages with numbered paragraphs from 1 to 9. The first page and most of the second page of the form are not numbered. There, you enter the basic information about your case.

Case No. Enter your workers' compensation case number if you have one. This would apply only if you previously filed documents with the appeals board, which is unlikely. If a case number has not yet been assigned, leave it blank.

Amended Application: Put a check in this box only if this form is for the purpose of amending (changing) a prior application that you have filed.

Venue choice: Most likely, you will check the first box that says you are filing in the jurisdiction based upon where you live. Then insert the three-letter abbreviation for the Workers Compensation Appeals Board you are filing your application with. A list of the Boards and their abbreviations is available on Nolo's website (See Chapter 29, "Online Appendixes" for the link to Appendix 1: Workers' Compensation Offices and Code Lists.)

Injured Worker: Enter the injured worker's full first and last name and middle initial. Enter the injured worker's home address, city, state, and zip code.

Applicant (if other than Injured Worker). This section is only relevant if someone other than the injured worker or the worker's attorney or representative is completing the form—this could be the insurance carrier, employer, or a lien claimant if the injured worker has not filed a claim and the entity wants to get a hearing before the workers' compensation appeals board on some issue. You as the injured worker do not need to be concerned with this section.

Employer Information. Check the box that applies, depending on whether your employer is insured, self-insured, legally uninsured, or uninsured. If you do not know or are unsure, do not check any of the boxes. "Insured" means employer has workers' compensation insurance. Enter the employer's full name, address, and zip code. If the employer has a corporate headquarters, it is best to use that address even if it isn't where you work.

Insurance Carrier Information. Enter the name of your employer's workers' compensation insurance company. If the insurance company uses a claims administrator, include the insurance company information anyway. If your employer is self-insured or uninsured, leave this part blank. By now you should have this information from the DWC-1 form that was completed by your employer. (See Section C2c, above, if you don't know the name of your employer's insurance company.) Enter its street address, city, state, and zip code on the designated lines.

Claims Administrator Information. Sometimes an insurance company or self-insured employer may hire a company, called a claims administrator, to handle claims processing. You should have this information from the DWC-1 form that was completed by your employer. Enter the address of the adjusting agency here.

The rest of the form is numbered from 1 to 9 and deals with the specifics of your claim.

Paragraph 1. Enter your birth date in the space provided. Next, enter your occupational title. If you have more than one title or do more than one job, it's very important that you list them all.

Put a check in the box that applies to whether you are claiming a specific injury or a cumulative injury (see the discussion of types of injuries, in Chapters 3 and 4). Enter the date of the injury if appropriate.

Next enter the address, city, state, and zip code where the injury occurred.

On the next five lines, list the parts of your body that have been injured, and the corresponding number. The list of numbers related to body parts is available on Nolo's website. (See Chapter 29, "Online Appendixes" for the link to Appendix 1, "Workers' Compensation Office Addresses and Code Lists."). If you're completing the form on the computer, the numbers will appear in a drop-down menu). Be sure to include *all* the parts of body you are alleging as injured. Be specific. For example, write "low back" instead of just "back," or "right knee" instead of just "knee." This information should be the same as listed on the DWC-1 form that you filled out using the instructions Section C2a, above.

Paragraph 2. In the box next to the words "The injury occurred as follows," enter a short description of how the injury occurred. Simply describe as best as you can how you were hurt, such as "lifting cartons of milk," "struck by falling boxes," "tripped and fell," or "computer programming."

Paragraph 3. Enter how much you were earning at the time of your injury. (If you have questions about how to compute your earnings, see Chapter 12, Section B1.) Check the box that applies as to how you computed your rate of pay and the number of hours you worked per week. Enter the value of tips, meals, lodging, or other nonsalary that you regularly received, and check the appropriate box as to how the value was calculated.

Paragraph 4. Fill in all the dates that you have been off work as a result of your injury. There are two lines provided in case you have more than one period of disability.

Paragraph 5. Check "Yes" if the insurance company has been or is paying you temporary disability benefits; otherwise check "No." On the next blank line, enter the total amount you have been paid to date if you know; otherwise enter "unknown." Next, enter the weekly amount you were paid by the insurance company. Finally, enter the date that you last received a check. (If you need more detailed information on temporary disability, see Chapter 12.)

Paragraph 6. Check the appropriate box as to whether you have received unemployment or state disability benefits. (See Chapter 17 for more about these benefits.)

Paragraph 7. On the first line, place an "X" or check mark in the "Yes" or "No" box indicating whether or not you received medical treatment for your injury from any source. On the next line, enter the date that you last received medical treatment from any source, or the words "not applicable."

Next, fill in the name of any person or agency, other than your employer, that provided or paid for any medical care. For example, you'd fill in the name of your group health insurance if it provided treatment. Enter "none" if appropriate, as would be the case if your employer paid for the whole thing.

Place an "X" or a check mark indicating whether Medi-Cal paid for any health care related to your claim. Finally, enter the name and address of any doctors or facilities that treated or examined you for your injury but were not paid by your employer or its insurance company. Enter "none" if appropriate.

Paragraph 8. On the blank line, enter "none" if you've never filed a workers' compensation claim. Otherwise, enter the case number of any other workers' compensation claims you have ever filed, whether in California or elsewhere. If you don't know the case number (or weren't assigned one), enter any information you have, such as "March 2, 1992 injury to right hand, filed in Los Angeles, CA."

It's possible that you're not sure whether you filed previous claims—perhaps because you started the claims process and your injury then resolved itself. List all claims you might have made. The insurance company will probably track them down later, and you could end up looking like you were trying to hide something.

Paragraph 9. Here you place an "X" or check mark for each issue on which you and the insurance company may disagree. Because a disagreement is always possible, and not in your control, check every line. On the blank line entitled "Other (Specify)," enter the words "penalties and interest" and "mileage (transportation)."

Next, check the box Yes or No stating whether you are represented by the lawyer. If you are represented, your lawyer will probably fill out this form, but just in case, if you checked "Yes," check the box as to whether your representation is by an attorney or a nonattorney and fill out the name of the law firm or company, address, city, state, and zip code. The form asks for the attorney's law firm number, which is a number assigned by the WCAB. You probably won't know the number, so just leave it blank and ask your lawyer to complete it. If you are not represented, sign the form where indicated and fill in the date and city where you signed.

4. How to File an Application for Adjudication of Claim

Follow the instructions below to file your application. You may also need to complete one or two other short documents that must be filed along with the application.

a. Prepare Declaration in Compliance With Labor Code Section 4906(g)

Along with the Application for Adjudication of Claim, you must file a Declaration in Compliance With Labor Code Section 4906(g). This form states, under penalty of perjury, that you have not bribed or otherwise induced any doctor or medical facility to write a fraudulent report on your behalf. A sample is below, and A downloadable copy of this declaration is available on Nolo's website. (See Chapter 29, "Online Appendixes" for the link to this and other forms in this book.) All you need to do is date and sign the form and check the box "Application."

b. Prepare Guardian ad Litem Papers If Injured Worker Is a Minor or Is Incompetent

SKIP AHEAD

If the injured isn't a minor. Skip this section unless the injured worker is a minor (under age 18) or an incompetent adult.

If the injured worker is a minor or is mentally unable to make legal decisions, you must prepare an additional form: a Petition for Appointment of a Guardian ad Litem and Trustee. This document requests that you, as the petitioner, be appointed to

STATE OF CALIFORNIA
DIVISION OF WORKERS' COMPENSATION
WORKERS' COMPENSATION APPEALS BOARD
APPLICATION FOR ADJUDICATION OF CLAIM

☐ Amended Application

GV7777
Case No.

555-55-5555
SSN (Numbers Only)

Venue choice is based upon (Completion of this section is required)

☑ County of residence of employee (Labor Code section 5501.5(a)(1) or (d).)

☐ County where injury occurred (Labor Code section 5501.5(a)(2) or (d).)

☐ County of principal place of business of employee's attorney (Labor Code section 5501.5(a)(3) or (d).)

LAO
Select 3 - Letter Office Code For Place/Venue of Hearing (From the Document Cover Sheet)

Injured Worker (Completion of this section is required)

JOHN
First Name

MI

WU
Last Name

111 NORTH HILL STREET
Street Address/PO Box (Please leave blank spaces between numbers, names or words)

Street Address2/PO Box (Please leave blank spaces between numbers, names or words)

International Address (Please leave blank spaces between numbers, names or words)

LOS ANGELES	CA	90012
City	State	Zip Code

Applicant (If other than Injured Worker)

☐ Insurance Carrier ☐ Employer ☐ Lien Claimant

Name (Please leave blank spaces between numbers, names or words)

Street Address/PO Box (Please leave blank spaces between numbers, names or words)

Street Address2/PO Box (Please leave blank spaces between numbers, names or words)

City State Zip Code

DWC/WCAB Form 1A (11/2008) - (Page 1) WCAB1

Employer Information (Completion of this section is required)

☑ Insured ☐ Self-Insured ☐ Legally Uninsured ☐ Uninsured

TBA INDUSTRIES
Employer Name (Please leave blank spaces between numbers, names or words)

415 W. OCEAN BOULEVARD
Employer Street Address/PO Box (Please leave blank spaces between numbers, names or words)

LONG BEACH	CA	90802
City	State	Zip Code

Insurance Carrier Information (If known and if applicable - include even if carrier is adjusted by claims administrator)

ABC INSURANCE
Insurance Carrier Name (Please leave blank spaces between numbers, names or words)

123 NORTH MAIN STREET, SUITE 3
Insurance Carrier Street Address/PO Box (Please leave blank spaces between numbers, names or words)

LOS ANGELES	CA	90018
City	State	Zip Code

Claims Administrator Information (If known and if applicable)

N/A
Name (Please leave blank spaces between numbers, names or words)

Street Address/PO Box (Please leave blank spaces between numbers, names or words)

City State Zip Code

IT IS CLAIMED THAT (Complete all relevant information):

1. The injured worker, born 10/06/1955 (DATE OF BIRTH: MM/DD/YYYY), while employed as a(n) WAREHOUSEMAN (OCCUPATION AT THE TIME OF INJURY)

(Choose only one)

suffered a :

☑ specific injury 9/9/20xx (Date of injury: MM/DD/YYYY)

☐ cumulative injury which began on (Start Date: MM/DD/YYYY) and ended on (End Date: MM/DD/YYYY)

The injury occurred at 415 WEST OCEAN BOULEVARD
Street Address/PO Box - Please leave blank spaces between numbers, names or words

LONG BEACH (City), CA (State) 90802 (Zip Code).

DWC/WCAB Form 1A (11/2008) - (Page 2)

WCAB1

(State which parts of the body were injured)

Body Part 1: 420 BACK

Body Part 2: 513 KNEE

Body Part 3: 450 SHOULDER

Body Part 4: 520 ANKLE

Other Body Parts: 300 UPPER EXT

2. The injury occurred as follows:

(EXPLAIN WHAT THE WORKER WAS DOING AT THE TIME OF INJURY AND HOW THE INJURY OCCURED)

SLIPPED ON GREASE WHILE WALKING ON WAREHOUSE FLOOR.

3. Actual earnings at the time of injury:

Rate of Pay $ 650.00 ☐ Monthly ☑ Weekly ☐ Hourly

State value of tips, meals, lodging, or other advantages, regularly received $ ______ ☐ Monthly ☐ Weekly ☐ Hourly

Number of hours worked per week 40

4. The injury caused disability as follows:

Last day off work due to injury: 01/06/20xx (MM/DD/YYYY)

First Period of Disability: Start Date 09/09/20xx (MM/DD/YYYY) End Date 04/06/xx (MM/DD/YYYY)

Second Period of Disability: Start Date ______ (MM/DD/YYYY) End Date ______ (MM/DD/YYYY)

5. Compensation:

Compensation was paid: ☐ Yes ☑ No

Total paid: ______

Weekly rate(s): ______

Date of last payment: ______ (MM/DD/YYYY)

6. Has the worker received any unemployment insurance benefits and/or any unemployment compensation disability benefits (state disability) since the date of injury? ☐ Yes ☑ No

DWC/WCAB Form 1A (11/2008) - (Page 3)

WCAB1

7. Medical treatment:

Medical treatment was received: ☐ Yes ☑ No

All treatment was furnished by the Employer or Insurance Carrier: ☐ Yes ☑ No

Date of last treatment: ____________ MM/DD/YYYY

Other treatment was provided/paid by: ____________________ (NAME OF PERSON OR AGENCY PROVIDING OR PAYING FOR MEDICAL CARE)

Did Medi-Cal pay for any health care related to this claim? ☐ Yes ☑ No

Names and addresses of doctor(s)/hospital(s)/clinic(s) that treated or examined for this injury, but that were not provided or paid for by the employer or insurance carrier:

NONE

Name of Doctor/Hospital/Clinic 1 (Please leave blank spaces between numbers, names or words)

____

Name of Doctor/Hospital/Clinic 2 (Please leave blank spaces between numbers, names or words)

8. Other cases have been filed for industrial injuries by this worker as follows:

NONE

Case Number 1

Case Number 3

Case Number 2

Case Number 4

9. This application is filed because of a disagreement regarding liability for:

☑ Temporary disability indemnity

☑ Permanent disability indemnity

☑ Reimbursement for medical expense

☑ Rehabilitation

☑ Medical treatment

☑ Supplemental Job Displacement/Return to Work

☑ Compensation at proper rate

☑ Other (Specify) ALL PER L.C.

DWC/WCAB Form 1A (11/2008) - (Page 4) WCAB1

Is the Applicant Represented? ☐ Yes ☑ No **If "No", applicant is to sign and date below.**

If "Yes", applicant's representative is to complete the following and is to sign and date below.

☐ Law Firm/Attorney ☐ Non-Attorney Representative

Law Firm or Company Name (If Applicable)

Law Firm Number (If Applicable)

Attorney/Representative First Name MI

Attorney/Representative Last Name

Street Address/PO Box (Please leave blank spaces between numbers, names or words)

City State Zip Code

Applicant Attorney/Representative Signature Applicant Signature

Dated at LONG BEACH, California
City

Date 05/24/20xx
MM/DD/YYYY

DWC/WCAB Form 1A (11/2008) - (Page 5) WCAB1

Declaration in Compliance With Labor Code Section 4906(g)

The undersigned swear under penalty of perjury that they have to the best of their information and belief not violated California Labor Code Section 139.3 and they have not offered, delivered, received, or accepted any rebate, refund, commission, preference, patronage, dividend, discount, or other consideration, whether in the form of money or otherwise, as compensation or inducement for any referred examination or evaluation.

4/4/20xx	Penelope Watson
Date	Employee
Date	Employee's Attorney
Date	Employer
Date	Insurer
Date	Employer's/Insurer's Attorney

The document filed is:

- ☑ Application
- ☐ Answer
- ☐ Case Opening Compromise and Release
- ☐ Case Opening Stipulations with Request for Award

act on behalf of the injured worker in the workers' compensation matter.

A Petition for Appointment of a Guardian ad Litem and Trustee can be filed by a parent or court-appointed guardian or conservator. You can get copies of these forms from the appeals board. If you need help completing them, contact an information and assistance officer.

c. Determine Where to File

You'll need to file the Application for Adjudication of Claim with a local Workers' Compensation Appeals Board. The appeals board will probably be located in the county where you currently live or where the injury occurred. If these are different, the choice is up to you.

For a list of the available cities (venues) in which to file your claim and for the code you will need for the application see Appendix 1 on Nolo's website. (See Chapter 29, "Online Appendixes" for the link to Appendix 1.)

In some larger counties, there are a number of appeals board offices. You can find out the correct office by calling the Workers' Compensation Appeals Board listed in the government section of your local telephone directory, under State of California, Industrial Relations Department. If you have questions about where to file, call the Information and Assistance Unit at 800-736-7401.

CAUTION

Any document that you file with the workers' compensation appeals board must include two (2) cover documents. The first is called a "Document Cover Sheet" and the second is called "Document Separator Sheet." The Document Cover Sheet is the top document for everything you file on a particular date. The Document Separator Sheet must be prepared for every document you file on a particular day. For example, if you file an application, a DWC-1 claim form. and a 4906 (g) form on April 4, 2009, you would have one Document Cover Sheet for the whole package and three Document Separator Sheets, one just before each separate document. Downloadable copies are available on Nolo's website. (See Chapter 29, "Online Appendixes" for the link to these and other forms in this book.) Instructions for how to fill them out are in Chapter 23 under "How to File Documents With the Workers' Compensation Appeals Board."

d. File Application and Other Documents With the Appeals Board

There is no fee for filing your documents. You may file the application and accompanying documents in one of two ways:

- Photocopy the documents and mail the originals to the Workers' Compensation Appeals Board, following the instructions in Chapter 23, Section B.
- Take the documents down to the appeals board, following the instructions in Chapter 23, Section C. If you're under time constraints to file (say you're nearing the filing deadline), you should file the application in person.

TIP

You may need to file more than one form. If you prepared separate applications for different injuries or different employers, remember to file all of these documents with the appeals board.

e. Amending an Application

If you need to make changes to the application form after you file it, you can follow the same general procedures covered in Section C2d, above, for amending a DWC-1 form.

Serve copies on all interested parties and file the amended application with the appeals board as if it were the original. If you amend the application, also amend the DWC-1 form if it's also incorrect.

Along with the above documents, you will need to file one Document Cover Sheet that goes on top of all the documents when you file them. (See Chapter 23, Section E2, for the form and how to fill it out.) You also need to place on top of EACH document (or between each document) a form called a Document Separator Sheet. (See Chapter 23, Section E2, for the form and how to fill it out.)

5. Preparing an Application for Adjudication of Claim for a Death Claim

Use the form below for filing an Application for Adjudication of Claim if you are filing a claim on behalf of a relative who died as a result of a work injury. Be sure you first read Chapter 15 on Death Benefits before doing so, because there are time limitations and other rules. Make sure you qualify for the death benefits before spending the time it takes to file a claim.

D. The Insurance Company's Answer

After you file your application, the Workers' Compensation Appeals Board will do one of two things:

- **If you don't have a lawyer.** The appeals board will serve (properly send) a copy of your date-stamped application to your employer's insurance company and all other interested parties. You will also receive a copy.
- **If you have a lawyer.** The appeals board will send your lawyer a copy of your Application for Adjudication of Claim, which shows the date of filing. Your attorney must then send copies of the file-stamped application to your employer, your insurance company, and all other interested parties.

Within 15 days after the appeals board serves the application on your employer's insurance company, the insurance company must file an answer with the appeals board. The answer should list any inaccuracies in the application and set forth any defenses. (LC § 5505, CCR § 10480.) You must be served with the answer.

Should the insurance company fail to answer in the required time, it may have waived its right to object. Check with an information and assistance officer for more information.

E. Take Steps to Protect Your Rights

As an injured worker, you should take steps to ensure that your rights under the workers' compensation system are protected. Although it shouldn't be true—and wouldn't be in a fairer system—your case may be jeopardized if you say or do the wrong thing. In short, while hoping for fair treatment (which you may receive), it is best to prepare yourself from the very start for a long and hard battle (which you may have to fight).

Once you've filed your claim, you'll find the following particularly helpful:

- **Keep good records.** How you keep track of your claim can make or break your case. (See Chapter 6.)
- **Be careful when dealing with the insurance company.** Look at everything the insurance company does from all possible angles. Keep in mind that the insurance company represents your employer, not you. (See Chapter 7.)
- **Know how to deal with your employer.** Regardless of whether or not you're hoping to return to your job, your employer can help or hurt your case. (See Chapter 8.)
- **Take charge of your medical care.** Which doctors you see and how actively you take charge of your medical care will affect both your health and your overall case. (See Chapter 9.)

STATE OF CALIFORNIA
DEPARTMENT OF INDUSTRIAL RELATIONS

SEE REVERSE SIDE FOR INSTRUCTIONS

WORKERS' COMPENSATION APPEALS BOARD

APPLICATION FOR ADJUDICATION OF CLAIM (Death Case) **CASE No.** 6V7777

(PRINT OR TYPE NAMES AND ADDRESSES)

Mrs. Susan Benson — (APPLICANT)
111 North Hill St., Los Angeles, CA 90012 — (APPLICANT'S ADDRESS AND ZIP CODE)

Mark Benson — (DECEASED EMPLOYEE)

Social Security No. 000-00-0000

TBA Industries — (EMPLOYER - STATE IF SELF-INSURED)
415 Ocean Blvd., Long Beach, CA 90802 — (EMPLOYER'S ADDRESS AND ZIP CODE)

ABC Industries — (EMPLOYER'S INSURANCE CARRIER OR, IF SELF-INSURED, ADJUSTING AGENCY)
123 N. Main St., L.A., CA 90018 — (INSURANCE CARRIER OR ADJUSTING AGENCY'S ADDRESS)

IT IS CLAIMED THAT:

1. Deceased employee, born 10/06/1955 (DATE OF BIRTH) while as employed as a Warehouseman (OCCUPATION AT TIME OF INJURY)

   on 09/09/2012 (DATE OF INJURY), at 415 Ocean Blvd, Long Beach, CA 90802 (ADDRESS) (CITY) (STATE) (ZIP CODE), by the employer sustained injury arising out of and in the course of employment to 198 Head (STATE WHAT PARTS OF BODY WERE INJURED)

2. The injury occurred as follows: he fell from ladder while fixing a light fixture and fractured his skull (EXPLAIN WHAT EMPLOYEE WAS DOING AT TIME OF INJURY AND HOW INJURY WAS RECEIVED) resulting in death on 12/26/20xx (DATE OF DEATH)

3. Actual earnings at time of injury were: $650.00 (GIVE WEEKLY OR MONTHLY SALARY OR HOURLY RATE AND NUMBER OF HOURS WORKED PER WEEK)

4. The injury caused disability as follows: died on 12/26/20xx (SPECIFY LAST DAY OFF WORK DUE TO THIS INJURY AND BEGINNING AND ENDING DATES OF ALL PERIODS OFF DUE TO THIS INJURY)

5. Compensation was paid ____ (YES) ✔ (NO) $ ____ (TOTAL PAID) $ ____ (WEEKLY RATE) ____ (DATE OF LAST PAYMENT)

6. Medical treatment was received ✔ (YES) ____ (NO) 12/26/20xx (DATE OF LAST TREATMENT). All treatment was furnished by the employer or insurance company ____ (YES) ____ (NO) other treatment was provided or paid by ____ (NAME OF PERSON OR AGENCY PROVIDING OR PAYING FOR MEDICAL CLAIM)

   Did Medi-Cal pay for any health care related to this claim ____ (YES) ____ (NO) Doctors not provided or paid for by employer or insurance company, who treated or examined for this injury are: ____ (STATE NAMES AND ADDRESSES OF SUCH DOCTORS AND NAMES OF HOSPITALS TO WHICH SUCH DOCTORS ADMITTED INJURED)

7. Defendants have paid burial expense ✔ (YES) ____ (NO) TOTAL PAID $4,600.00

8. The employee left surviving the following dependents:

NAME	DATE OF BIRTH (if under 18)	RELATIONSHIP TO THE EMPLOYEE	ADDRESS
Susan Benson		spouse	111 North Hill St., L.A., CA, 90012
Mildred Benson		mother	111 North Hill St., L.A., CA, 90012

WHEREFORE, applicant requests a hearing and an award of: Death benefit ____ Burial expense ____ Compensation accrued and unpaid ____ Unpaid medical bills ____ Other (specify) ____ and all other appropriate benefits provided by law.

Dated at Long Beach (CITY), California, 05/24/2011 (DATE)

____ (APPLICANT'S ATTORNEY)

____ (ADDRESS AND TELEPHONE NUMBER OF ATTORNEY)

____ (APPLICANT'S SIGNATURE)

DIA WCAB Form 2 (Rev. 7/81)
DIA-2

CHAPTER

6

Keep Good Records to Protect Your Claim

Keeping good records is one of the best ways you can protect your rights. By organizing the papers you accumulate in your workers' compensation case and keeping track of benefits you receive, you'll improve your chances of:

- receiving all benefits you're entitled to, especially if the insurance company disputes what you're owed or what you've been paid
- receiving a fair settlement, and
- being able to prove your case at trial, if it doesn't settle beforehand.

A. Set Up a Good Record-Keeping System

You will accumulate many papers in the process of handling your workers' compensation claim. Now is a good time to set up a system so that you can readily lay your hands on any document you need.

You may find it helpful to go to an office supply store or large stationery store to see what's available to organize your paperwork. File folders or large manila envelopes are a good start; even better is a cardboard accordion file with a top flap that can be tied securely. You might want an expandable file that holds separate file folders that are designated by category—such as medical reports, insurance company correspondence, medical benefits, vocational rehabilitation, and so on.

I suggest that you place your documents in each category in chronological order, with the oldest documents on the bottom. Then add current documents to the top of the stack, so your file will automatically be in chronological order.

B. Read and Understand What You Receive in the Mail

You may feel overwhelmed at the volume of the documents you receive and be tempted to file them away without careful study. Don't do it. It is imperative that you carefully read each and every letter, document, notice, and medical report you receive and understand what it says. If you put aside even one document, you run the risk of failing to meet a required deadline or losing track of an important aspect of your case.

If you do not understand the meaning of any letter, notice, or medical report you receive, immediately call the doctor, the insurance company's adjuster, or an information and assistance officer for clarification.

C. Gather Important Records Pertaining to Your Claim

It is crucial that you keep an accurate record of everything that happens from the moment your injury occurs until your case is finished, a period likely to span several years. So take some time now to gather the records listed below.

1. Papers Documenting Your Injury

Gather together any work accident reports, completed DWC-1 forms, and other records of your injury. For example, if you were a truck driver, you might have kept a log listing all your activities for each hour of the day. This might prove the date and time of injury.

2. Medical Reports and Records

Keep a chronological record of all medical reports and records you acquire directly from a medical facility, as well as those sent to you by the insurance company. If you request it, your employer and the insurance company must provide you with copies of all medical records and reports that come into their possession. We show you how to make a request in Section D, below.

3. Copies of Documents Filed With the Appeals Board

Include papers you or the insurance company filed in your case, including any Application for

Adjudication of Claim, Declaration of Readiness to Proceed, and Notice of Change of Address.

4. All Correspondence

Keep a chronological record of all your correspondence to and from your employer, the insurance company, doctors, and anyone else involved in your case, such as a lawyer.

If you sent documents by certified mail, keep copies of all return receipts. Also keep copies of any proofs of service showing that documents were served (properly sent).

5. Earnings Record

You'll need a record of your earnings if the insurance company disputes the amount you claim you earned (which in turn may affect the amount of your benefits). If available, gather together copies of your pay stubs for all jobs you held during the year prior to being injured. Also keep copies of your W-2 and 1040 tax forms for the last two years.

6. Record of All Income and Benefits Received

Keep track of all money you receive from the date of your injury until your case ends. Include any money received from the State of California Employment Development Department, the workers' compensation insurance company, Social Security, SSI, TANF (Temporary Assistance for Needy Families, previously known as AFDC), private disability policies, and any other source of income not mentioned here. Use the form entitled Record of Income and Benefits Received, which is available on Nolo's website. (See Chapter 29, "Online Appendixes" for the link to this and other forms in this book.) In addition, keep check stubs and any letters regarding payments you received.

7. Record of All Time You Are Off Work

Keep a chronological log of those periods for which you have a doctor's report or off-work order indicating that you are temporarily disabled. You can use a Record of Time Off Work for this purpose, which is available on the Nolo website. (See Chapter 29, "Online Appendixes" for the link to this and other forms in this book.)

8. Record of Any Out-of-Pocket Medical Expenses

Keep track of any expenses you directly incurred due to your injury. For example, you may have paid for (or made co-payments on) doctors' and chiropractors' bills, emergency room bills, medical tests, or prescriptions. Include all nonprescription medications you use. You may use the Record of Medical Expenses and Request for Reimbursement form, which is covered in Chapter 11, Section B1, and provided on Nolo's website. (See Chapter 29, "Online Appendixes" for the link to this and other forms in this book.)

9. Record of Your Medical-Related Mileage

You are entitled to be reimbursed at the rate of 55.5 cents per mile for the mileage involved in attending medical appointments and picking up medications any time after July 1, 2011. If you incurred parking or bridge tolls, list these as well. To keep track of the mileage, use the Medical Mileage Expense form which is available as a downloadable form on the Nolo website. (See Chapter 29, "Online Appendixes" for the link to this and other forms in this book.)

If you incurred mileage costs before July 1, 2011, here are the previous reimbursement rates:

7/1/11 to 12/31/11	55.5 cents per mile
1/1/11 to 6/30/11	51 cents per mile
1/1/10 to 12/31/10	50 cents per mile
1/1/09 to 12/31/09	55 cents per mile
7/1/08 to 12/31/08	58.5 cents per mile
1/1/08 to 6/30/08	50.5 cents per mile
1/1/07 to 12/31/07	48.5 cents per mile
1/1/06 to 12/31/06	44.5 cents per mile
Before 1/1/06	34 cents per mile

Record of Income and Benefits Received

Name: Denise Wilson Employer: World Designs

Insurance Carrier: Acme Insurance Claim Number: Acme Insurance

Date check received	Check number	Period (starting date through ending date)	Amount of check	Reason for check (temporary disability, permanent disability advance, vocational rehabilitation, unemployment, Social Security, etc.)
4/19/20xx	1234	4/1/20xx–4/15/20xx	$602	TD
5/2/20xx	1421	4/16/20xx–4/31/20xx	602	TD
5/17/20xx	1500	5/1/20xx–5/15/20xx	602	TD
5/21/20xx	1528	N/A	20	Travel to QME appointment
6/3/20xx	1599	5/16/20xx–5/30/20xx	602	TD
8/20/20xx	1904	8/7/20xx–8/15/20xx	300	TD

Record of Time Off Work

Name: Denise Wilson　Employer: World Designs

Insurance Carrier: Acme Insurance　Claim Number: Acme Insurance

Starting date	Ending date	Doctor's report or off-work order	Reason for time off work
4/19/20xx	5/30/20xx	off-work order	recovering from hip injury
8/7/20xx	8/20/20xx	off-work order	relapse of hip injury

10. A Diary of Your Pain and Day-to-Day Activities

Your employer or its insurance company may contend that you were not disabled or were not injured as seriously as you claim. Because it may be several years before your workers' compensation case is settled or goes to trial, it is helpful to have a written diary of the pain you experienced and the problems you encountered as a result of your injury. If necessary, the diary itself may be used later as evidence before a judge. (See "How to Keep a Pain Diary," below.)

11. Photographs, Videos, and Other Evidence

If the insurance company is claiming that you did not injure yourself at work, try to put together some physical evidence that will substantiate your position. This may include photographs of the job site where you were injured and photographs or videos of the part of your body you injured (as close to the date of injury as possible). If you sprained your ankle, for example, videos of you moving around with crutches might be helpful.

If you find something that can help prove your injury—such as a piece of equipment that contributed to your fall—by all means keep it (or a photograph) as evidence.

12. A Witness List

You may need to have witnesses testify on your behalf to help prove your case. For example, if the insurance company claims that you must have injured your back outside of work, you'd want to find a witness to testify to seeing you fall from a forklift at work. It is never too early to get the names and addresses of people who could serve as witnesses. This would include people who have firsthand knowledge of such things as:

- how the injury occurred
- the safety records of any equipment involved
- the fact that you reported the injury
- anything the employer may have done that contributed to the cause of your injury

How to Keep a Pain Diary

Keep your diary in a bound book (not a three-ring binder) and always use ink (not pencil), so the insurance company cannot claim you later inserted or changed pages. Keep your diary at least on a weekly basis, unless something unusual occurs (such as a fall brought on by severe pain), in which case you will want to make an additional entry for that day.

The diary should contain a detailed record of your day-to-day symptoms and pain. Do your best to rate your pain for the various parts of your body that were injured. A common scale is 1 to 10, 1 being only slight pain and 10 being excruciating pain. In addition, note particular problems or improvements you have performing day-to-day activities. If you are claiming emotional or physical injury due to stress, include a record of how your relationships and financial affairs are affected by the injury.

While it is important to be honest (don't exaggerate), it is also necessary to adequately document your pain or inability to do certain things. So don't minimize your problems.

Sample Pain Diary

Tuesday, 1/6/xx: Went to emergency room. Pain was a 7 plus.

Friday, 1/9/xx: Ankle is in a cast. I believe the fall has further injured my knee; the knee pain is an 8 and is constant and throbbing. The knee is red and swollen. I made a doctor's appointment to have it looked at next Wednesday. When I tried to watch TV tonight, I had to take four pain killers. The pain makes me edgy and nervous, and I'm afraid I've been taking it out on my kids, who continue to be upset.

Friday 1/16/xx: Knee feels better this week. Pain is on the average around a 5 or 6. Saw Dr. Jones yesterday, and he gave me pain medication.

- what your work duties consisted of (this may be relevant if issues of occupation and eligibility for vocational rehabilitation arise), and
- the amount of pain you have, as well as the activities you can no longer do (usually a family member can be helpful here).

TIP

Keep in touch with your witnesses. If you don't see your witnesses regularly, ask them to contact you in the event they move. While you don't want to pester your witnesses, it's also important not to lose track of them. For instance, make a point of calling your witnesses every few months just to stay in touch. It's common sense that it's much easier to locate someone who has recently moved than someone who moved several years earlier.

13. Notes of Conversations Regarding Your Claim

It is especially important to keep written notes of conversations you have with the insurance company, the defense attorney, and your employer.

14. Supplemental Job Displacement Benefit

If you were injured in 2004 or later and you're using the supplemental job displacement benefit, save all your records relating to education costs for which you hope to be reimbursed. This benefit may pay for tuition, books, and fees spent on retraining and skills enhancement, so save all of your receipts. The job displacement benefit is discussed in Chapter 14.

Sample Letter

[Date]

[Employer's name and address]

RE: Workers' Compensation Claim #12345
Injured worker: [Your name]
Injury date: [Date]
Certified mail, return receipt requested

Dear [Employer's name]:

I request that you, your insurance carrier, or your administrator send me copies of the following:

1. All of my medical reports
2. My wage statement
3. Any statements taken from me pertaining to my injury
4. Investigation reports regarding my injury
5. Copies of any videotapes, film, and/or photographs that have been taken of me
6. Any statements made by me with reference to my right or desire to participate in vocational rehabilitation
7. A history of all benefits paid, the dates, and the amounts
8. Any statements prepared by a qualified rehabilitation representative in my case
9. Any reports or statements prepared by a case management worker in my case.

Please consider this a *continuing demand*, and serve me with the above if you should receive them in the future.

Thank you for your anticipated cooperation.

Sincerely,

[Your name]

cc: [Insurance company]

D. Request Copies of Documents and Evidence

It's to your advantage to have copies of important documents and evidence your employer and its insurance company have on your case. Fortunately, you have the right to this information. If you make a written request, your employer and its insurance company must send you copies of all documents and evidence it has or acquires in your case. Mail a request to your employer (certified, return-receipt requested) with a copy to the insurance company. A sample is shown above and a form letter you can use for this purpose is provided on Nolo's website. (See Chapter 29, "Online Appendixes" for the link to this and other forms in this book.)

E. Keep Your Address Current

You are required to keep the appeals board and all opposing parties informed of any change in your address. If you move, send a Notice of Change of Address to the appeals board with a copy to all parties. A self-explanatory form you can use is available on Nolo's website. (See Chapter 29, "Online Appendixes" for the link to this and other forms in this book.) How to serve (send) copies to opposing parties is covered in Chapter 23.

CHAPTER

7

The Insurance Company's Role

Most employers pay premiums to a workers' compensation insurance company, which, in turn, pays any benefits due an employee who is injured at work. Your employer's workers' compensation insurance company, sometimes called the insurance carrier, will be responsible for managing and settling your workers' compensation claim, unless your employer is self-insured, as discussed in Section A of this chapter. In general, the insurance company makes most decisions on how the claim should be handled and ultimately resolved.

Although every workers' compensation case is unique, this chapter will give you some general guidelines about the most effective way to deal with the insurance company. By knowing what the insurance company expects and how it operates, you'll have a better chance of protecting your rights and being treated fairly.

Always keep in mind that your employer's insurance company is not in business to help you, but to represent your employer. This advice also applies to the State Compensation Insurance Fund (also called State Fund or SCIF), if that is your company's insurer. SCIF is a private insurance company set up by the state to make sure that workers' compensation insurance is available to all employers—including those unable to get coverage from a private company because of a poor safety history, and small businesses that can't find coverage elsewhere.

Insurance companies remain in business by paying out less in claims than they receive in premiums. Or, to put it more bluntly, the less the insurance company pays you, the more it gets to keep. Thus, the insurance company has no incentive to see that your rights are protected; if anything, the opposite is true.

Unfortunately, workers' compensation has evolved into an adversarial system. Insurance companies often rely upon, and take advantage of, the fact that most injured workers have no idea of how the system works. Many injured workers believe everything that an insurance adjuster tells them, thinking that the insurance company has their best interests at heart.

TIP

Record every contact with the insurance company. Keep accurate records of your dealings with the insurance company. This is important for a number of reasons, including the fact that the insurance company may switch the person in charge of handling your claim (the adjuster) many times throughout your case. If you don't have a written record of prior agreements, the new adjuster may not honor them. Section E, below, gives advice on how to keep a paper trail of your contacts with the insurance company.

The Many Names for Insurance Companies

In your dealings with the workers' compensation system, you will hear the terms "insurance company," "insurer," "insurance carrier," and "carrier." They all mean the same thing. The odd word "carrier" derives from insurance industry jargon, which refers to providing a person or business with insurance as "carrying" their insurance policy. Thus the ABC Insurance Company is said to be the insurance carrier (provider) for the Racafrax Company.

A. Self-Insured Employers

SKIP AHEAD

If your employer has a workers' comp insurance company. Skip to Section B, below, if an insurance company is handling your workers' compensation claim.

Some employers choose to "self-insure," rather than use an insurance company. This means that the employer handles its own workers' compensation claims and directly pays all benefits. Most self-insured employers hire an adjusting company that oversees and handles the day-to-day activities of workers' compensation claims. The adjusting agency may be an in-house agency (part of the company) or one that is hired by the employer.

Although you may believe that dealing directly with your employer instead of with an insurance company is an advantage, in my experience this is often not true. Your employer may bring to the negotiating table its opinions and biases regarding your claim and how it may affect your ability to remain a viable employee. Also, remember that a company that tries to save money by self-insuring is likely to be very concerned with the bottom line.

If you must deal directly with your company to settle your workers' compensation case, the general principles discussed in this chapter will still guide you. Where this book refers to the "insurance company," simply substitute "adjusting agency" or "employer" for a self-insured employer.

B. The Insurance Company's Responsibilities

The insurance company has three primary (and interrelated) responsibilities:

- to promptly handle all claims
- to provide benefits, and
- to deal with you in good faith.

All too often, however, an insurance adjuster will delay or deny benefits without any concrete evidence or proof that the claim is not valid. Typically, the insurance adjuster does so on information supplied by the employer that the injured worker "did not really get injured at work" or "is really not as hurt as the doctor says."

If you're subjected to such unfair behavior, you do have some recourse. There are financial penalties for not promptly paying a workers' compensation benefit. (See Chapter 19, Section C9.) In addition, if the insurance company takes action or uses tactics that are solely intended to cause unnecessary delay in paying your benefits, the workers' compensation judge may order the insurance company to pay any expenses, including attorney's fees and costs, that you incurred as a result of the delay. (Although rarely done, under LC § 5813, the judge may also order the insurance company to pay a penalty of up to $2,500 to the "general fund," the bank account for the State of California.)

Internal Utilization Review Process

Every employer (or its workers' compensation insurance company) must establish an "internal utilization review" process to approve, modify, delay, or deny treatment plans. This is discussed in more detail in Chapter 11, Section A3.

C. Your Responsibilities as an Injured Worker

As a person making a workers' compensation claim, you have certain legal responsibilities, namely, to cooperate with reasonable requests made by the insurance company in its investigation of your claim. Reasonable requests would entail such things as providing the insurance company with your medical history and a written authorization for release of your medical records.

TIP

Do not comply with unreasonable requests. Unless you filed a claim for psychiatric injury, your medical history and medical records pertaining to prior psychiatric treatment or counseling are irrelevant, and you don't have to turn them over.

You must attend all reasonable medical appointments scheduled by the insurance company. An examination every three months or so by the insurance company's doctor is reasonable.

Certainly, requiring you to be examined every week by the same doctor is not reasonable.

The insurance company must make reasonable accommodations for you to attend the medical examinations. If you do not have a car or can't drive, for example, the insurance company must pay your reasonable transportation costs. Medical appointments should also be set within your general geographic area. Requiring you to attend a medical appointment 100 miles away is not reasonable.

D. Who's Who in the Insurance Company

Let's back up a little and take a look at how workers' compensation insurance companies are set up. As your claim progresses, you'll deal with various people who work for the insurance company, including the following:

- insurance adjuster
- adjuster's supervisor
- attorney, house counsel, or hearing representative, and
- case management worker.

Knowing who the various players are and their respective roles will give you the best chance of resolving your claim fairly. Determine as soon as possible who is involved in your workers' compensation case. Keep a written list of their names, titles, addresses, and telephone numbers, as well as a written record of all contact you have with them.

1. The Insurance Adjuster

Assuming you do not have an attorney, your primary contact will be an insurance adjuster (claims adjuster), whose job is to settle your claim. It is important to do your best to establish a good working relationship with the adjuster. You'll likely have to do this with more than one person, as it is common for adjusters to leave or for cases to be rotated among adjusters.

Whatever the attitude of the adjuster (some can be uncooperative), remember that this person will decide when, and if, you get the various benefits you may be entitled to. A good approach is to treat the adjuster as you would want to be treated in business dealings. Start by making polite requests of the adjuster, but be willing to be more assertive (but not obnoxious) if need be, and confirm all agreements in writing.

If you get an adjuster who seems to be cooperative and kind, that's fine—it's always nice to deal with a pleasant person. But do remember that the adjuster was hired to bring your claim to a close as quickly and as cheaply as possible. Rule One: Never confide in the adjuster. For example, if yours is a back injury, don't tell the friendly adjuster about the mild strain you suffered a few weeks ago helping your brother lay a new roof. This information may be taken out of context, exaggerated, and used against you.

How to Negotiate With the Insurance Company

Successful negotiation is based upon requests and demands that are logical and reasonable and supported by the evidence. If you are requesting medical treatment authorization, point out the medical reports that support your request. If you are trying to negotiate a settlement, present sound medical evidence to back up a reasonable demand, not a request for an outrageous sum. If the insurance company realizes that you are well prepared and know what you are entitled to, your reasonable demands should get serious consideration.

2. The Adjuster's Supervisor

No matter how good your working relationship is with the insurance adjuster, there likely will be times when you cannot get this person to see things your way. If so, you may want to ask to speak to the adjuster's supervisor. The supervisor has authority to overrule any decisions made by the adjuster. Generally speaking, the supervisor has many more years of experience than does the adjuster. If your reasoning is sound, it is very possible that the supervisor will decide to grant your request and override the decision of the insurance adjuster on the case.

Going over the adjuster's head will probably negatively affect your future relationship, so only do this for important matters. In other words, don't complain to the supervisor if your $32 mileage check is late.

Before you call the adjuster's supervisor, think through your circumstances, what you want, and why it's reasonable. Then calmly and clearly explain your position, setting forth the medical and legal reasoning behind your request.

3. The Attorney, House Counsel, or Hearing Representative

If you cannot settle your workers' compensation claim with the insurance adjuster or supervisor, your matter will eventually be heard before the Workers' Compensation Appeals Board. If your case goes this direction, the adjuster will usually turn your file over to someone else, who will represent the insurance company at the appeals board hearing.

The person representing the insurance company may be an attorney, either house counsel (a lawyer who works only for the insurance company) or outside counsel (a lawyer hired by the insurance company to handle your particular case). Workers' compensation laws also allow nonattorneys to represent insurance companies at appeals board hearings. If the insurance representative is not an attorney, he or she will be referred to as a hearing representative, or hearing rep for short. The hearing rep acts like an attorney on behalf of the insurance company but is not licensed to practice law.

Who the insurance company uses is usually dictated by cost. Some companies find it cheaper to have an attorney working for them, while others find it less expensive to hire outside attorneys or nonlawyer hearing reps as needed. Regardless of who the insurance company decides to use, your case is going to be handled in much the same way.

4. The Case Management Worker

Some insurance companies hire outside case management workers to assist in the management of their workers' compensation claims. The case manager's job is to help you promptly get the medical care you need and report to the insurance company on how your medical treatment is progressing. Insurance companies hire case management workers for many reasons, such as efficiency, cost control, and goodwill. If you're offered this service, you have the option to accept or reject it. If you have an attorney, discuss the pros and cons of a case management worker if one is offered.

A case management worker can be a big help with things like scheduling medical appointments and even arranging to get to the doctor. But be sure you request copies of all of reports and other written materials the case management worker provides to the insurance company (discussed in Chapter 6, Section D). If you feel that the written documentation is not impartially stating everything that occurs, immediately terminate the services. Sometimes a case manager turns out to be little more than a "spy" for the insurance company, reporting to the insurance company anything that might be used against you. You do not need permission to terminate the services of a case manager; simply tell the case manager or the insurance company of your wishes.

E. How to Deal With the Insurance Company

If you are not represented by an attorney, you will eventually have to talk to someone from the insurance company about your claim. You may be contacted by an insurance adjuster, an attorney, or even a private investigator. This sets up a dilemma—if you don't cooperate with the insurance company, it has the legal right to immediately deny your claim and deny you benefits. However, if you say the "wrong" thing, you could jeopardize your case or delay the receipt of your benefits.

Your best approach is to keep your responses to the insurance company's questions as short as possible. Try to limit yourself to giving out the basic information about your claim.

Whenever you call the insurance company, be as prepared as possible. If the insurance company has assigned a claim number to your case, have it handy. Know exactly what you want to ask, and ask for your insurance adjuster by name if you know it. Otherwise, give your full name or claim number and ask to speak to whoever is handling your claim. Have a pen and paper handy so you can take notes of your conversation.

Questions to Watch Out For

The following types of questions are red flags and require well-thought-out and careful answers:

- questions that imply your injury was not caused by your employment or was caused by activities that were outside of your job duties
- questions that imply your injury happened because you were intoxicated or because you started a fight, and
- questions about prior injuries or accidents that imply you may be lying about the cause or extent of your present injury.

If you encounter any trick questions, answer them truthfully and in such a way as to leave no doubt that your injury occurred at work and was caused by your employment.

1. Initial Contact With the Insurance Company

The first contact you have with the insurance company will probably be by letter. By law, you must be sent a notice within 14 days after the insurance company receives your claim. This initial letter will advise you whether the insurance company is accepting or rejecting your claim, or whether it needs additional time (up to 90 days) to investigate before deciding. This letter will have the name and telephone number of the insurance adjuster who will be handling your case.

If the insurance company fails to advise you in writing within 14 days of receiving your claim that it is denying your claim or delaying its decision pending further investigation, your claim is presumed to be accepted. There is no penalty for the first 14 days of delay. However, there is a 10% penalty for any benefits due and not paid after the 14th day. (See Chapter 19, Section C9.)

If you do not receive any correspondence from the insurance company within 14 days of filing your workers' compensation claim, you should call the insurance company. Your first telephone contact with the insurance company is very important. In some instances, it will set the tone of your entire case. It's to your advantage to establish a cordial but firm working relationship with the insurance adjuster.

TIP

Insurance must pay for medical expenses. Within one day of your filing the DWC-1 claim form, your employer or its insurance company is required to authorize and agree to pay for medical treatment until the employer or insurance company either accepts or denies your claim. During this period, the employer or insurance company is liable for up to $10,000 in medical expenses. (LC § 5402 (c).)

Ask whether the insurance company intends to accept or reject your claim, and request that you be paid any benefits that are due. If the insurance company claims that it was not notified of the claim, send the insurance company a copy of the DWC-1 form you gave your employer.

2. Your Statement About the Injury

Even when an insurance company accepts a claim, it usually contacts the injured worker and asks for a statement about what happened (usually within the first 90 days). If the insurance company advises you by letter within 14 days that it is going to investigate your claim further before deciding whether or not to accept it, you can pretty much count on being asked to give a statement.

Before you are contacted, give some thought about what you want to say to the insurance company. Many people become nervous when interviewed and, as a result, do a very poor job of stating their case. Even if you feel confident about talking to the insurance company, you're best off writing out your statement ahead of time. That way, you can think through your case and avoid saying things that are inaccurate or misleading.

If you still don't feel comfortable giving an oral (spoken) statement, or feel too scared or shaky to do so, you may give a written statement instead. I give some guidelines below.

Whenever you give the insurance company any kind of statement, the most important thing is to tell the truth. As long as you follow this rule, you won't have problems with one statement contradicting another (unless you allow yourself to get confused or intimidated). Remember, you are the most important witness in your workers' compensation case, and you know more about the facts than anyone else.

a. Prepare Your Statement in Advance

As noted above, never give a statement on the spur of the moment. If you are contacted by phone and asked to give a statement before you have had a chance to prepare, tell the insurance company you don't have time just now, and make an appointment time for them to call you back for your statement. Or simply explain that you will send a written statement to the insurance company.

Whether you're planning to give your statement orally or in writing, take the time to write down all the important dates and times, as well as the names and addresses of the doctors you have seen. Include all important facts.

Also see Chapter 4, Section B3, for a sample statement regarding a cumulative trauma injury.

Sample Statement

1. Date of injury: 1/3/20xx.
2. How injury happened: I was carrying a box of supplies down some stairs when I tripped and fell, injuring myself. I think I fell down about five stairs onto the landing.
3. Parts of body injured: My back and left leg. *[Include all body parts that could possibly be injured, even if only slightly.]*
4. Witnesses: Coworkers Jim Walters and Sally O'Leary witnessed the accident.
5. Reporting the injury: I immediately told my supervisor, Ted Felding, of the injury. He had me fill out and sign a company injury report.
6. Medical treatment: Ted Felding told me to go to the Jason Medical Clinic at 3434 Smith St. in Los Angeles. I went there the same day of my injury at about 4:00 p.m. and they examined me and prescribed Naproxen, which I paid for and have been taking three times a day. No X-rays were taken.

b. Giving an Oral Statement

If you give the insurance company an oral statement, it will take one of three forms:

- an interview by phone, which will probably be recorded after you're informed of that fact and agree to it

- an in-person interview, which will probably be recorded, or
- a deposition, where you are asked questions under oath. In a deposition, a court reporter (a specially trained transcriber) records everything and later transcribes your testimony into a booklet, which can be used in any legal proceeding involving your case. Depositions are usually taken only if you have an attorney. (If you will be giving a deposition, refer to Chapter 21, Section C, which tells you how to prepare.)

If you don't have an attorney, you may decide to have a friend, family member, or other nonlawyer present at your interviews. Also, remember to have a written statement handy, as it will help prevent you from becoming confused or intimidated.

There is no reason to be afraid to have your statement recorded, as long as you get a written transcript of the recording. Begin your oral statement by specifically stating that the insurance company has agreed to provide you with a copy of the statement (the insurance company must give you a written copy of your statement upon request).

c. Changing Your Statement

For obvious reasons, you should try your best to give an accurate statement in the first place. Your statement is always suspect if you have to change it. However, if you made a mistake in your statement or left out something important, make arrangements to change your statement at the earliest opportunity. You can change your statement by writing the insurance company a letter setting forth your changes. Remember to sign and date the letter.

Sample Letter

12/8/20xx

Mr. Tom Smith
ABC Insurance Co.
33 W. Pine Avenue
Smithville, CA 99999

Re: Clyde Johnson v. Design Central
Claim No. 98765
Appeals Board No: BV 12345
Date of Injury: 9/9/20xx

Dear Mr. Smith:

On 11/21/20xx, I gave an oral statement to Jane Felsworth. I told her that the witness's name was Jose Flores. I have now learned that his name is Jose Torres.

Sincerely,

Clyde Johnson

Clyde Johnson
555 N. 12th Street
Smithville, CA 99999

3. Make Notes of Your Conversations

Make a written note of every conversation you have regarding your claim. Include the date, the time, who you talked with, and what the conversation was about. This will help to avoid any misunderstandings on your part. Also, a dated record, made at the time of the event, is excellent proof to substantiate what was said.

> **EXAMPLE:** December 7, 20xx, 10:15 a.m. Spoke with Tom Smith, insurance adjuster. He agreed to begin payments of temporary disability payments in the amount of $336 per week. He said the first check will be mailed this week.

4. Send Confirming Letters

If you reach any type of agreement with someone from the insurance company about your claim, it is best to follow up with a confirming letter. This may serve as a needed reminder to an overbusy adjuster. It also will avoid any misunderstanding about what you agreed upon, or claims that the conversation never took place.

Send a written or typed letter to the person you spoke with and keep a copy for your records. As the sample below shows, the letter can be very short.

Sample Letter

12/8/20xx

Mr. Tom Smith
ABC Insurance Co.
33 W. Pine Avenue
Smithville, CA 99999

Re: Clyde Johnson v. Design Central
Claim No. 98765
Appeals Board No: BV 12345
Date of Injury: 9/9/20xx

Dear Mr. Smith:

This will confirm our conversation of 12/7/20xx, where you agreed to begin making temporary disability payments of $336 per week. You indicated that you will mail the first check within a week. Thank you for your help and cooperation.

Sincerely,

Clyde Johnson

Clyde Johnson
555 N. 12th Street
Smithville, CA 99999

F. Tactics Insurance Companies Use to Deny or Minimize Claims

There are a number of techniques the workers' compensation insurance company may use to deny or delay your claim. By knowing what these are, you'll be better prepared to explore your options and protect yourself.

1. Private Investigators

The insurance company will not only monitor your medical progress, it may also assign an investigator to your case. An investigator is likely to search public records and other sources, collecting information on any prior workers' compensation claims, automobile accidents, and medical history. The investigator may interview your coworkers, witnesses, friends, relatives, neighbors, and past or present doctors, as well as you. (Before you consent to an interview, read Section E, above.)

Many insurance companies hire private investigators to follow and videotape injured workers. The goal is to catch you engaging in an activity that is inconsistent with your claimed disability, such as strenuous sports, household repair tasks, or other activities that contradict your doctor's orders. This type of surveillance (called a sub rosa investigation) is so common that some workers' compensation insurance companies have their own team of in-house investigators.

Typically, the investigator will hide in a van with one-way glass, parked quite a distance (up to about 150 yards) from the scene being filmed. The investigator will usually be equipped with at least one video camera with a telephoto lens. Filming may take place at a number of locations, and it may occur over a long period of time.

It's not uncommon for investigators to film injured workers attending medical appointments, shopping, going to family gatherings, or doing work around the house. Video clips may show you taking out the trash, picking up the mail (beware of large packages that you didn't order), changing a flat tire, lifting heavy items at a garage sale, or doing yard work.

Investigators are also fond of using the phone to get information or to find out whether you're home. They may pretend to conduct a survey or inform you that you're a prize winner. Instead of worrying about whether or not an investigator is calling, many injured workers use an answering machine to screen all calls. Be aware that if you're using a cordless phone, your calls can be monitored with a radio scanner.

Be prudent about your physical activities, and always follow your doctor's advice. If you claim you can't mow your lawn because of your injured back, don't allow yourself to be videotaped doing so—even if you're in pain the whole time and you're only giving the lawn a light trim because your mother-in-law is coming for dinner. Or, if you contend that you can't lift anything heavy, simply do not attempt to do so, no matter what the necessity. If you do, you're likely to find that it's all on videotape.

It's important to understand an investigation can happen for any case, and at any time in your workers' compensation case. You'd be foolish to think that an investigation won't happen to you because your injury is relatively minor, or you've moved, or your claim is proceeding smoothly. I once had a client who moved from California to a small Midwestern town (population of about 120), and was dumbfounded to discover that an investigator had filmed him doing farm work he said he could not do!

2. Delay Tactics

As mentioned, a favorite tactic used by workers' compensation insurance companies is to delay, and then delay some more. Even though you may be in pain and living from check to check, the insurance company is primarily interested in holding on to your money as long as possible. After all, the longer it delays paying you, the more interest it can earn on your money.

Some of the most common delay tactics include instances where the insurance company:

- delays in paying your temporary disability indemnity when due
- delays in accepting or rejecting your claim
- delays in authorizing medical treatment recommended by the treating doctor
- delays in setting up medical appointments for treatment or evaluation
- delays in authorizing vocational rehabilitation benefits after a doctor determines that you are entitled to them
- delays in the payment of valid medical or pharmaceutical bills, and
- delays in just about anything you ask the insurance company to do.

Your best approach is to always be diligent in making your demands. Don't let a deadline pass without making a phone call and sending a follow-up letter demanding that the insurance company promptly take appropriate action. If the insurance company fails to respond immediately, seek help from an information and assistance officer. You may even choose to have an appeals board judge hear the matter.

If your benefits or medical treatment are delayed, you may be entitled to an automatic 10% penalty under Labor Code § 4650 and, if the delay is unreasonable, you may be entitled to a 25% penalty on the entire amount of the benefits under Labor Code § 5814. In addition, an insurance company whose actions constitute "bad faith" may be responsible for expenses incurred as a result of that delay and penalties under Labor Code § 5813. See Chapter 19, Section C, for a more detailed discussion of penalties.

3. Intimidation

Let's say your adjuster tells you that you have no case, and if you don't accept what's being offered, you'll get nothing. The best defense to this tactic is to know your case. Assuming you have a legitimate claim, you should never allow yourself to be bullied into settling your claim prematurely.

Make a note of anything said to you that you consider unfair or outrageous. Then write a letter to your adjuster's supervisor protesting this treatment. Save a copy of the letter; you'll need it if your case later goes before the appeals board.

Sample Letter

> [Date]
>
> Dear [Name of supervisor]:
>
> I believe that I have been unfairly treated by *[Name of adjuster]* . On 9/3/20xx, I spoke with *[Name of adjuster]* and was told that, in her opinion, I have no case and that I could be prosecuted for filing a fraudulent claim if I do not drop my case.
>
> I feel these threats are a direct attempt to intimidate and constitute a failure to deal in good faith. I request that your company immediately discontinue such activities.
>
> Sincerely,
> [Your name]

G. Settling Your Case

The insurance company will do its best to settle with you for the least amount of money possible. Your goal is to receive the amount you are rightly entitled to.

Some insurance companies may try to wear you out by delaying settlement. Others may try for a quick settlement in the hope that you lack knowledge and will settle your claim for less than you are entitled to. No matter what, don't let yourself be pressured into settling before you're medically and vocationally ready.

Unless you're one of the lucky few for whom money is not a pressing concern, if you're on temporary disability, you must cut out all discretionary spending and put yourself on a tight budget. This will better prepare you to resist when the insurance company tries to tempt you to settle your case for less than it's worth.

Before you accept any settlement, take the time to carefully read Chapters 19 and 20 for details on how to figure out and negotiate a fair settlement.

CHAPTER

8

Dealing With Your Employer

Regardless of how well you and your employer get along, things can change—and often do—after a work injury. Especially if your injury is fairly serious, your employer can't count on your being able to resume your duties on a given date or at your old pace. It's very likely that your employer will fear that your injury will cause its workers' compensation insurance premiums to increase.

In the best of circumstances, your employer may support your efforts to get workers' compensation benefits so that you can recover and return to work. Unfortunately, it's probably more common for an employer to become unsympathetic, uncooperative, and even hostile. If this is your situation, you may feel very vulnerable and helpless. You may feel that your boss is unfairly turning against you.

Understand that regardless of your employer's attitude about your injury, your employer has certain legal obligations. This chapter provides information about what your employer can and can't do, as well as some possible explanations as to why it may try to limit your benefits. After reading this chapter you should be in a better position to protect your legal rights and deal with your employer in the best way possible.

Workplace Safety: The Best Way to Avoid Workers' Compensation Claims

The easiest and best way for employers to prevent employees from filing workers' compensation claims is to prevent workplace injuries in the first place. Oftentimes, a workplace injury could have been prevented had the employer implemented safety procedures or complied with ergonomic regulations promulgated by Cal-OSHA (California Occupational Safety and Health Administration).

Under LC § 6401.7, employers must establish an injury prevention program. Savvy employers will carefully study and track employee injuries, hold safety meetings and trainings, and involve employees in identifying safety hazards. Employers that adopt a proactive approach to making the workplace safer will find a marked decrease in employee work injuries and a corresponding decrease in their workers' compensation premiums. (For more on workplace safety, see *Your Rights in the Workplace*, by Barbara Kate Repa (Nolo), or *The Employer's Legal Handbook*, by Fred Steingold (Nolo).)

A. Self-Insured Employers

If an employer is large enough and meets certain requirements, it can legally be self-insured. This means that instead of paying premiums to an insurance company, the employer sets aside funds to pay workers' compensation claims directly to the insured worker. In other words, the employer becomes its own insurance company and is responsible for paying all workers' compensation claims. A self-insured employer has total control over every aspect of your claim.

In most cases, self-insured employers hire a claims adjusting service to manage and "adjust" (make recommendations regarding settlement) its workers' compensation claims. If so, you'll deal primarily with this entity. However, if the employer does not have a service, you will need to deal directly with the employer regarding all aspects of your claim, including settlement.

When we refer to the insurance company in this book, this also refers to self-insured employers who are acting as their own insurers.

B. The Employer/Insurance Company Relationship

It's important to realize from the onset that, unless the employer is self-insured, your employer is a separate business entity from its insurance company. Workers' compensation insurance works just like most insurance policies. Your employer pays the insurance company premiums that are determined by the number of workers, the amount of payroll paid, the type of work, and the number of workers' compensation claims. In return, the insurance company provides your employer with a workers' compensation insurance policy. If the employer's workers suffer industrial injuries, the insurance company pays benefits.

The insurance company continually reviews how many claims have been filed and adjusts the employer's insurance premiums accordingly. Not surprisingly, adjustments are usually upward, especially if there have been any workers' compensation claims.

1. How Your Employer Can Help

It is unfair to suggest that all employers turn against injured workers. Some employers may express a sincere concern for the welfare of their injured employees and will go out of their way to help. This positive attitude is probably more prevalent with smaller employers who have close working relationships with their employees. Unfortunately, many employers, especially large corporate ones, are so concerned with the bottom line that an injured worker is looked upon as a disposable commodity.

If you are fortunate enough to have an employer who wants you to be treated fairly by its workers' compensation insurance company, request that your employer contact the insurance company and speak up on your behalf. Although the employer technically has little say about the outcome of your claim (unless the employer is self-insured), it can use its economic clout on your behalf. After all, it's the employer who decides which workers' compensation company to deal with, and it can always switch to another if its loyal employees are being treated unfairly.

2. How Your Employer Can Hurt Your Case

How the insurance company decides to handle claims can affect the amount of money your employer has to pay for workers' compensation insurance. Because workers' compensation insurance is mandatory in the state of California, your employer has no choice but to pay for it or self-insure.

If a number of injured workers file claims for workers' compensation, the employer's workers' compensation premiums will increase if the injuries are very severe. Sometimes even one additional filing can trigger an increase. In addition, a workers' compensation claim may result in your employer's facing investigations or fines by state regulatory agencies, such as Cal-OSHA, for allowing unsafe work conditions.

While many employers will keep their noses out of their employees' workers' compensation claims, others will interfere.

a. Employer May Discourage Claims

Many employers realize that the only "real" control they have over costly insurance premiums is to try to limit the number of workers' compensation claims filed by injured workers. So a considerable number of employers, although they will not admit it, have unwritten (and illegal) policies designed to discourage their employees from filing claims. For example, some employers provide "bonuses" to all workers as a group if there are no workers' compensation claims filed during a quarter. If one employee files a claim, no one gets a bonus. This subjects employees to great peer pressure not to file a claim. When an employee files a workers' compensation claim, this type of employer may look upon the employee as a traitor, a troublemaker, or not a "team player."

A hostile employer may even attempt to harass or intimidate any employee who files a claim. The employer may attempt to make an example out of the injured employee to accomplish two things. First, the employer hopes to discourage other employees from filing a workers' compensation claim, even if they have serious injuries. Second, the employer wants to dissuade other employees from testifying on behalf of an injured employee at any workers' compensation hearing.

Illegal tactics employers sometimes apply include:

- reducing the number of the employee's work hours or overtime
- penalizing an employee, for example, by writing the employee up (or putting a bad performance report in his or her file) for things the employee did not do
- verbally harassing the employee, such as chastising the employee in front of coworkers
- firing or laying off the employee, or
- if the employee is working, assigning the most difficult, boring, or otherwise undesirable duties.

If you are injured, never let your employer dissuade you from filing a claim and seeking medical attention. These unfair tactics, and any similar ones that have the effect of punishing an employee, constitute illegal discrimination. Under LC § 132(a), you or another employee who may be a witness on your behalf may file a claim against your employer for discrimination. (See Chapter 16, Section C, for a complete discussion.)

b. Employer May Treat Claim as Fraudulent

Although most employers are responsible and treat their workers fairly, some employers take the position that employees' workers' compensation claims are almost always fraudulent and without merit. In rare instances, an employer may deliberately destroy an accident report and claim that the accident never occurred. I have even seen cases where the employer illegally threatened other employees by saying that they would be fired unless they testified against the injured worker.

Unfortunately, if your employer falsely advises its workers' compensation insurance company that your case is fraudulent, the insurance company is likely to investigate and possibly deny your claim. Although this will certainly be an inconvenience, it rarely will prevent you from ultimately getting benefits.

c. Employer May Prevent Settlement

Your employer has the right to veto or disapprove any settlement reached by you and the insurance company.

If your employer advises the insurance company that it disputes the validity of your workers' compensation claim, the employer must be notified of any workers' compensation hearings in your case. If your employer asks a workers' compensation judge in writing not to approve a proposed settlement agreement between you and the insurance company, the insurance company will probably not go forward with the settlement and your case will go to trial. If the insurance company proceeds with the settlement agreement over the employer's objection, it will not affect your settlement, but it could expose the insurance company to further proceedings by the employer.

For legitimate workers' compensation claims, employers will rarely try to prevent settlement. If your employer objects to a settlement without good reason, the court may impose a penalty upon the employer for acting in bad faith to cause unnecessary delay of the settlement of your claim. The employer may be required to pay you any expenses, including attorney fees and costs, that you incurred as a result of the delay. Although rare, under LC § 5813 the judge also has the power to order the insurance company to pay a penalty of up to $2,500 to the general fund (the checking account for the State of California). If it is found that your employer acted in bad faith, you will be entitled to payment of your expenses, including attorney fees, so you should give serious consideration to getting an attorney at this time.

If you have a legitimate claim, you should never be afraid to go to trial. You will generally gain more by going to trial because you did not give up anything to arrive at a compromised settlement figure.

C. The Employer's Responsibilities

An employer has a number of obligations under the workers' compensation system. If your employer does not fulfill these requirements, you may have legal recourse, ranging from being permitted to file a lawsuit to gaining control of your own medical treatment.

1. Employer Must Carry Workers' Compensation Insurance

If your employer doesn't have the workers' compensation coverage required by law, you may do either or both of the following:

- **File a lawsuit against your employer in civil court.** In this situation, you aren't limited to the benefits provided by workers' compensation. For example, you may sue for lost wages as well as pain and suffering that result from your industrial injury. Although this remedy may at first seem advantageous, its success depends on whether your employer is financially solvent enough to pay an eventual court judgment. Unfortunately, businesses that violate laws requiring them to maintain workers' compensation insurance are often close to insolvency.

  Winning a civil case against your uninsured employer should be merely a formality, as you don't need to prove that your employer was at fault for your injury. Uninsured employers are presumed responsible under the Labor Code. (LC § 3708.)
- **File a workers' compensation claim against the Uninsured Employers Benefits Trust Fund.** If you choose to file a workers' compensation claim, you'll need to follow the same paperwork procedures as with any other workers' compensation claim. However, also list the Uninsured Employers Benefits Trust Fund as a defendant. This fund is funded and run by the State of California to pay the claims of injured employees whose employers do not have workers' compensation coverage. (See Chapter 16, Section B.)

2. Employer Must Post Notices and Advise You of Your Legal Rights

Every employer must post certain notices in a convenient location frequented by employees during working hours. The notices contain important information about employees' rights and also:

- provide the name of the company's workers' compensation carrier or the fact that the employer is self-insured, as well as who is responsible for claims adjustment
- state that injured workers have the right to receive medical treatment and to select or change treating doctors,
- provide information about the employer's or its insurance carrier's medical provider network (MPN). This information should include the fact that the employer has an MPN and requires the injured employee to treat with a doctor within the network. The notice must provide the employee with information on how to determine which doctors are within the MPN and how to select a doctor from the network. (This information must also be provided to you by letter after you notify your employer of your injury.) The MPN network is discussed further in Chapter 9. If the employer fails to do any of the above, you may go to a doctor of your choice, and you do not need to select a doctor from the MPN. (See the case of *Knight v. United Parcel Service*, in Chapter 28.) And
- give details about available workers' compensation benefits. (LC § 3550, CCR § 9881.)

Employers must notify new hires of the above information no later than the end of the first pay period. (LC § 3551, CCR § 9880.) If an employee requests it, the employer must provide a form for designating a personal physician by whom the employee wishes to be treated if injured at work.

Some employers have contracts with at least two health care organizations to provide treatment for employees injured at work. At the time of hire, and at least once a year after, these employers must give employees an opportunity to designate a personal physician. (LC § 3552.)

If an employer fails to comply with all of these requirements, an injured worker is automatically allowed to choose which doctor will provide treatment for an industrial injury. (LC § 3550(a).) If your employer violated any posting or notice requirements, write a letter to the insurance company. Point out the violation and request that you immediately be allowed to treat with your doctor of choice. Remember to send the letter certified mail, return receipt requested.

3. Employer Must Provide Claim Forms and Pamphlet

If you were injured at work, your employer must provide you with a workers' compensation claim form DWC-1 within 24 hours of notification of the injury. (CCR § 10119.)

In addition, an employer has five days after it learns of a work-related injury to supply you with written information (usually a pamphlet) about your rights under the workers' compensation system. The written material explains your legal rights and provides details about available benefits, procedures for filing a claim, when and how to contact an information and assistance officer, and the fact that you're protected from discrimination. (CCR § 9882.) In addition, the material should include the fact that the employer has an MPN and that the injured employee must be treated by a doctor within the network. The notice must also provide the employee with information on how to determine which doctors are within the MPN and how to select a doctor from the network. If your employer fails to provide a DWC-1 form or give you written information on time, you may choose your personal doctor. Point out this fact in a letter to the insurance company and request that you immediately be allowed to treat with your doctor of choice. Remember to send the letter certified mail, return receipt requested.

D. If You're Out of Work Due to the Injury

SKIP AHEAD

This section applies only to employees who are off work because of their injuries. If you haven't lost work time, skip to Section E, below.

Being off work because of an injury can be a frightening and frustrating experience. Many injured workers cannot afford to lose much work time because temporary disability benefits paid under the workers' compensation system are not sufficient to live on. And of course, most employees have the reasonable fear of losing their jobs. While there are no hard and fast answers, the following suggestions should help you through this inevitably rough period.

Sick Leave and Vacation

If you've accumulated vacation and sick leave at your job, it's yours to take whenever you wish. You are not required to take or use your vacation and sick time before drawing temporary disability payments under workers' compensation.

If you want to receive sick leave or vacation pay, see the discussion in Chapter 12, Section C4.

1. Communicate With Your Employer

If you're disabled and out of work, you need to ask yourself two questions: Do you want to return to work for this employer? Are you able—or will you be able—to go back to your old job?

If your answer is "yes" to both questions, it's an excellent idea to open up a line of communication with your employer. An employer that does not hear from you may assume the worst, especially if you were upset when you left or if your accident or injury was your fault. Lack of communication may enforce an attitude that you are not a "team player" and that you only want to cost the company money. The employer may feel you are goofing off or trying to get a free ride.

If, on the other hand, you regularly check in with your boss, your employer is likely to see that you're still a loyal employee and you're doing your best to get better and get back to work. If possible, call your employer once a week and give an update about your condition and when you expect to return.

If you feel it is appropriate, you may even want to tell your employer one or more of the following:

- You didn't want to file a workers' compensation claim, but since you were legitimately injured, you filled out the paperwork as required by law.
- You are looking forward to returning to your old job.
- Your main concern is to get better and get back to work as soon as possible.
- Your treating doctor has found that you did indeed suffer an injury at work.

2. Will Your Employer Keep Your Job for You?

Unfortunately, there is no law or legal policy that requires your employer to hold your job for you if you are injured or ill. If there's no employment contract to the contrary, your employer can terminate you at any time. Your employer cannot, however, retaliate against you—including terminating you—for filing a workers' compensation claim. If your employer has notice of or knows about your injury and does terminate you, your right to receive workers' compensation for any injury that has already occurred will not be affected.

Common sense dictates that your employer would prefer to have you return to work, rather than incur the time and expense involved in finding and training a replacement. But whether or not your employer is willing—or can afford—to hold your job for you will depend upon a variety of factors, including:

- how irreplaceable your employer perceives you to be
- how long you've been out and when you expect to be able to return
- how critical your position is to the overall operation of the business—in other words, how long your employer can comfortably operate without filling your position
- your employer's financial well-being
- the requirements of your employment contract, if you have one; many employment contracts require that the employer hold a job for a set amount of days, weeks, or months, and
- your employer's willingness to put up with the inconvenience. How well you get along with your employer will likely contribute to its willingness to keep your job available. (See Section D1, above, on the importance of communicating with your employer.)

If you belong to a union, your union representative may be very helpful in negotiating on your behalf if your employer violated any provisions of your employment contract. Keep in touch with your union representative as your workers' compensation situation develops. That way, your representative can properly advise you of your rights under your employment contract and assist you in enforcing them.

3. If Your Employer Offers You an Alternate Job

If you can't ever return to the same type of work because of your injury, you may be entitled to vocational retraining.

You don't want to do anything that may jeopardize your future right to these benefits. This is an area where you need to be very careful.

If you cannot return to your old job because of your disability, your employer may offer you an alternative position once you can do some work, sometimes at less pay. If the job offers wages and compensation that are within 15% of those paid to you at the time of your injury, you must accept the job, or you will forfeit any future rights you have to vocational rehabilitation (this applies to workers injured in 2003 or earlier).

If your injury occurred in 2004 or later, your employer may, within 30 days of the end of your temporary disability benefits, offer you alternate or modified work accommodating your work restrictions. If you reject or fail to accept the offer and do not return to work within 60 days of the end of your temporary disability benefits, you might waive your right to the supplemental job displacement benefits. (For more on these benefits, see Chapter 14.)

Furthermore, if you were injured in 2005 or later and your employer offers you alternative or modified work, your permanent disability award may be reduced by 15% if you do not accept the offer. (This may also apply if you were injured before 2005 but your permanent disability is required to be determined by using the 2005 rating schedule for another reason.) See Chapter 13, Section E3, for the specifics.

4. If You Go Back to Work

It's likely that you will return to work long before your workers' compensation case settles. If that happens, you'll naturally be in close contact with your employer.

In most cases, going back to work is uneventful. You return and do your job, and everything is the same as before the injury. It's a good idea, however, to be careful about what you say to your employer regarding your injury. Until your case settles, you should do your best not to discuss your claim at work.

SEE AN EXPERT

If your employer harasses you. Sometimes an employer harasses a returning employee and starts laying a foundation for eventual termination. For example, the employer may single you out and write you up for things that other employees aren't being written up for. If you face problems with your employer, immediately see an information and assistance officer or consult a workers' compensation attorney.

E. Bankruptcy or Other Employer Financial Problems

As long as your employer had workers' compensation insurance coverage at the time of your injury, financial problems or bankruptcy by your employer will have no effect upon your workers' compensation case or your financial recovery. The insurance company makes decisions regarding settlement of your case and pays for the benefits you receive.

If, however, your employer did not have workers' compensation insurance or is permissibly self-insured and files for bankruptcy, you must file a claim with the bankruptcy court. You'll need to petition the bankruptcy court for what's called "relief from the automatic stay." (When a bankruptcy petition is filed, an "automatic stay" goes into effect, which precludes any potential creditor—the telephone company, landlord, or you—from proceeding with any actions, legal or otherwise, that would affect the bankruptcy.) As an injured worker, you may ask the bankruptcy court to lift the automatic stay as far as you are concerned so that you can collect your workers' compensation benefits. In situations such as these, it is best to get help from an information and assistance officer or contact a workers' compensation attorney.

CHAPTER

Taking Charge of Your Medical Case

As an injured worker, you are entitled to receive medical care needed to cure or relieve your injury or illness at no cost to you. (LC § 4600.) That's great, you say. But wait; it's important to fully understand that the doctors who treat your medical problem will also make important decisions about the fate of your workers' compensation case and may be able to deny you medical treatment.

To best protect your legal rights, you'll need to address two important aspects of your medical treatment:

- the medical care you receive—you obviously want the right kind of high-quality treatment, and
- how your medical treatment affects the legal status of your workers' compensation claim—you want to be sure your medical treatment supports, and doesn't undermine, your legal case.

Reimbursement for Travel and Medical Expenses

You are entitled to be reimbursed for costs of prescriptions, medical bills you paid, and other costs associated with your medical care. You are also entitled to be paid for your round trip mileage to and from doctors' examinations, physical therapy sessions, and trips to the pharmacy to pick up medications.

Keep copies of all medically related receipts and careful records of how much you travel. You'll need to submit these records to the insurance company when you request reimbursement. Chapter 11, Section B, gives step-by-step instructions.

A. What the Treating Doctor Does

The future of your workers' compensation case rests largely with the doctor who treats you or oversees your treatment until you completely recover or your condition reaches a plateau. In workers' compensation jargon, this person is usually called the "treating doctor" or "primary treating doctor."

Your treating doctor is important to your workers' compensation case because she or he will be reporting to the insurance company on the extent of your injury, your treatment, and your prognosis for recovery.

If your primary treating doctor thinks it's necessary, you may be referred to treating doctors in other specialties (a heart specialist or orthopedist, for example) for treatment and consultation, but you will also continue to see and treat with your primary treating doctor.

1. How the Treating Doctor Affects Your Case

Here are the main questions your primary treating doctor will answer for the insurance company:

- **Were you injured on the job?** If the treating doctor decides your injury or symptoms are consistent with your story of how the injury occurred, the insurance company will be more likely to accept your claim and agree to provide benefits.
- **What will be the type and extent of your treatment?** The treating doctor has the power to say you don't need any treatment. If you do need treatment, the doctor may prescribe the type of treatment and medication you need. It's up to the treating doctor to decide whether you need physical therapy, chiropractic care, or other types of help.
- **Do you need to see specialists?** It is up to the treating doctor to recognize when additional tests are necessary, or when you need to see a specialist in another medical field. If the treating doctor fails to live up to these responsibilities, you quite possibly won't receive the excellent medical treatment that you deserve.
- **Are you temporarily disabled?** The treating doctor determines whether you should return to work immediately or take some time off.

If you need time off from work as a result of your injury, you are entitled to temporary disability payments. The treating doctor also decides when you are well enough to go back to work. Some doctors are very reasonable when it comes to making this determination; others are not.

EXAMPLE: Joanne, who was working for a major grocery chain, injured her back when a heavy metal shelf gave way and fell on her. Although tests showed that Joanne had herniated (ruptured) two discs in her back, and she was in great pain, the treating doctor told her she could immediately go back to work. Eventually, Joanne required back surgery because of her injury.

If you feel you need time off work to recover, don't be reluctant to ask your doctor to prescribe it.

- **When is your condition "permanent and stationary" or when have you reached "maximal medical improvement"?** This bit of legal jargon means that your medical condition has reached a plateau, and your condition is not expected to improve over the next year. Your doctor makes this determination, which can have a big effect on your monetary benefits because it will cause your temporary disability payments to end.

  For injuries in 2005 or later, "permanent and stationary" may also be referred to as having reached maximal medical improvement (MMI). MMI technically means that the injured worker's condition is not expected to improve within the next year (with or without medical treatment).
- **Can you ever return to your former job?** The treating doctor is normally a crucial decision maker in determining whether or not you can return to your former job. If you can go back, the doctor may determine whether you can work full- or part-time and whether your job will need to be modified to accommodate your disability. The treating doctor's findings will also affect your qualification for additional workers' compensation benefits, such as vocational rehabilitation or job displacement benefits.
- **Do you have a permanent disability or need future medical care?** Your doctor's report will determine whether you have suffered permanent impairment. This determination will greatly affect your financial settlement. The treating doctor's opinions on issues of whether you have a permanent disability or need future medical care are important to your case.

TIP

You are entitled to a second opinion. If you or the insurance company objects to any of the treating doctor's findings, the objecting party may obtain another medical opinion. See Section D, below.

There can be only one *primary* treating doctor at a time. If you are seeing or have seen more than one doctor for treatment, you'll need to establish which one is your primary treating doctor. The primary treating doctor must have examined you at least once for the purpose of rendering or prescribing treatment and must have monitored the effect of the treatment afterward.

2. The Treating Doctor Decides Whether You Should Return to Work

Following your injury, the treating doctor will determine whether you need time off or may return to your job.

a. Off-Work Order

If the doctor determines that you need time off to recuperate, you'll get an off-work order, in the form of either a note or a written prescription. The off-work order will specify a set period of time, usually a week or two for fairly minor injuries, that you should not work. The order will also specify a return appointment date (before the expiration of the order), at which time the doctor will decide whether the off-work order needs to be extended.

You must give the off-work order to your employer or see that it's mailed or faxed. The off-work order specifies that you will be out due to an industrial injury and therefore will not be absent without reason.

b. Limited Duties Work Order (Restrictions)

The doctor may determine that you need to take it easy, but that it's okay to return to work with limited duties (restricting certain activities that you can do at work). If so, the doctor will give you a note—called a "limited duties," "light," or "modified" work order—indicating what those work restrictions are. A typical limited duties work order might be "no lifting at or above shoulder level," "no prolonged sitting," "no repetitive gripping or grasping," or "no climbing ladders." Make sure your employer gets this order promptly on the day you return to work; otherwise, you will be expected to do your normal duties.

c. Return to Work Order

Another possibility is that the doctor may issue a written note indicating that you may return to your work without any restrictions (or with restrictions that aren't meaningful, given your injury). In essence, this means that your injury doesn't affect your ability to perform your duties.

If, in fact, you have fully recovered, that's great! Your goal should be to return to work as soon as possible. Unfortunately, some doctors try to get employees back to work as quickly as possible to save the employer and its insurance company some money. Even if a doctor is acting in the best of faith and returns you to work without restrictions (or with restrictions that don't adequately protect you), always remember that this determination is only an opinion. *The doctor can be wrong!*

d. If You Disagree With the Doctor's Order

The safest way to cope with what you believe is an erroneous return to work order is to call the insurance company and explain the problem. Then report to work. If you don't show up at work, your employer may legally fire you because you failed to report to work without a good excuse. If this occurs, you'll face an uphill battle trying to convince your employer that your opinion is more reliable than the doctor's.

If, after returning to work, you believe you cannot do your job—even if you have only tried for a few minutes—inform your supervisor and ask that you be authorized to return to the doctor for further treatment and evaluation. By law, your employer must honor your request. When you see the doctor, explain that you returned to your job but could not continue working because of pain or an inability to perform the work. The doctor must reevaluate the assessment that you were ready to get back to work and will, in all probability, give you an off-work order.

If the doctor still refuses to take you off work or still insists on restrictions that are completely unhelpful (you can't lift your right arm without pain and the doctor says not to lift more than 50 pounds), immediately call the workers' compensation insurance company (ask for the adjuster handling your case) or your employer. Explain what happened and why you are dissatisfied, and demand another treating doctor.

If you are not being treated by a doctor in a medical provider network established by your employer, then by law, you are entitled to a one-time change of doctors within five working days of your request. If the insurance company does not provide you with the name of another doctor in that time, you may choose your own doctor, as discussed in Section D1, below.

If you are being treated by a doctor in a medical provider network established by your employer, you can request a second (and third) opinion within the network. See Section D2, below, for more information.

e. If You Are Reinjured or Your Condition Worsens

If you go back to work and reinjure yourself, in workers' compensation terms, the reinjury will be considered one of two things:

- **An aggravation**—a new injury. In this case, you should fill out the paperwork required to file a new workers' compensation claim—the same forms you used for your initial claim.
- **An exacerbation**—a worsening or flare-up of the same injury.

If your doctor concludes your new pain is an exacerbation of your original injury, your medical options depend on the status of your case.

If you have not yet settled your case, you're in luck. You can simply continue to be treated by your doctor until you are once again declared to be permanent and stationary and the doctor writes a final report setting forth your increased factors of disability.

If you have settled your case by stipulations with request for award (see Chapter 19, Section B), the insurance company will pay for the medical treatment you need. You may need to get prior approval from the insurance company.

If you have already settled your claim by compromise and release (see Chapter 19, Section B), you may be out of luck. The only way you can get workers' compensation benefits in this case is to file a new workers' compensation claim, and you can do this only if you can show that at least 1% of your current disability is due to your current employment, not your prior injury. If your doctor says your problems are due 100% to your prior injury, you may have to get a medical-legal evaluation to decide the issue. (See Chapter 10.)

Either way, you should immediately report any additional problems to your supervisor and request a medical appointment with your doctor.

3. The Treating Doctor's Reports

While you are being treated for your injuries, the treating doctor is required to send written reports to the insurance company to keep it apprised of your condition and prognosis. If you have more than one treating doctor, it's likely that each specialist will write a report and the primary treating doctor will write a comprehensive summary report.

TIP

Get copies of treating doctor's reports. If you send a request to your employer and the insurance company, they must send you copies of medical reports. See Chapter 6, Section D, for instructions on requesting documents. Read all reports carefully.

a. Doctor's First Report of Industrial Injury

Within five days of the initial examination, any doctor who treats an injured employee for an industrial injury must prepare a standard report that sets forth each treated occupational injury and illness. This is true for one-time treatments as well as emergency room treatments.

The first report of industrial injury is important because it is close to the date of injury. As such, the insurance company will often rely on it when initially determining whether to accept or deny your claim. The doctor will mail the first report of industrial injury to the insurance company, or, if the employer is self-insured, to the employer. (LC § 6409.)

b. Periodic Medical Reports

Assuming your claim is accepted, the treating doctor must file reports of your progress with the insurance company at least once every 30 days. If you're receiving temporary disability, the insurance company will stop paying if the reports indicate you have recovered or can return to work.

Sometimes insurance companies cut off temporary disability payments if the treating doctor fails to keep the insurance company informed as required. If this occurs, you may need to act as a go-between with your treating doctor and the insurance company. Do this by immediately calling and writing your doctor and urging the doctor to file the necessary reports.

c. Permanent and Stationary or MMI Report

When your treating doctor concludes that your condition is stable and is not likely to improve significantly over the next year, the doctor will write a "permanent and stationary report" or submit a finding that you have reached maximal medical improvement. From the date of this report, you are no longer judged to be temporarily disabled under the terms of the workers' compensation law, and any temporary disability payments you have been receiving will stop.

The permanent and stationary or maximal medical improvement report will incorporate the opinions of any specialists and will discuss such critical issues as the nature and extent of your permanent disability, your need for future medical treatment, and your qualification for vocational rehabilitation benefits.

Make sure you carefully review your permanent and stationary report with the help of Section E3, below.

TIP

Maximum medical improvement. For injuries that occurred on or after 1/1/2005, the doctor will use the term maximum medical improvement (MMI) instead of permanent and stationary (P&S). It means the same thing as permanent and stationary, and for our purposes in this book, anytime we refer to permanent and stationary (P&S) we also mean MMI.

d. What to Do If You Object to a Medical Report

Carefully review the first doctor's report and each and every interim medical report, as well as the permanent and stationary report. (See Section E3, below, for more information on the permanent and stationary report.)

If you object to a medical report, you can get a second opinion or switch doctors, but the rules differ depending on whether you have been labeled "permanent and stationary" yet (see Section E, below) and whether your employer has a medical provider network.

If you have not been declared permanent and stationary (or have not reached "maximal medical improvement") and you are being treated by a doctor in a medical provider network established by your employer, you may request a second and third opinion in the appropriate specialty within the network. If you are still not satisfied with these doctors' reports, you may submit an "independent medical review application" to the administrative director asking to be sent to another doctor outside of the network for an independent medical review (IMR). If the IMR decides the disputed issue in your favor, you may then go to any doctor you choose for treatment (you are not limited to your employer's provider network in this case). If the IMR decides against you regarding the disputed issue, you have no other recourse.

If you have not yet been declared permanent and stationary (or reached "maximal medical improvement"), and you are not being treated by a doctor in a medical provider network established by your employer, you may request a change of treating doctors and choose another doctor.

If you *have* been declared permanent and stationary or MMI, and you are objecting to your doctor's opinion stated in the permanent and stationary report regarding any of the following:

- whether you should be permanent and stationary
- the nature and extent of your permanent disability, or
- whether or not you are entitled to supplemental job displacement benefits

then you must make your objection within 30 days of receipt of the medical report (20 days if you have a lawyer) and request a medical-legal evaluation with a qualified medical evaluator (QME). For information on how to request a medical-legal evaluation to dispute the extent of your injury or whether you should have been made permanent and stationary, see Chapter 10, Sections C and D. For information on selecting a QME, see Chapter 10, Section E.

Sample Objection to Medical Report

[Date]

[Name of insurance company]
[Address]

Injured worker: [*Your name*]
Employer: [*Employer's name*]
Date of injury: [*Date*]
Claim number: [*Number*]

To Whom It May Concern:

Please be advised that I object to the findings of [*doctor's name*], my treating doctor, as set forth in her report of [*date*].

Specifically, I dispute the doctor's opinion regarding the following issues: [list those that apply]

1. My permanent and stationary status [or permanent and stationary date]
2. A finding that I no longer require medical treatment
3. My QIW status
4. The nature and extent of my permanent disability
5. My need for future medical treatment
6. Compensability of my injury
7. Apportionment
8. New and further disability
9. Other:

Please provide me with a form to request a QME panel.

Sincerely,
[Your name]

B. Choose Your Treating Doctor (Get Medical Control in Your Case)

Whoever selects your treating doctor obviously has great input and control over how your case will be handled. Unfortunately, as pointed out earlier, many employers and insurance companies pick doctors who will make decisions that will save them money, even if these decisions are not in your best interests. Doctors who are financially dependent on insurance company referrals quickly understand that if they want referrals to continue, they had better make workers'-compensation-related decisions cost-effective from the insurer's point of view.

And what makes employers and insurance companies appreciate a doctor so much that they make referrals? For one thing, getting you back to work as soon as possible. The sooner you're back to work, the less temporary disability indemnity the insurance company has to pay. Another thing that makes insurance companies happy is a diagnosis that you are 100% healed or have a very minimal disability as a result of your work injury. Finally, insurance companies are always pleased with a finding that you don't need any ongoing medical treatment.

Your employer (or its insurance company) may have in place a system called a medical provider network (MPN). If your employer does, it is required to advise you of its MPN at the time of your hire (if it was in existence then) or after you advise your employer of your injury. Your employer is also required to post a notice in a conspicuous place at your work, advising employees of the existence of the MPN and instructions on how to determine what doctors are within its MPN and how to choose a doctor within the MPN. The insurance carrier must also send you a letter advising you of its MPN and how to select a doctor from its network after you report an injury. If you have not previously predesignated a treating doctor (see below) and your employer has properly provided all of the required notices (see the case of

Knight v. United Parcel Service, in Chapter 28), then you must treat with a doctor within the employer's medical provider network.

What Is a Medical Provider Network?

One of the major changes in workers' compensation laws in 2004 was the establishment of an employer's (or insurance carrier's) right to set up a Medical Provider Network (MPN). An MPN is a group of doctors or medical clinics that are authorized by the employer or carrier to treat you if you have a work-related injury. If your employer or its workers' compensation insurance carrier has set up an MPN, you must treat with an MPN doctor or you run the risk of your doctor's not being paid. It's also possible that a non-MPN doctor's reports might not be considered by a judge if your case goes to trial.

How do you know whether you have to go to an MPN doctor? Simple—your employer or its insurance carrier is required by law to send you a letter advising you of the existence of the MPN and providing a list of in-network doctors within a reasonable distance of your residence (say 25 miles). They may also advise you how you can access the list on the Internet (or you can call your adjuster and ask). If you don't get a letter from the carrier, you can treat with any doctor of your choice.

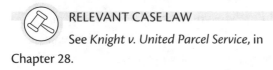

RELEVANT CASE LAW

See *Knight v. United Parcel Service*, in Chapter 28.

1. Designate Your Treating Doctor in Advance

The only sure way you will have immediate control of your medical care in case of a work injury is by giving your employer advance written notice of the treating doctor you wish to see in case you are injured at work. You can predesignate your treating doctor only if you meet all of the following conditions:

- Your employer provides group health coverage in a health care service plan or group health plan for nonoccupational purposes that's either licensed pursuant to Chapter 2.2 of Division 2 of the Health and Safety Code or as described in 8 CCR 9780.1.
- The predesignated doctor is your regular and primary care physician and has previously directed your medical treatment and retains your medical records, including your medical history.
- The physician agrees to be predesignated.

If you already reported an injury to your employer and did not previously designate your doctor, you are too late to do so for your present injury. It's still worthwhile to designate your doctor, however, in case you're ever injured again.

CAUTION

Designate your doctor before you report a gradually occurring injury. If you believe you have an injury that developed over time, such as a cumulative trauma injury, it's wise to designate your treating doctor before advising your employer of your injury.

To designate your personal physician as your treating doctor, simply notify your employer in writing. No special form is required, but you may wish to use the Employee's Designation of Personal Physician which is provided on Nolo's website. (See Chapter 29, "Online Appendixes" for the link to this and other forms in this book.) A sample is shown below. Keep a copy for your records.

Note that you are entitled to designate only one primary treating doctor. That doctor will have authority to refer you to other medical specialists if he or she feels that's appropriate.

TIP

Get referrals approved. It's best to call the insurance company to request authorization for any referrals made by your treating doctor.

Employee's Designation of Personal Physician
(California Labor Code Section 4600)

To: ____
Name of Employer

In the event I am injured at work and require medical treatment, I designate the following as my personal physician:

____
Name of Physician, Chiropractor, or Medical Facility

____
Address of Physician, Chiropractor, or Medical Facility

____
Telephone Number

______________________________ ______________________________
Date Signature of Employee

Given to: ____
Name of Employer Representative

2. Seeing Your Doctor of Choice Right After an Injury

CAUTION

If your employer has a medical provider network. If your employer has established a medical provider network, you must be treated by the doctors in that network. In certain circumstances, however (listed below), you may be able to choose your own doctor.

If you didn't designate your doctor in advance, you still may have the immediate opportunity to select your treating doctor rather than going to someone hand-picked by your employer. Generally, you can do this if your employer allows you to, doesn't follow the rules, or denies your claim. Specifically, you may choose your treating doctor from the start in any of these situations:

- Your employer leaves the decision up to you.
- Your employer denies your claim.
- Your employer has contracted with at least two health care organizations to provide medical treatment for employees injured due to work and you were not advised of your right to predesignate your treating physician in writing when you were hired, by the end of the first pay period, and at least once a year after.
- Your employer failed to post legally required notices of your workers' compensation rights, advise you of your right to predesignate your doctor when you were hired or by the end of your first pay period, or give you the required information about a medical provider network, if your employer has one.
- After being informed of your injury, your employer did not provide you with claim forms and information about workers' compensation benefits, as discussed in Chapter 8, Section C3.

- You require emergency medical care. In this case, you can go to the emergency room of your choice.

a. If Your Employer Leaves the Decision Up to You

If you gave your employer an opportunity to tell you what doctor to go to for medical treatment and your employer declined, you are free to go to whomever you want.

However, if your employer did not have a chance to name the doctor you should see (as might be the case where you first go to the emergency room), you haven't been given the go-ahead to choose doctors. Your employer can select a doctor at its first opportunity.

b. If Your Employer Won't Authorize Medical Treatment or Denies Your Claim

If your injury occurred in 2005 or later, your employer is required to pay for medical treatment (up to $10,000) until your injury is accepted or rejected.

If the insurance company denies your claim—claiming that your injury isn't work-related or that you are not injured and do not need treatment—it can be to your advantage. By refusing to authorize treatment, the insurance company waives the right to designate your doctor. You are therefore free to go to any doctor you choose who is willing to treat you.

If the insurance company denies your claim, you still have an excellent chance of getting workers' compensation coverage. Indeed, close to 90% of all claims or requests for medical treatment that are denied by employers or insurance companies are ultimately accepted or found to be valid by the Workers' Compensation Appeals Board.

The next question is, how do you get medical treatment when the insurance company won't pay? You may choose to seek treatment at a free medical clinic or county hospital. Barring that, there are generally four ways to obtain medical treatment:

- **Pay for treatment yourself.** If your workers' compensation case is later accepted, you are entitled to be reimbursed by the insurance company for all treatment that was reasonably necessary. Be sure you get reimbursed from the insurance company if your case settles. If the insurance company won't reimburse you, you'll have to make this an issue at your trial.
- **Use your group health insurance coverage.** If you have group health insurance coverage provided directly by a health maintenance organization such as Kaiser, or under a plan by which an insurance company reimburses doctors, use it. Your health insurance plan will provide or pay for treatment and file a "green lien" (discussed just below). The group company will be repaid by the workers' compensation insurance company at the end of the case. Be sure to tell your group insurance company that you were injured at work.
- **Find a doctor who is willing to file a "green lien."** You may ask the doctor you want to see if you can be treated without payment and instead file a lien form in your workers' compensation case. This is called a "green lien" in the jargon of the workers' compensation trade, because the form is green. By filing a green lien, the doctor is entitled to be paid if you are found to have a valid workers' compensation claim. In short, the doctor agrees to wait for payment until your workers' compensation case settles. The green lien can be filed by the doctor any time prior to settlement or a trial on the merits of your claim.

Unless the doctor is familiar with the workers' compensation system and has treated injured workers in the past, it is unlikely that he or she will agree to file a green lien. In short, you may have to call around to find a doctor's practice devoted at least partially to workers' compensation cases.

In the event you don't qualify for workers' compensation, it is possible that you may be personally responsible for payment of your medical treatment.

- **File for an appeals board hearing.** You may ask a workers' compensation judge to decide whether you are entitled to receive medical care. (See Chapter 22, Section B.)

Internal Utilization Review Process

All employers (or their insurance companies) must establish an internal utilization review process to review denials of treatment. Denials of treatment must be communicated in a timely manner to the requesting physician first by fax or telephone and then in writing, according to the following time frames:

For treatment waiting to be authorized, the decision must be communicated to the worker within five days from the receipt of information necessary to make the decision, but in no event more than 14 days from the treatment recommendation.

If the injured worker faces imminent and serious threat to his or her health or if further delay could jeopardize the worker's ability to regain maximum function of an injured body part, the decision must be communicated to the worker within 72 hours after the receipt of the information necessary to make the decision.

For retrospective review (for example, a review of whether to approve or deny payment for an MRI already taken), the decision must be communicated within 30 days from the receipt of all necessary information.

Once the utilization review doctor has made a decision, it must be communicated to the requesting physician within 24 hours (48 hours for prospective review). (See Chapter 11, Section A3, for more information.)

c. If Your Employer Failed to Post Proper Notices

Your employer is required by law to post a notice advising its employees about their rights under the California workers' compensation laws. If your employer failed to post such a notice prior to your injury, it forfeits its right to control your medical treatment, and you are free to choose your own doctor. You should therefore check your workplace (or ask a coworker or friend to do it) to see whether the proper notice is posted. Doing this is not a waste of time, as many small employers, particularly, don't bother to post notices, or post them in a place where employees never go. (See Chapter 8, Section C2, for a detailed explanation of the notice posting requirements.)

d. If Your Employer Failed to Advise You in Writing of Your Right to Predesignate Your Treating Doctor

In addition to posting notices, your employer is required to give you written notice of your right to predesignate your treating doctor in the event of an injury. This must be done at the time you are hired or by the end of the first pay period. (LC § 3551, CCR § 9880.)

Also, where your employer has contracted with at least two health care organizations to treat employees who suffer work injuries, your employer is required to place in your employment file either your choice of treating doctor or a signed statement that you declined to predesignate a treating doctor in the event of an injury. This must be done at the time you are hired, and at least once a year after that.

If your employer failed to advise you of your right to predesignate your treating doctor, you are free to choose your own doctor for treatment. (LC § 4600.3.) Because many employers fail to do this, it can be a valuable way to be sure you are treated by a doctor of your choice.

> **EXAMPLE:** Jacob is injured at work. He informs his employer and requests to see a doctor. His employer tells him to go see the industrial medical clinic doctor. Jacob tells his employer he wants to treat with his own doctor because he feels he'll get better treatment. He tells his employer (or its insurance company) that he has the right to choose his own doctor because the

employer failed to advise him of his workers' compensation rights in writing as required by LC § 3551. Jacob goes to his own doctor.

C. Be Sure You Receive Excellent Medical Care

You should be an active participant in your medical treatment and healing. After all, you are the only one with a 100% interest and commitment to your own health. The more you know about your condition and treatment, the better able you will be to get the best possible medical care.

1. Knowing What to Say to the Doctor

For most people, seeing a doctor can be an intimidating experience. This is especially true if the doctor was selected by your employer and you're worried that you may receive an inadequate diagnosis or treatment. Even if you selected your own medical clinic or doctor, you still may be a little concerned. This is not only understandable, it's sensible. But no matter who chose the doctor or how you feel about the doctor, you should always protect your legal rights.

a. Come to the Exam Prepared

If possible, bring a friend or family member to the initial examination. It's always nice to have support. In addition, that person may be called on later to verify what happened in the examination.

Take a pad and pencil with you and be prepared to keep a record of what is said. If the doctor appears to be hostile or asks intensive questions about your personal activities, jot down these questions along with your responses. Because it's obvious you are making a record, the doctor may be less likely to make an "erroneous" report.

b. Give a Complete Medical History

The medical history you provide should include the following:

- **How you were injured.** Give a complete and detailed description of the workplace-related events that led up to your injury. If you were outside the workplace itself (driving on an office-related errand or attending a seminar required by your job), make sure you emphasize the fact that you were doing your job.
- **All specific body parts you may have injured.** Make sure the doctor records information about all of the parts of your body you think you may have injured. Be as thorough as possible, even if you think you only injured a certain body part or you think something is only a minor problem. The workers' compensation insurance company is likely to deny coverage for any injured body part not reported promptly.

  EXAMPLE: Sally slips and falls at work, hitting both her head and right knee. The knee causes such extreme pain that Sally forgets to tell the doctor about her mild headache. A month and a half later, Sally realizes she's had constant and worsening headaches since the accident and she requests medical treatment. The insurance company claims that any head problems are not covered by workers' compensation, because Sally did not tell the doctor about them at the time of the accident.

- **An accurate history of any prior injuries.** Be sure to give a complete history about any prior related medical problems the doctor asks about. Do this even if you suspect that the information may be used to show that your present medical problems are due to prior medical problems. If you fail to mention possible related problems when asked (say, the fact that your back was injured before), you may end up in a bad situation. For example, the insurance company may get copies of prior medical reports and deny your claim altogether by attributing it to injuries you hid.

But don't get carried away. While you always want to be honest about your prior medical history, you also want to insist that your injury was caused by your current on-the-job injury, not by a flare-up of an old problem (if that's the truth). The best way to do this usually is to explain how the injury occurred in direct and, if necessary, graphic terms.

EXAMPLE: Tommy sees Dr. Wu after injuring his ankle while working in a cafeteria. Tommy had broken his ankle five years earlier playing basketball. He was treated at the emergency room at that time and had follow-up care with his family doctor. Dr. Wu asks Tommy if he ever injured his ankle before. Tommy should tell the doctor about his prior injury and explain that he made a complete recovery. Tommy has absolutely no incentive to cover up the earlier injury, because the insurance company will probably obtain Tommy's past medical records and learn about it anyway. What Tommy should do is to emphasize how the current injury occurred: "I slipped on a greasy spot in the cafeteria and had a hard fall. As I went down, I felt my ankle twist slowly and then felt an extremely painful moment when my whole ankle seemed to fly apart."

TIP

Report even embarrassing injuries. Never neglect to report an injury, even if you're embarrassed about the part of the body injured (you have a pain in your butt or genitals) or how the injury occurred.

c. What Not to Tell a Doctor

To avoid your workers' compensation claim's being denied, there are certain things you should never say:

Rule 1. Never speculate that it's possible that your injury may have occurred outside of work (unless it clearly did). To be eligible for workers' compensation benefits, your injury must have occurred as a result of your employment.

Rule 2. Never say that you are 100%, or completely, recovered from your injury, unless you're sure that's absolutely true. If you do, you will not receive a permanent disability award that you might otherwise be entitled to.

Rule 3. Never exaggerate your injury. Doctors are very good at spotting individuals who exaggerate their problems. If a doctor notes that you were exaggerating your pain or other symptoms, the insurance company may believe that you are faking your injury and deny a claim that might otherwise be allowed. (Don't understate your condition, either. As long as you are truthful, you will avoid most problems.)

Rule 4. Never say or do anything to antagonize the doctor. If you don't like the doctor's manner, either politely tell the doctor what's bothering you or don't say anything at all and exercise your right to change doctors (or, if the injury is serious, get a second opinion).

d. Watch Out for Inappropriate Questions by the Doctor

Some doctors, especially those selected by insurance companies or employers, may ask questions that seem to blame you for the injury. Although your actions rarely have anything to do with your entitlement to coverage (it's a no-fault system, remember), a doctor may try to establish the basis to deny you coverage. For example, a doctor may try to show that your injury was not work-related, was caused by something fairly outrageous you did, such as horseplay or starting a fight, or was the result of your intoxication or misuse of drugs. (It will help to read Chapter 3, Section C, which discusses when injuries may not be covered.)

A question like, "Isn't it possible your back hurts because of your gardening activities at home?" or "Do you ride horses or play an active sport like softball or soccer?" should be a red flag. Remember, the information you provide will be put in the doctor's report to the insurance company with an opinion on how you were injured. This report can make or break your claim.

If you face any hostile or trick questions by the doctor, slow down. Answer each question very carefully—and truthfully—so there can be no misunderstanding. For example, if you are asked, "Did you notice any increase in pain after gardening?" you should respond with something like, "Since the injury at work, my back has really been killing me. There are many activities I can no longer do since my injury at work, and gardening is now one of them." If you are convinced that a doctor is not treating you with your best interests in mind, request another treating doctor. (See Section D, below, on changing doctors.)

2. Stay Involved in Your Medical Treatment

For some injured workers, the treatment phase of the workers' compensation case seems to drag on forever. Especially if you are off work and in pain, you may feel very vulnerable at this time. It is not unusual to feel as though your world is falling apart and you can't do anything about it.

You must firmly believe that things will improve. Countless thousands before you have been through industrial injuries and have coped with the recovery and rehabilitation process. You can, too. With this in mind, you may want to consider the following suggestions:

- **Keep informed about your medical condition.** You have the right to know exactly what the doctor believes is wrong with you, what treatment the doctor thinks is appropriate, and why. It's your right and responsibility to ask questions about your treatment, recovery, and ultimate prognosis. For example, ask for the doctor's best estimate of the time frame for your treatment and recovery. This will help you plan your affairs better. Also, make it your goal to be sure you understand exactly what the doctor is saying. If you don't understand medical jargon, ask the doctor for a plain-English translation. If this doesn't clear it up, write down the confusing terms and take time to use the Internet or go to the library to do some research. Many libraries have access to computerized databases of medical articles and other information (check with the reference librarian). Always remember that the better informed you are, the easier it will be to discuss your treatment with your doctors.
- **Obtain copies of medical reports.** If you request it, the insurance company is required to give you copies of all medical reports it receives from the doctor. If you don't receive copies from the insurance company within a reasonable time after your appointment (say within 60 days), call or write and request copies. You can also obtain copies of your medical files from the doctor's office, although some doctors charge for this service. (A fill-in-the-blanks letter you may use to request your medical records is shown in Chapter 6, Section D, and a downloadable copy is provided on Nolo's website. (See Chapter 29, "Online Appendixes" for the link to this and other forms in this book.)
- **Keep a "pain diary" of your condition.** It is always a good idea to keep a diary of the pain you suffer and of how your condition is progressing. Because some workers' compensation cases can go on for years, it's very important that you start this record and faithfully continue it. Otherwise, you may not be able to recall accurately what your condition was like at a particular time. (See Chapter 6, Section C10, for details.)
- **Keep your medical appointments.** It is your responsibility to keep your medical appointments. If you must cancel an appointment, do so well in advance. Many

doctors require 48 hours' or more advance notice to avoid charges. The doctor's office may charge you directly for missed appointments. If the insurance company pays for any appointments you miss without advance notice, the cost of the missed appointment may be deducted from your final settlement. In short, missing appointments may be equivalent to finding several $100 bills and deliberately tearing them up.

- **Get a second opinion in important medical matters.** This is particularly necessary where a doctor is recommending surgery. Under workers' compensation laws, you are entitled to a second opinion if your injury is serious.
- **Seek alternative medical treatment if you want it.** Alternative medical treatment is available for workers' compensation injuries under certain conditions, such as where traditional treatment is not working. Examples of alternative medical treatments might include acupuncture, massage therapy, or biofeedback. You and the workers' compensation insurance company may agree on alternative healing practices in writing, with each party reserving the right to terminate the agreement upon seven days' written notice to the other party. (LC §§ 4600.3, 3209.7.) If you want alternative treatment and the insurance company won't authorize it, you may have to file for a hearing and request that a judge order the treatment. (See Chapter 22.)

Internal Utilization Review Process

Every employer (or its insurance company) must establish an internal utilization review process (UR) to approve, modify, delay, or deny treatment plans based on whether the proposed treatment is medically necessary to cure and relieve the industrial injury. This means that claims adjusters themselves can no longer overrule the treating doctor's recommendations. See Chapter 11, Section A3, for more information.

D. Changing Treating Doctors

If you weren't allowed to choose your own doctor initially, after you see the company's doctor you have the right to change treating doctors, subject to certain rules discussed below.

SKIP AHEAD

If the treating doctor wrote a permanent and stationary report. If your permanent and stationary report (discussed in Section A3, above) states that you don't need any more medical care, you no longer have the right to choose a different treating doctor. Instead, if you disagree with the permanent and stationary report, you must choose a "qualified medical evaluator" (QME) and go to a medical-legal evaluation. For information on selecting a QME, see Chapter 10, Section E, and for information on how to request a medical-legal evaluation to dispute the extent of your injury or your permanent and stationary status, see Chapter 10, Sections C and D.

Changing treating doctors is a very complicated area. The chart below may help you understand the different rules, which are discussed in detail, below.

1. Changing a Predesignated Treating Doctor

If you predesignated your treating doctor in the event of industrial injury, you are free to change doctors at any time. Simply notify the insurance company of the change.

Keep in mind that predesignating your doctor is allowed only if you meet all of the following conditions:

- Your employer provides group health coverage for nonoccupational purposes.
- The physician you predesignated is your regular and primary care physician who previously directed your medical treatment and retains your medical records, including your medical history.
- The physician has agreed to be predesignated.

Rules for Changing Your Doctor	
Circumstance	**Period of time you must wait before you can change doctors**
If you predesignated your doctor	None. You can change your doctor at any time.
If you are being treated by a doctor in a medical provider network established by your employer for the treatment of work injuries	After your initial examination, you can request a second and third opinion within the same network and then request an independent medical review (IMR).
If your employer did not establish a medical provider network for the treatment of work injuries, and:	
• your employer sent you to a specific doctor or clinic	30 days
• your employer gave you a choice of who to see for your injury, and your employer doesn't offer regular health insurance	90 days
• your employer gave you a choice of who to see for your injury, and your employer offers regular health insurance	180 days
• you don't mind the employer or insurance company choosing the new doctor	None. You can do this type of change for any reason, but only one time.

2. If Your Employer Has Established a Medical Provider Network

If your employer has established a medical provider network for the treatment of work injuries, you must use a network doctor unless you predesignated a doctor. The only exception to this rule is when you can show the insurance company failed to follow all the rules (if you think this is true, consult an attorney, as it's too complicated an issue to deal with yourself). If you treat with a nonpredesignated doctor outside the network and the insurance carrier objects, all medical reports by your doctor may be inadmissible and you may be personally liable for the doctor's bills. You may change treating doctors two times (you can see your original doctor and two others) within the network, and then one last time outside the network.

Specifically, if you dispute the doctor's diagnosis or treatment recommendations, you may request a second and a third opinion in the appropriate specialty within your employer's medical provider network. When you request a second (or third) opinion, the insurance company will present you with a list of available doctors in the medical network, and you must make an appointment with one of the doctors within 60 days.

If, after getting the third opinion, you are still not satisfied, you may submit an "independent medical review application" to the administrative director asking to be sent to a doctor outside of the network for an independent medical review (IMR). If the IMR decides the disputed issue in your favor, you may go to any doctor you choose for treatment (you are not limited to your employer's provider network in this case). If the IMR decides against you regarding the disputed issue, you have no other recourse.

RESOURCE

Medical provider network regulations. The final rules governing medical provider networks became effective September 9, 2005. If you are interested in the details, the rules are set forth in Administrative Rules

9767.1 through 9767.15, which can be viewed at www.dir.ca.gov/t8/9767%5F1.html.

The rest of this section applies only if your employer *did not* establish a medical provider network.

3. Automatic One-Time Change at Any Time

If you have not predesignated a doctor, the good news is that you may request a one-time change of doctors, without explaining the reason, from the insurance company at any time. (LC § 4601.) Unfortunately, there is also bad news. The doctor you change to will be selected by the insurance company if the company acts within five working days of your request. If you make your initial request by mail, you must allow an additional five days from the date of mailing, for a total of ten days.

The insurance company will provide you with the name and address of an alternative doctor as well as an appointment date. The information may be given to you by telephone, in writing, or by any other means.

Pay careful attention to the five-day deadline. Often you can use your right to an automatic one-time change of doctors to get a doctor of your own choosing. Here's why. The insurance company's paperwork backlog often means it can't respond to your request within five working days. If you aren't given the alternative doctor information within the five-day deadline, you are free to choose your own treating doctor. Do not count the day of the request in the five days. (See Section D7, below, for a sample letter to the insurance company on changing doctors.)

> **EXAMPLE:** Chris reports injuring his knee at work on Wednesday, July 18. The following day, the insurance company tells him to see Dr. Adelberg for treatment, which he does. Chris calls the insurance company on Monday, July 23, explains that he is not happy with Dr. Adelberg and requests a different treating doctor. The company does not give Chris the name of an alternative doctor within five working days, so on Tuesday, July 31, Chris sets up an appointment with Dr. Shell. Chris writes the insurance carrier a note explaining that he has decided to be treated by Dr. Shell because he wasn't given the name of an alternative doctor within the allotted time.

Your Right to a Second Opinion

In addition to the other rights discussed in this section, if yours is a "serious" injury, you have the right to the services of a consulting doctor or chiropractor. In other words, you can check the first doctor's diagnosis with a second opinion. (LC § 4601.) You do this by making a spoken or written demand on the insurance company.

What is considered a "serious" injury is anybody's guess and may be the subject of contention with the insurance company. But if you feel your injury is serious enough to require a second opinion, by all means, demand it.

4. If Your Employer Did Not Offer You a Choice Between Health Care Organizations for Treatment of Your Injury (30-Day Wait)

SKIP AHEAD

If your employer has contracted with at least two health care organizations to provide medical treatment for injured employees, skip to Section D5, below, to locate the rules that apply to you.

If your employer did not give you the choice of two health care organizations to go to for treatment of your injury, and instead referred you to a doctor or medical group after you reported an injury, you may usually change doctors after 30 days from the date of injury. You simply advise the insurance company that you are exercising your right to "free choice" and designate the doctor you want to treat with. From that point on, the company must honor your choice and pay your own doctor to treat you. (LC § 4600.3.) See Section D7, below, for a sample letter requesting a change of doctors.

If the doctor you saw has reported that you won't need further medical treatment in the future and that your condition is "permanent and stationary" (further medical treatment at this time will not improve your condition), you do not have the automatic right to change treating doctors. Instead, if you disagree, you must select a qualified medical evaluator (QME) to reevaluate your medical condition. (Chapter 10, Sections C and D, cover how to obtain a QME in this circumstance.)

5. If Your Employer Offered You a Choice Between Health Care Organizations for Treatment of Your Injury (90-, 180-, or 365-Day Wait)

SKIP AHEAD

If your employer did not offer you a choice between at least two health care organizations to treat your workplace injury, skip this section.

If your employer gave you a choice of seeing one of at least two health care organizations contracted to provide medical treatment to injured employees, and you chose one of the two, this organization now becomes your treating medical facility, and the doctor you see there will be your treating doctor. However, if you were given a choice and never exercised it, your employer or its insurance company has the right to choose which organization you must go to if you are injured.

When you go to one of the health care organizations your employer has contracted with, you usually will be assigned to one "primary care" doctor who will be considered your "treating doctor" for workers' compensation purposes. If you want to see another doctor or a specialist, you must first get permission from this primary care doctor.

You have the right to change doctors *within* the health care organization upon request. Within five days of a written or oral request, the health care organization must provide you with a list of participating doctors. (Although not specifically set forth in the law, I would argue that you have the right to go to a doctor of your own choice if you are not given the list of participating doctors within five working days of your request.) You also have the right to a second opinion from a participating doctor regarding a diagnosis from another participating doctor.

Even if your employer contracts with two health maintenance organizations and you were sent to one, you eventually have the right to stop going to the health care organization and instead to see an outside doctor of your choosing. But it gets even more complicated. When you may choose to switch doctors depends on whether your employer offers nonindustrial medical insurance (insurance for non-work-related injuries).

a. No Health Care Insurance Offered by Employer (90-Day Wait)

If your employer doesn't offer health insurance for nonindustrial needs (regular health insurance), you may change to a doctor of your choice after 90 days from the date you reported the injury to your employer.

> **EXAMPLE:** Jay is injured while working for Central Engineering. Central has contracted with two health care organizations to provide medical treatment to its employees only if they are injured on the job. Central provides no other health insurance for its employees. Jay must go to Central's health care organization for treatment for 90 days from the date he notified the employer of his injury. After that, he can freely choose another doctor.

b. Health Care Insurance Offered by Employer (180- or 365-Day Wait)

If you were injured in 2003 or later, and your employer offers health insurance for nonindustrial needs (regular health insurance), you may switch to your own doctor after 180 days. (This is true whether or not your doctor is participating in one of the health care organizations offered.)

If you were injured in 2002 or earlier, and your employer offers health insurance, your right to change doctors depends on whether or not your primary care physician (your family doctor) participates in the health care organization. (Your employer is deemed to have offered health insurance if it offers to pay more than half the costs of the coverage, or if the plan is established under a union collective bargaining agreement.)

- **If your doctor is not participating in the health care organization,** but you have been treated there for your industrial injury, you may exercise your right to choose a treating doctor 180 days from the date you reported your injury, or upon the date of contract renewal or open enrollment of the health care organization, whichever occurs first.

  EXAMPLE: Lori works for Beta Tools. Beta contracts with two health care organizations to provide health care coverage for its employees who are injured on the job. The contract also provides employees with the option of regular health insurance, with Beta picking up 50% of the monthly cost. Lori decides not to participate in the ordinary health care plan, because she's covered under her husband's health insurance. Lori suffers an industrial injury on March 3, 2011. The open enrollment for the health care plan is December 1, 2011. This means she doesn't have the right to choose her own doctor from outside the health care organization until 180 days from the date she notified her employer of the injury. (However, if the health care organization's next open enrollment date had been May 1, 2011, Lori could have chosen her own doctor then, after only 58 days.)

- **If your doctor is participating in at least one of the two health care organizations offered,** and you are treating with one of the health care facilities, you may choose a treating doctor of your choice after 365 days from the date your injury was reported, or upon the date of contract renewal or open enrollment, whichever occurs first.

  EXAMPLE: Let's take the same example given above with Lori. This time, however, Lori's doctor participates in one of the two health care organizations. Lori cannot choose another doctor until 365 days from the date she reported the injury to her employer.

6. Changing Doctors More Than Once

After the required waiting time has passed (30, 90, 180, or 365 days), you may change treating doctors as many times as is reasonably necessary until your doctor designates your condition as permanent and stationary and states that you don't need any more medical care. The insurance company may tell you that you only have the right to one "free choice" doctor. This is not true, as long as the change is reasonably necessary. (The insurance company will strenuously object if you change doctors for no reason.) "Reasonably necessary," in my opinion, would include such reasons as:

- The treating doctor is not readily available (you can't get appointments within a reasonable time).
- The treating doctor is not providing adequate treatment (you are in real distress, but the doctor doesn't seem to take your symptoms seriously).
- The treating doctor is prejudiced against you for some reason.
- You and the treating doctor simply don't get along.
- The treating doctor is insisting on unreasonable and unwarranted tests.

7. How to Request Change of Treating Doctors

If, after reading Sections D1–6, just above, you've concluded that you have the right to change treating doctors, you must notify the insurance company. It's wise to call the insurance company and then promptly send a confirming letter by certified mail, return-receipt requested. Legally, however, your request need not be in writing. (CCR § 9781.)

Sample Letter Requesting or Notifying of Change of Treating Doctors

February 4, 20xx

Acme Insurance
1200 Pepper Road
Anytown, CA 99999

Certified mail, return receipt requested

Injured employee: Perry Downing
Employer: Jeffrey Sporting Goods
Date of injury: 1/2/20xx
Claim No.: JT 372-B

To whom it may concern:

As discussed in our telephone conversation today, I have requested a one-time change of treating doctors pursuant to Labor Code Section 4601. Please provide the name and address of another doctor as required.

[*or*]

As discussed in our telephone conversation today, I am exercising my right of free choice of doctors. Accordingly, I select Dr. Joan Jenson, 3333 West 6th St., Anytown, CA 99999 as my treating doctor. Effective immediately, I will no longer be treating with Dr. Bruce Fellows.

Sincerely,
Perry Downing
Perry Downing

8. If the Insurance Company Refuses Your Request to Change Treating Doctors

If you have followed the rules set forth in this chapter and the insurance company will not recognize your right to change your treating doctor, immediately write a letter. Explain that under the law as set forth in the court case *Emporium-Capwell Co. v. WCAB (Tidwell)*, 48 CCC 801 (1983), you have the right to change treating doctors at any time after waiting the appropriate time from the date of injury. If the insurance company still refuses authorization, you have several ways to get medical treatment, as discussed in Section B2b, above.

RELEVANT CASE LAW

See *Ralph's Grocery Store v. WCAB (Lara)*, in Chapter 28.

E. When Your Condition Becomes Permanent and Stationary (P&S) or Has Reached Maximal Medical Improvement (MMI)

The single most important turning point in your workers' compensation case occurs when you are declared to be permanent and stationary. "Permanent and stationary" (P&S) describes a doctor's opinion that your condition has reached a plateau. It means that further medical treatment at this time will not help to improve your overall condition. It does not, however, mean that your medical condition will never improve.

For injuries in 2005 or later, "permanent and stationary" may also be referred to as having reached "maximal medical improvement" (MMI). The two terms mean pretty much the same thing, although MMI technically means that your condition is not expected to improve within the next year (with or without medical treatment). In the rating schedule for injuries occurring in 2005 or later, the term MMI is used. For our purposes, whenever we refer to permanent and stationary, or P&S, we are also referring to maximal medical improvement, or MMI.

Although a P&S or MMI determination is made in a doctor's medical report, the vast majority of injured workers are informed of their P&S status by the insurance company. Some receive a letter of explanation along with a final payment of temporary disability. Unfortunately, many injured workers find out they've been declared P&S only after calling the insurance company to find out why they didn't receive a temporary disability check.

1. What Happens Once You Are Permanent and Stationary or Have Reached MMI?

As soon as a doctor declares you P&S or MMI, a number of different things may happen. Depending on your health and, to some extent, on the attitude of your treating doctor and the insurance company, the most important changes may include:

- Your temporary disability payments will stop.
- Your current medical treatment may stop, depending on the doctor's opinion about your need for future medical treatment.
- You may be told to go back to work.
- You may be informed that your medical condition prevents you from returning to your former line of work.
- You may be told that you are entitled to a supplemental job displacement voucher.
- You may begin to receive permanent disability payments if the doctor considers you permanently disabled.

2. Who Determines When You Are Permanent and Stationary or Have Reached MMI?

Normally, your treating doctor determines when you are P&S or MMI. This is only logical, because it is the treating doctor's job to help you get better. As part of that process, at some point the doctor will decide that your condition isn't likely to improve much.

If you (or the insurance company) disagree with the treating doctor's opinion regarding your P&S status, such as whether you really are P&S or what date you became P&S, the objecting party may obtain a medical-legal evaluation from another doctor. (How and when to obtain a medical-legal evaluation in this situation is discussed in Chapter 10, Section D.)

3. Review the Permanent and Stationary or MMI Report

If the insurance company doesn't send you a copy of the P&S or MMI report within two weeks after you know the report was written, you should request a copy. Or you may request a copy directly from the treating doctor.

The treating doctor's P&S report contains critical information and opinions about your workers' compensation claim. It is important to review the report, because the treating doctor's opinions on all medical issues will determine your eligibility for various workers' compensation benefits. You and the insurance company may both rely on the P&S report in negotiating a settlement.

a. Review the Report for Accuracy

Carefully review your P&S report for accuracy, and write down any inaccuracies you may spot. As you go through the report, pay particular attention to the parts of it that cover:

- your employment history
- description of your job duties
- how the injury occurred, and whether your medical problems were caused by factors other than the work injury
- history of prior injuries
- diagnosis
- basis for the doctor's finding that you are P&S or have reached MMI
- subjective factors of disability (what type of pain you have as well as the frequency and intensity of the pain)
- objective findings of disability (what test results show—for example, test results for a

shoulder injury would include the range of motion of the shoulder)

- any work restrictions the doctor recommends, and
- the doctor's opinion as to whether you can return to the type of work you were doing when injured or whether you are a qualified injured worker (QIW)—someone who is eligible for vocational rehabilitation.

b. Review the Treating Doctor's Opinion on Critical Issues

In the P&S or MMI report, your treating doctor will render an opinion on certain issues that I term "critical." A critical issue is one that, in and of itself, may determine whether or not you're entitled to a major benefit in your workers' compensation case. If the treating doctor's opinion on a critical issue is not in your favor, you may lose any right to certain benefits unless you get a report from a qualified medical evaluator (QME) that is more favorable to you.

Take plenty of time to study your P&S report. On a separate piece of paper, note any areas of the report that you believe are wrong. As part of reviewing the report, pay very close attention to the doctor's opinion on the following critical issues. Answer the following questions very carefully:

1. Do you agree with the treating doctor's opinion that you are permanent and stationary or have reached MMI?
2. Do you agree with the treating doctor's opinion about your need—or lack of need—for medical care in the future?
3. Do you agree with the treating doctor's assessment of whether or not you can return to the type of work you did before the injury?
4. Do you agree with the treating doctor's opinion as to the nature and extent of your permanent disability? Note that you will need to get the report rated to make this determination; that is discussed in Section 5, just below.
5. Do you agree with the treating doctor's opinion on apportionment, if any? (Apportionment addresses the question of whether your permanent disability is due in whole or in part to factors other than your current job-related injury. For more on apportionment, see Chapter 3, Section B6.)

If you agree with the treating doctor on all critical issues, you can feel comfortable about contacting the insurance company to request benefits or to discuss settlement of your case.

If you disagree with the treating doctor's opinion, you have the right to object to the treating doctor's report within 30 days of receipt. (See Section A3d, above.)

You have the right to see additional doctors for evaluation of your condition if you disagree with the report. (The insurance company has the same right.) These additional doctors, called qualified medical evaluators (or QMEs), will review the P&S report and rely upon it to some extent in arriving at their opinion regarding your condition. Therefore, you will want to make them aware of any inaccuracies you found in the treating doctor's report. (See Chapter 10 for information on QMEs.)

TIP

Review all treating doctors' reports carefully. Review all treating doctors' reports, not just the P&S report. If any interim treating doctor's report contains a medical opinion that you disagree with, you must object within 30 days of receipt of the report. (See Section A3d, above, for more details.)

4. If the Permanent and Stationary Report Indicates a Permanent Disability

If, in the treating doctor's opinion, you have a permanent disability, the insurance company has three options.

Option 1: The insurance company may begin paying permanent disability benefits.

Option 2: The insurance company may dispute the conclusions of the P&S report and request a medical-legal evaluation, as discussed in Chapter 10. In the meantime, the insurance company must begin paying permanent disability benefits.

Option 3: The insurance company may object and promptly set the matter for trial before the Workers' Compensation Appeals Board to resolve the dispute. (LC § 4061(l).) In the meantime, the insurance company must begin paying permanent disability benefits.

TIP

How to get an attorney for free. If the insurance company decides to request a hearing with the appeals board, the insurance company must pay for your attorney's fees if you retain one. In this event, I strongly recommend that you seek a workers' compensation lawyer. There is no reason not to be represented, because your attorney will be paid by the insurance company. Be sure to tell any attorney you consult that you believe that the attorney's fee should be paid by the insurance company under LC § 4064 and explain why. Make sure the attorney gives you an opinion regarding this fee issue before you make a commitment to hire the lawyer.

5. Get the Permanent and Stationary Report Rated

After receiving and reviewing the treating doctor's permanent and stationary report, you need to arrange to have it rated. Rating is the process by which your permanent disability percentage is calculated. The insurance company will usually contact you about getting the report rated and will send you a form to do so. If you do not hear from the insurance company within 14 days after receipt of the P&S report, contact the company and request the form. See Chapter 18 for details on rating reports.

CHAPTER

10

Medical-Legal Evaluations

A medical-legal evaluation is used to resolve a legal dispute between an injured worker and the insurance company. The evaluation, done not to provide treatment but to provide evidence for your case, is performed by a doctor other than your treating doctor (see Section A1, below). The workers' compensation judge will review the doctor's medical-legal report and may rely upon it in making a decision regarding disputed issues.

The most important disputes that may require a medical-legal evaluation include:

- whether or not the injury is covered under workers' compensation (also known as compensability of the injury), covered in Section B, below
- the treating doctor's opinion on the nature and extent of your disability, the need for future medical treatment, and the nature of that treatment (see Section C, below), or
- opinions of the treating doctor regarding your permanent and stationary status, the extent and scope of your current medical treatment, the necessity of surgery, the existence of new and further disability, or any other medical issue (covered in Section D, below).

A. Rules for Medical-Legal Evaluations

Your decision to obtain a medical-legal evaluation will depend upon several factors, including whether the insurance company has accepted your case and what issues are in dispute.

- **If the insurance company denied your claim.** You may get a medical-legal evaluation to help establish that your injury is a result of your work and should be covered by workers' compensation.
- **If your claim was accepted by the insurance company.** If there is a dispute over a treating doctor's report, you or the insurance company may get a medical-legal report to prove your position.

Depending on your situation, you may need to obtain more than one medical-legal report in the course of your workers' compensation case.

1. Who Will Perform the Medical-Legal Evaluation?

A medical evaluator is a doctor who examines you and writes a comprehensive report (called a medical-legal report) commenting on various issues in your workers' compensation case.

A medical evaluator does not generally treat you; if you appear to need additional treatment, the evaluator will usually refer you back to your treating doctor. A medical evaluator need not be a medical doctor, and could be a chiropractor or other specialist.

a. Qualified Medical Evaluator (QME)

If you are not represented by a lawyer, you will select a qualified medical evaluator (QME), normally from a panel of three doctors. This rule applies when there is a dispute pursuant to LC § 4060 (see Section B, below), LC § 4061 (see Section C, below), or LC § 4062 (see Section D, below).

If there is a dispute over compensability, follow the rules in Section B3, below, for choosing a QME.

CAUTION

Consequences of picking a QME from a panel. If you don't have a lawyer and you select a QME from a three-physician panel, you may not select a new QME if you later hire a lawyer. (See LC §§ 4062(e) and 4062.2(e).) Therefore, if there is any possibility that you will be hiring a lawyer, it is important that you consult with an attorney before picking a QME from a three-physician panel.

If You're Satisfied With the Treating Doctor's Report

If the insurance company wants you to see a QME, it is important that you inform the insurance company that you are selecting a QME only because of its request. To do this, send the insurance company a letter similar to the following.

> 9/19/20xx
>
> Dear Sir/Madam:
>
> This letter will confirm that you have requested that I select a qualified medical evaluator pursuant to Labor Code Section 4061(d) because you disagree with the findings of the treating doctor, Dr. Hernandez, in his report of 3/3/20xx.
>
> Although I am doing so, please be advised that I do not dispute the findings of Dr. Hernandez in his report of 3/3/20xx, and that I will, in fact, be relying upon the findings contained in that report should this matter proceed to trial.
>
> Sincerely,
>
> *Terry Rose*
>
> Terry Rose

b. Agreed Medical Evaluator (AME)

If you have an attorney, the procedure is different. If a treating doctor has already written a report, your attorney and the insurance company will normally try to settle your case based on that report. If this can't be done, your attorney and the insurance company must mutually agree on an AME to make a medical evaluation. Generally speaking, the Workers' Compensation Appeals Board will follow recommendations of an AME, because the parties all found the AME acceptable.

If your date of injury is on or before December 31, 2004 and the attorney and the insurance company aren't able to agree on an AME, each will designate a QME, and two reports will be issued.

For injuries on or after January 1, 2005, if your attorney and the insurance carrier can't agree on an AME, either can request a list of three "panel QME" doctors from the medical unit. If the insurance carrier and the attorney can't agree on which of the three to choose, each will strike a doctor from the list. The remaining doctor will be your QME.

2. Who Pays for the Medical-Legal Evaluation?

The employer or its insurance company is liable for the cost of each reasonable and necessary comprehensive medical-legal evaluation you obtain pursuant to LC § 4060 (see Section B, below), LC § 4061 (see Section C, below), or LC § 4062 (see Section D, below).

3. Requirements of Medical-Legal Evaluations and Reports

The QME who examined you must prepare a report within 30 days of the evaluation. If the QME has good cause (such as a medical emergency, a death in the family, or a community catastrophe that interrupts the operation of the QME's business), this deadline may be extended by 15 days. Additional time may also be given where the QME has not received test results or consulting physician's evaluations in time to meet the 30-day deadline. (LC § 139.2 (j).)

In addition, for a medical-legal report to be valid, the doctor conducting the medical-legal evaluation must adhere to certain rules under the Labor Code. The report must satisfy all of the criteria listed below to be admissible evidence at any hearing on your case. (As a practical matter, however, if you don't object to a report that doesn't satisfy these requirements, it will be admitted as evidence.)

For starters, only the medical evaluator who signs the report may take a complete medical history, review and summarize prior medical records, and compose and draft the conclusions of the medical report. (LC § 4628.) If the evaluator delegates these tasks to anyone else, the report may be disregarded.

If you are already permanent and stationary (or have reached maximal medical improvement), the medical-legal report must contain the following information:

- your complaints
- all information received from the parties that the doctor reviewed in preparation of the report or relied upon to formulate an opinion
- the history of the injury, as well as your medical history (including any non-work-related medical issues and whether you are still experiencing any problems from them)
- what the doctor found upon examining you (also known as objective findings), as well as a diagnosis
- the cause of any disability and an opinion as to the extent of any disability and work limitations
- recommended medical treatment
- opinion as to whether or not permanent disability has resulted from the injury and whether or not it is permanent and stationary; if permanent and stationary, a description of the disability with a complete evaluation
- apportionment of disability, if any
- if the injury is alleged to be a psychiatric injury, a determination of the percent of the injury that resulted from the actual events of employment
- the reasons for the opinion, and
- the date of the examination and the signature of the physician. (CCR § 10978.)

Once you receive a report, check it for any defects; reports often lack one or more of the above items. Obviously, you will want to raise a fuss only if you want to discredit a medical-legal report you are not happy with, or where there is more than one report and you want to exclude a less favorable one from evidence. Later, at trial, you can tell the judge why you believe the report you don't like is defective under LC § 4628 and CCR § 10978. If the judge agrees, you can get a court order for a new medical-legal evaluation.

B. Compensability of Injury (Labor Code § 4060)

SKIP AHEAD

Skip this section if the insurance company accepts any part of your claim. For example, this might happen if the insurance company agrees that you injured your neck but does not agree that you injured your arm (assuming you claim both were injured). If the issue in your case is the nature and extent of your permanent disability or the need for future medical treatment, go directly to Section C, below. Skip to Section D, below, if the dispute involves any other medical issue.

This section covers what happens if the insurance company denies your claim—in other words, says that your claim is not compensable. Compensability is denied if the insurance company claims that your injury is not covered by workers' compensation *for any reason*. (LC § 4060(a).) If compensability (coverage) is an issue, any medical-legal reports you obtain to support your position must be done following the guidelines of LC § 4060. Here are the rules.

1. When to Get a Medical-Legal Report

If the insurance company denies your claim, it won't pay for medical treatment or temporary disability you might otherwise be entitled to receive. Whether you obtain a medical-legal evaluation immediately or wait a while will depend upon the circumstances in your case and your personal needs. Especially if you are out of work and lack other sources of income, you may need to act quickly to establish that your injury is covered by workers' compensation.

If you obtain a medical-legal report and it says your injury is compensable, the insurance company should begin providing benefits. If not, you can request a hearing before a Workers' Compensation Appeals Board judge.

If the insurance company wants a panel QME report to address the issue of whether your injury arose under your employment (AOE) or was in the course of your employment (COE), it must request the panel list of three doctors from the medical director within the 90 days time limit for admitting or denying your claim, and must make the request before denying your claim. Once a denial issues or the 90 days expires, the insurance carrier can no longer request a medical report under Labor Code section 4060 to address the issue of compensability of injury.

2. How to Qualify for a Medical-Legal Report

Before obtaining a medical-legal evaluation to address the issue of compensability, you must file your DWC-1 claim form and notify your employer that you have been injured. Then, your employer or the insurance company must either reject or postpone a decision on your claim. In either case, you are eligible to get a medical-legal report immediately.

Note: If the insurance company postponed a decision on your claim, the insurance company has 90 days from the time you filed your DWC-1 form to investigate your claim. However, you are entitled to get a medical-legal report immediately after you file your claim form. In addition, the insurance company must pay for all of your medical treatment up to $10,000 until it accepts or rejects your claim.

3. How to Get a Medical-Legal Evaluation When You Don't Have a Lawyer

If you are not represented by an attorney, the insurance company must notify you that you may request a medical-legal evaluation to determine compensability of your claim, or advise you that the insurance company is requesting a comprehensive medical-legal evaluation.

The medical-legal evaluation has to be set up by the procedure provided in LC § 4062.1. First, the insurance company will fax or mail you a form to request that the medical director assign a panel of three QMEs. LC § 4062.1 provides that the insurance company cannot submit the form itself unless you have failed to submit the form within ten days after the insurance company has given it to you with a request that you submit it. It's in your best interests to submit the form yourself. Whoever submits the form gets to designate the specialty of the physicians who will be assigned to the panel—for example, the insurance company may want a panel of surgeons, but you may want a panel of physiatrists (doctors of physical medicine and rehabilitation).

You will then receive a letter listing a panel of three QMEs. Within ten days, you must choose one of them to do your evaluation, schedule the appointment, and inform the insurance company of your selection. (See Section E, below, for more on picking a QME.) If you do not, the insurance company itself may select a QME from the panel.

You must attend the scheduled examination unless you believe the QME to be biased against you because of your race, sex, national origin, religion, or sexual orientation, or unless there is evidence that the QME is asking you to submit to unnecessary medical tests. In that case, you may ask for another panel of three QMEs to choose from. However, if the Workers' Compensation Appeals Board later determines that you did not have a good reason not to go to the original evaluation, the cost of the evaluation will be deducted from any award you receive.

Your employer or its insurance company must pay your estimated travel expenses after you submit written notice of your appointment arrangements, or if the employer arranged the appointment, after giving you notice of an appointment arranged by the employer.

Soon after that, the administrative director will set up the time frame in which the QME is required to complete the formal medical-legal evaluation. You will have the option to waive or extend the deadline for completion of the exam *if you want.* If the evaluation is not completed within the designated time frame, either party may obtain a new evaluation upon request as provided in LC

§ 4062.1 and LC § 4062.2. Neither the employer nor the employee will be responsible for payment for a formal medical-legal evaluation that was not completed within the required time frame unless the employee and employer, on forms prescribed by the administrative director, each waive the right to a new evaluation and elect to accept the original evaluation even though it was not completed within the required time frame. (LC § 4062.5.)

4. Getting a Medical-Legal Evaluation When You Have a Lawyer

If you have a lawyer and a medical-legal evaluation is required to determine whether your injury is covered by workers' compensation, your attorney may contact the insurance company and discuss the possibility of having you examined by a "neutral" agreed medical evaluator (AME).

If you have previously been evaluated by a panel QME pursuant to LC § 4062.1, your attorney will not be able to get an AME evaluation for you. You will be bound by whatever the QME said. Therefore, it is very important that if there is any chance that you are going to retain an attorney, you do so before you agree to a QME doctor.

The procedure for obtaining an AME for injuries in 2005 or later (set forth in LC § 4062.2) is roughly as follows: Either your attorney or the insurance company may start the selection process for an AME by making a written request naming at least one proposed physician to be the AME (this physician need not be a QME). If no agreement is reached, either party may request the assignment of a three-member panel of QMEs. Your attorney and the insurance company will then try to agree upon one doctor from the panel of QMEs. If they cannot agree on a doctor, each party may then strike one name from the panel, and the remaining QME will serve as the evaluating doctor. If your attorney or the insurance company fails to strike a name from the panel within three working days, the other party may select any physician who remains on the panel to serve as the evaluating doctor.

You are then responsible for arranging the appointment for the examination. If you get a medical-legal evaluation under this section and later fire or lose your lawyer, you aren't entitled to an additional evaluation.

For injuries in 2004 or earlier, your attorney and the insurance company will simply try to agree on a doctor to use as an AME. If they can't agree on an AME, they each will pick their own QME evaluator. Neither your attorney nor the insurance company is limited to the panel AME/QME doctors, however. They can use any qualified doctor.

5. Issues Covered by the Medical-Legal Report

Obviously, if coverage is being denied, the main reason you want a medical-legal evaluation is to get a determination that your injury will be covered under worker's compensation. But it's important to understand that the medical-legal evaluation will not be limited to the issue of compensability. It will also address other medical issues in dispute at the time of the examination. (LC § 4062.3.)

What issues will be addressed depends on your permanent and stationary status:

- **Permanent and stationary.** If, at the time of the medical examination, the doctor determines that you are permanent and stationary (or have reached maximal medical improvement), the doctor will also render an opinion on such issues as the extent of any permanent disability and whether or not you require future medical care.
- **Not permanent and stationary.** If you are not permanent and stationary when the medical evaluation occurs, the only other issues the QME will address are whether you are temporarily totally disabled and whether you are in need of current medical treatment.

Fortunately, the doctor who conducts your medical-legal evaluation is allowed to consult with any other doctors who have already treated you for injuries outside that doctor's field of expertise.

When compensability is an issue, you usually will already have seen one or more doctors.

C. Nature and Extent of Permanent Disability or Need for Future Medical Treatment (Labor Code § 4061)

SKIP AHEAD

If your claim was accepted by the insurance company but there is a dispute regarding the nature and extent of your permanent disability or your need for future medical treatment, read this section. Otherwise, skip ahead to Section D, below.

Most likely, you need a medical-legal evaluation because you and the insurance company disagree on the extent of your permanent disability. Or, your case may have reached this stage because the insurance company agreed that one part of your body is injured but denies that another is. It's also possible that the insurance company may have initially denied coverage (compensability) completely, but after getting medical evaluations and possibly going before the appeals board, you won and compensability is no longer an issue. Regardless of how you get here, any additional medical-legal report obtained to resolve the issues of permanent disability or need for future medical treatment must follow the rules under LC § 4061.

1. When to Get a Medical-Legal Report

Your need for a medical-legal evaluation under LC § 4061 will probably be triggered by an event such as one of the following:

- You receive a notice from the insurance company indicating that it disputes the opinion of the treating doctor on the nature and extent of your permanent disability or your need for future medical treatment.
- You review the treating doctor's medical-legal report and you disagree with the opinion given on the issues of permanent disability or need for future medical treatment.
- You receive your last payment of temporary disability indemnity from the insurance company along with a notice stating that you have no permanent disability—and you disagree.
- You receive your last payment of temporary disability from the insurance company along with a notice stating how much permanent disability it believes you are owed—and you disagree.

2. How to Get a Medical-Legal Evaluation When You Don't Have a Lawyer

If you do not have an attorney, medical-legal evaluations have to be set up by the procedure provided in LC § 4062.1. First, the insurance company will fax or mail you a form to request that the medical director assign a panel of three QMEs. LC § 4062.1 provides that the insurance company cannot submit the form itself unless you have failed to submit the form within ten days after the insurance company has given it to you and requested that you submit it. It's in your best interests to submit the form yourself. Whoever submits the form gets to designate the specialty of the physicians that will be assigned to the panel—for example, the insurance company may want a panel of surgeons, but you may want a panel of physiatrists (doctors of physical medicine and rehabilitation).

You will then receive a letter listing a panel of three QMEs. Within ten days of receipt of the panel, you must choose a QME to do your evaluation, schedule the appointment, and inform the employer or insurance company of your selection. (See Section E, below, for more on picking a QME.) If you do not inform your employer or the insurance company of your selection within ten days, one of them may select the QME from the panel itself.

If you inform the employer of your selection within ten days of the assignment of the panel of

QMEs but fail to make the appointment within that time, or if your employer or insurance company selects the physician pursuant to this subdivision, then the employer or insurance company is allowed to arrange the appointment.

You must attend the scheduled examination unless you believe the QME to be biased against you because of your race, sex, national origin, religion, or sexual orientation, or unless there is evidence that the QME is asking you to submit to unnecessary medical tests. In that case, you may ask for another panel of three QMEs to choose from. However, if the Workers' Compensation Appeals Board later determines that you did not have a good reason not to go to the original evaluation, the cost of the evaluation will be deducted from any award you receive.

Your employer or its insurance company must pay your estimated travel expenses after you submit written notice of your appointment arrangements, or if the employer arranged the appointment, after giving you notice of an appointment arranged by the employer.

The QME's report and the reports of the treating doctors are the only reports that can be presented by either side for consideration by a judge on the issues. (LC § 4061(i).) Any other reports obtained will be in violation of the Labor Code and will not be admissible in any hearing before the appeals board.

Soon after the appointment is arranged, the administrative director will set up a time frame in which the QME is required to complete the formal medical-legal evaluation. The time frames will allow for you to waive or extend the deadline for completion of the exam *if you want*. If the evaluation is not completed within the designated time frames, a new evaluation may be obtained upon the request of either party as provided in LC § 4062.1 and LC § 4062.2. Neither the employer nor the employee will be responsible for payment for a formal medical-legal evaluation that was not completed within the required time frames unless the employee and the employer, on forms prescribed by the administrative director, each waive the right to a new evaluation and elect to accept the original evaluation even though it was not completed within the required time frame. (LC § 4062.5.)

3. Getting a Medical-Legal Evaluation When You Have a Lawyer

Your attorney may contact the insurance company to discuss the possibility of having you examined by an agreed medical evaluator (AME). In that case, the reports of the treating doctor and the AME are the only reports that are admissible in any hearing before the appeals board.

The procedure for obtaining an AME for injuries occurring in 2005 or later (set forth in LC § 4062.2) is roughly as follows: Either your attorney or the insurance company may start the selection process for an AME by making a written request naming at least one proposed physician to be the AME (this physician need not be a QME). If no agreement is reached, either party may request the assignment of a three-member panel of QMEs. Your attorney and the insurance company will then try to agree upon one doctor from the panel of QMEs. If they cannot agree on a doctor, each party may then strike one name from the panel, and the remaining QME will serve as the evaluating doctor. If your attorney or the insurance company fails to strike a name from the panel within three working days, the other party may select any physician who remains on the panel to serve as the evaluating doctor. You are then responsible for arranging the appointment for the examination. If you get a medical-legal evaluation under this section and later fire or lose your lawyer, you aren't entitled to an additional evaluation.

For injuries in 2004 or earlier, your attorney and the insurance company will simply try to agree on a doctor to use as an AME. If they can't agree on an AME, they each will pick their own QME evaluator. Neither your attorney nor the insurance company is limited to the panel AME/QME doctors, however. They can use any qualified doctor.

4. Issues Covered by the Medical-Legal Report

The medical-legal report will address the issue in question as well as any other outstanding issues. For example, suppose you disagree with the treating doctor's permanent and stationary report on the extent of your permanent disability, and you request a qualified medical-legal evaluation pursuant to LC § 4061 to resolve the issue. (If you have been to a QME before, you must try to go back to the same QME if at all possible. LC § 4062.3(j).) The QME will first and foremost issue an opinion on the extent of your permanent disability, but then the doctor may address any other issues, such as your need for future medical care.

5. What Happens After You Attend the Medical-Legal Evaluation?

The QME will prepare a medical-legal report that addresses all issues in dispute at the time of your examination. The QME must mail the report and a one-page form that summarizes the medical findings to you, the insurance company, and the administrative director of the Workers' Compensation Appeals Board.

The QME who examined you must prepare a report within 30 days of the evaluation. If the QME has good cause (such as a medical emergency, a death in the family, or a community catastrophe that interrupts the operation of the QME's business), this deadline may be extended by 15 days. Additional time may also be given where the QME has not received test results or consulting physician's evaluations in time to meet the 30-day deadline. (LC § 139.2 (j).)

If the QME report indicates that all or part of your permanent disability is not due to your current job—for instance, you had a preexisting injury to the same body part—a portion of your disability may be legally allocated ("apportioned") to outside factors. (Apportionment is discussed in greater detail in Chapter 18, Section D1.)

Apportionment could allow the insurance company to reduce its payments to you, so special rules apply. The administrative director must first have the report reviewed by a workers' compensation judge. If the judge determines the proposed apportionment is inconsistent with the law, the report may be referred back to the QME for correction or clarification. (LC § 4061(f).)

Assuming no apportionment is indicated, within 20 days of receipt of the medical-legal evaluation the administrative director is supposed to calculate your permanent disability rating, which is used to determine the dollar value of your disability, and then mail the rating to you and the insurance company. (LC § 4061(e).)

Within 30 days after you receive the advisory rating, either you or the insurance company may request the administrative director to reconsider the recommended rating. Or you may obtain additional information from your treating doctor or the QME to address issues not addressed or improperly addressed in the original QME evaluation. (LC § 4061(g).) See Chapter 18, Section A6, for a sample letter.

SEE AN EXPERT

If you have an attorney. When the medical-legal report is issued, your attorney will evaluate and rate it. If you got a report from an agreed medical examiner (but not a QME), your attorney may agree with the insurance company to send the report to the rating bureau at the local appeals board for an opinion by a professional rater. See Chapter 18 for more on rating injuries.

If, after a medical-legal report is prepared, you or the insurance company objects to any *new* medical issue (one not covered in the QME's report), you must utilize the same QME to resolve the medical dispute, if possible. The insurance company pays for subsequent QME reports on different issues from those covered in the first QME report.

If a panel QME is required in a different specialty, you or your attorney, and the insurance carrier, must submit a joint letter to the medical director requesting a second panel in the required specialty.

6. If the Insurance Company Refuses to Pay Your Benefits

If a medical-legal evaluation resolves any issue so as to require the insurance company to provide compensation, the insurance company must begin payment of compensation or promptly start proceedings before the appeals board. (LC § 4061(h).)

SEE AN EXPERT

How to get an attorney for free. If the QME's medical-legal report finds that you are entitled to permanent disability payments, then the insurance company must start making payments to you or file an application for adjudication of claim (if you are unrepresented). (LC § 4063.) If the insurance company files an application for adjudication of claim instead of starting your payments, then you are entitled to have any attorneys' fees paid by the insurance carrier if you retain an attorney. (LC § 4064.) If this happens, I strongly recommend that you seek a workers' compensation lawyer. There is no reason not to be represented, because your attorney will be paid by the insurance company. If you decide to see an attorney, be sure to say why you believe that the attorney's fee should be paid by the insurance company. Make sure the attorney gives you an opinion regarding this fee issue before you decide to retain him or her.

D. Other Issues to Be Resolved by Medical-Legal Evaluations (Labor Code § 4062)

SKIP AHEAD

If your claim has been accepted and there are disputed issues other than the nature and extent of your permanent disability or your need for future medical treatment, read this section. Otherwise, skip ahead to Section E, below.

1. When to Get a Medical-Legal Report

The need to obtain a medical-legal evaluation may arise because you (or the insurance company) have objected to a determination made by the treating doctor concerning medical issues such as the following:

- whether or not you are permanent and stationary or have reached maximal medical improvement
- whether the medical treatment you are receiving is appropriate or necessary, or
- the existence of any new and further disability.

TIP

See specialists before the evaluation. Because the doctor performing the medical-legal evaluation may consult with other doctors who have already seen you, it is very important that you get treatment from doctors in each medical specialty for which you have alleged an injury before you obtain a medical-legal evaluation. Ask your treating doctor to refer you to the necessary specialists.

2. How to Get a Medical-Legal Report on Issues Other Than Spinal Surgery

Whoever objects to the treating doctor's report must notify the other side of the objection in writing within 30 days of receipt of the treating doctor's report if you are not represented by an attorney, or within 20 days if you are. (If any party fails to object within the appropriate time limitations, that party may have waived its right to obtain a medical-legal report on the issue. (LC § 4062(a).) But the time period may be extended for good cause by mutual agreement. As a practical matter, even if you miss the deadline, you should object. A judge may find that there was a good reason for the delay.

As soon as either party makes a timely objection, the insurance company must immediately provide you with a form with which to request the assignment of a panel of three qualified medical evaluators (QMEs).

The insurance company cannot submit the form itself unless you have failed to submit the form within ten days after the insurance company has given it to you and requested that you submit it. It's in your best interests to submit the form yourself, because whoever submits the form gets to designate the specialty of the physicians that will be assigned to the panel—for example, the insurance company may want a panel of surgeons, but you may want a panel of physiatrists (doctors of physical medicine and rehabilitation).

You will then receive a letter listing a panel of three QMEs. Within ten days of receipt of the panel of QMEs, you must choose a QME to do your evaluation, schedule the appointment, and inform the insurance company of your selection. (See Section E, below, for more on picking a QME.) If you do not, the insurance company may select the QME from the panel itself.

You must attend the scheduled examination unless you believe the QME to be biased against you because of your race, sex, national origin, religion, or sexual orientation, or unless there is evidence that the QME is asking you to submit to unnecessary medical tests. In that case, you may ask for another panel of three QMEs to choose from. However, if the Workers' Compensation Appeals Board subsequently determines that you did not have a good reason not to go to the original evaluation, the cost of the evaluation will be deducted from any award you receive.

Your employer or its insurance company must pay your estimated travel expenses after you submit written notice of your appointment arrangements, or if the employer arranged the appointment, after giving the employee notice of an appointment arranged by the employer.

Soon after the appointment is arranged, the administrative director will set up a time frame in which the QME is required to complete the formal medical evaluation. The time frame will allow for you to waive or extend the deadline for completion of the exam if you want. If the evaluation is not completed within the designated time frames, a new evaluation may be obtained upon the request of either party as provided in LC § 4062.1 and LC § 4062.2. Neither the employer nor the employee will be responsible for payment for a formal medical evaluation that was not completed within the required time frame unless the employee and the employer, on forms prescribed by the administrative director, each waive the right to a new evaluation and elect to accept the original evaluation even though it was not completed within the required time frame. (LC § 4062.5.)

Medical-Legal Reports and Treatment Issues

If the insurance carrier contests your doctor's recommendation for some sort of treatment for you, the carrier must submit the doctor's request to a utilization review process. Another doctor will review the treating doctor's reports and issue an opinion based upon American College of Occupational and Environmental Medicine (ACOEM) guidelines as to whether the treatment is reasonable and necessary. If not done within five days of insurance carrier's receipt of the medical report, the utilization report may be inadmissible in a hearing before the WCAB. If the report is timely and finds that treatment is appropriate, the carrier must authorize the treatment—in other words, the carrier may not dispute the utilization review findings. However, if the report finds the treating doctor's recommendations are not appropriate, you may object and request the issue be resolved by a panel QME examination.

3. Getting a Medical-Legal Evaluation When You Have a Lawyer

Your attorney may contact the insurance company to discuss the possibility of having you examined by an agreed medical evaluator (AME). In that case, the reports of the treating doctor and the AME are the only reports that are admissible in any hearing before the appeals board.

The procedure for obtaining an AME for injuries in 2005 or later (set forth in LC § 4062.2) is roughly as follows: Either your attorney or the insurance company may start the selection process for an AME by making a written request naming at least one proposed physician to be the AME (this physician need not be a QME). If no agreement is reached, either party may request the assignment of a three-member panel of QMEs. Your attorney and the insurance company will then try to agree upon one doctor from the panel of QMEs. If they cannot agree, each party may then strike one name from the panel, and the remaining QME will serve as the evaluating doctor. If your attorney or the insurance company fails to strike a name from the panel within three working days, the other party may select any physician who remains on the panel to serve as the evaluating doctor. You are then responsible for arranging the appointment for the examination. If you get a medical-legal evaluation under this section and later fire or lose your lawyer, you aren't entitled to an additional evaluation.

For injuries in 2004 or earlier, your attorney and the insurance company will simply try to agree on a doctor to use as an AME. If they can't agree on an AME, they each will pick their own QME evaluator. Neither your attorney nor the insurance company is limited to the panel AME/QME doctors, however. They can use any qualified doctor.

4. Issues Covered by the Medical-Legal Report

The medical-legal report will address the issue in question as well as any other outstanding issues. For example, suppose your treating doctor requests authorization to give you an injection and the insurance company denies it, and you request a qualified medical evaluation pursuant to LC § 4062 to resolve the issue. (If you have been to a QME before, you must try to go back to the same QME if at all possible. LC § 4062.3(j).) The QME will issue an opinion as to whether the injection requested by your treating doctor is necessary and appropriate, but then may go on to address any other treatment issues. If the QME decides that no further medical treatment is necessary and that you are permanent and stationary, the QME may issue an opinion on the extent of your permanent disability.

After you attend the medical-legal evaluation, the QME must mail a copy of the medical-legal report and a form that summarizes the doctor's medical findings to you, the insurance company, and the administrative director.

5. Disputes Regarding the Need for Spinal Surgery

If your doctor has recommended spinal surgery and the insurance company does not want to pay for it, the dispute is governed by LC § 4602(b), which is explained just below and is the only means to contest this issue.

The insurance carrier must submit the treating doctor's report requesting spinal surgery to a utilization review (UR) process (see Chapter 11, Section A4, for an explanation of the UR process). If the result of the UR process is an approval of the requested spinal surgery, or if the insurance company fails to timely complete the UR process, the insurance company must authorize the surgery. The insurance company must complete the UR process within ten days of its receipt of the treating physician's report, and the UR process must comply with AD Rule 9792.6.

If the result of the UR process is a denial of the spinal surgery request, the insurance company may object to the doctor's report recommending spinal surgery under section 4062(b), but any objection must use the form required by Administrative Director (AD) Rule 9788.11. (CCR § 9788.1.) This is DWC Form 233. In addition, if the UR process results in a denial of the requested surgery, the insurance company must make its section 4062(b) objection to the recommended spinal surgery within that same ten-day period.

If the insurance company fails to meet the ten-day timelines or comply with AD rules 9788.1 and 9788.11, the insurance company loses the right to a second opinion report, and it must authorize the spinal surgery. (See the case of *Jesus Cervantes v. El Aguila Food Products, Inc. et al.* in Chapter 28.)

What all this means is that if your treating doctor recommends spinal surgery, the insurance company has only ten days from receipt of the doctor's report to get its UR done AND object to the report under LC 4062(b). It is usually very difficult for the insurance company to meet these very short ten-day timelines, and they usually forfeit their rights to object to surgery and end up having to authorize it. Pay close attention to the ten-day timeline if you have this situation!

If the insurance company does complete the UR process and file an objection on Form 233 within the ten-day time period, only then can a second-opinion evaluator address the issue of whether spinal surgery should be approved.

The second-opinion surgical examination will be scheduled on an expedited basis, and the second-opinion report must be sent to the parties within 45 days of receipt of the treating physician's report. (There are no provisions for extending this time period, and no penalties set out for missing it. But if you have not received the second-opinion report within the 45 days, you should argue that the provisions of LC § 4062(b) have not been met and, therefore, that the surgery must be authorized.)

If the second-opinion report supports the need for the surgical procedure, then the insurance company must provide it.

If the second-opinion report does not recommend the surgery, an expedited hearing on the matter will be held. (The insurance company must call for a hearing by filing a Declaration of Readiness to Proceed—see Chapter 22, Section B4—whether or not you accept the second opinion.)

CAUTION

Wait until the second-opinion and UR process is complete. If the surgery is performed before the second-opinion process is completed, the insurance company (or employer) is not liable for the cost of the surgery or related temporary disability payments.

6. New Disputed Issues Arising After Report

If, after a medical-legal report is prepared, you or the insurance company objects to any new medical issue, you must utilize the QME who prepared the previous evaluation, if possible. (LC § 4062.3(j).) For example, if you get a QME to issue a medical-legal report on the issue of whether you are receiving proper medical treatment, and later a dispute arises as to whether your condition has become permanent and stationary, you would be entitled to an additional evaluation to resolve this issue, but you must try to use the same QME.

Subsequent QME reports on new issues are done at the expense of the insurance company. You are, however, limited to one QME report for each new issue.

E. Picking a Qualified Medical Evaluator (QME)

In many cases, the QME's report will make or break your case. For obvious reasons, it's in your best interests to be careful in selecting the doctor who will have this authority.

1. Assignment of the Panel

When a qualified medical evaluation is required to determine an issue in your case, either you or the insurance company will submit a form requesting the administrative director to assign a panel of three QMEs. (The insurance company is generally required to send you the form with which to request the assignment of a QME panel.) The QME panel form must advise you that you should consult with your treating doctor prior to deciding which type of specialist to request. (CCR § 101.)

You will then receive a letter that contains the names of three QMEs, as well as this information about each one:

- the doctor's name
- the doctor's address and telephone number
- the doctor's specialty and number of years in practice, and
- a brief description of the doctor's education and training, as provided by the administrative director. (CCR § 103.)

The three doctors for the panel are randomly selected from all QMEs who do not have a conflict of interest in the case (such as having a prior relationship with the employer or insurance company), who have the appropriate specialty selected by you, and who are within the general geographic area of your residence.

CAUTION

Consequences of picking a QME from a panel. If you don't have a lawyer and you select a QME from a three-physician panel, you may not select a new QME (or AME) if you later hire a lawyer. Therefore, if there is any possibility that you will be hiring a lawyer, it is important that you consult with one before picking a QME from the panel.

2. How to Pick a QME

Whether you are picking a QME from a panel of three doctors or from the entire QME list, it is obviously key that you pick someone who's competent and fair. You do not want to see a doctor who gets a great deal of workers' compensation business from insurance company referrals. Instead, you want a doctor who works at least half the time on referrals from injured workers' ("applicants'") attorneys.

The doctors you'll have to choose from are picked at random and are supposed to be neutral. But don't be complacent about which doctor to select. I have seen panels consisting of three doctors known to work primarily for insurance companies. But, in fairness, I have also seen well-balanced panels made up of doctors I consider to be caring and unbiased.

To know which doctor to pick, you have to take the time to investigate. Start by asking your treating doctor about the QMEs and whether they have the expertise to evaluate your injury. The information and assistance officer may have heard of the doctors in question and have some recommendations. You may even want to call each of the doctor's offices and try to determine what percentage of their workers' compensation examinations are done at the request of insurance companies. Often, if you tell a receptionist or other assistant why you are concerned, you will get a straight answer.

If you do not feel there is an acceptable doctor on the panel, write and request another panel; see the sample letter below.

Sample

July 2, 20xx

Administrative Director
P.O. Box 420603
San Francisco, CA 94142

Re:
Janice Clemens v. Johnson Masonry
Case No. BV 7777
Objection to QME panel

Dear Medical Director:

Please be advised that I object to the doctors provided on the QME panel I received on June 28, 20xx. The doctors provided are all known by reputation in the community to be defense medical evaluators. I do not feel I can get an impartial evaluation with any of these doctors.

Please provide me with a new panel from which I can select a doctor for my QME evaluation.

Sincerely,

Janice Clemens

Janice Clemens

3. Setting an Appointment With a QME

You must both select a QME and schedule your appointment within ten days of receipt of the QME panel letter, or the insurance company will be allowed to set the appointment for you. (LC § 4062.1(c).)

4. Exchange of Information

Once a QME has been selected by either you or the insurance company, the insurance company will want to provide the evaluator with any and all relevant documents that may help its cause—and so should you.

You or the insurance company may provide to the QME any of the following information:

- Records prepared or maintained by your treating doctor.
- Medical and nonmedical records relevant to the determination of the medical issue. Medical records that the insurance company may submit include records subpoenaed from doctors that you have seen in the past for work-related or non-work-related treatment. The insurance company may also submit nonmedical records such as movies taken of you doing certain activities, or your deposition testimony.

Oftentimes, the insurance company will also prepare a cover letter addressed to the doctor with a summary of your claim, advising the doctor of the issues to be addressed in his report, such whether you have any permanent disability or whole person impairment, AOE/COE issues, apportionment, the need for future medical treatment, and so on. This can either be a "joint letter" signed by both you and the insurance company (and printed on blank paper without letterhead, or you and the insurance company may each do your own letter to the doctor, called an "advocacy letter," which sets forth your particular positions about the issues.

Whether you do a joint letter or your own letter to the doctor, make sure it asks the doctor to address the issue of "*Almaraz-Guzman*" as discussed below.

Almaraz/Guzman Issues

This refers to the cases of *Mario Almaraz v. Environmental Recovery Services (aka Enviroserve); State Compensation Insurance Fund* and *Joyce Guzman v. Milpitas Unified School District, Permissibly Self-Insured; Keenan & Associates*, 74 Cal. Comp. Cases 1084. These cases were heard together because they involved the same issue, the issue of the injured workers' dispute with the scheduled permanent disability rating. The applicants contended that the impairment rating, based on the AMA Guides portion of the 2005 Schedule, resulted in an inequitable, disproportionate rating and was not a fair and accurate measure of the employee's permanent disability. The court held that the language of Labor Code § 4660(c), which provides that "the schedule ... shall be prima facie evidence of the percentage of permanent disability to be attributed to each injury covered by the schedule," unambiguously means that a permanent disability rating established by the schedule is "rebuttable." This means that if you feel your permanent disability should be higher, you can challenge the rating. (The burden of rebutting a scheduled permanent disability rating rests with the party disputing that rating.)

One way of rebutting a scheduled permanent disability rating is to successfully challenge one of the component elements of that rating, such as the injured employee's WPI (whole person impairment) under the AMA Guides. The court held, however, that when determining a person's WPI, it is not permissible to go outside the "four corners" of the AMA guides. However, a physician is allowed to utilize any chapter, table, or method in the AMA Guides that most accurately reflects the injured employee's impairment. Oftentimes, a doctor may find that under the AMA guides, using the required chapters and charts that apply to your injured part of body, you have little or no WPI, but by using another chapter or table by analogy, he or she can find you have a greater WPI.

Sample Joint PQME Letter

December 28, 20xx
Dr. Harvey Crane
231 Eucalyptus Avenue
Moreno Valley, CA 92553

RE: **John Wu v. ABC Controls, Inc.**
WCAB Case No.: ADJ999999
Claim No.: 9999-999
Exam Date: at ________ a.m., 1/30/20xx

Dear Dr. Crane:

Thank you for agreeing to examine the above-named applicant on ____________________ at _____ a.m. in your capacity as panel qualified medical evaluator in the field of Orthopedics. We are forwarding our complete medical file for your review.

This case involves [*explain how injury occurred and what body parts are impaired*].

Consistent with the new workers' compensation regulations, please use the AMA Guides on whole body impairment to determine the appropriate level that applicant is impaired, and by which injury and part of body, and also provide work restrictions under the pre-2005 guidelines.

We request that you examine the applicant, perform any noninvasive testing that you deem reasonable and necessary, take a complete history, and review the medical reports and records that are being provided. Based upon all of the information, please provide us with your medical opinion in the form of a narrative report.

Specifically, please consider the following:

1. Did the applicant sustain any injury in your field of expertise? If so, what is the diagnosis?
2. Is there a connection between the applicant's alleged injury and his work? If so, what is the connection?
3. Has the applicant sustained any periods of temporary total disability? If so, please outline the inclusive dates of all periods of temporary disability, and designate the injuries resulting in the temporary disability.
4. Has the medical treatment that the applicant received been reasonable and necessary, including self-procured treatment? If not, please outline those factors that you do not feel were reasonable and/or necessary.

   Is applicant's request for transportation services reasonable and/or necessary?
5. Is the applicant now permanent and stationary or MMI (maximum medical improvement)? If so, when did the applicant's condition become stable? Please differentiate between injuries, if possible.

   If not, what modalities of treatment are necessary for the applicant to become permanent and stationary, and how long do you believe it will be before the applicant's condition stabilizes?
6. If the applicant is now permanent and stationary or MMI, please address permanent disability under the workers' compensation standards as they existed

through that date. Please outline any factors of permanent disability, including all objective and subjective factors, as well as any applicable work restrictions.

In addition, please address permanent impairment by using the descriptions and measurements of physical impairments and the corresponding percentages of impairment published in the AMA Guides for the Evaluation of Permanent Impairment (5th Edition). Please refer to Chapter 2, Section 2.6, of the AMA Guides, 5th Edition, as to how to prepare a complete evaluation report.

Please ensure that you have separate portions of your report for any impairment of a body part/system rated under the separate categories in the AMA Guides, Chapters 3-18. As to each body part/system rated, please indicate the impairment rating that applies.

7. Please note that medical reporting on the issue of apportionment of permanent disability has changed per new Labor Code Sections 4663 and 4664. It is imperative that before completing your report, you address the issue of apportionment of permanent disability based on causation. Please note that it is now permissible to apportion to pathology.

   Please note the change in the law under Senate Bill 899. Please address the following concerning apportionment of permanent disability.

   Apportionment per Labor Code Section 4663(a), (b), and (c):

   - Labor Code Section 4663(a): "Apportionment of permanent disability shall be based on causation."
   - Labor Code Section 4663(b): "Any physician who prepares a report addressing the issue of permanent disability must now address the issue of causation of the permanent disability."
   - Labor Code Section 4663(c): (In part) "The physician shall make an apportionment determination by finding what approximate percentage of permanent disability was caused by the direct result of injury arising out of and occurring in the course of employment and what approximate percentage of the current disability was caused by other factors, both before and subsequent to the industrial injury, including prior industrial injuries."

   Labor Code § 4664(a), (b), (c)(l), and (c)(2) state in pertinent part, as follows:

   - Labor Code Section 4664(a): "The employer shall only be liable for the percentage of permanent disability directly caused by the injury arising out of and occurring in the course of employment."
   - Labor Code Section 4664(b): "If the applicant has received a prior award of permanent disability, it shall be conclusively presumed that the prior permanent disability exists at the time of any subsequent industrial injury. This presumption is a presumption affecting the burden of proof."
   - Labor Code Section 4664(c)(l): "Over the lifetime of an employee, he cannot receive more than 100% permanent disability to any one 'region of the body'."

- Labor Code Section 4664(c)(2): "The permanent disability rating for each individual injury sustained by an employee arising from the same accident, when added together, cannot exceed 100%."

Therefore, please note that when commenting in your apportionment section, make sure to follow these new guidelines and have them addressed as it pertains to apportionment of permanent disability based on causation, and make sure that your report addresses the issue of permanent disability by giving approximate percentages of permanent disability caused by the direct result of the injury as opposed to an approximate percentage of permanent disability caused by other factors, including prior and subsequent injuries.

8. Does the applicant need any further medical treatment? If so, what is the nature and extent of that treatment? Please explain both the frequency and duration that you would recommend.

   Are there contraindicated types of treatment in this case?

9. Is the applicant capable of performing the usual and customary work duties as described to you? If not, please outline those factors that the applicant is unable to do. Is this because of industrial or nonindustrial problems?

   If the applicant has returned to work, is the applicant physically capable of performing this new job?

Please send the original of your report to one of the undersigned who will accept responsibility for filing it with and serving it on the Board. Please provide each of the signatories below with copies and forward your bill for services to [*insert name and address of the insurance company*].

Again, the parties jointly thank you for acting in the capacity of a panel qualified medical evaluator.

Very truly yours,	Very truly yours,
John Wu 111 North Hill St. Los Angeles, CA 90012 310-555-1212	Sara Whiting, Representative Acme Insurance 123 Valley Dr. Los Angeles, CA 90210 310-555-1313
John Wu By: John Wu	*Sara Whiting* By: Sara Whiting

The insurance company must serve you with copies of all information it provides to the doctor 20 days before it is provided to the QME. You must also serve upon the insurance company any information you plan to provide to the doctor 20 days before you do so.

If you object within ten days to the QME's consideration of the nonmedical records to be provided by the insurance company, the insurance company may not provide the records to the QME. (This also applies to any records you serve on the insurance company that the insurance company objects to.)

If you find the *Almaraz-Guzman* issues complicated, all you need to worry about is to make sure that the doctor acknowledges in his medical report that he has considered "*Almaraz-Guzman*" in arriving at his opinions on the amount of your whole person impairment (WPI). If he did not, you need to send him a letter (making sure you send a copy to the insurance company and its attorney) requesting the following:

"Please issue a supplemental report addressing whether your previous opinions regarding the amount of WPI (whole person impairment) that you found considered the issues/concerns raised in the cases of *Almaraz-Guzman*, and if not, please do so. Please provide a detailed analysis to support your opinions, and please advise why or why not you feel or do not feel that the injured worker's WPI does or does not more accurately reflect the injured employee's impairment by using other chapters, tables, or methods (such as analogy to other conditions)."

If you are asked to prepare or participate in a letter to a doctor, such as a panel qualified medical evaluator (PQME), make sure similar language is included in the letter to the doctor.

An example of a joint PQME letter is shown above.

However, the insurance company is allowed to file for a hearing before a workers' compensation judge to request an order allowing the QME to consider your nonmedical records, and may use discovery to establish the accuracy or authenticity of the records.

If you have an attorney, then your attorney and the insurance company will agree on what information is to be provided to the agreed medical evaluator (AME).

In the medical-legal report, the QME (or AME) will identify all of the following:

- information received from you and the insurance company
- information reviewed in preparation of the report, and
- information relied upon in the formulation of the QME's opinion.

All communications with a QME (or AME) must be in writing, and any ex parte communication (communication without the knowledge of the other side) is prohibited. (But your communications with the QME in the course of the examination or at the request of the QME in connection with the examination are not considered ex parte communication.)

If the insurance company or your employer communicates with the QME in violation of these rules, you can cancel or terminate the medical evaluation and seek a new evaluation from another QME, to be selected according to LC § 4062.1.

5. Screening the QME

At the appointment, the QME must give you a brief opportunity to ask questions concerning the evaluation process and the evaluator's background. You must then participate in the evaluation unless you have good cause to discontinue it. "Good cause" includes evidence that the evaluator is biased against you because of your race, sex, national origin, religion, or sexual orientation, or that the evaluator requested that you submit to an unnecessary medical examination or procedure.

Take advantage of your right to discuss the examination procedure with the QME before starting the examination. Don't be afraid to ask questions regarding the QME's background, including where the majority of the QME's business comes from. If it comes from insurance company referrals, proceed with caution.

Try to get a feel as to whether the QME will give you a fair and impartial evaluation. If you don't think so, consider terminating the examination and requesting a new panel. If you decide not to proceed with the evaluation, you have the right to choose another QME from a new panel of three. However, if the appeals board later determines that you did not have good cause to terminate the original evaluation, the cost of the second evaluation will be deducted from any award you obtain. (LC § 4061(d).) This is usually a nonissue, however, because 90% of workers' compensation cases settle outside of court by agreement with the insurance company.

Part III

Workers' Compensation Benefits

CHAPTER

11

Medical Benefits

If you're an employee with a work-related injury, you are entitled to receive all the medical care that is reasonably required to cure or relieve your injury or illness. (See Section A, below, for limitations on treatment and what treatment is considered to be "reasonably required.")

The costs of your medical treatment must be paid for by your employer's workers' compensation company or by your employer, if self-insured. (LC §§ 4600–4603.) You don't pay any deductibles or co-pays.

Expenses that may be covered include medical, dental, surgical, psychiatric, and hospital treatment. Nursing care, physical therapy, chiropractic work, therapeutic massage, surgical supplies, crutches, apparatus (including artificial limbs), acupuncture, and the like may all be covered if they're necessary to cure or relieve the effects of the injury. (For limitations on chiropractic and physical therapy visits, see Section A1, below, and for a thorough discussion of medical care, see Chapter 9.)

In addition, you are entitled to costs associated with your medical treatment, including medications and round-trip mileage to medical appointments.

CAUTION

Payment for new or denied claims. Within one day of your filing the DWC-1 claim form, your employer or its insurance company is required to authorize and agree to pay for medical treatment until your employer or the insurance company either accepts or denies your claim. During this period, the employer or insurance company is liable for up to $10,000 in medical expenses. (LC § 5402 (c).)

If your employer's insurance company denies your workers' compensation claim, payment will not be authorized for your medical treatment. You need to pay for medical treatment yourself or make other arrangements for payment until your claim is settled. Your options are covered in Chapter 9, Section B2b.

A. Limitations on Medical Treatment

Legislation passed in 2003 and 2004 put new limits on medical treatment and required employers to set up a review process for the authorization and denial of medical treatment.

1. Chiropractic Visits and Physical Therapy Visits

If you were injured on or after January 1, 2004, you are entitled to no more than 24 chiropractic and 24 physical therapy visits for each work-related injury. But if you suffered two separate injuries to the same part of body that is being treated by the chiropractor or physical therapist—for instance, a continuous trauma injury and a specific injury—you are entitled to 24 visits for each date of injury.

This limitation can be exceeded if the claims adjuster authorizes further visits in writing.

This limitation is new and has not been challenged or tested, so it remains to be seen how some of the details will work. For instance, if a chiropractor performs both chiropractic and physical therapy services in one visit, does it count for one chiropractic and one physical therapy visit? As the law is not clear on this issue, you should argue that together they only count as one visit. Or, if you go beyond the 24 visits, can a chiropractor or physical therapist bill you for additional visits? Unless this is okay with you, make sure you have a clear understanding with your chiropractor or physical therapist that you will not be held responsible for any sessions beyond the 24 visits. You are entitled to more than 24 visits if you have had surgery and your doctor indicates that the treatment is necessary as a result of the surgery.

2. Medical Treatment Must Be Appropriate and Necessary

All employers or their insurance companies must now establish an internal utilization review process (UR) to approve, modify, delay, or deny treatment plans, based on whether the proposed treatment is medically necessary to cure and relieve the industrial injury. This means that claims adjusters themselves can no longer overrule the treating doctor's recommendations.

Employers and their insurance companies are required to provide medical treatment only if the treatment is considered by the medical community to be reasonable and appropriate for the medical condition. As of this writing, the standard being used for appropriateness and reasonableness is the "Occupational Medicine Practice Guidelines," published by the American College of Occupational and Environmental Medicine (ACOEM).

These guidelines are not currently available at most law libraries, but information and assistance offices should each have at least one copy you can borrow to read at the office. (See Chapter 29, "Online Appendixes" for a link to a listing of phone numbers for these offices) The guidelines are also available from www.acoem.org, but they are prohibitively expensive at $799, in hard copy or as an online subscription.

If the reason for medical treatment recommended by your doctor (or chiropractor, acupuncturist, or physical therapist) cannot be supported by scientific medical evidence as set forth in the guidelines, it is likely that your insurance company will not authorize it and that the appeals board would not require it in a hearing.

The utilization review schedule for medical treatment, and its recommended guidelines, are presumed correct on the issue of medical treatment. These guidelines are used to ensure that insurance companies' decisions to authorize or deny treatment are based on medical necessity to cure or relieve the effects of work injuries and are consistent from company to company. However, if you can show that a variance from the guidelines is required to cure you or relieve you from the effects of your injury, you may be able to beat this presumption.

These guidelines apply to all workers regardless of when they were injured.

RESOURCE

Permanent utilization review regulations. Permanent utilization review regulations became effective September 22, 2005. If you're interested in the details, the utilization review standards can be found in the California Code of Regulations, Sections 9792.6, 9792.7, 9792.8, 9792.9, and 9767.1. The full text can be downloaded at www.dir.ca.gov/dwc. Follow the links for "utilization review" until you get to the current regulations.

3. Required Review Process for Medical Authorizations

The utilization review, which insurance companies are required to do before they modify or deny treatment plans, must be directed by a California licensed physician. Only a physician competent to evaluate the specific clinical issues that are within the scope of the physician's practice can modify, delay, or deny treatment plans. (LC § 4610.)

Approvals, modifications, or denials of medical treatment must be communicated in a timely manner to the requesting physician first by fax or telephone and then in writing, according to the following time frames:

- For treatment waiting to be authorized (for example, a review of whether authorization for physical therapy should be given), the decision must be communicated to the worker within five days from the receipt of information necessary to make the decision, but in no event more than 14 days from the treatment recommendation.
- If the injured worker faces an imminent and serious health threat or if further delay could jeopardize the worker's ability to regain maximum function of an injured body part, the decision must be communicated to the worker within 72 hours after the receipt of the information necessary to make the decision.
- For retrospective review (for example, a review of whether to approve or deny payment of

an MRI already taken), the decision must be communicated within 30 days from the receipt of all necessary information.

Failure of the employer or the insurance company to comply with these time frames can result in administrative penalties being assessed. However, if the employer or insurance company has not received information sufficient to make a decision, or requires further testing before a decision can be made, it can notify the worker and the treating physician in writing that additional time is required, as long as it provides an estimate of the additional time needed to make a decision.

The above utilization review (UR) deadlines of LC § 4610(g)(1) are mandatory and, if the insurance carrier fails to meet these mandatory deadlines, it may not use the UR review procedure for the particular medical treatment dispute in question. If the insurance company does perform a UR that violates the deadlines, the UR report obtained is not usable (admissible) as evidence. In addition, the UR report cannot be forwarded to an AME or QME if the insurance company requests that the treatment dispute in question be submitted to an AME or QME under LC § 4062(a).

When an insurance company does not meet the LC § 4610(g)(1) deadlines, it may use the procedure established by LC § 4062(a) to dispute the treating physician's treatment recommendation (see Chapter 10, Section D). However, the insurance company (not the worker) is then the "objection party" and must meet the deadlines in LC § 4062(a), unless those deadlines are extended for good cause or by mutual agreement.

RELEVANT CASE LAW

See *Sandhagen v. Cox & Cox Construction, Inc.*, in Chapter 28.

If a request for treatment or payment is not approved in full, all disputes shall be resolved in accordance with LC § 4062. (See Chapter 10, Section D.)

4. Review Process for Spinal Surgery Requests

If your doctor has recommended spinal surgery and the insurance company does not want to pay for it, the dispute is governed by LC § 4602(b), which is discussed in Chapter 10, Section D5.

RELEVANT CASE LAW

See the case of *Jesus Cervantes v. El Aguila Food Products, Inc.; Safeco Insurance Co of Illinois; Superior National Insurance Co., In Liquidation; California Insurance Guarantee Association; and Broadspire (Servicing Facility)* in Chapter 28.

B. Payment for Current Medical Treatment and Evaluations

If your claim is accepted by your employer's insurance company, your doctor or the hospital should send your medical bills to the insurance company, which should pay them promptly. If the insurance company doesn't pay the bills promptly or disputes any charges, the doctor must look to the insurance company, not you, for payment. (LC §§ 4622, 4625, and 4621.)

Why Insurance Companies Sometimes Won't Pay Medical Benefits

Insurance companies do not always pay medical benefits voluntarily. You may run into nonpayment because the claims adjuster assigned to your case:

- does not know the law
- misplaces your file
- has not had time to work on your case
- does not believe your injury is work-related, or
- does not believe that you need medical treatment (yes, some claims adjusters really try to make medical decisions).

TIP

Request authorizations. To avoid disputes about payment, it's always best to contact the insurance company to request authorization for any additional tests or medical referrals made by your doctor. You can do this by telephone, but follow up any authorizations in writing.

1. Reimbursement for Medical Treatment and Supplies

You are entitled to be reimbursed by the insurance company for any out-of-pocket expenses you incur, such as:

- doctors' bills
- medications, both prescription and over-the-counter
- medical supplies, such as crutches and braces
- medical tests ordered by your doctors, and
- hospital bills.

To obtain reimbursement, you must submit copies of your receipts along with a request for reimbursement form. You can use a form provided by your insurance carrier or Nolo's Record of Medical Expenses and Request for Reimbursement (see the sample, below), which is available on Nolo's website. (See Chapter 29, "Online Appendixes" for the link to this and other forms in this book.) Periodically submit the request for reimbursement to the insurance company, remembering to keep a completed copy for your records.

2. Payment of Round-Trip Mileage

You are entitled to be reimbursed by the insurance company for the cost of your mileage to and from all doctors' appointments, physical therapy appointments, pharmacies to obtain medications, and special medical examinations. You are not, however, entitled to mileage reimbursement for attending court hearings or traveling to the insurance company's office. It doesn't matter whether you drive, take public transportation, or walk.

To determine the rate for mileage reimbursement, please see the chart below. Multiply the appropriate rate per mile by the number of miles you traveled. You may have to use different rates for different dates. Apply the rate that corresponds to the date you traveled.

Date	Mileage Rate
Prior to 1/1/06	34 cents per mile
1/1/06 to 12/31/06	44.5 cents per mile
1/1/07 to 12/31/07	48.5 cents per mile
1/1/08 to 6/30/08	50.5 cents per mile
7/1/08 to 12/31/08	58.5 cents per mile
1/1/09 to 12/31/09	55 cents per mile
1/1/10 to 12/31/10	50 cents per mile
1/1/11 to 5/31/11	51 cents per mile
6/1/11 to 12/31/11	55.5 cents per mile
On or after 1/1/12	55.5 cents per mile

You can keep track of your mileage using the Medical Mileage Expense Form provided on Nolo's website. (See Chapter 29, "Online Appendixes" for the link to this and other forms in this book). The form is self-explanatory and includes sample entries that will help you to provide the required information. There are forms for each year from 2006 to 2011, so make sure you use the right form for the year you incurred the travel expenses. (The form includes the proper mileage rate for that year.) If you need a form for a later year, you can download it from the Department of Industrial Relations website at this link: www.dir.ca.gov/dwc/I&A_mileageForm.pdf.

It's possible the insurance company will provide you with its own mileage record and reimbursement request form; you can use either one, as the purpose of the form is simply to notify the insurance company of your expenses so that you can be reimbursed. Submit the form every few months so that you keep up to date on your reimbursements.

Record of Medical Expenses and Request for Reimbursement

Name: William Johnson

Address: 19 Spring Lane, Anytown, CA 99999

Employer: Mel's Motor Co.

Claim Number: 00123 Today's Date: 8/8/20xx

To (Insurance Carrier): Allied Insurance Company

I have incurred the medical expenses listed below for prescriptions, medical treatment, and other medical costs. Receipts for these expenses are attached. Pursuant to the California Labor Code, I request immediate reimbursement. Please send the payment to me at the address listed above.

Date expense incurred	Specify expense	Reason for expense	Amount spent
6/6/20xx	Durant Pharmacy	Painkillers	$8.29
6/17/20xx	Durant Pharmacy	---------------------------	8.29
6/18/20xx	Downtown Medical	---------------------------	180.00
6/27/20xx	Ace Medical	---------------------------	42.94

Total expenses to be reimbursed $239.52

CAUTION

Special exam transportation costs must be paid in advance. If you are requested to attend a medical exam set up by the employer or its insurance carrier, you are entitled to be paid advanced transportation costs, which could include airfare or taxi fare. (LC § 4600.) See Section B3, below.

3. Payment of Expenses for Special Exams

From time to time, you may be asked to submit to a medical examination by a doctor chosen by your employer, its insurance company, or the workers' compensation judge. In addition to advance round-trip mileage for these appointments, you are also entitled to:

- all reasonable expenses of meals and lodging incidental to reporting for the examination, and
- one day of temporary disability indemnity for each day of wages lost in submitting to the examination. If you lose only a half-day, you are entitled to only a half-day of temporary disability.

These expenses must be paid to you in advance of the medical appointment, or you are not required to attend. Before attending the exam, you should contact the insurance company, give a reasonable estimate of the costs you will incur, and request payment.

C. Future Medical Care Costs

Future medical treatment, to be paid for by the insurance company, may be agreed upon in a settlement or awarded by the Workers' Compensation Appeals Board for an indefinite period, even for life, depending upon the facts of the case. You may, however, choose to waive your right to future medical care in exchange for a sum of money. See the discussion of settlement options in Chapter 19, Section B.

RELEVANT CASE LAW

See *Gardner v. WCAB*, *Stott v. WCAB*, and *Jensen v. WCAB*, in Chapter 28.

D. Penalties

If your doctor requires authorization for a medical procedure or treatment and the insurance company unreasonably delays or refuses to authorize it, you may be entitled to a penalty. Under LC § 5814, you may be entitled to a sum equal to 25% of the value of the treatment or service denied. (However, if the treatment has already been authorized, and the only dispute is payment of the bill, there is no penalty due for the late payment of medical treatment.)

If the insurance company discovers its violation before you claim a penalty, within 90 days of the date of discovery, the insurance company may pay a self-imposed 10% penalty of the amount of the payment unreasonably delayed or refused in lieu of the 25% penalty. (LC § 5814(b).)

CHAPTER

12

Temporary Disability Benefits

If your industrial injury temporarily prevents you from working at your previous job or for your previous hours, you are entitled to receive money to help replace your lost income. The payments you receive are called temporary disability indemnity (compensation), temporary disability benefits, or just "TD."

A. Qualifying for Temporary Disability

Depending on your injury and how it impairs your ability to work, your condition may fall into one of two temporary disability conditions:

- temporary total disability (TTD), or
- temporary partial disability (TPD).

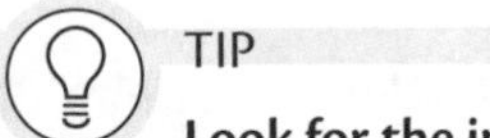

TIP

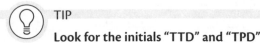

Look for the initials "TTD" and "TPD" on your checks. Many insurance companies use the abbreviations "TTD" and "TPD" on checks to describe which benefit they are paying. When looking to see whether you've been paid the correct amount, you'll need to know what payments you're receiving.

1. Temporary Total Disability (TTD)

You will qualify for temporary total disability benefits if you temporarily cannot do any kind of work as a result of your industrial injury. In this case, you are entitled to the full amount of any temporary disability benefits.

Your treating doctor usually decides whether you are temporarily totally disabled. If, however, you or the insurance company disputes the treating doctor's opinion, a qualified medical evaluator (QME) may evaluate you and render an opinion about the matter. (If you have an attorney, an agreed medical evaluator (AME) will perform the evaluation.)

If the insurance company still won't pay temporary disability payments following a QME's report that you are entitled to them, you will have to request a hearing before the Workers' Compensation Appeals Board. See Chapter 10 for a detailed explanation of how to use a QME.

For injuries that occurred before April 19, 2004, there is no time limit on how long you may collect temporary total disability benefits; you are entitled to payments for as long as you are off work and your treating doctor indicates that you are still being treated for your industrial injuries.

For injuries that occurred between April 19, 2004 and December 31, 2007, temporary total disability payments can last a maximum of two years from the date they began (technically, "104 compensable weeks within a period of two years from the date of the commencement of temporary total disability payments"). This means that even if you collect temporary total disability for only two weeks during the first two years, you may not collect any more temporary total disability payments once the two-year period expires. (LC § 4656.)

However, there are exceptions to this limitation. If you suffer from one of the following injuries or conditions, temporary total disability is extended to no more than 240 weeks within a period of five years:

- acute and chronic hepatitis B
- acute and chronic hepatitis C
- amputations
- severe burns
- human immunodeficiency virus (HIV)
- high-velocity eye injuries
- chemical burns to the eyes
- pulmonary fibrosis, or
- chronic lung disease.

For dates of injury on or after January 1, 2008, the maximum TTD payments you can receive are 104 weeks within five years of the date of injury. This means that if you were injured on 1/1/2011, you can collect a TOTAL of only 104 weeks, but in no event can you collect TTD benefits beyond 1/1/2016. The weeks do not have to be consecutive, they can be broken up. This means you should try to get all of your surgeries done before the five-year deadline expires, because if you have to have a surgery after the five years that takes you off work, you won't be able to collect temporary disability benefits.

In addition to the time limits discussed above, your right to temporary total disability benefits ends when you reach one of these workers' compensation milestones:

- You return to regular work.
- You are medically able to return to regular work (the doctor gives you a return to work order).
- You are determined to be permanent and stationary or to have reached maximal medical improvement—a determination by your doctor that you have reached a plateau and your condition is not expected to improve over the next year (see Chapter 9, Section E, for more about permanent and stationary status).

2. Temporary Partial Disability (TPD)

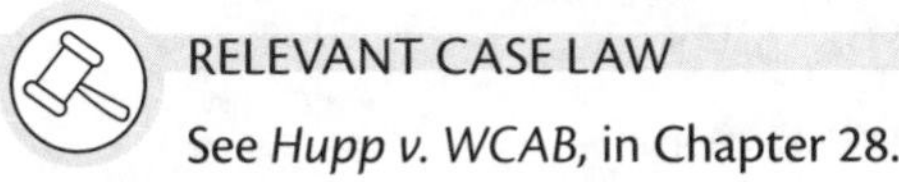

RELEVANT CASE LAW

See *Hupp v. WCAB*, in Chapter 28.

You may be entitled to temporary partial disability (TPD) if a doctor determines that you temporarily cannot carry out your full duties at work but you can work a limited number of hours. TPD is also payable if a doctor says you can return to work full time with restrictions but your employer says it does not have full-time work for you with your limitations and offers you restricted work only on a part-time basis.

For injuries that occur on or after April 19, 2004, TPD payments can last a maximum of two years from the date they began (technically, "104 compensable weeks within a period of two years from the date of the commencement of temporary total disability payments"). This means that even if you collect temporary partial disability for only two weeks during the first two years, you may not collect any more temporary partial disability payments once the two-year period expires. (LC § 4656.)

However, there are exceptions to this limitation. If you suffer from one of the following injuries or conditions, temporary partial disability payments may be extended to no more than 240 weeks within a period of five years:

- acute and chronic hepatitis B
- acute and chronic hepatitis C
- amputations
- severe burns
- human immunodeficiency virus (HIV)
- high-velocity eye injuries
- chemical burns to the eyes
- pulmonary fibrosis, or
- chronic lung disease.

For dates of injury on or after January 1, 2008, the maximum TPD payments you can receive are 104 weeks within five years of the date of injury. So, if you don't go on TPD until four years after your date of injury, you will only get 52 weeks of TPD. The 104 weeks start from the date of injury, not the first date you receive TPD payments.

For injuries that occurred before April 19, 2004, temporary partial disability payments cannot extend for more than 240 weeks within a period of five years from the date of injury.

As if this weren't already confusing enough, it is also possible to go from temporary total disability to temporary partial disability. For example, if your medical condition improves to the point where you can return to work on a limited basis, you might be entitled to some temporary partial disability benefits because you might not earn as much as you would on temporary total disability. Of course it is also possible to go from TPD to TTD if your condition were to deteriorate so that you could not work at all.

3. Off-Work Order or Medical Report Required

To qualify for temporary disability payments, you must have an off-work order or a medical report from a doctor specifying that you are temporarily totally or partially disabled. As soon as you get the off-work order, mail it to the insurance company with a written request for temporary disability payments.

It's possible that your treating doctor will authorize you to return to work with certain restrictions, such as no lifting more than 15 pounds or no repetitive bending and stooping. If you can't return to work because your employer has no job within these restrictions, you are entitled to be paid temporary disability benefits until your condition becomes permanent and stationary (or until you have reached maximal medical improvement).

If you are capable of doing the essential functions of your job with some reasonable accommodations from your employer but you feel your employer has not attempted to make those changes, you may be entitled to file a claim for discrimination. (See Chapter 16, Section C, and Chapter 17, Section D.)

B. Amount of Temporary Disability Payments

The temporary disability indemnity amount is computed at the rate of two-thirds of your average weekly earnings, with set maximum amounts. As you can see from the chart below, if you are reasonably well paid, you may receive less from workers' compensation than you did on the job.

EXAMPLE: Santiago earns $1,650 per week as a supervisor for a construction company. He is injured at work on June 22, 2011, and his doctor issues a report that says Santiago is temporarily totally disabled. His temporary disability amount is computed at two-thirds of his average weekly earnings. Two-thirds of $1,650 is $1,100. However, because the

Temporary Disability and Minimum/Maximum Rates for the First Two Years From Your Date of Injury

Date of Injury	Minimum Weekly Payment	Maximum Weekly Payment
7/1/96–12/31/02	$126 or 100% of your average weekly wages, whichever is less	$490 (based on weekly wages of $735 or more)
1/1/03–12/31/03	$126	$602 (based on weekly wages of $903 or more)
1/1/04–12/31/04	$126	$728 (based on weekly wages of $1,092 or more)
1/1/05–12/31/05	$126	$840 (based on weekly wages of $1,260 or more)
1/1/06–12/31/06	$126	$840 (based on weekly wages of $1,260 or more)
1/1/07–12/31/07	$132.35	$881.66 (based on weekly wages of $1,322 or more)
1/1/08–12/31/08	$137.45	$916.33 (based on weekly wages of $1,374.49 or more)
1/1/09–12/31/09	$143.70	$958.01 (based on weekly wages of $1,437.01 or more)
1/1/10 to 12/31/10	$148.00	$986.69 (based on weekly wages of $1,480.04)
1/1/11 to 12/31/11	$148.00	$986.69 (based on weekly wages of $1,480.04)
1/1/12 to 12/31/2012	$151.57	$1,010.50 (based on weekly wages of $1,515.75)

Notes: The amounts in parentheses ( ) are the equivalent gross weekly wage amounts needed to qualify for the benefit listed.

COLA stands for "cost of living adjustment." As of 1/1/2006, both the minimum and maximum weekly payments are adjusted annually, indexed to the state's average weekly wage.

For a table of temporary disability benefits refer to Appendix 2 on Nolo's website. (See Chapter 29, "Online Appendixes" for the link to the appendixes for this book). Remember that you cannot exceed the maximum weekly payment listed above.

maximum temporary disability rate for his date of injury is $986.69, that is all he is entitled to.

Remember, however, that temporary disability payments are not taxed as income.

You are locked into the temporary disability rate that applies to your date of injury for two years from your date of injury. If you are entitled to receive any temporary disability indemnity after two years from the date of injury (even if your disability has not been continuous), you are entitled to any higher rate in effect.

> **EXAMPLE:** Darlene was seriously injured on the job on May 5, 2003, and her doctor declared her temporarily totally disabled. When the injury occurred, her average weekly wage was $1,200. Two-thirds of $1,200 is $800, but Darlene is entitled only to the maximum rate of $602 per week. Darlene's temporary disability continues past May 5, 2005, so she is then entitled to the entire $800 per week, as the maximum disability rate in effect at that time is $840. (Because Darlene was injured before April 19, 2004, the two-year time limit does not apply to her temporary total disability benefits.)

1. How to Calculate Weekly Earnings

SKIP AHEAD

Maximum disability rate. If your temporary disability rate is the maximum weekly payment set forth in the chart, you do not need to read the rest of this section on how to compute your weekly wages. You'll receive the maximum weekly payment amount each week. Skip to Section 2, below.

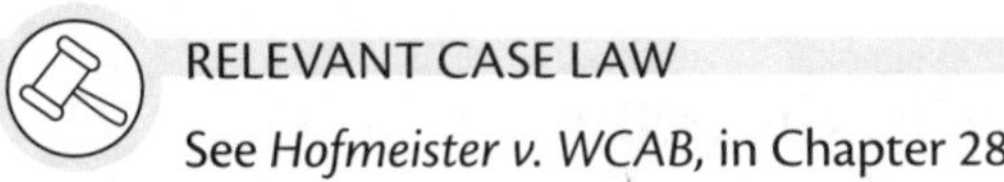

See *Hofmeister v. WCAB*, in Chapter 28.

It's important to know how your temporary disability rate is established so that you can make sure you're receiving the correct disability amount. Because it's fairly common for the insurance company to pay too little, it's important that you check this.

When you receive your first temporary disability check, the insurance company will advise you in writing how the amount you are getting was calculated. You will be told the average weekly wage used in calculating your weekly benefit.

Your weekly wage is figured at the gross amount (before taxes and other deductions are made) that you were earning at the time of your injury. This amount should include income from all jobs you held that were affected by your inability to work, such as any independent contract work you were doing, a second job, or a business you might own. You may also include overtime and the market value of board, lodging, fuel, and other perks you receive as part of your pay. (LC § 4454.) You should not include income such as alimony, dividends, or rental income, because these sources of income are not affected by your inability to work.

If you disagree with the insurance company's figure as to how much you earn per week, you will have to obtain evidence (actual documents) to prove your correct weekly wage.

The easiest way to get this evidence is to ask your employer for a wage statement setting forth how much you earned over the past 12 months (or for however long you worked there if less than 12 months). Divide the grand total by the number of weeks of pay to get your average weekly wage. If you can't get this information from your employer, you can get a good idea of your earnings from your pay stubs or W-2 tax form, provided by your employer.

TIP

How to qualify for a higher rate. It's possible that a recent raise or change in the number of hours you're working could help you qualify for a higher temporary disability rate. The insurance company should use the higher wage (rather than prior earnings) to compute your temporary disability rate.

Follow these guidelines to compute your average weekly earnings:

- **If you work for two or more employers at the time of the injury:** The average weekly wage is the total of these earnings from all jobs. If you're paid at different rates, you must calculate your pay at the rate at the job where the injury occurred.

  EXAMPLE: Tim works for employers A and B. He works 20 hours per week for employer A at $8 per hour, and 20 hours per week for employer B at $10 per hour. Tim is injured while working for employer A. Tim's average weekly wage is taken by multiplying 40 hours (the total from both jobs) by $8 (the wage paid at the job he was injured at). If Tim had been injured at the higher-paying job, he'd be able to use the higher wages for that job alone, and the lower wages from the other job (20 hours at $10 plus 20 hours at $8) to calculate the average weekly wage.

- **If your earnings are at an irregular rate (such as piecework), on a commission basis, or specified by week, month, or other period:** The average weekly wage is figured by averaging the actual weekly earnings for the previous year (or shorter period of time, if convenient, to determine an average weekly rate of pay).

  EXAMPLE: Bert has worked as a commissioned sales rep for XYZ Co. since February 2010. On August 6, 2012, he is injured on the job. Bert's wages depend upon his sales and are different every week. Bert's average weekly wage is computed by taking his total earnings for the period August 6, 2011 to August 6, 2012 and dividing by the total number of weeks he worked.

RELEVANT CASE LAW

See *Placer County Office of Education v. WCAB (Halkyard)*, in Chapter 28.

- **If you work fewer than 30 hours per week, or for any reason the previous methods of arriving at the average weekly wage cannot reasonably and fairly be applied:** The insurance company must use average weekly earnings that reasonably represent your average weekly earning capacity at the time of your injury. For example, if you just got a big raise, your average weekly wage would be your current weekly wage, not your average over the last 52 weeks. Consideration must be given to your actual earnings from all sources and jobs. (LC § 4453.)

2. Calculating the Partial Disability Benefit

If you go back to work for a limited number of hours, you are entitled to receive two-thirds of your weekly loss in wages, assuming your part-time work results in less pay than you'd receive if you received temporary total disability benefits and didn't work (TTD). (LC § 4654.)

Your "weekly loss in wages" is determined to be the difference between your average weekly wage (see Section B1, above, for the definition of average weekly wage), up to the maximum weekly payment as shown in the chart above, and the weekly amount you are able to earn part-time. (LC § 4657.)

EXAMPLE: Bonnie was injured in February 2006. Bonnie's average weekly wage of $1,300 qualifies her for the maximum TTD rate of $840 per week (for average weekly wages of $1,260 per week or more), as shown in the chart above. Bonnie returns to work on a part-time basis and earns only $500 per week. Her wage loss then is $660 per week (the maximum weekly wage of $1,260 minus the $500 she earns). The insurance company will pay Bonnie two-thirds of this $660 wage loss, or $440.

3. If You're Reinjured

If you return to work and are reinjured on the job, you need to know whether or not you have a new injury to determine your temporary disability rate.

If your injury is not new, but an exacerbation (flare-up) of your prior injury, the original injury date is used in figuring additional temporary disability (subject to any increase you are entitled to after two years—see the beginning of Section B, above).

If, however, the injury is new, you are entitled to the temporary disability minimums and maximums in effect at the time of the new injury. You must also follow procedures to file a claim for the new injury. (See Chapter 5, Sections B and C.)

C. How Payments Are Made

Temporary disability benefits are calculated weekly but must be paid every two weeks. The workers' compensation insurance company should begin sending temporary disability checks to you as soon as it determines that you:

- have a valid claim, and
- are temporarily disabled.

1. Special Rules for First Three Days Off Work

No temporary disability benefits are paid for the first three days off work unless the injury requires hospitalization or you are off work more than 14 days.

> **EXAMPLE:** Jerry is injured at work and takes 11 days off to recover. Because Jerry was neither hospitalized nor off work for more than 14 days, he is entitled to only eight days of temporary disability; he does not get paid for the first three days off work.

2. Payments Must Begin Within 14 Days

The first payment of temporary disability benefits must be made not later than 14 days after the employer learns of your industrial injury and temporary disability status. On that date, all benefits then due must be paid unless the employer denies liability for the injury.

If you do not receive your first temporary disability payment within two weeks after you forwarded the off-work order to the insurance company, follow up promptly. Call and request that payments begin immediately, retroactive to the date you were first taken off work. Always make a note of any telephone call and follow up with a written letter confirming what transpired in the phone call.

Sample Letter

April 22, 20xx

Katherine Bradford
ABC Insurance
333 West Third Street
Anytown, CA 99999

Re: Temporary disability payments for Henry Wilson
Employer: Brand X Corporation
Claim No: 11403-00-ABC

Dear Ms. Bradford:

On 4/5/20xx, I notified you by telephone, and then by letter, that Dr. Smith, my treating doctor, gave me an off-work order. The off-work order is dated 4/2/20xx and indicates that I will be temporarily totally disabled until at least 9/5/20xx.

It has been more than 14 days since you were advised of my disability status. Please begin temporary disability payments immediately and include all payments due since 3/29/20xx.

Sincerely,
Henry Wilson
Henry Wilson

3. Penalties for Late Payments

Temporary disability payments must be made every two weeks. If any payment is not made according to this time frame, you're entitled to an automatic 10% late fee in addition to the payment. (LC

§ 4650.) The insurance company probably won't pay the penalty unless you request it, although technically you're entitled to it automatically.

A 10% late penalty is not assessed if the insurance company cannot determine whether temporary disability payments are owed. To avoid liability for the penalty, the insurance company must advise you in writing within 14 days after you submit your DWC-1 form to your employer:

- why payments cannot be made within the 14-day period
- what additional information it requires to determine whether temporary disability payments are owed, and
- when it expects to have the information required to make the decision.

Most insurance companies pay temporary disability on time. If you are entitled to a 10% penalty and do not receive it with your next disability check, you may wait until your case settles to request the penalty. This is particularly advisable if it's not much money and you don't need it right away. After all, you don't want to alienate the claims adjuster with unnecessary demands. If, however, you want to receive the 10% penalty soon, call the insurance company and request payment. If you need to, follow up with a letter.

When a payment has been unreasonably delayed or refused by the insurance company, you are entitled to an extra penalty. The amount of the payment unreasonably delayed or refused is increased by up to 25%, or up to $10,000, whichever is less. For example, suppose Maria does not get her temporary disability check in the amount of $840 on time. It does not arrive until it is more than four weeks overdue. Maria may be entitled to a 25% penalty on the $840 that was late if it is determined that the delay was unreasonable. The penalty would be $210. This may or may not be in addition to the automatic 10% penalty Maria is entitled to under LC § 4650(d)—see the note below.

If, however, the insurance company discovers its violation before you claim a penalty, the insurance company, within 90 days of the date of discovery, may pay a self-imposed 10% penalty of the amount of the payment unreasonably delayed or refused, in lieu of the 25% penalty. (LC § 5814(b).) But if the insurance company pays a 10% penalty under LC § 4650(d) and then pays a 25% penalty for unreasonable delay under LC § 5814(a), it is then entitled to deduct the 10% paid under 4650(d) and pay only the 15% balance. However, if the carrier pays a 10% unreasonable delay penalty under LC § 5814(b) because the insurance company caught the penalty before the injured worker did, then no deduction is allowed for the penalty paid under LC § 4650(d).

Don't Unintentionally Waive Your Penalty Rights!

If you discover that you are entitled to a 25% penalty under LC § 5814 (see above), demand it from the insurance company immediately so that you'll get the full 25%.

Also, there is a two-year statute of limitations for collecting penalties due under LC § 5814. If you need to file for a hearing before the appeals board to collect a penalty or resolve a penalty issue, do not let more than two years pass (from the date of the event that gave rise to the penalty).

Finally, do not settle your case or go to trial without requesting all penalties due. If you settle your case by way of a compromise and release (see Chapter 19, Section B2), the appeals board will assume that all accrued penalty claims are included in your settlement unless you expressly exclude them. If your case goes to trial (see Chapter 24, Section C), the judge will assume that all penalties are resolved unless the penalty is listed as an issue at trial.

Problems Getting Paid

Unfortunately, not all injured workers get the temporary disability payments they're entitled to receive. The most common problems you are likely to encounter are:

- Your employer denies you have a workers' compensation claim and refuses to pay benefits.
- The insurance company claims your average weekly wage is less than it really is, so it pays you less than the amount you believe you are entitled to.
- The workers' compensation insurance company does not process your paperwork in a timely manner.

Most of these problems can be resolved by calling the insurance company or writing a letter (remember to keep copies). If you still cannot get results, you may have to file documents and set a hearing with the appeals board to have a judge determine whether you are entitled to benefits. (See Chapter 22, Section B.)

4. Sick Leave, Vacation, and Salary

If your employer pays you full wages in the form of sick leave or vacation pay during the time you are disabled, you're not entitled to temporary disability benefits. Even if you are paid less than your full salary, as long as it exceeds your temporary disability weekly rate, you are not entitled to temporary disability.

Some employers prefer that injured employees receive sick leave or vacation pay instead of temporary disability. If you have notified your employer that you have an industrial injury, the employer cannot make you take sick or vacation pay without your permission. (LC § 4652.) If your employer allows it, however, you might wish to receive sick leave or vacation pay if it gives you more money than temporary disability.

CHAPTER 13

Permanent Disability (and Life Pension)

When a doctor determines that further medical treatment at this time will not help you improve, your medical condition is referred to as "permanent and stationary," or as having reached "maximal medical improvement." This might mean you have fully recovered or simply that your condition has stabilized—meaning that the doctor doesn't think your condition will improve substantially over the next year.

After you're found to be permanent and stationary, it's time to determine whether you have a permanent disability as a result of your work injury. For workers' compensation purposes, a permanent disability is any disability or impairment that is expected to remain after you reach the maximum recovery or healing.

If you completely recover without any ill effects, you will not have a permanent disability. If, however, your maximum recovery from your injury is less than full and complete, you will have a permanent disability. Even if your injury has healed and you no longer experience pain, if the doctor gives you a physical restriction such as no heavy lifting, you are considered to have some percentage of permanent disability. This is because a permanent disability is defined as how your injury has affected your ability to participate in the open job market. If you have any restrictions on what you can do when you return to work, you have a disability, because the restriction might prevent you from taking certain types of jobs in the future.

TIP

New permanent disability schedule. A new permanent disability schedule (used to rate your amount of permanent disability—covered in Chapter 18) became effective January 1, 2005. Some of the changes in the schedule applied to all workers, regardless of when they were injured, while others applied only to workers injured in 2005 or later. In this new schedule, permanent disability percentages for severely injured workers were increased, and permanent disability percentages for workers with minor injuries were decreased.

Permanent Disability and Temporary Disability Compared

Do not confuse permanent disability with temporary disability (discussed in Chapter 12). A temporary disability exists if you temporarily can't perform your regular job. In that case, you'll receive temporary disability payments while you are off work getting medical treatment and recovering from the effects of your injury. Once you are finished with treatment, or can return to work, temporary disability payments end.

If you don't recover 100%, you are entitled to a specified amount as a permanent disability award. Permanent disability awards are over and above any temporary disability payments and medical care costs. You may receive permanent disability even if you are working again.

A. How Permanent Disability Payments Compensate You

If you have a permanent disability, you are entitled to a limited sum of money, referred to as a permanent disability award. The money is intended to compensate you for your diminished future earning capacity. In other words, if your permanent disability limits which jobs you can do, you at least get some money as compensation.

If you qualify for permanent disability, payments are due even if you:

- return to work
- do the exact work for which you had previously been employed, or
- didn't suffer any wage loss.

In fact, the vast majority of injured workers who receive a permanent disability award return to their former jobs.

EXAMPLE: Wesley falls and injures his right knee while working as a bank teller. After his condition stabilizes, his doctor gives a work restriction of "no very heavy lifting." Wesley is entitled to a permanent disability award because his inability to lift heavy objects would make it harder for him to find employment on the open job market. The fact that Wesley's current job as a bank teller (to which he returned) does not require very heavy lifting is irrelevant for permanent disability purposes. After all, Wesley may not work for the bank forever. Wesley will receive a small permanent disability award.

In case you're thinking that a permanent disability award is a pretty good deal, you should know that it's actually quite limited. For example, a permanent disability award does not compensate you for pain and suffering stemming from your injury, nor does it account for past or present wages lost because of your injury or financial damage as a result of your injury, including loss of creditworthiness (if, for example, you don't have enough money to pay your bills). In addition, permanent disability awards are usually very small compared to court awards.

Finally, there is no right of survivorship to permanent disability awards. In other words, if you die before you receive the amount due, your survivors will not get your permanent disability payments.

B. Kinds of Permanent Disability Awards

If you have a permanent disability, you should be entitled to at least one of the following types of monetary awards:

- **Permanent partial disability award.** The vast majority of injured workers with permanent disabilities have permanent partial disabilities. Any permanent disability that is ultimately determined to be less than 100% is considered to be a partial disability.
- **Life pension award.** Injured workers with permanent partial disabilities of 70% to 99.75% are paid, in addition to permanent partial disability payments, a nominal lifelong pension. (LC § 4659.) This weekly amount is paid to you after your normal weekly permanent disability indemnity ends. The life pension is paid until you die, even if your condition improves.
- **Permanent total disability award.** If it is ultimately determined that you have a total permanent disability (100%), you are entitled to lifetime payments at your temporary disability rate. This is similar to a life pension, but it is paid at a much higher rate. A total disability means you aren't expected to be able hold down any type of gainful employment whatsoever.

C. Establishing Your Permanent or Maximal Medical Improvement Disability Status

It typically takes months or years to reach a final determination of a permanent disability or maximal medical improvement. First, your doctor must say that your condition is permanent and stationary—that your medical condition has plateaued. For injuries after 2005, reaching permanent and stationary status is also known as having reached "maximal medical improvement" (MMI), meaning that your condition is well stabilized and unlikely to change substantially in the next year, with or without medical treatment.

After your condition has stabilized, your doctors (treating doctors and perhaps qualified medical evaluators) will write medical reports in which they set forth whatever limitations have resulted from your industrial injury. These opinions are usually contained in a permanent and stationary medical report, which is "rated" to convert the doctors' opinions on your limitations into a percentage of disability. (See Chapter 9, Section E, for more on reviewing your permanent and stationary report.)

Unless you have an attorney, the rating process will be done for you automatically by the administrative director of the Workers' Compensation Appeals Board (called an advisory rating, or summary rating). Fortunately, advisory ratings are usually reliable and rarely contain errors.

The percentage of permanent disability will be rated anywhere from 0.25% to 100% (in increments of 0.25). The advisory rating will also convert the percentage of disability into the amount of money you are entitled to based upon the percentage of disability. (See Chapter 18 for more on rating your permanent disability.)

1. Notification of Your Permanent Disability Status

If you were never temporarily disabled—for example, you continued to work while you were getting medical treatment—you will receive notice from the insurance company regarding permanent disability when your medical condition is determined to have stabilized (is permanent and stationary).

If you were receiving temporary disability payments, the insurance company will give you notice of your permanent disability status when it stops making temporary disability payments to you. Temporary disability payments stop either when your medical condition is determined to be permanent and stationary or when you return to work full time. At this point, the insurance company must send your last payment of temporary disability along with a notice stating one of the following:

- **No permanent disability benefits will be paid because the insurance company believes that you don't have a permanent disability from the injury.** The notice must include information on how you can get a formal medical evaluation if you disagree with the insurance company's opinion. (LC § 4061(a)(1).)
- **The insurance company believes you have a permanent disability.** The insurance company must state the amount of permanent disability benefits that are payable, the basis on which the determination was made (usually your treating doctor's permanent and stationary report), and whether you'll need future medical care. (LC § 4061(a)(1).) The notice must include information on how you can get a formal medical evaluation if you disagree with the insurance company's opinion.
- **Permanent disability benefits may be or are payable, but the amount cannot be determined yet because your medical condition is not permanent and stationary.** You may get this notice if you return to work but are still receiving treatment for your injury or illness. In this case, the insurance company will monitor your treatment until the treating doctor says that you are permanent and stationary. Within 14 days of that time, the insurance company will send you notice of its position regarding your permanent disability, as discussed just above. (LC § 4061(a)(2).)

2. Check the Basis for Your Permanent Disability Status

Insurance companies almost always base their decisions about whether you are entitled to permanent disability benefits on the treating doctor's permanent and stationary report or the advisory rating of that report if it has been rated. Sometimes, however, an insurance company reviews a medical report and then makes its own estimate of the amount of permanent disability compensation to which you are entitled.

You should carefully review the treating doctor's permanent and stationary report and any advisory rating to see what the treating doctor says about the nature and extent of your permanent disability. (See Chapter 9, Section E, for an explanation on how to analyze the doctor's report.)

Note that for permanent and stationary reports written in 2004 and earlier, the doctor's opinion about permanent disability was generally set forth as "work restrictions" or as "subjective complaints."

For most permanent and stationary reports written in 2005 and later, the doctor is required to include an "impairment number" for your injury and your amount of "whole person impairment" (WPI)—your basic disability rating before being adjusted for your age, occupation, and loss of future earning capacity (you'll learn about these adjustments in Chapter 18).

Note: Do not be surprised if you see subjective complaints and work restrictions in your doctor's report rather than a WPI and an impairment number. Even if your doctor wrote your permanent and stationary report in 2005 or later, the doctor is not required to include a WPI if all of the following are true:

- Your injury occurred in 2004 or earlier.
- You didn't receive a medical-legal evaluation report or any other doctor's report before January 1, 2005 that indicated that you had some permanent disability.
- The insurance company was not required to provide you with notice required by LC § 4061. (An LC § 4061 notice is notice either that permanent disability may be payable but the amount cannot be determined because your medical condition is not yet permanent and stationary, or that no permanent disability will be paid.) This means that there has not yet been a dispute as to the nature and extent of your permanent disability or your need for future medical treatment.

These are really the same standards for determining whether your permanent disability must be rated using the new rating schedule or the old rating schedule. For more information, see Chapter 18, Section B1.

If your doctor did include an impairment number and a WPI in the report, note the number and the WPI rating and read the objective findings to make sure the doctor didn't leave anything out. (You may want to look at the new rating schedule to decipher the impairment number and to adjust your WPI; see Chapter 18, Section B2, for information on the new rating schedule). Also see Chapter 9, Section E, for an explanation of how to analyze permanent and stationary reports in general.

If the treating doctor's permanent and stationary report hasn't been rated yet, immediately submit it to the Disability Evaluation Unit for calculation of a permanent disability rating. (See Chapter 18, Section A2, on how to do this.) If the insurance company wants to discuss settlement based upon the opinion of the treating doctor's report only, insist that the report be rated first. (If the insurance company reviews the treating doctor's report and thinks it has a low rating, it will request an advisory rating to help convince you to settle, knowing that the rating will be low. But if the insurance company thinks the report will rate fairly high, it might not request an advisory rating.)

If you agree with the insurance company's opinion regarding the nature and extent of your permanent disability (how much disability you have), you may begin settlement negotiations. (See Chapter 19.)

3. Dispute Your Permanent Disability Status If Necessary

If you disagree with the doctor's permanent and stationary report or any advisory rating, call or write the insurance company within 30 days of receipt of the report or rating. If you call, always follow up with a written confirmation of your telephone conversation.

Explain that you dispute the determination of your permanent disability rating. Give your reason for disagreeing (see Chapter 18). If your explanation makes sense to the insurance company, it may agree and improve its offer. If it doesn't, and you dispute the treating doctor's report, the insurance company will send you the necessary paperwork to select a qualified medical evaluator (QME) to resolve the dispute. (This process is covered in Chapter 10.)

The insurance company also has the right to object to the treating doctor's opinion or the advisory rating, and if it does, it must notify you of its objection. The insurance company will then provide you with a form to request a QME panel. (Again, this process is covered in detail in Chapter 10.)

Permanent Disability Is Sometimes Arbitrarily Denied

If the insurance company has a valid medical basis for denying permanent disability, it should willingly tell you. If it refuses to tell you, you should suspect that your benefits are being arbitrarily denied.

Workers' compensation insurance companies cannot legally deny permanent disability benefits without a legitimate reason. If the insurance company won't explain why it refuses to pay you permanent disability benefits, you may request that a workers' compensation judge resolve the matter. Under LC § 5814, the judge may find that the insurance company owes you a 25% penalty payment on the entire permanent disability award for arbitrarily denying you benefits.

D. How Permanent Disability Benefits Are Paid

Unless you request that payments be postponed, the insurance company must begin paying your permanent disability benefit within 14 days after the date your temporary disability payments cease. (LC § 4650(b).)

The insurance company must begin paying you permanent disability payments regardless of whether the extent of your permanent disability has been determined. The insurance company must continue to pay these permanent disability payments until a reasonable estimate of your permanent disability can be determined, and then must continue the payments until you have been compensated for that amount. (LC § 4650(b).)

Incidentally, don't worry about getting more money in permanent disability payments than you are entitled to. The insurance company is very good at underestimating how much your permanent disability award will be. In addition, it will probably withhold 12%–15% to cover possible attorney fees, even if you don't have a lawyer. In the unlikely event that you're overpaid, the insurance company could ask you to repay the overpayment, but in many years of practice I have yet to see this happen.

1. Biweekly Permanent Disability Payments

The insurance company must make payments to you at least twice in each calendar month; typically, payments are made every two weeks. (LC § 4650(c).) For permanent partial disabilities, payments end after a set amount of time based on a system that rates the dollar value of your injury. For permanent total disability, you will be entitled to receive permanent disability payments for the rest of your life.

These biweekly payments are also referred to as permanent disability advances, because they will be deducted from any final settlement check you receive.

2. Lump Sum Permanent Disability Advances

In addition to receiving your biweekly payments, if you need money due to financial hardship, you can ask the insurance company for a lump sum advance such as $500 or $1,000. Most insurance companies are willing to advance some permanent disability money against your final settlement check if you have a good reason for requesting the advance. The request may be made by phone or by letter. It generally takes the insurance company several weeks to act upon the request.

Whether you eventually settle out of court or go to trial and receive a monetary award from a workers' compensation judge, the insurance company is entitled to subtract any money it has paid you for lump sum permanent disability advances, as well as any biweekly payments it has made, from the settlement or award.

EXAMPLE: Barbara received $1,000 in lump sum permanent disability advances and $7,000 in biweekly permanent disability payments. Her total permanent disability settlement is $10,000. At the time of final settlement, she will be entitled to receive $2,000 for her permanent disability ($10,000 – $1,000 – $7,000 = $2,000). Any amounts that she was paid for temporary disability are not credited against the final settlement.

The following questions should help you decide whether or not to request a lump sum permanent disability advance or accept the biweekly permanent disability payments:

- Do you need the money now?
- Will you need the majority of your money later?
- Do you have the discipline to save or invest the money without touching it? If so, you may be better off having the money working for you now, rather than letting the insurance company use the money.

CAUTION

Permanent disability advances may affect other disability policies. Most long-term disability policies, as well as Social Security disability, take a credit or offset for any workers' compensation benefits you receive. You are required by law to advise these agencies of any money you get in your workers' compensation case. If you may receive disability payments other than workers' compensation, it is better not to accept any permanent disability advances (either weekly or lump sum) to avoid having the other benefits reduced by a like amount. If your case later settles, you may be able to insert special language in your settlement agreement to minimize the amount of credit taken against your workers' compensation settlement by these agencies. (See Chapter 20, Section D2c.)

3. Penalties for Late Payments

If any biweekly payment is not made on time, the amount of the payment must automatically be increased by 10%. (LC §§ 4650(c) and (d).) The insurance company is supposed to include the penalty with the payment of any benefit that is late. If the insurance company does not, you may send a letter demanding the penalty or wait until your case settles.

When a payment has been unreasonably delayed or refused by the insurance company, you are entitled to an extra penalty. The amount of the payment unreasonably delayed or refused is increased by up to 25%, or up to $10,000, whichever is less. For example, suppose Jason does not get his permanent disability check in the amount of $340 on time. It does not arrive until it is more than four weeks overdue. Jason may be entitled to a 25% penalty on the $340 that was late. The penalty would be $85, less credit for any penalty paid pursuant to LC 4650(d) for the same delay.

If, however, the insurance company discovers its violation before you claim a penalty, the insurance company, within 90 days of the date of discovery, may pay a self-imposed 10% penalty of the amount of the payment unreasonably delayed or refused, in lieu of the 25% penalty. (LC § 5814(b).)

4. Resolving Problems With the Insurance Company

If the insurance company refuses to provide you with biweekly permanent disability payments and it has not denied that the money is owed to you, you may need to appear before the Workers' Compensation Appeals Board for a hearing to obtain an order that the insurance company must pay you these benefits.

Before taking this action, however, try calling or writing the insurance company and demanding the benefits to which you are entitled. (If you need to set a hearing before the appeals board, see Chapter 22.)

E. Amount of Permanent Partial Disability Benefits

SKIP AHEAD

Permanent partial disability awards are made for permanent disabilities that are rated 99.75% or less. If you have a 100% (total) disability, skip to Section G, below.

RELEVANT CASE LAW

See *Benson v. The Permanent Medical Group, Parker v. WCAB*, and *The Home Depot v. WCAB*, in Chapter 28.

A permanent partial disability benefit is determined by:

- your permanent disability rating, which converts from a percentage into the number of weekly payments you are entitled to, multiplied by
- your permanent disability indemnity rate, which is based upon your average weekly wage at the time you were injured.

It is always wise to double-check the insurance company to make certain that it is paying you at the correct rate and for the proper amount of time. Here's how.

The first factor in determining the amount of money you are entitled to receive is your permanent disability rating—that is, the percentage of disability. This is expressed as a percentage in increments of 0.25, such as 26.75%.

This figure will be based on some or all of the following:

- the percentage of disability determined by your treating doctor
- the percentage of disability determined by a qualified medical evaluator, and/or
- an advisory rating, discussed in Section C2, above.

The percentage of disability is subject to negotiation. If you and the insurance company cannot agree upon a permanent disability rate, the judge will decide on a rate after hearing evidence at your trial. (Disability ratings are discussed in Chapter 18.)

1. How Many Weeks of Benefits Will Be Paid?

Once you have your disability rating (percentage of disability), it must be converted into the number of weeks of payments. It's easy to do this. Refer to the Permanent Disability Indemnity Chart on Nolo's website. (See Chapter 29, "Online Appendixes" for the link to Appendix 3: Permanent Disability Indemnity Chart.) Find your percentage of disability in the first column, and then find the corresponding number of weeks of payments in the column to its immediate right. The number of weeks to which you are entitled changes with the date of injury, so make sure you find the correct "Total Weeks" column (there are two) that corresponds to your date of injury. For example, 26.75% for an injury date of July 30, 2005 would entitle you to 111.25 weeks of payments.

2. What Is the Weekly Rate of Payment?

You are entitled to up to two-thirds of your average weekly wage, according to your date of injury, within the minimum and maximum amounts allowed by law. (LC § 4658.) Refer to the Permanent Partial Disability Rates chart, below, to determine the rate you're entitled to. (See Chapter 12, Section B1, if you're not sure how to compute your average weekly wage.)

EXAMPLE 1: Brad is injured at work on August 3, 2011 and gets a 50% disability rating. Two-thirds of his $600 average weekly earnings is $400 per week. The maximum average weekly amount allowed for an injury occurring in 2011 is $230 for a permanent disability rating under 70%. Brad is entitled to the maximum weekly amount, or $230.

EXAMPLE 2: Jason is injured at work in January 2003 and gets a 25% disability rating. Two-thirds of his weekly earnings of $210 is $140 per week. Jason does not get the maximum weekly payment of $185 shown in the chart, below. Instead, he gets $140 per week, which becomes his permanent disability rate.

3. Determining the Amount You Are Entitled To

If you are entitled to the maximum weekly permanent disability amount, such as $185 for a

The New Permanent Disability Schedule

A new permanent disability schedule (which is used to rate your amount of permanent disability—covered in Chapter 18) became effective January 1, 2005. In this new schedule, permanent disability percentages for severely injured workers have been increased, and permanent disability percentages for workers with minor injuries have been decreased.

For injuries that occurred before 2005, there is a question of which rating manual applies to your date of injury. This is important, because using the new rating manual may substantially reduce the amount of money you will get as your permanent disability award.

Unfortunately, the case law on this subject (see Chapter 28) clearly indicates that the new rating manual applies to *all* dates of injury (even those occurring before January 1, 2005) unless *one* of the following three exceptions apply:

- there is a comprehensive medical-legal report (see Chapter 10) indicating the existence of permanent disability
- there is a report from the treating physician indicating the existence of permanent disability, or
- the employer or insurance carrier is required to give you the notice required under LC § 4061, which provides that "together with the last payment of temporary disability indemnity, the employer shall ... provide the employee one of the following:
  1. Notice either that no permanent disability indemnity will be paid because the employer alleges the employee has no permanent impairment or limitations resulting from the injury or notice of the amount of permanent disability indemnity determined by the employer to be payable ... or
  2. Notice that permanent disability indemnity may be or is payable, but that the amount cannot be determined because the employee's medical condition is not yet permanent and stationary. (See Labor Code Sections 4061 and 4660(d)."

Without one of these exceptions, your case will be rated under the new manual.

rating of up to 69.75% for injuries in 2003 (this would be your weekly payment if your average weekly wages are at least $277.50), to find your lump sum permanent disability award you can simply look up your disability rating in the Permanent Disability Indemnity Chart. Find your disability percentage and then follow the figures across to the column that corresponds to your date of injury. There, you will find the total dollar amount you are entitled to for your maximum weekly disability rate.

If your weekly permanent disability rate is below the maximum, you'll need to do this calculation without the chart. To determine the amount of money you are entitled to, multiply the total number of weeks to which you are entitled by your permanent disability rate. For example, 33.25 weeks multiplied by $140 = $4,655.

Returning to Jason's example, remember that he has a disability rating of 25% and his permanent disability rate is $140 per week. Jason looks in the Permanent Disability Indemnity Chart in on Nolo's website and finds that a 25% disability from an injury in 2003 is entitled to 95.75 weeks of permanent disability payments. His lump sum permanent disability amount is $13,405 ($140 x 95.75 weeks).

New rules for 2005 and later. There are some new rules that went into effect for workers injured in 2005 or later and that apply only to employers who employ 50 or more workers. First, if within 60 days of your condition's becoming permanent and stationary (see Chapter 9, Section E) your employer does not offer you regular work, modified work, or alternative work (in the form and manner prescribed by the administrative director) for at

Permanent Partial Disability Rates		
Date of Injury	**Minimum Weekly Payment**	**Maximum Weekly Payment**
7/1/94–6/30/95	$70 [$105 wages]	$140 for PD under 15% [$210 wages] $148 for PD 15% to 24.75% [$222 wages] $158 for PD 25% to 69.75% [$237 wages] $168 for PD 70% and over [$252 wages]
7/1/95–6/30/96	$70 [$105 wages]	$140 for PD under 15% [$210 wages] $154 for PD 15% to 24.75% [$231 wages] $164 for PD 25% to 69.75% [$246 wages] $198 for PD 70% and over [$297 wages]
7/1/96–12/31/02	$70 [$105 wages]	$140 for PD under 15% [$210 wages] $160 for PD 15% to 24.75% [$260 wages] $170 for PD 25% to 69.75% [$255 wages] $230 for PD 70% and over [$345 wages]
1/1/03–12/31/03	$100 [$150 wages]	$185 for PD under 70% [$277.50 wages] $230 for PD 70% and over [$345 wages]
1/1/04–12/31/04	$105 [$157.50 wages]	$200 for PD under 70% [$300 wages] $250 for PD 70% and over [$375 wages]
1/1/05–12/31/05	$105 [$157.50 wages]	$220 for PD under 70% [$330 wages] $270 for PD 70% and over [$405 wages]
On or after 1/1/06	$130 [$195 wages]	$230 for PD under 70% [$345 wages] $270 for PD 70% and over [$405 wages]
Note: The amounts in brackets [ ] are the equivalent weekly wage amounts needed to qualify for the benefit listed.		

least one year, your permanent disability payments will be increased by 15% (for the payments remaining to be paid to you, and starting from the end of the 60-day period).

Second, if within 60 days of your condition's becoming permanent and stationary your employer *does* offer you regular work, modified work, or alternative work for at least one year—regardless of whether you accept or reject the offer—each disability payment remaining to be paid to you from the date the offer was made will be decreased by 15%.

If you accept the offer of work and your employer terminates it before the end of the period for which disability payments are due to you, the amount of each of the remaining payments will be increased by 15%. If you voluntarily terminate your employment, you will not be eligible for the 15% increase.

The modified or alternative work must be something that you are able to perform, must offer compensation that is at least 85% of what you were being paid at the time of your injury, and must be located within a reasonable commuting distance of your residence at the time of injury.

4. Combining Injuries for Disability Rating Purposes

In Chapter 18, Section C, Step 7, we discuss combining multiple injuries to come up with a higher permanent disability rating. Here we'll explain how it works so that you can plan ahead if you have multiple injuries.

For rating purposes, it is often (but not always) to your advantage to combine successive injuries. This tactic can increase your overall monetary award, because one injury with a high permanent disability rating often pays more benefits than two or three smaller injuries.

EXAMPLE: While working for Ajax Cleaning, Joe injures his lower back on March 23, 2005. He files a workers' compensation claim and is seen by Dr. Smith, who treats Joe and sends him back to work with certain modifications to his activities. Joe returns to work for the same employer, and while still being treated for his back injury of March 23, 2005, he suffers another back injury. Joe files a second workers' compensation claim and is treated for that injury. Eventually the doctor releases Joe back to work and writes a report stating that Joe's back became permanent and stationary on January 2, 2006 and that Joe has some permanent disability, caused half by the first injury and half by the second injury. The doctor gives Joe a work restriction of "no heavy work." This restriction works out to an approximate rating of 30% permanent disability. (We discuss how to rate injuries in Chapter 18.)

Joe's insurance company tries to say that Joe has two separate injuries, each rated at 15% disability. This would result in two separate settlements for permanent disability of $8,040 each (see the Permanent Disability Indemnity Chart on Nolo's website), for a total of $16,080. However, Joe demands that his injuries be combined for rating purposes, resulting in one permanent disability of 30%. This would result in one settlement for permanent disability of $21,420 instead of two settlements for $16,080—an increase of $5,340.

The legal justification for combining injuries can be found in the case of *Wilkinson v. WCAB.* (See Chapter 28.) The court in this case said that if an employee has two successive injuries to the same part of the body that occur with the same employer, and those injuries become permanent and stationary at the same time, the injuries can be combined. And in a subsequent case (*Rumbaugh v. WCAB*; see Chapter 28), the court threw out the requirement that the injuries need to occur with the same employer. It remains in controversy whether the injuries must involve the same part of the body and must become permanent and stationary at the same time to be combined.

A later case, *Benson v. The Permanente Medical Group*, 72 CCC 1620, has now overturned the *Wilkinson* rule—bad news for the injured worker. Now, if you have two dates of injury, even if they become permanent and stationary at the same time, the amount of the permanent disability is determined separately for each.

F. Life Pension Benefits

SKIP AHEAD

Skip this section if you are not eligible for a life pension (available only for injuries rated between 70% and 99.75%). For injuries that result in 100% total disability, there is no life pension, but you are entitled to permanent total disability benefits; skip to Section G, below.

If you have a permanent partial disability of 70% to 99.75%, you are entitled to a relatively small life pension in addition to permanent partial disability payments you receive. Life pension payments usually are paid biweekly and begin after all permanent partial disability payments have been made.

Don't get overly excited if you qualify for a life pension. It is a small amount of money, and certainly not enough to support you. For example, if you were injured in 2010, the most you could possibly be entitled to would be a weekly payment of about $316—and that would be for an injury of 99%!

1. How to Compute a Life Pension

To compute your life pension, you may want to seek help from an information and assistance officer. If you want to compute your life pension yourself, here are the steps; an example follows.

Step 1: Multiply your average weekly earnings on your date of injury, up to the maximum allowed as the "Maximum average weekly wage" in the chart below, by 1.5%. If your average weekly wage is less than the maximum shown in the chart, use your average weekly wage.

Step 2: Subtract 60% from your percentage of disability to get a multiplier. For example, a disability of 70% would have a multiplier of 10, computed: 70% – 60% = 10.

Step 3: Multiply the number you calculated in Step 1 by the multiplier in Step 2.

Maximum Wages for Calculating Life Pension Rates

Date of Injury	Minimum Average Weekly Wage
7/1/94–6/30/95	$157.69
7/1/95–6/30/96	$207.69
7/1/96–12/31/04	$257.69
1/1/05–12/31/05	$262.63
1/1/06–12/31/06	$273.16
1/1/07–12/31/07	$540.94
1/1/08–12/31/08	$562.21
1/1/09–12/31/09	$587.78

Note: COLA stands for "cost of living adjustment." Beginning 1/1/2006, the maximum average weekly wage has been adjusted annually, indexed to the state's average weekly wage.

EXAMPLE: Jim's industrial injury occurred on June 2, 2002. His permanent partial disability was 72.25%, entitling Jim to a life pension in addition to his permanent partial disability award. At the time of his injury, Jim's average weekly wage was $480. Because his average weekly wage exceeds the maximum for his date of injury, Jim must use the maximum allowable average weekly wage of $257.69 (see chart just above). Jim multiplies $257.69 by 1.5% to get $3.86535. Multiplying $3.86535 by 12.25 (the difference between Jim's disability of 72.25% and 60%), Jim comes up with $47 (rounded to the nearest penny) per week. In addition to all other benefits, Jim is entitled to $47 per week for life after his permanent disability award has been paid in full.

G. Permanent Total Disability Benefits

SKIP AHEAD

Skip this section if your injury does not result in a 100% total disability rating. Go on to Chapter 14.

If you are 100% disabled, you are considered to be "totally" disabled for workers' compensation purposes.

Any one of these work injuries will automatically entitle you to a total permanent disability award:

- loss of, or loss of sight in, both eyes
- loss of, or loss of use of, both hands
- an injury resulting in a practically total paralysis, or
- an injury to the brain resulting in incurable mental incapacity or insanity. (LC § 4662.)

Other injuries, or combinations of injuries, may result in total permanent disability. This determination must, however, be made by doctors. If it is agreed between the parties or determined by a judge after a trial that you cannot do any work at all, you are considered totally disabled.

1. Permanent Total Disability Rate

Note that permanent total disability payments are paid at your temporary disability weekly payment rate. (See Chapter 12, Section B.) This rate is significantly higher than the rate paid for permanent partial disabilities, so don't confuse the two.

Unlike temporary disability benefits, however, if your injury occurred in 2003 or earlier you are not entitled to an increase after two years to whatever maximum temporary disability rate is in effect two years from the date of your injury. Your total permanent disability rate is based upon your temporary disability rate in effect on the date of your injury, and remains the same.

If your injury is on or after January 1, 2003, however, your temporary disability rate begins at the temporary disability rate in effect at the time of your injury but increases each January 1 based on a cost of living adjustment (COLA), which is tied to the average weekly wage in California.

See the total temporary disability chart in Chapter 12, Section B, to determine the maximum permanent total disability rate (based upon two-thirds of your average weekly wage).

2. How Long Payments Last

If you have an injury serious enough to result in a permanent total disability, you are generally entitled to disability payments for the rest of your life. Permanent total disability is the only award other than life pension that is not capped at a set amount. How much you will receive depends upon how long you live.

Your survivors will not be entitled to receive any of your permanent total disability payments after you die.

CHAPTER

14

Supplemental Job Displacement Benefit

If your doctor determines that you should not return to your former type of work because of your work injury, you may qualify for supplemental job displacement benefits. These benefits can help you gain new skills to return to work.

If you have already returned to your former job, you may choose to skip this chapter. But be careful. If you reject an offer of modified or alternate work with the same employer, this may result in termination of your right to job displacement benefits. This means that if you change your mind after working a few months and you want to leave your job, you may not be able to get benefits at that point. At the very least, carefully read Section A, below.

TIP

Rejecting offers of work may affect permanent disability payments, too. Besides possibly making you ineligible for job displacement benefits, rejecting offers of modified or alternative work can lower your permanent disability payments. For more information, see Chapter 13, Section E3.

Employers Subsidized for Giving You Alternative or Modified Work

Your employer may be reimbursed for up to 50% of wages paid to you (up to $2,500) for alternate or modified work during the period that you are temporarily disabled. The reimbursement can be for no more than 90 days, or until you are released by your doctor to return to the full duties of your usual occupation, or until your condition becomes permanent and stationary, whichever occurs first. To be eligible for this subsidy, the job must be compatible with your work restrictions as imposed by the treating physician.

The employer may also be eligible for reimbursement up to $1,250 for modifications made to the workplace to allow you to return to work. The maximum reimbursement for both of the above subsidies is $2,500 total. (LC § 139.48.)

A. Supplement Job Displacement Benefits and Offers of Alternative or Modified Work

Your employer or its insurance company does not have to provide supplemental job displacement benefits if the employer offers you at least 12 months of the following:

- **Modified work.** This is a return to your former job with modifications made so that you can work with your disability. If you voluntarily quit prior to the end of the 12 months, you won't be entitled to job displacement benefits.
- **Alternative work.** This is work that is different from your previous job. The work must meet several requirements. Given your disability, you must have the physical ability to perform the job. The job must offer wages and compensation that are not more than 15% below those paid to you at the time of your injury. In addition, the job must be located at your present worksite or within reasonable commuting distance of your residence at the time of the injury, generally no more than 25 to 50 miles, one way.
- **Any work at all, if you fail to reject the offer of work in the proper manner.** If you are not offered modified or alternative work that is acceptable to you, your rejection of your employer's unsatisfactory offer must meet certain requirements, or you will not be eligible for supplemental job displacement benefits.

CAUTION

Only U.S. citizens and legal residents are entitled to retraining. If you are offered modified or alternative work on DWC Form RU-94, but your employer subsequently learns that you do not have legal work status, the employer (or insurance company) is not required to provide supplemental job displacement benefits.

B. Supplemental Job Displacement Benefit

Since 2004, injured workers who are unable to return to their employer are eligible for a tuition or retraining voucher.

Within ten days of your last temporary disability payment, your employer must send you notice of your job displacement benefit rights by certified mail.

1. Eligibility

This job displacement benefit is available to injured workers who:

- are injured on or after January 1, 2004
- have sustained a permanent partial disability, and
- do not return to work for the at-injury employer within 60 days after the termination of temporary disability.

An injured worker does not qualify for supplemental job displacement benefit if either of the following conditions exist:

- Within 30 days of the termination of temporary disability payments, the employer offers, and the employee fails to properly accept, modified work that accommodates the employee's work restrictions and that lasts at least 12 months.
- Within 30 days of the termination of temporary disability payments, the employer offers, and the employee fails to properly accept, alternative work that meets all of the following conditions:
  - The employee has the ability to perform the essential functions of the job provided.
  - The job provided is a regular position lasting at least 12 months.
  - The job provided offers wages and compensation that are within 15% of those paid to the employee at the time of injury.
  - The job is located within reasonable commuting distance of the employee's residence at the time of injury.

2. Benefits

The supplemental job displacement benefit consists of a nontransferable voucher for education-related retraining or skill enhancement, or both, at state-approved or accredited schools. The voucher may be used to pay for tuition, books, fees, and other expenses required by the school.

The voucher can also be used for hiring a vocational retraining counselor or to pay for work counseling, but no more than 10% of the voucher can be used this way.

The amount of the voucher depends on the amount of permanent disability:

Permanent Disability	Voucher Amount
Less than 15%	$4,000
15%–25%	$6,000
25%–49%	$8,000
50%–99%	$10,000

For small disabilities, the "value" of an otherwise paltry claim increases substantially if you qualify for supplemental job displacement benefits. For example, a 1% disability would have a permanent disability value of $800. However, the supplemental job displacement benefit for a 1% disability is worth up to $4,000 for retraining.

CHAPTER

15

Death Benefits

When a work injury or illness causes or contributes to the death of an employee, the surviving dependents are entitled to recover death benefits. (LC § 4703.) These benefits consist of:

- a fixed sum of money; the amount depends on the number of surviving dependents and the date the injury occurred
- actual burial expenses up to $5,000, and
- retroactive temporary disability and accrued permanent disability payments (dependents get these only if they are also the worker's legal heirs).

Surviving dependents may also be eligible for benefits outside the workers' compensation system, such as Social Security; refer to Chapter 17 for details.

CAUTION

Make sure you receive all benefits. Insurance companies sometimes try to pay less than a death claim is worth. Read this chapter carefully to make sure you (or any dependents) are not shortchanged.

A. Who May Receive Death Benefits

You are entitled to death benefits if you are a surviving dependent of the deceased employee. This includes most surviving spouses (or registered domestic partners) and children under 18. In addition, for employees injured in 2003 and later, if the employee had no spouse or children, any surviving parents can be considered dependents. (LC § 3501.) (For injuries before 2003, surviving parents are not considered dependents even if there are no other dependents living.)

While you do not have to be in these categories to be legally considered a surviving dependent, you must be able to prove that you were either totally or partially dependent upon the deceased employee for financial support. The date of the injury that resulted in death—not the date of death—is used to determine whether or not you qualify as a dependent.

Here's the difference between total and partial dependency:

- **Total dependent.** This person is presumed to have completely depended upon the deceased worker for support.
- **Partial dependent.** This person depended to some degree, but not totally, upon the deceased worker for support.

There are a few situations where a surviving relative is conclusively presumed to be totally dependent for support upon the deceased employee. This means that the insurance carrier cannot deny total dependency, even if there is evidence to the contrary:

- **Spouse or registered domestic partner.** If a deceased employee was married or a partner in a registered domestic partnership at the time of death, and the surviving spouse or partner earned $30,000 or less in the 12 months immediately preceding the death, the surviving spouse or partner is conclusively presumed to be totally dependent for support upon the deceased employee. (LC § 3501(b).)
- **Children (by blood or adoption).** A minor child (under age 18), or an adult child who cannot earn a living due to physical or mental incapacity, is conclusively presumed to be totally dependent for support upon a deceased employee-parent if that child was living with the employee-parent at the time of injury. (LC § 3501.)

EXAMPLE: Tom and his mother were living with his father when his father was killed in a freak accident at work. Tom was 12 years old at the time of his father's death, and his mother did not work. Both Tom and his mother are total dependents.

- **Parent or parents.** For employees injured in 2003 or later who do not have a partially or totally dependent spouse or partially or totally dependent children, any surviving parents are conclusively presumed to be total dependents. (LC § 3501(c).)

If none of the situations listed above exist, the surviving relative must prove financial dependence on the deceased employee.

> EXAMPLE: Trevor is 22 years old and still lives with his parents. His father, John, dies as a result of an on-the-job injury. Because Trevor is over 18 and not physically or mentally incapacitated, to be entitled to any death benefit he must prove that at the time of injury he was totally or partially dependent upon his father for support. If Trevor was not working on the date of his father's injury and had no source of income, he may be able to show total dependency upon his father, even if his mother was also working. If Trevor was working part-time, he may be able to show partial dependency upon his father for support.

B. Death Benefit Amount

The fixed-sum death benefit that surviving dependents are entitled to depends upon:

- the date of the injury that resulted in death, and
- the number of total and partial dependents the deceased wage earner had. (LC § 4702.)

The accompanying chart and following discussion cover how much total and partial dependents may be entitled to receive.

RESOURCE

Minor children may receive more. Totally dependent minor children will also receive weekly death benefits. See Section C, below.

Total Amount of Death Benefits

Date of Injury	One total dependent or partial dependent only	More than one total dependent or one total dependent and one or more partial dependents
7/1/94–6/30/95	$115,000	$135,000 for 2 dependents $150,000 for 3 or more dependents
7/1/96–12/31/05	$125,000	$145,000 for 2 dependents $160,000 for 3 or more dependents $250,000 to the estate if no dependents*
01/01/06–present	$250,000	$290,000 for 2 dependents $320,000 for 3 or more dependents $250,000 to the estate if no dependents

* For injuries in 2004 and later.

1. No Dependents

For injuries occurring after 2003, if there are no surviving dependents, the estate of the deceased employee receives $250,000.

2. One Total Dependent Only

If you are the sole surviving total dependent, and there are no partial dependents, you are entitled to the entire death benefit amount. Look at the accompanying chart and locate the date of injury. The amount you are entitled to is listed in the second column, entitled "One total dependent or partial dependent only." For example, if the date of injury was October 23, 2005, you would be entitled to $125,000.

3. Two or More Total Dependents

When there are at least two surviving total dependents, they will split the amount of money in the third column of the chart. In this situation, if there are any partial dependents, they are not entitled to anything.

> **EXAMPLE 1:** Woody is injured on December 5, 2000 and dies a month later, leaving a surviving wife and a small daughter, who were totally dependent on him. Woody's wife and daughter are entitled to split $145,000, or to receive $72,500 each.

> **EXAMPLE 2:** Assume the same facts, with the exception that Woody and his wife had two young daughters who were totally dependent on him. In addition, Woody had a son from a previous marriage who partially depended on him for support. His surviving wife and two daughters are entitled to a third of $145,000, or $48,333 each. The son doesn't get anything.

4. One Total Dependent and One or More Partial Dependents

If there is only one total dependent, but one or more partial dependents, the total dependent is entitled to the entire sum of money in the second column, entitled "One total dependent."

The partial dependents are also entitled to benefits. Calculating the benefits for these partial dependents is a little more complicated. These partial dependents receive four times the amount that the deceased employee annually devoted to their support, up to the difference between the second and third columns in the chart. If the amount that partial dependents would be entitled to exceeds that difference, then each takes a proportionate share of the maximum amount available.

> **EXAMPLE:** Charlie dies as a result of an October 21, 2000 work injury, leaving one son from his current marriage and two sons from a previous marriage. His son from his current marriage, Larry, is found to be a total dependent and is entitled to $125,000. Mo and Curly, who each received $6,000 per year in support before their father died, are determined to be partial dependents. They are entitled to a maximum of $24,000 each (four times $6,000), based upon four times the amount annually devoted to their support by their father. However, because only $35,000 is available between them ($160,000 – $125,000), Mo and Curly receive $17,500 each.

5. Partial Dependents Only

If there are no total dependents, the partial dependents are entitled to four times the amount annually devoted to their respective support by the deceased employee, not to exceed the amount in the second column, entitled "one total dependent or partial dependent only." If the amount that partial dependents would be entitled to exceeds the amount in the second column, each takes a proportionate share of the maximum amount available.

> **EXAMPLE 1:** Lori received a total of $10,500 per year from Ed for her support. Upon Ed's work-related death, Lori may be entitled to receive $42,000 (four times $10,500) if she qualifies as a partial dependent.

> **EXAMPLE 2:** Sean partially supported his three college-aged children, Mike ($15,000 per year), Cathy ($7,000 per year), and Donna ($5,000 per year). Sean dies in an injury at work on November 20, 2000. The maximum amount available to dependents is $125,000. Mike may receive $60,000, Cathy may receive $28,000 and Donna may get $20,000. The total Sean's three children will receive is $108,000.

Whether the dependents are partial or total, in order to qualify for benefits they must provide proof of the support provided by the deceased worker.

C. Additional Payments for Dependent Minor Children

RELEVANT CASE LAW

See *Wright Schuchart-Harbor v. WCAB (Morrow, deceased)* and *Foodmaker v. WCAB (Prado-Lopez, deceased)*, in Chapter 28.

In addition to any payments made according to the chart in Section B, above, weekly death benefits will be paid on behalf of any totally dependent minor children (by blood or adoption) until the youngest child reaches the age of 18. (LC § 4703.5.) Minor children who did not live with the deceased employee are eligible for death benefits if they were totally dependent upon the deceased employee for support. However, these children (or their guardians) must prove their dependence.

This is a very valuable benefit that can be worth a lot of money. Weekly payments are paid in the same amount and manner as temporary disability payments would have been made to the deceased employee, except that no weekly payment will be less than $224. Any increases in benefit amounts to which the deceased employee would have been entitled two or more years after the date of injury would apply. (See Chapter 12, Section B, for a discussion of temporary disability amounts.)

EXAMPLE: Juanita dies as a result of a work-related injury in December 2001, leaving three children, ages 17, 11, and 2. In addition to any fixed-sum payments made according to the chart in Section B, above, the children will receive weekly payments of the greater of $224 or Juanita's temporary disability rate. Juanita's average weekly wage at the date of her injury that resulted in her death was $960, so she qualified for the maximum temporary disability rate in 2001 of $490 (two-thirds of $960 equals $640, well above the maximum of $490). The three children split $490 per week for the first two years. In December 2003, the temporary disability rate increases, because it has been two years since the date of injury. (See Chapter 12, Section B.) The amount to be split among the three children increases to the 2003 maximum of $602, because Juanita's wage of $960 qualifies for the increase (two-thirds of $960 equals $640, still above $602). On January 1, 2004, the temporary disability rate increases again. However, the temporary disability rate does not increase to the maximum of $728, because Juanita's wages weren't high enough. Instead, the temporary disability rate increases only to $640 (two-thirds of $960). The rate remains at $640 for good, because Juanita's wages weren't high enough to qualify for any additional increases. This benefit will be divided three ways until the oldest child reaches age 18. It will then be divided equally between the remaining children until the middle one turns 18. After that point, the youngest child will continue to get weekly payments until age 18.

D. Burial Expense for Deceased Worker

In addition to any other benefits, actual burial expenses must be paid by the insurance company, up to $5,000. (LC § 4701.)

E. Unpaid Temporary or Permanent Disability Payments

RELEVANT CASE LAW

See *Manville Sales Corporation v. WCAB*, in Chapter 28.

If the deceased employee was entitled to any unpaid temporary or permanent disability benefits at the time of death, that amount is due and payable to the surviving heirs. Surviving heirs are those entitled to the estate of the deceased either by will or, if there is no will, by state law. As a matter of course, the surviving heirs are often, but not necessarily, the same as the surviving dependents discussed in Section B, above.

Overdue disability amounts (and possibly penalties due, if payments were late) must be paid in addition to the other death benefits. See Chapter 12 for a discussion of temporary disability payments and Chapter 13 for information about permanent disability payments.

> **EXAMPLE:** Martha was owed temporary disability payments in the amount of $12,500 at the time of her death. The insurance company had not been paying Martha her temporary disability checks, claiming she was not temporarily disabled for the period claimed. After Martha's death, the insurance company agreed to pay the past-due amount. Martha's heirs are entitled to the $12,500 plus any penalties due.

F. How Death Benefits Are Distributed

All agreements between an insurance company and the dependent beneficiaries of a deceased worker regarding settlement of death benefit claims must be drafted in a settlement document. If the parties cannot agree on settlement of the death claim, a workers' compensation judge will hear the case in a trial and make a decision.

Although the appeals board generally distributes the death benefits according to the rules we have discussed, it may distribute death benefits in any manner that it deems fair and equitable. The appeals board also determines whether the death benefit should be paid directly to the dependents or to a trustee appointed by the appeals board for the benefit of the dependents. (LC § 4704.)

If Dependent Is a Minor

If a claim is being made for death benefits on behalf of a minor (person under age 18), the appeals board must designate an adult to represent the minor's interests in the claim. In legal jargon, this person is referred to as a guardian ad litem. Typically, but not always, the person appointed is the parent or legal guardian of the minor. A Petition for Appointment of Guardian ad Litem and Trustee is available from the Workers' Compensation Appeals Board. Check with an information and assistance officer if you need help filling it out.

SEE AN EXPERT

If your death benefits claim is denied. If the insurance carrier disputes your entitlement to death benefits as a surviving dependent of a deceased worker, you should immediately see an information and assistance officer or a competent workers' compensation attorney.

CHAPTER

16

Extraordinary Workers' Compensation Benefits and Remedies

The benefits and remedies discussed in this chapter are "extraordinary" because they are above and beyond a typical workers' compensation claim. The circumstances that give rise to these benefits are unusual in a workers' compensation case, but they do occur. If you think that you may be entitled to one or more of these benefits, you should see a qualified workers' compensation attorney or consult an information and assistance officer.

Before we go on, let's define some terms. When I mention "benefits" that are over and above what is normally allowed in the workers' compensation system, I'm referring to additional awards of money or the reestablishment of certain rights, such as getting your job back after being fired.

When I refer to "remedies," I mean legal actions you may be able to take. These usually consist of additional claims you can file within the workers' compensation system to recover damages you suffered as the result of someone else's improper actions.

The benefits and remedies discussed in this chapter will be relevant to you only if one of these fairly unusual situations applies:

- You had a prior injury or illness before your present workers' compensation injury; it does not matter if it happened at work. (Read Section A.)
- Your employer does not have workers' compensation insurance and is not self-insured. (Turn to Section B to learn about the Uninsured Employers Benefits Trust Fund.)
- You believe that your employer discriminated against you because you asserted your right to file a workers' compensation claim—for example, you were harassed or fired after you filed or threatened to file a workers' compensation claim. (Read Section C, on discrimination benefits.)
- You believe that your employer's seriously improper action or inaction, such as the failure to remedy an obvious safety violation, contributed to or caused your work injury. (Read Section D.)

SKIP AHEAD

If your situation isn't unusual. If none of the situations described above applies to you, skip the rest of this chapter.

A. Subsequent Injuries Benefits Trust Fund

The state-run Subsequent Injuries Benefits Trust Fund is designed to provide a remedy for employees with preexisting physical impairments who sustain a new injury at work. It allows these workers to recover benefits for their entire disability—the preexisting disability and the new workers' compensation injury considered together. The prior impairment need not be work-related, but it could be a previously compensated workers' compensation injury.

A little background is in order. In the event that a previously disabled worker sustains an injury at work, an employer is liable only for that percentage of the overall disability resulting from the new work injury—not for any portion of the injury that resulted from the prior disability. (LC § 4750.) This is fair, as most employers are not allowed to inquire as to the nature and extent of any prior disabilities while interviewing a prospective job applicant. (See a discussion of the Americans with Disabilities Act in Chapter 17, Section D.) This policy of holding employers liable only for the present injury also encourages employers to hire physically disabled applicants without fear of incurring workers' compensation liability for a preexisting disability.

An injured worker with a permanent disability caused by the work injury will receive money from the insurance company for the part of the injury caused by work. In addition, the worker may qualify for a money award that takes the entire disability into account, paid by the Subsequent Injuries Fund.

> **EXAMPLE:** Jane injured her left leg in a horseback riding incident when she was a child. She injures her right leg on the job, which results in a permanent disability. Jane qualifies for workers' compensation, and her present employer's insurance company pays for the permanent disability to her right leg (none of this injury was the result of her prior condition). In addition, she should be entitled to money from the Subsequent Injuries Benefits Trust Fund for the disability to her left leg, because the work injury has now increased her overall disability. In short, without the Subsequent Injuries Benefits Trust Fund, Jane would have suffered a permanent disability greater than that for which the employer is liable, yet be unable to get compensated for her greater overall disability.

An injured worker with a prior disability may even be entitled to a life pension from the Subsequent Injuries Benefits Trust Fund if the combined effect of the work injury and the earlier disability equals a permanent disability rating of 70% or more. (See Chapter 18 for more on rating disabilities.) To be entitled to a life pension, at least one of the following must apply:

- The present work injury rates 35% or more when considered alone, without any adjustment for the employee's age or occupation.
- The prior disability was to an eye, arm, hand, leg, or foot, and the present work injury is to the opposite member (the other eye, for example). The new disability must rate 5% or more when considered alone, without adjustment for the employee's age or occupation.

The time limitation for filing an application for Subsequent Injuries Benefits Trust Fund benefits is the same as with workers' compensation benefits: one year from the date of injury. If, however, you did not know of your right to Subsequent Injury Benefits Trust Fund benefits, you may have an extension to the filing deadline. This extension is typically for a "reasonable time" after learning about your right, even if more than one year has passed since the date of injury.

You generally will not know whether you have a Subsequent Injuries Benefits Trust Fund claim until after the doctors have determined your overall disability, as well as what portion of your disability is work-related. Once this has been determined, file right away if you think you qualify.

SEE AN EXPERT

See a lawyer if you intend to make a claim against the Subsequent Injuries Benefits Trust Fund. Because this is a complicated area, I highly recommend that you get help from an information and assistance officer or see an attorney.

B. The Uninsured Employers Benefits Trust Fund

The Uninsured Employers Benefits Trust Fund, which is set up and funded by the State of California, pays an injured employee's workers' compensation benefits if both of the following are true:

- The employer did not have workers' compensation insurance.
- The employer is not permissibly self-insured. (LC §§ 3715, 3716.)

If you suffer an injury at work and find out that your employer did not carry workers' compensation insurance, you may pursue your workers' compensation claim against the Uninsured Employers Benefits Trust Fund.

SEE AN EXPERT

Seek assistance if your employer is uninsured. If you opt to file a claim against the state Uninsured Employers Benefits Trust Fund, it's likely you will need help, as you must meet very strict procedural requirements that are not covered in this book. Start by consulting with an information and assistance officer. You may also want to see a workers' compensation lawyer and possibly a civil litigation attorney, who should be able to provide you with information about whether you are likely to obtain a substantial recovery if you file a civil case.

You may also sue your uninsured employer in civil court to recover damages suffered as a result of your work injury. If your injury is serious, you may be able to recover more money through a civil suit than you could through a workers' compensation claim. But there are downsides to lawsuits—they're time-consuming, emotionally draining, and costly. In addition, before you proceed on this track, make sure your employer is financially sound. You won't be able to collect from a bankrupt or defunct employer.

C. Discrimination Benefits (Labor Code § 132(a))

If you believe your employer discriminated against you because you filed a workers' compensation claim, you may have certain legal remedies within the workers' compensation system. (You may also have rights outside of the workers' compensation system; see Chapter 17.)

If your employer discriminates against you, you may file a Petition Alleging Discrimination against your employer. (LC § 132(a).) You must file the petition with the Workers' Compensation Appeals Board within one year from the date of the discriminatory action.

You may have a legitimate discrimination claim against your employer if you file or plan to file a workers' compensation claim and any of the following events occur:

- **You are terminated from your job.** You are fired or laid off without good cause—that is, without a legitimate business reason.
- **You are harassed.** Your employer "writes you up," embarrasses you in front of other employees, or otherwise makes your work life more difficult without a legitimate business reason for doing so.
- **You are threatened.** Your employer threatens to terminate you or make your work life difficult if you proceed with your workers' compensation case.
- **You are subjected to an unreasonable change at work.** For example, your shift is changed to a less desirable one or you're given extra work to do without a reasonable business necessity.
- **You are demoted or given a cut in pay.** Your seniority is taken away or your pay is decreased without a reasonable business necessity for doing so.
- **You are subjected to any other type of discriminatory action.** This may apply if other employees in like circumstances are not subjected to these actions or if your employer fails to offer reasonable accommodations for your disability.

If the Workers' Compensation Appeals Board determines that your employer discriminated against you, your employer will be guilty of a misdemeanor and you will be entitled to:

- a 50% increase in your workers' compensation award (all the benefits you receive), but in no event more than an additional $10,000
- costs and expenses not to exceed $250, and
- reinstatement in your job and reimbursement for lost wages and work benefits caused by your employer's actions.

All of this sounds great. But now for a reality check. An action for discrimination against an employer is difficult to prove under the best of circumstances. You must be able to show that the reason your employer discriminated against you was solely because you filed, or threatened to file, a workers' compensation action. For example, you will probably not be successful in your discrimination petition if your employer can show that you were fired partially because you had a history of being late, your work was sub par, or the company needed to cut back. This is true even if you are sure you were really terminated because you filed a workers' compensation claim.

Which Discrimination Claims Are Likely to Succeed

A discrimination case with a reasonable chance of success contains most of the following factors:

- The employee has a clean work record, with few, if any, written warnings. If, however, the written warnings are made *after* a workers' compensation claim was filed, this may be evidence of an employer's plan to retaliate.
- The employee's file contains written commendations about a job well done.
- The employee has been employed for at least several years—the longer the better.
- The employer's reasons for terminating the employee do not make sense. For example, the employer claims the layoff was because of a lack of business yet hires someone to replace the employee.
- The employer's discriminatory action occurs within a short time period of the employee's filing of a workers' compensation claim—for example, a week or two after the employee files a DWC-1 form.

D. Employer's Serious and Willful Misconduct

In unusual cases, a work injury or death may have been caused by an employer's serious and willful misconduct. (LC § 4553.) In legal jargon, serious and willful misconduct is behavior that goes well beyond the realm of negligence (carelessness). In short, the employer's actions must approach criminal conduct. Violations of certain health and safety codes, such as those promulgated by the California Occupational Safety and Health Administration (Cal-OSHA), may be considered serious and willful misconduct. Similarly, tampering with or removing safety devices on equipment would probably be viewed as serious and willful misconduct.

Many other actions would not, however, fall into this category. For instance, an employer who insists that employees work too many hours, or who speeds up the work process to a point where it causes injury to an employee, is certainly negligent. But those actions would probably not constitute serious and willful misconduct on the employer's part.

To be liable, the employer must be responsible for the serious and willful misconduct. In other words, the misconduct generally must be committed by:

- the owner
- the store or business manager or supervisor
- if the employer is a partnership, one of the partners, or
- if the employer is a corporation, an executive officer, managing officer, or general superintendent (supervisor).

A petition alleging serious and willful misconduct of an employer must be filed with the Workers' Compensation Appeals Board within 12 months from the date of the action in question. If it's successful, the employer may have to pay:

- a 50% increase in workers' compensation benefits (no limit on the amount), and
- costs and expenses not to exceed $250.

SEE AN EXPERT

Successful petitions based on serious and willful misconduct are rare. Petitions based on employer misconduct are complicated, with procedures and rules much like going to civil court. If you suspect that you have a serious and willful misconduct claim against your employer, I strongly recommend that you consult with a workers' compensation attorney.

CHAPTER

17

Benefits and Remedies Outside the Workers' Compensation System

The workers' compensation system does not exist in a vacuum. It's quite possible that you may be entitled to benefits and remedies that fall beyond the scope of workers' compensation. Here we shift gears and talk about different state and federal agencies that may offer benefits to injured workers. We also discuss circumstances under which you may be entitled to legal recourse outside the workers' compensation arena.

If you're out of work or receiving a reduced income, it will be important for you to obtain all of the benefits to which you are entitled. Very few people can afford to be out of work without suffering some financial hardship. Your best approach will be to learn about your options and obtain all of the benefits you're entitled to. This chapter discusses:

- state disability insurance, or "SDI" (Section A)
- Social Security benefits (Section B)
- personal injury claims and lawsuits (Section C), and
- claims or lawsuits based on discrimination due to your disability (Section D).

Other Sources of Help

In addition to what's covered in this chapter, you may want to investigate the following important sources of income and benefits:

- Medicare
- Medi-Cal
- pensions
- disability policies
- vocational rehabilitation through the State Department of Rehabilitation, and
- public assistance (welfare).

A discussion of these additional benefits is beyond the scope of this book. You may find useful information in *Social Security, Medicare & Government Pensions*, by Joseph Matthews and Dorothy Matthews Berman (Nolo).

A. State Disability Insurance (SDI)

California employees who work for private employers have money automatically deducted from their paychecks to cover state disability insurance (SDI). A few groups of workers, such as state or federal employees, may not have this deduction taken and are therefore not eligible for SDI benefits. If you aren't sure whether you are covered, ask your employer or look at one of your pay stubs. Look for a deduction entitled "SDI," which is usually only a few dollars per week.

The money you pay into the SDI system goes into your own personal "account." When you have paid in enough money over the required number of quarters (three-month increments), you normally are entitled to benefits if you're injured or ill. The amount of state disability benefits is roughly equivalent to workers' compensation temporary disability payments. You are paid out of your account until it is exhausted, at which time your payments stop.

Before we go on, let's emphasize the difference between SDI benefits and workers' compensation benefits. Only persons with a work-related injury are entitled to workers' compensation benefits. However, anyone who paid into the state disability system for the required period of time is entitled to state disability benefits if they cannot work due to any injury or illness, even if it's not work related. A doctor must certify that you are unable to work because of your injury or illness.

If you sustained an injury at work, you should immediately apply for state disability, even if you are receiving temporary disability payments from the workers' compensation insurance company or have gone back to work. If you are receiving workers' compensation temporary disability, you will initially be denied SDI benefits, but that's okay. By filing for state disability as soon as possible, you "lock in" the date you applied. If you later need to reapply because your workers' compensation benefits terminate, your qualification will be determined by the original date you applied.

Although this sounds like a technical point, it is extremely important. Eligibility for state disability benefits is based upon previous quarters worked from the date of application. If, for example, you fail to apply soon after your injury and have to apply nine months later because you lost workers' compensation coverage, you may find that you do not qualify for benefits—simply because you did not work for the last nine months (three quarters).

CAUTION

You can't receive temporary disability benefits and SDI at the same time. You're allowed to get SDI during periods when you're not receiving workers' compensation benefits, but you can't get both for the same period of time.

Why You May Need SDI

As mentioned, it's important to apply for SDI as soon as possible to "lock in" the benefit date in case you are not covered by workers' compensation. This is because of the following possibilities:

- The insurance company may deny your workers' compensation claim.
- The insurance company may interrupt your temporary disability benefits for some reason.
- Your doctor may claim that you are not temporarily disabled for workers' compensation purposes.
- The insurance company may pay you at an incorrect rate and refuse to pay you at the correct rate; in that event, you may be able to receive the difference between the correct rate and the rate you're being paid for temporary disability.

1. How to Apply for State Disability

Contact your local office of the California Employment Development Department (EDD) to apply for state disability benefits. You can find the number in the front of the phone book under state agencies, or call directory assistance.

2. If You Later Qualify for Workers' Compensation Benefits: The SDI Lien

It is not uncommon to receive state disability benefits for a few weeks or months and then discover that you should have been receiving temporary disability from the workers' compensation insurance company.

To recover its money, the state will file a lien (legal claim) in your workers' compensation case. At the time your case is resolved, the workers' compensation insurance company will have to negotiate with the state about how much money, if any, it must reimburse the state for state disability payments made to you. Money that is repaid to the state by the workers' compensation insurance company goes directly back into your SDI account, and you are free to apply for those benefits again if needed. In fact, you may immediately qualify for state disability indemnity if a doctor certifies that you are unable to work. This may be for a disability as a result of your present workers' compensation case (which you settled), a new workers' compensation case, or a nonindustrial injury.

CAUTION

Settlement documents may address SDI liens. If you received SDI payments for any periods of time that you were entitled to receive permanent disability payments, the Employment Development Department (EDD) can have that amount deducted from your final permanent disability award. (LC § 4904.) This is usually a problem if your case goes to trial and the judge determines that you received SDI benefits after you were permanent and stationary. An information and assistance officer or workers' compensation attorney should be able to help. In addition, we discuss the settlement language that requires the insurance company to be responsible for the SDI lien (available if you settle by compromise and release) in Chapter 20, Section D2.

B. Social Security Benefits

Social Security provides, among other things, benefits for seriously injured workers and their families. To qualify for Social Security benefits because of a disability, all of the following must be true:

- You must have a physical or mental impairment.
- The impairment must prevent you from doing any "substantial gainful work."
- The impairment must be expected to last, or have lasted, at least 12 months, or must be expected to result in death.

Of course, these terms are subject to different interpretations. Guidelines developed by Social Security and the courts provide details about the qualifications for disability.

Social Security disability will, over the long run, provide more benefits than workers' compensation, so contact your local Social Security department if you think you may meet the above requirements.

If you receive Social Security benefits, such as Social Security disability or SSI (Supplemental Security Income), any money you later receive from your workers' compensation case may be credited against your Social Security benefits. In other words, if you settle your workers' compensation claim after you have received Social Security benefits, the Social Security department will want to offset the benefits it pays you against your workers' compensation benefits. Your Social Security benefit may be reduced by the amount of your workers' compensation settlement.

CAUTION

Address offset in settlement documents. If it turns out that an offset may be taken against your workers' compensation claim, you should include some special language in your workers' compensation settlement documents. This language (which is available only with a compromise and release) is designed to minimize the amount of credit that Social Security will take against your workers' compensation award. You may want to consult with an information and assistance officer or see a workers' compensation attorney to make sure the appropriate language is included. (We discuss the required language in Chapter 20, Section D2c.)

C. Claims or Lawsuits for Personal Injuries

In fairly unusual circumstances, you may have the right to sue a third party (someone other than your employer or a coworker), in addition to pursuing your workers' compensation remedies. This usually applies when a person or entity outside the employment arena caused or contributed to the cause of your injury.

The right to sue a third party may arise if you were injured because of circumstances such as these:

- **negligence** (for example, a careless driver with no relationship to your job hit you while you were on company business)
- **products liability** (for example, you were injured at work when a defective aerosol can blew up in your face)
- **intentional torts** (for example, a customer physically assaulted you), or
- **malpractice** (for example, you are further injured due to the malpractice of a doctor who treated you for your work injury).

It is usually advantageous to pursue a personal injury claim, because the amount you may recover is not restricted by workers' compensation rules. Unlike workers' compensation, you may be entitled to compensation for your pain and suffering, property damage (such as damage to your car in an auto accident), loss of monetary support caused by the death or injury of a loved one, lost wages (past, present, and future), and punitive damages where appropriate. However, unlike the workers' compensation system, which basically is a "no-fault" system, you can only recover damages for personal injuries if you can show that the outside individual or entity caused or contributed to your injury.

You usually start by making a demand and trying to settle with the responsible party or that party's insurance company. If settlement negotiations fail, you must file a lawsuit within certain time frames (called the "statute of limitations"):

- You generally have one year from the date of your injury to sue third parties that may have caused or contributed to your injury. (Lawsuits against governmental agencies may require much quicker action on your part, often requiring an initial written claim within 180 days, and sometimes sooner.)
- You must bring a medical malpractice lawsuit within one year from the date the injury is discovered or three years from the date the medical malpractice was committed, whichever date occurs first.
- For a negligence or products liability lawsuit, you must file within one year from the date of injury (except for government agencies, which may require you to file an initial written claim within about 180 days).

CAUTION

Don't miss the filing deadline. If you don't file your lawsuit within the applicable statute of limitations, you could be forever barred from making any kind of recovery. See an attorney immediately if you think you have a personal injury claim.

RESOURCE

Settle the claim yourself. If the third party is covered by insurance, *How to Win Your Personal Injury Claim,* by Joseph Matthews (Nolo), can help you through the insurance claims system. This book can help you protect your rights, understand what your claim is worth, and negotiate a fair settlement.

You cannot recover twice for the same injury. Each person you sue will be entitled to claim a credit against any settlement or recovery you receive from anyone else. This is called "subrogation."

EXAMPLE 1: Jenny is a driver for a courier service. While delivering a package, Jenny is seriously injured when another driver runs a red light and hits her van. She files a workers' compensation claim against her employer and a civil suit against the driver of the car that hit her. Jenny settles her civil suit first for $15,000. The workers' compensation insurance company is entitled to a credit of $15,000 (the net amount Jenny received from her third-party case) against any money Jenny may be entitled to in her workers' compensation case. If her workers' compensation case settles for less than $15,000, Jenny would keep the $15,000 but would not get any additional money.

EXAMPLE 2: Let's assume the same facts as above, but this time Jenny settled her workers' compensation case first for $10,000. Now the insurance company in the third-party case would be entitled to a credit of $10,000 (from Jenny's net recovery from her workers' compensation case) against any money it might have to pay her for her third-party case. If Jenny now settles her third-party case for $15,000, she would only be entitled to an additional $5,000.

SEE AN EXPERT

Consider hiring a civil attorney. Consider seeking representation by both a workers' compensation attorney and a civil attorney. Both attorneys will need to work together to maximize your recovery. If you go this route, you won't normally have to pay your lawyers up front. The civil attorney will probably receive at least a third of any recovery in the form of the lawyer's "contingency fees," and the workers' compensation attorney will receive a percentage of your final workers' compensation settlement.

D. Claims or Lawsuits Based on Discrimination

Several laws may protect you if a current employer or potential employer discriminates against you because of your industrial injury and any resulting permanent disability. For example, if you are refused a new job and you believe it is because you have a disability, you may have a claim under the Americans with Disabilities Act or the California Fair Employment and Housing Act. Or, if you are terminated from your present job because of your disability, you may have a discrimination claim.

1. The Americans with Disabilities Act

The Americans with Disabilities Act (ADA) applies to private employers, state and local governments, employment agencies, labor unions, and joint labor-management committees with 15 or more employees.

Here are the basics of the ADA. Employers cannot discriminate against people with disabilities in any aspect of the employment process. This includes application, testing, hiring, assignment, evaluation, disciplinary actions, training, promotion, medical examinations, layoff/recall, termination, compensation, leave, and benefits.

Penalties for violation of the ADA include job reinstatement, back pay, payment for loss of future earnings, and payment of legal fees, expert witness fees, and court costs. Compensatory and punitive damages between $50,000 and $300,000 may also be awarded.

A charge of discrimination on the basis of disability must be filed with the Equal Employment Opportunity Commission (EEOC) within 180 days of the alleged discriminatory act. Call 800-669-4000 to file a claim over the phone or to find out the location of the nearest EEOC office. After the EEOC issues a right-to-sue letter, you have one year to file a complaint in civil court.

RESOURCE

Discrimination based on disability is a complicated area of the law and generally requires legal representation. You may also want to consult *Your Rights in the Workplace,* by Barbara Kate Repa (Nolo), for more detailed information on the ADA.

2. The California Fair Employment and Housing Act

In addition to the ADA, you may have similar rights under a California law known as the California Fair Employment and Housing Act (FEHA). The FEHA has recovery provisions very similar to the ADA discussed above. It requires that a claim be filed with the California Department of Fair Employment and Housing (DFEH) within one year from the alleged discriminatory act. After you receive a right-to-sue letter, you have one year to file a complaint in civil court. You can find the local DFEH address in your phone book under government agencies.

SEE AN EXPERT

See a lawyer for a discrimination case. If you believe you were discriminated against because of your disability, you should contact an attorney immediately. An in-depth discussion of your rights in this area is beyond the scope of this book.

Part IV

Settling Your Case

CHAPTER

18

Rating Your Permanent Disability

SKIP AHEAD

If you don't have a permanent partial disability. This chapter does not apply if you've recovered fully from your work injury with no disability whatsoever. This chapter also does not apply if you and the insurance company agree that you have a permanent disability rating of 100%, in which case you are entitled to receive payments at your temporary disability rate for the rest of your life. This chapter only applies if you have a permanent partial disability. If you're not sure, review Chapter 13.

If you have a permanent disability, your disability will have to be "rated"—that is, assigned a numerical value, or percentage. The rating, in turn, is plugged into a chart, which is the basis for determining the amount of money you'll receive. The process of rating disabilities is rather long and complicated. But it's also extremely important, because your rating determines how much money you'll be awarded for your permanent disability.

TIP

Different permanent disability schedules. A new permanent disability schedule (which is used to rate your amount of permanent disability) became effective January 1, 2005. Some of the changes in the schedule apply to all workers, regardless of when they were injured, while other changes apply only to workers who were injured in 2005 or later. In this schedule, permanent disability percentages for severely injured workers were increased, and permanent disability percentages for workers with minor injuries were decreased.

This chapter gives you an overview of the process involved in rating permanent disabilities. For most readers, the advantage of learning the basic principles involved in rating injuries lies in better understanding of how the administrative director's result is arrived at (although some readers may wish to rate their own injury). Gaining a basic understanding of the process will:

- **Help you preserve your rights when seeking medical care.** All ratings are arrived at by analyzing medical reports. By understanding the process, you'll get a good idea of what a favorable medical report should contain. This may help you understand what the doctor is looking for and enable you to communicate better with the doctor. (See Chapter 9 for more on your medical case and Chapter 10 for information on the medical-legal evaluation process.)
- **Help you determine whether the rating in your case is fair and equitable.** You'll have a good chance of spotting an unreasonably low rating, and will learn the tools you'll need to challenge it.
- **Provide you with the basis for negotiating a fair settlement.** Understanding the rating process will help you negotiate with the insurance adjuster. If the adjuster realizes that you understand your disability rating and how it was arrived at, he or she is much more likely to take your demands seriously.

TIP

Don't confuse permanent disability and temporary disability. If the doctor gives you an off-work order for a period of time, you have a temporary disability and you'll receive temporary disability payments while you're off work. If you don't recover 100% from your injury, you are entitled to permanent disability in the form of a monetary "award" to compensate you for your decreased earning capacity. Permanent disability payments are over and above any temporary disability payments and medical costs. You can receive permanent disability payments even if you are working again.

A. Obtaining a Rating

When and how an injury will be rated varies significantly from case to case. You may take an active role in getting your injury rated, or you may choose to sit back and wait until the system gets around to you. The following is an overview of how a rating is typically arrived at.

1. Reach Permanent and Stationary or MMI Status

Your permanent disability cannot be rated until you have been declared permanent and stationary by your treating doctor. (See Chapter 9, Section E, for a discussion of permanent and stationary status.) Reaching "permanent and stationary" status (in the old rating schedule) is known as having reached "maximal medical improvement" (MMI) in the 2005 rating schedule.

2. Request an Advisory Rating

After you've been designated as permanent and stationary or MMI by the treating doctor, you may request that your disability be given an "advisory" rating, also referred to as a "summary" or "consultative" rating. The rating is "advisory" because it is not legally binding. In other words, it is an opinion only. If your case goes to trial, the judge may use a different rating.

Although you may request a rating of the treating doctor's permanent and stationary report at any time, it is in your best interest to do so as soon as possible to expedite settlement of your case.

To request your advisory rating, you'll need a copy of the treating doctor's permanent and stationary report. If for some reason you haven't received a copy, request one from the doctor or the insurance company. Then send the report and a request for a calculation of your permanent disability rating to the administrative director —the person responsible for overseeing the worker's compensation system. (LC § 4061(i).) Check with the clerk's office at your local Workers' Compensation Appeals Board to get the administrative director's correct address. The following is a sample of the form you'll use to request an advisory rating.

3. Administrative Director Prepares Advisory Rating

Within 20 days of receipt of the treating doctor's medical evaluation, the administrative director is supposed to calculate the advisory rating based upon that report and mail a copy to you and your employer. As a practical matter, however, it often takes months to get a rating back.

The advisory rating may be titled "Summary Rating" or something similar. At first, it will probably seem incomprehensible, with a phrase such as: "7.713-50%-11-H-56%-58:0%." Fortunately, this chapter will help you make sense out of that gobbledygook. Section C, below, takes you through the step-by-step process to rate relatively simple injuries yourself.

4. If You Agree With the Rating

If both you and the insurance company agree with the rating of the treating doctor's report, you can comfortably begin settlement negotiations. See Chapters 19 and 20 for more on settlement negotiations.

5. If You Disagree With the Rating

You may disagree with the rating of the treating doctor's report because of either of the following:

- The rating was done incorrectly and is inaccurate.
- Although the rating was accurate, you disagree with the basis for the rating—that is, the treating doctor's report itself.

If you arrived at a different rating altogether by rating your own disability, realize that unless you find a very basic error in the advisory rating, there is probably a good reason why it differs from yours. There are many advanced rating procedures, such as "overlap" and "pyramiding," that are simply beyond the scope of this book.

State of California
Division of Workers' Compensation
Disability Evaluation Unit

DEU Use Only

REQUEST FOR CONSULTATIVE RATING

Indicate type of request:

☐ Mail-in ☐ Walk-in

INSTRUCTIONS FOR MAIL-IN'S:

1. Attach a photocopy of the medical report(s) for which a rating is being requested, if not previously on file. Do not send original reports.
2. Serve a copy of this request on the representative for the opposing party

INSTRUCTIONS FOR WALK-IN'S:

1. Attach this request form to copies of the medical reports that you wish to have rated.
2. List below the doctor's names and dates of reports to be rated.
3. If a deposition is to be rated, mark or list the pages to be reviewed by the rater.

SSN (Numbers Only) ____________ Date of Birth ____________ MM/DD/YYYY

Case Number 1 ____________ Date of Injury 1 ____________ MM/DD/YYYY

Case Number 2 ____________ Date of Injury 2 ____________ MM/DD/YYYY

Case Number 3 ____________ Date of Injury 3 ____________ MM/DD/YYYY

Case Number 4 ____________ Date of Injury 4 ____________ MM/DD/YYYY

Case Number 5 ____________ Date of Injury 5 ____________ MM/DD/YYYY

Injured worker

First Name ____________ MI ____

Last Name ____________ Suffix(Jr,Sr,etc) ____

Occupation (attach description if unclear) ____________

DWC-AD form104 (DEU) (Rev. 11/2008) (Page 1)

RCR

Insurance Claim Number ______________________________

Date of report(s) to be rated and doctor's name:

______________ MM/DD/YYYY ______________________________

______________ MM/DD/YYYY ______________________________

______________ MM/DD/YYYY ______________________________

This case has been set on for: ______________ MM/DD/YYYY for the type of hearing checked below:

☐ Rating MSC

☐ Trial

☐ Conference

Rating requested by:

____
Name of firm

Representing the

☐ Employee ☐ Employer

A copy of this request has been served on

____
Firm Name

____
Firm Address 1/PO Box (Please leave blank spaces between numbers, names or words)

____
Firm Address 2/PO Box (Please leave blank spaces between numbers, names or words)

______________________________ ______ ______________
City State Zip Code

DWC-AD form104 (DEU) (Rev. 11/2008) (Page 2)

RCR

Common Reasons to Dispute a Rating

Ratings may be disputed for one or more of these reasons:

- work restrictions were not taken into account or wrong work restrictions were given by the doctor
- not all injuries were taken into account
- wrong occupation or occupational group was specified
- age was not correctly taken into account
- standard disability rating doesn't use best choice of work restrictions or subjective findings—using other restrictions would result in a higher disability
- treating doctor's report contained disputed physical findings
- medical history relied upon by the treating doctor was incomplete or inaccurate
- treating doctor did not review relevant tests or prior medical opinions in arriving at conclusions, or
- treating doctor did not correctly state subjective complaints.

RESOURCE

Further information. Check with the rating specialist at your local Workers' Compensation Appeals Board, who may be able to refer you to a seminar or educational course on rating disabilities. You may also find helpful information in *California Workers' Compensation Practice*, by Charles Laurence Swezey (California Continuing Education of the Bar), discussed in Chapter 27, Section B1. Or, consider trying to find a lawyer to take your case and rate your disability.

You can start by letting the insurance company know that you don't agree with the advisory rating. See whether you and the adjuster can agree to a rating. If you can't, the judge will decide what the correct rating is at trial. The judge has a great deal of latitude, and may agree with your rating or that of the insurance company, find that the rating is somewhere between the two, or find that the rating is higher or lower than either of you is arguing.

If you review the treating doctor's report and disagree with the medical findings, you can get a second opinion. You'll need to attend a panel qualified medical evaluation and get a medical-legal report. (To learn more, see Chapter 10, Section C.)

The panel qualified medical evaluator (PQME), a doctor or chiropractor, examines you and prepares a formal medical evaluation. The doctor mails the evaluation report, along with a form summarizing its conclusions, to the insurance company, you, and the Disability Evaluation Unit for a new calculation of your permanent disability rating (independent of, and unrelated to, the rating of the treating doctor's report).

The administrative director must calculate the permanent disability rating based upon the PQME's medical evaluation report and mail a copy to you and the insurance company. To request a rating of the PQME report, use the same form used for requesting a rating of the treating doctor's report, "Request for Consultative Rating."

6. If You Disagree With the New Rating of the QME

If you disagree with the new advisory rating of the QME's report, you have 30 days to request that the administrative director reconsider the recommended rating or obtain additional evaluations from a QME to address issues not dealt with or inadequately addressed in the QME report.

You must explain your reasons in a written request to the Disability Evaluation Unit, and send a copy to the defendants. The following is an example.

Sample

8/29/20xx

Administrative Director
[Address]

Re: Rating of Dr. Jones's qualified medical evaluation report dated 6/6/20xx

To whom it may concern:

I would appreciate a reevaluation by the QME doctor, Dr. Jones, because he did not obtain an opinion from a neurologist regarding the nerve loss I sustained, as evidenced by the EMG test performed by Dr. Smith on 3/3/20xx (copy enclosed). I believe that an opinion from a neurologist regarding my disability is absolutely necessary to determine the nature and extent of my permanent disability.

Sincerely,

Jane Smith

Jane Smith

cc: [*Insurance company*]

B. What Is Involved in the Rating Process?

Your disability is rated according to rules and percentages in a rating schedule. A new rating schedule became effective on January 1, 2005. This means there are now three rating schedules in existence:

- **New rating schedule.** The "new" rating schedule, published in 2005, will be used to rate your permanent disability if you were injured in 2005 or later, and also in a few other circumstances (explained in Section 1, below).
- **"Old" rating schedule.** The "old" schedule, published in 1997, applies if your date of injury was before 2005 and there was a comprehensive medical-legal evaluation report or a treating doctors' report before 2005 indicating that you had a permanent disability (and the insurance company was not required to provide you with notice required by LC § 4061—explained below, in Section 1).
- **Pre-1997 rating schedule.** This schedule, published in 1988, applies to injuries that occurred before April 1, 1997.

1. When the "New" Rating Schedule Is Used

If you were injured in 2005 or later, your permanent disability will be determined by using the 2005 rating schedule. (LC § 4658, CCR § 9805.) The new rating schedule may also apply to you if either of the following is true:

- Your injury occurred before 2005 but your case had not moved too far along before January 1, 2005. Specifically, if the first doctor's report (or medical-legal evaluation report) that indicates you have a permanent disability is dated in 2005 or later, the new rating schedule will apply to you.

RELEVANT CASE LAW

See *Joseph Baglione v. Hertz Car Sales and AIG, Adjusting by Cambridge Integrated Services*, in Chapter 28.

- There is a dispute as to the nature and extent of your permanent disability or your need for future medical treatment, and your employer is required to provide you with notice as required by LC § 4061. (An LC § 4061 notice is notice either that permanent disability benefits may be payable, but that the amount cannot be determined because your medical condition is not yet permanent and stationary, or that no permanent disability benefits will be paid.) This notice is sent together with the last payment of temporary disability indemnity.

If the last payment of temporary disability was made for any period of temporary disability ending before January 1, 2005, the new rating schedule will apply, because LC § 4061 requires the employer or insurance company to provide the injured worker with a notice regarding permanent disability "together with the last payment of temporary disability indemnity."

RELEVANT CASE LAW

See *Josh Pendergrass v. Duggan Plumbing and State Compensation Insurance Fund*, in Chapter 28.

Often questions arise as to which schedule to use. The Division of Workers' Compensation publishes a helpful set of frequently asked questions (FAQs) giving examples of when to use the old schedule and when to use the new schedule. It can be found at www.dir.ca.gov/dwc/faq/deu_faq.html.

2. The New Rating Schedule

The new rating schedule calls for the treating or evaluating doctor to use rating procedures set forth in the American Medical Association's *Guides to the Evaluation of Permanent Impairment*, 6th edition, to come up with the basic disability rating.

Your doctor is required to rely solely on objective medical tests rather than subjective factors (such as a patient's complaints of pain) or work restrictions (such as a doctor saying "no heavy lifting") to come up with the rating. (By contrast, the old rating schedule allowed all three types of evidence—objective findings, subjective complaints, and work restrictions—to be used to rate a disability.)

While basing diagnoses and disability ratings on objective tests alone will make ratings more consistent across the board, the new rating schedule may make it more difficult for workers with repetitive stress injuries to prove their inability to do certain kinds of work.

Most injured workers will get a lower permanent disability rating if their permanent disability is rated with the new rating schedule than they would have under the old schedule. Although the new rating schedule should result in an increase in the permanent disability ratings for severely injured workers, most injured workers suffer from moderate to minor injuries, and it's their permanent disability ratings that will be reduced.

Rating a disability under the new rating schedule is quite complicated. The fact is, most workers' compensation attorneys do not know how to rate disabilities under the new rating schedule. I recommend that you do what most attorneys do (and what I do), and have your medical report rated by the rating bureau at the Workers' Compensation Appeals Board. See Section A2, above, for how to request an advisory rating.

Fortunately, as mentioned above, your doctor is required to provide a basic rating in the permanent and stationary report. This basic rating is also known as the "whole person impairment," or WPI.

When a doctor's report is sent to the rating bureau at the Workers' Compensation Appeals Board, the rater will check the report for accuracy and make sure the doctor used the correct procedure in arriving at the WPI. The rater will then adjust the WPI for your age, occupation, and your loss of future earning capacity to arrive at a final permanent disability rating.

See Section C, below, for instructions on using the new rating schedule to adjust your whole person impairment on your own (or to understand the rating given to you by your doctor or the appeals board).

The new rating schedule can be viewed for free on the Internet at www.dir.ca.gov/dwc/pdr.pdf.

The new schedule will base the amount of your disability rating on several new factors. First, the disability rating will take into consideration your diminished future earning capacity. Second, in considering the nature of your physical injury or disfigurement, the disability will incorporate the descriptions and percentages of impairments published in the American Medical Association's *Guides to the Evaluation of Permanent Impairment*, 6th edition.

3. The Old Rating Schedule

If the old rating schedule applies to you, you'll need to get a copy of it in order to rate your own injury. You can view it or print it from the Internet at www.dir.ca.gov/dwc/PDR1997.pdf (it was published in 1997). Or, if you'd like to order a hard copy, see the ordering information in Chapter 27, Section B1. For information on using the old rating schedule to rate your permanent disability, see Section E, below.

The old rating manual contains various charts and graphs necessary to rate a permanent disability. However, many disabilities and ratings are not contained in the rating manual and are learned by many years of working in the workers' compensation field.

In Section E, below, I include much of the information that I have gathered and developed over the years in my practice. You should know, however, that rating your own disability is not for the faint of heart. Remember that you can always request an advisory rating from the rating bureau at the Workers' Compensation Appeals Board if you'd rather leave the rating to someone else (see Section A2, above, for instructions).

C. How to Rate a Disability Using the 2005 Rating Schedule

Again, rating a disability under the new rating schedule is very complicated, and I recommend you have your medical report rated by the rating bureau at the Workers' Compensation Appeals Board. (See Section A2, above, for how to request an advisory rating.) But if you want to double-check the rating you received, or "adjust" your basic rating (the whole person impairment number from your doctor's report) for your age, occupation, and your loss of future earning capacity, read on.

If the new rating schedule applies to your injury (see Section B1, above), you'll need to get a copy. You can view it or print it from the Internet at www.dir.ca.gov/dwc/pdr.pdf. You may also be able to locate a copy at a law library.

The process of adjusting your doctor's basic rating is similar to adjusting a rating under the old rating schedule. Let's look at an example:

Step 1: Whole Person Impairment Rating

To help you understand the process of adjusting a basic WPI rating, we'll use a hypothetical example involving a woman named "Amy," who has suffered a back injury.

Let's assume the final report from Amy's treating doctor finds that Amy has a disability impairment formula that reads "15.02.02.04-15%." (Your treating doctor's opinion on your percentage of whole person impairment (WPI) is required to be in the permanent and stationary report.)

The beginning part of the formula, 15.02.02.04, indicates that Amy has a thoracic spine injury with range of motion loss and stenosis following an operation. This sounds complicated, but it comes straight from Section 2 of the rating schedule, "Impairment Number/Earning Capacity Adjustment."

The last numeral following the hyphen refers to Amy's percentage of whole person impairment (WPI). The doctor determined Amy's WPI based on AMA guidelines. Her WPI means that she has lost 15% of her overall functionality, taking into consideration her thoracic spine problems. Assuming that the doctor's report has correctly determined the WPI, we can now adjust the WPI for Amy's age, occupation, and loss of earning capacity.

Remember, the formula at this point reads 15.02.02.04-15%.

Step 2: Determine Your Loss of Future Earning Capacity (FEC)

The first step to adjusting the WPI is to determine the likely loss of future earning capacity (FEC) for the specific type of injury (this has been standardized in the new rating schedule). At the end of Section 2 of the new rating schedule, we look up the "FEC rank." The FEC rankings go from 1 to 8. The higher the number, the greater the increase in the disability rating will be. We look up 15.02.02.04 on page 2-3 of the schedule and see that the FEC rank for Amy's injury is a "5."

We then turn to the "Future Earning Capacity (FEC) Adjustment Table" beginning on page 2-6. We find on that page that, for an FEC rank of 5, a 15% whole person impairment standard adjusts upward to 19%.

The formula at this point reads: 15.02.02.04-15-(5)-19.

Step 3: Determine Your Occupational Group

Next, you need to adjust the disability rating for your occupation. The first step is to find your occupational group number. This is done in Section 3 of the new schedule, which begins on page 3-1. Amy is an accountant, so we look up "accountant" on page 3-3 and see that it has a group number of 111.

The formula at this point reads 15.02.02.04-15-(5)-19-111.

Step 4: Determine Your Occupational Variant

Next, you need to look for your appropriate occupational group characteristic, or variant. We see on page 3-29 that a spine injury for group 111 takes an occupational group characteristic of "C." This can also be determined by the chart on page 4-6, where you can see that a 15.02.02.04 injury with a group number of 111 has an occupational variant of "C."

The formula at this point reads 15.02.02.04-15-(5)-19-111C.

Step 5: Adjust the Rating for Your Occupation

Next, using your occupational variant, you adjust the rating again (the rating that you have already adjusted for loss of future earning capacity). In Amy's case, her rating, adjusted for loss of future earning capacity, is 19%. She looks at the chart on page 5-1 to find the cross-section of 19% and her occupational variant "C," to come up with a newly adjusted rating of 14%.

The formula at this point reads 15.02.02.04-15-(5)-19-111C-14.

Step 6: Adjust the Rating for Your Age

The final step is adjusting the rating for your age. In Amy's case, the age is 42. The rating is adjusted by using Section 6 of the schedule. On page 6-2, we see that a 14% rating adjusts up to 15% for age 42.

So the final formula for Amy's permanent disability reads 15.02.02.04-15-(5)-19-111C-14-15% PD.

The final percentage for Amy's disability rating is 15%.

Although Amy's rating of 15% is the same as the one her doctor gave her, this won't always be true—you may come up with a different number, which is why you bother doing the rating.

Step 7: Determine a Dollar Value for the Disability

Now that your disability rating is complete, you can determine the dollar value of your permanent disability. The new rating schedule uses the same chart as the old rating schedule to convert a permanent disability percentage to a dollar amount—the Permanent Disability Indemnity Chart, which is available on Nolo's website (See Chapter 29, "Online Appendixes" for the link to this chart.). For instructions on using the chart, please refer to Chapter 13, Section E.

For dates of injury on or after January 1, 2005 and for employers with more than 50 employees, if the employer does not offer you regular, modified, or alternate work within 60 days of your being found to have reached maximal medical improvement (MMI), then each disability payment from the date of the end of the 60-day period shall be increased by 15%. (LC § 4658.)

EXAMPLE: Barry is found to be MMI by Dr. Smith on April 3, 2009. The report is received by the insurance company on April 10, 2009. Barry's employer, which has over 50 employees, does not offer him any type of work. Any permanent disability that is owed to Barry from June 10, 2009 on is increased by 15%.

On the flip side, if under the same circumstances you are offered regular, modified, or alternate work, then beginning 60 days from the date the report is received by the insurance company, your permanent disability will be decreased by 15% whether or not you accept or reject the offer.

Step 8: Combine Disabilities Using the Combined Values Chart

When you've injured more than one body part on the same injury date, you combine the percentages of disability (using a formula, not by simple addition).

The above steps are done for each part of your body for which the doctor finds that you have a whole person impairment (WPI) number. The above example took you through the steps to rate a whole person impairment to your thoracic spine (15.02.02.04).

If you also had a knee injury, for example, depending on what the doctor says, the impairment number could be 17.05.01.011 (for muscle atrophy). Let's say you followed all of the above steps for the knee injury and came up with a final whole person impairment for the knee of 8%. To get your final overall disability, you would go to Section 8 of the rating manual, the Combined Values Chart (see below).

Start with the highest disability first, 15% for the thoracic spine, and find it in the left-hand column. Then find the next disability from along the bottom of the chart (8%), and where the two numbers intersect is the final disability value: 22%. You would continue to do this for each part of your body. If you had a third part of your body that had a whole person impairment of, say 3%, you would then take the 22% from the left-hand column and 3% from the bottom row, and find the intersection, for a total of 24%. Continue this process until you have combined all parts of your body for which you have a whole person impairment.

SKIP AHEAD

Life pension available for disabilities of 70% or more. If you have a permanent disability rating of at least 70%, you are entitled to a life pension in addition to your permanent disability benefits. A life pension consists of a small amount of money that is payable every two weeks for as long as you live. See Chapter 13, Section F, on how to compute your life pension.

D. Other Considerations in Rating a Permanent Disability

This section flags several more complicated issues that may come up when you're rating your disability. Although you will most likely need to see a lawyer or an information and assistance officer to deal with these, this overview will help you spot problem areas.

1. Apportionment of the Disability

RELEVANT CASE LAW

See *Bakersfield City School District v. WCAB (Robertson)*, *Ashley v. WCAB*, *Pullman Kellogg v. WCAB (Normand)*, and *Tanenbaum v. IAC*, in Chapter 28.

Sometimes an insurance company will tell you that all or part of a permanent disability is being "apportioned" to outside factors. "Apportionment" is basically a concept the insurance company uses to claim it is not responsible for paying full permanent disability because the disability is not entirely attributable to the work injury. The insurance company is liable only for the percentage of permanent disability directly caused by your work injury.

Combined Values Chart, page 1

DIRECTIONS: To combine any two values, locate the larger value on the left side of the chart, and the smaller value at the bottom of the chart. The intersection of that row and column contains the combined value.

	1	2	3	4	5	6	7	8	9	10	11	12	13	14	15	16	17	18	19	20	21	22	23	24	25	26	27	28	29	30	31	32	33	34	35	36	37	38	39	40	41	42	43	44	45	46	47	48	49	50
1	2																																																	
2	3	4																																																
3	4	5	6																																															
4	5	6	7	8																																														
5	6	7	8	9	10																																													
6	7	8	9	10	11	12																																												
7	8	9	10	11	12	13	14																																											
8	9	10	11	12	13	14	14	15																																										
9	10	11	12	13	14	14	15	16	17																																									
10	11	12	13	14	15	15	16	17	18	19																																								
11	12	13	14	15	15	16	17	18	19	20	21																																							
12	13	14	15	16	16	17	18	19	20	21	22	23																																						
13	14	15	16	16	17	18	19	20	21	22	23	23	24																																					
14	15	16	17	17	18	19	20	21	22	23	23	24	25	26																																				
15	16	17	18	18	19	20	21	22	23	24	24	25	26	27	28																																			
16	17	18	19	19	20	21	22	23	24	24	25	26	27	28	29	29																																		
17	18	19	19	20	21	22	23	24	24	25	26	27	28	29	29	30	31																																	
18	19	20	20	21	22	23	24	25	25	26	27	28	29	29	30	31	32	33																																
19	20	21	21	22	23	24	25	25	26	27	28	29	30	30	31	32	33	34	34																															
20	21	22	22	23	24	25	26	26	27	28	29	30	30	31	32	33	34	34	35	36																														
21	22	23	23	24	25	26	27	27	28	29	30	30	31	32	33	34	34	35	36	37	38																													
22	23	24	24	25	26	27	27	28	29	30	31	31	32	33	34	34	35	36	37	38	38	39																												
23	24	25	25	26	27	28	28	29	30	31	31	32	33	34	35	35	36	37	38	38	39	40	41																											
24	25	26	26	27	28	29	29	30	31	32	32	33	34	35	35	36	37	38	38	39	40	41	41	42																										
25	26	27	27	28	29	30	30	31	32	33	33	34	35	36	36	37	38	39	39	40	41	42	42	43	44																									
26	27	27	28	29	30	30	31	32	33	33	34	35	36	36	37	38	39	39	40	41	42	42	43	44	45	45																								
27	28	28	29	30	31	31	32	33	34	34	35	36	36	37	38	39	39	40	41	42	42	43	44	45	45	46	47																							
28	29	29	30	31	32	32	33	34	34	35	36	37	37	38	39	40	40	41	42	42	43	44	45	45	46	47	47	48																						
29	30	30	31	32	33	33	34	35	35	36	37	38	38	39	40	40	41	42	42	43	44	45	45	46	47	47	48	49	50																					
30	31	31	32	33	34	34	35	36	36	37	38	38	39	40	41	41	42	43	43	44	45	45	46	47	48	48	49	50	50	51																				
31	32	32	33	34	34	35	36	37	37	38	39	39	40	41	41	42	43	43	44	45	45	46	47	48	48	49	50	50	51	52	52																			
32	33	33	34	35	35	36	37	37	38	39	39	40	41	42	42	43	44	44	45	46	46	47	48	48	49	50	50	51	52	52	53	54																		
33	34	34	35	36	36	37	38	38	39	40	40	41	42	42	43	44	44	45	46	46	47	48	48	49	50	50	51	52	52	53	54	54	55																	
34	35	35	36	37	37	38	39	39	40	41	41	42	43	43	44	45	45	46	47	47	48	49	49	50	51	51	52	52	53	54	54	55	56	56																
35	36	36	37	38	38	39	40	40	41	42	42	43	43	44	45	45	46	47	47	48	49	49	50	51	51	52	53	53	54	55	55	56	56	57	58															
36	37	37	38	39	39	40	40	41	42	42	43	44	44	45	46	46	47	48	48	49	49	50	51	51	52	53	53	54	55	55	56	56	57	58	58	59														
37	38	38	39	40	40	41	41	42	43	43	44	45	45	46	46	47	48	48	49	50	50	51	51	52	53	53	54	55	55	56	57	57	58	58	59	60	60													
38	39	39	40	40	41	42	42	43	44	44	45	45	46	47	47	48	49	49	50	50	51	52	52	53	54	54	55	55	56	57	57	58	58	59	60	60	61	62												
39	40	40	41	41	42	43	43	44	44	45	46	46	47	48	48	49	49	50	51	51	52	52	53	54	54	55	55	56	57	57	58	59	59	60	60	61	62	62	63											
40	41	41	42	42	43	44	44	45	45	46	47	47	48	48	49	50	50	51	51	52	53	53	54	54	55	56	56	57	57	58	59	59	60	60	61	62	62	63	63	64										
41	42	42	43	43	44	45	45	46	46	47	47	48	49	49	50	50	51	52	52	53	53	54	55	55	56	56	57	58	58	59	59	60	60	61	62	62	63	63	64	65	65									
42	43	43	44	44	45	45	46	47	47	48	48	49	50	50	51	51	52	52	53	54	54	55	55	56	57	57	58	58	59	59	60	61	61	62	62	63	63	64	65	65	66	66								
43	44	44	45	45	46	46	47	48	48	49	49	50	50	51	52	52	53	53	54	54	55	56	56	57	57	58	58	59	60	60	61	61	62	62	63	64	64	65	65	66	66	67	68							
44	45	45	46	46	47	47	48	48	49	50	50	51	51	52	52	53	54	54	55	55	56	56	57	57	58	59	59	60	60	61	61	62	62	63	64	64	65	65	66	66	67	68	68	69						
45	46	46	47	47	48	48	49	49	50	51	51	52	52	53	53	54	54	55	55	56	57	57	58	58	59	59	60	60	61	62	62	63	63	64	64	65	65	66	66	67	68	68	69	69	70					
46	47	47	48	48	49	49	50	50	51	51	52	52	53	54	54	55	55	56	56	57	57	58	58	59	60	60	61	61	62	62	63	63	64	64	65	65	66	67	67	68	68	69	69	70	70	71				
47	48	48	49	49	50	50	51	51	52	52	53	53	54	54	55	55	56	57	57	58	58	59	59	60	60	61	61	62	62	63	63	64	64	65	66	66	67	67	68	68	69	69	70	70	71	71	72			
48	49	49	50	50	51	51	52	52	53	53	54	54	55	55	56	56	57	57	58	58	59	59	60	60	61	62	62	63	63	64	64	65	65	66	66	67	67	68	68	69	69	70	70	71	71	72	72	73		
49	50	50	51	51	52	52	53	53	54	54	55	55	56	56	57	57	58	58	59	59	60	60	61	61	62	62	63	63	64	64	65	65	66	66	67	67	68	68	69	69	70	70	71	71	72	72	73	73	74	
50	51	51	52	52	53	53	54	54	55	55	56	56	57	57	58	58	59	59	60	60	61	61	62	62	63	63	64	64	65	65	66	66	67	67	68	68	69	69	70	70	71	71	72	72	73	73	74	74	75	75

Combined Values Chart, page 2

	1	2	3	4	5	6	7	8	9	10	11	12	13	14	15	16	17	18	19	20	21	22	23	24	25	26	27	28	29	30	31	32	33	34	35	36	37	38	39	40	41	42	43	44	45	46	47	48	49	50
51	51	52	52	53	53	54	54	55	55	56	56	57	57	58	58	59	59	60	60	61	61	62	62	63	63	64	64	65	65	66	66	67	67	68	68	69	69	70	70	71	71	72	72	73	73	74	74	75	75	76
52	52	53	53	54	54	55	55	56	56	57	57	58	58	59	59	60	60	61	61	62	62	63	63	64	64	64	65	65	66	66	67	67	68	68	69	69	70	70	71	71	72	72	73	73	74	74	75	75	76	76
53	53	54	54	55	55	56	56	57	57	58	58	59	59	60	60	61	61	61	62	62	63	63	64	64	65	65	66	66	67	67	68	68	69	69	69	70	70	71	71	72	72	73	73	74	74	75	75	76	76	77
54	54	55	55	56	56	57	57	58	58	59	59	60	60	60	61	61	62	62	63	63	64	64	65	65	66	66	66	67	67	68	68	69	69	70	70	71	71	71	72	72	73	73	74	74	75	75	76	76	77	77
55	55	56	56	57	57	58	58	59	59	60	60	60	61	61	62	62	63	63	64	64	64	65	65	66	66	67	67	68	68	69	69	69	70	70	71	71	72	72	73	73	73	74	74	75	75	76	76	77	77	78
56	56	57	57	58	58	59	59	60	60	60	61	61	62	62	63	63	63	64	64	65	65	66	66	67	67	67	68	68	69	69	70	70	71	71	71	72	72	73	73	74	74	74	75	75	76	76	77	77	78	78
57	57	58	58	59	59	60	60	60	61	61	62	62	63	63	63	64	64	65	65	66	66	66	67	67	68	68	69	69	69	70	70	71	71	72	72	72	73	73	74	74	75	75	75	76	76	77	77	78	78	79
58	58	59	59	60	60	61	61	61	62	62	63	63	63	64	64	65	65	66	66	66	67	67	68	68	69	69	69	70	70	71	71	71	72	72	73	73	74	74	74	75	75	76	76	76	77	77	78	78	79	79
59	59	60	60	61	61	61	62	62	63	63	64	64	64	65	65	66	66	66	67	67	68	68	68	69	69	70	70	70	71	71	72	72	73	73	73	74	74	75	75	75	76	76	77	77	77	78	78	79	79	80
60	60	61	61	62	62	62	63	63	64	64	64	65	65	66	66	66	67	67	68	68	68	69	69	70	70	70	71	71	72	72	72	73	73	74	74	74	75	75	76	76	76	77	77	78	78	78	79	79	80	80
61	61	62	62	63	63	63	64	64	65	65	65	66	66	66	67	67	68	68	68	69	69	70	70	70	71	71	72	72	72	73	73	73	74	74	75	75	75	76	76	77	77	77	78	78	79	79	79	80	80	81
62	62	63	63	64	64	64	65	65	65	66	66	67	67	67	68	68	68	69	69	70	70	70	71	71	72	72	72	73	73	73	74	74	75	75	75	76	76	76	77	77	78	78	78	79	79	79	80	80	81	81
63	63	64	64	64	65	65	66	66	66	67	67	67	68	68	69	69	69	70	70	70	71	71	72	72	72	73	73	73	74	74	74	75	75	76	76	76	77	77	77	78	78	79	79	79	80	80	80	81	81	82
64	64	65	65	65	66	66	67	67	67	68	68	68	69	69	69	70	70	70	71	71	72	72	72	73	73	73	74	74	74	75	75	76	76	76	77	77	77	78	78	78	79	79	79	80	80	81	81	81	82	82
65	65	66	66	66	67	67	67	68	68	69	69	69	70	70	70	71	71	71	72	72	72	73	73	73	74	74	74	75	75	76	76	76	77	77	77	78	78	78	79	79	79	80	80	80	81	81	81	82	82	83
66	66	67	67	67	68	68	68	69	69	69	70	70	70	71	71	71	72	72	72	73	73	73	74	74	75	75	75	76	76	76	77	77	77	78	78	78	79	79	79	80	80	80	81	81	81	82	82	82	83	83
67	67	68	68	68	69	69	69	70	70	70	71	71	71	72	72	72	73	73	73	74	74	74	75	75	75	76	76	76	77	77	77	78	78	78	79	79	79	80	80	80	81	81	81	82	82	82	83	83	83	84
68	68	69	69	69	70	70	70	71	71	71	72	72	72	72	73	73	73	74	74	74	75	75	75	76	76	76	77	77	77	78	78	78	79	79	79	80	80	80	80	81	81	81	82	82	82	83	83	83	84	84
69	69	70	70	70	71	71	71	71	72	72	72	73	73	73	74	74	74	75	75	75	76	76	76	76	77	77	77	78	78	78	79	79	79	80	80	80	80	81	81	81	82	82	82	83	83	83	84	84	84	85
70	70	71	71	71	72	72	72	72	73	73	73	74	74	74	75	75	75	75	76	76	76	77	77	77	78	78	78	78	79	79	79	80	80	80	81	81	81	81	82	82	82	83	83	83	84	84	84	84	85	85
71	71	72	72	72	72	73	73	73	74	74	74	74	75	75	75	76	76	76	77	77	77	77	78	78	78	79	79	79	79	80	80	80	81	81	81	81	82	82	82	83	83	83	83	84	84	84	85	85	85	86
72	72	73	73	73	73	74	74	74	75	75	75	75	76	76	76	76	77	77	77	78	78	78	78	79	79	79	80	80	80	80	81	81	81	82	82	82	82	83	83	83	83	84	84	84	85	85	85	85	86	86
73	73	74	74	74	74	75	75	75	75	76	76	76	77	77	77	77	78	78	78	78	79	79	79	79	80	80	80	81	81	81	81	82	82	82	82	83	83	83	84	84	84	84	85	85	85	85	86	86	86	87
74	74	75	75	75	75	76	76	76	76	77	77	77	77	78	78	78	78	79	79	79	79	80	80	80	81	81	81	81	82	82	82	82	83	83	83	83	84	84	84	84	85	85	85	85	86	86	86	86	87	87
75	75	76	76	76	76	77	77	77	77	78	78	78	78	79	79	79	79	80	80	80	80	81	81	81	81	82	82	82	82	83	83	83	83	84	84	84	84	85	85	85	85	86	86	86	86	87	87	87	87	88
76	76	76	77	77	77	77	78	78	78	78	79	79	79	79	80	80	80	80	81	81	81	81	82	82	82	82	82	83	83	83	83	84	84	84	84	85	85	85	85	86	86	86	86	87	87	87	87	88	88	88
77	77	77	78	78	78	78	79	79	79	79	80	80	80	80	80	81	81	81	81	82	82	82	82	83	83	83	83	84	84	84	84	84	85	85	85	85	86	86	86	86	86	87	87	87	87	88	88	88	88	89
78	78	78	79	79	79	79	80	80	80	80	80	81	81	81	81	82	82	82	82	82	83	83	83	83	84	84	84	84	84	85	85	85	85	85	86	86	86	86	87	87	87	87	87	88	88	88	88	89	89	89
79	79	79	80	80	80	80	80	81	81	81	81	82	82	82	82	82	83	83	83	83	83	84	84	84	84	84	85	85	85	85	86	86	86	86	86	87	87	87	87	87	88	88	88	88	88	89	89	89	89	90
80	80	80	81	81	81	81	81	82	82	82	82	82	83	83	83	83	83	84	84	84	84	84	85	85	85	85	85	86	86	86	86	86	87	87	87	87	87	88	88	88	88	88	89	89	89	89	89	90	90	90
81	81	81	82	82	82	82	82	83	83	83	83	83	83	84	84	84	84	84	85	85	85	85	85	86	86	86	86	86	87	87	87	87	87	87	88	88	88	88	88	89	89	89	89	89	90	90	90	90	90	91
82	82	82	83	83	83	83	83	83	84	84	84	84	84	85	85	85	85	85	85	86	86	86	86	86	87	87	87	87	87	87	88	88	88	88	88	88	89	89	89	89	89	90	90	90	90	90	90	91	91	91
83	83	83	84	84	84	84	84	84	85	85	85	85	85	85	86	86	86	86	86	86	87	87	87	87	87	87	88	88	88	88	88	88	89	89	89	89	89	89	90	90	90	90	90	90	91	91	91	91	91	92
84	84	84	85	85	85	85	85	85	85	86	86	86	86	86	86	87	87	87	87	87	87	88	88	88	88	88	88	88	89	89	89	89	89	89	90	90	90	90	90	90	91	91	91	91	91	91	92	92	92	92
85	85	85	85	86	86	86	86	86	86	87	87	87	87	87	87	87	88	88	88	88	88	88	88	89	89	89	89	89	89	90	90	90	90	90	90	90	91	91	91	91	91	91	91	92	92	92	92	92	92	93
86	86	86	86	87	87	87	87	87	87	87	88	88	88	88	88	88	88	89	89	89	89	89	89	89	90	90	90	90	90	90	90	90	91	91	91	91	91	91	91	92	92	92	92	92	92	92	93	93	93	93
87	87	87	87	88	88	88	88	88	88	88	88	89	89	89	89	89	89	89	89	90	90	90	90	90	90	90	91	91	91	91	91	91	91	91	92	92	92	92	92	92	92	92	93	93	93	93	93	93	93	94
88	88	88	88	88	89	89	89	89	89	89	89	89	90	90	90	90	90	90	90	90	91	91	91	91	91	91	91	91	91	92	92	92	92	92	92	92	92	93	93	93	93	93	93	93	93	94	94	94	94	94
89	89	89	89	89	90	90	90	90	90	90	90	90	90	91	91	91	91	91	91	91	91	91	92	92	92	92	92	92	92	92	92	93	93	93	93	93	93	93	93	93	94	94	94	94	94	94	94	94	94	95
90	90	90	90	90	91	91	91	91	91	91	91	91	91	91	92	92	92	92	92	92	92	92	92	92	93	93	93	93	93	93	93	93	93	93	94	94	94	94	94	94	94	94	94	94	95	95	95	95	95	95
91	91	91	91	91	91	92	92	92	92	92	92	92	92	92	92	92	93	93	93	93	93	93	93	93	93	93	93	94	94	94	94	94	94	94	94	94	94	94	95	95	95	95	95	95	95	95	95	95	95	96
92	92	92	92	92	92	92	93	93	93	93	93	93	93	93	93	93	93	93	94	94	94	94	94	94	94	94	94	94	94	94	94	95	95	95	95	95	95	95	95	95	95	95	95	95	96	96	96	96	96	96
93	93	93	93	93	93	93	93	94	94	94	94	94	94	94	94	94	94	94	94	94	94	95	95	95	95	95	95	95	95	95	95	95	95	95	95	96	96	96	96	96	96	96	96	96	96	96	96	96	96	97
94	94	94	94	94	94	94	94	94	95	95	95	95	95	95	95	95	95	95	95	95	95	95	95	95	96	96	96	96	96	96	96	96	96	96	96	96	96	96	96	96	96	97	97	97	97	97	97	97	97	97
95	95	95	95	95	95	95	95	95	95	96	96	96	96	96	96	96	96	96	96	96	96	96	96	96	96	96	96	96	96	97	97	97	97	97	97	97	97	97	97	97	97	97	97	97	97	97	97	97	97	98
96	96	96	96	96	96	96	96	96	96	96	96	96	97	97	97	97	97	97	97	97	97	97	97	97	97	97	97	97	97	97	97	97	97	97	97	97	97	98	98	98	98	98	98	98	98	98	98	98	98	98
97	97	97	97	97	97	97	97	97	97	97	97	97	97	97	97	97	98	98	98	98	98	98	98	98	98	98	98	98	98	98	98	98	98	98	98	98	98	98	98	98	98	98	98	98	98	98	98	98	98	99
98	98	98	98	98	98	98	98	98	98	98	98	98	98	98	98	98	98	98	98	98	98	98	98	98	99	99	99	99	99	99	99	99	99	99	99	99	99	99	99	99	99	99	99	99	99	99	99	99	99	99
99	99	99	99	99	99	99	99	99	99	99	99	99	99	99	99	99	99	99	99	99	99	99	99	99	99	99	99	99	99	99	99	99	99	99	99	99	99	99	99	99	99	99	99	99	99	99	99	99	99	100

Combined Values Chart, page 3

	51	52	53	54	55	56	57	58	59	60	61	62	63	64	65	66	67	68	69	70	71	72	73	74	75	76	77	78	79	80	81	82	83	84	85	86	87	88	89	90	91	92	93	94	95	96	97	98	99
51	76																																																
52	76	77																																															
53	77	77	78																																														
54	77	78	78	79																																													
55	78	78	79	79	80																																												
56	78	79	79	80	80	81																																											
57	79	79	80	80	81	81	82																																										
58	79	80	80	81	81	82	82	82																																									
59	80	80	81	81	82	82	82	83	83																																								
60	80	81	81	82	82	82	83	83	84	84																																							
61	81	81	82	82	82	83	83	84	84	84	85																																						
62	81	82	82	83	83	83	84	84	84	85	85	86																																					
63	82	82	83	83	83	84	84	84	85	85	86	86	86																																				
64	82	83	83	83	84	84	85	85	85	86	86	86	87	87																																			
65	83	83	84	84	84	85	85	85	86	86	86	87	87	87	88																																		
66	83	84	84	84	85	85	85	86	86	86	87	87	87	88	88	88																																	
67	84	84	84	85	85	85	86	86	86	87	87	87	88	88	88	89	89																																
68	84	85	85	85	86	86	86	87	87	87	88	88	88	88	89	89	89	90																															
69	85	85	85	86	86	86	87	87	87	88	88	88	89	89	89	89	90	90	90																														
70	85	86	86	86	87	87	87	87	88	88	88	89	89	89	90	90	90	90	91	91																													
71	86	86	86	87	87	87	88	88	88	88	89	89	89	90	90	90	90	91	91	91	92																												
72	86	87	87	87	87	88	88	88	89	89	89	89	90	90	90	90	91	91	91	92	92	92																											
73	87	87	87	88	88	88	88	89	89	89	89	90	90	90	91	91	91	91	92	92	92	92	93																										
74	87	88	88	88	88	89	89	89	89	90	90	90	90	91	91	91	91	92	92	92	92	93	93	93																									
75	88	88	88	89	89	89	89	90	90	90	90	91	91	91	91	92	92	92	92	93	93	93	93	94	94																								
76	88	88	89	89	89	89	90	90	90	90	91	91	91	91	92	92	92	92	93	93	93	93	94	94	94	94																							
77	89	89	89	89	90	90	90	90	91	91	91	91	91	92	92	92	92	93	93	93	93	94	94	94	94	94	95																						
78	89	89	90	90	90	90	91	91	91	91	91	92	92	92	92	93	93	93	93	93	94	94	94	94	95	95	95	95																					
79	90	90	90	90	91	91	91	91	91	92	92	92	92	92	93	93	93	93	93	94	94	94	94	95	95	95	95	95	96																				
80	90	90	91	91	91	91	91	92	92	92	92	92	93	93	93	93	93	94	94	94	94	94	95	95	95	95	95	96	96	96																			
81	91	91	91	91	91	92	92	92	92	92	93	93	93	93	93	94	94	94	94	94	94	95	95	95	95	95	96	96	96	96	96																		
82	91	91	92	92	92	92	92	92	93	93	93	93	93	94	94	94	94	94	94	95	95	95	95	95	96	96	96	96	96	96	97	97																	
83	92	92	92	92	92	93	93	93	93	93	93	94	94	94	94	94	94	95	95	95	95	95	95	96	96	96	96	96	96	97	97	97	97																
84	92	92	92	93	93	93	93	93	93	94	94	94	94	94	94	95	95	95	95	95	95	96	96	96	96	96	96	96	97	97	97	97	97	97															
85	93	93	93	93	93	93	94	94	94	94	94	94	94	95	95	95	95	95	95	96	96	96	96	96	96	96	97	97	97	97	97	97	97	98	98														
86	93	93	93	94	94	94	94	94	94	94	95	95	95	95	95	95	95	96	96	96	96	96	96	96	97	97	97	97	97	97	97	97	98	98	98	98													
87	94	94	94	94	94	94	94	95	95	95	95	95	95	95	95	96	96	96	96	96	96	96	96	97	97	97	97	97	97	97	98	98	98	98	98	98	98												
88	94	94	94	94	95	95	95	95	95	95	95	95	96	96	96	96	96	96	96	96	97	97	97	97	97	97	97	97	97	98	98	98	98	98	98	98	98	99											
89	95	95	95	95	95	95	95	95	95	96	96	96	96	96	96	96	96	96	97	97	97	97	97	97	97	97	97	98	98	98	98	98	98	98	98	98	99	99	99										
90	95	95	95	95	96	96	96	96	96	96	96	96	96	96	97	97	97	97	97	97	97	97	97	97	98	98	98	98	98	98	98	98	98	98	99	99	99	99	99	99									
91	96	96	96	96	96	96	96	96	96	96	96	97	97	97	97	97	97	97	97	97	97	97	98	98	98	98	98	98	98	98	98	98	98	99	99	99	99	99	99	99	99								
92	96	96	96	96	96	96	97	97	97	97	97	97	97	97	97	97	97	97	98	98	98	98	98	98	98	98	98	98	98	98	98	99	99	99	99	99	99	99	99	99	99	99							
93	97	97	97	97	97	97	97	97	97	97	97	97	97	97	98	98	98	98	98	98	98	98	98	98	98	98	98	98	99	99	99	99	99	99	99	99	99	99	99	99	99	99	100						
94	97	97	97	97	97	97	97	97	98	98	98	98	98	98	98	98	98	98	98	98	98	98	98	98	99	99	99	99	99	99	99	99	99	99	99	99	99	99	99	99	99	100	100	100					
95	98	98	98	98	98	98	98	98	98	98	98	98	98	98	98	98	98	98	98	99	99	99	99	99	99	99	99	99	99	99	99	99	99	99	99	99	99	99	99	100	100	100	100	100	100				
96	98	98	98	98	98	98	98	98	98	98	98	98	99	99	99	99	99	99	99	99	99	99	99	99	99	99	99	99	99	99	99	99	99	99	99	99	99	100	100	100	100	100	100	100	100	100			
97	99	99	99	99	99	99	99	99	99	99	99	99	99	99	99	99	99	99	99	99	99	99	99	99	99	99	99	99	99	99	99	99	99	100	100	100	100	100	100	100	100	100	100	100	100	100	100		
98	99	99	99	99	99	99	99	99	99	99	99	99	99	99	99	99	99	99	99	99	99	99	99	99	100	100	100	100	100	100	100	100	100	100	100	100	100	100	100	100	100	100	100	100	100	100	100	100	
99	100	100	100	100	100	100	100	100	100	100	100	100	100	100	100	100	100	100	100	100	100	100	100	100	100	100	100	100	100	100	100	100	100	100	100	100	100	100	100	100	100	100	100	100	100	100	100	100	100

EXAMPLE: Kathleen injured her left knee at work, and the treating doctor says she has a work restriction of no prolonged standing. The doctor also reports that prior medical records show that she injured the same knee while playing soccer in high school. The doctor concludes that 50% of Kathleen's present work restrictions are due to the prior sports injury. If she has a 30% disability rating for her knee, the insurance company would argue that it is really a 15% disability because only half is due to Kathleen's work injury.

Your doctor will determine whether factors other than your work injury are involved in your current disability and will discuss the apportionment in his medical reports. In fact, the law requires that any doctor who writes a report that addresses permanent disability must speak to the issue of what caused the disability. Was it caused solely by your work injury? Did other factors in your medical history contribute to your overall disability?

In order to make this determination, your doctor (or any QME or AME) may request your medical history, and you must disclose any previous impairments or disabilities you have had. The doctor's report will note any prior injuries or illnesses. In deciding whether these prior injuries or illnesses have contributed to your disability, the doctor considers such factors as the amount of time between your current work injury and the prior injuries and whether you fully recovered from the prior injuries.

Note that if you have received a prior award of permanent disability from the workers' comp system, the doctor must find that your prior permanent disability still exists at the time of your current work injury, whether or not you have actually recovered. (LC § 4664(b).)

The doctor can also consider injuries that take place *after* your work injury. For example, if you are involved in an auto accident a year after you fall off a ladder at work, it is possible that your doctor could apportion part of your disability to the subsequent auto accident, and the insurance company would not be responsible for that part.

If the doctor considers any prior or subsequent injuries or impairments to be factors in your disability, the doctor's report will contain an opinion on what approximate percentage of the permanent disability is a direct result of your work injury alone. The doctor will also estimate what approximate percentage of the permanent disability was caused by other factors, both before and after your work injury.

A doctor who is unable to give an opinion on apportionment must give specific reasons as to why not and then must consult with other doctors or refer you to another doctor in order to make such a determination.

Under the apportionment laws as they now stand, the doctor may even be able to apportion part of your disability to preexisting conditions such as arthritis, obesity, or age. If the doctor can give an opinion within reasonable medical probability as to how much disability you would have had as a result of these other factors if there had been no industrial injury, the apportionment may be factored in to your rating. For example, if the doctor says that absent the industrial injury you would have 50% of your current disability because of your preexisting arthritis, then 50% of your overall disability may be determined to be non-industrial and therefore noncompensable.

Previous Permanent Disability Awards

If you have received a permanent disability award or awards in the past, the total amount of the permanent disability ratings with respect to any one region of the body, as set out below, cannot exceed 100% over your lifetime (unless your injury or illness is considered as a total permanent disability, which is the case with the loss of sight in both eyes, the loss of the use of both hands, total paralysis, and severe brain injury resulting in incurable imbecility or insanity). The separate regions of the body are considered to be:

- your upper extremities, including the shoulders
- your lower extremities, including the hip joints
- your spine
- your hearing
- your vision
- mental and behavioral disorders, and
- your head, face, cardiovascular system, respiratory system, and all other systems or regions of the body not listed in the above.

CAUTION

If apportionment becomes an issue in your case, you should try to get the help of an experienced workers' compensation attorney or consult an information and assistance officer.

2. *"Benson"* Issues

Until 2009, if you had a permanent disability from one or more different injuries (with different dates of injury), you could "combine" them to arrive at one "total" amount of permanent disability. For example, if the doctor said you had a 31% disability for your back due to an injury in March and another 31% disability for a knee injury in June, you could combine them for a total disability of, say, 57%. This would equate to a permanent disability award of $75,267.50. This was called the *Wilkinson* doctrine from the case of *Wilkinson v. Worker' Comp. Appeals Board*, 19 Cal.3d 491 (1977).

In 2009, in another case, *Benson v. Workers' Comp. Appeals Board,* the Workers' Compensation Appeals Board overturned the long-standing case of *Wilkinson*. Now, because of the *Benson* decision, you can't combine awards. Instead, you get two separate awards (which will turn out to be lower).

In the above example, the awards for the back injury and the knee injury would each be for 31%. That equates to $31,750 for each 31% award. This would give you a total of $63,500, or about $11,767.50 less than you would have gotten before under *Wilkinson*. So, this is not good news, but it is now the law.

As a result, if the doctor says that you have more than one injury that contributed to your disability, he is now required to "apportion" the disability amongst the various dates of injury. If the doctor does not do this, however, don't raise the issue, as you will get more money if you don't. Make it the responsibility of the insurance company—if they don't do it, great!

RELEVANT CASE LAW

See *Benson v. Workers' Comp. Appeals Board,* in Chapter 28.

3. *"Almaraz-Guzman"* Issues

If you think your rating is lower than it should be, and that perhaps your doctor should have used a different chapter or chart in calculating your WPI, you can challenge the rating. *Almaraz-Guzman* refers to the cases of *Almaraz v. Environmental Recovery Services* and *Guzman v. Milpitas Unified School District.* The injured workers in these cases contended that the impairment rating, based on the AMA Guides portion of the 2005 Schedule, resulted in an inequitable, disproportionate rating and was not a fair and accurate measure of the employee's permanent disability. The court held that the language of Labor Code § 4660(c), which provides that "the schedule ... shall be prima facie evidence of the percentage of permanent disability," means that if you feel your permanent disability should be higher, you can challenge the rating.

One way of rebutting a scheduled permanent disability rating is to successfully challenge the WPI (whole person impairment). Oftentimes, a doctor may find that under the AMA guides, using the required chapters and charts that apply to your injured part of body you have little or no WPI, but by using another chapter or table by analogy, he can find you have a greater WPI. The court in the *Almaraz-Guzman* cases held that a physician is allowed to utilize any chapter, table, or method in the AMA Guides that most accurately reflects the injured employee's impairment.

Make sure the doctor who wrote the report acknowledges in the report that he has considered "*Almaraz-Guzman*" in arriving at his opinions on the amount of your whole person impairment (WPI). If he did not, you need to send him a letter, as discussed in Chapter 10, Section E4.

RELEVANT CASE LAW

See *Almaraz v. Environmental Recovery Services* and *Guzman v. Milpitas Unified School District*, in Chapter 28.

4. "Ogilvie" Issues

You may disagree with your impairment rating because of the doctor's Diminished Future Earnings Capacity (DFEC) adjustment. The case of *Wanda Oglivie v. City and County of San Francisco* involved the DFEC adjustment in the rating formula. The injured worker in this case contended that the DFEC adjustment did not adequately represent the worker's Diminished Future Earnings Capacity, which the worker contended was much greater. The Appeals Board held that an individualized DFEC adjustment factor must be consistent with LC § 4660(b)(2), the RAND data to which § 4660(b)(2) refers, and the numeric formula adopted by the Administrative Director (AD) in the 2005 rating schedule, and it also must constitute substantial evidence that the Worker's Compensation Appeals Board (WCAB) determines is sufficient to overcome the DFEC adjustment factor component of the scheduled permanent disability rating.

Now, don't be upset if you don't understand any of this. I can tell you many workers' compensation attorneys are still trying to figure it all out. From experience, I know that most challenges to the rating schedule are based upon the "*Almaraz-Guzman*" issues discussed above, and very few are challenged using "*Ogilvie*." If you are successful, however, it can substantially raise the amount of your WPI.

To challenge a rating under *Ogilvie*, I believe you or your attorney will have to hire a "vocational rehabilitation expert" who must do a study and prepare a thorough report using the parameters set forth in this case. There are companies and individuals who now hold themselves out as experts in this field. If you believe this issue applies to your case, I recommend you contact a voc rehab expert or a workers' comp attorney for further information.

RELEVANT CASE LAW

See Wanda Ogilvie v. City and County of San Francisco, Permissibly Self-Insured, in Chapter 28.

5. Employee Dies Before the Case Is Rated

If you are the surviving spouse or other dependent of a deceased worker who had an industrial injury, a determination will have to be made as to the nature and extent of the disability prior to death. This can be difficult if the injured worker passed away before undergoing medical examinations. In this situation, you should seek the help of a workers' compensation attorney.

E. How to Rate a Disability Using the Old Rating Schedule

A quick review of the old rating schedule reveals that it contains seven main sections:

Section 1—Introduction and Instructions
Section 2—Disabilities and Standard Ratings
Section 3—Occupations and Group Numbers
Section 4—Occupational Variants
Section 5—Occupational Adjustment
Section 6—Age Adjustment
Section 7—Appendices.

The rating process consists of eight basic steps. You'll need to use the rating schedule in conjunction with the medical report being rated.

Step 1: Read Section 1 of the rating schedule for an overview of the rating process and a guide to rating your disability.

Step 2: Determine the disability number and standard rating for your disability.

Step 3: Determine your occupational group number.

Step 4: Determine the occupational variants for your disability and your occupation.

Step 5: Adjust the disability rating for your occupation.

Step 6: Adjust the disability rating for your age.

Step 7: Refer to the appendixes to make final adjustments to the disability rating where necessary and to combine multiple disabilities, if applicable.

Step 8: Determine a dollar value for the disability rating.

Think of arriving at the disability formula and the value of your permanent disability as solving a puzzle. The puzzle has seven equally important pieces. Once you have all seven pieces (Steps 2 through 8) in place, you will know your "disability formula," which tells you your "disability rating."

We will now look at how to find and use each of the seven pieces of the puzzle. To help you through the process, we'll use a hypothetical case involving a woman named "Mary," who has suffered three common industrial injuries: a back injury, arm injuries, and a leg injury.

Mary was injured while working as a meat wrapper for a major grocery chain. Her duties required her to regularly lift up to 25 pounds of meat at once. In addition, Mary constantly used machinery to measure and prewrap various meats, which required repetitive gripping and grasping motions.

Mary is claiming two dates for her injuries. The first was October 23, 1999, when she slipped on some grease in the meat department and fell, injuring her back and right knee. The second injury is for continuous trauma (pain and disability) to both arms as a result of the repetitive meat-wrapping motions. After the fall, Mary's doctor diagnosed carpal tunnel syndrome in both wrists and an ulnar nerve neuropathy in the left elbow. Mary has not worked since her fall on October 23, 1999. For the second injury, she uses the dates of October 23, 1998 to October 23, 1999 as the period of injury. (See Chapter 5, Section C1b, for details on how to determine the injury date for a continuous trauma.)

Mary was 42 years old on the date of her fall. She was declared permanent and stationary by her treating doctor. Mary received copies of both the treating doctor's medical report and an advisory rating of her injury. (See "Mary's Advisory Rating," below.)

Mary wants to determine her own disability rating for the injuries set forth in the treating doctor's report. She wants to understand how the advisory rating was arrived at, to be better prepared to deal with doctors and the insurance company's lawyers in the future.

Because Mary has injuries to three different parts of her body, she will have to figure out a disability formula for each body part. She'll then combine them using the multiple disability rating table (explained in Step 7, below).

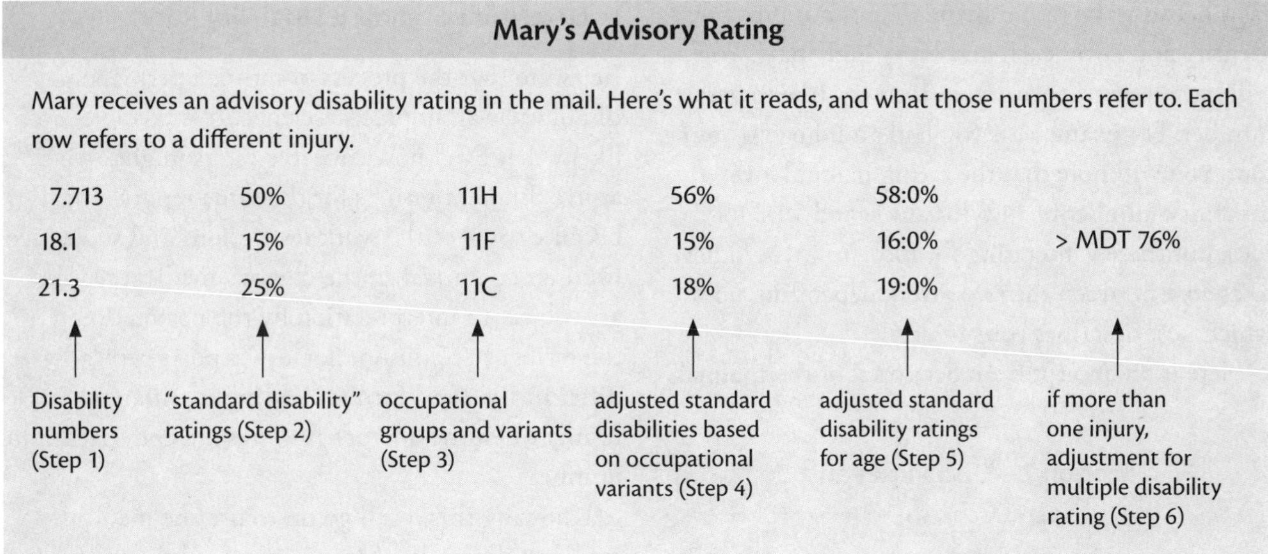

Mary's Advisory Rating

Mary receives an advisory disability rating in the mail. Here's what it reads, and what those numbers refer to. Each row refers to a different injury.

Disability numbers (Step 1)	"standard disability" ratings (Step 2)	occupational groups and variants (Step 3)	adjusted standard disabilities based on occupational variants (Step 4)	adjusted standard disability ratings for age (Step 5)	if more than one injury, adjustment for multiple disability rating (Step 6)
7.713	50%	11H	56%	58:0%	
18.1	15%	11F	15%	16:0%	> MDT 76%
21.3	25%	11C	18%	19:0%	

TIP

Disability rating means the same thing as disability percentage. The rating is usually expressed as a percentage. We use these terms interchangeably in this chapter.

Understanding Standard Disability Percentages

Leave it to workers' compensation to complicate even the way percentages are expressed. Percentages of disability are listed as a whole number followed by a colon (:), and then another number from 0 to 3. Here's what the numbers following the colon mean:

- the number 1 means 0.25%
- the number 2 means 0.50%, and
- the number 3 means 0.75%.

For example, 25:1% is equivalent to 25.25%, 25:2% is equivalent to 25.5%, and 25:3% is equivalent to 25.75%. 25:0% means there's no fraction.

Step 1: Read Section 1 of the Rating Manual

Reading this section in the rating manual will give you a good overview of the rating process. It discusses the various factors used in rating a disability and the indexes you'll be using to calculate the components of your disability.

Step 2: Determine Standard Ratings for Parts of Body Injured

This step consists of two parts: determining a disability number for the part of your body that's injured and assigning the standard rating to that disability.

a. Determine the Disability Number

The rating manual contains a section entitled "Section 2—Disabilities and Standard Ratings." Disabilities are listed by number ranging from 1 to 14. The smaller the number, the higher the injury is located on the body. Headaches, for example, are 1.7, while a toe injury is 14.7. Your objective is to find the number of the body part that most closely matches the injury location. This is not always easy, because the rating manual does not precisely identify and cover each and every body part. You will have to extrapolate from time to time to get a number. For example, if you had an injury to your foot, you will note that the rating manual gives a disability number of 14.6 for ankle and 14.7 for toes, but there is no rating for foot. You would have to choose between the two given, depending upon which best describes your injury.

Here is an excerpt from Section 2 of the manual:

Section 2—Disabilities and Standard Ratings

7.7 IMPAIRMENT OF FUNCTION, WRIST

Immobility of wrist joint in favorable position

7.711	Major	20%
7.712	Minor	17%
7.713	Both	50%

Note that the term "major" applies to the hand/wrist you are most proficient with (most people are right-handed) and "minor" applies to the less proficient hand/wrist.

Mary injured both arms, her back, and her right knee. The disability number that most closely covers Mary's arm injuries is 7.713, which is "impairment of function" for both wrists. Section 2 also shows that the disability number for a back injury is 12.1, and the disability number for an injury to one knee is 14.511. Great, we have the first piece of our puzzle: Mary's disability numbers.

EXAMPLE: The first part of Mary's disability rating:

arms.....7.713
back.....12.1
knee.....14.511

b. Determine Standard Disability Rating

Be aware that the process of rating a permanent disability is an imprecise science. It is possible, even likely, that five knowledgeable raters might arrive at five different ratings for the same report. This is because some of the work restrictions and subjective findings contained in the doctor's medical report are subject to interpretation by the person doing the rating. In addition, doctors' reports typically differ in style and format, leading to different results when the doctor's findings are converted into numbers.

Knowing this, we'll go on to use the medical report to determine Mary's "standard disability" for each injured part of the body. Or, to put it another way, we now need to find out how disabled the doctor thinks Mary is.

You should take several factors into consideration to arrive at any standard disability:

- **subjective complaints**—how much pain the doctor believes the patient is in
- **objective findings**—medical test results and examinations, and
- **work restrictions**—how the doctor feels the patient is limited in the open labor market as a result of the injury.

All three factors may be used to determine a standard disability, but often only one of the three is used. After you find separate standard ratings based upon subjective complaints, objective findings, and work restrictions, you will compare the three and use the highest rating as your standard.

Mary's medical report covers objective and subjective factors of her disability and work restrictions, as do most medical reports that provide opinions on permanent disability. (If you're having trouble finding factors of disability, see "Where to Find Factors of Disability in a Medical Report," below.) Here's how her report reads:

Factors of Disability

A. Subjective
   1. **Right & Left Arms:** Intermittent moderate pain.
   2. **Low Back:** Intermittent slight to moderate pain.
   3. **Right Knee:** Intermittent moderate pain.

B. Objective
   1. **Left Elbow:** History of surgery with residual surgical scar.
   2. **Right & Left Wrists:** (a) Decrease of grip bilaterally; (b) History of surgery bilaterally with residual scars.
   3. **Low Back:** Positive MRI.
   4. **Right Knee:** (a) Atrophy of the right calf; (b) History of surgery with residual surgical scars.

C. Work restrictions
   1. **Right & Left Arms:** The patient should be prophylactically [preventively] restricted from heavy lifting, repetitive pushing and pulling with both arms, and repetitive and forceful gripping with both hands.
   2. **Low Back:** The patient should be prophylactically restricted from very heavy work.
   3. **Right Knee:** The patient should be prophylactically restricted from prolonged weight bearing.

i. Determine Subjective Standard Rating of Disability

The first basis for arriving at a standard disability rating is the doctor's opinion regarding subjective complaints. Some standard disability ratings for subjective complaints are set out in the rating manual—see the chart below. In addition, I have added a few extra ratings to help you rate your doctor's comments on your subjective complaints. I have compiled these extra ratings, which say "author's addition," on the basis of attending many courses and lectures on rating permanent disabilities, and I believe them to be accurate.

Although the chart contains standard disability ratings for the most common subjective complaints, it does not list all possible variations. This means that sometimes you must extrapolate or modify the doctor's subjective factors to "fit" the chart.

Standard Disability Ratings for Subjective Complaints

Complaint	Rating
occasional slight pain (author's addition)	3%
intermittent minimal to slight pain (author's addition)	3%
intermittent slight pain (author's addition)	5%
frequent slight pain (author's addition)	8%
constant slight pain	10%
constant slight to moderate pain	30%
constant moderate pain	50%

Mary uses the medical report to match her disabilities with the standard disability ratings of subjective factors. To do this, she must rate each of her disabilities separately, using the description from the medical report. Here's the process Mary undertakes:

- **Right & Left Arms: "intermittent moderate pain."** There is no listing for "intermittent moderate pain" on the chart. However, by looking at the chart we see that, in one instance at least, "intermittent" means one-half of "constant" pain. ("Constant slight pain" is a 10% disability, while intermittent slight pain is a 5% disability.) Therefore it's probably reasonable to extrapolate that if "constant moderate pain" is a 50% standard in the chart, "intermittent moderate pain," should be a 25% standard. So Mary lists her subjective arm standard at 25%.
- **Low Back: "intermittent slight to moderate pain."** Mary compares the subjective factors of disability given by the doctor to the standard disability ratings contained in the chart. By

Where to Find Factors of Disability in a Medical Report

Most doctors who write reports for workers' compensation set out the factors of disability in a separate section. However, you may receive a report that is not well organized. If so, you'll have to locate language that deals with objective findings, subjective complaints, and work restrictions. Here are some suggestions.

Objective findings. In a typical report, objective factors are found throughout the report, and are summarized under the heading "Factors of Disability." Look for terms such as these:

- "objective findings of disability include ..."
- "upon examination, the patient showed ..."
- anything that supports the doctor's findings of "subjective factors of disability" or "work restrictions," including such terms as "loss of motion," "test results," or descriptions of "tenderness" or "pain" upon examination.

Subjective findings. Subjective factors of disability are found under a heading entitled "Subjective Factors of Disability." Look for terms such as these:

- "subjective complaints include ..."
- "upon examination I would describe the patient's pain as ..."
- language that deals with the doctor's opinion as to the type of pain you have in each part of the body you injured. The pain may be described as the type of pain you have all the time, the type of pain you have upon doing certain activities, or both. For example, "the patient has constant slight pain in the right upper extremity which increases to moderate upon heavy lifting."

Work restrictions. Work restrictions are often listed under "Disability," "Permanent Disability," or "Work Restrictions." In some instances, however, you may have to read the report carefully to find where the doctor lists the work restrictions, such as:

- "work restrictions include ..."
- "the patient should be precluded from doing the following types of activities ..."
- language that describes limitations or things you can't do. These may be described as "actual" things the doctor says you physically can't do or "prophylactic" (preventive) things the doctor says you shouldn't do.

doing this, Mary finds she has a standard disability rating of 15% based on the same procedure that she used for her arms.

- **Right Knee: "intermittent moderate pain."** Comparing the subjective factors of disability given by the doctor for her right knee to the chart's ratings, Mary finds that she has a standard disability rating of 25%.

Here are Mary's subjective disability standards:

- 25% subjective standard (arms)
- 15% subjective standard (back), and
- 25% subjective standard (knee).

ii. Determine Standard Rating for Objective Findings

The rating manual lists standard disabilities and their ratings based on objective findings of the severity of a physical injury. As discussed in Section 2a, above, these are listed under "Section 2—Disabilities and Standard Ratings" in the rating manual. Because of the infinite number of possible objective findings, not all disabilities are in the rating manual.

Your specific disability may be listed in Section 2 of the rating manual. If, when you found your disability number (see Step 2a, above), your exact disability was listed, you only need look at the corresponding standard rating to the right of the disability number. For instance, if you have severe mobility problems in both of your wrists, you could use a standard disability of 50%. (See the chart in Step 2a, above, entitled "Section 2—Disabilities and Standard Ratings.")

For some injuries where you have lost only partial use of a body part, you'll have to take a fraction of the objective rating percentage given in Section 2 of the manual by using the charts in the appendix of the manual. This may apply to injuries involving vision; limitation of motion of finger, shoulder, hip, or knee; reduction of grip strength; or thigh or calf atrophy (loss of muscle tissue).

Most of Mary's objective findings do not have a standard rating listed in the rating manual. This is not unusual. I would estimate that 80% of all injuries are rated based upon work restrictions, 15% on subjective findings, and only 5% on objective findings. And in almost all cases, the rating based upon work restrictions, discussed in Subsection b(iii), below, will be greater. Mary will not use the objective findings for her elbow, low back, or right knee to rate her disability.

Mary's loss of grip strength can be rated with the manual, by using the objective rating percentage in Section 2 of the manual and a chart in the appendix of the manual. Let's look at Mary's objective findings for grip loss.

Mary's doctor's report said she sustained grip loss bilaterally—for both hands. (See Mary's sample "Factors of Disability," above.) If you look in Section 2 of the rating manual, entitled Disabilities and Standard Ratings, you find that injuries to the grip are assigned the disability number 10.511, which is in turn assigned a disability percentage of 85%. (This percentage of disability applies to those who have lost *all* grip strength bilaterally.)

To find out how much grip strength she has lost, Mary should call or write the doctor for a supplemental report stating the percentage of grip loss the doctor estimates that she has sustained. When Mary receives the doctor's supplemental report on loss of grip strength, she'll refer to Table 4 in the appendix of the rating manual (on page 7-6) to find her percentage of disability. If the doctor's supplemental report states that Mary has lost approximately 50% of her gripping capacity bilaterally, by reference to the table (reproduced below) we see that a 50% loss amounts to one-third of the disability percentage. Therefore, a medical opinion that the applicant has lost 50% of her gripping capacity bilaterally results in one-third of 85%, or a 28.5% disability. We'll see in the section below that a disability rating based on Mary's work restrictions will actually give a higher rating for her arms (50%), so she won't use this 28.5% rating.

Table 4—Hand: Reduction of Grip Strength (Disability Nos. 10.511, 10.512)

Percentage of Grip Strength Lost	Fraction
10%	0
15	1/20
20	1/12
25	1/8
30	1/6
35	1/5
40	1/4
45	3/10
50	1/3
55	2/5
60	4/9
65	1/2
70	3/5
75	2/3
80	3/4
85	4/5
90	5/6
95	1

I know all this sounds confusing—believe me, it can be! The good news is, it is much simpler to come up with a disability percentage using your work restrictions (see immediately below). And often a rating based upon work restrictions will be greater than one based on objective findings.

Objective Findings Should Support Work Restrictions

Objective findings are used not only to find the existence of a particular disability and to give a standard rating, but also to support subjective complaints and work restrictions. For instance, an objective finding of an amputation of a finger on the right hand would support a work restriction of "no fine dexterous activities using the right hand."

In our example, Mary looks at the medical report to see whether any of the objective findings can be rated for a standard disability. Mary has some very significant objective findings: a history of surgery to the left elbow, a decrease of grip strength in both hands, a history of surgery to both hands, a positive MRI for the back, and a history of surgery for the right knee, as well as atrophy of the right calf. These findings strongly support the doctor's conclusions and opinions on subjective factors of disability, as well as recommended work restrictions.

But if you're satisfied with a medical report, don't worry if objective findings don't support subjective findings and work restrictions unless the insurance company raises this issue. Most insurance companies do not examine medical reports carefully enough to discover such inconsistencies. If the insurance company points out that the report does not contain objective findings to support the doctor's conclusions, you should write the doctor and request more detailed comments upon the objective findings. Hopefully, the doctor's report is only defective because of an oversight. But if the doctor simply can't find any objective findings, do your best to downplay this, because your subjective factors will, or should, support the doctor's work restrictions.

iii. Determine Standard Rating for Work Restrictions

RELEVANT CASE LAW

See *Capistrano Unified School District v. WCAB,* in Chapter 28.

The doctor's medical report will explain that work restrictions are based on a combination of the subjective complaints of the patient as well as the objective findings.

Work restrictions can be of two types:

- **actual,** meaning you physically cannot do the restricted activity, and
- **prophylactic,** meaning that although you could do a certain activity, you should not do so prophylactically (preventively), because there is a high likelihood you will either reinjure yourself or exacerbate your injury.

No matter how the doctor arrives at the restrictions (actual or prophylactic), the rating is the same.

Obviously, work restrictions are different for different parts of the body. For example, if you have an eye problem, what you can't or shouldn't do would differ from what someone with a bad knee shouldn't do. Similarly, there are different percentages of disability and various levels of restrictions for each body part.

The rating manual lists disability percentages for two types of work restrictions. Listed in Section 2, the rating manual has work restriction guidelines in "Spine and Torso Guidelines," page 2-14, and in "Lower Extremity Guidelines," page 2-19. The spine and torso guidelines can be used for injuries involving the abdomen or rib cage, problems with the neck, back, or pelvis, or pulmonary or heart disease. The lower extremity guidelines can be used for any injuries involving the legs, knees, feet, ankles, or toes. Whether you have an injury to one or both legs, the disability percentages listed in the lower extremities chart are taken at full value. To put it another way, one leg gets the full value of the disability listed.

These charts are reprinted below. Note that these charts contain a few extra restrictions and corresponding percentages that are followed by the words "author's addition." I developed these ratings on the basis of workers' compensation lectures and seminars, on years of experience rating permanent disabilities, and by extrapolating information from other disability percentages in the rating manual.

They are believed, but not guaranteed, to be accurate.

Lower Extremity Guidelines Ratings for Work Restrictions	
Disability precluding repetitive squatting, kneeling, or crawling (author's addition)	3%
Disability precluding squatting and/or kneeling	5%
Disability precluding work at unprotected heights (author's addition)	8%
Disability precluding climbing	10%
Disability precluding descending (author's addition)	10%
Disability precluding walking over uneven ground	10%
Disability precluding very heavy lifting	10%
Disability precluding prolonged sitting (author's addition)	10%
Disability precluding prolonged walking (author's addition)	10%
Disability precluding prolonged standing (author's addition)	20%
Disability precluding climbing, walking over uneven ground, squatting, kneeling, crouching, crawling, and pivoting	20%
Disability precluding prolonged weight bearing (can bear weight 75% of time)	10%
Disability precluding heavy lifting	20%
Disability precluding heavy lifting, squatting, kneeling, crawling, pushing, pulling, or twisting (author's addition)	30%
Disability precluding heavy lifting, climbing, walking over uneven ground, squatting, kneeling, crouching, crawling, and pivoting	30%
Disability precluding heavy lifting, prolonged weight bearing, climbing, walking over uneven ground, squatting, kneeling, crouching, crawling, and pivoting	40%
Disability resulting in limitation of weight bearing to half time	40%
Use of cane required for work (author's addition)	40%
Disability resulting in limitation to semisedentary work	60%
Disability resulting in limitation to sedentary work	70%

Spine and Torso Guidelines Ratings for Work Restrictions	
Disability precluding very heavy lifting	10%
Disability precluding very heavy work	15%
Disability precluding very heavy lifting and repeated bending and stooping (author's addition)	15%
Disability precluding repetitive motions of the neck or back	15%
Disability precluding heavy lifting	20%
Disability precluding heavy lifting and repeated bending and stooping	25%
Disability precluding heavy work	30%
Disability precluding substantial work	40%
Disability resulting in limitation to light work	50%
Disability resulting in limitation to semisedentary work	60%
Disability resulting in limitation to sedentary work	70%

If your injury is to your spine or torso or your legs or feet, you use the ratings, or disability percentages, in one of the charts printed above.

If your injury is to one or both arms, you may have a bit more difficulty rating your disability. The rating schedule does not set forth any standards for rating work restrictions for upper extremities, so they must be determined by analogy to other scheduled disabilities. However, on the basis of lectures and seminars, experience in rating permanent disabilities, and extrapolation from other disability percentages in the rating manual, I have developed my own set of ratings for work restrictions involving the arms. Again, they are believed, but not guaranteed, to be accurate. Note that the term "major" applies to the arm/hand you are most proficient with (for example, most people are right-handed), and "minor" applies to the less proficient arm/hand.

Upper Extremity Guidelines Ratings for Work Restrictions	
Disability precluding pushing and pulling	
major arm/hand	10%
minor arm/hand	8%
both	18%
Disability precluding gripping and grasping	
major hand	15%
minor hand	13%
both	30%
Disability precluding very heavy lifting	
one arm	5%
both	10%
Disability precluding very heavy work	
one arm	8%
both	15%
Disability precluding heavy lifting	
one arm	10%
both	20%

One last rule: For disabilities above 24%, you need to round off to the nearest 5%. For instance, 58% rounds off to a 60% disability standard.

Now let's return to Mary and start by seeing how her doctor described her work restrictions, which were covered under a "Factors of Disability" category in her medical report:

C. Work Restrictions

1. **Right & Left Arms:** The patient should be prophylactically restricted from heavy lifting, repetitive pushing and pulling with both arms, and repetitive and forceful gripping with both hands.
2. **Low Back:** The patient should be prophylactically restricted from very heavy work.
3. **Right Knee:** The patient should be prophylactically restricted from prolonged weight bearing.

Now we'll see how all of these technicalities work out in arriving at a disability rating.

Arms. Using the work restrictions given by the doctor for Mary's right and left arms in the upper extremities chart, Mary finds that she has a standard work restriction for her arms of 50%. Whoa! How did Mary arrive at 50%? A step-by-step look at how she did this will not only make this clear, it will also introduce a very important rating principle known as "pyramiding." (See "Pyramiding: Multiple Work Restrictions for One Body Part," below.)

Pyramiding: Multiple Work Restrictions for One Body Part

If you have more than one work restriction to the same body part, you are allowed to "pyramid" the restrictions—that is, apply more than one work restriction to the same part of the body. To do this, you take 100% of the greatest work restriction and add 50% of the combined total of all the other work restrictions.

For example, work restrictions of no heavy lifting (20%), no prolonged walking (10%), and no climbing (10%) would be 30%, a total of the entire amount of the greatest restriction (20%), plus half of the total of the other restrictions ((10% + 10%) × ½ = 10%).

According to the doctor's report, Mary should be "prophylactically restricted from heavy lifting, repetitive pushing and pulling with both arms, and repetitive and forceful gripping with both hands." Although this may seem like one large restriction, it is in fact three, as far as the workers' compensation rating system is concerned. This means Mary has to determine three different disability standards for her upper arms. Using the upper extremity chart, Mary finds:

- No heavy lifting with both arms is a 20% standard.
- No pushing and pulling with both arms is 18%.

- No gripping and grasping with both hands is 30%.

You might logically think that the standard disability would be the total of all three, or 68%. However, this is where the concept of pyramiding comes in. As discussed above, if you have more than one work restriction to the same part of the body, you first take the greatest restriction and then add to it one-half of the total of the remaining restrictions.

For Mary, the greatest of the three restrictions above is 30%. To this, she adds 19%, which is one-half of the total of the remaining restrictions (20% + 18% = 38%; 38% × ½ = 19%). Adding 30% and 19% together gives Mary a 49% standard disability for her upper extremities. Finally, because disabilities above 24% are rounded off to the nearest 5%, Mary rounds off 49% to a 50% disability standard.

Low back. Finding the work restriction given by the doctor for Mary's back (no very heavy work) in the spine and torso chart, Mary finds that she has a standard work restriction for her back of 15%.

Right knee. Mary's doctor gives a work restriction of "no prolonged weight bearing," which is a 10% standard according to the lower extremity chart.

Mary comes up with the following work restrictions:

- arm restrictions: 50%
- back restrictions: 15%
- knee restrictions: 10%

If you aren't pleased with the medical report, study it carefully. If you can argue that the doctor's work restrictions are not correct based upon the objective findings, you may be able to convince the insurance company that the injury is, in fact, more severe than the doctor finds.

iv. Determine Which Standard to Use

Usually, you are not entitled to a work restriction rating based upon both subjective complaints and work restrictions. Instead, you are limited to the higher of the two for each body part. Of course, to know which is higher, you need to rate both, as covered above.

EXAMPLE: A comparison of Mary's subjective disabilities to her work restrictions shows:

Part of body	Subjective disabilities	Work restrictions
Arms	25%	50%
Back	15%	15%
Right knee	25%	10%

Taking the higher of the two ratings for each injury, Mary will use a standard of 50% for her upper arms, 15% for her back, and 25% for her right knee.

Sometimes the same or similar work restrictions may be imposed on different body parts. This concept is called "overlap," and works like this: If you have the same work restriction for two or more parts of the body, you are not entitled to total the two. Instead, you get one work restriction that covers both parts. In Mary's case, she already has a work exclusion based on her arm problems of no heavy lifting, so it does her no further good to claim a work restriction based on her back injury of no very heavy work (a restriction with a lesser disability percentage). In other words, Mary is already precluded from lifting for her arms, so an additional lesser lifting restriction would be irrelevant.

If asked by the insurance company how she arrived at her rating, Mary should explain that she used the 15% subjective findings for her back instead of the 15% work restriction. (She did this to avoid the overlapping work restrictions from her low back.)

Finally, Mary puts together the disability numbers (from Step 1, above) and the standard disability ratings she just came up with:

EXAMPLE: Mary's standard disability rating now consists of two parts:

arms ....7.713 - 50%
back ....12.1 - 15%
knee ....14.5 - 25%

Overlap

Overlap occurs when a work restriction for one part of the body also benefits another part of the body. If you are restricted from heavy lifting because of your back, your injured knees will also benefit from that restriction. Therefore a restriction of no very heavy lifting to the knees is absorbed in the no heavy lifting restriction for the back.

Overlap is not always easy to spot, and if your rating differs from that arrived at by an advisory rating, it is quite likely due to the application of this concept. The only way to spot overlaps is to check whether there are similar work restrictions to different parts of the body. If so, you must determine whether you included both restrictions in your rating. Because this is impermissible, you must subtract the duplicate rating. To avoid overlap, it is best to use subjective ratings for the body part that has no work restrictions or that has overlapping work restrictions.

Step 3: Determine Your Occupational Group Number

RELEVANT CASE LAW

See *Kochevar v. Fremont Unified School District,* in Chapter 28.

The next factors in the formula are based upon your occupation. Different occupations will affect (increase or decrease) the standard rating for the same injury differently. For example, a cashier will be adversely affected by a hand injury to a greater degree than a restaurant hostess.

You need to search Section 3 of the rating manual, called "Occupations and Group Numbers," to find your occupation (the list is not reprinted here due to size limitations). Occupations are listed in alphabetical order, and each has a corresponding group number. In Mary's case, looking up "meat clerk" in the rating manual tells us that the group number is 322. The occupation you use does not have to be the same one you listed in your Application for Adjudication of Claim.

Many occupations are not contained in the rating manual's list of occupations, with the result that you sometimes have to be creative and take a group number from a similar occupation. You should determine the basic activities of the occupation and relate it to a comparable occupation in the manual. If you find more than one group that your occupation could fit into, note all of them.

TIP

Advantages to changing occupational group numbers. You may be entitled to a larger permanent disability payment if you use a more advantageous occupational group number. This is covered below, in Step 4.

Your occupational group number will be the third figure in your rating formula (see below).

Step 4: Determine Your Occupational Variant

Next, we turn to Section 4 in the rating manual, entitled "Occupational Variants." This chart has the disability number (Step 2, above) down the left side of the page, and the occupational group numbers (Step 3, just above) across the top of the page. Where the two columns intersect, you will find a letter of the alphabet from "C" to "J." This letter is known as the "occupational variant," which is placed next to the occupation group number in the formula (see below).

With this occupational variant, you will be able to tell whether one occupational group is better for you than another. The closer the letter is to "Z," the higher your disability rating will be. Here is the breakdown:

- **Occupational variant of "F" is neutral**—it will neither raise nor lower your standard disability rating.

Occupational Variant Table

		110	111	112	120	210	211	212	213	214	220	221	230	240	250	251	290	310	311	320	321	322	330
1.1	Paralysis	D	F	G	G	E	F	E	F	F	G	G	F	E	F	E	G	F	G	H	G	G	G
1.3	Epilepsy	H	G	I	I	H	G	H	I	H	I	H	F	F	J	I	H	I	I	I	G	H	H
1.4	Psychiatric	J	I	I	H	I	H	J	I	I	J	F	F	G	H	I	H	I	J	H	F	G	F
1.5	Post-trauma head	I	H	H	H	H	H	H	I	H	H	G	F	G	H	H	G	H	H	H	F	G	F
1.6	Vertigo	D	D	D	D	E	D	E	H	F	F	F	F	E	G	F	E	F	F	F	F	F	F
1.7	Headaches	I	H	H	H	H	H	H	I	H	H	G	F	G	H	H	G	H	H	H	F	G	F
1.8	Cognitive dis	I	H	H	H	H	H	H	I	H	H	G	F	G	H	H	G	H	H	H	F	G	F
2.1	Sight-cosmetic	I	I	J	J	J	I	I	I	J	J	H	G	G	I	I	J	I	J	I	H	H	G
2.2-2.6	Vision	H	I	J	J	I	I	I	I	I	J	H	G	F	I	H	I	I	I	I	H	G	G
2.7	Lacrimation	I	I	J	J	J	I	I	I	J	J	H	G	G	I	I	J	I	J	I	H	H	G
3.1	Hearing loss	J	H	I	F	J	H	I	H	J	H	D	E	H	H	J	I	J	J	E	D	H	E
4.1	Cosmetic	I	I	I	H	J	I	I	H	J	J	G	E	J	H	J	J	I	J	E	E	H	E
4.3-4.4	Skull	C	C	C	C	D	C	C	F	C	C	D	F	D	F	D	C	C	D	F	F	F	F
4.5	Jaw	I	H	H	F	J	H	I	H	J	I	F	F	G	G	I	H	H	I	F	F	G	F
4.7	Nose	H	H	H	F	J	H	H	H	H	G	F	F	F	F	F	H	F	F	F	F	F	F
5.2	Speech	J	I	I	F	J	I	I	H	J	I	D	D	H	H	J	I	I	I	D	C	G	D
5.31	Smell	F	F	F	F	F	F	F	F	F	F	F	F	F	F	F	G	F	F	F	F	H	F
5.32	Taste	F	F	F	F	F	F	F	F	F	F	F	F	F	F	F	F	F	F	F	F	F	F
5.33	Smell, taste	F	F	F	F	F	F	F	F	F	F	F	F	F	F	F	G	F	F	F	F	H	F
6.1	Skin-outside	F	F	F	F	F	F	F	H	F	F	F	F	G	G	G	F	F	F	F	F	F	F
6.2	Skin-wet wk	F	F	F	F	F	F	F	F	F	G	F	F	F	F	F	H	F	G	G	F	H	F
7.1	Arm amp	E	G	H	H	E	G	F	E	G	H	G	G	E	F	F	G	F	G	H	G	G	G
7.3	Shoulder	C	D	D	E	C	D	E	E	F	F	F	F	D	F	D	G	F	F	F	F	F	F
7.5	Elbow	D	F	G	G	D	F	E	E	F	G	G	F	E	G	F	G	F	G	H	G	G	G
7.6	Forearm	D	G	H	H	D	G	F	E	G	H	G	F	E	F	E	H	F	G	I	H	G	F
7.7	Wrist	D	G	H	H	D	G	F	E	G	H	G	F	E	F	E	H	F	G	I	H	H	F
8.11	Thumb amp	F	G	G	H	E	G	F	F	G	H	H	G	E	F	F	H	F	G	H	G	H	G
8.12	Index amp	F	H	I	I	E	H	G	F	H	I	H	G	E	F	F	H	G	H	I	H	H	G
8.13	Middle amp	F	H	I	I	E	H	G	F	H	I	H	G	E	F	F	H	G	H	I	H	H	G
8.14	Ring amp	F	G	I	G	E	G	F	F	G	G	G	F	E	F	F	F	F	G	H	G	G	F
8.15	Little amp	F	G	I	G	E	G	F	F	G	G	G	F	E	F	F	F	F	G	H	G	G	F

- **Occupational variant of "C," "D," or "E"** will decrease your standard disability rating (C the most and E the least). This will result in a lower disability rating and thus less money.
- **Occupational variant of "G" through "J"** will increase your standard disability rating (G the least and J the most). This means you'll end up with a higher disability rating and thus more money.

Mary finds that the occupational variant for wrists (only the variant for the wrists can be found in the excerpt reprinted above) is G, the variant for her back is F, and the variant for her knee is F.

EXAMPLE: Mary's standard disability formula now consists of three parts:
arms..... 7.713 - 50% - 322H
back..... 12.1 - 15% - 322F
knee..... 14.5 - 25% - 322F

TIP

Decide whether to change occupational groups. As mentioned, oftentimes a change in your group number can make a significant difference in your disability rating and thus the amount of disability that you are entitled to. That is because various work restrictions affect different occupations in different ways. For example, someone who has a work restriction of "no fine hand manipulations" will find that their standard rating goes up in value if their occupation requires fine hand manipulations, such as a typist or jeweler, and will go down for such occupations as a laborer, where fine hand manipulations are not required.

Just because your job title is listed in the section of the rating manual under occupational group numbers does not necessarily mean that you must use that group number. Look more to your job duties rather than your job title to determine your group number(s). And don't be afraid to be creative. If your job title is "assembler" but your duties are really that of a "warehouseman," use the job classification that results in the most favorable occupational variant.

If it is possible that your job qualifies you for more than one group number, follow the instructions above and check all possible occupational groups to see which one results in an occupational variant that is best for you. Again, the point is that you want to locate and use the occupational group that gives you the greatest increase in your standard rating.

Step 5: Adjust the Rating Based on Your Occupational Variant

The next step is to determine the percentage of disability after "adjustment" for your occupation. As discussed in Step 4, just above, the adjustment is based upon how your disability affects your ability to work in your general occupation classification. Different occupations are affected differently by the same disability. (See "Decide whether to change occupational groups," just above, for information on how to decide which occupational group is best for you.)

Turning to Section 5 in the rating manual, entitled "Occupational Adjustment," Mary takes the standard ratings for each part of her body and finds the corresponding adjustment for her occupational variant using the occupational adjustment table.

The occupational adjustment table below has the standard disability rating (up to 50%) down the left side, and the occupational variants from "C" through "J" across the top of the page. You need to find the intersection of the standard disability rating (from Step 3) and the occupational variant (from Step 4).

Looking up her disability rating for her arms, 50%, with an occupational variant of H, Mary finds that it adjusts to 56%. Looking up 15%, for her back, with an occupational variant of F, Mary finds that it remains at 15%. Looking up 25%, for her knee, with an occupational variant of F, Mary finds that it also remains at 25%.

EXAMPLE: Mary's standard disability formula now consists of four parts:
arms..... 7.713 - 50% - 322H - 56%
back..... 12.1 - 15% - 322F - 15%
knee..... 14.5 - 25% - 322F - 25%

Occupational Adjustment Table

Standard rating percent	C	D	E	F	G	H	I	J
0	0	0	0	0	0	0	0	0
1	1	1	1	1	2	2	2	2
2	1	2	2	2	3	3	4	4
3	2	2	3	3	4	5	5	6
4	3	3	4	4	5	6	7	8
5	3	4	4	5	6	7	8	9
6	4	5	5	6	7	8	9	11
7	5	5	6	7	8	10	11	12
8	6	6	7	8	9	11	12	14
9	6	7	8	9	11	12	14	15
10	7	8	9	10	12	13	15	16
11	7	9	10	11	13	14	16	18
12	8	10	11	12	14	16	17	19
13	9	10	12	13	15	17	18	20
14	10	11	13	14	16	18	20	22
15	11	12	14	15	17	19	21	23
16	11	13	14	16	18	20	22	24
17	12	14	15	17	19	21	23	26
18	13	15	16	18	20	22	24	27
19	14	15	17	19	21	24	26	28
20	15	16	18	20	22	25	27	29
21	16	17	19	21	23	26	28	31
22	16	18	20	22	24	27	29	32
23	17	19	21	23	26	28	31	33
24	18	20	22	24	27	29	32	34
25	18	21	23	25	28	30	33	36
26	19	22	24	26	29	31	34	37
27	20	23	25	27	30	33	35	38
28	21	24	26	28	31	34	36	39
29	22	24	27	29	32	35	37	40
30	23	25	28	30	33	36	38	41
31	24	26	29	31	34	37	40	43
32	25	27	30	32	35	38	41	44
33	25	28	30	33	36	39	42	45
34	26	29	31	34	37	40	43	46
35	27	30	32	35	38	41	44	47
36	28	31	33	36	39	42	45	48
37	29	32	34	37	40	43	46	49
38	30	32	35	38	41	44	47	50
39	31	33	36	39	42	45	48	51
40	32	34	37	40	43	46	49	52
41	33	35	38	41	44	47	50	54
42	34	36	39	42	45	48	51	55
43	35	37	40	43	46	49	52	56
44	36	38	41	44	47	50	53	57
45	36	39	42	45	48	51	54	58
46	37	40	43	46	49	52	55	59
47	38	41	44	47	50	53	56	60
48	39	42	45	48	51	54	57	61
49	40	43	46	49	52	55	58	62
50	41	44	47	50	53	56	59	62

Step 6: Adjust the Rating for Your Age

The older a worker is at the time of injury, the greater will be the disability after adjustment for age. Age 39 is the median. For ages younger than 39, the disability will be adjusted downward, and above that age it will go up.

Here's the reasoning behind this. The younger someone is, the longer that person has to figure out how to adjust to the disability and become a productive worker. The older a worker is, the less chance the worker will adapt to the disability in the workforce.

In our example, Mary was 42 at time she was injured. In the rating manual, under Section 6, entitled "Age Adjustment," we find a table where the adjusted standard disability rating (from Step 5) is listed down the left side of the page, and ages are listed across the top of the page. Where the two figures intersect on the page is the corresponding age-adjusted rating. (Only adjusted ratings up to 25% are excerpted here from the manual.)

Looking up 56% (the adjusted rating for her arms, not shown here), Mary finds that it adjusts to 58:0% for age 42. Looking up 15%, Mary finds that it adjusts to 16:0% for her age. Looking up 25%, Mary finds that it adjusts to 27:0% for her age.

Age Adjustment Table

	Age at Time of Injury									
Rating	**21 and under**	**22–26**	**27–31**	**32–36**	**37–41**	**42–46**	**47–51**	**52–56**	**57–61**	**62 and over**
1	1	1	1	1	1	1	1	1	1	1
2	2	2	2	2	2	2	2	3	3	3
3	2	2	3	3	3	3	3	4	4	4
4	3	3	3	4	4	4	5	5	5	6
5	4	4	4	5	5	5	6	6	6	7
6	5	5	5	6	6	6	7	7	8	8
7	5	6	6	7	7	8	8	9	9	10
8	6	6	7	7	8	9	9	10	10	11
9	7	7	8	8	9	10	10	11	12	12
10	8	8	9	9	10	11	11	12	13	13
11	8	9	10	10	11	12	13	13	14	15
12	9	10	10	11	12	13	14	15	15	16
13	10	11	11	12	13	14	15	16	16	17
14	11	11	12	13	14	15	16	17	18	19
15	12	12	13	14	15	16	17	18	19	20
16	12	13	14	15	16	17	18	19	20	21
17	13	14	15	16	17	18	19	20	21	22
18	14	15	16	17	18	19	20	21	23	24
19	15	16	17	18	19	20	22	23	24	25
20	16	17	18	19	20	21	23	24	25	26
21	17	18	19	20	21	22	24	25	26	27
22	17	18	20	21	22	23	25	26	28	29
23	18	19	20	22	23	24	26	27	29	30
24	19	20	21	23	24	25	27	28	30	31
25	20	21	22	24	25	27	28	29	31	32

EXAMPLE: Mary's standard disability formula now consists of five parts:

arms.....7.713 - 50% - 322H - 56% - 58:0%
back.....12.1 - 15% - 322F - 15% - 16:0%
knee.....14.5 - 25% - 322F - 25% - 27:0%

Step 7: Make Final Adjustments Where Necessary and Combine Multiple Disabilities

If Mary had an injury to just one part of her body, say her back, she'd have figured out her permanent partial disability in Step 6, above. In our example, it would be 16% (her formula would be 12.1-15%-322F-15%-16:0%), and she could skip this step.

However, where there are disabilities to more than one part of the body, as in Mary's case, the individual disability totals must be combined into one grand total. This is done by referring to the "Multiple Disabilities Table" (also known as the MDT table), the last table in the appendices of the rating manual. This table has the disability rating across the top of the page in increments of 5%, as well as down the left side of the page in increments of 1%. (See table below.)

Here's how Mary proceeds. First, she takes her largest disability, 58%, and finds the nearest number at the top of the page. The numbers are set forth in 5% increments, so Mary locates 60%.

Next, Mary will take her second-largest disability and find it down the left side of the page. Although Mary's second largest disability was to her knee, at 27%, we must subtract the 2% we added to the largest disability above when we rounded the number up (from 58% to 60%). So Mary actually uses the 25% on the left side of the table. (If Mary needed to round her disability number down, she could have added it into one of her lower disability ratings.)

Now Mary is ready to compute the combined disability rating for the two disabilities. She does this by looking to see where the two numbers intersect. The number at the intersection is the percentage of disability for both injuries. In this instance, where 60% on top and 25% on the left intersect, the figure is 73%.

Now Mary must combine the 73% disability (gotten by combining her 58% and 27% disabilities) with her smallest disability of 16%. She follows the same procedure. Mary finds 75% (the closest 5% increment) across the top of the page for her biggest rating. Next, Mary will take her smallest disability and find it down the left side of the page. Although Mary's smallest disability was to her knee at 16%, we must subtract the 2% that we added to the largest disability above when we rounded the number up to the closest increment (from 73% to 75%). So Mary actually uses the 14% (16% minus 2%) on the left side of the table. She finds that these two percentages intersect at 80%.

After applying the multiple disability table to her three different disabilities, Mary finds that her permanent partial disability is 80%.

EXAMPLE: Mary's completed disability formula:

arms.....7.713 - 50% - 322H - 56% - 58:0%
back.....12.1 - 15% - 322F - 15% - 16:0%
knee.....14.5 - 25% - 322F - 25% - 27:0%
Multiple Disability Rating (MDT) = 80%.

Step 8: Determine a Dollar Value for the Disability

Now that your disability rating is complete, you're ready to determine the dollar value of your permanent disability. To do this, please refer to Chapter 13, Section E, for an explanation on how to use the permanent disability table located in Appendix 3 of this book to determine the dollar value of your permanent disability.

TIP

Life pension available for disabilities of 70% or more. If you have a permanent disability rating of at least 70%, you are entitled to a life pension in addition to your permanent disability benefits. A life pension consists of a small amount of money that is payable every two weeks for as long as you live. See Chapter 13, Section F, on how to compute your life pension.

Multiple Disabilities Table

Rating for Secondary Disability—Percent	Rating for Major Disability—Percent																		
	5	**10**	**15**	**20**	**25**	**30**	**35**	**40**	**45**	**50**	**55**	**60**	**65**	**70**	**75**	**80**	**85**	**90**	**95**
5	10	15	20	25	29	34	39	44	48	53	58	63	67	72	77	82	86	91	96
6	11	16	21	25	30	35	40	44	49	54	58	63	68	72	77	82	87	91	96
7	12	17	22	26	31	36	40	45	50	54	59	64	68	73	77	82	87	91	96
8	13	18	23	27	32	36	41	46	50	55	59	64	69	73	78	82	87	92	96
9	14	19	24	28	33	37	42	46	51	55	60	65	69	74	78	83	87	92	96
10	15	20	25	29	33	38	43	47	52	56	61	65	70	74	79	83	88	92	97
11	16	21	25	30	34	39	43	48	52	57	61	66	70	74	79	83	88	92	97
12	17	22	26	31	35	40	44	48	53	57	62	66	70	75	79	84	88	92	97
13	18	23	27	32	36	40	45	49	53	58	62	67	71	75	80	84	88	93	97
14	19	24	28	33	37	41	46	50	54	58	63	67	71	76	80	84	89	93	97
15	20	25	29	34	38	42	46	51	55	59	63	68	72	76	80	85	89	93	97
16				34	39	43	47	51	55	60	64	68	72	76	81	85	89	93	97
17				35	39	44	48	52	56	60	64	69	73	77	81	85	89	93	98
18				36	40	44	49	53	57	61	65	69	73	77	81	85	90	94	98
19				37	41	45	49	53	57	61	65	70	74	78	82	86	90	94	98
20				38	42	46	50	54	58	62	66	70	74	78	82	86	90	94	98
21					43	47	51	55	59	63	67	71	74	78	82	86	90	94	98
22					44	48	52	55	59	63	67	71	75	79	83	87	91	94	98
23					45	48	52	56	60	64	68	72	75	79	83	87	91	95	98
24					45	49	53	57	61	64	68	72	76	80	83	87	91	95	99
25					46	50	54	58	61	65	69	73	76	80	84	88	91	95	99
26						51	55	58	62	66	69	73	77	80	84	88	92	95	99
27						52	55	59	63	66	70	74	77	81	84	88	92	95	99
28						52	56	60	63	67	70	74	78	81	85	88	92	96	99
29						53	57	60	64	67	71	75	78	82	85	89	92	96	99
30						54	58	61	65	68	72	75	79	82	86	89	93	96	100
31							58	62	65	69	72	76	79	82	86	89	93	96	100
32							59	62	66	69	73	76	79	83	86	90	93	96	100
33							60	63	66	70	73	77	80	83	87	90	93	97	100
34							61	64	67	70	74	77	80	84	87	90	94	97	100
35							61	65	68	71	74	78	81	84	87	91	94	97	100
36								65	68	72	75	78	81	84	88	91	94	97	100
37								66	69	72	75	79	82	85	88	91	94	97	100
38								67	70	73	76	79	82	85	88	91	95	98	100
39								67	70	73	76	80	83	86	89	92	95	98	100
40								68	71	74	77	80	83	86	89	92	95	98	100
41									72	75	78	81	83	86	89	92	95	98	100
42									72	75	78	81	84	87	90	93	96	98	100
43									73	76	79	82	84	87	90	93	96	99	100
44									74	76	79	82	85	88	90	93	96	99	100
45									74	77	80	83	85	88	91	94	96	99	100
46										78	80	83	86	88	91	94	97	99	100
47										78	81	84	86	89	91	94	97	99	100
48										79	81	84	87	89	92	94	97	100	100
49										79	82	85	87	90	92	95	97	100	100
50										80	83	85	88	90	93	95	98	100	100
51											83	86	88	90	93	95	98	100	100
52											84	86	88	91	93	96	98	100	100
53											84	87	89	91	94	96	98	100	100
54											85	87	89	92	94	96	99	100	100
55											85	88	90	92	94	97	99	100	100
56												88	90	92	95	97	99	100	100
57												89	91	93	95	97	99	100	100
58												89	91	93	95	97	100	100	100
59												90	92	94	96	98	100	100	100
60												90	92	94	96	98	100	100	100
61													92	94	96	98	100	100	100
62													93	95	97	99	100	100	100
63													93	95	97	99	100	100	100
64													94	96	97	99	100	100	100
65													94	96	98	100	100	100	100
66														96	98	100	100	100	100
67														97	98	100	100	100	100
68														97	99	100	100	100	100
69														98	99	100	100	100	100
70														98	100	100	100	100	100

As you can see, the process of properly rating a permanent disability requires both time and effort. However, I believe that if you commit yourself to doing it, you will increase your chances of negotiating a fair settlement. By understanding your rating, you will be in a position to discuss your disability with the insurance claims adjuster intelligently and with confidence.

CHAPTER

19

Figure Out a Starting Settlement Amount

The vast majority of workers' compensation cases settle without a trial. Settling means you and the insurance company agree that you'll accept a certain amount of money (and perhaps future medical treatment) instead of having a workers' compensation judge decide these issues in a trial. This chapter will help you establish the value of your workers' compensation case so that you can fairly assess any settlement offers made by the insurance company. Chapter 20 explains how to take this starting figure and negotiate a fair settlement.

A. What You May Receive in a Settlement

As you undoubtedly know by now, the sky is not the limit when it comes to how much you will receive to settle your workers' compensation case. You may, however, be entitled to cash amounts for some or all of the following:

- **Permanent disability award.** This amount is based upon doctors' reports and a complicated rating system (described in Chapter 18) that puts a dollar value on your injuries.
- **Life pension.** Your award may also include a small life pension if you have a severe disability of over 70%.
- **Retroactive (past-due) temporary disability payments.** If you weren't paid all of the temporary disability payments you were entitled to receive while out of work and temporarily disabled, you are entitled to that amount.
- **Reimbursement for mileage.** You are entitled to reimbursement for mileage to and from your doctors' appointments.
- **Medical expenses you paid.** You are entitled to be reimbursed for out-of-pocket expenses you incurred for medical treatment, hospital bills, and doctors' fees, as well as costs of tests, prescriptions, and medical supplies.
- **Future medical expenses.** You may choose to be paid a sum of money in exchange for relieving the insurance company of the responsibility of paying for your future medical expenses. If, however, you want the insurance company to be responsible for those expenses, you can forgo settlement money for future medical costs.
- **Your right to petition to reopen your case.** If, within five years from the date of your injury, your medical condition deteriorates further as a result of your work injury (known in workers' compensation jargon as "new and further disability" stemming from your original injury), you may petition the Workers' Compensation Appeals Board for an additional permanent disability award. You may either reserve this right or negotiate an additional sum of money in exchange for giving up this right.
- **Penalties.** In some cases, the insurance company may be required to pay penalties for nonpayment or late payment of your workers' compensation benefits.

In Section C, below, we'll take a look at how to calculate the value of each of the above components of your settlement. But first, you'll need to understand your settlement options.

B. Two Kinds of Settlements

If you settle your case, you have two settlement alternatives:

- stipulations with request for award (also referred to as "stips"), or
- compromise and release (also known as C&R).

How much your case will settle for depends both on the severity of your injury and on which settlement option you use. In this section, we explain what this jargon means and how to decide which settlement option is best for you.

1. Stipulations With Request for Award (Stips)

As discussed in Section A, above, every case that settles is made up of several components. Here's what's unique to a settlement by stipulations with request for award.

a. Permanent Disability Award Usually Paid Biweekly

Permanent disability is paid to you based on a weekly amount and is actually paid every two weeks—not in a lump sum—until the maximum amount is reached or until you die, whichever comes first. If you die, your surviving dependents (spouse or children, for example) are entitled to any unpaid permanent disability payments due as of the date of your death, but not afterward.

There are two exceptions to the biweekly payment schedule. First, remember that the insurance company is required to begin paying permanent disability starting the 14th day after the last payment of temporary disability. (LC § 4650.) Any permanent disability that wasn't paid and should have been is payable retroactively in one lump sum. Second, it's possible that an appeals board judge may grant a "commutation," where weekly payments are "commuted" to a lump sum payoff (but judges usually don't favor commutations).

If you received any permanent disability advances from the insurance company, the advances will be deducted from your award. (See Chapter 13, Section D2, for more on permanent disability advances.)

> **EXAMPLE:** Tom and the insurance company have agreed on the value of his permanent disability claim: 50 weeks of indemnity payable at $140 per week for a total of $7,000. Tom has already received 16 weeks of permanent disability advances paid at $140 per week, for a total of $2,240. Tom is entitled to receive the difference between the total amount due him and what he has already been advanced, or $4,760. The amount paid to Tom as permanent disability advances will be deducted from his total amount, and instead of 50 weeks of payments, Tom will receive 34 weeks of payments.

b. Future Medical Expenses Will Be Paid by Company

With a settlement by stips, the insurance company agrees to pay for any future medical treatments needed to cure or relieve your workplace injury, as indicated in your medical reports. You don't receive any settlement money for this benefit. Future medical expenses may include prescriptions, examinations, tests, physical therapy, and surgery, if the doctor has indicated that these may be necessary. If the doctor simply states that you may need future medical treatment and does not specify the type, you should be entitled to reasonably necessary treatment.

Note that the reasonableness or necessity of your medical treatment is always subject to challenge by the insurance company, and it may be necessary to file for a hearing in the future to enforce your right to medical treatment.

c. Right to Petition to Reopen Your Case

If you settle by stips and your disability level increases (you have a new and further disability stemming from the original injury) within five years from the date of your injury, you may reopen your case. In other words, if your medical condition becomes worse and results in an increase in your permanent disability, you may be entitled to additional money.

2. Compromise and Release (C&R)

Unlike stips, with a compromise and release (C&R) the insurance company pays you your entire settlement in one lump sum. You agree to give up all rights to future medical treatment and the right to reopen your case. Here's how a C&R differs from stips:

- **Permanent disability award.** Your basic permanent disability value is computed in exactly the same way as in stips, but it's paid in a lump sum.
- **Future medical expenses.** With a C&R, the insurance company pays you a sum of money

to buy out your right to future medical treatment. You add this amount to your settlement.

- **No right to reopen your case.** With a C&R, the insurance company may buy out your right to reopen your case.

3. Which Is Right for You: Stips or Compromise and Release?

Whether it's best to settle by stips or C&R depends upon your situation. There is no hard and fast answer that will fit everyone. However, there are several considerations that will tend to tilt your decision one way or the other. This chapter will help you figure out the settlement value of your case based upon both stips and C&R to help you decide.

a. Your Need for Future Medical Treatment

If your injury is likely to require expensive surgery or other treatment in the future, and you have no other insurance to pay for it, you will likely want to settle by stips to reserve your right to future medical treatment. It makes no sense to take a lump sum now only to find out later that your medical treatment will cost many times what you received.

On the other hand, you might opt to cash out your future medical with a C&R in situations such as these:

- You have medical insurance that you're not in danger of losing anytime in the future.
- You are sure your injury will not require much in the way of future medical treatment.

The main reason for stips instead of a C&R is to provide for future medical treatment. If you are fully recovered and unlikely to need future medical treatment, you would probably be better off with a C&R, which entitles you to a little more money, sooner.

b. If You Need All the Money at Once

If your financial situation is such that you need to have your entire settlement paid to you in a lump sum instead of weekly payments, you may want to settle by C&R, as this is the only type of settlement that will give you a lump sum settlement. But don't jump to conclusions.

First of all, you don't want to make bad decisions to give up your future rights because you're desperate for money now. Second, you may have a fair chunk of change coming to you in a lump sum with stips if either of the following is true:

- You're owed a lot of retroactive temporary disability payments or reimbursement for medical expenses.
- You stopped receiving temporary disability quite a while ago, and permanent disability payments did not commence 14 days after your last payment of temporary disability.

c. If You Have Other Sources of Disability Income

Some disability programs, such as Social Security and certain private disability policy providers, will ordinarily take a credit or offset for money you receive in your workers' compensation settlement. In other words, if you're receiving benefits through these programs, your benefits may be reduced if you also receive money in your workers' compensation case.

A C&R is the only type of settlement that allows you to insert language into the settlement document that may avoid or limit how much credit the disability provider may take. You do this by designating part of the settlement as future medical expenses, which won't ordinarily affect your disability benefits. If you're receiving Medicare or Medi-Cal, however, these programs may also take an offset against your settlement, even if the funds are earmarked for future medical expenses. (See Chapter 20, Section D2c, for a discussion.)

d. If You May Need to Reopen Your Case

If your disability worsens, settling by stips preserves your right to reopen your workers' compensation case within five years from the date of injury. This is done by filing a petition to reopen (a procedure beyond the scope of this book). The right to reopen your case is extremely important if there's a good possibility of either of the following:

- You will undergo surgery or other serious medical procedures sometime in the future. (Your permanent disability may be greater following the procedure.)
- The medical reports on which your settlement was based aren't current (usually over 18 months old), and your condition has worsened since then.

> **EXAMPLE:** Sid is injured on the job on October 6, 2011. He settles his workers' compensation claim by stips on January 3, 2012. Sid has until October 5, 2016 to file a petition to reopen his case for new and further disability. If Sid's condition gets worse during that period, he can have another chance at getting a bigger award. However, after five years from the date of injury, he can no longer reopen the case.

If you settle by C&R, you'll give up the right to reopen your case.

The closer you already are to the five-year anniversary of your injury, the less this becomes a major consideration. Also, if your injury (say, a broken wrist) has healed with no problems for a year or more, there is little chance of needing to reopen your case. But, obviously, if your injury is less certainly behind you (say a respiratory problem that keeps flaring up), it would not be wise to give up the right to reopen your case.

e. Stipulate Now, C&R Later

Another option is to enter into stips now with the knowledge that you can always C&R your right to future medical treatment any time in the future. The insurance company should always be willing to C&R your case, because it does not want to keep your file open indefinitely.

This option may be attractive if you don't have private health insurance or your coverage calls for high deductibles. Should you later acquire health insurance that will cover your industrial injury (a preexisting condition), you can contact the insurance company and negotiate a settlement (C&R) of your future medical benefits.

The disadvantage of doing this is that you probably will not be able to get as much money if you negotiate for your future medical treatment later. This is because the insurance company is anxious to C&R your case now. If you wait several years, and especially if you need little or no medical treatment during that time, the insurance company will not pay much to C&R because it will perceive its future liability to be very small.

Comparison of Ways to Settle Your Workers' Compensation Case

	Stipulations with Request for Award	Compromise and Release
Permanent Disability	Paid biweekly at permanent disability rate until settlement is paid off.	One lump sum payment made for the full value of permanent disability.
Medical Benefits	Paid as long as reasonably necessary; you must make written demand on company for authorization for treatment. May later negotiate buyout of right to future medical treatment.	Money for future medical treatment is included in the lump sum settlement.
Right to Reopen Case	No later than five years from date of injury, you may petition to reopen your case for new and further permanent disability.	Money for waiving right to reopen case is included in the lump sum settlement.

C. Determine the Value of Your Claim Using the Settlement Worksheet

Before you try to settle your workers' compensation case, you need an accurate idea of what it's worth. Armed with this information, you can confidently negotiate a fair settlement without worrying about being bamboozled into settling for less than you should.

As you go through this section, use the form titled Settlement Worksheet: Value of Workers' Compensation Claim, provided on Nolo's website. (See Chapter 29, "Online Appendixes" for the link to this and other forms in this book.) The settlement worksheet will help you keep track of all the components that make up the total value of your claim. You can also use the settlement worksheet to compare the two ways to settle your claim—by stipulations with request for award or by compromise and release.

Below are line-by-line instructions for filling in the settlement worksheet.

TIP

If you have a lawyer. Your attorney will enter into settlement negotiations with the insurance company. However, it's a good idea for you to go through the process in this chapter. You'll not only understand what your lawyer is doing but will also be in a more confident and informed position when it comes to discussing final decisions with your attorney.

Top of form. Fill in your name and the names of your employer and its insurance company. Provide the insurance company's claim number. If you have a disability rating, fill it in. (See Chapter 18.) Also, insert the appeals board case number if you have one.

1. Permanent Disability

The most important building block for any workers' compensation settlement is the permanent disability award. If you have a permanent work injury that affects your ability to participate in the open job market, you are entitled to a sum of money. How much you are entitled to is set by law.

Your permanent disability is expressed as a percentage of disability. Your permanent disability will be either partial (somewhere between 0.25% and 99.75%) or total (100% disability). The percentage of permanent disability is computed through a process called "rating." This procedure, which is discussed in detail in Chapter 18, arrives at a percentage of permanent disability by converting the various restrictions on your ability to work into numerical values.

For a permanent partial disability, you are entitled to be paid the appropriate number of weeks (determined by the extent of your disability) at your permanent disability rate—which is usually less than your temporary disability rate. If you haven't already calculated your permanent disability rate, turn to Chapter 13, Section E, for a detailed explanation.

In addition, if you were injured in 2005 or later (or your disability was rated using the new rating manual for another reason (see Chapter 18, Section B1)) and your employer employed 50 or more workers, your permanent disability award will be adjusted up or down depending on whether your employer offers you modified or alternative work. See Chapter 13, Section E3, for details.

Once you have determined the value of your permanent partial disability, you will have a basic figure to work from. Insert this figure into the blank spaces on Line 1 on your settlement worksheet.

2. Life Pension

SKIP AHEAD

Skip to Section 3, below, unless you have a permanent disability rating between 70% and 99.75%.

For any permanent disability of 70% to 99.75%, you are entitled to a small lifetime pension that is paid to you at a weekly rate (but actually paid every two weeks.) Please refer to Chapter 13, Section F, to learn how to figure out your weekly rate. Then take these steps:

Step 1: Determine your life expectancy using the Expectation of Life chart, below.

Step 2: Multiply your life expectancy figure in Step 1 by 52 to get the total number of weeks the actuaries say you will live.

Expectation of Life

Age	Male	Female	Age	Male	Female	Age	Male	Female
0	74.8	80.1	34	42.8	47.3	68	14.8	17.5
1	74.3	79.6	35	41.9	46.4	69	14.1	16.8
2	73.4	78.6	36	40.9	45.4	70	13.5	16.0
3	72.4	77.6	37	40.0	44.5	71	12.9	15.3
4	71.4	76.7	38	39.1	43.5	72	12.2	14.6
5	70.4	75.7	39	38.2	42.6	73	11.7	14.0
6	69.5	74.7	40	37.3	41.6	74	11.1	13.3
7	68.5	73.7	41	36.4	40.7	75	10.5	12.6
8	67.5	72.7	42	35.5	39.7	76	10.0	12.0
9	66.5	71.7	43	34.6	38.8	77	9.5	11.4
10	65.5	70.7	44	33.7	37.9	78	9.0	10.8
11	64.5	69.7	45	32.8	37.0	79	8.5	10.2
12	63.5	68.7	46	31.9	36.0	80	8.0	9.6
13	62.5	67.7	47	31.1	35.1	81	7.6	9.1
14	61.6	66.8	48	30.2	34.2	82	7.2	8.6
15	60.6	65.8	49	29.3	33.3	83	6.7	8.1
16	59.6	64.8	50	28.5	32.4	84	6.4	7.6
17	58.6	63.8	51	27.7	31.5	85	6.0	7.2
18	57.7	62.8	52	26.8	30.6	86	5.7	6.7
19	56.8	61.9	53	26.0	29.7	87	5.3	6.3
20	55.8	60.9	54	25.2	28.9	88	5.0	5.9
21	54.9	59.9	55	24.4	28.0	89	4.7	5.5
22	54.0	58.9	56	23.6	27.1	90	4.4	5.2
23	53.1	58.0	57	22.8	26.3	91	4.1	4.8
24	52.1	57.0	58	22.0	25.4	92	3.9	4.5
25	51.2	56.0	59	21.2	24.6	93	3.6	4.2
26	50.3	55.1	60	20.4	23.8	94	3.4	3.9
27	49.4	54.1	61	19.7	22.9	95	3.2	3.7
28	48.4	53.1	62	18.9	22.1	96	3.0	3.4
29	47.5	52.2	63	18.2	21.3	97	2.8	3.2
30	46.5	51.2	64	17.5	20.5	98	2.6	3.0
31	45.6	50.2	65	16.8	19.8	99	2.4	2.8
32	44.7	49.3	66	16.1	19.0	100	2.3	2.6
33	43.7	48.3	67	15.4	18.2			

Source: *National Vital Statistics Reports*, Vol. 54, No.14, April 2006.

Step 3: Multiply the figure in Step 2 by the weekly rate of your life pension to get a basic figure.

Step 4: To determine the present value of that money, you must then reduce (discount) it. You must figure out what amount invested today would give you your weekly life pension amount per week for the rest of your life. The accepted interest rate in the workers' compensation community seems to be around 3% for purposes of this investment calculation. I will leave the actual computation of this figure to you.

SEE AN EXPERT

Discounted life pension. If you don't have a workers' compensation lawyer to help you compute the discounted value of your life pension, check with an information and assistance officer. Or, see if your banker or life insurance agent can help with this computation.

Once you have determined the value of your life pension, insert that figure into line 2 of the settlement worksheet.

TIP

You can receive life pension payments all at once. A life pension is paid biweekly only if you settle your case by stipulations with request for award or you are awarded a life pension after a trial. If, however, you settle your case by a compromise and release, you will receive all your pension payments in one lump sum.

3. Total Disability

If you have a 100% permanent total disability, you are entitled to receive payments at your temporary disability rate for the rest of your life. To determine the value of a lifetime permanent total disability, you need to determine the number of years you are expected to live; see the Expectation of Life chart, above. Multiply the number of years by 52 (the number of weeks in the year) and then by your temporary disability rate (See Chapter 12,

Settlement Worksheet

Value of Workers' Compensation Claim

Name: ______________________ Employer: ______________________

Insurance Company: ______________________ Claim Number: ______________________

Rating: _______–_______–_______–_______–_______ Appeals Board Case Number: ______________________

	Stipulations with Request for Award (permanent disability and life pension paid biweekly)	**Compromise and Release** (lump sum payment)
1. Permanent disability (determined by rating) _________ weeks x $ ____________ per week	$ ____________	$ ____________
2. Life pension (available if rating is between 70% and 99.75%)	$ ____________	$ ____________
3. Total disability	$ ____________	$ ____________
4. Past-due temporary disability	$ ____________	$ ____________
5. Reimbursement for mileage	$ ____________	$ ____________
6. Reimbursement for medical expenses	$ ____________	$ ____________
7. Future medical expenses, calculated at _____% of actual costs: $ __________ medical examinations and hospital bills (including surgery, physical therapy, etc.) $__________ temporary disability (figured at _______ weeks x $__________ per week) $__________ medical costs (including prescriptions, tests, wheelchairs, hearing aids, braces, etc.)	No cash value _____	$____________
8. Right to reopen case (five years from date of injury)	No cash value _____	$____________
9. Penalties (specify)	$____________	$____________
10. Other (specify)	$____________	$____________
11. Total value of claim (sum of 1–10 above)	$____________	$____________
12. Attorney fees	$(____________)	$(____________)
13. Permanent disability advances	$(____________)	$(____________)
14. **Total you'll receive (11 minus sum of 12 and 13)**	$____________	$____________

Section B). Insert those values into the blank spaces on Line 1 of the settlement worksheet.

SEE AN EXPERT

If you are 100% disabled. When you are discussing settlement of a 100% disability case, you are going to be talking about significant amounts of money, and it would be prudent to solicit the help of a workers' compensation attorney as well as an accountant or investment counselor. An attorney can help you calculate the dollar value and figure out the interrelationship with other benefits, such as Social Security.

4. Past Due Temporary Disability Payments

Next, you'll need to add in the value of any retroactive (past-due) temporary disability payments. We discuss how to arrive at your temporary disability rate in Chapter 12, Section B. If you have been keeping accurate records, you can refer to your Record of Income and Benefits Received to verify the periods you received temporary disability. (See Chapter 6, Section C.) You may also ask the insurance company for a printout of temporary disability benefits you've received.

Here's how to compute the amount you are owed. First, determine the number of weeks you should have been paid but were not. Then multiply the number of weeks by your weekly temporary disability rate to arrive at the total. If you received state disability insurance, subtract the amount you received from the total.

> EXAMPLE 1: Jed was temporarily disabled for approximately one year. Jed looks through his records and finds that during that time he was not paid temporary disability payments from the insurance company for a period of two weeks. During this period, Jed did not receive state disability. Jed's temporary disability rate was $336 per week; $336 per week multiplied by two weeks is $672. In figuring the settlement value of his case, Jed should insert $672 in Line 3 of the settlement worksheet.

> EXAMPLE 2: Let's take the same facts, but let's assume that during the two weeks, Jed was receiving state disability in the amount of $250 per week. The value of the retroactive temporary disability would be the difference between what Jed was entitled to from the insurance company ($336 per week) and what he actually received from the state ($250). This amounts to $86 per week for two weeks, or $172. Jed should insert $172 on Line 3 of the settlement worksheet.

The insurance company may be required to pay you penalties as a result of its delay. We discuss that later, in Section C9.

CAUTION

You are entitled to recover past due VRMA only if you have a final order from the rehab unit or the WCAB establishing the amount to which you are entitled. A final order is an order that was not appealed, or if appealed was finalized before January 1, 2009.

5. Reimbursement for Mileage

You're entitled to reimbursement for your mileage expense for travel to and from doctor's appointments, physical therapy, and pharmacies to pick up medication.

If you haven't been reimbursed for these costs, tally them up using the Medical Mileage Expense form and instructions described in Chapter 11, Section B2. There is a copy of this form on Nolo's website. (See Chapter 29, "Online Appendixes" for the link to this and other forms in this book.) Fill in this amount on your settlement worksheet on Line 5.

6. Reimbursement for Medical Expenses

The insurance company must reimburse you for any reasonable and necessary medical expenses you paid, including costs of prescription drugs and health aids.

If the insurance company refused to provide medical treatment and you had to pay for it yourself, you're entitled to be repaid as long as it was later determined that yours is an industrial injury. This would include, for example, an MRI exam requested by your treating doctor that you paid for because the insurance company refused to authorize it.

It's unlikely that you would have paid your own medical expenses. Many injured workers cannot afford to pay for treatment themselves, and most doctors and medical facilities want payment in advance before providing treatment. But if you've paid for any medical expenses, add them up using the Record of Medical Expenses and Request for Reimbursement form discussed in Chapter 11, Section B1. Be sure to include any medical expenses you are responsible for, even if you have not yet paid the bill. Otherwise, the insurance company will only be responsible for paying doctors and medical facilities that treated you without payment and instead filed a lien form with the appeals board.

CAUTION

If you obtained treatment that has not been paid for. Contact the doctors or medical facilities and request they file liens with the Workers' Compensation Appeals Board. (See Chapter 9, Section B2b.) If they do, you need not include their bill in this section, because the insurance company will have to pay or adjust their bill as part of the settlement documents you sign. However, if the doctor or the medical facility refuses or neglects to file a lien by the time you negotiate your settlement, those outstanding bills will be your responsibility. Because you will have to pay them out of your settlement proceeds, you should include them in your demand. Enter the total on Line 6 of the settlement worksheet.

7. Value of Future Medical Treatment

SKIP AHEAD

If you plan to settle your case by stips. If you do not want to settle your case by compromise and release, you may skip this section. Remember, in Section B of this chapter, above, we discussed that future medical treatment will be paid for by the insurance company if you settle by stips. That means you won't be paid any cash for future medical treatment if you settle by stips.

The only time you add in the value of your future medical treatment is if you are negotiating a settlement of your case by compromise and release, which is a full and complete settlement of your workers' compensation case. The value of your future medical treatment is the most difficult item to put a price tag on, because you must estimate (or guess) what the cost of various medical treatments will be.

Future medical costs are certain to be a point of negotiation between you and the insurance company. You can pretty much expect that the insurance company will not agree to pay you up front for the full value of future medical treatment you and your doctor believe may be necessary. That's because no one knows for sure whether you will ever have the treatment and what it will actually cost. For example, from the insurance company's point of view, just because your doctor says that you may need surgery in the future does not mean that you will ever decide to have it.

As a general rule, you can expect that an insurance company will try to pay no more than 25% to 35% of the value of your anticipated future medical treatment as part of a settlement. But there are no hard and fast rules. For example, you well may be able to negotiate as much as 75% of the value of your future medical treatment if your doctors present a strong opinion that you will need treatment. (See Chapter 20 for more on negotiating a settlement.)

How much you will end up with often depends on the words used in your doctor's reports. Even seemingly similar reports can produce very different results. For example, there is a big difference between a medical opinion that "the patient may need a laminectomy in the future if symptoms significantly worsen" and one that states "the patient is presently a definite candidate for a laminectomy but has decided not to undergo this procedure at this time.

Do You Require a Medicare Set-Aside (MSA) Opinion?

The Social Security Disability Department and Medicare have become concerned in recent years about injured workers who receive lump sums for future medical treatment and then use the money for purposes other than medical treatment and rely on Medicare to pay the medical expenses when they arise. For example, imagine that an injured worker receives $50,000 as a workers' compensation settlement to buy out future medical treatment, which the doctor says includes a total knee replacement. Five years go by and the injured worker has spent the $50,000 on nonmedical expenses, but now requires the total knee replacement. The injured worker applies for Social Security Disability benefits and Medicare, which ultimately pay for the surgery.

To avoid this scenario, new rules require that an injured worker must, when required (see list below), obtain a Medicare Set-Aside (MSA) Opinion—an independent analysis paid for by the workers' compensation insurance company. The report gives an opinion as to the estimated cost of the injured workers' future medical care, and this figure must be taken into account in any settlement that includes a future medical component. For example, if the MSA comes back at $110,000 for lifetime future medical care, that amount must be included in any Compromise and Release and Set-Aside—and that $110,000 can be used only to pay for future medical treatment. Once the $110,000 is used up by the injured worker, from that point on Medicare will pay any medical treatment needed as a result of the injury.

In addition to getting the MSA, under certain circumstances the Compromise and Release agreement must be approved by the Center for Medicare Services (CMS) before it is approved by a judge. Failure to get either an MSA or CMS approval may subject all parties (you, the insurance carrier, and the attorney for the injured worker) to personal liability for any future medical treatment paid by Medicare.

So, do you require a Medicare Set-Aside and/or CMS approval? Here are the guidelines:

1. If you, the injured worker, are Medicare-eligible at the time of settlement:
   a. and the settlement is under $25,000, you need an MSA, but do not require CMS approval
   b. and the settlement is over $25,000, you need an MSA and you must get CMS approval.
2. If you, the injured worker, are not on Medicare at the time of settlement:
   a. and the settlement is under $250,000 and you are not entitled to Medicare in the next 30 months, no MSA is required and no CMS approval is needed
   b. and the settlement is under $250,000 and you will be on Medicare in the next 30 months, you need an MSA but CMS approval of the Compromise and Release is not needed
   c. and the settlement is over $250,000 and you will not be on Medicare in the next 30 months, no MSA is required and no CMS approval is needed.
   d. and the settlement is over $250,000 and you will be on Medicare in the next 30 months, you will need an MSA and CMS approval.

If any of this applies to you, you must contact the insurance company and request an MSA Opinion. You will not have any problem getting this as it is very much aware of these issues and will insist that an MSA and or CMS approval be obtained where needed because it does not want to be sued by Medicare in the future to recover the cost of your medical treatment that Medicare paid for.

However, this option must be kept open for the future." The first opinion will probably entitle you to no more than 30% (and probably much less) of the cost of a laminectomy and other related future medical expenses. The latter opinion is probably good for somewhere around 75% of the cost.

Don't forget to add in the value of any other related expenses due to the various medical treatments you may require. For instance, you might be entitled to an additional period of temporary disability payments if you have back surgery within five years from the date of your injury. (See Chapter 12, Section B, to figure out the amount of your temporary disability benefits.)

In addition to temporary disability, other future medically related expenses to consider include:

- prescriptions
- nonprescription painkillers and other over-the-counter medications
- physical therapy
- doctors' visits
- the cost of tests, and
- the cost of apparatus, such as wheelchairs, hearing aids, and braces.

You should also contact various hospitals and doctors' offices to get estimates regarding the cost of the type of medical treatment you may need in the future. This will give you a reliable dollar amount, and it will impress the insurance adjuster if your figures are valid.

In deciding on a value to insert on your settlement worksheet for future medical treatment, I recommend starting in the 75% to 80% range of the actual cost you estimate for future medical treatment. Indicate the percentage of actual costs you're using to come up with this figure. If you try demanding 100%, the insurance adjuster will not take you seriously and will categorize you along with all those other unrepresented workers who don't know what they're doing. By starting at 75% to 80% and being willing to negotiate, the insurance adjuster should recognize that you understand how the system works and should take you seriously.

Once you determine the value of your future medical treatment, enter it on your settlement worksheet on Line 7 by first breaking it down into the three elements listed, and then putting the total in the far right column under "Compromise and Release." If you are settling your case by stipulation, put a check on other line next to "No cash value."

8. Value of Waiving Your Right to Reopen Your Case

SKIP AHEAD

If you don't want to settle by compromise and release. You may choose to skip this section if you are only interested in settling your case by stips. Stips gives you the right to reopen your case and ask for more money if your condition gets worse within five years from the date of injury. (See Section B1c, above, for more on your right to reopen your case.) In that case, check the line next to "No cash value."

If you settle your case by compromise and release, you will give up your right to reopen your case should your condition get worse. For example, if you now have a 10% permanent partial disability, and six months after you settle by compromise and release your disability worsens to a 50% disability, you will not be able to ask for any more money.

There's no set formula to follow in determining the amount you should get for waiving your right to reopen your case. The amount you'll receive depends upon two factors:

- **Whether your disability is likely to get worse in the future.** For example, if you have a progressive disability such as a lung disease, you can expect to get more money for waiving your right to reopen than if you have an ankle fracture that has healed with a good result. That is because the ankle probably won't get any worse and require future care, while the lung disease probably will.
- **How much time is left to petition the Workers' Compensation Appeals Board to reopen your case.** If, at the time of settlement, there are

only five months left until the five-year anniversary date of your injury, you will not get nearly as much money as if there are three years until the five-year anniversary date of your injury.

In general, unless your condition is very likely to require lots more treatment (in which case you probably shouldn't waive your right to reopen your case in the first place), you should figure on getting anywhere from nothing to several thousand dollars to waive this right. As in all settlement figures, this amount is negotiable, and some insurance companies include it in future medical expenses. Insert the estimated value of this figure on Line 8 of the settlement worksheet.

9. Penalties

RELEVANT CASE LAW

See *Pierce Enterprises, Argonaut Insurance Company, Petitioners v. WCAB and George Colchado, Respondents; Rhiner v. WCAB; Ready Home Health Care, Inc. v. WCAB (Sharp)*; and *Christian v. WCAB*, in Chapter 28.

If the insurance company failed to pay you benefits, or failed to pay them in a timely manner, you may be entitled to additional money in penalties unless the insurance company has a good reason for its action (or inaction).

- **Delay or failure to provide benefits.** If the delay was unreasonable, the appeals board may assess a 25% penalty, calculated on the amount of the particular benefit that was delayed, including temporary disability, permanent disability, and medical treatment. (LC § 5814.) (See Chapter 11, Section D.)
- **Late payment of temporary disability or permanent disability allowance.** There is an automatic 10% penalty on the delayed payment of these biweekly payments. (LC § 4650.) Make sure the insurance company hasn't already paid the penalty (discussed in Chapter 12, Section C3) before you ask for it in your settlement. (Note that an additional 25% penalty on all benefits may also apply under LC § 5814, as discussed just above and in Chapter 11, Section D.)
- **Employer's illegal hiring of a minor under age 16.** The appeals board may award a 50% penalty on the workers' compensation award unless the minor furnished falsified identification. (LC § 4557.)
- **Employer's serious or willful misconduct.** If your employer intentionally did something seriously wrong, such as endangering employees by violating Cal-OSHA regulations, the workers' compensation award can be increased by 50%, excluding costs of medical treatment. (LC § 4553.) We cover this in Chapter 16, Section D. To qualify for this penalty, you must file a separate application with the appeals board within one year of the date of injury. (CCR §§ 10440, 10445.) See a lawyer; the procedure is beyond the scope of this book.
- **Employer's discrimination against worker for filing claim.** As discussed in Chapter 16, Section C, an employer who fires, threatens to discharge, or otherwise discriminates against an employee for filing a workers' compensation claim is subject to a 50% penalty on the award, up to $10,000. (LC § 132(a).) See a lawyer; you must file an application with the appeals board within one year from the date of the employer's discriminatory action.

Enter the value of any penalties on Line 9 of the settlement worksheet.

10. Other

Specify any other expenses you may be entitled to and fill in the amounts. Here are some possibilities:

- costs of depositions, if you held any (Chapter 21, Section C)
- costs of serving subpoenas or subpoenas duces tecum (Chapter 21, Section D), and
- costs of having subpoenaed documents photocopied by an attorney service.

11. Total Value of Your Claim

Add the total of Lines 1 through 10 above. This is the figure you will use in starting your settlement negotiations. Enter the total on Line 11 of the settlement worksheet. To determine how much you can expect to actually keep, complete Lines 12 through 14, below.

12. Attorney Fees

If you do not have an attorney, enter 0 in this space. If you have or had an attorney, you'll need to enter the amount of the attorney fee on Line 12. This is usually 12% to 15% of your settlement (the figure you ultimately agree to settle for). For starters, calculate 12% to 15% of the Line 11 total.

13. Permanent Disability Advances

If you received permanent disability advances, explained in Chapter 13, Section D2, enter the total amount you received on this line. You are subtracting already paid permanent disability advances to see how much "new money" you will get. Many injured workers forget this fact and pass up reasonable settlement offers because they will not net enough money.

EXAMPLE: Tom gets an offer of $3,000 to settle his case, which is reasonable. Tom has received $2,500 in permanent disability advances. Tom erroneously thinks that he is only going to get $500 for his case. While it is true that Tom will only get $500 in "new money" when his case settles, Tom will in fact receive $3,000 to settle his case. It's just that he already got most of his settlement in advances.

14. Total You'll Receive

Subtract the total of Lines 12 and 13 from Line 11. This is what you can expect to receive in new money if you settle for the amount listed on Line 11.

D. What to Do Next

Remember that the total represented on Line 11 of your settlement worksheet is just the starting point for settlement negotiations. It is doubtful that you will get an offer from the insurance company at this figure. Armed with the information in the settlement worksheet, you may now begin the negotiating process to try to arrive at a final figure that you are willing to accept. Chapter 20 explains how to use your newfound knowledge to negotiate a fair settlement of your case.

CHAPTER

20

Negotiating a Settlement

This chapter covers what most people need to know about settling a workers' compensation claim. If you do not have an attorney, you will learn how to negotiate and settle your workers' compensation case. If you do have an attorney, this chapter will help you to understand what your attorney is going to do on your behalf, which should help you to better communicate your goals and desires. Finally, you will learn how to review settlement documents and get your settlement finalized.

If you've decided to negotiate the settlement of your case, you probably feel a little nervous. That's normal. Just remember that the insurance adjuster is as eager as you are to settle your case, even if it doesn't seem that way.

You also have the element of surprise on your side. Insurance adjusters often deal with injured workers who represent themselves. However, it's rare for an injured worker to know as much about how the system works as you probably do, having read this book. The claims adjuster may underestimate your ability to assess the value of your case and may be somewhat flustered when you're able to justify your demands with facts and figures.

Thousands of people have negotiated settlements of their cases even without the benefit of a self-help book. You should be able to do the same. If you feel overwhelmed, or feel you're not getting the results you want, you may seek the assistance of a workers' compensation attorney at any time. If you can't find a lawyer to represent you, or if you choose not to hire one, bear in mind that an appeals board judge will be reviewing your settlement documents. The judge will look particularly closely at a settlement negotiated by an unrepresented worker and will approve it only if it's in your best interests.

A. Deciding Whether to Negotiate Your Own Settlement

There are many different negotiating styles. Some people can achieve more with a smile and a nod than others can by banging the table—but, of course, the reverse is also true. In the last analysis, your negotiating style should be an extension of your personality, not something you put on for the day.

That said, it's also important to realize that good negotiating is a skill, and that the amount of your workers' compensation settlement will depend, to some degree, on your negotiating ability. If you are generally pretty good at bargaining for a good deal in other contexts (such as buying a car or getting a raise), you may want to negotiate your own workers' compensation settlement. But if you break out in a sweat and can't open your mouth to speak at the thought of even calling the insurance adjuster, you will want to seriously consider getting a lawyer. See Chapter 26 for help finding a lawyer. As an alternative, you may have a knowledgeable nonlawyer friend negotiate on your behalf.

Some of the factors that come into play in determining your negotiating ability include:

- **Personality.** Are you comfortable talking to people? Or do you avoid confronting difficult personal and business situations?
- **Communication skills.** Are you able to effectively communicate in business transactions generally? Will you be able to make the adjuster understand your position?
- **Confidence.** Do you feel confident in business dealings? When you speak, will the insurance adjuster be likely to take you seriously, or will you come across as being afraid or unsure?
- **Objectivity.** Are you so angry or bitter about how your claim was handled that you can't talk about it without getting upset? If so, you'll probably have a hard time negotiating an equitable settlement.
- **Knowledge.** When it comes to your workers' compensation claim, do you know what you're talking about? Have you read this book carefully and followed the suggestions to prepare your case?

Of all of the above factors, the most important is knowledge of the law and facts in your case. If you adequately study and prepare your case, the knowledge you acquire should help give you the confidence and the ability to persuade the insurance adjuster that you have correctly assessed your case.

If You Fired Your Lawyer

A workers' compensation lawyer will generally be entitled to a fee of 12% to 15% of your settlement. If you previously had an attorney, but you dropped that attorney ("substituted him out of your case," in legal jargon), the attorney must file a lien on your case for the reasonable value of services provided. The lien will require you to negotiate a settlement of attorney's fees with your former lawyer at the time you settle your case. If your former attorney did not file a lien, you don't need to pay the attorney to get your settlement approved. In that situation, the attorney can't collect a fee from your settlement, but could sue you in civil or small claims court (although that rarely happens) to collect the fees.

How much you end up paying your former attorney will depend on how long the lawyer represented you, what was accomplished, and how much better you did after you dropped the attorney. The worst you can do is to owe what the attorney would have been entitled to originally: 12% to 15% of your settlement. If you had two or more attorneys who worked on your case, don't worry. The most you can owe is a total of 12% to 15% of your settlement. It is up to the attorneys to decide how that fee is to be split among them.

If you negotiate your own settlement, you will probably be able to negotiate an amount in the area of 6% or less of your settlement as attorney fees. If, however, hardly any work was done on your case, the attorney might even be willing to waive a fee. Once an agreement has been reached, request that your former attorney send you a letter confirming the agreed-upon amount for satisfying the lien, or send the attorney a letter to sign and return that states your agreement.

RESOURCE

Books on negotiating. Several books that can help you hone your negotiating skills are: *Getting to Yes: Negotiating Agreement Without Giving In*, by Roger Fisher, William Ury, and Bruce Patton (Houghton Mifflin), *Getting Past No: Negotiating Your Way from Confrontation to Cooperation*, by William Ury (Bantam Books), and *You Can Negotiate Anything*, by Herb Cohen (Bantam Books).

B. The Concept of Compromising

The basis for any out-of-court settlement is a principle known as compromising. Compromising is giving up something you want in return for the other side's giving up something it wants. In other words, each side gives a little to reach a settlement. If one or both sides are unwilling to compromise, there is little chance of settling the case without a trial. A willingness to compromise is the basis for any realistic and fruitful negotiation.

Sometimes—fortunately not very often—an insurance adjuster refuses to negotiate in good faith or takes an outrageous position. In these rare situations, you will be left with no alternative but to proceed to trial. Don't worry or be discouraged; sometimes these things happen. We cover what to do in Section C4, below.

C. How to Negotiate a Settlement

Before you begin the actual negotiating process, you need to take two important steps:

Step 1: Have a good grasp of how much your claim is worth. Chapter 19, Section C, takes you step by step through the process of determining a value of your claim. Once you have come to an educated estimate as to the value of your case, you will be in a position to begin settlement negotiations.

Step 2: Learn about the different ways to settle your case. If you haven't done so already, you need to decide what type of settlement you want: stipulations with request for award or compromise and release. In Chapter 19, Section B, we discuss the advantages and disadvantages of each settlement approach. But it's important to understand that even after studying this material carefully, you may still be undecided. If so, you should make settlement demands based upon both types of settlements, and include both demands in the same letter.

1. When to Settle

The best time to settle your workers' compensation claim is when there is nothing else left to do on your case except settle it or go to trial. In other words, the following should all apply:

- Your doctors have all said you are permanent and stationary—in other words, your medical condition has stabilized and your condition is not likely to improve in the next year. (See Chapter 9, Section E.)
- You have obtained the medical reports you need to determine the nature and extent of your permanent disability and your need for future medical treatment, and have attended any medical appointments requested by the insurance company.
- You have determined a starting figure for the settlement value of your case and completed a settlement worksheet. (See Chapter 19, Section C.)

Sometimes financial circumstances may pressure you to try to settle your case in a hurry. Do your best to get financial assistance or seek permanent disability advances rather than rushing into a settlement that's not to your advantage. (Chapter 13, Section D2, discusses asking for an advance.)

2. How to Initiate Settlement Negotiations

It is very possible that the insurance company will initiate settlement negotiations. If so, you may receive a telephone call or a letter from the insurance adjuster setting forth an initial settlement offer. In fact, the insurance company may send you a filled-out Stipulations with Request for Award form with a permanent disability percentage and a cover letter saying that you must sign the agreement to ensure your rights to medical treatment, or even with a simple Post-It note saying, "Please sign and return." You do not have to sign and return it—this is just the insurance company's first settlement offer.

If you don't hear from the insurance company, then when you're ready to begin settlement negotiations you should take the initiative. Contact the person you have been dealing with all along—the insurance adjuster, the insurance company's attorney, or the insurance company's hearing representative.

The quickest method of beginning settlement negotiations is by making a telephone call. Before you call, be prepared to discuss the basis for your demand in detail on the phone. You should have your settlement worksheet (Chapter 19, Section C) and all your figures and computations in front of you. Sometimes it is difficult to reach the person you need to discuss settlement with, in which case you should make your demand in writing.

Even if you do reach someone and discuss settlement, you should follow up the call with a letter to that person, setting forth your demand and any agreements you reached. I recommend sending all letters certified, return-receipt requested, and keeping copies for your records. Make sure that your letter covers all the figures in your settlement worksheet. Also make sure your demand is reasonable, but not too low, as discussed in Section C3, below. You'll want some room to negotiate the settlement figure.

You should not expect any response to your correspondence in fewer than 30 days. It generally takes this long for the insurance adjuster or attorney to receive your letter, read it, obtain some authority to counter your settlement offer, and respond. However, after about 30 days, you should follow up with another letter or a phone call. The follow-up letter should be short and have a deadline for

Sample Demand Letter

12/1/20xx

Mr. Mark Washington
Acme Insurance Co.
333 Tenth Ave.
Bartville, CA 99999

Applicant: Jean Mills
Employer: Ace Manufacturing
Date of injury: 3/12/20xx

Claim No: 12345
Appeals Board Case No: 99999

Dear Mr. Washington:

Please be advised that I have received the advisory rating of the qualified medical evaluator's report, which indicates that I have a permanent partial disability of 33.5%. This is equivalent to $20,979, as I am a maximum earner for purposes of permanent disability.

In addition, I believe that I am owed retroactive temporary disability for the period 6/7/20xx through and including 2/2/20xx. As you know, Dr. Jones, the QME, states that I was temporarily totally disabled during this period of time, and you failed to pay me temporary disability benefits. This is equivalent to 241 days at $58 per day, or $13,978. I am also entitled to a 10% penalty of $1,398 under Labor Code Section 4560.

My records reflect that you did not pay me mileage reimbursement as I requested in my letter of 5/30/20xx. This amounts to $182.35.

Dr. Jones has indicated that I will require future medical treatment, including a possible laminectomy (surgery). I believe the value of my future medical treatment to be approximately $40,000. However, for settlement purposes, I am willing to accept $30,000 to waive my right to future medical treatment and my right to petition to reopen my case.

I am therefore willing to settle my workers' compensation claim by signing a Compromise and Release in the sum of $66,537.

If I have not heard from you within 30 days, I plan to file a Declaration of Readiness to Proceed to get this matter resolved before the Workers' Compensation Appeals Board. If I do, I will, of course, ask for the entire amount I believe I am owed. I look forward to your anticipated cooperation in resolving this matter.

Sincerely,
Jean Mills
Jean Mills
[Address]
[Telephone number]

the insurance company to respond. For example: "May I please have a response to my July 3, 20xx letter? If I don't hear from you within ten days, I will have no alternative but to set this matter for hearing." If you don't get a satisfactory response, you should probably set your matter for a hearing. Don't delay, as it may take months to get on the court's calendar. (See Chapter 22, Section D, for instructions.)

3. Settlement Negotiation Tips

Here are some tips you should keep in mind when negotiating your settlement.

Expect to negotiate the amount of permanent disability. The main area of dispute between you and the insurance adjuster will probably concern the value of your permanent disability. A dispute is likely to arise if you and the insurance adjuster are relying on the rating of different medical reports. The best way to negotiate the value of your permanent disability is to consider both reports (called "splitting the reports") and agree to a figure somewhere between the two. For example, if the treating doctor's report rates at 30% disability and the QME report rates at 20% disability, a reasonable compromise may be a 25% permanent partial disability.

Use the settlement worksheet to recalculate your award. Remember that your claim is made up of many different components. Once you've agreed to a particular part of the award, such as permanent disability, plug the agreed amount into your settlement worksheet (Chapter 19, Section C) and recompute your demand.

Your first demand should be more than you expect to receive. How much of a premium over your bottom-line offer you should ask for initially depends on the situation, but 10%–25% is usually about right. Thus, if you figured out in the settlement worksheet (Chapter 19, Section C) that you are entitled to $20,000, you may want to ask for between $22,000 and $25,000 (again, depending on the circumstances). While your demand should be high, make sure it's reasonable or you'll damage your credibility.

Never negotiate with yourself. Never make two demands in a row without first having received a counteroffer from the insurance adjuster or attorney. Here's an example. You demand $15,000. The claims adjuster says, "I don't think I can get that much authority, what's the least you will take?" Don't reduce your demand! Explain that $15,000 is your demand and you would appreciate a response. The claims adjuster will either accept your demand (unlikely) or make a counterproposal.

If the insurance company raises its offer, use that figure as the new "floor" for negotiating. If you ask for $5,000 and the insurance adjuster offers $4,000, would you be willing to split the difference and accept $4,500 if the other side proposes it? If so, you have lots to learn about negotiating. Instead of accepting, you would be smarter to come back with $4,750 or $4,800. After all, the other side has already let you know they will pay $4,500, so you can probably get more.

You should not need to come down more than one or two times. In our example above, where your initial demand is $15,000, if the insurance adjuster makes a counterproposal of $10,000, you might consider making a demand at $13,000. If your $13,000 demand is supported by facts and figures, this should be the end of the negotiations and the case should settle. If the insurance company makes yet another counterproposal at, say, $11,000, you will have to reevaluate just how strong your case is and then decide whether to accept the $11,000 or, more likely, make a last counteroffer at $12,000.

Don't be intimidated. A good insurance adjuster will make it sound like you have the worst case in the world. It's the adjuster's job to try and punch as many holes in your case as possible and make you believe that you should accept the figure being offered. Most (if not all) of what the adjuster says is just "smoke" without substance. Stick to your guns unless you are presented with indisputable evidence to the contrary.

In addition, after you make a demand or a counteroffer, the insurance company may send you a letter saying that it is forwarding your file to an attorney to take over the case, or that if you do not agree to its offer, the insurance company will subpoena you or your doctor to come in for a deposition (a formal legal interview). These are normal procedures and shouldn't intimidate you. Don't be tempted to agree to their offer to avoid the legalities that may follow.

If you want any special provisions, ask for them. Some disability programs, such as Social Security, Medicare, and certain private disability policy providers will ordinarily take a credit or offset for money you receive in your workers' compensation settlement. In other words, if you receive benefits from these disability providers, your benefits may be reduced after you receive your settlement. With a compromise and release settlement, you may designate part of the settlement as future medical expenses, which won't ordinarily affect your disability benefits (although it may affect Medicare and Medi-Cal benefits). Section D2c, below, covers this issue in more detail.

4. If You Can't Settle

If you don't settle your case, it will go to trial before a judge at the Workers' Compensation Appeals Board. Here are some issues to weigh if you're considering going to trial instead of settling.

a. Advantages of Going to Trial

There are several benefits of going to trial, including:

- Your case is decided on the true value of your situation; neither side gives up something to arrive at a settlement.
- If you are entitled to future medical treatment, you will get it.
- If your condition worsens within five years from the date of injury, you may petition the court to reopen your case for a determination of new and further disability.
- It is possible that you'll get more than has been previously offered by the insurance company.

b. Disadvantages of Going to Trial

Going to trial is time-consuming and complicated. In addition:

- You will not get your money as quickly by going to trial as you would by settling.
- You could end up getting less than the amount previously offered by the insurance company.
- If the insurance company has denied your claim, there is the possibility that you could lose and get nothing.
- Payments are made weekly at the maximum rate payable on the date of your injury, rather than in the lump sum available if you settle by compromise and release. You will be entitled, however, to receive a lump sum of any past-due payments that weren't paid beginning 14 days after your last payment of temporary disability.
- You will not receive settlement money for future medical treatment, so your cash award will usually be less than a settlement by a compromise and release. (Of course, this can be fine if you may need medical treatment in the future—the insurance company will have to pay for it.)
- If you know that your case is going to trial, you may decide to get an attorney who will be entitled to a percentage (usually 12% to 15%) of your recovery. The attorney will be paid even if you end up settling without going to trial.

Chapters 21 through 24 cover the step-by-step process of preparing for and going to trial.

TIP

Don't let your attorney push you to settle. Workers' compensation lawyers don't get paid until your case settles or a Findings and Award is entered after trial. Although most workers' compensation lawyers are honest, you would be foolish if you did not pay attention to the fact that your lawyer will do a lot less work and get paid sooner if your case settles. In addition, your attorney will probably receive more money if you settle by a compromise and release. Don't feel bound to accept a settlement without question just because your lawyer recommends it. If you have done your numbers and are convinced you should get more, discuss your concerns with your attorney.

D. Review and Sign Settlement Documents

Whether you're settling by stipulations with request for award or by compromise and release, the insurance company will probably prepare the actual settlement document. There is no advantage to drafting the document yourself. It is, however, your responsibility—and to your advantage—to make sure the document correctly reflects what you've agreed to.

If you find a mistake in the settlement document, or discover a waiver or disclaimer you didn't agree to, contact the insurance company immediately and point out the error. Ask if you can handwrite the correction in the document or whether the insurance company should make the necessary changes and send you a new set of papers for signing.

If the insurance company refuses to make the change and insists on proceeding with the settlement as presented, you have two choices: You can agree to do it the insurance company's way, or you can refuse to sign the settlement papers and be ready to proceed to trial. If you want to make substantial changes, you will need to discuss them with the insurance representative to get approval. This may require some additional negotiations.

1. Reviewing Stipulations With Request for Award (Stips)

The document your insurance company provides will already have some information filled in. Here are the important issues to look for in stips. A sample is below, and a downloadable copy is available on Nolo's website. (See Chapter 29, Online Appendixes" for the link to this and other forms in this book.)

Top portion of form. At the top of the form, fill in your case number. This is the number that was assigned by the Workers' Compensation Appeals Board when you filed your Application for Adjudication of Claim (covered in Chapter 5, Section C3). The case number will be in this format: ADJ 2743660. You will note there is only a place for one case number. Don't worry: there is a place to put in your other case numbers, if you have more than one, below. For now just put in your first case number. Also fill in your Social Security number and your date of injury.

Venue Choice is based upon: In most cases you'll check the first box—venue is based upon the county where you reside. Select the three-letter Office Code and make sure it is correct. A complete list of codes is available on Nolo's website on this book's. See Chapter 29, "Online Appendixes" for the link to Appendix 1: Workers' Compensation Offices and Code Lists

Applicant. Make sure your name is spelled correctly (it should be the same name you used when you filed your claim) and that your address is correct.

Employer #1 Information: Check to make sure your employer's name and address are correct. If you know and it's not already completed, check the box that applies as to whether your employer had workers' compensation insurance, was self insured, legally uninsured, or uninsured.

Insurance Carrier Information: The insurance carrier's name and address go in here. Generally this will have been filled in by the insurance company. If there is a separate claims administrator (usually when the employer is self insured), that information will also be included.

The next two and a half pages—down to the bottom of page 4—provide blanks to enter the name of any additional employers, insurance carriers, or

Sample Stipulations With Request for Award (Page 1)

STATE OF CALIFORNIA
DIVISION OF WORKERS' COMPENSATION
WORKERS' COMPENSATION APPEALS BOARD
STIPULATIONS WITH REQUEST FOR AWARD

ADJ 888888
Case No.

Date of Injury 08/20/20xx
MM/DD/YYYY

999-99-9999
SSN (Numbers Only)

Venue Choice is based upon: (Completion of this section is required)

- [x] County of residence of employee (Labor Code section 5501.5(a)(1) or (d).)
- [ ] County where injury occurred (Labor Code section 5501.5(a)(2) or (d).)
- [ ] County of principal place of business of employee's attorney (Labor Code section 5501.5(a)(3) or (d).)

LAO
Select 3 Letter Office Code For Place/Venue of Hearing (From the Document Cover Sheet)

Applicant (Completion of this section is required)

BETTY
First Name

R
MI

WHITE
Last Name

1970 CANYON DRIVE
Address/PO Box (Please leave blank spaces between numbers, names or words)

LOS ANGELES
City

CA
State

90012
Zip Code

Employer #1 Information (Completion of this section is required)

- [x] Insured
- [ ] Self-Insured
- [ ] Legally Uninsured
- [ ] Uninsured

HOME RETAIL
Employer Name (Please leave blank spaces between numbers, names or words)

1234 FRANKLIN STREET
Employer Street Address/PO Box (Please leave blank spaces between numbers, names or words)

HOLLYWOOD
City

CA
State

90018
Zip Code

DWC-CA form 10214 (a) Page 1 (Rev 11/2008)

Sample Stipulations With Request for Award (Page 2)

Insurance Carrier Information (if known and if applicable - include even if carrier is adjusted by claims administrator)

ABC INSURANCE
Insurance Carrier Name (Please leave blank spaces between numbers, names or words)

5544 SANTA MONICA BOULEVARD
Insurance Carrier Street Address/PO Box (Please leave blank spaces between numbers, names or words)

LOS ANGELES	CA	90004
City	State	Zip Code

Claims Administrator Information (if known and if applicable)

Name (Please leave blank spaces between numbers, names or words)

Street Address/PO Box (Please leave blank spaces between numbers, names or words)

City State Zip Code

Employer #2 Information (Completion of this section is required)

☐ Insured ☐ Self-Insured ☐ Legally Uninsured ☐ Uninsured

Employer Name (Please leave blank spaces between numbers, names or words)

Employer Street Address/PO Box (Please leave blank spaces between numbers, names or words)

City State Zip Code

Insurance Carrier Information
(if known and if applicable - include even if carrier is adjusted by claims administrator)

Insurance Carrier Name (Please leave blank spaces between numbers, names or words)

Insurance Carrier Street Address/PO Box (Please leave blank spaces between numbers, names or words)

City State Zip Code

DWC-CA form 10214 (a) Page 2 (Rev 11/2008)

Sample Stipulations With Request for Award (Page 3)

Claims Administrator Information (if known and if applicable)

Name (Please leave blank spaces between numbers, names or words)

Street Address/PO Box (Please leave blank spaces between numbers, names or words)

City State Zip Code

Employer #3 Information (Completion of this section is required)

☐ Insured ☐ Self-Insured ☐ Legally Uninsured ☐ Uninsured

Employer Name (Please leave blank spaces between numbers, names or words)

Employer Street Address/PO Box (Please leave blank spaces between numbers, names or words)

City State Zip Code

Insurance Carrier Information
(if known and if applicable - include even if carrier is adjusted by claims administrator)

Insurance Carrier Name (Please leave blank spaces between numbers, names or words)

Insurance Carrier Street Address/PO Box (Please leave blank spaces between numbers, names or words)

City State Zip Code

Claims Administrator Information (if known and if applicable)

Name (Please leave blank spaces between numbers, names or words)

Street Address/PO Box (Please leave blank spaces between numbers, names or words)

City State Zip Code

DWC-CA form 10214 (a) Page 3 (Rev 11/2008)

Sample Stipulations With Request for Award (Page 4)

Employer #4 Information (Completion of this section is required)

☐ Insured ☐ Self-Insured ☐ Legally Uninsured ☐ Uninsured

Employer Name (Please leave blank spaces between numbers, names or words)

Employer Street Address/PO Box (Please leave blank spaces between numbers, names or words)

City State Zip Code

Insurance Carrier Information
(if known and if applicable - include even if carrier is adjusted by claims administrator)

Insurance Carrier Name (Please leave blank spaces between numbers, names or words)

Insurance Carrier Street Address/PO Box (Please leave blank spaces between numbers, names or words)

City State Zip Code

Claims Administrator Information (if known and if applicable)

Name (Please leave blank spaces between numbers, names or words)

Street Address/PO Box (Please leave blank spaces between numbers, names or words)

City State Zip Code

The parties hereto stipulate to the issuance of an Award and/or Order, based upon the following facts, and waive the requirements of Labor Code section 5313:

1. BETTY
Employees First Name

WHITE ,
Employees Last Name

birth date 04/19/1963 ,
MM/DD/YYYY

while employed at HOME RETAIL , CA
State

as a(n) ACCOUNTANT , iii in
Occupation Group

DWC-CA form 10214 (a) Page 4 (Rev 11/2008)

Sample Stipulations With Request for Award (Page 5)

☐ More than 4 Companion Cases

☑ Specific Injury

ADJ 888888
Case Number 1

☐ Cumulative Injury

08/28/20xx
(Start Date: MM/DD/YYYY)

11/02/20xx
(End Date: MM/DD/YYYY)

(If Specific Injury, use the start date as the specific date of injury)

Body Part 1: 300 UPPER EXT Body Part 2: 420 BACK Body Part 3: 513 KNEE

Body Part 4: 450 SHOULDER Other Body Parts: 520 ANKLE

☐ Specific Injury

Case Number 2 ☐ Cumulative Injury (Start Date: MM/DD/YYYY) (End Date: MM/DD/YYYY)
(If Specific Injury, use the start date as the specific date of injury)

Body Part 1: ______ Body Part 2: ______ Body Part 3: ______

Body Part 4: ______ Other Body Parts: ______

☐ Specific Injury

Case Number 3 ☐ Cumulative Injury (Start Date: MM/DD/YYYY) (End Date: MM/DD/YYYY)
(If Specific Injury, use the start date as the specific date of injury)

Body Part 1: ______ Body Part 2: ______ Body Part 3: ______

Body Part 4: ______ Other Body Parts: ______

☐ Specific Injury

Case Number 4 ☐ Cumulative Injury (Start Date: MM/DD/YYYY) (End Date: MM/DD/YYYY)
(If Specific Injury, use the start date as the specific date of injury)

Body Part 1: ______ Body Part 2: ______ Body Part 3: ______

Body Part 4: ______ Other Body Parts: ______

by the employer(s) and their insurer(s) listed above and who sustained injury(ies) arising out of and in the course of employment to

LOW BACK, RIGHT KNEE, RIGHT SHOULDER, RIGHT UPPER EXTREMITY

(Please list all body parts injured)

DWC-CA form 10214 (a) Page 5 (Rev 10/2008)

Sample Stipulations With Request for Award (Page 6)

2. The injury (ies) caused temporary disability for the period 08/28/20xx (MM/DD/YYYY) through 11/02/20xx (MM/DD/YYYY) for which indemnity has been paid at $ 406.00 (Indemnity Paid) per week.

2(a).The injury(ies) caused additional temporary disability for the period ________ (MM/DD/YYYY) through ________ (MM/DD/YYYY) at the rate of $ ________ (Rate) in the amount of $ ________ (Indemnity Paid)

3. The injury(ies) caused permanent disability of 25 % for which indemnity has been paid at $ 230.00 (Indemnity Paid) per week beginning 03/02/20xx (MM/DD/YYYY) in the sum of $ 23,172.50 , less credit for such payments previously made. ☐ And a life pension of $ ________ (Life Pension) per week thereafter.

Labor Code §4658(d) adjustment:

☐ Increase rate to $ ________ as of ________ (MM/DD/YYYY)

☐ Decrease rate to $ ________ as of ________ (MM/DD/YYYY)

☑ Not Applicable

An informal rating ☑ has / ☐ has not (Select one) been previously issued in case no(s) ADJ 888888 .

4.There ☑ is ☐ is Not a need for medical treatment to cure or relieve from the effects of said injury (ies).

5. Medical-legal expenses and/or liens are payable by defendant as follows:

DEFENDANTS TO PAY, ADJUST, OR LITIGATE ALL LIENS OF RECORD WITH WCAB RESERVING JURISDICTION

6. Applicant's attorney requests a fee of $ 0.00

☐ Fees to be commuted as follows:

7. Liens Against compensation are payable as follows:

DWC-CA form 10214 (a) Page 6 (Rev 10/2008)

Sample Stipulations With Request for Award (Page 7)

8.Any accrued claims for Labor Code section 5814 penalties are included in this settlement unless expressly excluded.

9.Other stipulations:

APPLICANT AGREES TO WAIVE ALL INTEREST WITHIN 25 DAYS AFTER ISSUANCE OF THE AWARD

Dated 07/10/20xx
MM/DD/YYYY

Applicant

Applicant's Attorney or Authorized Representative:

☐ Law Firm/Attorney ☐ Non Attorney Representative

First Name

Last Name

Firm Number

Law Firm name

Address/PO Box (Please leave blank spaces between numbers, names or words)

City State Zip Code

Dated
MM/DD/YYYY

Applicant Attorney Signature

DWC-CA form 10214 (a) Page 7 (Rev 11/2008)

Sample Stipulations With Request for Award (Page 8)

Defendant's Attorney or Authorized Representative:

☐ Law Firm/Attorney ☐ Non Attorney Representative

First Name

Last Name

Firm Number

Law Firm Name

Address/PO Box (Please leave blank spaces between numbers, names or words)

City State Zip Code

Dated MM/DD/YYYY

Defense Attorney Signature

Defendant's Attorney or Authorized Representative:

☐ Law Firm/Attorney ☐ Non Attorney Representative

First Name

Last Name

Firm Number

Law Firm Name

Address/PO Box (Please leave blank spaces between numbers, names or words)

City State Zip Code

Dated MM/DD/YYYY

Defense Attorney Signature

DWC-CA form 10214 (a) Page 8 (Rev 11/2008)

Sample Stipulations With Request for Award (Page 9)

Defendant's Attorney or Authorized Representative:

☐ Law Firm/Attorney ☐ Non Attorney Representative

First Name

Last Name

Firm Number

Law Firm Name

Address/PO Box (Please leave blank spaces between numbers, names or words)

City State Zip Code

Dated ____________ MM/DD/YYYY ____________ Defense Attorney Signature

Interpreter Licence Number:

Interpreter Name Interpreter License Number

DWC-CA form 10214 (a) Page 9 (Rev 11/2008)

claims administrators. You'll only use these blanks if you have more than one claim or if one claim involves more than one employer and each employer has an insurance carrier or claims administrator. For example, if you have a continuous trauma claim and over the last year of exposure there are two different insurance carriers that insured your employer, you would put in the information for the second carrier in the next blank area.

At the bottom of the fourth page is where the parties enter the facts upon which the stipulation and award is based, and waive the requirements of LC § 5313, meaning you agree that it's okay that you're not going to get a judge's decision on your case.

Check to make sure that your name, birth date, address, and employer information are correct. Also check to make sure your occupational title and group number are correct as this can affect the amount of your settlement (see Chapter 18, Section C).

At the top of page 5, there is a box to check if you have more than four companion cases (unlikely, but check it if it's true for you). Most people only have one or two case numbers. You might have a case number for a specific injury that occurred on a particular date while you were lifting something and injured your back, and at the same time you may have filed a second case number for a continuous trauma to your back from your date of hire to a particular date, alleging that the day-to-day activities of your employment injured your back.

Carefully check the date(s) of injury listed. Sometimes the insurance company will try to expand the time period or include additional dates of injury to preclude any other potential claims you may have. For example, the insurance company may list all dates you were employed or list the entire year before your injury as a continuous trauma date of injury.

> **EXAMPLE:** Assume the date of your injury was September 9, 2012. The stips lists September 9, 2012, as well as a date of injury of September 9, 2011 to September 9, 2012. Unless your injury was caused in part by a cumulative trauma that occurred over this period of time, it's best not to accept this.

Check to make sure that your case number or numbers are correctly entered and that for each case number the correct box is checked based upon whether the injury for that case number is a specific injury or a continuous trauma.

Finally, make sure that all parts of your body that were injured are listed correctly. Because stips include a provision for payment of your future medical treatment, the insurance company may try to omit a body part. Let's say that you injured your back, left leg, left shoulder, and right arm. If the insurance company omits the right arm in the settlement documents and you don't argue, the insurance company may later refuse to provide medical treatment for that part of the body. To get the correct number for each part of body you are settling on, see the Body Part List on Nolo's website (See Chapter 29, "Online Appendixes" for the link to Appendix 1: Workers' Compensation Offices and Code Lists.)

Paragraph 2. Make sure the dates are correct for the periods you were temporarily disabled. Check that the weekly indemnity amount you have been paid is accurate. If you had more than one period of temporary disability (separate times off work), there is a place for entering the amount you were paid and the periods paid for each time you were off work.

Paragraph 3. Make certain that the correct percentage of permanent disability is listed, as well as your correct indemnity rate and total sum due.

In the blank after the words "per week beginning," you should see a date of 14 days after you last received temporary disability. Make sure this date is correct, and that it is *not* the date of the settlement agreement. This is important, because you'll receive weekly payments (actually, every two weeks, but based on a weekly amount). If you last received temporary disability on September 1, 2011 and you sign the settlement documents (stips) on March 15, 2012, you are already owed 24 weeks of permanent disability payments, which you will get in a lump sum check if you haven't already received it. Insert the weekly amount you are entitled to for a life pension if your permanent disability is 70% or greater (see Chapter 19, Section C).

The next line of text, "Labor Code § 4658(d) adjustment," refers to offers of alternative or modified work. This line applies to you only if you were injured in 2005 or later and your employer has more than 50 employees.

If, within 60 days of your condition's becoming permanent and stationary, your employer offers you modified or alternative work, your permanent disability payments will be decreased by 15%. If your employer doesn't offer you modified or alternative work, your permanent disability payments will be increased by 15%. (For more information, see Chapter 13, Section E3.)

If this applies to you, fill in the increased or decreased rate and the date that is 60 days from the date you were designated permanent and stationary.

> **EXAMPLE 1:** Suzanne, a teacher at a Montessori preschool, injures her knees from constantly kneeling down to help her students. She is designated permanent and stationary in her doctor's report dated March 2, 2012, with a 15% permanent disability, which is payable at $230 per week. Her employer does not offer her any type of modified or alternative work by May 2, 2012, so her payments increase by 15% ($34.50) on May 2, 2012. Her ongoing permanent disability payments are now $264.50.

> **EXAMPLE 2:** Paul injures his knees fighting wildfires, and is designated permanent and stationary in his doctor's report dated August 17, 2011, with a 15% permanent disability, which is payable at $230 per week. On September 1, 2011, Paul's employer offers Paul an office job that will not require field work, and Paul accepts the job. Paul's payments decrease by 15% ($34.50). His ongoing permanent disability payments are now $195.50.

Paragraph 4. This paragraph is extremely important. Assuming there is a possibility you may need future medical treatment, it must be reflected here. Unless all of the medical reports relied upon to arrive at your settlement state that you are fully recovered, you will want the paragraph to read, "There *is* need for medical treatment ...."

CAUTION

Beware of other statements on medical treatment. If you sign an agreement stating that there is no need for any future medical treatment, you are out of luck if your injury flares up (although you may still reopen your case if your condition worsens and you have a "new and further disability").

Paragraph 5. This paragraph addresses the liens for medical-legal evaluation reports written by QMEs or AMEs (see Chapter 10), if there are any. See the discussion regarding Paragraph 7, below, and follow the precautions covered there, as they apply to medical-legal liens as well. Paragraph 5 directs the insurance carrier to pay for any liens filed by treating doctors, hospitals, clinics, chiropractors, physical therapists, or other medical professionals for treatment they provided to you without payment. Include the following sentence, which will allow any disputes over liens to be settled by the WCAB in the future: "Defendants to pay, adjust, or litigate all liens of record with WCAB reserving jurisdiction." You should also ask the judge for a printout of "lien claimants of record" that will list all the doctors, hospitals, and clinics that are seeking payment from the insurance company for their services. Compare this list with the doctors and other providers you know you have seen. If there are any missing, contact them and find out whether they have been paid—and if they haven't, request that they file a lien with the WCAB so that they can get paid by the insurance company. This will keep you from having providers come looking for payment from you several years down the road.

If there are outstanding medical bills for which no liens have been filed, you should do one of the following:

- Contact those doctors or companies and request that they file a lien before you sign the stips. Then negotiate with the insurance company to agree to pay the bills by specifically listing them in the stips.
- Get the insurance company to include language that it will pay or negotiate any outstanding bills that are a result of your injury. (Most insurance companies probably won't agree to this, because there's no way to know what might be outstanding.)

CAUTION

Outstanding bills may be your responsibility. If you do not make these specific arrangements for the insurance company to agree to be responsible for the bills, any bills that are outstanding after you sign the stips will be your responsibility, and the creditor could sue you in civil court for the money.

Paragraph 6. If you have a lawyer, the lawyer will list the attorney fee here. This must be in the percentage range listed on the Attorney Fee Disclosure Statement you signed—usually between 12% and 15%. The attorney may choose to list "reasonable fees," to be approved by the appeals board, and may check the box "Fees to be commuted as follows:" and insert something similar to this: "Off the far end of the award." This means that if your stipulated settlement would be payable over 350 weeks, than the attorney fees are paid from the back (farthest away) end of your award, and the number of weeks you will get paid is reduced accordingly.

Paragraph 7. This paragraph is extremely important. Liens against compensation are any liens that will be paid out of your settlement proceeds rather than by the insurance company. For example, if the district attorney has filed a child support lien in your workers' compensation case, then that lien amount will be listed here and the amount stated will be deducted from your settlement before you get your money. If you're not aware of any such liens but there's something in this box, peruse it with care.

CAUTION

The SDI lien. If you received SDI (state disability insurance) payments from the EDD for any periods of time that you were entitled to receive permanent disability payments, the EDD can have that amount deducted from your final permanent disability award. (LC § 4904.) This is usually a problem only if your case goes to trial and the judge determines that you received SDI benefits after you were permanent and stationary. If your case settles, however, make sure the insurance company agrees to be responsible for the SDI lien.

You may also request that the following language be included in Paragraph 7: "The company agrees to hold the applicant harmless therefrom." This means that if the insurance company can't successfully resolve the outstanding lien with the creditor, and the creditor attempts to sue you in civil court, the insurance company will agree to defend you. Many insurance adjusters won't agree to add this language, but it's worth asking. If yours refuses, press the issue but don't blow your settlement over the company's refusal to do so.

Paragraph 8. This statement reminds you that you are settling any penalty issues even if they have not been written into the document and you have not received any money for them. Therefore, if you are claiming penalties under LC § 5814 (see Chapter 19, Section C9), make sure that in Paragraph 9, "Other stipulations," you reserve your right to pursue these penalties, or set forth the amount the insurance company has agreed to pay you to resolve the issue.

Paragraph 9. Any miscellaneous agreements between you and the company can, and usually should, be set out here. Here are some examples:

- Any agreement you have with the insurance company regarding waiving or declining vocational rehabilitation benefits should be explained in detail. Be sure to include any amount of money the insurance company has agreed to pay you, if appropriate.
- If you have agreed to accept cash to resolve a past-due temporary disability issue, you and the insurance company might set forth your understanding that "retroactive temporary disability in the sum of [amount] is to be paid outside of this agreement within 25 days of approval."
- Include any agreement that the insurance company will reimburse you for your out-of-pocket mileage or medical expenses. This could include prescription as well as nonprescription drugs you paid for.

Signature. You must sign the Stipulations with Request for Award. There is no need to have it witnessed or notarized. Insert the date you signed the document.

Applicant's Attorney or Authorized Representative. If you have an attorney this is where the attorney's identifying information and signature will go.

Defendant's Attorney or Authorized Representative. This is where the defense attorney who represented the insurance company will include identifying information and sign the document. Note that there is room for up to three different defense attorneys or firms.

Last, if you've used a language interpreter, that person will enter a name and license number.

Once you sign the document, make a copy for your records and send the original to the insurance company. The stips must be approved by a Workers' Compensation Appeals judge, and a document entitled "Award" must be signed by the judge.

If the judge does not believe the agreement adequately compensates you, or finds other problems, the judge will point them out to you and ask you if you still want to proceed with the settlement. (See Section E, below, for more on the hearing to approve your settlement.)

2. Reviewing a Compromise and Release (C&R)

It's extremely important to make sure all of the information in the Compromise and Release (C&R) document is correct. Understand that by signing this settlement document, you make a complete and final settlement of your workers' compensation claim. In other words, when you settle by C&R, you will no longer have any right to have your medical treatment paid by the insurance company, nor will you have the right to file a petition to reopen your case. What you agree to receive in the C&R will be the only money you'll get in your case.

Following is a sample Compromise and Release form; there's a downloadable copy on Nolo's website. (See Chapter 29, "Online Appendixes" for the link to this and other forms in this book.) In this sample, we've included only the pages on which there's information filled in; the blank form in the appendix has all nine pages.

Most likely, you'll receive this from the insurance company with much of the information already filled in. Here are the important issues to look for.

Top Portion of Form. At the top of the form, fill in your case number or numbers if they are not already there. Your case number was assigned by the Workers' Compensation Appeals Board when you filed your Application for Adjudication of Claim (covered in Chapter 5, Section C3). This number will be in this format: ADJ 274366. You will see that there are lines for up to five case numbers. For each case (claim or date of injury), you have to put in the corresponding case number. If you have only one date of injury, just put the one case number on the line "Case Number 1." Also fill in your Social Security number.

Venue Choice is based upon. Usually you'll check the first box, stating that you're filing in your county of your residence. Fill in the three letter Office Code for the Workers Compensation Appeals Board where your case was filed. A list of the boards and their office codes can be found on Nolo's website. (See

Chapter 29, "Online Appendixes" for the link to Appendix 1: Workers' Compensation Offices and Code Lists.)

Applicant: If they're not already there, fill in your name and address.

Employer Information: If they're not already there, fill in your employer's name and address.

Applicant Attorney or Authorized Representative: If you have an attorney, the attorney's office will fill out this entire form for you, including this information. If you don't have an attorney, leave this blank.

Defendant's Attorney or Authorized Representative: This is where the name and contact information for the attorney representing the insurance company go. The insurance company will provide all this information.

Insurance Carrier Information: Once again, the insurance company will fill in the information.

Claims Administrator Information: If your insurance company or employer had a third-party administrator, someone who managed the claim for them, they will fill in the name and address of that party here.

Paragraph 1. Fill in or verify your date of birth and your occupation. Make certain the correct case number is listed for Case Number 1. This is a number that is preceded by the letters ADJ. Check the box that corresponds to your type of injury, specific or continuous trauma. Make sure the dates for the start and end of your injury are correct—sometimes the insurance company will try to include additional dates of injury to preclude any other potential claims you may have. For example, the insurance company may list all dates you were employed or list the entire year before your injury as a continuous trauma date of injury.

> **EXAMPLE:** Assume the date of your injury was September 9, 2012. The C&R lists September 9, 2012, as well as a date of injury of September 9, 2011 to September 9, 2012. Unless your injury was caused in part by a cumulative trauma that occurred over this period of time, it's best not to accept this.

If your injury was a cumulative injury, put the date it began on the "start date" and the date it ended (if any) on the "end date" line.

After the date of injury, make sure the insurance company has listed only the parts of your body that you have injured. There are spaces for up to four parts of the body and then a space to include additional body parts if you've injured more than four. Along with the body parts listed, you must include the corresponding number for each one; these are available on Nolo's website. (See Chapter 29, "Online Appendixes" for the link to Appendix 1: Workers' Compensation Offices and Code Lists.) For example, if you injured your back, the form should include under "Body Part 1:" the words "Back 420."

Some companies try to list body parts that you did not claim as injured, to preclude your filing for injuries to these body parts later. For example, if you only claimed you injured your right leg, don't allow the insurance company to add "back." If at a later date you want to file a claim for a back injury, you might have waived your right to do so.

Next, fill in the address where the injury occurred.

If you have more than one date of injury, you must list each date of injury and the parts of your body injured on those dates on separate lines. That is why there are spaces for up to five different case numbers on the form.

Paragraph 2. This is a statement that requires no input by you. It tells you that you are settling all aspects of your workers' compensation claim, including any and all injuries that resulted from your injuries or that may arise in the future as a result your injuries. In other words, if you later learn of a new body part that was injured on the same date(s) of injury, you can't file a new claim. It further states that the settlement does not apply to any claims outside the jurisdiction of the Workers' Compensation Appeals Board.

Paragraph 3. This is a statement that requires no input by you. It says that the settlement is limited to the body parts injured and the conditions listed in Paragraph 1 and for the dates of injury in Paragraph 1.

Sample Compromise and Release (Page 1)

STATE OF CALIFORNIA
DIVISION OF WORKERS' COMPENSATION
WORKERS' COMPENSATION APPEALS BOARD
COMPROMISE AND RELEASE

ADJ 777777
Case Number 1

Case Number 4

ADJ 777778
Case Number 2

Case Number 5

Case Number 3

999-99-9999
SSN (Numbers Only)

Venue Choice is based upon: (Completion of this section is required)

☑ Residence of employee (Labor Code section 5501.5(a)(1))

☐ Location where injury occurred (Labor Code section 5501.5(a)(2))

☐ Principal address of employee's attorney (Labor Code section 5501.5(a)(3))

LAO
Select 3 Letter Office Code For Place/Venue of Hearing (From Document Cover Sheet)

Employee(Completion of this section is required)

BETTY
First Name

R
MI

WHITE
Last Name

1970 CANYON DRIVE
Address/PO Box (Please leave blank spaces between numbers, names or words)

LOS ANGELES
City

CA
State

90012
Zip Code

Employer Information (Completion of this section is required)

☑ Insured ☐ Self-Insured ☐ Legally Uninsured ☐ Uninsured

HOME RETAIL
Employer Name (Please leave blank spaces between numbers, names or words)

1234 FRANKLIN STREET
Employer Street Address/PO Box (Please leave blank spaces between numbers, names or words)

HOLLYWOOD
City

CA
State

90018
Zip Code

DWC-CA form 10214 (c) (Rev. 10/2008) (Page 1 of 9)

Sample Compromise and Release (Page 2)

Applicant's Attorney or Authorized Representative:

☐ Law Firm/Attorney ☐ Non Attorney Representative

First Name

Last Name

Law Firm Number

Law Firm Name

Address/PO Box (Please leave blank spaces between numbers, names or words)

City | State | Zip Code

Defendant's Attorney or Authorized Representative:

☑ Law Firm/Attorney ☐ Non Attorney Representative

MARY
First Name

DEROSA
Last Name

4444
Law Firm Number

BIX & WORTH
Law Firm Name

4000 SANTA MONICA BOULEVARD
Address/PO Box (Please leave blank spaces between numbers, names or words)

LOS ANGELES | CA | 90003
City | State | Zip Code

Insurance Carrier Information (if known and if applicable - include even if carrier is adjusted by claims administrator)

ABC INSURANCE
Insurance Carrier Name (Please leave blank spaces between numbers, names or words)

5544 SANTA MONICA BOULEVARD
Insurance Carrier Street Address/PO Box (Please leave blank spaces between numbers, names or words)

LOS ANGELES | CA | 90004
City | State | Zip Code

DWC-CA form 10214 (c) (Rev. 11/2008) (Page 2 of 9)

Sample Compromise and Release (Page 3)

Claims Administrator Information (if known and if applicable)

Name (Please leave blank spaces between numbers, names or words)

Street Address/PO Box (Please leave blank spaces between numbers, names or words)

City State Zip Code

IT IS CLAIMED THAT:

1. The injured employee, born 04/19/1963 (DATE OF BIRTH: MM/DD/YYYY), alleges that while employed as a(n)

ACCOUNTANT (OCCUPATION AT THE TIME OF INJURY), sustained injury arising out of and in the course of employment at the locations and during the dates listed below:

(State with specificity the date(s) of injury(ies) and what part(s) of body, conditions or systems are being settled.)

☑ Specific Injury

ADJ 888888
Case Number 1

☐ Cumulative Injury

08/28/20xx (Start Date: MM/DD/YYYY) 08/28/20xx (End Date: MM/DD/YYYY)

(If Specific Injury, use the start date as the specific date of injury)

Body Part 1: 300 UPPER EXT Body Part 2: 420 BACK Body Part 3: 450 SHOULDER

Body Part 4: 520 ANKLE Other Body Parts: 513 KNEE

The injury occurred at 2500 WILSHIRE BOULEVARD
(Street Address/PO Box - Please leave blank spaces between numbers, names or words)

SANTA MONICA (City), CA (State) 90018 (Zip Code).

Body parts, conditions and systems may not be incorporated by reference to medical reports.

DWC-CA form 10214 (c) (Rev. 10/2008) (Page 3 of 9)

Sample Compromise and Release (Page 4)

☐ Specific Injury

ADJ777778
Case Number 2

☑ Cumulative Injury

08/20/20xx (Start Date: MM/DD/YYYY) 12/30/20xx (End Date: MM/DD/YYYY)
(If Specific Injury, use the start date as the specific date of injury)

Body Part 1: 300 UPPER EXT Body Part 2: 320 WRIST Body Part 3: ______

Body Part 4: ______ Other Body Parts: ______

The injury occurred at 2500 WILSHIRE BLVD.
(Street Address/PO Box - Please leave blank spaces between numbers, names or words)

SANTA MONICA (City), CA (State) 90018 (Zip Code).

Body parts, conditions and systems may not be incorporated by reference to medical reports.

☐ Specific Injury

______
Case Number 3

☐ Cumulative Injury

______ (Start Date: MM/DD/YYYY) ______ (End Date: MM/DD/YYYY)
(If Specific Injury, use the start date as the specific date of injury)

Body Part 1: ______ Body Part 2: ______ Body Part 3: ______

Body Part 2: ______ Other Body Parts: ______

The injury occurred at ______
(Street Address/PO Box - Please leave blank spaces between numbers, names or words)

______ City, ______ State ______ Zip Code.

Body parts, conditions and systems may not be incorporated by reference to medical reports.

☐ Specific Injury

______
Case Number 4

☐ Cumulative Injury

______ (Start Date: MM/DD/YYYY) ______ (End Date: MM/DD/YYYY)
(If Specific Injury, use the start date as the specific date of injury)

Body Part 1: ______ Body Part 2: ______ Body Part 3: ______

Body Part 4: ______ Other Body Parts: ______

The injury occurred at ______
(Street Address/PO Box - Please leave blank spaces between numbers, names or words)

______ City, ______ State ______ Zip Code.

Body parts, conditions and systems may not be incorporated by reference to medical reports.

DWC-CA form 10214 (c) (Rev. 10/2008) (Page 4 of 9)

Sample Compromise and Release (Page 5)

☐ Specific Injury

Case Number 5 ☐ Cumulative Injury ____ (Start Date: MM/DD/YYYY) ____ (End Date: MM/DD/YYYY)

(If Specific Injury, use the start date as the specific date of injury)

Body Part 1: ____ Body Part 2: ____ Body Part 3: ____

Body Part 4: ____ Other Body Parts: ____

The injury occurred at ____
(Street Address/PO Box - Please leave blank spaces between numbers, names or words)

____ City, ____ State ____ Zip Code.

Body parts, conditions and systems may not be incorporated by reference to medical reports.

2. Upon approval of this compromise agreement by the Workers' Compensation Appeals Board or a workers' compensation administrative law judge and payment in accordance with the provisions hereof, the employee releases and forever discharges the above-named employer(s) and insurance carrier(s) from all claims and causes of action, whether now known or ascertained or which may hereafter arise or develop as a result of the above-referenced injury(ies), including any and all liability of the employer(s) and the insurance carrier(s) and each of them to the dependents, heirs, executors, representatives, administrators or assigns of the employee. Execution of this form has no effect on claims that are not within the scope of the workers' compensation law or claims that are not subject to the exclusivity provisions of the workers' compensation law, unless otherwise expressly stated.

3. This agreement is limited to settlement of the body parts, conditions, or systems and for the dates of injury set forth in Paragraph No. 1 and further explained in Paragraph No. 9 despite any language to the contrary elsewhere in this document or any addendum.

4. Unless otherwise expressly stated, approval of this agreement RELEASES ANY AND ALL CLAIMS OF APPLICANT'S DEPENDENTS TO DEATH BENEFITS RELATING TO THE INJURY OR INJURIES COVERED BY THIS COMPROMISE AGREEMENT. The parties have considered the release of these benefits in arriving at the sum in Paragraph 7. Any addendum duplicating this language pursuant to Sumner v WCAB (1983) 48 CCC 369 is unnecessary and shall not be attached.

5. Unless otherwise expressly ordered by the Workers' Compensation Appeals Board or a workers' compensation administrative law judge, approval of this agreement does not release any claim applicant may have for vocational rehabilitation benefits or supplemental job displacement benefits.

6. The parties represent that the following facts are true: (If facts are disputed, state what each party contends under Paragraph No. 9.)

EARNINGS AT TIME OF INJURY $ 800.00

TEMPORARY DISABILITY INDEMNITY PAID 32,200.19 Weekly Rate $ 533.33

Period(s) Paid 01/02/20xx (Start Date: MM/DD/YYYY) 12/10/20xx (End Date: MM/DD/YYYY)

PERMANENT DISABILITY INDEMNITY PAID 5,040.00 Weekly Rate $ 230.00

Period(s) Paid 11/11/20xx (Start Date: MM/DD/YYYY) End date 07/09/20xx (End Date: MM/DD/YYYY)

TOTAL MEDICAL BILLS PAID $ 32,220.00 Total Unpaid Medical Expense to be Paid By: DEFENDANT

Unless otherwise specified herein, the employer will pay no medical expenses incurred after approval of this agreement.

DWC-CA form 10214 (c) (Rev. 10/2008) (Page 5 of 9)

Sample Compromise and Release (Page 6)

7. The parties agree to settle the above claim(s) on account of the injury(ies) by the payment of the SUM OF

$ 175,355.00
Settlement Amount

The following amounts are to be deducted from the settlement amount:

$ 5,040.00 for permanent disability advances through 07/09/20xx subject to proof

$ 3,000.00 for temporary disability indemnity overpayment, if any.

$ 105,355.00 payable to APPLICANT TO PLACE IN MSA TRUST ACCO

$ ______ payable to ACCOUNT

$ ______ payable to ______

$ ______ payable to ______

$ ______ requested as applicant's attorney's fee.

LEAVING A BALANCE OF $ 61,960.00, after deducting the amounts set forth above and less further permanent disability advances made after the date set forth above. Interest under Labor Code section 5800 is included if the sums set forth herein are paid within 30 days after the date of approval of this agreement.

8. Liens not mentioned in Paragraph No. 7 are to be disposed of as follows (Attach an addendum if necessary):

DEFENDANTS TO PAY, ADJUST, OR LITIGATE ALL LIENS OF RECORD WITH JURISDICTION RESERVED TO WCAB.

Sample Compromise and Release (Page 7)

9. The parties wish to settle these matters to avoid the costs, hazards and delays of further litigation, and agree that a serious dispute exists as to the following issues (initial only those that apply). ONLY ISSUES INITIALED BY APPLICANT AND HIS/HER REPRESENTATIVE AND DEFENDANTS, REPRESENTATIVES ARE INCLUDED WITHIN THIS SETTLEMENT.

Applicant	Defendant	
BW		earnings
BW		temporary disability
BW		jurisdiction
BW		apportionment
BW		employment
BW		injury AOE/COE
		serious and willful misconduct
		discrimination (Labor Code §132a)
		statute of limitations
BW		future medical treatment
		other ______
BW		permanent disability ______
BW		self-procured medical treatment, except as provided in Paragraph 7
		vocational rehabilitation benefits/supplemental job displacement benefits

COMMENTS:

Any accrued claims for Labor Code section 5814 penalties are included in this settlement unless expressly excluded.

10. It is agreed by all parties hereto that the filing of this document is the filing of an application, and that the workers' compensation administrative law judge may in its discretion set the matter for hearing as a regular application, reserving to the parties the right to put in issue any of the facts admitted herein and that if hearing is held with this document used as an application, the defendants shall have available to them all defenses that were available as of the date of filing of this document, and that the workers' compensation administrative law judge may thereafter either approve this Compromise and Release or disapprove it and issue Findings and Award after hearing has been held and the matter regularly submitted for decision.

Sample Compromise and Release (Page 8)

11. WARNING TO EMPLOYEE: SETTLEMENT OF YOUR WORKERS' COMPENSATION CLAIM BY COMPROMISE AND RELEASE MAY AFFECT OTHER BENEFITS YOU ARE RECEIVING TO WHICH YOU BECOME ENTITLED TO RECEIVE IN THE FUTURE FROM SOURCES OTHER THAN WORKERS' COMPENSATION, INCLUDING BUT NOT LIMITED TO SOCIAL SECURITY, MEDICARE AND LONG-TERM DISABILITY BENEFITS.

THE APPLICANT'S (EMPLOYEE'S) SIGNATURE MUST BE ATTESTED TO BY TWO DISINTERESTED PERSONS OR ACKNOWLEDGED BEFORE A NOTARY PUBLIC

By signing this agreement, applicant (employee) acknowledges that he/she has read and understands this agreement and has had any questions he/she may have had about this agreement answered to his/her satisfaction.

Witness the signature hereof this ________ day of ______________, _______________ at ______________________

Timothy Lindsey	*7/5/20xx*	*Betty White*	*7/5/20xx*
Witness 1	(Date)	Applicant (Employee)	(Date)
Randi Winters	*7/5/20xx*	*Mary DeRosa*	*7/5/20xx*
Witness 2	(Date)	Attorney for Applicant	(Date)
Andrea Dawson	*7/5/20xx*		
Interpreter	(Date)	Attorney for Defendant	(Date)
		Attorney for Defendant	(Date)
		Attorney for Defendant	(Date)
		Attorney for Defendant	(Date)

DWC-CA form 10214 (c) (Rev.10/2008) (Page 8 of 9)

Paragraph 4. This is a standard clause that states that you are waiving any right that your dependents may have to recover death benefits in the event that you die as a result of this injury. In the vast majority of cases, this is fine, because the injury isn't that serious.

If, however, your injury is life-threatening (you may die within 240 weeks of the injury date), you should not agree to this paragraph unless the insurance company pays you for doing so. How much extra money you can get will depend upon how likely it is that you will die, and how soon you may die, and whether or not you have any dependents. Settling your death claim rights in a C&R will allow you, rather than your dependents, to get the money, if that's what you want.

If you don't waive your death benefits by agreeing to this paragraph, and you should die as a result of your injury, your dependents may be entitled to recover death benefits. Especially if you have dependents under the age of 18, this can entail a significant amount of money. (Chapter 15 explains what you or your dependents would be entitled to.) If there is any possibility that you could die as a result of your industrial injury, you should seriously consider seeing a workers' compensation attorney.

Paragraph 5. This standard paragraph states that unless otherwise stated in the C&R, you are not waiving any rights you may have to supplemental job displacement benefits (for more information, see Chapter 14).

Paragraph 6. Carefully check this paragraph for accuracy. If you find any inaccuracies, you may contact the insurance company to make the correction or you may handwrite or type in the words "in dispute" in the appropriate place.

Make sure your correct average weekly wage is filled in on the line titled "EARNINGS AT TIME OF INJURY." This figure will determine how much permanent disability you qualify for (see Chapter 13, Section E). If you don't agree with the figure the insurance company inserted, contact the claims adjuster at the insurance company and ask for the correct amount to be inserted. If the claims adjuster won't agree, this should read "in dispute." The same goes for your last day off work due to the injury.

After "TEMPORARY DISABILITY INDEMNITY PAID," review the insurance company's figures on the amount of temporary disability indemnity paid to you, the weekly temporary disability rate, and the periods you were paid for. If you disagree with any of the figures or dates, you can request that "in dispute" be inserted. Any amounts listed for temporary disability will not be deducted from your settlement.

On the line titled "PERMANENT DISABILITY INDEMNITY PAID," the insurance company should have inserted the amount it has paid you in permanent disability advances, the weekly permanent disability rate, and the periods for which you were paid. Because all permanent disability advances will be deducted from the amount listed in Paragraph 7, make sure these figures and dates are correct. To allow for the possibility that the total is wrong and to allow for later adjustments if a different amount is found to be correct, write or type in "subject to proof" after the amount.

If you don't know how much you've received. You can ask the insurance company for a computer printout of permanent disability advances (dates and amounts) or copies of canceled checks, and they must provide it to you within 20 days of the date of your request. You should always make such request in writing.

The next section of Paragraph 6 is "TOTAL MEDICAL BILLS PAID." Make sure that the insurance company has inserted the amount it has paid for hospital and medical bills on your behalf. If you disagree with the figure, you can have "in dispute" handwritten or typed in. Amounts listed for medical treatment paid will not be deducted from your settlement.

After the phrase "Total Unpaid Medical Expense to Be Paid By," you will want to make sure that "Defendant" is inserted. If the insurance company will not agree to this, ask to speak to the judge.

Finally, if there is a dispute about any of the amounts or figures under Paragraph 6, you must state your contentions under Paragraph 9 under "Comments."

Paragraph 7. Make certain that the correct amount that you are settling your claim for is listed on the first line: "SUM OF $______." Under "The following amounts are to be deducted from the settlement amount," the insurance company will type in any amounts that it will take as a credit or deduction from the settlement amount. This will include any known amounts for money already advanced to you based on your permanent disability (also set forth in Paragraph 6 under "PERMANENT DISABILITY INDEMNITY PAID"). In addition, sometimes the insurance company will be entitled to take a credit for overpayment of temporary disability indemnity. That is set forth on the second line of Paragraph 7. For example, if the doctor's report says your condition reached "maximal medical improvement" (see Chapter 9, Section E) on February 2, 2012, and the insurance company paid you temporary total disability payments through May 2, 2012, the insurance company could take credit for the three months of temporary total disability paid to you in error. The last deduction is for your attorney fee, if you have an attorney; the fee will be listed and deducted from your settlement amount.

Finally, under the section that begins "LEAVING A BALANCE OF __________," the insurance company will type in the amount you will receive after deducting credit for any permanent disability advances, any temporary disability indemnity overpayment, any attorney fee, or any other deductions agreed upon. This is the amount of "new money" you will receive. Make sure this is the correct amount.

Paragraph 8. This paragraph is extremely important. It lists all of the outstanding liens (debts) the insurance company agrees to pay as part of the settlement, other than attorney fees and amounts for unpaid medical and hospital bills listed in Paragraph 7.

Make sure no doctor, medical facility, or anyone else who has provided you with medical treatment, tests, examinations and reports, or other services to help prove your case has been overlooked.

Make sure the following language is inserted in the box: "DEFENDANT SHALL PAY, ADJUST, OR LITIGATE ALL LIENS OF RECORD WITH JURISDICTION RESERVED TO THE WCAB." This will ensure that the insurance company will pay all legitimate medical legal bills, whether listed or not.

Even if the insurance company claims it paid a particular lien claimant, it is best to list it anyway, with the provision that "jurisdiction is reserved to the appeals board to resolve any disputes."

If there are outstanding medical bills for which no liens have been filed, you should do one of the following:

- Contact those doctors or companies and request that they file a lien before you sign the C&R. Then negotiate with the insurance company to agree to pay the bills by specifically listing them in the C&R.
- Get the insurance company to include language that it will pay or negotiate any outstanding bills that are a result of your injury. (Most insurance companies probably won't agree to this because there's no way to know what might be outstanding.)

CAUTION

Outstanding bills may be your responsibility. If you do not make these specific arrangements for the insurance company to agree to be responsible for the bills, any bills that are outstanding after you sign the C&R will be your responsibility, and the creditor could sue you in civil court for the money.

Make sure that the Employment Development Department (EDD) is listed here if it filed a lien in your case for reimbursement for money paid to you for disability periods that should have been the responsibility of the workers' compensation insurance company.

CAUTION

The SDI lien. If you received SDI (state disability insurance) payments from the EDD for any periods of time that you were entitled to receive permanent disability payments, the EDD can have that amount deducted from your final permanent disability award. (LC § 4904.) This is usually a problem only if your case goes to trial and the judge determines that you received SDI benefits after you were permanent and stationary. If your case settles, however, make sure the insurance company agrees to be responsible for the SDI lien.

You may request that the following language be included in Paragraph 8: "Defendant agrees to hold the applicant harmless therefrom." This means that if the insurance company can't successfully resolve the outstanding lien with the creditor and the creditor attempts to sue you in civil court, the insurance company will defend you. Many insurance adjusters won't agree to add this language, but it's worth asking. If yours refuses, press the issue but don't blow your settlement over the company's refusal to do so.

Paragraph 9. Both you and the representative for the insurance company must initial each of the issues being settled by compromise and release. The insurance company will usually do this first and then have you initial on the same line they did. IF YOU ARE NOT SETTLING A PARTICULAR ISSUE, DO NOT PLACE YOUR INITIAL NEXT TO THAT ISSUE! For example, if you filed a petition claiming that the employer discriminated against you for filing a workers' comp claim (under LC § 132(a)—see Chapter 16, Section C), and you did not include any money in the settlement to resolve that claim but you wish to pursue it, do not initial by the line "discrimination (Labor Code § 132a)," as your initials indicate you are giving up that claim.

In the "Comments" section of paragraph 9, you can list anything you want to clarify or concerns you have. The insurance company will usually put the basis of the calculation of your permanent disability here. For example, the box may say something like "Permanent disability of 30% is based upon the report of Dr. Smith dated 12/5/2012." If you have comments you want to add, put in the words "Applicant's comments:" followed by your comments, so the judge will know who has made which comments.

Paragraph 10: This requires no input from you. It simply states that in the event you never actually filed an application for adjudication of claim, the C&R constitutes an application for jurisdictional purposes.

Paragraph 11: This requires no input from you. It is a warning to you that you are settling out all your benefits by signing this document.

Due to the limited amount of space on the form for comments, the insurance company may refer to attached addenda in the "Comments" section of Paragraph 9. The following are samples of the most common addenda you'll likely run into. Although each C&R may be arranged a little differently, most will cover the issues presented below, although not necessarily in the same order.

CAUTION

Addenda should be prohibited. The addenda discussed below are no longer supposed to be allowed by the Worker's Compensation Appeals Board, but some judges still allow them, and that's why they're addressed here in detail. If the insurance company tries to include an addendum, ask the judge to remove it. Addenda rarely benefit the worker.

a. Addendum A (Waivers and Agreements)

This addendum sets forth the various waivers and miscellaneous agreements between the parties.

Paragraph 1 explains the reasons you and the defendants have decided to settle your case.

Paragraph 2 is called a "*Sumner* waiver" in workers' compensation jargon. It is standard in almost all workers' compensation settlements and is always referred to by its name. The *Sumner* waiver waives your dependents' right to any workers' compensation death benefits in the event you

ADDENDUM "A"

1. A bona fide dispute exists between the parties as to injury, nature, extent, and duration of permanent disability, occupation, employment, need for future medical treatment, liability for self-procured medical treatment, medical/legal costs, earnings, temporary disability, rehabilitation, apportionment, transportation expenses, penalties, and all other issues. All parties desire to avoid the hazards and delays of litigation. Applicant wishes to receive a lump sum settlement and to control all future medical care; defendants by this settlement are buying their peace.

2. The parties have taken into consideration the release of any and all claims of applicant's dependents to death benefits relating to the injury covered by this Compromise and Release. The parties have considered the release of these benefits in arriving at the amount of this Compromise and Release, and the attention of the judge is directed to this fact.

3. In the event applicant elects to participate in vocational rehabilitation at some future date and is found to be a qualified injured worker, applicant expressly waives any potential claims for ordinary compensation benefits and medical treatment for any injury that may be sustained while participating in vocational rehabilitation in compliance with *Rogers vs. WCAB,* 168 Cal.App.3rd (1985), *Carter vs. County of L.A.,* 51 CCC 255 (1985), *Weatherspoon vs. St. Ferdinand's School,* 51 CCC 255 (1985), and *Constancio vs. L.A. County,* 51 CCC 255 (1986).

4. The only lien claims in existence are stated in this agreement. The applicant guarantees and warrants there are no other or further lien claims and thereby agrees to hold defendants harmless from any claims or cause of action commenced or presented by any lien claimants other than those accounted for herein.

5. This agreement represents full and final settlement of any liability on account of [*employer*] and the carrier [*insurance company*] with respect to any and all employment at [*employer*] during any period when [*insurance company*] was the workers' compensation insurance carrier, and further is based upon any cumulative trauma or specific injuries that may have occurred during such employment at [*employer*].

6. Applicant agrees that this release will apply to all unknown and unanticipated injuries and damages resulting from such accident, and all rights under § 1542 of the Civil Code of California are hereby expressly waived. Applicant agrees that this release extends and covers employees of the defendants. This clause applies only to this claim.

By: ______________________________

Applicant

should die as a result of your industrial injury. This is really just a restatement of Paragraph 4 of the main body of the C&R. If there is any possibility that your injury may result in your death (within 240 weeks from the date of injury), you should not allow a *Sumner* waiver. You should also seek the advice of an attorney.

Paragraph 3 of addendum A is what is referred to in workers' compensation jargon as a "*Rogers* waiver" or a "*Carter* waiver." We'll refer to it as a *Rogers* waiver. A *Rogers* waiver is only significant if you are going to participate in vocational rehabilitation training. This waiver states that if you are injured or need treatment while participating in your vocational rehabilitation plan, you will not be able to file a workers' compensation claim for a new injury.

If you are participating in vocational rehabilitation, consider the likelihood of getting injured and decide whether or not you want to agree to a *Rogers* waiver. If you don't sign the waiver and you suffer a new injury while participating in vocational rehabilitation, that injury is covered by workers' compensation; if you sign a *Rogers* waiver, it isn't. The insurance company will probably want a *Rogers* waiver to settle your case if you are still participating in vocational rehabilitation. But this is a matter for negotiation. Workers' compensation lawyers consider a *Rogers* waiver to be worth some money (up to a couple of thousand dollars), depending upon how badly the insurance company wants to settle. On the other hand, the insurance company may refuse to settle until you complete vocational rehabilitation or sign a *Rogers* waiver. This is where negotiating skills will prove valuable.

Paragraph 4 is an agreement that the defendants are only responsible for those liens (debts) that are listed in the C&R. We already discussed this issue for Paragraph 7 of the main text of the document. If the insurance company includes this paragraph, make doubly sure that all doctors and others who provided you services have been paid or are listed, and that no outstanding bills remain unaccounted for.

Paragraph 5 is a catchall clause waiving claims to any and all injuries and claims (such as discrimination or wrongful termination) you may have sustained while working for your employer. This is a sneaky way an insurance company may try to get you to unknowingly give up all other potential claims against your employer for which you have not yet filed, including cumulative trauma injuries. Ordinarily, you should not allow a catchall waiver in the agreement unless the defendants pay additional money for it. The C&R is a settlement of this claim; it should not be used to settle potential future claims you may have. If, however, you are certain that you will not be filing any more claims against your employer, you should try to negotiate some additional money for the waiver. The amount is entirely negotiable, but a figure of up to $1,000 or so is probably reasonable for a waiver where you really don't have any potential claims outstanding. If you may have a legitimate claim, the amount should be much higher, if you agree to it at all. Of course, the statute of limitations may determine whether you have the right to file any other claim. In short, in many cases you'll be waiving little by agreeing to waive all future claims.

Paragraph 6 is a standard clause that most insurance companies put in compromise and release agreements. This clause says you agree to waive your rights under § 1542 of the Civil Code of California. By agreeing to this waiver you are confirming that the compromise and release settles any and all claims you may have against this employer for this date of injury, and that you are giving up your right to file for any additional injuries that you might discover later. For example, if you have a back injury and you sign a C&R for the date of injury in which you injured your back, then you later find out that you injured your liver as a result of the same injury, you can't file a new claim.

This is standard procedure for settlement by compromise and release, and it really shouldn't present any problem as, by the time of settlement, any and all parts of body that you injured on

ADDENDUM "B"

1. This Compromise and Release and attachments contain the entire agreement between the parties hereto, and the terms of this release are contractual in nature and not merely a recital.

2. THE CONSIDERATION FOR THIS COMPROMISE AND RELEASE SET FORTH IN PARAGRAPH 2 INCLUDES ANY INTEREST WHICH MAY OTHERWISE BE DUE PRIOR TO THE 25th DAY AFTER APPROVAL THEREOF.

3. The undersigned hereby affirms and acknowledges that he has read the foregoing Compromise and Release agreement, or had it fully explained to him, and fully understands and appreciates the foregoing words and terms and their legal effect, and that this is a full, final compromise, release, and settlement of all claims, demands, actions, or causes of action, known or unknown, suspected or unsuspected, arising out of his employment with the employer set forth within this Compromise and Release. Further, it is agreed this Compromise and Release shall extend to and pertain to any and all injuries known or unknown, to any and all parts of the body, whether by way of specific injury or continuous trauma, arising out of the employment with the employer set forth herein.

4. In further consideration of the payment of the aforesaid sum, applicant agrees that this release extends to and covers the executors, administrators, representatives, heirs and successors, assigns, officers, directors, agents, servants, and employees of the defendants, and each of them, and the physicians, surgeons, and nurses retained by the defendants, and each of them, whether acting individually or on behalf of them, or either of them.

5. THE PERSON WHOSE SIGNATURE APPEARS BELOW HAS READ AND UNDERSTOOD EACH ATTACHMENT AND FURTHER TERMS OF COMPROMISE AND RELEASE AND HEREBY AGREES TO ALL PROVISIONS.

By: ______________________________

Applicant

that particular date of injury should have been determined and treated. However, because this clause may also bar any other claims for damages you may have outside the workers' compensation claim (see *Jefferson v. California Department of Youth Authority,* in Chapter 28), you should always add the following language to the end of that clause: "This clause applies only to this claim."

b. Addendum B (Standard Agreements and Waivers)

Addendum B contains standard language that further clarifies the understanding of the parties. The paragraphs may not appear in the same order or be in the same wording as discussed here.

Paragraph 1 explains that the C&R you are signing is a contract and is the only agreement between you and the defendants on this subject. This is additional legal jargon that is really not needed, but if the insurance company wants to put it in, it's no problem.

Paragraph 2 gives the insurance company 25–30 days to mail your settlement check before they are responsible for paying you any interest on the money you settled for. This standard paragraph is okay.

Paragraph 3 tells the Workers' Compensation Appeals Board that you have read the entire C&R, understand it, and are aware of its legal effect. If you are settling a claim for a cumulative trauma (see Chapter 4), the language as set forth in Paragraph 3 is okay.

However, if you are settling a specific injury, such as a broken leg, you should strike out the language that reads "arising out of his employment with the employer" and the language that reads "whether by way of specific injury or continuous trauma, arising out of the employment with the employer set forth herein."

CAUTION

If you anticipate future problems. As I have repeatedly emphasized, if you don't want to sign away your right to future claims because you believe you later may have problems arising out of your injury, you should not agree to a compromise and release. Instead, you should settle by way of stipulations with request for award. (See Section D1, above.)

Paragraph 4 states in legal lingo that you are settling your claim on behalf of not only yourself, but anyone else who may have any future claim to these benefits. This is okay.

Paragraph 5 simply states that you have read and understood the agreement and agree to be bound by its terms and provisions.

c. Addendum C (Characterization of Settlement Proceeds)

If you are receiving or expect to receive Social Security disability, Supplemental Security Income, payments from a private disability policy, or Medicare, it may be extremely important that your C&R addresses how your settlement proceeds are to be characterized.

Let's back up just a bit. Some disability programs will take a credit or offset for moneys you receive in your workers' compensation settlement and reduce or limit the disability benefits you're entitled to. Many disability policy providers will not, however, take credit for money that is earmarked to help pay your future medical expenses (although Medicare and Medi-Cal may take a credit for those payments).

For these reasons, it may be prudent to designate in the C&R that a certain sum of the settlement is for future medical expenses and is being paid to you at a designated monthly rate.

Addendum C explains how the money you will receive is to be classified. That means you may designate part of the settlement as future medical expenses. Accompanying Addendum C is a supplemental order to be signed by a judge. This order reiterates the characterization of settlement proceeds set forth in Addendum C.

ADDENDUM "C"

CHARACTERIZATION OF SETTLEMENT

(A) After negotiation between the parties, the following items have been reached in regard to the settlement proceeds being received:

(1) Total amount of Compromise and Release: $25,000.

(2) Temporary disability should have been paid to the applicant between 3/1/20xx and 9/7/20xx.

(3) Temporary disability should have been paid at the rate of $336/week.

(4) Total temporary disability benefits that should have been paid to the Applicant: $10,000.

(5) Applicant was actually paid temporary disability benefits in the amount of $7,000.

(6) Of the above-referenced Compromise and Release amount, $3,000 is being paid to applicant for temporary disability.

(7) Included in the Compromise and Release is the sum of $10,000 to be used for future medical care, in accordance with the recommendation of Dr. Shirley Smith.

(8) After deduction for attorney fees, medical care, and temporary disability, the sum of $12,000 remains. This sum is being paid to applicant Jane Dowry due to lifelong permanent disability which will interfere with applicant's ability to engage in gainful employment for the remainder of her life. This sum is being paid to applicant in a lump sum based upon a life expectancy of 25 years and payments at the rate of $40/week beginning on 11/1/20xx at the rate of $173 per month. This is based upon *Sciarotta vs. Bowen*, 837 F.2d 135, using the "Hartman" formula.

(B) The specific characterization of the settlement proceeds in this matter, as set forth above, is an essential element of the Compromise and Release in this matter and it is specifically requested that the judge reviewing this Compromise and Release make a specific finding in the order of approval as to the characterization of the benefits set forth in this Compromise and Release.

(C) A finding is requested as to the life expectancy of the employee based upon the life expectancy tables found in the *Vital Statistics of the United States*, 1988, Life Tables Volume 2, Section 6, DHHS Pub. No. (OHS) 89-1147, to wit; Employees' life expectancy as a female, as of 11/1/20xx, is 25 years.

(D) It is agreed between the parties that this settlement shall be paid in a lump sum, but it shall be prorated over the life expectancy of the employee since this is a lifetime settlement. The rate per week would be found by dividing the net lump sum amount to the employee by the number of weeks of her life expectancy. Proration shall start the month of receipt of the lump sum and will continue into the future.

(E) Paragraph D referring to the proration has been noted and is approved. As of this date, the employee's life expectancy is 25 years. Paragraph A is noted and approved.

Medicare Set-Aside Trusts

Before you settle your claim by compromise and release you must consider the interest of Medicare, especially if you feel that at some time in the future you may need Medicare assistance to pay for your treatment. If your settlement violates Medicare rules, you can be held liable for the cost of medical treatment paid for by Medicare. The government has become much more aggressive in recent years about pursuing these claims. See Chapter 19, Section C8, to learn the details of the Medicare rules.

Some injured workers settle their rights to future medical care for their work injuries by signing a compromise and release. (See Chapter 19, Section C7.) These workers hope that if they need future medical care, Medicare will pay for it. However, if your settlement violates Medicare rules, you can be held liable for the cost of medical treatment paid for by Medicare.

EXAMPLE: Fred had a severe back injury at work. He has already had one back surgery, and his doctors say that he is likely to need additional surgeries in the future. He is settling his case by compromise and release. The permanent disability amount for his back is worth $50,000. To avoid paying upwards of $60,000 per surgery in the future, the insurance company offers to pay Fred an additional $20,000 in cash to "buy out" his future medical rights. Fred is willing to do this because he is currently getting Social Security disability and Medicare benefits. Fred rationalizes that he can always get his surgery paid for in the future by Medicare, so he might as well take the extra cash. BUT WAIT! Medicare doesn't think that is fair. If Fred takes this settlement and later tries to get Medicare to pay for his back surgery, Medicare will probably ask to see his compromise and release settlement. After seeing that Fred received $20,000 for future medical care costs, Medicare will force Fred to pay the first $20,000 of his surgery costs before Medicare will pay anything!

This can be avoided by doing what is called a "Medicare set-aside trust." The set-aside trust determines a portion of your settlement that is put in trust to pay for your future medical treatment. Medicare agrees that once that amount is used up, they will pay for your future medical treatment regardless of the cost. (Usually, the amount put in the trust is less than the amount you receive in cash to "buy out" your future medical treatment.) There are companies that put these trusts together as part of your settlement, and the insurance company will pay for it.

If you are getting Medicare, you should do a set-aside trust regardless of the amount of your settlement. If you are not getting Medicare now, you should do a set-aside trust only if you have a reasonable expectation of getting Medicare within the next 30 months and only if your total settlement is more than $250,000.

Situations where Medicare rules say you are deemed to have a "reasonable expectation" of Medicare enrollment within the next 30 months include the following.

- You have applied for Social Security disability benefits.
- You have been denied Social Security disability benefits but anticipate appealing that decision.
- You are in the process of appealing or refiling for Social Security benefits.
- You are 62 years old (you may be entitled to Medicare within 30 months based upon your age).
- You have an end-stage renal disease (ESRD) condition but you do not yet qualify for Medicare based upon ESRD.

SEE AN EXPERT

Research credit or offset rules. To find out whether your workers' compensation settlement will affect other benefits you're currently receiving, contact the appropriate disability providers or agencies. You may also wish to consult with an information and assistance officer or a workers' compensation attorney to make sure you're making the best possible arrangements in your settlement.

If you will need a Medicare set-aside trust (see "Medicare Set-Aside Trusts," above), the insurance company will send you some releases to sign so that they can hire a company to prepare a Medicare set-aside analysis. The insurance company must pay for the Medicare set-aside analysis. Sign the forms and send them back to the insurance company.

The insurance company will send in all of your medical reports from all the doctors you have seen and you will get back an analysis of the projected costs of your future medical expenses (an example of an analysis is included below). Your analysis will state an amount that represents their estimate of your future medical costs. Don't be surprised to see the figures that come back; they can be very high because of the cost of medications and any surgeries that you may need.

Let's take an example. Say your analysis comes in at $105,355 (this is the amount you should hope to get). This is now the minimum amount you demand for settlement of your future medical costs. There are other future medical costs that Medicare will not cover, such as in-home care, so if you have those costs, or think you may in the future, you'll want to add those to your settlement demand as well.

To determine the value of a compromise and release when you have an MSA, you add the value of the MSA to the value of your permanent disability (PD). Continuing the example from above, if your PD is determined to be $70,000, you add $105,355 for the MSA, and any other amounts you can negotiate, to the $70,000. Let's keep it simple and for our example say no other amounts are added, and the total C&R is $175,355. On one of the lines in paragraph 7 of the C&R, the MSA amount will be inserted as a deduction, as follows: $105,355 payable to applicant to be placed in a Medicare set-aside trust account.

You are supposed to put the money set aside for your MSA in a bank account for the sole purpose of paying for your future medical bills as they arise for your injury. Then, once all this money is used up, Medicare will pay for your medical treatment for your injured body parts for the rest of your life. If you use part or all of the money for other purposes, Medicare will not pay for your medical treatment (for the body parts injured and listed in the compromise and release) until you make up the difference.

Some people don't care about having Medicare pay for their treatment, and they use the money as they want. That is perfectly legal, even though, technically, you don't get this money to do with as you wish. Just know that if you need to get medical treatment in the future for your injuries,

When Is an MSA Needed?

	Settlement amount	On Medicare in next 2½ years?	MSA Required?	CMS Approval Required?
Injured worker on Medicare	Under $25,000	n/a	recommended	No
	Over $25,000	n/a	needed	Yes
Injured worker not on Medicare	Under $250,000	no	no	No
	Under $250,000	yes	recommended	No
	Over $250,000	no	no	No
	Over $250,000	yes	needed	Yes

Medicare Set-Aside Summary

A Medicare Set-Aside Allocation has been prepared for the settlement of the following injury claim:

Case Information:

RE: Tom Jones

SS# 123-45-6789 **DOB:** 10/01/xx **DOI**: CT 20xx-03/03/xx

WC Jurisdiction: CA **Claim #:** 88888888

Employer: Ace Accounting

Residence: 555 Blakely Street, Sacramento, CA

Diagnosis: Bilateral Wrist Pain

ICD-9 Codes: 719.43

Medical Cost Projections Prepared by: Dwight & Parker, LLC **Date Prepared: 2/16/20xx**

Rated Age: **53**	**Life Expectancy: 28** years Remaining LE years based upon the U.S. Dept. of Health and Human Services, National Center for Health Statistics, National Vital Statistics Reports, Vol. 58. No. 21. Released June 28, 20xx, Life Expectancy Tables.

Note: Releases are required to complete SS/Medicare Status, COB Notification, Lien Research and CMS Submissions

Medical Cost Analysis:

The proposed Medicare Set-Aside (MSA) Allocation was determined through the completion of a life care plan. **The annual estimated Medicare covered expenses** related to the following injury were calculated at $718.68 per year for future medical treatment and $3,495.02 per year for future prescription drug treatment.

Initial expense of $7,999.00 is anticipated for the **first surgery, first procedure and/or replacement.**

Initial expense of $0.00 is anticipated for **additional or one-time prescription costs.**

Annuity Funding Parameters:

If a structured settlement is utilized to fund the MSA Account, the annuity should provide:

Initial Deposit:	
Future Medical	$9,436.36
Future Prescription	$6,990.04
Total Initial Deposit	$16,426.00

Annual Payments:	
Future Medical	$692.06 per year
Future Prescription	$3,365.57 per year
Total Annual Payments	$4,057.63 per year

Note: Initial Deposit equals seed money, and the 1st annuity payment is expected to occur 1 year postsettlement. This amount has been rounded to the nearest dollar to reflect CMS processes.

MSA Allocation Detail:

Total proposed Future Medical treatment (Part A & B):	$28,142.00
Total proposed Future Prescription Drug treatment (Part D):	$97,860.56
Total proposed MSA Exhaustion Amount:	$126,002.68

Life Care Plan–Financial

	Service	Frequency	Every X Years	No. of Years	Price Per Service	Total Lifetime Expenses	Medicare Coverage	Total Lifetime Expenses Covered by Medicare
Physician Evaluations	Orthopedic surgeon	4	1	28	57.00	$6,384.00	1	$ 6,384.00
Therapy	Physical therapy	24	28	28	33.00	792.00	1	792.00
Diagnostics	Standard lab work (general health panel)	1	1	28	44.00	1,232.00	1	1,232.00
	Urine drug test	1	1	28	123.00	3,444.00	1	3,444.00
	EMG/NCS (bilateral upper extremities)	1	28	28	533.00	533.00	1	533.00
	MRI (left and right shoulder)	4	28	28	1,393.00	5,572.00	1	5,572.00
	X-rays (left and right shoulder)	9	28	28	107.00	983.00	1	983.00
	X-rays (left and right wrist)	2	28	28	69.00	138.00	1	138.00
Equipment	Wrist brace (left and right)	1	28	28	814.00	814.00	1	814.00
Medical Procedures	Intramuscular injections (left and right shoulder)	3	28	28	53.00	159.00	1	159.00
	Steroid injections (left and right wrist)	2	28	28	46.00	92.00	1	92.00
Mileage	Mileage	4	1	28	14.00	1,568.00	NC	
	Additional mileage	24	28	28	14.00	336.00	NC	
Surgeries, Replacements, & Procedures (1 time or 1st replacement costs to be included in seed money)	Right carpal tunnel release revision	1	28	28	2,523.00	2,523.00	1	2,523.00
	Left ulnar nerve release (includes: facility fee, surgeon and assist. fee, anesthesia, pre- and post-op diagnostics, and physical therapy)	1	28	28	2,738.00	2,738.00	1	2,738.00
	Right ulnar nerve release (includes: facility fee, surgeon and assist. fee, anesthesia, pre- and post-op diagnostics, and physical therapy)	1	28	28	2,738.00	2,738.00	1	2,738.00
	Estimated Total Lifetime Expenses					**$30,046.00**		
	Estimated Total Lifetime Expenses Covered by Medicare							**$ 28,142.00**

Future Prescription Drug Treatment

Estimated Prescription Drug Expenses over Life Expectancy

	Prescription Name, Dosage, & Form	NDC Number	Frequency & Duration	No. of refills per year	No. of Years	Price per refill	Total Lifetime Expenses	Medicare Coverage	Annual Medicare Covered Expenses	Lifetime Medicare Covered Expenses
Medications	Hydrocodone/APAP 7.5/750 mg tablets	00591038705	QID RPN 120 6x/year	6	28	$ 7.91	$1,328.88	1	$47.46	$1,328.88
	Morphine Sulfate ER 80 mg tablets	00591374201	BID 60/month	12	28	119.09	40,014.24	1	1,429.08	40,014.24
	Gabapentin 800 mg tablets	68462012605	BID 60/month	12	28	151.74	50,984.64	1	1,820.88	50,984.64
	Cyclobenzaprine 10 mg tablets	00591565810	BID 80 8x/year	6	28	4.88	816.48	1	29.16	816.48
	Ketoprofen 10% cream	38779007800	PRN 1 gm 4x/year	4	28	42.11	4,716.32	1	168.44	4,716.32
	Capsaicin .1% cream	51927180700	PRN 1 gm 4x/year	4	28	267.00	29,904.00	NC		
	Total Estimated Lifetime Prescription Drug Treatment						**$127,764.56**			
	Total Estimated Annual Medicare Covered Prescription Drug Treatment								**$3,495.02**	
	Total Estimated Lifetime Medicare Covered Prescription Drug Treatment									**$97,860.56**

and you spent all the MSA money on other things, Medicare will not pay for your treatment.

The final issue to be determined is whether or not you have to have the MSA that was prepared by the outside company approved by the Center for Medicare Services (called CMS approval). See the chart below to determine when CMS approval is required (and whether an MSA is needed or not). Generally, if you are on Medicare or expect to be on Medicare in the next 30 months, you should have an MSA.

If you do need to get CMS approval per the chart above, your compromise and release form must be sent to CMS for approval along with the MSA addendums. The insurance company will handle this.

Supplemental Order Approving Compromise and Release and Findings of Facts

Compromise and release having been submitted in the above-referenced matter, and order approving having been issued this date, the following additional findings are made:

(1) That the terms of the compromise and release agreement set forth herein are incorporated in whole in this order approving.

(2) That applicant Jane Dowry will receive, after attorney's fees are deducted, the sum of $25,000. That amount is to be construed as follows:

(a) $3,000 is to be construed as temporary disability benefits that should have been provided during the period of 3/1/20xx to 9/7/20xx.

(b) $10,000 is to be construed as payments for future medical care as deemed necessary by the treating doctors.

(c) The lump sum remainder of the compromise and release amount is to be construed as periodic payments of permanent disability at the rate of $40 per week for the remainder of Applicant's lifetime.

__________ ____________________________

Date Workers' Compensation Judge

d. Signing the C&R

Make sure you review the entire C&R agreement carefully, including all the addenda. If you've received permission from the insurance company to cross out any language or write anything in, initial each instance.

Your signature must either be witnessed by two people who are not related to you, or it must be notarized. Legally, it doesn't matter which route you follow—do whichever is easier. If you're having two witnesses sign, they must be over age 18 and not be related to you or entitled to receive money from your workers' compensation case.

If you want your signature notarized, you can look in the phone book under "notary public" to find a notary. Notaries may charge up to $10 to notarize a document. Or check with your bank or a real estate office, which may do the notarization for free.

Once you sign the C&R, make a photocopy for your records and send the original back to the insurance company.

E. Attend an Adequacy Hearing

You will need to attend an adequacy hearing at the Workers' Compensation Appeals Board. This is a short meeting in which a judge reviews the proposed settlement documents and decides whether they are adequate. (See Chapter 24, Section B2, for more on adequacy hearings.)

Part V

The Workers' Compensation Appeals Board

CHAPTER

21

Preparing Your Case

If your workers' compensation case goes to trial, you and the insurance company will appear before a Workers' Compensation Appeals Board judge. If you don't have a lawyer, the judge will walk you through the trial process. Appeals board trials (called hearings) are relatively informal, and the judge will give you the benefit of the doubt.

What Are Trials and Hearings?

The terms "trials" and "hearings" are often used interchangeably in this book. But in case you are thinking that, for once, workers' compensation terms have been made easy to understand, think again. It turns out that while a trial is always a hearing, a hearing is not necessarily a trial. Here's how to differentiate between the two:

- **Hearing.** This refers to any time your claim is set before the Workers' Compensation Appeals Board for any reason. A hearing would include a pre-trial conference or mandatory settlement conference to try to settle your case, a "lien conference" to deal with the payment of medical bills, or a hearing in which a judge orders a party to do something prior to trial (such as to attend a medical appointment or pay benefits), as well as an actual trial.
- **Trial (which, by definition, is also a hearing).** A trial refers to a proceeding heard before a workers' compensation judge where both sides offer evidence and put on witnesses trying to prove or disprove issues regarding a workers' compensation claim. You may have more than one trial in the course of your case. See Chapter 22, Section A, for more about types of hearings and trials.

During the trial, you will probably need to present evidence—information you want the judge to consider as the basis for making decisions in your favor. Evidence may take many forms, including your oral (spoken) testimony, testimony of witnesses, medical reports, and documents such as wage statements and injury reports. You won't need to follow the rules of evidence lawyers love to spout in court trials (for example, "I object, your honor, on the basis that no foundation has been laid for the introduction of that document").

Now, here is a crucial point. *From the moment you file your claim, you should begin preparing your case as if it were going to result in a contested trial.* This is true even though most cases settle and never actually go to trial. It's only common sense to ask, "Why prepare for a trial that may never occur?" Because if you wait until you realize that settlement won't be possible, it will be too late to gather and organize the necessary evidence.

If you've followed the suggestions in Chapter 6, you probably have the evidence you need. In this chapter, you'll learn how to put your evidence in the context of the possible issues that are likely to be decided at your trial. You'll also learn about legal procedures for obtaining any evidence you may be missing. Finally, you'll find out how to prepare for your upcoming hearing.

A. Identify Possible Issues in Dispute

To prepare effectively for your trial, it will help to identify and understand all issues that may be in dispute (not agreed upon). Disputed issues may be raised by the insurance company at the outset of your case. However, it's quite likely that some disputed issues will be added and others eliminated as your case proceeds. For this reason, until you know for certain otherwise, it's wise to assume that the insurance company may contest all aspects of your claim. This will allow you to be prepared for all possible contingencies.

The two-page "Issues That May Be in Dispute" chart, below, lists the key issues that may be resolved at workers' compensation hearings. Scan the first column and check all issues that are in dispute. Then look over the second column to see whether you have the evidence to back up your claims. If you don't, you'll need to do your best to find documentation or testimony that will help prove your case.

Issues That May Be in Dispute	
Issues in dispute (and where to get more information)	**Evidence that may support your position**
Coverage of Claim	
☐ **AOE/COE:** whether injury arose out of and occurred in the course of employment (Chapter 3, Section C8)	injury reports, emergency room records, medical reports, your testimony, testimony of witnesses who saw the injury occur
☐ **Insurance company at time of injury:** which company is responsible for paying benefits (Chapter 1, Section C2; also see Chapter 8, Section C1, if employer was not insured)	search by Workers' Compensation Insurance Rating Bureau (WCIRB), letters from insurance companies
☐ **Employment:** whether you were an employee or an independent contractor (Chapter 3, Section A2)	witnesses who can attest to your job duties, employment contracts, your testimony, W-2 tax forms
Job and Wages	
☐ **Wages at time of injury:** how much you earned determines your disability rates	pay stubs (last 12 months of employment), W-2 tax forms from previous year, your personnel records, employer's testimony, your testimony, testimony of coworkers
☐ **Occupation:** determines your employment group number, which affects your permanent disability rating	testimony of coworkers, your testimony, documents that describe your job duties (if you agree with the description)
Injury and Treatment	
☐ **Date of injury:** determines your disability rate	completed DWC-1 form, work accident report, medical records, employee's personnel records, your testimony, testimony of witnesses who saw the injury occur
☐ **Part(s) of body injured:** whether all of your injuries will be covered	medical reports, your testimony, testimony of witnesses who saw the injury occur, completed DWC-1 form
☐ **Nature and extent of injury:** whether you injured yourself as badly as you claim	medical reports, your testimony (as long as the insurance company doesn't have photos or videotapes of you doing activities you claim you can't do)
☐ **Date of permanent and stationary status:** determines when temporary disability ends (Chapter 9, Section E)	medical reports, your testimony
☐ **Type of current medical treatment needed:** determines reasonableness and necessity of treatment when disputed	medical reports, your testimony
Benefits	
☐ **Past due-temporary disability**	medical reports, your testimony, EDD certifications of disability
☐ **Temporary disability rate**	wage statements for last year of employment, W-2 tax forms from previous year, employer's testimony, personnel records, your testimony, testimony of coworkers

Issues That May Be in Dispute (continued)	
Issues in dispute (and where to get more information)	**Evidence that may support your position**
☐ **Permanent disability amount**	wage statements for the last year of employment, W-2 tax forms from previous year, employer's testimony, personnel records, your testimony, testimony of coworkers, collective bargaining agreement showing scheduled wage and salary increases
☐ **Medical costs and mileage paid for and not reimbursed**	your testimony, receipts, canceled checks, requests for reimbursement, mileage logs
☐ **Need for particular medical treatment**	medical records, medical reports, your testimony, letters from insurance carrier
☐ **Need for future medical treatment**	medical reports, test results, your testimony
☐ **Penalties for late payment of benefits** (Chapter 19, Section C9)	your testimony, postmarked envelope showing when checks were sent, copies of bills from medical providers showing unpaid balances
☐ **Entitlement to supplemental job displacement voucher**	letters from insurance company advising that they do not have a job for you, whether regular, modified, or alternate work
Liens and Attorney Fees	
☐ **Medical liens**	copies of green liens, your testimony, bills
☐ **Other liens,** including Employment Development Department (EDD) liens and liens by attorneys	copies of liens, copies of EDD goldenrod liens, your testimony
☐ **Attorney fees,** if you previously had a lawyer and there is dispute over how much the lawyer is entitled to	copies of liens, your testimony, prior signed Attorney Fee Disclosure Statements
Other Matters	
☐ **Apportionment:** where insurance company claims your medical condition is partially or all due to a preexisting or subsequent condition or event	medical reports, medical records, your testimony *(See an information and assistance officer or a lawyer; this is beyond the scope of the book)*
☐ **Statute of limitations:** where insurance company alleges you did not file your workers' compensation claim on time	your testimony, DWC-1 form, medical reports *(See an information and assistance officer or a lawyer; this is beyond the scope of the book)*
☐ **Death case:** who are your total and partial surviving dependents?	copies of tax returns, birth certificates, marriage certificates
☐ **Death case:** amount of burial expenses or death benefits	copies of bills for burial expenses, canceled checks
☐ **Rehabilitation appeal**	*(See an information and assistance officer or a lawyer; this is beyond the scope of the book)*
☐ **Unlawful discrimination**	*(See an information and assistance officer or a lawyer; this is beyond the scope of the book)*
☐ **Other**	

TIP

Periodically review issues in dispute. As your case progresses, the issues in dispute may change. Do your best to keep track of what's in dispute. This will allow you to always know what you may have to deal with at trial, and therefore help you be prepared.

B. How to Prove (or Disprove) Disputed Issues

If there are any issues in dispute, the parties (you and the workers' compensation insurance company) will have to provide evidence to prove or disprove a particular point of view.

At trial, you, as the injured worker, will testify first. This should allow you to establish your basic case. Only after you testify (and call witnesses to support your position) may the insurance company offer evidence that your claim is not true. If you're not represented by a lawyer, make sure you have your evidence organized and readily accessible. A judge will help you through the process.

> EXAMPLE: Raphael claims that he injured himself at work and therefore is entitled to workers' compensation benefits. The workers' compensation insurance company disputes this, claiming he hurt himself playing football. It's up to Raphael to introduce at least some evidence that what he claims is true. Once he establishes his basic case, the insurance company will have a chance to offer evidence that he did not suffer an injury at work.

1. Ways to Prove Your Case

"Proving your case" simply refers to establishing—by 51% of the evidence—that the issues you are trying to prove at your hearing are true. Proving your case can be accomplished in a variety of ways. These are the most common methods:

- presumptions—this sounds complicated, but presumptions are simply facts or legal issues that are considered to be true unless they are proven otherwise (Section B3, below, covers this)
- your testimony in court
- testimony of other witnesses in court
- documents such as payroll slips, W-2 forms, employment records, and injury reports
- medical evidence such as doctor's reports, other medical records, and test results, and
- deposition testimony—prior testimony of witnesses taken under oath in front of a court reporter and then transcribed and signed by the witness under penalty of perjury.

2. Insurance Company May Raise Affirmative Defenses

The insurance company may try to raise issues that are known as "affirmative defenses"—issues that, if proven, will either defeat or limit your entitlement to some workers' compensation benefits.

The insurance company may try to raise some of these affirmative defenses:

- **Independent contractor status.** The insurance company may try to show that you were an independent contractor, not an employee, and therefore you are excluded from receiving workers' compensation benefits. (To help prepare your response, see Chapter 3, Section A2.)
- **Intoxication.** The insurance company may try to prove that your injury was caused by intoxication from alcohol or misuse of drugs, thereby making you ineligible for workers' compensation benefits. (See Chapter 3, Section C1.)
- **Willful misconduct.** The insurance company may try to show that you are ineligible for workers' compensation benefits because your injury was caused by intentional misconduct, such as horseplay or disobeying a company policy. (To help prepare your defense if this issue is raised, see Chapter 3, Section C4.)
- **Aggravation of injury by unreasonable conduct.** The insurance company may try to show that your actions unreasonably contributed to or aggravated your injury. If it is determined

that your conduct was unreasonable, the insurance company is entitled to subtract whatever percentage of permanent disability your misconduct contributed to the overall disability. For example, this might be a situation where you unreasonably refused medical treatment, which resulted in further injury.

- **Failure to report the injury.** The insurance company may try to prove that you failed to notify your employer of the injury as required by law, thereby making you ineligible for workers' compensation benefits. (LC §§ 5400, 5401, 5705.) Chapter 5, Section B, explains how and when to report an injury.
- **Apportionment of permanent disability.** The insurance company may try to prove that part or all of your permanent disability is not due to an injury on the job. For instance, the insurance company may try to say that your disability is due to a preexisting condition or prior injury. (See Chapter 3, Section B6, for more information.)
- **Statute of limitations.** The insurance company may try to show that your claim for workers' compensation benefits is barred by the statute of limitations—in other words, that you filed your claim too late.

3. Identify Presumptions in Your Favor

Simply put, a "presumption" is a belief established by law that something is considered to be true unless evidence is presented that proves otherwise. If you have a presumption in your favor, it's like having a head start in a race—and if the other side can't present convincing evidence to overcome the presumption, it can amount to winning the race by default.

Note: In the past, the opinion and report of your treating doctor was "presumed to be correct." This is no longer the case. Now, your doctor's opinion is no more important than that of a qualified medical evaluator (QME) to whom your insurance company may send you.

a. Identify Conclusive Presumptions

A conclusive presumption (also called an irrebuttable presumption) cannot be disproved. In other words, if you can show that the presumption applies to you, no evidence—no matter how strong—can overturn this presumption. Unfortunately, there are very few of these and it's unlikely that one will apply to your case. But look over this list to be sure:

- These are conclusively presumed to be total (100%) permanent disabilities: (a) loss of both eyes or sight in both eyes, (b) loss of both hands or the use of both hands, (c) an injury resulting in practically total paralysis, or (d) an injury to the brain resulting in incurable imbecility or insanity (the inability to manage one's own affairs due to being mentally incompetent). (LC § 4662.)
- A spouse who earned less than $30,000 in the year preceding a worker's death is conclusively presumed to have been a dependent of a deceased spouse. (LC § 3501.)
- A minor (person under age 18), or an adult who is physically or mentally incapable of performing work for wages, is conclusively presumed to be wholly dependent for support upon a deceased employee-parent if the person was living with the employee-parent at the time of an injury that resulted in the parent's death. (LC § 3501.)

b. Identify Rebuttable Presumptions

RELEVANT CASE LAW

See *SCIF v. WCAB (Welcher)* and *Rodriguez v. WCAB*, in Chapter 28.

A rebuttable presumption (also known as a disputable presumption) stands unless it is invalidated by evidence to the contrary or by a stronger presumption.

Here are the main rebuttable presumptions that may apply to a workers' compensation case:

- If you filed a workers' compensation claim and more than 90 days passed with no rejection of the claim by your employer or its insurance company, there is a rebuttable presumption that the claim is compensable—that is, that the insurance company will compensate you for your injury. The 90 days start to run from the date that you filed a DWC-1 claim form, or first requested the DWC-1 form if your employer did not provide it to you within 24 hours of making the request.

The insurance company can rebut this presumption only with evidence discovered after the 90-day period. (LC § 5402.) In other words, any evidence that the employer should have been able to obtain prior to the expiration of 90 days cannot be used to deny the claim.

- If you were injured in 2003 or earlier, you are temporarily totally disabled, and you are off work due to the industrial injury for more than 365 days, there is a rebuttable presumption that you are a qualified injured worker (QIW)—that is, you're medically eligible for vocational rehabilitation services.
- Peace officers, firefighters, and safety officers who suffer from heart disease, tuberculosis, hernia, pneumonia, and cancer that manifests itself during their employment (and for a limited time after retirement) are presumed to have a condition that arose out of the employment. (LC §§ 3212–3214.)
- Any person rendering service for another is presumed to be an employee unless the person is an independent contractor or is expressly excluded as an employee by the Labor Code. (LC § 3357.)

c. When to Raise Presumptions

Although the judge could raise a presumption or give you the benefit of it without being asked, it's unwise to leave something this important to chance. The appropriate time and place to make the judge aware of any presumptions is before your case goes to trial, at a pre-trial conference (discussed in Chapter 22, Section A1, and Chapter 24, Section B).

C. Depositions

A deposition is a proceeding in which a party or a witness answers questions orally under oath so the other side can determine what the person knows before calling the person to testify at a trial. Depositions take place at a location away from the court, often at a lawyer's or doctor's office. Each lawyer asks questions, and if you represent yourself, you may ask questions, too. A court reporter (someone who makes a permanent record of the deposition by means of an electronic device) records the testimony and later prepares a written transcript of the entire proceeding.

Depositions are expensive. The court reporter is paid several hundred dollars. In addition, if you are conducting the deposition, you may be required to pay witness fees, which can range from under $100 for nonexperts to much more for experts such as doctors. You are usually required to pay these amounts up front. If you conduct and pay for a deposition, however, you may be entitled to recover deposition costs when your case settles or goes to trial.

1. Reasons for You to Conduct a Deposition

Injured workers rarely conduct depositions. However, it may make sense to take the deposition of a witness to your case in instances such as these:

- You feel that information gained at the deposition might persuade the insurance company to settle your case or change its position on a particular issue. For example, suppose the insurance company disputes that your injury really occurred. If you take the deposition of a witness who testifies to seeing you injure yourself as you claimed, it may persuade the insurance company to accept your claim.

- A witness is out-of-state or likely to be unavailable at trial due to poor health or inability to travel. If you take the deposition of a witness who is later unavailable for trial, the deposition transcript can be entered into evidence.

RESOURCE

If you need to take a deposition. A deposition of a doctor will not be necessary unless the doctor's report is very bad for your case. If you decide to conduct a deposition, please refer to *Nolo's Deposition Handbook*, by Paul Bergman and Albert Moore. This book will give you guidance on depositions, whether you're being deposed or are deposing someone else. Or you may choose to see an attorney and discuss the possibility of having representation for the rest of your case.

2. Attending Your Own Deposition

In workers' compensation cases, the insurance company usually takes the injured worker's deposition. That way, the insurance company can determine the facts of the case and the extent of its liability. In most workers' compensation cases, the injured worker is the only person who is deposed. Attending your own deposition shouldn't be a problem as long as you always tell the truth. If things get out of hand, you can always stop the deposition and get a lawyer.

If you receive a notice that your deposition will be taken, read it carefully. Make sure you can appear at the date, time, and place it's scheduled. If you can't attend, call the other side well in advance and make arrangements for a new date. If you don't show up, your benefits may be cut off immediately, and you may need to arrange for a hearing at the appeals board to get benefits. This may cause a delay of up to several months.

On the day of the deposition, show up a little early. Do not bring any documents with you unless you have been instructed to do so. Such a request may be made in advance in a document from the insurance company: either a Notice to Produce or a Deposition Subpoena for Personal Appearance and Production of Documents and Things.

To begin the deposition, the court reporter will ask you to raise your right hand and take the same oath to tell the truth that you would in a court of law. This oath carries with it criminal penalties if you knowingly tell a falsehood.

The attorney will then advise you of some ground rules that will be followed in the deposition. These instructions will mainly be about how to best answer the questions so that the court reporter can understand you.

The first questions the attorney will ask probably will cover the following areas:

- your personal history, including your name, current home address, Social Security number, and driver's license number
- where you have lived for the past ten years
- your educational background and family members, and
- whether you have ever been convicted of a felony.

TIP

How to handle the felony question. The other side is allowed to ask you whether you have ever been convicted of a felony (a crime punishable by a jail sentence of more than one year). The purpose of this question is to lessen your credibility if you have had a felony conviction, with the idea being that someone convicted of a felony presumably might not tell the truth. If you've been convicted of a felony, limit your answer to yes or no and the type of felony conviction. You should refuse to answer all other questions regarding this issue.

The lawyer will then move on to other topics:

- your employment history from the time you got out of school to the present, including questions about your various job duties, why you left each job, and whether or not you had any injuries at those jobs
- your claim of industrial injury, including how it happened, whether you reported it, and whether there were witnesses

- your past and current medical history, including the names and addresses of doctors you have seen, who sent you to which doctors, what they did for you, and whether or not you are still being treated by a doctor, and
- your current complaints regarding your industrial injury. You will probably be asked to state the various parts of your body that still bother you, what kinds of activities and movements you can no longer do, and what types of pain you have.

CAUTION

When not to answer psychiatric or stress-related questions. Unless you have some kind of a stress-related injury, do not answer any questions regarding psychiatric problems, personal problems (alcoholism, divorce, and the like), or treatment. This includes questions about whether you have ever seen a psychiatrist and any questions of a very personal nature that would have to do only with your emotional welfare. Simply state that you object to the question as being irrelevant, and don't answer.

a. Rules to Follow at Your Deposition

At a deposition, it's always a good idea to abide by these general rules:

- **Tell the truth.** Always tell the truth, even if you feel it might be detrimental to your case. But it's fine to frame the truth in its most favorable light to you. For example, you are asked, "Can you lift heavy objects without experiencing pain?" If the truth is that yes, at the time you don't feel pain, but the next day you'll have severe stiffness and pain, make both points in your answer.
- **Be polite and courteous.** Don't argue with or be rude to the person asking the question, no matter what you privately think about that person.
- **Make sure you understand the question.** If you aren't certain that you understand the question, ask that it be repeated or explained. Always make sure you fully understand the question before you start answering.
- **Answer only the question asked.** If you can comfortably answer a question with a "yes," "no," "I don't know," or "I don't remember," give that answer. This will make for a clear record, as well as prevent you from providing information that your opponent may have never thought to ask. If the questioner wants an explanation, you'll be asked for it.
- **Don't guess.** You may give your best estimate if you really have one, but don't guess. If your answer is a guess, just say, "I don't know."
- **Take a break when you need one.** You may take as many breaks as you need. For example, you may want time to use the rest room, or simply take time to regain your composure if you find yourself getting tired or angry. Try to limit a break to five or ten minutes.

b. Potential Problems at Your Deposition

In 90% of workers' compensation cases, the attorney asking the questions will be polite and will not try to trick you. You should be on guard, however, for the other 10%. Here are the kinds of questions to watch out for:

- **Questions about irrelevant information.** If you're asked for information not relevant to your case, first say, "For the record, I object to this question as being irrelevant." By objecting for the record, you can later object to your answer being admitted into evidence at the time of trial. Wait and see whether the attorney asks you to answer the question anyway. If the attorney does, you may choose to answer it if the question is harmless. But if you refuse to answer, the attorney's only recourse is to seek a hearing before a judge and get an order for you to answer at a later date.
- **Repetition of the same question.** If the attorney badgers you by repeatedly asking the same question, you have the right to object. Simply say, "The question has been asked and answered," and refuse to answer it again.

- **Trick questions.** Watch out for questions that tend to box in your testimony, such as "Please tell me *everything* that bothers you, that you attribute to your injury." If you testify at trial to something you failed to include in your answer, the defendants may try to discredit your testimony by pointing out that you testified differently at your deposition. You should answer these types of questions by first qualifying your answer, such as "As best as I can recall at this time" or "At this moment, the following things bother me …." Or, if the question is phrased in such a way as to elicit a certain response, answer in such a way as to make your limitations known. For instance, when you are asked if you can walk 50 feet, and the answer is yes, but you know you can't walk 100 feet, make sure to include that as part of your answer.

c. Terminating the Deposition

It's quite common to end a deposition because of health reasons. If at any time during the deposition you do not feel capable of continuing because you feel lousy, inform the attorney of this, and say that you are willing to finish it at a later date.

You may also end a deposition if the attorney is harassing you (say, by asking offensive personal questions). Be aware, however, that the insurance company could use this as an excuse to cut off benefits. So before taking such a drastic move, follow the suggestions in Section C2b, above, for handling problem questions. If the attorney continues to harass you, you may choose to end the deposition. Inform the attorney that you will no longer tolerate such actions and that you are leaving.

The attorney may threaten to obtain a judge's order to force you to complete the deposition. Tell the attorney that is fine. If the attorney gets such an order, you will be notified of the time and place. You will have an opportunity to tell the judge what happened at the deposition and to request that the judge order the attorney to stop harassing you.

If you terminate a deposition, you should agree to a subsequent deposition only if you get a lawyer or first obtain an order from a workers' compensation judge restraining the defense attorney from harassing you.

D. Subpoenaing Witnesses and Documents

In this section, we show you how to use legal procedures to require someone to show up at a deposition or hearing or provide you with copies of documents that will help you win your case:

- **Subpoena.** A subpoena requires someone to appear at a deposition or hearing to answer questions.
- **Subpoena duces tecum.** A subpoena duces tecum requires a person to produce documents.

To require both someone's personal appearance and the production of documents, you'll need both a subpoena and a subpoena duces tecum.

When one party wants another party to produce documents, a Notice to Produce Documents is generally used instead of a subpoena duces tecum. To require another party to attend a deposition or hearing, a Notice of Deposition is usually used instead of a subpoena. You may, however, use a subpoena duces tecum or subpoena with a party such as the insurance company and your employer.

1. Subpoena Duces Tecum

SKIP AHEAD

If you want documents from a party. If you want your employer or insurance company to give you documents, send them a copy of the letter provided in Chapter 6, Section D. You don't need to use a subpoena duces tecum.

A subpoena duces tecum is a powerful tool. You may use it to require any person or business to produce books, accounts, papers, and other documents relevant to your workers' compensation case. In addition, you may require the production of not only documents that you know about, but also any relevant documents that you don't even know exist!

You can get a subpoena form by making a written request to the Workers' Compensation Appeals Board, or by going to the appeals board office and asking a clerk for one. There's also a copy on Nolo's website (see Chapter 29). If you need help filling it in, see an information and assistance officer. This document must be signed by a judge or stamped with a judge's signature. Generally the form you pick up at the WCAB office will be pre-signed by the judge.

The person being served will have a minimum of 15 days to comply with the subpoena duces tecum. As a practical matter, you will want to issue your subpoena duces tecum long before your case is set for trial. This allows you to use it to discover any possibly relevant information that may help you to settle your case or that may point to other documents that you may want to obtain.

2. Subpoena

To be sure witnesses will actually show up at your workers' compensation hearing, you need a court order requiring their presence, called a subpoena. You can get a subpoena by making a written request to the Workers' Compensation Appeals Board, or by going to the appeals board office and asking a clerk for one. There's also a copy on Nolo's website (see Chapter 29). This document must be signed by a judge or stamped with a judge's signature.

Most subpoenaed witnesses may request $35 for a day's appearance, plus transportation expenses (at the mileage rate in effect at the time of the hearing) from their home to the place of the hearing. In the unlikely event that you subpoena an expert witness, such as your treating doctor, you must pay that person an expert witness fee. (Government Code § 68092.5.) Expert witness fees can easily total hundreds of dollars and must be agreed upon in advance. That is why doctors' medical reports are routinely admitted into evidence in workers' compensation cases without the necessity of having the doctor appear at the hearing. In fact, I have never had to subpoena an expert witness to a trial.

a. Which Witnesses to Subpoena

The issues that are contested by the insurance company in your case will usually determine what witnesses you will need to subpoena to help prove your case. They may include:

- your supervisor
- coworkers who witnessed the accident
- anyone who can substantiate your physical or mental limitations, and
- coworkers or others who know what your job duties were.

There are some restrictions as to who may be forced to appear with a subpoena. A witness is not required to attend a Workers' Compensation Appeals Board hearing if it's located out of the county in which that person lives, unless the distance is less than 75 miles from the witness's place of residence to the place of the hearing. (Evidence Code § 1989.) If you can't subpoena someone because the distance is too great, you could take the person's deposition. (See Section C1, above.)

If the witness is "friendly" to your case—that is, someone who will voluntarily appear in court when needed and give testimony in your favor, you may think you won't need to serve a subpoena. This is risky, however, because witnesses can change their minds. Here are some reasons to subpoena even friendly witnesses:

- If something "better to do" comes up on the date of your hearing, a witness will be less likely to decide not to attend your hearing.
- The witness must still appear even if the person gets cold feet or is pressured by the employer or others not to testify.
- If the witness fails to show up, the judge is more likely to postpone ("continue") the hearing rather than proceed without the person's testimony.
- The subpoena can provide a witness with the necessary reason or excuse to get time off from work to testify.

b. How to Fill In a Subpoena

If you want someone to appear at a hearing, you should serve a subpoena only after you've received a Notice of Hearing in the mail. You'll use information from the Notice of Hearing to complete the subpoena. If you've received but misplaced the Notice of Hearing, you can get another by contacting the Workers' Compensation Appeals Board where your case was filed. (A sample Notice of Hearing is provided in Chapter 22, Section F.)

You may type in the information or neatly handwrite the subpoena. Here's how to fill it out.

County. In the blank line after the words "Workers' Compensation Appeals Board," fill in the name of the county in which your matter has been filed. For example, "San Bernardino County, California."

Case Number. Fill in your case number, which is the number assigned to your claim when you file an Application for Adjudication of Claim.

Applicant. That's you; fill in your name.

Defendant. Fill in the name of both your employer and its insurance company.

The People of the State of California Send Greetings to. Fill in the name and address of the witness you wish to have present at your hearing. You must use a separate subpoena for each witness. If you don't know the person's full legal name, provide enough identifying information that the person serving the subpoena can find the right person. For example, "Mary, Dispatcher for Anderson Trucking."

In the next blank, after the sentence "YOU ARE HEREBY COMMANDED to appear before a Workers' Compensation Judge of the WORKERS' COMPENSATION APPEALS BOARD OF THE STATE OF CALIFORNIA at," fill in the name of the appeals board that appears on the Notice of Hearing. For example, "Workers' Compensation Appeals Board, Long Beach," and give the address.

Next, insert the date and time the witness is to appear. For example, "on the 3rd day of September, 2012, at 10:00 a.m."

Finally, fill in your name and telephone number as the requesting party.

Leave the rest of the form blank.

3. Serving a Subpoena or Subpoena Duces Tecum

How to serve (provide copies) of documents to witnesses and others is covered in Chapter 23. You'll follow different rules depending on whether you're serving a subpoena or a subpoena duces tecum:

- **Subpoena duces tecum.** The easiest way to serve a subpoena duces tecum is by mail, although it may also be served personally. You must give the recipient at least 20 days to comply with the subpoena duces tecum. For example, if you mail the subpoena duces tecum on October 1, the person served has until October 21 to produce the documents. (If the subpoena duces tecum is served personally, the person has only 15 days to comply.)
- **Subpoena.** A subpoena must be personally served no fewer than ten days before the hearing. If, at the time of service, the witness demands a witness fee, the person serving must immediately pay $35 for one day's appearance plus transportation expenses to the Workers' Compensation Appeals Board. (Government Code § 68093.) In the rare event that you are using an expert witness, that person must be contacted in advance and a fee agreed upon.

After you serve documents, you'll need to complete a proof of service form, which states when and how service occurred. For more on completing proofs of service, see Chapter 23, Sections B and C.

E. Preparing for a Pre-Trial Hearing

If settlement efforts by phone or mail prove fruitless, you will have to move into high gear when it comes to getting ready for your day in court. Before you go to trial, however, you will have at least one, and possibly more, pre-trial hearings.

You may have a status conference, a mandatory settlement conference, a rating MSC (mandatory settlement conference), or a priority conference. See Chapter 22, Section A, for a description of these various pre-trial hearings.

You may receive a Notice of Hearing advising you of what type of hearing is being held, and the date and time (a sample Notice of Hearing is provided in Chapter 22, Section F), or you may take the initiative and file a Declaration of Readiness form yourself to request a hearing date. See Chapter 22, Section D, for a sample Declaration of Readiness form and instructions on how to complete and file the document.

1. Review Issues in Dispute

About 30 days before the pre-trial conference date, you should figure out which issues are still in dispute. You may find that some of the issues you originally listed as disputed have been accepted by the insurance company, while others you thought were accepted are now in dispute. Turn to Section A, above, for a chart listing issues that may be in dispute.

Review the letters from the insurance company, notes about your conversations with the insurance adjuster, and any answer filed by the insurance company to your application. (As explained in Chapter 5, Section D, the insurance company can file a document called an "Answer," which sets forth the issues it is agreeing to or disputing.)

If any issues are in dispute at this stage, you'll need to organize the evidence that you are going to offer at the trial. You will be required to list all of your evidence at the pre-trial conference.

CAUTION

Any evidence you don't list will not be allowed. If you need evidence—including doctor's reports—you should get it before you go to the pre-trial conference or lose the right to present it at trial. If you don't have a medical report you need, make an appointment with your doctor before the hearing so you can list the report as evidence.

2. Review Your File and Serve Documents

Take a thorough look through your file, from beginning to end. Make sure you have all of the documents you're using as evidence to prove your case. Also check to see that you have not overlooked anything, such as a demand for mileage that was never paid.

File and serve upon the appeals board and the insurance company any documents you intend to use at the trial that have not been previously filed. All written documents must be filed and served within 20 days of the conference, or the judge may not allow them into evidence. (How to do this is covered in Chapter 23.)

Special Rules for Medical Reports

Medical reports are important because they are used as evidence to prove (or disprove) medical issues in your case. A party files medical reports with the Workers' Compensation Appeals Board along with a Declaration of Readiness to Proceed to Trial. The opposing party has six days from service of a Declaration of Readiness (11 days if service is by mail) to file medical reports with the appeals board. (CCR § 10879.)

In most cases, you will have already served most, if not all, of your medical reports on opposing parties and lien claimants. Once a request for medical reports has been made, it is considered an ongoing request, and the party to whom the request was directed must serve and file any new doctors' reports within five days of receipt.

Remember, there is a difference between medical reports and medical records. You are required to file and serve medical reports, not medical records. Do not send X-rays or other records, such as the results of tests, to the appeals board unless the board requests it.

Issues Likely to Arise After You Become Permanent and Stationary

After you have been declared permanent and stationary, you should be looking for one or more of the following new issues:

- **Retroactive temporary disability payments.** Determine whether the insurance company owes you temporary disability payments for any periods off work due to your work injury. If so, organize all medical reports and records that would show that you were temporarily disabled during the periods you have claimed.
- **Permanent disability payments.** You or the insurance company may dispute the doctor's opinion regarding the nature and extent of your permanent disability. Review the treating doctor's opinion to determine whether you will be relying on the doctor's report or a QME's evaluation.
- **Need for future medical treatment.** How much, and what kind of, medical treatment you will need in the future are almost always disputed. As with permanent disability indemnity, you will need to rely on the treating doctor's report or a medical-legal opinion to substantiate your need for future medical treatment. (See Chapter 10, Section D.)
- **Self-procured medical treatment.** If you had to pay for any medical expenses yourself, you should acquire copies of all receipts and canceled checks and add up the total amount you spent. (See Chapter 11, Section B.)
- **Liens.** Make a list of all the medical facilities, doctors, the Employment Development Department, attorneys, and any others who have filed liens (formal requests for payment) against your case. You should have received copies of all liens filed in your case. If you know that any particular medical facilities failed to file a lien, contact them and see that they do so. You will want to make sure that the insurance company pays these off.
- **Apportionment.** If any medical reports indicate that part of your present disability is due to preexisting conditions or other outside factors, obtain, if possible, medical-legal reports to substantiate that all of your present disability is due to your industrial injury.

TIP

If you didn't receive documents from the insurance company. If you made a request to the insurance company to send you medical reports or other documents and you didn't receive them, write a letter to the judge before the pre-trial conference and send a copy to the insurance company. Request that the judge issue an order asking for the documents. It's unlikely that the judge will comply with your request, but it will be a big help for the judge to know that you requested, but weren't sent, certain evidence.

3. Review Your Witness List

Check over your list of witnesses, if any. You will be required to list all your witnesses at the pre-trial conference. There's no harm in listing witnesses you may not end up calling to testify; you can always decide not to call them. But if you neglect to list someone, you will not be permitted to call that person to testify.

F. Preparing for a Trial

Once you've received your Notice of Hearing for your trial, you should be in a "countdown mode." For the first time, you know the exact date and time of your trial. (See Chapter 22, Section F, for more on the Notice of Hearing.)

At least 30 days before the trial, you should prepare your case for presentation to the judge. As we discuss in Chapter 24, Section B, you may have attended a pre-trial conference (where you were unable to settle your case) and completed the Pre-Trial Conference Statement, listing all the evidence and witnesses you intend to present at trial. Now it is just a matter of organizing your medical reports, witnesses, and documentary evidence for the actual trial.

Get a Head Start by Watching a Trial

You'll want to be sure you know what you're up against. If possible, go to the Workers' Compensation Appeals Board to observe a trial, preferably by the judge who will be hearing your case. Ask the clerk to direct you to courtrooms where trials are going to begin. Before the trial gets started, walk up to the judge at a free moment and ask whether it would be okay for you to sit in and watch. As long as you check with the judge first, you should have no problem sitting in on a workers' compensation trial to get a feel of what is going to happen in your case.

When you observe a trial, take some notes as to how things proceed. Note the order in which people testify, what kinds of questions are asked, and what types of testimony are most effective.

1. Prepare Your Evidence

Organize all of the medical reports that you listed at the pre-trial conference and wish to admit into evidence. They should be organized in chronological order, with all the proofs of service attached to each report indicating when it was served. All of your original medical reports should have already been filed and served upon the Workers' Compensation Appeals Board.

Have an extra copy of every piece of evidence you intend to offer at your trial, so that in the event that anything was misplaced, you can provide the judge with another copy.

Write out all the issues you need to offer evidence on at the trial, using the "Issues That May Be in Dispute" chart in Section A, above. Decide what issues you and any other witnesses will offer testimony on. You will generally testify first. Decide in what order you will call your remaining witnesses, and write out a list.

CAUTION

Make certain that you have subpoenaed all your witnesses. If you haven't, subpoena your witnesses now. Your witnesses must be served at least ten days before the trial. (See Section D, above, for instructions.)

2. Consider Trying to Exclude Medical Reports

In some cases, the insurance company will have obtained medical evidence in violation of the rules or regulations of the Labor Code. If it did, the medical evidence may be inadmissible at a workers' compensation hearing. In other words, you may be able to persuade the judge to not allow those reports into evidence at trial.

For example, unless there has been a qualified medical evaluation by a doctor you chose from a panel of three doctors, generally no medical reports, other than those of the treating physician, may be admitted into evidence in a proceeding before the Workers' Compensation Appeals Board. (See Chapter 10, Sections D and E.) The practical application of this comes into play when the insurance company attempts to offer into evidence medical reports from doctors they have sent you to without having complied with the requirements of the Labor Code.

TIP

Review LC §§ 4060, 4061, 4062, and 4062.1. These Labor Code sections are critical when it comes to admissibility of medical evidence. If at all possible, you should carefully review those code sections. (See Chapter 27, on legal research.)

CHAPTER

22

Arranging for a Hearing or Trial

This chapter discusses the how, what, when, and why of getting a hearing or trial date set with the Workers' Compensation Appeals Board.

Let's back up a bit and explain some legal jargon. Cases heard before the Workers' Compensation Appeals Board are sometimes referred to as "conferences," sometimes "trials," and sometimes "hearings." And, unlike with a civil court case, you may have more than one trial during the course of your workers' compensation case. Don't let the legal lingo throw you; it's not that difficult to sort it out, and once you do, you'll realize that even lawyers are prone to jumble it up.

A. Kinds of Hearings

"Hearing" is a generic term that refers to any matter set before the Workers' Compensation Appeals Board. A workers' compensation hearing usually takes one of two forms: a conference or a trial.

1. Pre-Trial Conferences

Pre-trial conferences, or pre-trial hearings, are hearings held at the Workers' Compensation Appeals Board prior to the actual trial on the merits of your case. These conferences are an opportunity to discuss disputed issues face-to-face with a representative from the insurance company to see if the issues can be resolved by mutual agreement. There are four types of pre-trial conferences.

a. Status Conference

A status conference is an opportunity to have a face-to-face meeting with the insurance company's representative to discuss open issues in the case. For example, if you have multiple insurance carriers in your case and you need to meet to sort out which insurance carrier had coverage for your date(s) of injury, you may need a status conference.

To request a status conference, you file a Declaration of Readiness to Proceed and check the box "Declarant requests: (x) Status Conference." (See Section D1, below.)

You will receive a Notice of Hearing as to the date and time of the status conference and where it will take place. No evidence or testimony is allowed at a status conference. If you aren't represented by a lawyer, the judge may facilitate a discussion about the issues in your case. Otherwise, you and the insurance company will meet in the courtroom to discuss the issues.

Once the status conference is over, no further action will be taken by the judge and your case will not be set for any further hearings unless another Declaration of Readiness is filed.

b. Rating MSC (Mandatory Settlement Conference)

If the issues in your case are only the extent of permanent disability (see Chapter 13) and the need for future medical treatment, and you have not yet requested and received a rating of your disability (see Chapter 18), you can request a rating mandatory settlement conference (MSC). The purpose of the rating MSC is to obtain a rating on the various medical reports so that you and the insurance company can see how much permanent disability each of the reports assigns to your injuries. This should help facilitate settlement. A rating MSC should be requested only if you are ready to proceed to trial.

To request a rating MSC, you file a Declaration of Readiness to Proceed and check the box "Declarant requests: (x) Rating MSC." (See Section D1, below.) You will receive a Notice of Hearing advising you of the date, time, and place of the rating MSC.

At the conference you will be given a copy of the ratings (percentages of permanent disability) for each of the medical reports submitted, to help facilitate settlement discussions. If you aren't represented by a lawyer, a judge may facilitate a discussion about the issues in your case. No evidence or testimony is allowed at a rating MSC. If you reach an impasse and the judge can't help, the matter will be set for trial.

c. Mandatory Settlement Conference

A mandatory settlement conference (MSC) should be requested only when you are ready to proceed to trial on every one of the issues in your case. A trial will not be scheduled unless you have attended a mandatory settlement conference.

To request a mandatory settlement conference, you file a Declaration of Readiness to Proceed and check the box "Declarant requests: (x) Mandatory Settlement Conference." (See Section D1, below.) You and the insurance company will receive a Notice of Hearing setting forth the date, time, and place of the hearing.

No evidence or testimony is allowed at a mandatory settlement conference. If you aren't represented by a lawyer, a judge may facilitate a discussion about the issues in your case. Otherwise, you and a representative from the insurance company will meet in a courtroom to discuss the issues. If you reach an impasse and the judge can't help, the matter will be set for trial.

d. Priority Conference

A priority conference can be requested only if you have an attorney and the insurance company has denied your case because it says the injury did not arise out of your employment or occur in the course of your employment (referred to as AOE/COE issues; see Chapter 3, Section C). The purpose of asking for a priority conference is to get an expedited conference date to try to resolve these issues as soon as possible.

To request a priority conference, your attorney will file a Declaration of Readiness to Proceed and check the box "Declarant requests: (x) Priority Conference." (See Section D1, below.) You and the insurance company will receive a Notice of Hearing setting forth the date, time, and place of the priority conference.

No evidence or testimony is allowed at a priority conference, and the only issues that can be discussed are AOE/COE. At the conference the judge will determine whether the matter is ready to proceed to trial on the limited issues of employment and/or injury AOE/COE.

If the AOE/COE issues can't be resolved at the conference, the judge will either set the matter for trial, or, if further discovery is required, the judge will determine a plan for the completion of discovery. If further discovery is required, the matter will also be set for a status conference date to check on the progress of discovery or confirm its completion. Once discovery is complete (or the judge feels the parties have had enough time to complete discovery), the matter will be set for trial.

TIP

Request computer printout of all benefits paid. At all mandatory settlement conferences and rating MSCs, the insurance company is required to produce a computer printout of all benefits paid to date. In addition, you can demand at any time a computer printout of all benefits paid, and the insurance company must produce such a printout within 20 days of your demand. You can make such a demand up to five times per year. (See Rule 10607.)

2. Pre-Trial Discovery Motions

A pre-trial discovery motion requests that the workers' compensation judge issue an order requiring the other side to take, or stop taking, a particular action in connection with the evidence in your case.

For example, you could file a pre-trial discovery order to compel the insurance company to stop harassing you at your deposition or to comply with your request to produce documents.

Insurance companies might file a pre-trial discovery motion to compel you to:

- attend a deposition if you failed to appear for your deposition at least once before
- attend a medical examination scheduled by the insurance company where you have failed to appear at a scheduled appointment at least once before, or

- produce certain documents, if you have refused to do so.

If a hearing is set to discuss the discovery motion, you will receive notice of the place, date, and time to appear. This will be a short hearing where each side will tell the judge why the order should be granted or denied.

3. Trials on Preliminary Issues and Trial on the "Case-in-Chief"

A "trial" refers to any hearing before a workers' compensation judge in which you have an opportunity to present your case and to have a decision rendered on issues in dispute. As noted earlier, a trial may also be referred to as a hearing. Trials come in two broad varieties:

- minitrials, to resolve a particular preliminary issue that develops as you go along, such as eligibility for medical treatment, and
- your main trial, to deal with the final value of your case. Lawyers often call this the trial on your case-in-chief.

B. Trial on Preliminary Issues

As your case progresses, you may find it necessary to have one or more minitrials to resolve important preliminary issues, but not to settle the entire case. For example, if the insurance company refuses to pay for surgery recommended by the treating doctor, you may need a trial to have a judge decide whether the surgery is reasonable and necessary. At a trial on preliminary issues, evidence is presented and testimony given before a workers' compensation judge, who then makes a decision on the issues.

1. Kinds of Preliminary Issues

A minitrial on preliminary issues may be necessary if you believe you are entitled to certain benefits, such as medical treatment or temporary disability payments, and the insurance company refuses to provide them. A hearing may also be needed if the insurance company is denying your claim altogether.

a. Preliminary Issue of Whether Injury Is Compensable

"Compensability" is a broad term that means your claim is valid and therefore you are entitled to benefits. If the insurance company asserts that you don't have a compensable injury, it is denying your claim altogether. (LC § 4060(a).) We cover compensability issues in Chapter 3, Section B.

You are entitled to set a matter for trial at any time to resolve the issue of compensability. If the insurance company claims your injury is noncompensable (denies your claim), you will always have other issues as well, such as the insurance company's failure to pay you temporary disability or provide medical treatment. So, as a practical matter, there is no point in requesting a trial solely on the issue of compensability; you'll want to resolve the other issues as well.

SEE AN EXPERT

If your claim is disputed. If the insurance company disputes the basic issue of whether you have a compensable injury (whether or not you are entitled to any workers' compensation benefits), obtain the help of a competent workers' compensation attorney, if possible. If this issue is decided against you, you will be precluded from obtaining any workers' compensation benefits whatsoever.

b. Other Preliminary Issues

It's possible that your claim was accepted by the insurance company, but you and the insurance company disagree over one or more preliminary issues, such as these:

- What should be the extent and scope of your present medical treatment?
- Are you entitled to receive temporary disability indemnity?
- How much temporary disability should the insurance company be paying?
- Are you entitled to medical treatment that the insurance company refuses to authorize?

2. When to File for a Hearing on Preliminary Issues

Before you file for a hearing before the Workers' Compensation Appeals Board to deal with any preliminary issues, consider whether it may make more sense to wait and resolve these issues when your entire case is ready for trial. Consider the following criteria in deciding whether to get a separate hearing (trial) date on a preliminary issue:

- **How serious is the issue?** For example, if the issue is your entitlement to temporary disability payments and you have no other source of income, you probably need a hearing to resolve that issue. However, if the issue is your right to $22.95 for mileage reimbursement, you should wait to resolve this issue when your case is ready to settle.
- **Do you have any alternatives?** There's no point in going through the hassles of an extra trial if there are easy options that will solve your problem. Let's say the issue is your entitlement to a particular medical treatment. If your doctor is willing to file a "green lien," you might decide to wait to resolve the issue when your case is ready to settle.
- **How strong is your position?** If you proceed to trial on an issue, what are your chances of winning? The best way to make an educated guess is to carefully read the appropriate sections of this book on the particular issue to first determine what you must convince the judge of at a trial. Then carefully consider whether you will be able to do so.

3. Medical Examination Requirements for Hearing on Preliminary Issues

Before you may request a trial on any preliminary issues, you must satisfy certain medical requirements. No disputed medical issue (preliminary issue) may come before a workers' compensation judge unless there has first been an evaluation of the injured worker by:

- the treating doctor
- a qualified medical evaluator (QME), if the employee does not have a lawyer, or
- an agreed medical evaluator (AME), if the employee is represented by an attorney. (LC § 4062(e).)

If the insurance company has denied compensability, you may need to use your group medical insurance doctor as the treating doctor or find a doctor willing to treat you on a lien. (See Chapter 9, Section B2b.) You are still entitled to a QME evaluation, however. (See Chapter 10, Section B.)

4. Regular and Expedited Preliminary Hearings

A regular preliminary hearing (trial) usually does not occur for 45–80 days after you request it. Because trials on preliminary issues are generally urgent in nature, that just won't do. For example, preliminary issues may cover authorization for medical treatment or granting of temporary disability payments to help pay bills. As a result, preliminary issues may sometimes be decided earlier, using what is known as an expedited hearing procedure.

a. Regular Preliminary Hearing

Any hearing (trial) set on the regular trial calendar will first be set for a pre-trial conference date, typically 30 to 60 days after the hearing is requested.

If the issue can't be resolved at the pre-trial conference, a trial will then be set, usually 60 to 120 days after the pre-trial conference date.

TIP

When will your trial be set? Check with your local Workers' Compensation Appeals Board to find out how quickly it is setting hearings. How long it will take will vary greatly depending upon how heavy the particular appeals board calendar is, and how many judges are available to hear workers' compensation cases. If regular hearings are being set fairly quickly, you may not need to request an expedited hearing.

b. Expedited Hearings

An expedited hearing (trial) is given priority over regular trial dates, and is usually set for trial within 30–90 days of request. No pre-trial conference is scheduled.

There are certain limits on your right to an expedited hearing. You're only entitled to an expedited hearing if the insurance company has accepted your workers' compensation claim—in other words, the issue of whether you're covered (compensability) cannot be determined in an expedited hearing. In general, only the following issues may be resolved in an expedited hearing:

- entitlement to medical treatment
- entitlement to temporary disability payments or the amount of those payments
- enforcement or termination of vocational rehabilitation, or
- dispute between employers or insurance companies as to liability for payment of benefits.

How to file the documents to obtain an expedited hearing is covered in Section D2, below.

c. Hardship Hearings

When you can't qualify for an expedited hearing, the appeals board may grant a hearing on a priority basis if waiting for the regular hearing date would cause you undue hardship. The hearing will probably be set sooner than a regular hearing, but not as quickly as an expedited hearing. There are no hard and fast rules on what constitutes a hardship; requests are considered on a case-by-case basis. (We discuss how to request a hardship hearing in Section D3, below.)

d. Priority Conference Calendar for AOE/COE Disputes

RESOURCE

AOE/COE issues explained. See Chapter 3, Section C, for an explanation of AOE/COE issues.

If the issues in dispute are whether the injury arises out of employment or in the course of employment (AOE/COE), and you have an attorney, a hearing must be conducted by a workers' compensation administrative law judge within 30 days of a party's filing a declaration of readiness to proceed.

If the dispute cannot be resolved at the hearing, a trial must be set as expeditiously as possible, unless discovery is not complete (for good reason), in which case "status" conferences will be held at regular intervals. The case will be set be for trial when discovery is complete, or when the administrative law judge determines that the parties have had enough time to complete discovery. A determination as to the insurance company's and employee's rights concerning the AOE/COE issues must be made and filed within 30 days after the conference. (For dates of injury in 2002 or earlier, these issues must be heard at a regular conference or trial.)

C. Trial on Entire Case (the Case-in-Chief)

When your entire case is ready to be heard, it's referred to as the "case-in-chief" in workers' compensation jargon. Generally speaking, the main issue that must be resolved at a hearing is the settlement value of your case. The hearing centers around the nature and extent of the permanent disability and your need for future medical treatment. It also addresses any other unresolved issues, such as your right to retroactive temporary disability.

At a trial on the case-in-chief, evidence is presented and testimony given before a workers' compensation judge, who then makes a decision on the issues.

1. When to Set a Trial on the Case-in-Chief

A hearing on the case-in-chief generally occurs when all of the following apply:

- You have been declared permanent and stationary.
- You are no longer receiving temporary disability payments.
- You have been unable to reach a settlement with the insurance company on the remaining issues in your case. (Issues that may remain unresolved are set forth in Chapter 21, Section A.)

2. Medical Examination Requirements for Setting a Trial on the Case-in-Chief

Any disputed medical issue regarding the existence or extent of permanent disability and limitations or the need for continuing medical care may be decided in a trial on the case-in-chief only if there has been an evaluation of the injured worker by:

- the treating doctor
- a qualified medical evaluator (QME), if the employee is not represented, or
- an agreed medical evaluator (AME), if the employee is represented by an attorney. (LC § 4061(m).)

D. File a Declaration of Readiness to Proceed to Set Your Case for Hearing

To set your case for hearing (whether on preliminary issues or the case-in-chief), either you or the insurance company will need to file and serve a Declaration of Readiness to Proceed (also called a DOR). There is one DOR for a regular hearing and a separate DOR if you are requesting an expedited hearing.

1. Complete the Declaration of Readiness to Proceed for a Regular Hearing

In a Declaration of Readiness to Proceed, the person completing the document states under penalty of perjury that the person is ready to proceed to a hearing on the issues specified. The document also indicates what efforts were made to resolve the issues before asking for a hearing. (CCR § 10414.)

It's easy to complete a Declaration of Readiness to Proceed. Start by locating the form Nolo's website (see Chapter 29, "Online Appendixes" for the link to this and other forms in this book.). Following are step-by-step instructions as well as a completed sample. You may either type or neatly print the information. You can also find the form online at www.dir.ca.gov/dwc/DOR.pdf, where you can fill it out using your computer. You won't be able to save the form to your own computer, so it's a good idea to print out a copy first, handwrite a draft so that you know exactly what you want to fill in, and then type in the responses on the computer and print a final draft.

Case No. When you filed an Application for Adjudication of Claim, a number was assigned to your case. Insert the number here. It will be in the form ADJ999999.

Applicant. Fill in your name. This should be the same name you listed on the Application for Adjudication of Claim.

Declarants: Please designate your role. Check the box before the words "Employee or Applicant." This indicates that you—the employee/applicant—are filing the Declaration of Readiness to Proceed. Use Employee if you are the injured employee.

Declarant requests: Check one of the following boxes:

Mandatory Settlement Conference. Check this box if you are ready to proceed to trial on all issues in your case. If you can't settle the issues in your case at the mandatory settlement conference, your case will be set for trial.

Status Conference. If you are not yet ready for trial but want to meet with the insurance company face-to-face at the Workers' Compensation Appeals Board to discuss certain issues, check this box.

Rating MSC. Check this box if you are ready to set your matter for trial and the only remaining issues to be decided are the extent of permanent disability and the need for future medical treatment. Also, a rating MSC should be requested only if you have not yet requested or received a rating on one or more medical reports in your case. All ratable doctors' reports (reports that discuss the extent of permanent disability or the patients' subjective complaints), including the reports of the treating physician, QME, and AME, must be filed with the Declaration of Readiness, unless they have been previously filed.

Priority Conference. Your attorney will check this box only if the insurance company has denied your case based on the claim that your injury did not arise out of your employment or occur in the course of your employment (referred to as AOE/COE issues; see Chapter 3, Section C), or for lack of coverage.

Lien Conference. You won't ever check this box.

At the present time the principal issues are: Be sure to check all issues that apply, as follows:

Compensation Rate. Put an "X" in this box only if there is an issue over how much per week you made at your employment. Your average weekly wage affects your temporary disability and permanent disability rates.

Rehabilitation/SJDB. Check this box if you are requesting supplemental job displacement benefits (SJDB) that the insurance company is denying.

Temporary Disability. Put an "X" in this box if you believe that there were periods of time when you were off work as a result of your injury for which the insurance company failed to pay you temporary disability benefits. Also check this box if you are currently temporarily disabled and not getting paid.

Self-Procured Medical Treatment. Check this box if the insurance company has not repaid you for all out-of-pocket expenses you incurred for medical treatment or medication. This includes prescription drugs as well as over-the-counter medication. For example, check this box if you paid $500 for an MRI test and $32 for over-the-counter painkillers and were not reimbursed.

Permanent Disability. Check this box if you have been declared permanent and stationary, your case is ready to settle, and you need a determination by the appeals board as to the nature and extent of your permanent disability.

Future Medical Treatment. Check this box if you are in need of medical treatment for your injury and the insurance company refuses to authorize it, or there is a dispute as to the nature of the present or future treatment you require.

AOE/COE. Check this box if the insurance company or your employer disputes that you sustained an injury while on the job or while working for the employer.

Discovery. Check this box if you are requesting a hearing over a dispute concerning discovery, such as the insurance company's refusal to comply with a subpoena for records benefit printouts, and the like.

Employment. Check this box if the insurance company or your employer disputes that you were an employee at the time of injury

Other. On these lines, describe any other issues you want resolved, such as:

- penalties and interest (Chapter 19, Section C9), or
- mileage reimbursement (Chapter 11, Section B2).

Declarant relies on the report(s) of Doctor(s). Fill in the name of the doctor who wrote the medical report upon which you are relying, usually the one who determined permanent disability most favorably for you.

Date. Enter the date of the medical report upon which you are relying to establish your permanent and stationary date.

Declarant states under penalty of perjury ...: On this line, briefly explain what efforts you have made to settle your case with the insurance company. If possible, list the dates of letters and phone calls made to the insurance company, as well as the results of those efforts. Then state, "Assistance of the appeals board is required to resolve the issues in dispute." For example: "Defendant has failed to respond to applicant's settlement offers of March 11, 20xx and April 20, 20xx. Assistance of the appeals board is required to resolve the issues in dispute."

Declarant's Signature. Sign your name with your usual signature.

Sample Declaration of Readiness to Proceed (Page 1)

STATE OF CALIFORNIA
DIVISION OF WORKERS' COMPENSATION
WORKERS' COMPENSATION APPEALS BOARD
DECLARATION OF READINESS TO PROCEED

NOTICE: Any objection to the proceedings requested by a Declaration of Readiness to proceed shall be filed and served within ten (10) days after service of the Declaration.

ADJ777777
Case No.

Applicant

JOHN
First Name

MI

WU
Last Name

VS

Employer Information

TBA INDUSTRIES
Employer Name (Please leave blank spaces between numbers, names or words)

415 W OCEAN BLVD
Employer Street Address/PO Box (Please leave blank spaces between numbers, names or words)

LONG BEACH — City
CA — State
90802 — Zip Code

Declarants: Please designate your role (Please Select Only One)

☑ Employee ☐ Applicant ☐ Defendant ☐ Lien Claimant

Declarant requests: (Please Select Only One)

☑ Mandatory Settlement Conference ☐ Status Conference ☐ Rating MSC* ☐ Priority Conference
☐ Lien Conference

At the present time the principal issues are: (Check all that apply)

☑ Compensation Rate ☐ Rehabilitation/SJDB ☐ Temporary Disability ☐ Self-Procured Medical Treatment
☑ Permanent Disability ☑ Future Medical Treatment ☐ AOE/COE ☐ Discovery
☐ Employment ☐ Other ______

Declarant relies on the report(s) of:

Doctors (s) DR. SMITH date 12/02/20xx
MM/DD/YYYY

*For a Rating MSC, all ratable medical reports, including treating physician, QME and AME reports, must be filed with this Declaration of Readiness, unless they have been previously filed. A Rating MSC will be set only where the issues are limited to permanent disability and the need for future medical treatment.

DWC-CA form 10250.1 Page 1 (Rev. 6/2011)

DWC-CA form 10250.1

Sample Declaration of Readiness to Proceed (Page 2)

Declarant states under penalty perjury that he or she is presently ready to proceed to hearing on the issues below and has made the following specific, genuine, good faith efforts to resolve the dispute(s) listed below:

MY LETTER TO INSURANCE COMPANY PROPOSING SETTLEMENT DATED 03/12/20XX HAS GONE UNANSWERED. WCA ASSISTANCE IS REQUIRED.

Unless a status or priority conference is requested, I have completed discovery on the issues listed above, and that all medical reports in my possession or control have been filed and served as required by the rules promulgated by the Court Administrator.

Copies of this Declaration have been served this date as shown on the attached proof of service.

Declarant's Signature ______________________________

JOHN WU
Name of declarant or name of the law firm of the declarant (Print or Type)

111 NORTH HILL STREET LOS ANGELES CA 90012
Address (Please leave blank spaces between numbers, names or words)

(213) 270-1233
Phone Number

Date 12/21/20xx
MM/DD/YYYY

DWC-CA form 10250.1 Page 2 (Rev. 6/2011)

DWC-CA form 10250.1

Name of Declarant or Law Firm (Print or Type). Enter your name.

Address. Enter your current mailing address.

Phone. Fill in your current home telephone number.

Date. Enter today's date.

2. Complete the Declaration of Readiness to Proceed to Expedited Hearing (Trial)

SKIP AHEAD

If you do not wish to request an expedited hearing, you can skip this section. (See Section B4, above, for guidelines on when to request an expedited hearing.)

If you qualify for an expedited hearing, you'll need to complete a Declaration of Readiness to Proceed to Expedited Hearing (Trial). A downloadable copy of this simple form is available on Nolo's website. (See Chapter 29, "Online Appendixes" for the link to this and other forms in this book.) Either type or neatly print the information. You can also find the form online at www.dir.ca.gov/dwc/forms.html.pdf, where you can fill it out using your computer. You won't be able to save the form to your own computer, so it's a good idea to print out a copy first, handwrite a draft so that you know exactly what you want to fill in, and then type in the responses on the computer and print a final draft.

Case No. Fill in the number assigned to your case.

Applicant. Enter your name.

Employer Information. Enter the name, address, city, state, and zip code of the employer you worked for when you were injured.

Next, you will check off the issues that are the subject of the expedited hearing:

Entitlement to medical treatment per L.C. § 4600. Check this line if you want a judge to resolve your need for medical treatment and the insurance company's refusal to provide it.

Entitlement to temporary disability, or disagreement on amount of temporary disability. Check this line if this is an issue to be resolved at the expedited hearing.

Appeal from determination of the rehabilitation Unit. Check this line if you are appealing or requesting enforcement of a decision and order of the rehabilitation unit. (This issue is beyond the scope of this book.)

Entitlement to compensation in dispute because of disagreement between employers and/or carriers. Check this line if you're involved in a situation where there is more than one employer and/or insurance company possibly liable for your industrial injury, and each is claiming the other is responsible, with neither providing you any benefits.

Declarant states under penalty of perjury ...: State the reason why you need the assistance of the Workers' Compensation Appeals Board. If you can, you should refer to specific dates where you contacted the defendants either by phone or letter and attempted to resolve the dispute. For example, "Defendants failed to respond to my letter proposing settlement of April 5, 20xx and the assistance of the appeals board is necessary to resolve the issues in dispute."

Declarant's Signature. Sign your name.

Name and law firm (Print or Type). Enter your name.

Address. Enter your address.

Phone. Enter your phone number.

Date. Enter the date on which you are signing the document.

Service. At the bottom of this page, type or print the names and addresses of the insurance company or its attorney (if it has one). If your employer is self-insured, list your employer or its attorney (if it has one).

3. Attachment Letters

You will need to attach a letter to your Declaration of Readiness to Proceed in situations such as these:

- **You are requesting that your matter be set on a priority basis.** If, because of hardship or other good cause (discussed in Section B4c,

Sample Declaration of Readiness to Proceed to Expedited Hearing (Trial) (Page 1)

STATE OF CALIFORNIA
DIVISION OF WORKERS' COMPENSATION
WORKERS' COMPENSATION APPEALS BOARD
DECLARATION OF READINESS
TO PROCEED TO EXPEDITED HEARING (TRIAL)
[Labor Code section 5502(b)]

NOTICE: Any objection to the proceedings requested by a Declaration of Readiness to proceed shall be filed and served within ten (10) days after service of the Declaration.

ADJ 222222
Case No.

Applicant

KENNETH — First Name
T — MI

GOMEZ — Last Name

VS

Employer Information

A-1 TECHNOLOGIES
Employer Name (Please leave blank spaces between numbers, names or words)

4242 LAKESHORE DRIVE
Employer Street Address/PO Box (Please leave blank spaces between numbers, names or words)

SAN JOSE — City
CA — State
92244 — Zip Code

The Declarant requests that this case be set for expedited hearing and decision on the following issues:

- [x] Entitlement to medical treatment per Labor Code section 4600.
- [x] Entitlement to temporary disability, or disagreement on amount of temporary disability.
- [ ] Appeal from a determination of the Rehabilitation Unit finding entitlement to or terminating liability for rehabilitation services, or enforcement of an order of the Rehabilitation Unit.
- [ ] Entitlement to compensation is in dispute because of a disagreement between employers and/or carriers.

Declarant states under penalty of perjury that he or she has made the following specific, genuine, good faith efforts to resolve the dispute(s) listed above:

DESPITE DEMANDS FOR AUTHORIZATION FOR SURGERY AND PAYMENT OF TEMPORARY DISABILITY BENEFITS, DEFENDANTS HAVE FAILED TO AUTHORIZE NECESSARY SURGERY AND PAY DISABILITY INDEMNITY. THE ASSISTANCE OF THE APPEALS BOARD IS NECESSARY TO RESOLVE THE ISSUES IN DISPUTE.

DWC-CA form 10252.1 Page 1 (Rev. 11/2008) DWC-CA form 10252.1

Sample Declaration of Readiness to Proceed to Expedited Hearing (Trial) (Page 2)

Declarant states under penalty of perjury that there is a bona fide dispute; that he/she is presently ready to proceed to hearing; that his/her discovery is complete on said issues.

Declarant's Signature ______________________________

KENNETH GOMEZ
Name of declarant or name of the law firm of the declarant (Print or Type)

1212 FIRST STREET SAN JOSE CA 94421
Address (Please leave blank spaces between numbers, names or words)

(408) 555-1212
Phone Number

Date 02/07/20xx
MM/DD/YYYY

DWC-CA form 10252.1 Page 2 (Rev. 11/2008)

DWC-CA form 10252.1

above), you want an earlier hearing, write a letter specifying in detail the nature of the hardship and the reason why an early hearing is required. This would be important, for example, if the insurance company has denied your case (therefore you are not entitled to file for an expedited hearing) and you are experiencing financial hardship due to the insurance company's failure to provide benefits.

- **You want to bypass the pre-trial settlement conference procedure because you have previously been to one.** The appeals board may schedule you for another pre-trial conference unless you attach a letter explaining that you have previously attended a pre-trial conference and you would prefer to have your matter set directly for trial.

E. Copy, Serve, and File Documents

Once you've prepared the documents necessary to request a hearing (Declaration of Readiness to Proceed or Declaration of Readiness to Proceed to Expedited Hearing), you'll need to make copies, serve the defendants and lien claimants, and file the papers with the court.

You may serve the defendants by mail or fax. Faxing is an acceptable alternative to mailing for serving the defendants and lien claimants, and the same time limits for reply apply. (CCR §§ 10505 and 10506.) However, faxing and emailing are never acceptable for filing documents with the WCAB. Chapter 23 explains how to file and serve documents.

Upon the filing of a Declaration of Readiness to Proceed by any party, all of the medical reports in your possession that have not been previously served must be served on all the parties (including lien claimants). This includes even medical reports that you do not intend to introduce into evidence. The medical reports do not have to be filed until the date of the mandatory settlement conference. (See Section A, above.) Failure to serve the medical reports is subject to mandatory sanctions pursuant to CCR § 10561 and may result in the exclusion of the report at trial. (CCR §§ 10616 and 10622.)

If you or the insurance company requested an expedited hearing, the appeals board must review the request within two business days. If approved, the request will be referred to the presiding workers' compensation judge for placement on a separate and faster trial schedule. (CCR § 10136.)

F. Receiving Notice of a Hearing

After you (or the insurance company) files a Declaration of Readiness to Proceed with the Workers' Compensation Appeals Board, you will receive a notice in the mail called a Notice of Hearing. This document contains important information about your case that will assist you at the time of your hearing. Carefully look over the Notice of Hearing and find:

- the type of hearing you are set for, such as a pre-trial settlement conference
- the date and time of your hearing (often several weeks or months away)
- the address of the Workers' Compensation Appeals Board where your matter will be heard, and
- the department or judge who will hear your matter.

Depending on the calendar (schedule) at your local Workers' Compensation Appeals Board, your matter will be set for either a pre-trial conference (mandatory settlement conference) or a trial. Typically, you will go directly to trial only if you have requested an expedited hearing or, sometimes, if a pre-trial conference has already been held.

1. If the Insurance Company Requested the Hearing

If the insurance company filed a Declaration of Readiness to Proceed on any issues (preliminary or on the case-in-chief), you will be served with a copy of the document.

Sample Notice of Hearing

DIVISION OF WORKERS' COMPENSATION

WORKERS' COMPENSATION APPEALS BOARD

NOTICE OF HEARING

DATE OF SERVICE: 12/16/20xx

WCAB CASE NBR(s): XX 0000

EMPLOYEE: Allen Mar

EMPLOYER: Sandy's Restaurant

INSURER: AAA Insurance Company

TYPE OF HEARING:	MANDATORY SETTLEMENT
DATE OF HEARING:	02/22/20xx TUESDAY
TIME OF HEARING:	9:00 A.M.
LENGTH OF HEARING:	
LOCATION:	303 W. Third Street #640 SAN BERNARDINO CA 92401
JUDGE:	John Justice (909) 555-2222

You are hereby notified that the above-entitled case is set for hearing before the Division of Workers' Compensation of the State of California. Continuances are not favored and will be granted only upon clear showing of good cause. Please arrive before scheduled appearance time.

NOTICE TO INSURER: The employer will not receive notice of hearing.

SPECIAL COMMENTS/INSTRUCTIONS:

WC01

Within six days of being served with a Declaration of Readiness to Proceed (11 days if it was mailed to you), you must file with the Workers' Compensation Appeals Board and serve upon opposing parties any medical reports that you have in your possession or under your control, unless they've been previously filed in the proceeding. (CCR § 10979.) (For more information, see "Special Rules for Medical Reports," in Chapter 21, Section E2.)

2. How to Object to a Hearing

It's possible that you won't be ready to go to trial for reasons such as these:

- You are still receiving medical treatment and are not yet permanent and stationary.
- You have not yet seen a QME to determine the nature and extent of your permanent disability.
- You are still participating in a vocational rehabilitation program and do not want to settle your case until it is completed.

If you are served with a Declaration of Readiness to Proceed, you can object to the hearing's being set. Here's how to object to having the hearing set for trial: Write and file an "objection letter," which must be signed under penalty of perjury. In the letter, explain the specific reasons why you feel your matter is not yet ready to be heard.

Your objection to the matter being set for a hearing must be sent to the Workers' Compensation Appeals Board (and a copy served upon opposing parties) within ten days (15 days if you were mailed a copy) of the date of service of the Declaration of Readiness to Proceed by the insurance company. If you don't object within the time allotted, your case will be set for a hearing on the issues listed in the Declaration of Readiness to Proceed and you will be treated as if you waived any objections to proceeding on the issues specified in the DOR. You will have to appear and try to request that the case be taken off calendar at that time or be prepared to set the matter for trial.

File your objection letter with the appeals board and serve copies on all opposing parties in your case within the required time limits. (See Chapter 23, Section E, for instructions). You should receive a response from the appeals board within 30 days.

Sample Objection Letter

June 12, 20xx

Presiding Judge Workers' Compensation Appeals Board[Address]

Re: Donna Goldstein v. SQ Industries, A & A Insurance Company
Case # BV 0000
Objection to Defendants' Declaration of Readiness to Proceed

Your Honor,

I have been served with a copy of a Declaration of Readiness to Proceed filed by A & A Insurance Company, a copy of which is attached to this letter.

I object to the Declaration of Readiness and request that this case not be set for a hearing at this time because I am still treating with Dr. Smith for my back injury, and have not yet been declared permanent and stationary.

I respectfully request that the Declaration of Readiness filed by A & A Insurance Company be set aside.

I declare under penalty of perjury under the laws of State of California that the facts contained in this letter are true and correct to the best of my knowledge.

Sincerely,

Donna Goldstein

Donna Goldstein
[Address]

cc: A & A Insurance Company
[Address]

3. Prepare for the Hearing

Turn to Chapter 21 for information on how to prepare for the hearing. Then read Chapter 24 to learn what to expect when you attend a hearing.

CHAPTER

23

How to File and Serve Documents

If you're handling your own workers' compensation case, you're legally required to serve opposing parties with copies of all important documents. You'll also need to file certain documents with the Workers' Compensation Appeals Board.

Various rules govern who must be served with which documents and whether or not copies must be filed with the appeals board. Why are all these procedures so important? Because most of the key issues of your case will be determined on the basis of written documents, such as medical reports, your DWC-1 form, your Application for Adjudication of Claim forms, and work injury reports.

This chapter gives step-by-step instructions on how to:

- serve (provide) the other side with copies of documents pertaining to your case, and
- file documents with the Workers' Compensation Appeals Board to ensure that all relevant evidence in your case is part of your appeals board file.

A. What Is Service of Documents?

"Serving papers" refers to the process of providing copies of documents to people in a way that complies with legal requirements. In a workers' compensation case, documents are usually served by sending them via regular U.S. mail. Documents may also be served if they are personally handed or faxed to someone. (See CCR §§ 10505 and 10506.)

1. Who Must Be Served?

We refer to your employer and the workers' compensation insurance company as opposing parties, because their interest in the process is directly opposed to yours.

Every document that you file with the appeals board (and some that you don't) must be served on opposing parties. If your employer is represented by an insurance company, you need to serve the insurance company only, unless you're advised differently.

If a party (such as the insurance company) hires an attorney, service should be made on the attorney rather than the party. (CCR § 10510.)

You must also serve any persons or entities who have an interest in the outcome of your claim. This would include any doctors, hospitals, or others yet to be paid (called lien claimants).

2. What Documents Must Be Served and When?

All documents that are filed with the Workers' Compensation Appeals Board must also be served on opposing parties. This includes all of the documents in the chart below.

You must also serve opposing parties with certain documents that are not filed with the appeals board if either of the following is true:

- The documents require action on the part of the other party.
- You intend to submit the documents into evidence at your trial.

Examples of documents that are not initially filed with the appeals board but that must be served on opposing parties include medical reports, subpoenas, and subpoenas duces tecum. See the chart below, "Documents to Be Served and Filed," for details.

After the filing of an Application for Adjudication of Claim, if the insurance company or a lien claimant requests you to serve copies of physician's reports relating to the claim, you must serve copies of the medical reports within six days of the request. (Similarly, if you ask the insurance company for reports, it must serve them on you within six days.)

Once this request has been made, the duty to serve medical reports becomes a continuing one, and you (or the insurance company) have six days from the date you receive any new reports to serve a copy upon the requesting party. Failure to properly serve copies of the medical reports within these time limits can result in the WCAB's disregarding the report.

Documents to Be Served and Filed

Document	When to Serve Defendants	When to File With Workers' Compensation Appeals Board
Application for Adjudication of Claim	Appeals board will serve if you don't have a lawyer	Within one year of the date of injury
DWC-1 form	Within one year of the date of injury	At the time you file a Declaration of Readiness
Declaration of Readiness to Proceed	At the time you file the Declaration of Readiness with the appeals board	When you're ready to set your matter for a hearing
Subpoena	At the time you serve a subpoena on individual being subpoenaed	Only if (and when) you need to get an order enforcing the subpoena
Subpoena duces tecum	At the time you serve a subpoena duces tecum on the individual or entity you want to produce records	Only if (and when) you need to get an order enforcing the subpoena duces tecum
Medical reports	Within five days of receipt	At the time you file a Declaration of Readiness or Application for Adjudication of Claim
Medical records	Not required if you don't intend to submit as evidence	If you intend to submit as evidence, serve records at the time you file a Declaration of Readiness or Application for Adjudication of Claim
Written evidence to be presented at trial, such as W-2 forms, pay stubs, letters, pain diaries	Not less than 20 days before hearing	At the time you file a Declaration of Readiness
X-rays	Not required	Not required; judges generally don't want to see X-rays
Letters you write to the appeals board judge regarding your matter	At the time you send letter to the appeals board	Not applicable

3. Who Is Responsible for Serving Documents?

As a general rule, each party has the responsibility of serving documents on the other parties. In some instances, the Workers' Compensation Appeals Board may serve parties with documents filed there. You should not, however, rely on this. Get into the practice of always serving the parties with copies of any documents that are listed in the accompanying chart. Serving documents consists of putting copies in the mail and filling out a simple proof of service form, so there is really no reason not to do it as a matter of course.

B. How to Serve Documents by Mail

Documents other than subpoenas may all be served by mail. (See Section C, below, for instructions on how to serve documents personally.) Subpoenas duces tecum may be served either personally or by mail.

1. Complete Proof of Service Form

A proof of service is simply a form in which you state that you mailed a certain document to a particular person or entity on a certain date. Any time you serve the opposing parties with a document, you must prepare a proof of service and staple one copy to the document you are serving. (CCR § 10324.)

The proof of service must give the names and addresses of all persons served, specify how service was made, provide the date of service, and either the place of personal service or the address to which mailing was made. Refer to the sample proof of service, below, as a guide. A downloadable copy of this form is available on Nolo's website. (See Chapter 29, "Online Appendixes" for the link to this and other forms in this book.)

After you've completed the proof of service form, proceed to Section B2, below, for instructions on how to copy and serve the legal documents.

Five Days Added for Service by Mail

The time limitations for serving documents is extended by an additional five days if the documents being served are in response to documents received by mail. (CCR § 10507; California Code of Civil Procedure § 1013.)

> **EXAMPLE:** Craig receives a Declaration of Readiness to Proceed in the mail. He has a total of 15 days from the date he received the Declaration to object if he wants to—that is, the normal ten days plus five additional days because the document was served by mail.

2. Copy and Mail Documents

Here's what you need to do to serve papers through the mail:

Step 1. Gather together the papers you want to serve.

Step 2. Make photocopies of all papers, including the signed proof of service. You'll need one copy of each set of papers for every opposing party, plus two copies for filing, and at least one to keep for your own records.

Step 3. Staple the signed proof of service form to the top of the documents you are mailing.

Step 4. Put a copy of the papers, including a copy of the proof of service, in an envelope addressed to each party being served. If there is an attorney of record, remember to serve the attorney instead of the party.

Step 5. Put sufficient postage on each envelope for first-class delivery.

Step 6. Deposit the envelope in the mailbox. Or, if you are mailing the papers from work, you may deposit them in the business's mail if it will be taken for collection that day.

Step 7. Keep the original signed documents and proof of service. You may need to file these with the appeals board. Section E, below, has instructions on filing documents.

C. How to Serve Documents Personally

Subpoenas for a witness to appear must be served personally—that is, personally handed or delivered to the person being served. Subpoenas duces tecum and other documents may be served either personally or by mail. (How to serve documents by mail is covered in Section B, just above.)

In a workers' compensation case, you (the injured worker) or any adult may serve documents. If it's convenient, have someone other than you serve the documents. Here's how to serve papers personally:

Step 1. Gather together the papers you want served.

Step 2. Fill in a proof of service form, provided Nolo's website. (See Chapter 29, "Online Appendixes" for the link to this and other forms in this book.) Follow the sample shown, and check the appropriate box to indicate personal service rather than service by mail. If more than one person is being personally served, fill out a separate proof of service for each. Don't sign the proof of service yet.

Step 3. Make copies of the papers, including the proof of service. You'll need one set for the person being served, one set for every opposing party, two copies for filing, plus the original.

Step 4. Staple the proof of service to the top of the documents you are serving.

Step 5. Shortly before serving the person (perhaps outside the person's home or office), fill in the date and time of service and sign and date the proof of service. Simply hand a completed proof of service and documents to the person being served. The person need not accept the documents. It's fine to put them as near as possible to the person being served and say "This is for you" or "These are legal documents."

Step 6. If you served someone other than the opposing parties (a witness, for example), you'll also need to serve the opposing parties with copies of the documents you served, including the completed proof of service. Follow the directions in Section B, above, for serving documents by mail.

Step 7. Keep the original signed documents and proof of service. You may need to file these with the appeals board. Section E, below, has instructions on filing documents.

TIP

If you anticipate problems serving someone. For people who are difficult to serve—for example, it's hard to find them or they don't want to be served and are trying to avoid the papers—your best bet may be to hire a professional process server. Check in the yellow pages of the telephone directory under "process servers" or "attorney services." Process servers generally charge around $25–$50 for personal service and sometimes more, especially if service is difficult. I highly recommend using professionals for personal service.

D. How to Serve Documents by Fax

You are allowed to serve a copy of a medical report or other document by fax, but if you do, I recommend that you telephone the parties you are serving and verify that they are willing to accept a faxed copy of the document as if it were served by mail. If they are not, serve them by mail to be safe.

If you choose to serve a document by fax, include a proof of service form, as discussed in Section B, above. Also, add a cover sheet addressed to the party you are serving, describing the items being faxed and the number of pages in the fax, including the cover page. Keep a copy of the fax confirmation for your records.

E. How to File Documents With the Workers' Compensation Appeals Board

To file a document with the Workers' Compensation Appeals Board, take or mail it to the appeals board, where it is recorded (date-stamped as received) and placed in your official case file. Before any document can be reviewed and considered by a judge, it must first be filed with the appeals board. Documents may be filed either in person or by mail.

You'll file all papers and documents at the appeals board office where your case is being heard. This office is usually located in the county where you live. If you're not sure which office to file in, see Chapter 5, Section C4c, for an explanation of how to find this out.

1. What Documents Must Be Filed and When to File Them

Before you file any documents with the Workers' Compensation Appeals Board, turn to the chart above, "Documents to Be Served and Filed." Make sure that you have done all of the following:

- You have served the opposing parties.
- You are filing the document at the appropriate time.

Sample Proof of Service for Service by Mail or Personal Service

STATE OF CALIFORNIA

DEPARTMENT OF INDUSTRIAL RELATIONS

WORKERS' COMPENSATION APPEALS BOARD

Sara Gonzalez
Applicant

vs.

ABC Corporation and AIG Insurance
Defendants

Case No. POM 345670

Proof of Service

I declare that:

1. At the time of service I was at least 18 years of age.
2. My business or residence address is: 18818 El Camino Real, San Diego, CA
3. If service is by mail, I am a resident of or employed in the county where the mailing occurred.
4. I served copies of the following papers *(list exact titles of papers served)*: Declaration of Readiness to Proceed
5. Manner of service *(check one box)*:

   ☒ a. By placing true copies in a sealed envelope with postage fully prepaid and depositing the envelope in the United States Mail on August 1, 20xx, at *(city and state)*: San Diego, CA

   ☐ b. *(If deposited at a business)*: By placing true copies for collection and mailing following ordinary business practices. I am readily familiar with the business's practice for collection and processing of correspondence for mailing with the United States Post Office. The correspondence is/was scheduled to be deposited with the United States Post office in the ordinary course of business on ________, 20___, at *(city and state)*: ________

   ☐ c. By personally delivering true copies on ________, 20___, at ______ *(time)*.
6. Name and address of each party/person served:

   Joe Nolo

   Attorney at Law

   123 Central Ave, Suite 230

   San Diego, CA 90123
7. I declare under penalty of perjury under the laws of the State of California that the foregoing is true and correct.

Date: 8/2/20xx

Signature: Sara Gonzalez

Printed Name: Sara Gonzalez

- You are permitted (or required) to file the document with the appeals board.

If you aren't certain whether or not to file particular documents, check with an information and assistance officer.

Some Documents Cannot Be Filed With the Appeals Board

Certain documents cannot be filed with, or sent to, the Workers' Compensation Appeals Board. If you try to file these documents, the appeals board may send them back to you. Worse yet, the appeals board could simply discard them and not tell you. Do not try to file:

- letters to opposing parties or lawyers
- subpoenas or subpoenas duces tecum
- notices of taking deposition, or
- medical appointment letters.

2. Requirements for Filing Documents

CAUTION

All documents filed with the Workers Compensation Appeals Board are now scanned into their computer and then destroyed. It is very important that you keep copies of all documents you file so that you can refer to them at hearing—they will no longer be available to you in a hard copy file after you submit them to the WCAB.

All legal documents (such as completed forms, letters, petitions, briefs, and notices) filed with the Workers' Compensation Appeals Board must meet certain requirements. First, you must include a sheet called a Document Separator Sheet between each document you file with the WCAB. If you are filing an Application for Adjudication of Claim and a DWC-1 notice (or any other form), each must have its own Document Separator Sheet on top. A downloadable copy of the Document Cover Sheet is available on Nolo's website. (See Chapter 29, "Online Appendixes" for the link to this and other forms in this book.). Here's how to use it:

- On the line for Product Delivery Unit, insert "ADJ."
- On the line for Document Type, include a general description of the document—medical report, legal document, correspondence, and so forth.
- On the line for Document Title, simply put in the title of the document, such as C&R.
- Fill in the date of the document—not the filng date, but the date the document was created—on the document date line.
- The Author is whoever prepared the document; this may be you or, for example, a doctor who prepared a medical report.

A list of all the possible document types and document titles for ADJ cases is included as part of the Document Separator Sheet form, available on Nolo's website. (See Chapter 29, "Online Appendixes" for the link.)

Next, you must include a "Document Cover Sheet" on top of the full package that includes all documents that you file. For example, if you are filing an Application for Adjudication of Claim and a DWC-1 form, the Document Cover Sheet would go on top of all the documents (including the two Document Separator Sheets and the two documents themselves).

Although the form allows for up to 15 cases to be listed, you only need to use enough pages to cover all your claims—there's no need to file blank pages. (You also don't need to worry about pages 6 and 7, which contain information addressed elsewhere in this book.) Here's how to fill it out:

- Check yes or no to indicate whether this is a new case (that is, a first-time filing). If there is a companion case (an additional date of injury), check the appropriate box. If you are just filing the documents and are not presenting them to a judge directly, check the box "no" for walkthrough.
- Put in the date you are filing the form on the left along with the case number (ADJ number) and your Social Security

Document Separator Sheet

DOCUMENT SEPARATOR SHEET

Product Delivery Unit ADJ

Document Type LEGAL DOCS

Document Title DWC-1 CLAIM FORM

Document Date 12/20/xx
MM/DD/YYYY

Author BETTY WHITE

Office Use Only

Received Date ____________
MM/DD/YYYY

DWC-CA form 10232.2 Rev. 9/2010 Page 1

Document Cover Sheet

STATE OF CALIFORNIA
DWC DISTRICT OFFICE

DOCUMENT COVER SHEET

Is this a new case? Yes ☐ No ☑ Companion Cases Exist ☐ Walkthrough Yes ☐ No ☐

More than 15 Companion Cases ☐

10/08/20xx
Date:(MM/DD/YYYY)

SSN: 123-45-6789

☑ Specific Injury

ADJ777777
Case Number 1

☐ Cumulative Injury (Start Date: MM/DD/YYYY) (End Date: MM/DD/YYYY)
(If Specific Injury, use the start date as the specific date of injury)

Body Part 1: 420 Body Part 3: 450

Body Part 2: 513 Body Part 4: 520

Other Body Parts: 300

Please check unit to be filed on (check only one box)

☑ ADJ ☐ DEU ☐ SIF ☐ UEF ☐ INT ☐ RSU

Companion Cases

☐ Specific Injury

Case Number 2

☐ Cumulative Injury (Start Date: MM/DD/YYYY) (End Date: MM/DD/YYYY)
(If Specific Injury, use the start date as the specific date of injury)

Body Part 1: 420 Body Part 3: 450

Body Part 2: 513 Body Part 4: 520

Other Body Parts: 300

DWC-CA form 10232.1 Rev. 7/2010 - Page 1 of 8

number, and check the box for Specific Injury or Cumulative Injury (see Chapter 3, Section B1). If it is a specific injury you will only complete the "start date" and leave the end date blank. For a cumulative injury, the start date goes on the first line and the end date on the last line.

- List your body parts affected in the "body parts" section. (See Chapter 29, "Online Appendixes" for the link to the body part list.)
- Check the appropriate box for the unit to be filed in. Almost all of the time this will be ADJ.
- If you are filing a request for a rating you will check the box DEU.
- All the other boxes are for complicated issues for which an attorney is recommended.

If you have any additional dates of injury (companion cases) fill out the same boxes and lines for each of those.

- Documents must be on 8.5" x 11" white paper, with no holes.
- No staples are allowed—use only paper clips to secure documents.
- All documents must have a heading that includes the name of the injured employee and the Workers' Compensation Appeals Board case number, if one has been assigned.
- Copies must be served on opposing parties, either by mail or in person. To show that service was made, you must include a proof of service. (See Sections B and C, above.)

3. How to File Documents in Person

Make at least one extra copy of the documents (and proofs of service) you're planning to serve. There are two ways to file a document in person:

- You or someone else may take the document to the clerk's office at the Workers' Compensation Appeals Board. Simply ask the clerk to file the documents. Some appeals boards have baskets where you drop documents off for filing the next day. Before placing the document in the basket, you need

Proof of Service Rule

Where does the proof of service go in the packet when filing workers' comp forms? The answer depends on how many forms or documents you are listing on the same proof of service. If you are listing only one form, with no attachments, the proof of service goes directly under the form, as though it were part of the form, without a separator sheet between the form and the proof of service.

If you're filing a form with accompanying documents, and listing the form and the documents on a single proof of service, the proof of service will come at the end of the form and documents, with a document separator sheet before the proof of service.

Here's how the proof of service is placed in filings with multiple documents and separator sheets—this example is for an Application for Adjudication of Claim.

- Document separator sheet
- Application for adjudication of claim
- Document separator sheet
- Declaration in compliance with L.C. section 4906(g)
- Document separator sheet
- DWC-1 form
- Document separator sheet
- Fee disclosure statement
- Document separator sheet, and
- Proof of service of the above documents.

Here's how the proof of service is placed in filings with a single document and only one separator sheet—this example is for a Notice and Request for Allowance of Lien.

- Document cover sheet
- Document separator sheet
- Notice in request for allowance of lien
- Itemized billing statement (this doesn't get a separator sheet because it's appended to the lien), and
- Proof of service.

Sample Letter to Appeals Board

Date August 29, 20xx

State of California

Workers' Compensation Appeals Board

Oakland Office

1111 Jackson Street

Oakland, CA 94602

Re: Workers' Compensation Claim

Injured Worker: Juan Martinez

Employer: Creekside Development

Insurance Company: SCIF

Appeals Board Case Number: BD 121

To whom it may concern:

Enclosed please find the original and 1 copy/copies of the following documents *(list exact title and date of each document):*

Medical report and bill of Dr. Smith dated June 1, 20xx.

Please file the original documents and return date-stamped copies to me. I have enclosed a self-addressed, stamped envelope. Thank you.

Signature: Juan Martinez

Printed Name: Juan Martinez

Mailing Address: P.O. Box 101010

City, State, Zip: Oakland, CA 94606

Telephone Number: (510) 555-8181

to "file stamp" it. There will be a machine similar to a time clock. Insert your document for stamping. Remember to file stamp an extra copy for your records.

- If you're going to a settlement conference, hearing, or trial, file stamp your documents as discussed just above. You'll then need to take the original file stamped document to the courtroom for filing in your board file. Do not leave your documents with the clerk, as they won't make it into your file in time for the hearing.

Make sure you get back an extra copy of every document you file, file stamped for your records. Also get an extra file-stamped copy for the opposing parties if they have not yet been served.

4. How to File Documents by Mail

Make at least two extra copies of each document (and proof of service or service letter) you're filing by mail. If you mail two or more documents in the same case at one time, you must staple them to a cover letter which includes your name and appeals board case number and lists each document by name and date. (CCR § 10392.)

A downloadable copy of a form cover letter to the appeals board is available on Nolo's website. (See Chapter 29, "Online Appendixes" for the link to this and other forms in this book.) There is a sample copy above.

Mail the documents to the Workers' Compensation Appeals Board. Include a self-addressed, stamped envelope, because you're asking the appeals board to send you a file-stamped copy. Documents filed by mail are deemed filed on the date they are received by the Workers' Compensation Appeals Board, not on the date the stamp on the envelope is "canceled." (CCR § 10390.) It is best to send important mail like this by certified mail, return-receipt requested.

TIP

Appeals boards aren't rigid on filing and service of evidence. Most appeals board judges are lenient about the rules for filing and serving medical reports and other evidence. Unless the other side objects, any evidence you file—even on the day of a hearing—will generally be allowed. Even if the other side objects, there is a good chance the judge will allow you to present your evidence anyway, cutting you some slack because you don't have an attorney.

CHAPTER

24

Going to the Hearing or Trial

This chapter assumes the necessary papers have been filed with the Workers' Compensation Appeals Board and your case is scheduled for a hearing or trial. (How to complete the required paperwork is covered in Chapter 22.)

If you do not have an attorney, this chapter will take you through the basics of handling your own hearing. Your lawyer, if you have one, will handle the procedural details for you, but this chapter will still be useful.

Prior to reading this chapter, you should review Chapter 21 and make sure that you've adequately prepared for your hearing. If you've followed our advice, you will have already observed a workers' compensation hearing to get a feel for what goes on.

It is a good idea to read this chapter at least twice. Read it a minimum of several weeks before your hearing date so you have plenty of time to prepare. Then reread this chapter shortly before your hearing, to keep the information fresh in your mind.

Here's what this chapter covers:

- Section A discusses practical aspects of appearing at the Workers' Compensation Appeals Board. This information applies to all types of hearings and trials. You'll learn, among other things, how to check in, find your hearing room, locate your file, and find the insurance company representative.
- Section B covers pre-trial conferences (often called mandatory settlement conferences or pre-trial hearings). You will find out how to go about settling your case and what to do if you can't settle.
- Section C discusses trials. You'll find material on final negotiations, as well as advice on when to proceed to trial and when to "continue" (postpone) your case. You'll learn how to submit medical evidence and other exhibits, stipulate (agree with your opponent) to issues, and generally set the stage for the trial. Finally, you'll learn about the trial itself: questions you will be asked and how best to cross-examine witnesses.
- In Section D, we cover the judge's decision, which will be set out in a document called the Findings and Award.

TIP

Judge or referee: It makes little difference. Whenever I use the term "judge," I refer to people who may technically be classified as either a judge or a referee in the workers' compensation bureaucracy. But as far as you are concerned, workers' compensation referees and judges have the same basic responsibilities, and therefore it makes no difference who hears your case. Out of respect, I refer to both referees and judges as judges, and suggest you do the same.

A. Finding Your Way Around the Appeals Board

By now, you have prepared your case for the hearing, filed and served appropriate documents, notified any witnesses, and collected all necessary paperwork.

1. Several Days Before Your Hearing

Double-check that your paperwork and evidence are in order. Leave yourself enough time to get and make copies of anything that's missing. You won't want to be in a rush before your hearing. Organize your papers so that you can easily lay your hands on any documents you may need.

2. The Day Before Your Hearing

The night before your big day, lay out the clothes you plan to wear. If possible, men should wear a dress shirt and tie. Women should wear appropriate clothing, as if attending a business meeting. Finally, get to bed early, and get a good night's sleep.

3. Getting to the Appeals Board

If you have never been to the appeals board before, be sure to call well in advance and get directions.

You will have enough on your mind on the day of your hearing; you don't need to worry about directions.

Plan on arriving at the appeals board at least 30 minutes before your designated hearing time. This will allow you time to get oriented and find out where you're supposed to be. (Information about the hearing date, time, and location are contained in the Notice of Hearing. See Chapter 22, Section F.)

Expect to spend the better part of the day at the appeals board (although you will probably end up staying for a shorter time, such as a morning or an afternoon). For example, park your car where you won't have to move it, and don't make appointments you'll need to rush to.

Your promptness at hearings is a reflection on you, so be on time unless an emergency arises. If you can't avoid being late (flat tire or some other unavoidable reason), call the appeals board and leave a message telling when you can be expected. The appeals board operates rather informally, so if you have a good reason for being late, it shouldn't be a problem as long as you notify the board.

4. Checking In at the Appeals Board

When you arrive at the appeals board, job one is to check in. Almost all appeals boards have a main assembly area, with posted lists of matters to be heard that day.

Look at the list of cases under the name of the judge who has been assigned to your case (the judge's name is on your Notice of Hearing). The list should have your name and the name of your employer, as well as the name of attorneys representing any of the parties. Sign or initial next to your name. This will notify anyone checking the list that you are present. Also look to see if a representative from the insurance company has signed in and make a note of the person's name.

If there is no list, check with a clerk at the main desk (clerk's office) and inquire whether you need to sign in anywhere. If your name is not on the list of matters to be heard that day, find out from the clerk's office why you're not scheduled to appear.

5. Find the Courtroom

After checking in, you'll need to find the courtroom where your matter will be heard. Many appeals boards take security precautions to prevent entry by anyone carrying weapons or who is otherwise unauthorized to enter. As a party to a proceeding, you are permitted to enter the security area, but, of course, you must comply with all required security measures.

Individual courtrooms are often identified by the name of the judge or referee, rather than a room number. The sign-in sheet will have the judge's room number listed if room numbers are used.

If you have any difficulty finding the courtroom, don't hesitate to ask a clerk at the main desk. Or you might ask someone in a suit with a briefcase. Chances are that person is an attorney who is familiar with the appeals board.

Once you find the courtroom, enter and take a moment to get acquainted with the room. The hearing room is generally small. At some appeals boards, there will be an office room adjoining the hearing room, known as the judge's chambers. Judges sometimes hear matters that can be resolved quickly in their chambers. At other appeals boards, the judge's chambers and the hearing room are one and the same. If there is a judge's chambers, don't enter it.

The time for your hearing will be listed on your Notice of Hearing. Most morning calendars (schedules) begin at 9:00 a.m. and finish by noon, while the afternoon calendar generally begins at 1:30 p.m. and finishes by 4:30 p.m. You will probably not see much activity in the courtroom until it's time to begin. If no hearing or trial is in progress, you can sit anywhere.

6. Find the Minutes of Hearing

The minutes of hearing is a form that everyone who appears at the hearing must sign to show the judge who is present. At the hearing, there will be numerous minutes of hearing forms on the table, one for each case the judge has that day, so search through them until you find your name.

It is a three-page document, but you only sign on the first page under "Appearances." Check the box for "Applicant present" and print your name. That's it, you're done. The representative for the insurance company (usually its attorney) will sign in on the line for "Defendant represented by..."

If you can't find your minutes of hearing form, ask the judge when he or she appears if there is a sign-in sheet for your case. Simply walk up to the judge when he is seated at his desk, or at some boards you will have to knock on the door to his office and wait for him to call you in.

A copy of the Minutes of Hearing form is below.

CAUTION

Bring all paperwork to the hearing. Since the WCAB has gone paperless, everything is electronically filed, which means the WCAB doesn't keep any paper copies of your forms. That means that you have to bring all of your papers with you to all hearings, because there will be no copies at the hearing for you to look at. The judge will look up all of the documents he needs to see on his computer.

7. Find the Opposing Parties

If the insurance company representative or attorney has checked in, you'll want to locate that person.

Announce to those persons in the courtroom, "Is anyone here on the (your name) matter?" Do this every so often until you find the representative.

Unless your employer is permissibly self-insured, or has been asked to appear as a witness in your case, it is rare for the employer to appear at appeals board hearings.

8. Propose a Settlement

You will probably want to make one last effort to settle your case before going before the judge. You might try opening up the lines of communication by saying something about the issues to be resolved. For example, if you are trying to settle your overall case, you might say something like, "Have you had an opportunity to review my file?" or "Do you have any settlement authority today?"

If there is room in the courtroom, you and the insurance company's representative (whom we'll refer to as "the representative") can sit down and discuss your case. You can leave the courtroom if you'd like. You should not need to take the board file with you if you leave the room, but if you wish to, get permission from the judge or the judge's secretary first.

Don't be afraid to tell the representative what you want and why you feel you are entitled to it. Listen very carefully to the representative's opinion regarding the issues you are trying to resolve. If anything said casts a new light on your case, you will need to make a quick analysis to see if you wish to change your position. The key to doing this is to understand your case very well in the first place.

If you are dealing with an attorney, don't let the lawyer intimidate you. If you ever had any suppressed desires to be an actor, use them now. Even if you're nervous, act with authority and confidence. Demonstrate your knowledge of the case and your determination to see it through. If you clearly know what you are talking about, the person you're dealing with is less likely to try to put something over on you.

Above all, don't cave in to what you know to be an unreasonable proposal. Representatives often use the tactic of waiting till the last moment before trial begins to settle—hoping that you will be too nervous to go to trial and will settle on their terms. So make up your mind in advance that you are fully prepared to try your case if necessary. Remember, the judge will help you through the hearing or trial.

B. Pre-Trial Conferences

The type of pre-trial conference you will attend depends upon which box you or the insurance

Minutes of Hearing

STATE OF CALIFORNIA
DEPARTMENT OF INDUSTRIAL RELATIONS
DIVISION OF WORKERS' COMPENSATION

MINUTES OF HEARING

ADJ777777
Case No.

Date of Hearing (MM/DD/YYYY) ____________

Hearing Information

☐ Before ☐ AT ☐ Trial ☐ Conf ☑ MSC ☐ EXP. HEARING ☐ Lien

Request Date (MM/DD/YYYY) ____________

Applicant

JOHN
First Name

MI

WU
Last Name

VS

Defendants

HOME INC
Employer Name (Please leave blank spaces between numbers, names or words)

Appearances

Applicant ☑ Present ☐ Not Present

	Attorney	Hearing Rep
Applicant Represented By JOHN WU PRO PER	☐	☐
Defendant Represented By ____________	☐	☐
Others Appearing ____________	☐	☐

Interpreter ____________ Cert. No. ____________

Party Making Request

☐ Joint ☐ Applicant ☐ Defendant ☐ Other ____________

Request For: ☐ Continuance ☐ OTOC Request By: ☐ Letter ☐ Telephone

Position of Opposing Party

☐ Agree ☐ Oppose ☐ Unreachable ☐ Unknown

DWC-CA form 10245 (11/2008) (Page 1)

company checked on the Declaration of Readiness to Proceed. (See Chapter 22, Sections A and D.)

Regardless of the type of hearing, the purpose of all pre-trial conferences is to help the parties settle the issues in dispute, rather than having a judge resolve them. A pre-trial conference is really just a meeting at the appeals board between you and the insurance company.

By the time your pre-trial conference rolls around, you should have already considered the key issues in your case. (See Chapter 21, Sections A and E1, for a more detailed discussion.) You should be able to answer all of the following questions:

- Do you have all the medical reports you require, or do you need to see other doctors and get more reports?
- Have you collected all your documentary evidence, such as pay stubs and W-2 forms?
- Do you know who your witnesses will be, if any?
- Has your permanent disability been rated?
- Do you have a settlement amount (often called a demand) in mind? (See Chapter 19 for a step-by-step approach to figuring out this amount.)

Expect to spend the entire morning or afternoon at your pre-trial conference, as the case may be. With a little luck, you might wrap things up in less than two hours, but plan on spending at least three. As you'll learn, it's to your advantage to set aside plenty of time for your pre-trial conference.

At the pre-trial conference, you cannot offer evidence or testimony, and although a judge will be present, the judge will not decide the issues in your case. (That will come later, at a trial if you're unable to settle.) Instead, the judge's function is to informally assist you and the insurance company in arriving at a settlement.

TIP

Settlement conference procedures can vary. The procedures at your pre-trial conference may be a little different from what's described below. Don't worry—just follow the judge's instructions.

1. Try to Settle Your Case

You will usually be discussing settlement with an attorney or a hearing representative—a nonattorney who acts as a representative for the insurance company. Sometimes an insurance company will send a claims adjuster (whose job is to settle workers' compensation claims), possibly the same adjuster you have been dealing with all along. No matter who you are dealing with, don't be intimidated. As discussed earlier, put on your best acting face and pretend that you also are entirely comfortable.

The best way to describe the atmosphere is to say the hearing room often looks like a crowded bus. It is not uncommon for there to be 20 or more people in a 10' x 10' room, all trying to find a place to sit and discuss their case. Typically, there will be at least half a dozen conversations taking place at once.

The judge will probably not participate in the actual settlement discussions, so you and the insurance company's representative may discuss the matter there in the courtroom or go anywhere else in the building. Because you may need help from the judge, however, you probably won't want to stray too far from the courtroom. If you need to take the board file with you for any reason, remember to first get permission.

a. If the Representative Is Pressed for Time

Often lawyers and insurance adjusters are in a hurry. This is because once an agreement—or impasse—is reached, it must be presented to the judge, which is done on a first-come, first-served basis. Lawyers, anxious to get back to their offices, want to be at the front of the line.

If you sense that the insurance company's representative is eager to get going, use it to your advantage. For starters, make a demand that is slightly higher than what your opening demand was going to be and see what the response is. You may very well end up with extra cash simply because the insurance company representative wants to get back to the office.

You also might let the representative know you've set aside the whole day to settle your case. The rule here is, don't be rushed. By taking your time, you have everything to gain and nothing to lose.

b. Settlement Tips

Before you attend a pre-trial conference, spend a little time reviewing Chapter 20 on the art of negotiating a settlement. Remember that once the insurance company raises the offer to a new high, that figure becomes the new "floor" for your case. Any further negotiations between your demands and their offer should begin with the new floor, not with the insurance company's original offer.

Be clear about your goal at the pre-trial conference. Understand that there is no urgency to settle the case now. There will be plenty of time between the pre-trial conference and the trial date to try to settle your case. In addition, you will have one final opportunity to settle before your hearing begins on the trial date. And if you just can't settle, there should be no harm in going to trial.

You might expect the insurance company to sweeten its previous offer to try and arrive at a fair compromise at a pre-trial conference. While this sometimes happens, it's also very possible that the insurance company will play hardball and, hoping that you will want to avoid a trial, make an inferior offer. Oftentimes, the insurance company will wait until the day of trial to offer a reasonable settlement, and will do so only after realizing that you're perfectly willing to go to trial.

TIP

Don't be swayed by hardball tactics! It is the insurance representative's job to convince you that your case is weak in order to scare you into settling for less than you want. Don't allow yourself to be intimidated! If you are adequately prepared, you will know when the representative is "blowing smoke." If you're not sure, set the matter for trial (refuse to settle) and then research the points brought by the representative.

Some attorneys may initially refuse to negotiate with you, claiming that your demand is unreasonable or that they don't have any settlement authority from their client (the insurance company). Don't believe it! If the attorney refuses to talk to you about settlement, take your time. Say that you have all day if necessary, and that you want the lawyer to seriously consider your demand or make a reasonable counteroffer.

At any time during the pre-trial conference, you may ask the judge to help you. Judges have an interest in seeing that matters are settled at the pre-trial conference if at all possible, and they are often helpful in assisting parties to reach settlement. For example, if the attorney is uncooperative, walk up to the judge and explain that the attorney is unwilling to negotiate a settlement in good faith and ask for the judge's help. Tell the judge you want to settle your case today if at all possible.

CAUTION

Both parties must be present when speaking with the judge. Any time you speak to the judge, you must do so in the presence of the insurance company representative and vice versa. Talking to a judge outside the presence of the other side is called "ex parte communication" and is not allowed.

Resolving a Disagreement Over an Advisory Rating

At some appeals boards, the Rating Bureau will allow parties to come in on certain days and have their medical reports rated on an informal basis. If there has not previously been an advisory rating in your case or if a disagreement over your permanent disability rating is hindering settlement, try to see whether the rater is available to give you and the insurance representative an advisory rating.

If you are at a hearing, you can inquire of the judge or ask the appeals board clerk about its policy for getting advisory ratings done at the appeals board.

2. If You Settle Your Case

If you and the insurance company reach an agreement, you must sign the appropriate settlement documents: a Compromise and Release or Stipulations with Request for Award. A line-by-line look at these settlement documents is in Chapter 20, Sections D1 and D2.

You may want to have the signed settlement documents submitted to the judge at a pre-trial conference, because the judge's immediate approval will expedite the receipt of your check by at least 30 days. Assuming the settlement documents are prepared to your satisfaction, you and the insurance representative will get in line to see the judge. The judge must review the settlement documents to ensure they are fair and adequate.

TIP

Settlements must always be approved by a judge. A great advantage you have when you are not represented by an attorney is that the judge will look very carefully at any settlement proposal you and the insurance company present for approval. If the judge does not feel that it is fair, it will not be approved. This is a kind of security blanket. Don't be afraid to ask the judge for an opinion regarding the adequacy of the settlement. This will ensure that the judge reviews the medical reports upon which the settlement is based, as well as the settlement amount and terms.

If you feel uncomfortable because things are just going too fast and you want to review the settlement documents at home, don't sign. It's perfectly reasonable to accept a slight delay in receiving your check in exchange for being able to carefully review the settlement documents at your leisure.

It's also possible that the representative will state that the documents cannot be completed at the board (sometimes this happens, and there is really nothing you can do about it). If you've reached a settlement, you and the insurance representative should inform the judge. Explain that the matter has been settled and request that the pre-trial conference be taken off calendar pending receipt of the settlement documents, usually within 30 days. In workers' compensation jargon, this is referred to as "30 days for C&R" or "30 days for stips." Ask for a hearing date at which the judge will review the settlement documents, also known as an "adequacy hearing." You will need to come back to the appeals board for the adequacy hearing, discussed below.

Adequacy Hearings

If you have agreed to settle your case by stipulations or compromise and release, the insurance company will file a Declaration of Readiness to Proceed and request that your matter be set on calendar for a hearing to approve your settlement. The notice may be titled "Pre-Trial Conference," followed by wording in the document such as "Hearing is set over issue of adequacy of C&R" or something similar.

The adequacy hearing is a short meeting with a judge at the Workers' Compensation Appeals Board. At the hearing, the judge reviews the proposed settlement documents and decides whether, in the judge's opinion, they are adequate. If they are, the judge will approve the settlement. If not, the judge will instruct the insurance company to make changes to the agreement, which could even include more money for you.

You should always attend this hearing, even though some boards may allow you to waive this procedure. This is a good way to find out whether you have negotiated a fair settlement. At the hearing, bring up any questions or concerns you have and ask the judge for an opinion.

3. If You Cannot Settle Your Case

If you and the insurance representative cannot agree to a settlement, you may request the judge's assistance. As mentioned earlier, the judge wants you and the representative to settle and will do everything possible to help you do so. If you feel the insurance representative is being unreasonable or won't agree to your demand because of a belief that your demand is not supported by the facts or the law, tell the representative that you want to ask the judge's opinion. You have this right—and should use it—even if the insurance representative doesn't want you to. Stand in line and wait to see the judge.

When your turn comes to see the judge, you'll be directed to a seat. The insurance representative will also be present. If you have the board file, hand it to the judge. Always remember to address the judge as "Your Honor." Answer the judge's questions clearly, giving all the necessary information and no more. Don't ramble or get off track into irrelevant issues. Above all, be calm, courteous, and patient.

Tell the judge the one or two main points in your case that are preventing you and the insurance company from reaching a settlement. For example, let's say the insurance representative contends that, based on the medical reports, your case is only worth $3,000 in permanent disability, while you contend that it is worth $10,000. The judge will review the reports and probably give an opinion on the value of your permanent disability. Depending on what the judge says, you (or the insurance company) may decide to reconsider settlement.

By law, the judge must protect your best interests. The judge's point of view will give you very valuable information about the true value of your case as well as the likely outcome of crucial issues if your case proceeds to trial. The judge may make suggestions to you or the insurance representative about settlement. Listen carefully and, if possible, take notes on the judge's comments.

If you cannot settle your case, even with the assistance of the judge, you must do one of the following:

- **Set your case for trial.** This means you and the representative will get a date to have the issues decided by a judge. This requires that you and the insurance representative fill out a Pre-Trial Conference Statement, perhaps with a judge's assistance. (See Section B4, below, for instructions.)
- **Ask the judge to take the matter off calendar (postpone the trial).** This means that you want your case taken off the court's system for setting trials at this time.
- **Ask the judge to "continue" the pre-trial conference to another date.** This means that you can't resolve your matter at the present time but may be able to do so in the future.

Let's look at these options in more detail.

a. Set Your Case for Trial

If you can't settle your case at the pre-trial conference, you may choose to set your case for trial. At this time, you and the insurance company's representative must fill out a pre-trial conference statement, perhaps with the judge's assistance (as discussed in Section B4, below).

Some judges may assign a trial date themselves. Sometimes the trial will be set "on notice," which means that you won't find out the date and time of the trial until you receive a Notice of Hearing in the mail. It's also possible that the judge will give you the board file and send you and the insurance company representative down the hall to the calendar clerk, who will assign a trial date and note it on the board file.

b. Take the Matter Off Calendar

On the basis of what you learn prior to or at the pre-trial conference, you may want to delay your trial date. This may be necessary because you realize that your situation has changed since your case was set for hearing and other things need to be done before the case is ready for trial. For example, your medical condition may have deteriorated since you last saw a QME, and you may need to be reexamined to substantiate your medical condition.

The workers' compensation jargon for taking your matter off the trial calendar is "order taken off calendar," or OTOC (pronounced "Oh-tock"). This amounts to a request that the judge take your case out of the loop and not set it for a new pre-trial conference or trial date. (If you OTOC your case, you do not need to fill out the Pre-Trial Conference Statement form covered in Section B4, below.)

To OTOC your case, you must get the judge's permission. How to proceed depends on who set the matter for trial—that is, who filed the Declaration of Readiness to Proceed:

- **If you set the matter for trial.** Ask the judge in the presence of the insurance company representative that the matter be OTOCed, and state your reasons.
- **If the insurance company set the matter for trial.** In this case, it is more difficult to get the matter taken off calendar. Because the insurance company has requested that the matter be set for trial, it probably will object to your OTOC request. If you previously objected to the insurance company's filing of the Declaration of Readiness to Proceed, you should point that out to the judge. (See Chapter 22, Section F2.) If you did not object, your position is much weaker. However, if your reasons are good, the judge nevertheless may OTOC the matter.

c. Request a Continuance of the Pre-Trial Conference

A continuance means you are rescheduling your pre-trial conference to a later date. The reasons and factors discussed above regarding OTOCing also apply to continuing (postponing) the pre-trial conference. This makes sense. They both accomplish the same objective: to acquire additional time to do something before the matter is set for a trial. (If you continue the pre-trial conference, you do not need to fill out a Pre-Trial Conference Statement, covered in Section B4, below.)

Continuing the pre-trial conference has the advantage of keeping your case in the pre-trial conference/trial loop. You'll save time because you won't need to file another Declaration of Readiness to Proceed. However, not all judges will allow you to continue the pre-trial conference, so you may be required to either OTOC it or set your case for trial.

TIP

Continuance to a "rating calendar." If one of the stumbling blocks in settling your case is a dispute about the rating of any medical report, request that the judge continue your pre-trial conference to a "rating calendar." At the next pre-trial conference, you will be able to get the report in question rated by the appeals board rater.

4. How to Complete the Pre-Trial Conference Statement

RELEVANT CASE LAW

See *Early California Foods v. WCAB (Ellis)* and *Henley v. I.I.*, in Chapter 28.

SKIP AHEAD

A pre-trial conference statement is required only when a matter is set for trial. You need not complete the pre-trial conference statement if you have settled your case, OTOCed your case, or requested a continuance of the pre-trial conference. This form is required only if you are setting your matter for a trial date.

The pre-trial conference statement gives basic information about your injury and employment. In addition, you and the insurance company's representative must each list every piece of evidence you want to offer at your trial, as well as the names of any witnesses you will be calling. The pre-trial conference statement also sets out all issues that you and the insurance company agree upon, as well as all issues that the judge will be required to decide.

It is important to take as much time as you need to complete the pre-trial conference statement, even if it means that the insurance company has to wait for you. In fact, you should have a pre-trial conference statement completed BEFORE the hearing, if possible. (Always assume that your case is going to be set for trial.) A downloadable copy of this statement is available on Nolo's website (see Chapter 29, "Online Appendixes" for the link to this and other forms in this book) or from the Department of Workers' Comp website at http://www.dir.ca.gov/dwc/forms.html.

Above all, don't sign anything that you haven't had the time to review carefully. If you don't have a lawyer, the judge may help you fill out the pre-trial conference statement. If this happens, feel free to ask the judge to explain anything you don't understand.

CAUTION

Filling out a pre-trial conference statement has important legal consequences. When you fill out your pre-trial conference statement, you must make certain that you list all the issues you want resolved and all evidence and witnesses you plan to present at trial. Anything that you fail to list on this statement may be excluded from consideration at the trial.

If the judge does not help you fill out the pre-trial conference statement, ask the insurance company representative to complete it first, as this is routine. Then carefully review the form and fill in any blanks or make changes.

If you attempt to complete the pre-trial conference statement first, realize that the form asks for some information that only the insurance company may know, such as the total amount of benefits paid. Leave these questions blank if you don't know the answer, and the insurance company representative will fill them in.

Follow these instructions and the sample below when filling out the statement.

Case No. Insert your appeals board case number(s) here and any other place where the form asks for your case number(s). You will find this on your Notice of Hearing. Remember, you will have a separate case number for each date of injury.

Heading. Insert your name before APPLICANT, and your employer's name and its insurance company before the word DEFENDANTS. Enter the location, time, and date of the pre-trial conference.

Settlement Conference Judge. Enter the name of the judge.

Appearances. Check the box before "Injured Worker" and insert your name.

If you have an attorney, insert the attorney's name after "Injured Worker's Attorney." Otherwise, insert "None."

If you know someone besides you or the insurance company representative will appear at the hearing, list the name under "Others Appearing." For example, this might be a lien representative—someone representing the interests of a doctor or medical group that has filed a lien for payment. If you know of no one, fill in "None."

Stipulations

This section lists all the facts that you and the insurance company agree on. If any fact is in dispute, insert "in dispute" on the line provided. *Do not admit to facts you disagree with or aren't sure about.*

1. Insert your name here.

Born. Insert your date of birth here.

While. Check the box "Employed."

Next, you'll list your injury date or period of injury. Check one or two boxes, depending on your situation:

- Check the first box if your injury—or one of your injuries—was a specific injury. (See Chapter 3, Section B1, if you're not sure about the type of injury.) After the word "on," insert the date of your injury.
- Check the second box if your injury—or one of your injuries—was a cumulative trauma injury. (See Chapter 3, Section B2, if you're not sure about the type of injury.) After the words "during the period," insert the date of injury—for example, December 2, 2011 to December 2, 2012.

As a(n). Put in your job title as of the date you were injured. After the word "at," list the city in which you were working when injured. This may not necessarily be the same city as your employment address. For example, if you were a truck driver and reported to Los Angeles each morning to get your truck, and were involved in an accident in Banning, California, the city of your injury would be Banning, not Los Angeles.

By. Insert the name of the employer you were working for at the time of your injury. If you had other jobs, you need not list them unless you are claiming that they caused your injury.

Sustained injury/Claims to have sustained injury. If the insurance company has admitted that your injury arose out of and was sustained in the course of your employment, check the first box. (See Chapter 3, Section C8, for more on AOE/COE.)

If the insurance company is denying that you were injured on the job (AOE/COE is an issue), check the second box. Sometimes the insurance company may admit injury to some parts of your body and deny injury to other parts you have claimed. It may be appropriate in some cases to check both boxes.

In the blank, list all of the parts of your body you claim to have injured.

2. If your employer was insured, insert the name of the workers' compensation insurance company in the blank.

Or, if your employer did not have a workers' compensation insurance company, check the appropriate box to indicate that the employer was either permissibly self-insured or was uninsured.

3. In the first blank, if you and the insurance company agree on how much you were earning at the time of your injury, fill in the amount. If you and the insurance company are in disagreement over this figure, enter "in dispute."

In the second blank, insert how much per week you would be entitled to for temporary disability payments, based upon your average weekly wage. If you and the insurance company agree upon a figure, insert it here. If not, insert "in dispute." (See Chapter 12, Section B, for information on how to compute your temporary disability rate.)

In the last blank, insert how much per week you would be entitled to for permanent disability indemnity based upon your average weekly wage. If you can agree upon a figure, insert it here. If not, insert "in dispute." (See Chapter 13, Section E, for information on how to compute your permanent disability indemnity.)

4. Here you list the various types of compensation you have been paid by the insurance company. It's generally best to let the insurance company fill this part out, since they usually have a computer printout of all benefits paid to date.

Check the box before the words, "The employee has been adequately compensated for all periods of T/D claimed," only if you agree that you have been paid for all periods of temporary disability that you claimed. *Do not check this box if you believe the insurance company owes you some retroactive temporary disability payments.*

5. Check the appropriate box before the word "all," "some," or "no" to indicate whether the insurance company has paid for all, some, or none of your medical treatment. Enter the name of your treating doctor.

6. Check this box if no attorney fees have been paid and you do not have an attorney fee agreement. If you had a prior attorney, you should check this box.

7. Other stipulations. Check this box and write in other stipulations (agreements) you and the insurance company want to make, if any. For example, you might list an agreement that the issue of retroactive temporary disability owed is resolved for the sum of $1,100.

Issues

In this section of the form, you indicate which issues are to be resolved at the trial. Check each relevant box if there is a dispute on a given issue. Do not check the box if you and the insurance company agree on the facts involving that issue. Following are possible issues in dispute.

Employment. Check this box if the insurance company is denying that you were an employee.

Insurance coverage. Check this box only if the insurance company is denying that it insured your employer for the date of injury you have claimed.

Sample Pre-Trial Conference Statement (Page 1)

STATE OF CALIFORNIA
DEPARTMENT OF INDUSTRIAL RELATIONS
WORKERS' COMPENSATION APPEALS BOARD

JOHN WU
APPLICANT
V.
HOME INC, ABC INSURANCE
DEFENDANT(S).

CASE NO. ADJ777777

PRE-TRIAL CONFERENCE STATEMENT §5502 (e) (3)
☐ NOTICE OF HEARING

LOCATION: ______ DATE: ______ TIME: ______

SETTLEMENT CONFERENCE JUDGE: ______

APPEARANCES:

☑ INJURED WORKER: JOHN WU

☐ INJURED WORKER'S ATTORNEY ______ ☐ATTY ☐HRG REP

(FIRM NAME AND PERSON APPEARING)

☐ DEFENDANT'S ATTORNEY ______ ______ ☐ATTY ☐HRG REP
☐ATTY ☐HRG REP
☐ATTY ☐HRG REP
☐ATTY ☐HRG REP
(FIRM NAME AND PERSON APPEARING) (DEFENDANT)

☐ OTHERS APPEARING:
(L.C., INTERPRETERS, ETC.) ______

☐ ADDRESS RECORD CHANGES: ______

BOX BELOW TO BE COMPLETED ONLY BY WORKERS' COMPENSATION JUDGE

DISPOSITION: SET FOR REGULAR HEARING: ☐ WCAB NOTICE ☐ NOTICE WAIVED
☐ 1 HOUR ☐ 2 HOURS ☐ ½ DAY ☐ ALL DAY
☐ BEFORE ANY WCJ ☐ BEFORE WCJ ______ ☐ BEFORE ANY WCJ OTHER THAN ______
☐ CASE(S) SET ON ______ (DATE) AT ______ (TIME) WCJ ______ IN ______ (LOCATION)

☐ **OTHER DISPOSITION AND ORDERS:** ______

SERVICE AS ORDERED ON PAGE 4

______
WORKERS' COMPENSATION
ADMINISTRATIVE LAW JUDGE

DWC CA form 10253.1 (Rev 9/2010)

Sample Pre-Trial Conference Statement (Page 2)

PRE-TRIAL CONFERENCE STATEMENT **CASE NO.** ADJ777777

STIPULATIONS

THE FOLLOWING FACTS ARE ADMITTED:

1. JOHN WU, BORN 03 / 31 / 1966

WHILE ☒ EMPLOYED ☐ ALLEGEDLY EMPLOYED

☑ ON 08/18/20XX

☐ DURING THE PERIOD(S) ______

AS A(N) ACCOUNTANT, OCCUPATIONAL GROUP NUMBER 111

AT LONG BEACH, CALIFORNIA,

BY HOME INC

☑ SUSTAINED INJURY ARISING OUT OF AND IN THE COURSE OF EMPLOYMENT TO BACK

☑ CLAIMS TO HAVE SUSTAINED INJURY ARISING OUT OF AND IN THE COURSE OF EMPLOYMENT TO LEFT ELBOW

2. AT THE TIME OF INJURY THE EMPLOYER'S WORKERS' COMPENSATION CARRIER WAS ABC COMPANY

☐ THE EMPLOYER WAS ☐ PERMISSIBLY SELF-INSURED ☐ UNINSURED ☐ LEGALLY UNINSURED

3. AT THE TIME OF INJURY, THE EMPLOYEE'S EARNINGS WERE $ 800.00 PER WEEK, WARRANTING INDEMNITY RATES OF $ 533.33 FOR TEMPORARY DISABILITY AND $ 230.00 FOR PERMANENT DISABILITY.

4. THE CARRIER/EMPLOYER HAS PAID COMPENSATION AS FOLLOWS: (TD/PD/VRMA)

TYPE	WEEKLY RATE	PERIOD	TYPE	WEEKLY RATE	PERIOD

☐ THE EMPLOYEE HAS BEEN ADEQUATELY COMPENSATED FOR ALL PERIODS OF T/D CLAIMED THROUGH ______

5. THE EMPLOYER HAS FURNISHED ☐ ALL ☑ SOME ☐ NO MEDICAL TREATMENT.
THE PRIMARY TREATING PHYSICIAN IS DAVID KELL, M.D.

6. ☐ NO ATTORNEY FEES HAVE BEEN PAID AND NO ATTORNEY FEE ARRANGEMENTS HAVE BEEN MADE.

7. ☐ OTHER STIPULATIONS ______

APPLICANT DEFENDANT LIEN CLAIMANT/OTHER

PAGE 2

(This issue is both unusual and beyond the scope of this book; seek the help of a workers' compensation lawyer. For more information on hiring a lawyer, see Chapter 26.)

Injury arising out of and in the course of employment (AOE/COE). Check this box if AOE/COE is an issue. (See Chapter 3, Section C8.) AOE/COE is a critical issue, so if this relates to your case, you should consider seeking the help of an information and assistance officer or a workers' compensation lawyer.

Parts of body injured. Check this box only if the insurance company is disputing your claim that you injured certain parts of the body. If you do check this box, list all parts of the body that the insurance company either admits or denies. For example, "defendant admits back but denies knees."

Earnings. Check this box if you and the insurance company cannot agree on a figure for your average weekly earnings. After the words "Employee claims," insert the amount you believe you earned on a weekly basis at the time of your injury. Then fill in the basis for your claim, such as pay stubs, W-2s received from employer, or a recent raise. Let the insurance company fill in what it claims to be the amount you earned.

Temporary disability. Check this box if you claim that the insurance company owes you any retroactive temporary disability. Then fill in the dates for which you should have received temporary disability. (See Chapter 12 for more on temporary disability benefits.)

Permanent and stationary date. Check this box if there is a dispute as to the date your medical condition became permanent and stationary (discussed in Chapter 9, Section E). This is important for determining when the insurance company's obligation for payment of temporary disability payments ended (unless you returned to work on an earlier date). After the words "Employee claims," insert the date you claim you became permanent and stationary and the reason. Let the insurance company insert the date it claims you became permanent and stationary.

Permanent disability. Check this box if permanent disability is an issue to be resolved.

Occupation and group number claimed. Check this box if you and the insurance company cannot agree on your occupational group number. Fill in the group number you claim, and let the insurance company fill in the group number that it claims. The occupational group number is the number assigned according to your occupational duties.

Need for further medical treatment. Check this box if the insurance company is denying that you should be entitled to future medical treatment.

Liability for self-procured medical treatment. Check this box if the insurance company disputes that it should be required to pay for any expenses you incurred getting medical treatment. Note that this refers to money actually spent for medical treatment. Mileage is not included.

Liens. Check this box if there are any outstanding liens to be paid in your case, such as liens filed for payment of medical treatment, medical tests performed, interpreter fees, and pharmaceutical liens. List each of the liens on the lines provided. Also, check the board file and make sure that copies of all of the liens are in the file.

Attorney fees. Check this box if you have or previously had an attorney who claims attorney fees on your case. If you do not know, leave this blank.

Other issues. Check this box to list any other issues in your case not covered above. This might include reimbursement for mileage, or penalties for nonpayment or late payment of benefits. (See "You May Be Required to Submit Your Rating Formula," below, for information on why you may want to list additional issues.)

Exhibits. Under the section entitled "Exhibits," list all of the medical reports and other documents you want the judge to consider in your case. Make sure you list everything you want to present at your trial. If you leave anything out, the judge may not allow you to present it at trial if the defendants object, unless you can give a good reason why you failed to list it here.

Sample Pre-Trial Conference Statement (Page 3)

PRE-TRIAL CONFERENCE STATEMENT **CASE NO.** ADJ777777

ISSUES

- ☐ EMPLOYMENT
- ☐ INSURANCE COVERAGE
- ☐ INJURY ARISING OUT OF AND IN THE COURSE OF EMPLOYMENT
- ☑ PARTS OF BODY INJURED: LEFT ELBOW
- ☐ EARNINGS: EMPLOYEE CLAIMS ______ PER WEEK, BASED ON ______
  EMPLOYER/CARRIER CLAIMS ______ PER WEEK, BASED ON ______
- ☑ TEMPORARY DISABILITY, EMPLOYEE CLAIMING THE FOLLOWING PERIOD(S): DATE OF INJURY TO P&S DATE
- ☑ PERMANENT AND STATIONARY DATE:
  EMPLOYEE CLAIMS ___/___/___, BASED ON ______
  EMPLOYER/CARRIER CLAIMS ___/___/___, BASED ON ______
- ☑ PERMANENT DISABILITY ☐ APPORTIONMENT
- ☐ OCCUPATION AND GROUP NUMBER CLAIMED: BY EMPLOYEE ______
  BY EMPLOYER/CARRIER ______
- ☑ NEED FOR FURTHER MEDICAL TREATMENT
- ☑ LIABILITY FOR SELF-PROCURED MEDICAL TREATMENT
- ☐ LIENS:

LIEN CLAIMANT	TYPE OF LIEN	AMOUNT AND PERIODS PAID

- ☐ ATTORNEY FEES
- ☐ OTHER ISSUES:

John Wu
APPLICANT

DEFENDANT

LIEN CLAIMANT/OTHER

PAGE 3

Sample Pre-Trial Conference Statement (Attachment)

PRE-TRIAL CONFERENCE STATEMENT **CASE NO.** ADJ777777

EXHIBITS

☑ APPLICANT
☐ DEFENDANT
☐ LIEN CLAIMANT
☐ APPEALS BOARD

DESCRIPTION	DATE
Wage Statements	01/01/2011
Dr. Kell's medical report	03/24/2011
Dr. Kell's medical report	08/01/2011
Dr. Kell's medical report	04/22/2011
xx	
1/1/20xx–12/31/20xx	

WITNESSES

Mark Nakayama
Brian Davidson
John Wu

ABOVE LISTINGS OF EXHIBITS AND WITNESSES REVIEWED BY ALL PARTIES.

John Wu
APPLICANT

DEFENDANT

LIEN CLAIMANT/OTHER

PAGE ___ OF ___

Witnesses. List all witnesses. Make certain you list yourself as a witness, as well as anyone else you will call to testify at your trial. If you fail to list a witness here, the judge may not allow that witness to testify at your trial if the defendants object, unless you can give a good reason why you failed to list that person here.

You May Be Required to Submit Your Rating Formula

It's common for an insured worker and the insurance company to have arrived at different rating formulas. If you rated your disability yourself, you may be required to submit your rating formula to the judge at the pre-trial conference if the trial is to resolve either or both of these two issues (and no other issues):

- the amount of your permanent disability, and/or
- your need for future medical treatment.

If any other issues are to be resolved, you do not have to submit your rating formula. (LC § 4065.) To avoid having to submit your rating formula, it's best to list on the pre-trial conference statement any other issue still in dispute at the pre-trial conference, such as temporary disability payments, mileage, or reimbursement for medical expenses.

Beware of "baseball" arbitration. By law, a judge may be required to choose either your rating or the rating submitted by the insurance company for injuries before 2003. (This is required if a worker is represented by an attorney.) The judge may not be allowed to choose a rating somewhere in between the two. Like an arbitration hearing in baseball, the arbitrator (judge) must choose one party's figure; nothing in between is allowed. This is where the name "baseball arbitration" comes from. Because of this all-or-nothing possibility, be certain your rating is reasonable.

C. Trial

If you have already been to a pre-trial conference, covered in Section B, above, your matter may be set for trial. You'll be notified of the hearing date either by mail or at the pre-trial conference.

When you arrive at the appeals board, look for any witnesses you have subpoenaed and do your best to keep them advised of when your case will be ready to be heard. You might suggest that they wait in the designated assembly room or in the coffee shop, if there is one.

TIP

Send subpoenas before trial date.

Immediately upon learning of your hearing date, send out any subpoenas you need, to assure the attendance of any witnesses. (See Chapter 21, Section D, for instructions.)

1. Try (Again) to Settle Your Case

Before your case is heard by a judge, you should try to settle it one last time. For the most part, you'll follow the same settlement procedures discussed in Section B1, above.

By now, you should know whether you want to settle your case by "compromise and release" or by "stipulations with request for award." (These forms of settlement are discussed in detail in Chapter 19, Section B.) If a lump sum settlement is important to you, this is your last chance to negotiate one. You can get a lump sum settlement only by a compromise and release. If you proceed to trial, you will be paid in the same manner as if you negotiated a settlement by stips.

Your case will probably be one of several set for trial that day. Therefore, the sooner you can determine whether you can settle your case or will need to go to trial, the better. That is because the judge will generally only have time to put on one or two trials.

It is possible that if you take too long in settlement negotiations, the judge may start another trial. If you see the judge is preparing to start a trial, you and the insurance company's representative should ask the judge whether you can interrupt if you come to an agreement or decide to go to trial. However, don't allow yourself to be rushed if you feel additional discussion may settle the case. Be prepared to stay for a few hours, if necessary.

The pressure to settle at this stage is more intense than at the pre-trial conference, as both sides realize that trial is imminent. If you have done your homework, you will know the strength of your case. The stronger your case, the firmer your position should be to settle at, or close to, your terms. Bear in mind that the insurance company does not really want to go to trial. It's quite common for insurance companies to settle at the last moment.

How much you are willing to come down from your original demand will depend upon many factors, including what you expect if you proceed to trial. When I have gotten as far as the day of trial without being able to settle the case, it is usually because the insurance company has not been willing to negotiate in good faith. My attitude is that they have forced me to do all the work and preparation necessary to prepare for a trial and as long as I am at the appeals board and ready, I'll go ahead—unless I can get an offer pretty close to my demand or my case is really weak. I recommend that you take the same approach. Remember, if you don't have a lawyer, the appeals board judge will help you through the trial.

Be aware that the insurance company representative may not be well prepared. It is not unusual for the insurance company to turn over a file to the attorney the day before the case goes to trial. Rarely is everything in order, which gives you a big advantage. If you are fully prepared and determined to try the case if necessary—and more important, your opponent realizes that you are willing to do so—you will have a strong advantage in final settlement negotiations.

When to Continue (Postpone) Your Trial

You or the insurance company may ask the judge for a "continuance" (postponing your trial to a later date) in situations such as these:

- Your physical condition has significantly changed since the pre-trial conference, and you need an additional medical exam and report. For example, if your medical condition has become much worse, you might want to be reevaluated to see whether the medical examiner thinks your permanent disability has increased.
- One or more witnesses for either side did not appear even though they were subpoenaed.
- One of the parties is ill and unable to proceed.

But be forewarned: Simply not being prepared is *not* an acceptable reason for a continuance. And don't agree to a continuance if you think the insurance company representative is asking for it due to lack of preparation.

2. Appearing Before the Judge

By the time you and the insurance representative make the decision to proceed to trial, there will probably be a line of people waiting to see the judge. Take your place in line and wait.

When your turn comes, explain to the judge that you and the insurance company cannot settle your case, so you will need to go to trial. The judge may ask questions of both of you and make recommendations about settlement. Most judges will try to get you to settle first.

Neither of you is under any obligation to follow the judge's recommendations, but as the injured worker, realize that the judge is supposed to have your best interests in mind. In fact, it is the judge's legal duty to assist you and only to approve fair settlement agreements you reach with the insurance company. If the judge tells you that you should settle because the insurance company's offer is higher than what you are likely to get at trial, you'll probably be wise to settle. Unless you have very strong evidence the judge has not yet considered, you run the risk that the judge will render a decision that awards you less than what was offered in the settlement proposal.

If it is clear to the judge that you're not going to be able to settle the case (the parties are too far apart on the amount, or one or the other side is being stubborn and won't negotiate in good faith), the judge will advise you of the status of the trial calendar that day. It is not uncommon for three or more trials to be set for a particular day, as well as many pre-trial conferences. It's likely that you'll have to wait a few hours while the judge takes care of the pre-trial conferences first.

If other cases set for trial in addition to yours do not settle, the judge will have to decide which cases to hear that day and which to delay until a future date. If you are asked to return on a different day for your trial, and you have subpoenaed any witnesses, ask the judge to order that those witnesses appear at the postponed trial.

If the judge agrees to hear your case that day, the judge or the clerk will tell you when to report back to chambers or the courtroom for your hearing. Be sure to arrive at least 15 minutes prior to the designated time. Bring your file, documents, and witnesses.

3. Setting the Groundwork for the Trial

At the designated time, the judge will take you and the insurance company through several pre-trial procedures.

a. Submit Medical Evidence

The judge may go through the board file and read off the reports that are in the file for consideration. The judge may then ask you whether any reports that you previously listed were omitted. It's also possible that the judge will ask you and the representative to review the board file and sort out any medical evidence you want considered when the judge makes a decision. This is all done rather informally.

TIP

Preparation pays off. Anticipating the judge's request, you should have reviewed all medical reports before your hearing. Be prepared to tell the judge what you believe is the key medical evidence. Also, bring extra copies of every medical report you want to submit to the judge. If, for any reason, a particular report is not in the file, let the judge know, and provide a copy of the missing report.

b. Submit Additional Exhibits

Tell the judge what nonmedical exhibits (documents) to examine before making a decision. (For a list of what evidence to use, see the "Issues That May Be in Dispute" chart in Chapter 21, Section A.)

c. When to Object to the Insurance Company's Evidence

If the representative for the insurance company offers something into evidence that was not listed on the pre-trial conference statement, you should object. You do this by speaking up and saying, "Objection, Your Honor. This evidence was not previously listed on the pre-trial conference statement."

d. Identify Stipulated Issues

The judge will ask each of you what issues can be stipulated to (agreed upon). The judge will go through the potential issues and ask each of you if there is any agreement. If not, the judge will designate that issue as something to be decided at trial.

Once all the issues to be decided at trial have been identified, the judge will enter the various medical reports and exhibits into evidence. This simply means that after the hearing, the judge will read and consider each of those pieces of information before rendering a decision in your case.

e. Final Preparations Before the Trial

The judge will then call for a court reporter. The court reporter uses a machine to make a written record of every word that is said in the courtroom as part of the proceeding. When the court reporter arrives, most people will leave the room. Unless there is an objection by the other side, you may have your witnesses (if any) sit in the back of the room so you may call them as needed. If the other side objects, the judge may instruct them to wait in the hallway, where they'll be called as needed.

TIP

If the insurance company has witnesses. Ask the judge to exclude the insurance company's witnesses from the courtroom until they testify. This will prevent any possibility of one witness's testimony being influenced by another's.

4. The Trial Begins

The judge will start things off by asking you to call your first witness. Tell the judge that you will testify first. It's important for you to do so, even if you have other witnesses. That way, you can state the facts that may be substantiated by other witnesses.

The judge will instruct the court reporter to swear you in. An advantage to representing yourself is that the judge will almost always act as your attorney and ask you all the necessary questions to establish and prove your case.

TIP

If you don't have a lawyer. Take advantage of your right to get help from the judge. Ask for an explanation of anything you don't understand. For example, you may want an explanation of issues, stipulations, and what evidence may be admitted.

a. Questions a Judge Usually Asks

The following questions are typical of the questions you can expect. Some questions may not be asked if you and the insurance company have stipulated to (agreed upon) the issue concerning those questions.

TIP

Bring these questions with you. Have a copy of these questions handy at your trial. In the event the judge does not ask you specific questions (not likely), you can simply go down this list and answer the relevant questions. Skip over any questions that deal with issues that are not disputed.

1. By whom were you employed on the date of injury?
2. When were you first employed by your employer?
3. How did your injury occur?

   Hint: *Take your time and carefully explain how the injury occurred. You want to make sure the judge knows why your injury is work related.*
4. What symptoms did you notice?

   Hint: *Describe what you felt immediately after the accident. You want the judge to understand that your problems were a result of the work injury.*
5. Did you request—and did your employer provide—medical treatment?
6. Did you seek medical treatment on your own? If so, when?
7. Who treated you?
8. What was the reason for any delay in obtaining medical treatment?
9. Who paid for your medical treatment?
10. Were you reimbursed for any medical expenses you personally incurred?
11. Did you report the injury? If so, when and to whom?
12. Did you lose time off from work due to the injury?
13. What dates were you off work, and for how long were you off work as a result of your injury?
14. Did you receive any compensation while you were off work?

15. Who paid you compensation while you were off work?
16. How much per week did you receive while you were off work?
17. Are there any periods that you were off work as a result of your injury for which you did not receive payment from the insurance company?
18. Had you ever injured your [part of body injured] before? If so, when and how?

    Hint: *Be truthful. Explain to the judge why you feel that the prior injury (or a subsequent injury) has nothing to do with your present problems.*
19. As a result of your prior injury, did you have to limit your work activities in any way before your current date of injury?
20. Did you see a qualified medical examiner on [*date of the exam*]?
21. Did you give that doctor an accurate and complete history of your injuries and problems?
22. Did you read the report of [name of doctor] dated [date of the report]?
23. Do you consider the report to be accurate? If not, in what way is the report inaccurate?

    Hint: *Hopefully your report is accurate and you agree with it. If you disagree with any part of the report, say so and explain why.*
24. Did you have to pay [name of doctor] anything?

    Note: *The judge will probably ask the same questions (#20 to #24) for each doctor you saw who rendered a medical opinion about your injury.*
25. What current complaints do you attribute to your injury?

    Hint: *Slowly and carefully tell the judge all of your present complaints. Start with the top of your head and go down to your toes, discussing each body part that still bothers you.*
26. What can't you do now that you used to be able to do?

    Hint: *Explain your physical limitations. If you used to play sports and now you can't, say so. If the QME report says you shouldn't lift more than 30 pounds, tell what happens if you do. Or tell the judge you really can't lift more than 20 pounds if that's true.*
27. On a scale of 1 to 10, with 1 being minimal pain, and 10 being terrible pain, how would you describe your pain to your [part of body injured] on a typical day?

    Hint: *Don't be a whiner, but don't underrate your condition either. Be truthful.*
28. Depending upon the part of body injured, the judge may ask particular questions about your ability to do such things as lift heavy objects, bend, stoop, walk for extended periods, stand for extended periods, and grip and grasp items.

    Hint: *Again, don't be a crybaby, but make sure you let the judge know your new limitations.*
29. What was the date you last worked?
30. When were you last able to work?
31. Are you currently employed? If so, by whom, and what are your duties? If you're not working, why not?
32. Could you return to your former job duties? If not, why not?
33. Have any doctors told you that you will need additional medical care? If so, which doctors?
34. What kind of treatment do the doctors say you need?

b. Cross-Examination

When the judge has finished asking you questions, the attorney or other representative for the insurance company will ask you questions about your testimony. This is called "cross-examination." When answering the questions proposed by the insurance representative, be calm, courteous, and truthful. Do not become upset or hostile.

What questions the representative will ask depends entirely upon the contested issues. For example, if the main issue involves the nature and extent of your permanent disability, you may be asked very specific questions about whether or not you can do certain things. The insurance representative can only ask you questions on cross-examination that deal with your original testimony. You should object to any questions that deal with subjects you didn't cover.

Sometimes the insurance company will plan to show a video of you doing certain things you claim you cannot do. If you're asked very specific questions like "Can you change a flat tire?" you should suspect that they have film on you. If the representative did not list the videotape on the pre-trial conference statement, object to it being shown. The insurance company is required to provide you with a copy of the videotape for review upon request before the trial. If the insurance company representative plans on showing a film to the judge, the person who took the film must testify as to its authenticity. If this witness was not listed on the pre-trial conference statement, object to the testimony.

After the attorney has finished questioning you, you may comment or explain anything you want to clear up regarding what the representative asked you. This is called "redirect examination." The insurance representative may then ask you additional questions, within the scope of what you just testified to. This is called "recross examination."

TIP

Ask the judge for help if you need it. If you feel you or any of your witnesses are being badgered by the representative for the insurance company, don't be afraid to ask the judge for help. Simply tell the judge that you (or any of your witnesses) feel you are being unreasonably badgered and request that the judge tell the representative to be civil.

c. Witnesses Testify

When you are done with your testimony, you may call any other witnesses you have. The order in which they are called to testify is not really important. Ask each witness the questions you have prepared and practiced in advance.

For example, if you have called a coemployee who saw your injury occur as your witness, your questions might go like this:

1. Please state your name.
2. Where do you work?
3. Were you working on [date of injury]?
4. Did you witness anything unusual? [Your witness will describe what he or she saw.]
5. Ask any other relevant questions regarding what was seen, such as what happened immediately after the accident and how you reacted.

After you are done questioning the witness, the insurance representative may ask the witness additional questions. After the representative has finished, you may do the same. This process continues until each of you indicates that you have no more questions for that witness.

After all your witnesses have testified, the insurance company representative may call witnesses. You have the right to question each one after the insurance representative finishes asking questions. You will have to make an on-the-spot decision as to whether or not you want to ask a defense witness questions. It is not necessary unless, in your opinion, the testimony has hurt your case. Even then, do so only if you feel you have questions that will show the witness to be mistaken or to be biased. Otherwise, you may just reinforce the witness's testimony.

The following are reasons you may want to cross-examine a defense witness:

- **You want to discredit the witness.** You might ask whether anyone told the witness that the appearance to testify was mandatory, or whether the witness will be receiving payment for testifying.
- **The witness has made a statement that directly contradicts another credible witness.** You might ask for an explanation of the discrepancy.
- **The witness has contradicted himself.** You should point out the witness's self-contradiction.

You can also recall any of your witnesses to rebut (refute) any damaging testimony. Put your witness back on the stand and ask questions that will clear up any damaging testimony that the insurance company's witness gave.

d. Judge Takes Matter Under Submission

When the defendants are done presenting their witnesses, the trial is over and the matter will stand submitted. That means the judge will review notes and consider the exhibits and medical evidence and then make a decision within 30–90 days. The judge will rarely make a decision the same day.

The judge should tell you that prior to receiving the decision, you will be mailed a copy of the judge's summary of evidence, which consists of notes the judge took on the trial. The judge will also tell you how many days the parties will have to review the summary of evidence before the judge issues a decision. Make careful note of this deadline.

When you receive the summary of evidence, read it very carefully. If you think the judge failed to note important testimony or evidence or noted something incorrectly, immediately write the judge a letter and explain the omission or error. Be sure to serve (mail) a copy of your letter to the insurance company.

D. Findings and Award

The judge's decision, called the Findings and Award, will be mailed to you. It will generally include a summary of evidence and an explanation of the rationale that the judge relied upon to make a decision on each disputed issue. The Findings and Award also sets forth the benefits to which you are entitled. Short of an appeal, it's the final decision in your case. There's a sample below.

Petition for Commutation

The only sure way to get your settlement in one lump sum check is by settling your case with a compromise and release. If you settle your case by stipulation, or you get a Findings and Award following a trial, you will receive your permanent disability award in weekly payments (paid every two weeks) until paid in full. If you want a judge to "commute" payments into a lump sum, you'll need to file a Petition for Commutation. The process is beyond the scope of this book; check with an information and assistance officer or see a lawyer.

Sample Findings and Award

STATE OF CALIFORNIA

DIVISION OF WORKERS' COMPENSATION

[*name of injured worker*], Applicant, vs. [*name of employer and insurance company*], Defendants	CASE No. [number] JOINT Findings, Award, & Order

[*name of attorney*], Attorney for Applicant

[*name of attorney*], Attorney for Defendants.

The above-entitled matter having been heard and regularly submitted, the Honorable [judge's name], Workers' Compensation Judge, makes his/her decision as follows:

Re: Case No. [*number*]

FINDINGS OF FACT

1. [Name of injured worker], born April 29, 1944, while employed during the period of May 30, 20xx, through March 30, 20xx, as an irrigation specialist, occupational group number of 5, at Crockett, California, by [employer], insured by [insurance company], sustained injury arising out of and in the course of said employment to his low back and neck.
2. Average weekly earnings at injury were $336 per week for temporary disability and $148 per week for permanent disability.
3. There is need for medical treatment to cure or relieve the effects of said injury.
4. Said injury caused temporary total disability as follows: Beginning May 30, 20xx, to and including August 24, 20xx, payable at weekly rate of $336 per week.
5. Said injury caused permanent disability of 61 percent.
6. Applicant is entitled to unapportioned award.
7. All self-procured medical treatment costs shall be paid.
8. All medical-legal costs shall be paid pursuant to the current provisions of the Labor Code.
9. The reasonable value of services and disbursements of applicant's attorneys is $7,000, payable to [name of present attorneys] and $200 to [name of prior attorney].
10. The following liens are found to be reasonable and necessary and ordered paid: Bayside Medical Group, $5,237.32; Signal Radiology Medical Group, $1,327; Parker Pharmacy, $560.30; and Barry Bradstreet, D.C., $945.30.
11. The lien of Dalton Drug Company in the sum of $1,982 is excessive and unreasonable.

Sample Findings and Award (continued)

AWARD

AWARD IS MADE in favor of [injured worker] against [insurance company], of temporary disability indemnity of $336 per week for the periods specified in Finding of Fact 4; of permanent disability indemnity of $____________________, payable at the rate of $148 per week, beginning ____________________, for 279.50 weeks, less attorneys fees in the sum of $_______________ to [*name of present attorneys*] and $200 to [name of prior attorney]; together with further medical treatment as set forth in Finding of Fact 3; together with reimbursement for self-procured medical treatment as set forth in Finding of Fact 7; together with reimbursement for medical-legal costs as set forth in Finding of Fact 8; and payment of liens as set forth in Finding of Fact 10.

ORDER

IT IS HEREBY ORDERED that Defendants adjust or litigate the lien of Dalton Drug Company.

FINDINGS OF FACT

1. Applicant did not sustain an injury to his left shoulder and psyche while employed as an irrigation specialist at [employer], during the period of May 30, 20xx, through March 30, 20xx.
2. All other issues are moot.

ORDER

IT IS HEREBY ORDERED that Applicant takes nothing further herein.

Filed and Served by mail on: MARCH 4, 20xx

On all parties on the official address record — ____________________ WORKERS' COMPENSATION JUDGE

By: ____________________

CHAPTER

25

Appealing a Workers' Compensation Decision

This chapter gives an overview of your right to appeal, the possible grounds (basis) for an appeal, and the appeals process. The step-by-step procedure involved in appealing a workers' compensation case is, however, beyond the scope of this book.

SEE AN EXPERT

Seek outside help if you plan to appeal. If you think you have grounds for appealing a decision that went against you in your workers' compensation case, check with an information and assistance officer or try to find a workers' compensation attorney who is interested in taking your case. Bear in mind that most attorneys will not be interested. If you do find a lawyer, at least 15% of any judgment you win on appeal will go to the attorney.

Workers' Compensation Appeals Board

Many people are confused about the different uses of the term "Workers' Compensation Appeals Board." The confusion is for good reason. The appeals board may refer to the place where you file your papers and your case is heard by a judge or referee. It's not an appeal at all—just your first chance to go to court. But these terms also refer to the actual seven-member appeals board located in San Francisco that hears the first step in an appeal if you are unhappy with how your case was initially decided and you file a Petition for Reconsideration.

A. The Three-Step Appeal Process

There are three separate and distinct levels of appeal in a workers' compensation case. You must start with the first level; if you lose, you may appeal to the next level, and so on. The three levels are:

- the Petition for Reconsideration
- the Writ of Review in the appellate court, and
- the Writ of Review in the California Supreme Court.

The Appeal Process

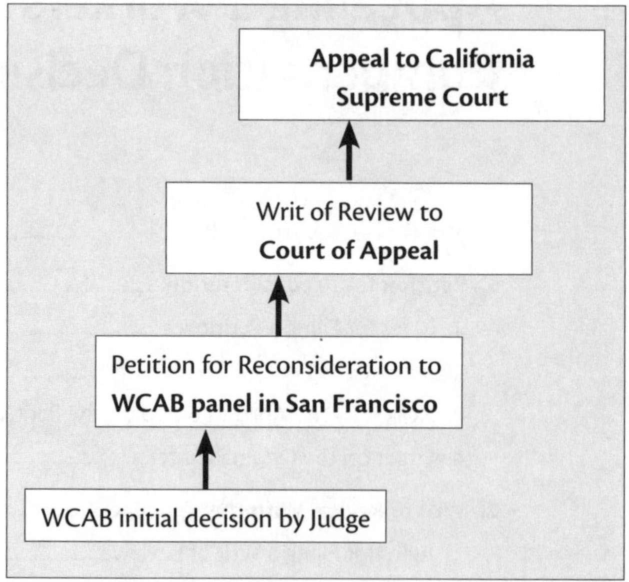

A decision by a higher authority supersedes and takes precedence over that of a lower court or authority. For example, a decision by the Court of Appeal would take precedence (would be followed by later courts) over that of an opposite decision by the WCAB.

B. Petition for Reconsideration

Any person who is affected by a final decision, award, or order made by a workers' compensation judge, referee, or arbitrator may petition the Workers' Compensation Appeals Board for reconsideration on any matter covered by the order. (CCR § 10988, LC § 5900.) This would be you, the employer, the insurance company, a lien claimant (such as a doctor who filed a green lien), or anyone else who is legally bound by the order.

To appeal your case, you must file a document called a Petition for Reconsideration with the Workers' Compensation Appeals Board where your case was heard. The petition is directed to the seven-member appeals board panel in San Francisco. Usually, only three members of the panel will handle a given appeal.

It is not hard to file a Petition for Reconsideration. An information and assistance officer should be able to provide you with a form and help you complete it. You must act fast, though, as you'll only have 20–25 days from the date you received your decision, award, or order to file the petition.

Vocational Rehabilitation Appeals

A vocational rehabilitation appeal differs from an appeal of an order of the appeals board. This is because the initial order in a vocational rehabilitation matter is made by the rehabilitation unit, not the appeals board.

If you decide to appeal, you must request that the issue be heard by a judge or referee at the local board (not the appeals board panel in San Francisco). To do this, you file a petition in which you give your reasons for the appeal. Next, you file a Declaration of Readiness to Proceed. (CCR § 10992.) You must serve copies of all pleadings, notices, and orders on the Office of Benefit Determination, Vocational Rehabilitation Unit.

1. Rules for Filing a Petition

You must file a Petition for Reconsideration within 20 to 25 days of the date that the judge signs the order, decision, or award. (LC § 5903.) When you receive your copy of the signed order, check for the date the judge signed it and calculate 20 days from that date. If you received your notice in the mail (rather than receiving a copy of the order in person), you may add five days, giving you a total of 25 days to file your petition.

Don't miss this deadline. If you fail to file your petition within the 20 to 25 days, the appeals board will probably not hear your appeal, especially if the insurance company files an opposition to your appeal pointing out that you failed to file on time.

To win your appeal, you must have a sound reason why the appeals board decision is unjust or unlawful. Your petition may be made upon one or more of the following grounds—and no others:

- The appeals board acted without power or in excess of its powers when it made the order, decision, or award.
- The order, decision, or award was procured by fraud.
- You discovered important new evidence, which you could not, with reasonable diligence, have discovered and produced at the hearing.
- The evidence presented before the appeals board does not justify the appeals board's Findings and Award. This means that the judge's opinion on the facts of your case is mistaken, given the evidence presented at your trial. For example, if the judge listed in the Findings and Award that you purposefully jumped off a roof at work, there would have to be some evidence to support that finding. If there was testimony or any other evidence to indicate that in fact you fell off the roof, the evidence would not justify that finding. (A sample Findings and Award is provided in Chapter 24, Section D.)
- The Findings and Award by the appeals board judge does not support the order, decision, or award. (LC § 5903.) In short, given the facts of the case as found by the judge, the order is plainly incorrect. For example, if the judge found that you sustained an injury at work, and then issued a decision that your injury is not industrial, the Findings and Award would not support the decision.

Don't get bogged down by these categories. Just list each reason why the judge made a mistake on a given issue. Your petition must identify every issue you want the appeals board to consider. Then point to the evidence that supports your viewpoint and explain why it does.

The petition must contain a general statement of any evidence or other matters upon which you rely to support your petition. (LC § 5902.) Finally, the petition must be verified under oath, meaning that you are stating under penalty of perjury that the facts contained in your petition are true and correct to the best of your knowledge.

2. Serving the Petition and Answer

You must immediately serve a copy of the Petition for Reconsideration on all opposing parties; you may serve by mail. (Instructions for serving papers are in Chapter 23, Section B.)

Any opposing party may file an Answer to your petition within ten days of the date of service and serve a copy on you. An Answer is the opposing party's position regarding the merits of your petition. The Answer must also be verified.

3. Action by the Appeals Board on the Petition

Once you file a Petition for Reconsideration, the appeals board usually must decide to accept it or deny it within 60 days from the date of the filing, otherwise the petition is automatically considered denied.

The appeals board has the power to affirm, rescind, or change the original decision, order, or award upon which your Petition for Reconsideration is based. The appeals board may proceed by either:

- going ahead and deciding the appeal without further notice to you or without any further proceedings, or
- scheduling a hearing to take additional evidence. In this rare situation, you'll be mailed a notice of the time and place of any hearing. Information on the hearing will also be sent to opposing parties.

A majority of the appeals board members assigned to hear it (usually two out of three) must sign the decision to grant or deny your petition or otherwise uphold, cancel, or change the original order. The board must state the evidence it relied upon for the new decision and specify in detail the reasons for making it. (LC § 5908.5.) All parties are mailed a copy of the decision.

4. Effect on the Original Order

If you file a Petition for Reconsideration, the order, decision, or award that you're appealing is automatically suspended for ten days, unless otherwise ordered by the appeals board. (LC § 5910.) A suspension means that no action need be taken on the order. Let's say an order required the insurance company to immediately pay you retroactive temporary disability benefits. If the insurance company appeals, the automatic suspension means that it does not have to comply with the order yet. The appeals board may delay the order, decision, or award for as long as it takes to act on the petition.

Any order the appeals board makes after reconsideration will not affect the original order or its enforceability unless the appeals board says so. (LC § 5908.) In other words, the appeals board must specifically state that the original order or decision is changed or no longer enforceable. Normally, the original order is suspended until after the appeal, meaning the insurance company does not have to pay during that time.

C. Writ of Review With the Appellate Court

If you or the insurance company is unhappy with the appeals board's decision on the petition, a second appeal is possible, this time to the appellate court (also called the State Court of Appeal) for a Writ of Review. The appellate court is the same court that you would appeal a regular court case to; it is not part of the workers' compensation court system.

The purpose of the Writ of Review is to inquire into, and determine the lawfulness of, the original order, decision, or award if the petition was denied, or of the order, decision, or award following reconsideration if the petition was granted and a subsequent order issued. (LC § 5950.)

The appellate court can't make its own determination of what the facts are in the case—for example, it cannot hold a new trial, take evidence, or exercise its independent judgment on the evidence. (LC § 5952.) It must assume that the facts found by the appeals board are correct. (The entire record of the appeals board will be certified as true and correct by the appeals board.) However, the court can look into whether, given the facts, the appeals board could have reasonably arrived at its decision.

The overwhelming majority of appealed cases are affirmed by the appellate court, so you really need to consider carefully before you file an appeal. It's a good idea to talk to an attorney to evaluate your chances of winning

1. Rules for Filing a Writ of Review

The application for Writ of Review must be filed:

- within 45 days after a Petition for Reconsideration is denied, or
- within 45 days after the filing of an order, decision, or award after a Petition for Reconsideration was granted. (LC § 5950.)

The only issues that can be determined on appeal are whether:

- the appeals board acted without or in excess of its powers
- the order, decision, or award was procured by fraud
- the order, decision, or award was unreasonable
- the order, decision, or award was not supported by substantial evidence, and
- findings of fact, if made, do not support the order, decision, or award under review.

2. Service of Pleadings

You must serve a copy of every pleading that was filed with the appellate court by any party on:

- the appeals board, and
- every opposing party who appeared in the action.

Instructions for serving papers are in Chapter 23.

3. Suspension of Previous Appeals Board Decision

By filing a Writ of Review with the appellate court, previous appeals board orders, decisions, or awards are not automatically suspended. The court before which the petition is filed may, however, choose to suspend part or all of a previous decision. (LC § 5956.)

4. Right to Appear and Judgment

The appeals board, and each party to the action or proceeding before the appeals board, have the right to have their positions heard in the review by the appellate court.

There are no deadlines set forth in the Labor Code regarding when you must be notified or when a hearing by the appellate court must be scheduled. It typically takes six to 12 months.

At the hearing, the court will enter judgment either affirming or canceling the order, decision, or award, or the court may return the case for further proceedings to the original appeals board where the case was considered in the first place. If the case is returned to the original appeals board, further proceedings will be held according to the instructions given by the appellate court. In other words, you may need to have a new trial on one or more issues in your case.

D. Writ of Appeal to the California Supreme Court

The final step in the appeal process is to appeal your case to the California Supreme Court if you are not satisfied with the decision of the appellate court. Appeals to the Supreme Court are almost never granted. Carefully consider whether the remote chance of success makes an appeal worthwhile.

All of the rules and procedures set forth under Section C, above, apply to Writs of Appeal to the Supreme Court of California. The only difference is that the Supreme Court will decide the issue instead of the appellate court.

Part VI

Beyond This Book

CHAPTER

26

Lawyers and Other Sources of Assistance

Although this book covers the basic information you need to handle your own workers' compensation case, a unique situation or issue in your particular case may require that you seek assistance from:

- a workers' compensation information and assistance officer, and/or
- a lawyer.

This chapter discusses how to best use these resources.

A. Information and Assistance Officers

Each Workers' Compensation Appeals Board has a minimum of one information and assistance officer available to help you pursue your workers' compensation claim. Information and assistance officers not only help workers but also provide information and help to employers, lien claimants, and other interested parties. They are an excellent source of free assistance in such areas as:

- providing legal information
- contacting the insurance company to determine why benefits were not provided
- filling out forms
- resolving disputes, and
- reviewing settlement documents.

Because information and assistance officers are very busy, you may have to be extremely patient and persistent in order to get the help you need. If possible, you may want to meet with your local information and assistance officer, explain your case, and establish a good working relationship. This may prove helpful later if you require assistance at a critical stage in your case.

To reach a local information and assistance officer, find the number to your local workers' compensation office on Nolo's website. (See Chapter 29, "Online Appendixes" for the link to Appendix 1, "Workers' Compensation Offices and Code Lists.") You may also reach the Workers' Compensation Information and Assistance Unit at 800-736-7401. This unit at this toll-free number can answer your questions and refer you to the information and assistance officer closest to you.

B. Hiring a Lawyer

If you meet with a workers' compensation lawyer to discuss your case, your initial consultation must be free. Fees must be awarded on a contingency basis and are paid out of your settlement after approval by a workers' compensation judge. (LC § 4906.) Typically, fees will amount to 12% to 15% of your permanent disability recovery.

1. Where to Find a Good Workers' Compensation Lawyer

Any attorney who is licensed to practice law in California may represent you in your workers' compensation matter. However, you should limit your search to attorneys who practice exclusively in this area. Workers' compensation has become a very complicated area of the law and requires an attorney who is knowledgeable regarding the many new laws and procedures. Here are some suggestions.

Personal referrals. Seek out information from friends or acquaintances who hired attorneys to handle a workers' compensation case. Give serious consideration to an attorney who gets rave reviews. Watch out for the "I have a friend whose second cousin is a workers' compensation attorney"-type recommendation. Also, pay attention to who is making the recommendation. Is this person really savvy, or is it someone whose judgment you often question?

Professional workers' compensation organizations. Several organizations provide a regular forum for the exchange of ideas and for learning new developments in the workers' compensation field. Because participation by lawyers is voluntary, membership can be a good indication that the attorney is willing to put forth the extra effort required to be at the forefront of the field. Ask any prospective attorney about membership in either of these professional organizations:

- **The California Applicants' Attorneys Association (CAAA).** The CAAA is an organization of lawyers affiliated for the purpose of protecting the legal rights of California's injured workers. These lawyers usually work exclusively for injured workers (applicants). You can write to the CAAA at 801 12th Street, Suite 201, Sacramento, CA 95814 or call 916-444-5155 to request a list of workers' compensation applicant attorneys in your area, or go online at www.caaa.org.
- **The Workers' Compensation Division of the California State Bar.** Contact your local bar association. You can find the number in the telephone book or online. If you request a list of attorneys in your area, make sure you contact applicant attorneys only (defense attorneys represent insurance companies and employers).

Information and Assistance Office. This office may have a list of applicant attorneys who practice workers' compensation in your area.

Nolo's lawyer directory. nolo now has a lawyer directory at www.nolo.com. The directory features advertising profiles of attorneys and contains extensive information about the attorney's education, background, and practice. You can search by zip code and legal specialty to find lawyers who specialize in workers' compensation law.

Yellow pages. While not highly recommended, a careful reading of the various ads can alert you to attorneys who specialize in workers' compensation and have been in practice for many years. But be wary here; the fact that a lawyer bought a splashy ad promising big recoveries is no guarantee of competence. Be sure you carefully check up on and interview any lawyer you find this way.

2. What to Look for in a Lawyer

Again, you should do your best to find a lawyer with substantial experience in the workers' compensation field. When you interview an attorney about your case, do not be afraid to ask about the attorney's experience. Find out how long the lawyer has been practicing in the workers' compensation field, as well as what organizations the attorney belongs to, such as the California Applicants' Attorneys Association (CAAA) and the Workers' Compensation Division of the California State Bar.

In my opinion, you should limit your choices to attorneys who practice workers' compensation law full time as applicants' (injured worker) attorneys. If an attorney you speak to also practices family law, real estate, or anything else, move on. Assuming the lawyer practices only in the workers' compensation area, ask whether the lawyer exclusively represents injured workers. If the answer is "No, I also represent insurance companies," it's my opinion that you should look elsewhere.

3. Interview Prospective Lawyers

Once you have an attorney in mind, call the law office and explain that you have a workers' compensation case. The secretary, paralegal, or other staff person will ask you some preliminary questions, designed to determine whether or not the attorney would be interested in talking to you. This will often depend on whether or not you have suffered a permanent disability. As mentioned, workers' compensation attorneys generally work on a 12% to 15% contingency fee, so they will rarely accept workers' compensation cases where there is little or no permanent disability. If they do, the final settlement will be too low to reasonably compensate them for their time.

> **EXAMPLE 1:** James severed the tip of his little finger at work. Since this will generally result in a permanent disability of 5% or less, most attorneys will not be interested in representing James.

> **EXAMPLE 2:** Marna fractured her hip in a fall at work. She had a total hip replacement. This injury will result in a substantial permanent

disability, so any attorney should be interested in representing Marna.

EXAMPLE 3: Antonio hurt his elbow from repetitive use of a hammer at work. The doctor suspects ulnar nerve entrapment. Because Antonio's permanent disability is an unknown quantity, some attorneys will and some won't want to represent Antonio.

As pointed out earlier, you cannot be charged a fee for an initial consultation with a workers' compensation attorney. If a lawyer attempts to charge you a fee for a consultation, do not make an appointment. The lawyer is either unethical or does not know the law regarding workers' compensation fees. Either way, you don't want to be represented by that person.

In addition to asking the lawyer the questions discussed just above, ask yourself whether you like the attorney you are considering hiring. You are going to have to work together, perhaps for several years. Make certain that you are at ease and feel comfortable with your choice. Are you able to communicate with the lawyer? Does the lawyer take the time to answer your questions to your satisfaction?

Ask the attorney about office policy regarding returning your phone calls and answering your letters. Any workers' compensation attorney who is being up-front and honest with you should say

The Attorney's Interview of You

The better workers' compensation lawyers can afford to turn down three or four cases for every case they accept. At the same time you are interviewing a lawyer, you are also being interviewed! Put bluntly, the lawyer wants to determine whether you are someone he or she would feel comfortable representing and whether your case will produce a large enough settlement to be worth the time.

With this in mind, here are some ground rules about how to approach your initial interview if you want an attorney to take your case:

- Show up on time for your appointment. Be sure you are neat and presentable. (If you can't keep an appointment, call ahead of time to cancel.)
- If possible, have a copy of your DWC-1 form and all correspondence and paperwork from the insurance company and your employer.
- Answer questions honestly and specifically. Be prepared to tell the lawyer exactly how you injured yourself and what you did afterward. Have a concise history of your medical treatment to date. Because of the relatively low fees, workers' compensation lawyers have many clients, and they don't have time for people who ramble on and on.
- Completely and accurately fill out any questionnaires given to you by the attorney.
- Don't sound like a know-it-all. While it is true that if you've read this book you will know a great deal about workers' compensation law, don't use the interview as a way to impress the lawyer.
- It is usually a mistake to say that you have spoken to another attorney, unless you can't avoid it. Even if you decided not to hire the other attorney, you may be perceived as having been turned down. This can be a red flag to a lawyer who may wonder why the other lawyer rejected your case.
- Be reasonable with regard to your case. Avoid making belligerent statements such as, "I won't settle for anything less than ..." or "I don't care if I ever get a dime, I just want to get back at them ...." The attorney is looking for someone who is realistic and willing to listen to good advice. It's fine to be knowledgeable and want to be involved in your case, but an attorney who sees you as uncontrollable will probably decide not to represent you.

that because of a large caseload, it is very difficult to return all phone calls immediately. But the lawyer should promise to either return your call or have someone from the office capable of answering your questions call you as soon as possible, usually within five days.

4. How Workers' Compensation Attorneys Are Paid

The only way an applicant's workers' compensation attorney can earn money is by a contingency agreement or contract. That means that the attorney earns a fee based upon a percentage of your recovery. If you do not get a recovery, you do not owe the attorney a penny. If the attorney asks you for a retainer or any money up front, get up and leave! This is a violation of the law. You may also want to consider reporting the attorney to the State Bar. You can find the number of the local State Bar by calling information or referring to the telephone directory.

The lawyer's fee percentage of your recovery varies slightly from county to county and depends in part on the complexity of your case. For example, in some counties, a judge may award 10% for a very easy case, 12% for an average case, and 15% where the attorney has done a bang-up job in a highly complex situation.

Considering the amount of work involved in a typical workers' compensation case, a 12% to 15% fee based upon the amount the attorney recovers for you is a bargain. If you had another kind of case, you wouldn't be as lucky. For instance, contingency fees in auto accident and other types of personal injury cases usually run from 25% to 40% of the recovery.

The amount of the attorney's fee is calculated on:

- the amount of your permanent disability award
- the amount of any retroactive temporary disability payments (future payments are excluded)
- any money received to settle your future medical treatment
- any money you receive by way of retroactive vocational rehabilitation maintenance allowance, and
- any penalties you recover.

EXAMPLE: Nina's case settles for $10,000 for permanent disability plus $3,000 for past-due temporary disability payments. Her attorney's fee is based upon a percentage (10%, 12%, or 15%) of the $13,000. Fees are not calculated on amounts she receives for current temporary disability payments or payment of her outstanding medical bills and related costs. If, prior to Nina's retaining an attorney, the insurance company had offered Nina $13,000 to settle her case, and she settles for $13,000 after hiring an attorney, the attorney still would be entitled to a fee based on the $13,000 settlement. The fee in Nina's case will be between $1,300 and $1,950.

In addition to charging a fee based on your permanent disability award and retroactive benefits recovered, most lawyers will also insist on representing you if you are entitled to and want vocational rehabilitation benefits. If you don't want representation and want to handle your own vocational rehabilitation case, you will have to find an attorney willing to take only the workers' compensation portion of your case. Vocational rehabilitation is an additional service for which the attorney is entitled to another fee (usually about 12%) based upon the temporary maintenance allowance you receive while you are being retrained. For example, if you are receiving $246 per week maintenance allowance while participating in retraining, 12% (or $29.52) would be deducted each week and set aside for attorney fees.

TIP

Out-of-pocket legal expenses are paid by the attorney and the insurance company. Any legal expenses such as costs of depositions or subpoenas are advanced by your attorney and will be reimbursed by the insurance company when your case settles.

5. Pro Per Advice Only

Unlike other areas of the law, workers' compensation attorneys are not allowed to charge an hourly rate for representing you in a workers' compensation matter. (LC § 4906.) This apparently includes giving advice to pro pers (people representing themselves), as all workers' compensation fees received must first be approved by a workers' compensation judge.

If you want to hire a lawyer by the hour to help or advise you on a difficult issue in your case, it's possible that a judge would allow you to do so. If a judge approves an hourly fee, you are then free to find an attorney willing to help. You might also try asking a judge to issue an order allowing an attorney you chose to bill for services for a few hours. You'd make this request by filing documents with the appeals board and arranging for a hearing before a judge, as described in Chapter 22.

6. How to Work With a Lawyer

Because workers' compensation lawyers have very high caseloads, their time is at a high premium. Against this background, let's look at how to keep in touch with your lawyer so that you stay informed, provide help as needed, but respect the fact that your lawyer likely has hundreds of other cases to attend to.

Most offices specializing in workers' compensation cases have sophisticated systems to process a case from beginning to end. Very often, the attorney relies on trained paralegals and other support personnel to handle the routine aspects of each case. The lawyers devote most of their time to appearing in court, attending depositions, negotiating with defendants, and interviewing clients.

In most offices, legal assistants are trained to answer routine questions. They are likely to be more up-to-date on the status of your case than your lawyer. So as long as you get reasonably prompt and solid answers to your questions, do not feel neglected or slighted if you have more contact with a legal assistant than with your lawyer.

If you simply must communicate with your lawyer, and your request is ignored, realize that it is much easier to get in touch by writing than by telephone. Write your attorney a letter and address it "personal and confidential." This will assure that your letter goes directly to your lawyer. Keep your letter polite, short, and to the point, such as the following example.

Sample

March 10, 20xx

Dear Ms. Watson:

I have been trying to reach you for several weeks regarding an issue that is very important to me. [*State problem.*]

Your legal assistant, Darlene Gray, while very competent, is unable to answer my questions to my satisfaction.

I realize you are very busy. However, I would appreciate speaking with you at your earliest convenience. If I haven't heard from you by March 29, I will call your office for an appointment. I would very much appreciate if you would leave word with your assistant to set an appointment date for me when I call.

Sincerely,

Susan Sheridan

Susan Sheridan

[*Address and phone number*]

You naturally want to know the status of your case at all times. However, don't let this fact cause you to be overly anxious or concerned if you haven't heard from your attorney for several months. As you know from reading this book, the workers' compensation system is very slow, and it is not unusual for months to go by without hearing anything—because nothing significant has happened.

Make use of the knowledge you've gleaned from this book and ask specific questions of your lawyer. If you ask, "How is my case going?" you're liable to get a response such as "Fine." However, if you ask, "Now that Dr. Smith has declared me to be permanent and stationary, are you planning to set up an agreed medical examination and, if so, when?" you should get a solid answer to your question or at least a call back within a day or two.

Make sure you advise your lawyer of any changes in your address or phone number, and always advise the lawyer of any letters you receive from the insurance company, such as notices of medical appointments or changes in benefits.

How to Work With a Law Firm

If you retain an attorney from a law firm with more than one partner, realize that you are hiring the firm and not that particular attorney. It is common practice for attorneys within the same firm to appear on each other's cases. For example, if "your" attorney is on vacation or has a calendar conflict, another attorney from the firm may show up to cover a deposition, settlement conference, or a trial. Also, the attorney who handles your case may leave the firm and another attorney may be assigned to your case.

Don't let the fact that you may have several different attorneys throughout your case upset you. They should all become completely familiar with your case and capable of representing your interests. You won't be responsible for additional attorney fees.

TIP

Set an appointment when necessary. Asking to have an appointment with your attorney should be a last resort. However, it may be necessary if you have a new injury, your employer fires you, or some other major event occurs in your case. When all else fails, set an appointment to review your concerns.

7. How to Fire Your Attorney

Getting rid of your lawyer is fairly simple. Simply advise the lawyer in writing that you no longer want that law office to represent you. This is your right; the lawyer can't continue to represent you if you don't want that.

Once notified that you wish to end the relationship, the lawyer should mail you a self-explanatory substitution of attorney form to fill out and return. You may also get a substitution of attorney form from the appeals board. Your old attorney and your new attorney (or you, if you will be representing yourself) must sign. Your old attorney must file the substitution of attorney form with the Workers' Compensation Board and send you your file.

In those rare cases where the attorney will not cooperate with you, you'll need to fill out a Withdrawal of Attorney Fee Disclosure form and Dismissal of Attorney form. You can get these forms from the Workers' Compensation Appeals Board. Go to the law office you are firing, present them with a copy and request your file, or mail your lawyer copies by certified mail, return-receipt requested. If your lawyer won't cooperate, call the State Bar of California and lodge a complaint. This will generally get you quick results.

If you fire an attorney, you still have to pay a reasonable fee based upon the amount of work done prior to termination. To guarantee payment, the lawyer will likely file a lien with the Workers' Compensation Appeals Board asking for a "reasonable fee." When your case is ready to settle, you—or your new lawyer—will have to negotiate your prior attorney's lien. Obviously, you will want to convince the attorney to accept as little as possible, as the fee will come out of your settlement.

TIP

Don't fire your lawyer without good reason. If your case was sufficiently complex that your attorney agreed to take it on, you likely will benefit from formal legal representation. Once you fire an attorney, finding a new one may be very difficult, particularly if the original attorney is well regarded in the community. Workers' compensation attorneys often have far more injured workers seeking their services than they can accept as clients. They can be, and are, very selective about the cases they take. If you are seen as a difficult, demanding client, you will likely be turned down, even if you have a good case. Some attorneys have a rigid "two attorney" rule—if you have fired two prior attorneys, they will not accept your case under any circumstances.

CHAPTER

27

Figure Out a Starting Settlement Amount

A number of books aimed at lawyers have been written about workers' compensation. Most of these are dry and technical but, nevertheless, can be gold mines of useful information. Although these books often cost upwards of $100, most are available for use at a good law library. Going that extra mile to look up the law on a troublesome issue in your case can sometimes mean the difference between receiving or losing important workers' compensation benefits.

A. Find a Law Library

All California counties have at least one law library open to the public, usually located in the main county courthouse where the Superior Court is headquartered. Publicly funded law schools at UCLA, UC Berkeley, UC Davis, and Hastings College of the Law (San Francisco) also have excellent law libraries open to the public.

While you will be able to find laws and regulations online (see Section B2, below), to find cases and background sources on workers' compensation law, you'll need to go to the law library.

B. The Basics of Legal Research

The law library contains four very important sources of information on workers' compensation law. They are:

- California Labor Code (this is also available at many larger public libraries and online)
- California Code of Regulations, which defines and interprets the Labor Code (also available online)
- case law (court decisions), and
- background resources (textbooks) that cover California workers' compensation law.

RESOURCE

Step-by-step method for answering legal questions. Please refer to *Legal Research: How to Find & Understand the Law*, by Stephen Elias and the Editors of Nolo (Nolo). This excellent book covers in detail how to find statutes, regulations, and cases.

The first step in doing legal research is to figure out what you are looking for. Formulate one or more questions that deal with your subject. For example, if the insurance company raised the statute of limitations (the time period in which you have to take a particular action) as a defense to your workers' compensation case, you may want to know:

- What is the statute of limitations?
- Does it apply to my case?
- Are there any exceptions to the statute of limitations that may apply?

Next, you will want to break down your subject into key words or phrases that will allow you to easily find your topic in various indexes to statutes, cases, or background resources. For example, statute of limitations might be categorized in an index under such headings as statute of limitations, statute/limitation of, limitation of actions, or time limitations. Use the indexes in the various background resources listed below to find the information you are looking for.

1. Find a Good Background Resource

When starting a legal research task, it's often best to get an overview of how the legal issues connected with your question fit into the larger legal fabric. Assuming you need a more detailed treatment of the subject than presented here, you'll want to refer to other books written by experts on the subject.

In order of importance or usefulness, here is a list of good resources for researching workers' compensation topics or issues:

- ***Workers' Compensation Laws of California*** (Matthew Bender). This soft-bound book contains the various laws governing workers' compensation, such as the Labor Code, Insurance Code, and Rules and Regulations. It does not, however, give any comments or discussions on the laws. Most workers' compensation attorneys (including myself) use this book on a daily basis. It contains an excellent index that allows you to easily find the law that applies to your situation. If you can afford it (the cost is about $80 plus tax), consider purchasing a copy. (Call the publisher at 888-285-3947 for ordering information or go to www.lexisnexis.com.)

- ***California Workers' Compensation Practice,*** by Charles Laurence Swezey (California Continuing Education of the Bar). This 900+ page book contains a good treatment of California workers' compensation laws set out by subject matter. This book is written to assist the practicing workers' compensation attorney. It is comprehensive (and expensive) and includes sample forms. It offers good treatment of the appeals and rating processes.
- ***California Workers' Compensation Law and Practice,*** by Newman, Wong, Dobrin, and St. Clair (California Compensation Seminars). This two-volume set gives a very thorough discussion by subject matter. St. Clair is considered to be an authority on the subject and is often cited as law.
- ***The California Workers' Compensation Handbook: A Practical Guide to Workers' Compensation Laws of California,*** by Stanford D. Herlick (Matthew Bender). A thorough and readable treatment of California workers' compensation laws. This book gives a detailed discussion on all subject matter, and includes references to applicable case law. Order at www.lexisnexis.com or 888-285-3947.
- ***Schedule for Rating Permanent Disability Under the Labor Code of California,*** by the Division of Industrial Accidents, State of California. A must-have manual on rating permanent disabilities, discussed in Chapter 18. You can view the new schedule on the Internet for free at www.dir.ca.gov/dwc/pdr.pdf. If you don't have online access, you may order a copy from the California Applicants' Attorneys Association, 801 12th Street, Suite 201, Sacramento, CA 95814, 916-444-5155, for $25. The old rating schedule can be found at www.dir.ca.gov/dwc/PDR1997.pdf. The association also sells both old schedules—for injuries occurring before 2005 and for injuries occurring before April 1, 1997—for $65.
- ***California Law of Employee Injuries and Workers' Compensation,*** by Warren L. Hanna (Matthew Bender). A three-volume set containing the Rules and Regulations, sample forms, tables, and an index as well as a thorough discussion of the law by subject matter. (This is similar in scope and depth to the Matthew Bender book mentioned above; try the other book first.)
- ***California Workers' Compensation Claims and Benefits,*** by David O'Brien (Parker and Son). A large three-binder manual containing over 1,100 pages of information, featuring a thorough discussion of each workers' compensation law. Includes references and citations to applicable case law. A great way to find out whether courts have ruled on any of the key legal issues in your case. But make sure to look at updates to the 1990 edition.
- ***California Civil Practice—Workers' Compensation,*** by Judge Alan Eskenazi, Raymond E. Frost, and Lynn Pearce Peterson (Bancroft Whitney). A two-volume set containing a very good discussion of workers' compensation laws. This book is set out by subject matter, starting with an overview and proceeding through various topics. It is similar in scope to the O'Brien book, listed above.

2. Read California Workers' Compensation Laws and Rules

After you review background resources, you will want to proceed to the law itself. In most instances, you'll start by consulting statutes and rules organized into groups of laws known as codes.

I estimate that 95% of all laws you will be concerned with in your workers' compensation case are either in the California Labor Code or in the

California Code of Regulations (also referred to as CCR or Rules and Regulations).

a. Statutes (Codes)

You can find the Labor Code, which is published by a number of different publishers, in most larger public libraries as well as all law libraries. You will find various divisions, each of which covers a different aspect of the general subject of labor. Division 4 specifically deals with workers' compensation laws. It is subdivided into chapters, which are set out in a very logical fashion. When it comes to workers' compensation, you will almost always work with the Labor Code.

To find California statutes online, go to www.leginfo.ca.gov/calaw.html. Check the box for Labor Code. Go to the bottom of the page to the "search for keywords" box. If you know the number of the code section (for example, LC § 5412), you can put the number into the box. Otherwise, enter a word or two describing your topic (for example, for the date of injury, enter "date" and "injury"). Click on "Search." A page will come up with a list of the laws that contain the keywords you entered. The laws at the top of the list have more instances of those keywords than the ones at the bottom of the list. Click on the law at the top of the list and browse through it to see whether it answers your question (your keywords will be in bold type). If it doesn't answer your question, go to the next law. If you get too many laws, you may want to refine your search. Go back to the previous search screen and either add another word or change one of the words to be more specific. If you get too few laws, or none, go back to the previous search screen and either remove a keyword or change a keyword to be more general. Click on "Search" again.

Occasionally you may need to refer to another code, such as the Code of Civil Procedure or the Insurance Code. All of these codes are available at most of the larger public libraries and at all law libraries, or you can search the codes online at the same URL above, by checking the box for the appropriate code.

Whenever you look up a code section in the library, make sure you always check the pocket inside the back cover of the code book to see whether there is a current supplement. The supplement, which is also organized numerically by code section, will contain the latest version of the law.

If possible, refer to the annotated version of the Labor Code (and any other relevant codes), which is available in law libraries. In addition to the actual words of the statute, annotated codes contain extremely valuable references to related court cases, other relevant code sections, key law journal articles, commentaries on the statute, and a discussion of how the code section has been interpreted.

b. California Code of Regulations (CCR)

You will often hear the California Code of Regulations (CCR) referred to as the "Rules and Regulations" or the "Rules and Regs." The Rules and Regulations that apply to workers' compensation are an extension of the Labor Code. They mostly expand upon and clarify the procedural aspects of processing a workers' compensation claim.

You can find all the regulations that apply to workers' compensation online at www.dir.ca.gov/samples/search/querydwc.htm.

The best way to understand the purpose of the Rules and Regulations is to review the synopsis in the front. The section that is applicable is Title 8. Like the Labor Code, it is set forth in a very logical manner.

Always check the pocket part of the Rules and Regulations to see if there is a current supplement that contains the latest version of the law.

3. Find Relevant Cases

Most of the laws you will deal with in workers' compensation can be found in the Labor Code, the Rules and Regulations, and a few other codes, discussed just above. Additional laws have come about as a result of court decisions made by the California Appellate Courts or California Supreme

Court. You may need to research this case law to see how various issues have been decided by the courts. The process of referring to a case as precedent for a legal point is known as "citing a case" or "case citation."

Workers' compensation cases generally fall into one of three categories:

- Workers' Compensation Appeals Board decisions that have been denied judicial review
- California appellate court opinions. Certain decisions are certified for publication in the official reports and may be cited as law to the court. Those cases that have not been certified for publication in the official reports may not be cited as law to the court.
- California Supreme Court decisions.

Before you do the legal research necessary to find court decisions that may help you win your case, you'll need to know how cases are referred to, or "cited." Citations start with the name of the case, usually in italics or underlined. For example: *Massey v. WCAB*. (In this case Massey is the injured worker and, of course, WCAB stands for Workers' Compensation Appeals Board.) Immediately following the name are the locations (books) where the case can be found. For example: 58 CCC 367, 21 CWCR 189. CCC refers to a set of books called *California Compensation Cases*, which is available in many law libraries; 58 refers to the volume number, and 367 the page number where the *Massey* case starts. CWCR refers to *California Workers' Compensation Reporter*, another set of books where the same court decision can also be found; 21 refers to the correct volume, and 189 to the page where the *Massey* decision begins.

Finally, in parentheses, some cites will tell you the court that made the decision. Sometimes this information will be very easy to understand, as would be true for (California Supreme Court) or (Court of Appeal, First Appellate District). But you will also encounter the more confusing term (Writ denied). This means that the Court of Appeal decided not to consider a case, which has the effect of leaving the decision of the Workers' Compensation Appeals Board intact. (See Chapter 25, Appealing a Workers' Compensation Decision, for an explanation of the workers' compensation appeals process.)

Case law can also be very helpful at the time of trial if your right to certain benefits turns upon an interpretation of a particular section of the Labor Code. If you know how to do case research, you have the opportunity to find and call the judge's attention to helpful decisions. And if the judge asks each side to submit "points and authorities" (jargon that means citations to relevant cases), you'll know how to respond.

Fortunately, because workers' compensation is a relatively narrow field, it's not difficult to locate significant court decisions. In fact, most of the collection work has already been done for you by the authors of the books listed in Section B1, above. In addition, the following books, which are available in law libraries, contain virtually every case relevant to workers' compensation:

- ***California Compensation Cases (CCC)*** (Matthew Bender). This is probably the best source of case law for workers' compensation. All cases are grouped by year from 1936 to the present. New cases are set forth in monthly advance sheets (loose-leaf publications usually found in a three-ring binder near the bound volumes). Best of all, the cases are grouped in the index by subject matter, which allows you to easily find cases relevant to your situation. Each case is discussed, including what the case held or stands for under workers' compensation law.
- ***California Workers' Compensation Reporter*** (CWCR, P.O. Box 520, Berkeley, CA 94701). A monthly bulletin of key developments in workers' compensation law. (Some information is available online for free at www.cwcrwitt.com.)
- ***West's California Reporter*** (West Publishing Co.). This multivolume set contains cases of the Supreme Court, courts of appeal, superior court, and appellate courts of California.

- ***Shepard's Citations for Statutes*** contains cross-references to all relevant case law that supports or gives an opposing opinion to a particular case.
- ***California Appellate Reports*** (Bernard and Whitney Company), 1st through 4th series. A multivolume set containing all appellate court decisions.

a. How to Find a Case

Here are several methods or sources for finding relevant case law:

- **Annotated codes.** As mentioned, if you look up a particular law in an annotated version of the Labor Code (available in law libraries), you'll find short summaries of all the court cases that interpret the statute directly following the notes on the statute's history. Annotated codes also provide information on the statute's history (when it was adopted and modified) and case law interpretation. (See Section B2a, above, for more on using annotated codes.)
- **Background resources.** Most of the workers' compensation texts discussed in Section B1, above, are copiously footnoted with citations to cases that discuss specific points of law covered in the main discussion. Thus, if you read the commentary about legal issues that affect your case, you'll almost surely find that key court cases are mentioned.
- ***Shepard's Citations for Statutes.*** This resource provides a complete listing of each time a particular statute, regulation, or constitutional provision has been referred to and perhaps interpreted by a published decision of a federal or state court. We are, of course, interested only in California state court citations. To Shepardize state statutes, note the year the statute you wish to Shepardize was passed. Find the *Shepard's* volume of California's statutes, and select all volumes covering the years since the statute was passed. Next, find the Labor Code in the upper margin in boldface. Locate the section number of the statute. Finally, note the citations under the section number. These citations are to the book and pages where the statute is referred to. Follow this process for all volumes and pamphlets up to the most recent case.

TIP

Using *Shepard's*. It is not always easy for a novice to use *Shepard's*. Fortunately, the complete ins and outs of how to do it are covered in detail in *Legal Research: How to Find & Understand the Law,* by Stephen Elias and the Editors of Nolo (Nolo). You can also ask a law librarian to help you.

- **Case digest subject index.** Digests are collections of brief summaries (called headnotes) from cases, which are organized according to subject and indexed. It's easy to use the subject index or table of contents in a case digest to find the court cases that deal with your legal questions. For example, look up "statute of limitations" (or other appropriate words or phrases) to find a long list of cases on that subject. The two main digests are *Shepard's California Citations* and *West's California Citations.*
- **Case digest table of cases.** It is common to hear well-known cases referred to by name only. For example, a letter advising that an employee may have a workers' compensation claim is known as a "*Reynolds*" letter because of the case of *Reynolds v. Appeals Board*, 12 Cal.3d 726, 39 CCC 768 (1974). If you know the name of a case only, you'll need to find its citation to find the book and page where it's located. To do this, the *West* digest system is extremely helpful. Each digest (collection of summaries of cases) is accompanied by a table of cases that lists all the cases referred to in that digest.
- ***California Reporter.*** The *California Reporter* is a multivolume set of books listing all the California cases in detail. Each *California Reporter* has a subject index, usually at the

back, as well as a table of cases, usually at the front. This table contains a listing of all cases in that volume of the report and their page references.

Chapter 28—Case Law Review

In addition to the sources for finding relevant workers' compensation case law listed here, please refer to Chapter 28, Case Law Review. That chapter digests many court decisions in key legal areas. You may find case law on your legal issue in that chapter. For easy reference, the cases have been arranged by topic and refer to the chapter and page in the book where the material is discussed.

b. How to Find Related Cases

Once you've found a relevant case, you may find similar cases or cases that affect the validity of the case you've found. The tools used to find these cases are *Shepard's Citations for Cases* and the *West* digest system. Explaining exactly how to use these systems is beyond the scope of this book. You may want to ask the law librarian for assistance, or turn to *Legal Research: How to Find & Understand the Law*, by Stephen Elias and the Editors of Nolo (Nolo).

CHAPTER 28

Case Law Review

Most of the laws you will deal with in workers' compensation can be found in the California Labor Code, the California Code of Regulations, and a few other codes. All important ones are discussed in this book as part of our detailed review of the process of applying for workers' compensation benefits. But in many substantive legal areas we have not had the space to discuss how courts have applied the law to particular fact situations. This is where case law comes in.

If you have a particular problem in your case, it is likely that others have faced a similar situation. This means by finding a prior reported case that deals with your problem or issue—or even a similar one—you can often learn whether the court that will consider your case is likely to agree or disagree with your position. In addition, you will be in a position to tell the court about the existence of the earlier case, something they may or may not discover on their own. The process of referring to a court case as precedent for a legal point is known as "citing a case" or a "case citation." (See "Precedent: Why One Court Follows the Decisions of Another," below.)

Case law is not magic. It doesn't just "appear" one day for everybody to read and benefit from. It is created by people, just like you, who are not willing to accept a decision by a workers' compensation judge. When faced with what they believe to be a wrong interpretation of a particular code or regulation, these people appeal their cases to a higher court. (See Chapter 25, Appealing a Workers' Compensation Decision.) The resulting court opinions then act as precedent to be applied by workers' compensation judges in the future.

The rest of this chapter identifies and briefly discusses what I believe to be the most important recent workers' compensation cases, following the same subject organization as used in the book itself. By important, I mean a case that casts light beyond what can be found in a statute or regulation on a fact situation that many injured workers face. But please understand that there are thousands of other cases I do not discuss. So treat the cases discussed in this chapter as only a starting place for your case law research. (See Chapter 27 for more on legal research.)

CAUTION

Read the case, not just my comments. In a very short space below I summarize what I believe each noteworthy case means. By definition this sort of legal shorthand is an imperfect science—if you think a case may have a bearing on your situation, look it up and read it in its entirety.

Chapter 3—Is Your Injury Covered by Workers' Compensation?

The cases discussed here deal with issues involving whether or not your injury is covered by workers' compensation in the first place. Please refer to Chapter 3 for a detailed review of this subject.

Area of Law #1

The issue is whether an injured worker can file a workers' compensation claim after the worker has been terminated or laid off. If a claim for workers' compensation benefits is not filed until after the injured worker has been laid off or fired, the claim will not be allowed unless the worker can prove one or both of the following:

- The worker received medical treatment for the work-related injury prior to receiving the notice of layoff or termination.
- The employer had knowledge of the injury prior to the notice of layoff or termination.

Jeffrey Mabe v. Mike's Trucking and California Indemnity Insurance Company, 26 CWCR 381

This case says: An injured worker can file a claim for workers' compensation benefits after he quits, provided that the worker did not have prior notice of a potential for layoff or termination.

Precedent: Why One Court Follows the Decisions of Another

In any hearing before a workers' compensation judge (as well as any other court of law), the judge will base a decision on the written laws and regulations. Sometimes, however, the meaning of the law is not absolutely clear but instead is subject to different interpretations given the facts of a particular case.

To avoid confusing an issue by making different decisions on the same or similar fact situations, the judge will look to how other judges have "interpreted" the meaning of the law by looking at other case decisions. The procedure of deciding a case based upon an interpretation of the law as made by another judge is known as "case law precedent." Previous cases set "precedents" to be followed by other judges. In order for precedent to apply, however, the facts in the two cases must be the same or very similar. In addition, to understand whether a second court *must* follow a previous court's decision (precedent is binding) or *may* consider it, but nevertheless can arrive at a different decision (precedent is advisory), it is necessary to understand the hierarchy or pecking order of the courts.

- As the state's highest court, decisions by the California Supreme Court must be followed by lower state courts and the Workers' Compensation Appeals Board.
- The Court of Appeal must follow cases (precedent) decided by the California Supreme Court but can treat opinions at the WCAB level as being advisory.
- The judges at the Workers' Compensation Appeals Board must follow the decisions of both the Court of Appeal and the California Supreme Court.

For instance, when Labor Code § 4600 was written to provide the level of medical treatment an injured worker is entitled to, it was only a matter of time before judges were faced with deciding whether particular injured workers qualified for benefits under its terms; they "interpreted" and "defined" its meaning. And each time a higher court did this, it created new case law, or precedent, for lower courts to follow when faced with the same fact situation. Another way of saying this is that when courts make law, they are fitting statutes to real-life situations. And because this is true, you will often want to check to see whether any of this judge-made law affects you.

EXAMPLE: Your doctor states in writing that you can hire someone to do your housekeeping for you because you are physically unable to do it yourself. But the insurance adjuster claims that under the law you are not entitled to this benefit. You disagree, and the dispute ends up in court. You do some legal research and locate a previous court case where a court said that an injured worker was entitled to payment of housekeeping services. (See *Gardner v. WCAB*, 20 CWCR 295.) You call this precedent to the attention of the judge hearing your case.

Area of Law #2

Psychiatric injury—is it covered by workers' compensation?

Jargon note: For workers' compensation purposes, a psychiatric and a psychological injury are the same thing. In different cases, you will see one or the other term used—there is no real difference.

Rodriguez v. WCAB, 59 CCC 14, 22 CWCR 12

Rodriguez claimed that he suffered a psychiatric injury as a consequence of dealing with a physical injury. (This case does not involve a claim of a psychiatric injury due to the stress and strain of the job.) The case holds (rules) that psychological stress and strain from dealing with the workers' compensation process (dealing with court hearings, coping with results of medical reports, etc.) is not compensable (recoverable) under workers' compensation. However, it also says that workers' compensation does cover a situation where a psychiatric injury results from a work injury. For example, under the reasoning of this case, you can qualify for workers' compensation if you establish that as a result of the stress and strain of dealing with the consequences of your severe back injury, you have sustained a psychological injury. It follows that you should advise your doctor that, if possible, the doctor's report should contain language to the effect that your psychiatric problems are due to the frustrations of dealing with the pain and limitations of the *injury,* not as a result of the many frustrations inherent in the workers' compensation litigation process.

California Youth Authority v. WCAB (Walker), 60 CCC 1099

This case plows some of the same ground as the *Rodriguez* case, discussed just above, but deals with psychiatric stress injuries. It holds that when an original injury is psychiatric in nature, the need for additional temporary disability and medical treatment is compensable as a combined effect of the industrial injury and the workers' compensation litigation process. In this case the applicant had an admitted psychiatric injury covered by workers' compensation and had been receiving disability payments. (See Chapter 12, Section A.) The applicant then requested a permanent disability advance in order to pay for his sons' college education. The carrier delayed payment (whether or not the delay was reasonable or not is of no consequence) of the lump sum advance pending an agreed medical evaluator's (AME) evaluation. (See Chapter 10, Section A.) As a result of the delay, the applicant suffered a significant depressive episode and required a new period of temporary disability. (See Chapter 12, Section A.) The insurance carrier argued that because the aggravation of the condition was a result of the worker's compensation litigation process, it should not be responsible for the additional temporary disability. The court stated that this case involved "an original injury to the psyche and need for medical treatment should major recurrent depressive episodes and/or psychological reversal occur" and that "since the original industrial injury triggered the employee's psychiatric condition, the employee's later need for treatment and temporary disability is on an industrial basis." In other words, if the original injury is psychiatric in nature (not purely physical as in *Rodriguez,* above), the aggravation due to the workers' compensation litigation process is compensable.

Area of Law #3

A normal personnel action by the employer, such as writing the employee up for alleged misconduct, cannot give rise to psychiatric injury covered by workers' compensation. And this is true even if the action was unfair. To recover, an employee who suffers a psychological injury must show that the employer acted in bad faith—that is, from an ulterior motive or reason, outside of the immediate needs of the job. For example, a bad faith action by an employer might consist of a supervisor's writing up an innocent employee for stealing because the supervisor did not like the employee.

Cristobal v. WCAB, 61 CCC 65

In this case the injured worker claimed a psychiatric injury as a result of a verbal altercation with a supervisor related to a change in the applicant's work shift. The court decided that the source of the stress that caused the psychiatric injury was a good faith personnel action by the employer, so the applicant's injury was determined to be nonindustrial and, therefore, not covered by workers' compensation. In other words, a personnel action by the employer undertaken in good faith (the employer was motivated by needs of the job) does not give rise to an injury arising out of or occurring in the course of employment based on Labor Code § 3208.3.

Chapter 5—What to Do If You're Injured

The cases that follow deal with what happens when you are injured at work. Please refer to Chapter 5 for a more complete discussion of this subject.

Area of Law #1

Failure to report the injury on time. As discussed in Chapter 5, Section C1, if you fail to promptly report your injury and file a timely workers' compensation claim, your right to receive benefits may be barred by the statute of limitations.

Reynolds v. Workmen's Comp. Appeals Bd. (1974), 12 Cal.3d 726, 39 CCC 768 (California Supreme Court case)

This case says: If your employer fails to follow the law and advise an injured worker in writing of the right to file a workers' compensation claim, the employer is not allowed to assert that the claim has been filed too late (is barred by the statute of limitations). But once you have actual knowledge that you may be entitled to benefits under the workers' compensation system, the statute of limitations period (usually one year from the date of your injury) can begin to be counted.

Area of Law #2

Date of injury for continuous trauma injuries. The date of injury you use can affect the disability rate at which you are paid for both temporary disability (see temporary disability rates table in Chapter 12, Section B) and permanent disability (see the permanent disability rates table in Chapter 13, Section E2). The later your date of injury, the higher your disability rate will be. But for a continuous trauma injury, your insurance carrier will probably want to make the date of injury the day you first started having symptoms, saw a doctor, or filed a claim. As discussed in Chapter 5, Section C1b, the date of injury should be the first day you took off work. The following cases clarify Labor Code § 5412, which says that the date of injury is when you first suffered a disability *and* knew (or should have known) that the disability was caused by your employment.

Globe Indemnity Co. v. IAC, 125 Cal.App.2d 763

This case says: For purposes of compensation in a progressive disease case, the injury date is measured from the time when the condition culminated in incapacity to work. Therefore, if you worked for several months or years after the beginning of symptoms, your rate will be that in effect on your first day off work, not on the first day you experienced symptoms.

Thorp v. WCAB, 153 Cal.App.3d 327

This case says: The date of injury is when bodily impairment results in impairment of earnings capacity. This can be the day you are eligible to receive temporary total or partial disability or permanent disability.

Dickow v. WCAB, 34 Cal.3d 762, 33 CCC 664

This case says: To calculate your disability rate, you use the rate that is in effect on the date of your disability.

Chapter 9—Taking Charge of Your Medical Case

The cases that follow deal with issues involving the treating doctor. Since this doctor determines many of the issues in your case, it is very important that you control who this person is. Please read Chapter 9 for a review of this subject matter.

Area of Law #1

You are entitled to change treating doctors after the first 30 days (a longer wait is required in certain circumstances).

Ralph's Grocery Store v. WCAB (Lara), 45 Cal.Rptr.2d 197, 38 Cal.App.4th 820, 60 CCC 840, 23 CWCR 249

This case dispels the myth that you are only allowed to change your treating doctors once. In fact, you can have more than one change of treating doctors if reasonably necessary.

Tenet/Centinela Hospital Medical Center v. Carolyn Rushing and WCAB, 80 CalApp.4th 1041, 2 WCAB Rptr. 10, 205

This case involves a situation that occurs quite often, if you are initially sent to the company doctor for treatment (because your employer generally has the right to control your medical treatment for the first 30 days; see Chapter 9, Section C). Before you have a chance to change treating doctors, the company doctor may write a report saying that you are permanent and stationary (see Chapter 9, Section E) and that you do not need ongoing or continuing medical treatment, but you may need future medical treatment. This case says that you cannot change treating doctors because the first doctor says you don't need treatment. If you dispute the treating doctor's opinion that you are permanent and stationary and that you don't need current treatment, you must advise the insurance company, pursuant to Labor Code §§ 4061 and 4062, that you want to see a QME. (See Chapter 10.) You should dispute the original treating doctor's report within 30 days of receiving it. Only if the QME says you need more treatment can you change doctors and get more treatment.

If the insurance company tries to tell you that you can't change treating doctors, you should cite the next case (*Krueger*), which appears to give workers the right to change treating doctors at any time, in support of your right to do so.

Another way to overcome this problem would be to demand the insurance company in writing that you be seen again by the original treating doctor because you feel you need treatment pursuant to the future medical provisions of his report. If the doctor refuses to see you, or the insurance company refuses to authorize treatment, you can advise the insurance company that you can change treating doctors. If the doctor agrees to see you and puts you back on a treatment program, you can then change treating doctors because you are currently being treated. If the doctor examines you and again says you are not in need of treatment, then you will have to dispute his findings pursuant to Labor Code §§ 4061 and 4062 (see above).

Krueger v. Republic Indemnity Company of America, 28 CWCR 44

This case says: You have the right to change treating doctors at any time pursuant to Labor Code § 4060. It also rules that the Administrative Director (AD) Rule 9785 is invalid. AD Rule 9785 provides:

"There shall be no more than one primary treating physician at a time. Where the primary treating physician discharges the employee from further medical treatment and there is a dispute concerning the need for continuing treatment, no other primary treating physician shall be identified unless and until the dispute is resolved. If it is determined that there is no further need for continuing treatment, then the physician who discharged the employee shall remain the primary treating physician. If it is determined that there is further need for continuing treatment, a new primary treating physician may be selected."

This AD Rule 9785 (codified as CCR § 9785) was the basis for the *Tenet* decision, above. This case says AD Rule 9785 is invalid because it is inconsistent with the right of an injured worker to the "free choice of physician" guaranteed by Labor Code § 4600. Therefore, under this case, you do not need to request a QME evaluation, and you can change treating doctors. Rule 9785 is still the law but you can make the argument under *Krueger* that it shouldn't apply.

Area of Law #2

Medical Provider Network.

Knight v. United Parcel Service and Liberty Mutual Insurance Company, 71 CCC 1423

In this case, the Board held that an employer or insurer's failure to provide required notice to an employee of rights under the medical provider network (MPN) that results in a neglect or refusal to provide reasonable medical treatment renders the employer or insurer liable for reasonable medical treatment self-procured by the employee.

Elayne Valdez v. Warehouse Demo Services; Zurich North America, Adjusted by ESIS, 76 Cal. Comp. Cases 970

This case says: Where an injured employee obtains unauthorized medical treatment for an industrial injury outside a validly established and properly noticed medical provider network (MPN), the resulting non-MPN treatment reports are inadmissible. This applies to the non-MPN treating doctor reports and any reports of doctors that the treating doctor refers the injured worker to for treatment.

Area of Law #3

Utilization Review Process.

Brice Sandhagen vs. WCAB and State Compensation Insurance Fund, 74 CCC 835.

In this case the court held that when deciding whether to approve or deny an injured employee's request for medical treatment based upon a doctor's report, the insurance company must timely conduct utilization review pursuant to Labor Code § 4610 and only the injured employee may challenge the determination of the review board under Labor Code § 4602. In other words, if the utilization review determines that the treatment is appropriate, the insurance company cannot challenge the decision and must provide the treatment. However, if the utilization review concludes the treatment is not appropriate, the injured worker may challenge it and request a decision from an agreed medical evaluator or panel QME under Labor Code § 4602.

Chapter 10—Medical-Legal Evaluations

The cases that follow deal with the area of law concerning your right to have a doctor of your choice determine whether or not you are entitled to workers' compensation benefits (a process that is called a medical-legal evaluation). Remember, as discussed in Chapter 10, different rules apply when you are represented by an attorney or represent yourself.

Area of Law #1

Whether an insurance company can require an injured worker to attend a rebuttal medical evaluation in a situation in which the self-represented applicant obtained and relied on a board panel qualified medical evaluator. (Please refer to Chapter 10, Section E, for a detailed discussion regarding the QME process.)

Regents of University of California, Lawrence Berkeley Laboratories v. WCAB (Ford), 60 CCC 1246

This case says: The court concludes that the defendant insurance company was not entitled to obtain a rebuttal report to the board panel QME under Labor Code § 4050. The important point here is that if you have already gone to a panel QME and are relying on that report, you do not have to attend another exam set by the defendants. Instead, you should set your case for hearing by filing a Declaration of Readiness or an Application for Adjudication of Claim. (See Chapter 22, Section D.)

Area of Law #2

Whether you are entitled to obtain multiple medical-legal evaluations at the insurance company's expense, when the insurance company has obtained multiple medical-legal evaluations to address allegations arising from a single injury to multiple body parts.

Donald W. Gubbins v. Metropolitan Insurance Company, Travelers Indemnity Company (Board panel decision), 62 CCC 946

This case says: The WCAB concluded that when the insurance company has set up three separate medical-legal evaluations because there are three separate and distinct body parts involved, the injured worker can obtain three similar evaluations at the insurance company's expense. In its decision, the WCAB acknowledged that it would not be possible to obtain an opinion from any one of the physicians to cover all the aspects of the claim. (Labor Code §§ 4060, 4064, and 4621.)

Area of Law #3

A party who disagrees with a report issued by the treating physician has to object within a reasonable time, or may lose the right to obtain a qualified medical evaluation (QME) report.

Strawn v. Golden Eagle Insurance Company, 28 CWCR 105

In this case the insurance company objected to a treating doctor's report and obtained a qualified medical evaluation four months after the report was issued. The court stated that despite the absence of a specific time limit set forth in Labor Code § 4061, an objection to the treating doctor's report is required within a reasonable period of time. In this case, the judge found a four-month delay in objecting to the report to be unreasonable.

Chapter 11—Medical Benefits *(Treatment)*

The cases that follow deal with the subject of payment of medical benefits. Please see Chapter 11 for a detailed discussion of this important subject.

Area of Law #1

If the doctor(s) say you will need future medical care for your injuries, you are entitled to it.

Gardner v. WCAB, 20 CWCR 295

This case says: An unrestricted award for future medical treatment covers any psychiatric problems that develop later as a result of the original injury. It also appears that this case requires that where there is a nonspecific award (or a general medical award), virtually any medical need that is a direct result of the industrial injury is to be covered. Therefore, based on this reasoning, when you are negotiating a settlement by stipulation (see Chapter 20, Section C), it makes sense to try to include very general language covering the need for future medical treatment, such as "Applicant will need future medical treatment." Unfortunately, it also means that the insurance company will likely be bargaining for language that is very limiting, such as "Applicant's medical treatment is limited to medications and physical therapy as needed."

Stott v. WCAB, 57 CCC 22, 26 CWCR 3

This case says: If an industrial injury aggravates a preexisting condition, then further medical treatment should be awarded. In this case the injured worker's industrial injury aggravated preexisting multiple sclerosis. The court held that the defendants were responsible for treating the preexisting multiple sclerosis for life because there is no way to apportion treatment between the applicant's current injury and the multiple sclerosis in a situation where the multiple sclerosis is made worse by the industrial injury. Of course the defendants are also responsible for treating the industrial injury.

Area of Law #2

Can future medical treatment also include paying for housekeeping services?

Jensen v. WCAB, 57 CCC 19, 20 CWCR 10

This case says: If the doctor says housekeeping services are a medical necessity, the insurance carrier must pay for them.

Area of Law #3

Utilization review process.

Sandhagen v. Cox & Cox Construction, Inc., 69 CCC 1452

This case says: The utilization review time deadlines of Labor Code § 4610(g)(1) are mandatory and, if a defendant fails to meet these mandatory deadline, it can't use the utilization review procedure for the particular medical treatment dispute in question. If a defendant undertakes an untimely utilization review procedure, any utilization review report obtained as to the particular treatment in dispute is not admissible in evidence, and any utilization review report obtained cannot be forwarded to an AME or QME if Labor Code § 4062(a) procedures are timely pursued. Finally, when a defendant does not meet the Section 4610(g)(1) deadlines, it may use the procedure established by Section 4062(a) to dispute the treating physician's treatment recommendation; however, the defendant (not the applicant) is then the "objecting party" and the defendant must meet the Section 4062(a) deadlines, unless those deadlines are extended for good cause or by mutual agreement.

Willette v. AU Electric Corporation and State Compensation Insurance Fund, 69 CCC 1298

This case says: If an employer's utilization review physician does not approve an employee's treating physician's treatment authorization request in full, then an unrepresented employee who wants to dispute the utilization review physician's determination must object in a timely manner, after which a panel qualified medical evaluator (QME) must be obtained to resolve the disputed treatment issue(s). Once the panel QME's evaluation has been obtained, neither the treating physician nor the utilization review physician may issue any further reports addressing the utilization review treatment dispute. The panel QME should consider both the reports of the treating physician and the utilization review physician regarding the disputed issue, and if a postutilization review medical treatment dispute goes to trial after the panel QME issues his or her report, both the treating physician's and the utilization review physician's reports are admissible in evidence. When a Workers' Compensation Judge or the Appeals Board issues a decision on a postutilization review medical treatment dispute, the reports of the panel QME, the treating physician, and the utilization review physician will all be considered, but none of them is necessarily determinative.

Area of Law #4

If the injured worker (you) fails to get medical treatment within a validly established and properly noticed medical provider network (MPN), any medical reports generated by those doctors are inadmissible.

Elayne Valdez v. Warehouse Demo Services; Zurich North America, Adjusted by ESIS, 76 Cal. Comp. Cases 970

This case says: Where unauthorized treatment is obtained for an industrial injury outside a validly established and properly notice medical provider network (MPN), the resulting non-MPN treatment reports are inadmissible. This applies to the non-MPN treating doctor reports and any reports of doctors to whom the treating doctor refers the injured worker for treatment.

Area of Law #5

Insurance company's failure to authorize spinal surgery as recommended by the treating physician.

Jesus Cervantes v. El Aguila Food Products, Inc.; Safeco Insurance Co. of Illinois; Superior National Insurance Co., In Liquidation; California Insurance Guarantee Association; and Broadspire (Servicing Facility)

This case says: The Appeals Board held that the procedures and timelines governing objections to a treating physician's recommendation for spinal surgery are contained in Labor Code §§ 4610 and 4062 and in Administrative Director (AD) Rules 9788.1, 9788.11, and 9792.6(o), and are as follows: (1) when a treating physician recommends spinal surgery, the insurance carrier must begin a utilization review (UR); (2) if the UR approves the requested spinal surgery, or if the insurance company fails to timely complete the UR, the insurance company must authorize the surgery; (3) if the UR denies the spinal surgery request, the insurance company may object to the surgery under Section 4062(b), but any objection must comply with AD Rule 9788.1 and use the form required by AD Rule 9788.11; (4) the insurance company must complete its UR process within ten days of its receipt of the treating physician's report, which must comply with AD Rule 9792.6(o), and, if the UR denies the requested surgery, the insurance company's Section 4062(b) objection must be made within that same ten-day period; and (5) if the insurance company fails to meet the ten-day timelines or comply with AD Rules 9788.1 and 9788.11, the insurance company loses the right to a second-opinion report and it must authorize the spinal surgery.

Chapter 12—Temporary Disability Benefits

The cases that follow deal with temporary disability benefits payable to the injured worker while that person cannot work as a result of a work-related injury. Please refer to Chapter 12 for a detailed review of this subject.

Area of Law #1

Establishing the amount of temporary disability benefit. Generally, as discussed in Chapter 12, this benefit is payable at two-thirds of the worker's average weekly wage with certain minimum and maximum amounts based upon the date of injury. (See chart in Chapter 12, Section B, "Temporary Disability and Minimum/Maximum Rates for the First Two Years From Your Date of Injury.")

Hofmeister v. WCAB (1984), 49 CCC 438, 12 CWCR 155

This case says: Temporary disability benefits, whether paid on time or past due, that are paid more than two years after the date of injury, must be paid at the current temporary disability rate. For example, assume the date of injury is May 2, 1994 and the injured worker is entitled to the maximum temporary disability rate of $336. But because of procedural delays, benefits are not paid. More than two years later the applicant finally receives temporary disability payments. They would be paid at the maximum rate of $448 as of 1996 (or at two-thirds of actual wages for workers who don't qualify for the maximum).

Placer County Office of Education v. WCAB (Halkyard), 60 CCC 641

This older case, which is still good law, concerns how the amount of temporary disability is determined for people who ordinarily work less than a full year. It is important to teachers and seasonal workers. Here the applicant was a teacher who was off during the summer and therefore only worked ten months out of the year. She earned a total salary of $12,400 for the year. The insurance company tried to argue that during the summer months, when the teacher ordinarily received no income, it should not have to pay her anything. The court disagreed, ruling that the teacher is entitled to temporary disability for the entire year because it is her earning capacity that is being replaced, not her actual lost wages. The court then went on to compute the teacher's benefits based on two different rates. The first rate, payable during the ten months when she would ordinarily be working, was based on the $12,400 divided by the 40.71 weeks of the school year. It worked out to a weekly wage of $304.59. (The teacher got two-thirds of this figure, or $203.06 per week, for temporary disability.) The court then ruled that during the remaining 11.29 weeks when she did not teach, she would be entitled to a temporary disability rate of $158.97. This was computed by taking the $12,400 and dividing it by 52 weeks for an average weekly wage of $238.40. Two-thirds of this figure produced the temporary disability rate of $158.97 payable during the summer months. Despite this case, an insurance carrier will probably try to pay disability based on the 52-week average wage (in this case, $158.97). Don't let them get away with it.

Area of Law #2

Defendant's right to deduct any money earned by the injured worker from temporary disability amounts owed to the worker. Please see Chapter 12, Section A2, for a detailed discussion of temporary partial disability.

Hupp v. WCAB, 60 CCC 928, 45 Cal.Rptr.2d 859, 23 CWCR 275

This case says: When the injured worker is engaged in a self-employment activity, the defendant insurance carrier is only entitled to offset (take credit for) the *net* income earned from the injured worker's self-employment after all necessary business expenses are deducted. The defendant argued that they should be entitled to deduct applicant's gross receipts (money received from self-employment before the cost of doing business was subtracted) from the amount of temporary disability owed. The court obviously did not agree.

Area of Law #3

Applicant's right to receive temporary disability while receiving treatment for a nonindustrial condition that must be treated before applicant's industrial injury can be properly treated. (Please refer to Chapter 11 for a detailed discussion of medical treatment.)

Fremont Medical Center v. WCAB (Easley), 61 CCC 110

This case says: Applicant was scheduled for shoulder surgery for an industrial injury. During the surgery work-up it was discovered that applicant had anemia that needed to be controlled before surgery could proceed. Applicant was entitled to receive temporary disability payments during the period it took to cure the anemia so that surgery could take place.

Area of Law #4

Entitlement to temporary disability after retirement age.

Gonzales v. WCAB, 63 CCC 147

This case says: An injured worker is not entitled to temporary disability benefits after retirement unless the worker has made known the intention to return to the labor market. In this case, the injured worker turned 65 while on temporary total disability and had previously made known her intention to retire at age 65. The court said that the injured worker had removed herself from the labor market, so she was not entitled to temporary disability benefits. If you are close to age 65 and still temporarily totally disabled (see Chapter 12), make sure your employer and the insurance company know you intend to keep working after age 65 or retirement.

Chapter 13—Permanent Disability (and Life Pension)

The cases that follow deal with the permanent disability benefit payable to an injured worker. Specifically, they concern the issue of how the permanent disability affects the worker's future ability to participate in the labor market. Please refer to Chapter 13 for a review of the permanent disability benefit.

Area of Law #1

You are entitled to up to two-thirds of your average weekly wage as a permanent disability benefit, according to your date of injury, within the minimum and maximum amounts allowed by law.

Wilkinson v. WCAB, 42 CCC 402, 5 CWCR 87, 19 Cal.3d 491

This case says: Where there are two separate injuries with the same employer and the condition resulting from the first injury became permanent and stationary after the date of the second injury, the appeals board, rather than calculating the amount of benefits payable on the percentage of disability assigned to each injury separately, must calculate the amount on the combined total disability resulting from both injuries (but also see the *Parker* case, just below, which limits the *Wilkinson* rule to only injuries involving the same body part).

TIP

Always cite this case when you have two or more injuries to the same body part. You should definitely refer to this famous and often-cited case if you have two or more injuries to the same body part that become permanent and stationary at the same time. Under its reasoning, you will get more money for your permanent disability because of the progressive escalation in your benefit amount as your percentage of disability goes up. Example: Two separate injuries to the same body part, each by themselves having a 10% disability, result in a larger disability payment if computed as an overall 20% disability—as required by the *Wilkinson* case (rather than 10% plus 10%). Also, the fact that the date of the last injury is used for computational purposes is another reason why you may end up with a higher permanent disability rate.

Parker v. WCAB, 57 CCC 608, 12 Cal.Rptr.2d 370

This case says: The use of the *Wilkinson* case doctrine discussed just above applies only to situations where the same part of the body is involved in a successive injury. So if you have an ankle injury and a back injury that both become permanent and stationary at the same time, *Wilkinson* does not apply and you have two separate permanent disability awards (they can't be combined). However, if you have two successive back injuries that become permanent and stationary at the same time, they can be combined for a higher permanent disability rating. (Although not definitively determined, this is probably true if the injuries are to a part of the body covered by the same workers' compensation number—a back injury and a neck injury, for example, are both classified under the number 18.1 for workers' compensation purposes (see Chapter 18, Rating Your Permanent Disability), and therefore should be able to be combined under *Wilkinson*.

Benson v. The Permanente Medical Group, 72 CCC 1620 (2007)

This case overturns the *Wilkinson* rule—bad news for the injured worker. Now, if you have two dates of injury, even if they become permanent and stationary at the same time, the amount of the permanent disability is determined separately for each.

Rumbaugh v. WCAB, 87 Cal. App.3d 907, 43 CCC 1399

In this case, an injured worker had two successive injuries to the same part of his body that became permanent and stationary at the same time. However, the injuries did not occur at the same employer. The court said that the worker can combine those injuries for rating purposes even if the injuries did not occur with the same employer, abandoning the same-employer rule from the *Wilkinson* case, above.

Nuelle v. WCAB, 92 Cal.App.3d. 239, 44 CCC 1399

This case says: When a worker is injured on two separate dates, the worker is entitled to all permanent disability benefits at the rate in effect as of the last date of injury.

Harold v. WCAB, 100 Cal.3d. 772, 45 CCC 77

This case says: Where a worker is injured on two separate dates and both of the injuries become permanent and stationary at the same time, the injuries may be combined for permanent disability rating purposes even if the injuries were to different parts of body. The court said that what matters is not the parts of the body injured, but what parts are causing the permanent disability.

LeBoeuf v. WCAB (1983), 48 CCC 587

This case says: The amount of your permanent disability may be determined by factors in addition to the medical reports. Specifically, evidence can be considered at trial to the point that the injured worker is precluded from receiving rehabilitation benefits because the injury is so serious the worker is found to be nonfeasible (noneligible) for vocational rehabilitation. Similarly, evidence that the applicant can't function in the open labor market and is in fact 100% disabled can also be considered.

Sandlin v. WCAB, 55 CCC 277

This case says: Permanent disability encompasses not only impairment of the normal use of a portion of the body, but also impairment of earning capacity and the diminished ability of the injured worker to compete in an open labor market. In this case the injured worker was unable to perform more than two hours of work at a stretch due to back pain and was not a feasible candidate for vocational rehabilitation, and was therefore found to be permanently and totally disabled.

Area of Law #2

Challenging the new permanent disability rating schedule in the new rating manual on the basis that the calculation of loss of earning capacity in the formula is inaccurate. Allows applicant to hire expert to testify to loss of future earning capacity and also allows applicant to recover costs of hiring expert.

Costa v. Hardy Diagnostic and State Compensation Insurance Fund, 72 CCC 1492 (2007)

In this case, the Board reaffirmed its prior holding that Labor Code § 4660 continues to allow the parties to present evidence on, and/or in rebuttal to, a permanent disability rating under the new permanent disability rating schedule, and that the costs of such evidence may be allowable (reimbursable). Additionally, the Board noted that the standards for allowing such cases will be the same as in cases about medical-legal costs—whether such costs are reasonable and necessary when they are incurred.

Wanda Oglilvie v. City and County of San Francisco, 74 CCC 1127

This very important case holds that the person challenging a scheduled permanent disability rating must provide evidence showing that the rating is wrong. One way to do this is to challenge the rating's evaluation of the worker's diminished future earning capacity (DFEC) factor by showing that the individualized adjustment factor reflects your DFEC more accurately than the one used by the manual. You can show this by hiring a vocational rehabilitation expert to give an expert opinion on your actual DFEC, or by presenting evidence of your actual postinjury earnings using EDD wage data. This sounds complicated because it is. If you feel you are not getting a fair amount for your injury, read this case and consider getting an attorney to pursue this issue for you.

Mario Almaraz v. Environmental Recovery Services (a.k.a. Environserve); and ***State Compensation Insurance Fund and Joyce Guzman v. Milpitas Unified School District, Permissibly Self-Insured and Keenan & Associates, Adjusting Agent,*** 74 CCC 201

These very important cases show a second way of challenging the permanent disability rating under the new 2005 rating manual by challenging the injured employee's whole person impairment (WPI) under the AMA guides. You can ask the doctor who gave the WPI to determine whether the WPI is reasonable and appropriate considering all of the medical evidence; the doctor may use any charts or analogies to any part of the AMA guides to support an increase in the WPI. If you feel your WPI Is too low you should consider getting an attorney to represent you and pursue additional permanent disability under this case as well as *Ogilvie,* above.

Area of Law #3

Credit for payment of prior disability award. When you file a petition to reopen your case based on a new and further disability (see Chapter 19, Section B), the defendant is entitled to a credit (deduction) for prior payments. You are entitled to additional permanent disability payments for any increase in your disability as a result of the natural progression of your prior injury. For example, if your prior permanent disability award was 20% and you now (within five years of the date of your injury) have a permanent disability of 40%, you are entitled to additional benefits. But in computing them, the insurance carrier is entitled to deduct the money already paid based on your 20% disability from the 40% you are now entitled to, with the result that you get an additional permanent disability award of 20%.

This is also true when you have a new injury. For example, let's say you injured your back in 2010 and settled that case in 2012 for a permanent disability of 30%. You now have a new injury to your back (not a natural progression from your prior injury) that results in a permanent disability of 50%. The defendant is entitled to deduct the money already paid for the disability from what is now due for the 50% disability—unless you can show that you rehabilitated yourself from the prior injury. In other words, if, since 2012, you exercised and strengthened your back to the point where your back was no longer disabled (or, for example, improved it to be only 10% disabled), the insurance carrier would not be entitled to deduct the prior 30%. In the case of your strengthening it so you only had a 10% disability from the first injury, that's the amount they could deduct from the subsequent amount.

The Home Depot v. WCAB (Smith), 60 CCC 449

This case says: If the original award is for a partial disability (let's say 20%) and after petitioning to reopen the case you are found to have a larger overall disability (say, 36%), the defendant will argue that your disability should be figured by simply subtracting the original percentage from the higher percentage of your overall disability (36% – 20% = 16%). This case says the correct way to do this is to take the dollar value of 36% and subtract the dollar value of the prior award. Although this sounds like a highly technical distinction, it's important, because doing it this way will always result in more money in your pocket.

> **EXAMPLE:** Using the figures above for a July 2, 1997 date of injury, 16% disability is equivalent to $8,680. So if the subtraction method above were used (36% – 20% = 16%), the injured worker would get $8,680. However, the dollar value of 36% disability is $28,560. Subtracting the worker's prior award of 20% ($11,280) leaves $17,280. As you can see, this results in substantially more money ($17,280, as compared to $8,680).

Area of Law #4

Where you have more than one injury and suffer a separate permanent disability to each injured body part, the important principle known as "overlap" may apply. Simply stated, overlap occurs when a work restriction for one part of the body also benefits another part of the body. For example, if you are restricted from heavy lifting because of your back, your injured knees will also benefit from that restriction. Unfortunately, because the restriction of no heavy lifting with regards to your knees is "absorbed" in the no heavy lifting restriction for your back, the insurance carrier will use this principle to reduce the amount of disability you get. In response, you should claim that the doctrine of overlap doesn't apply and you are entitled to a permanent disability award for each part of your body that you injured. Please see Chapter 18, Section E, for a detailed review of this subject matter.

County of Los Angeles v. WCAB (McLaughlin), 56 CCC 510

This case says: If a nonindustrial medical condition develops concurrently with an industrial condition (injury), the doctrine of overlap will not apply. In this case, the applicant developed nonindustrial obstructive lung disease due to smoking. At the same time, due to exposure to asbestos at work the applicant developed a restrictive lung condition that was not as severe as the nonindustrial condition. The insurance carrier argued that the less severe work-related condition was completely absorbed (complete overlap occurred) by the nonindustrial condition. Their point was that absent the industrial injury the applicant would have still had at least this amount of disability and that therefore the industrial injury didn't really cause any additional disability. The court did not agree, holding that there can be no apportionment (overlap) between a medical condition covered by workers' compensation and one that developed off the job (a nonindustrial condition) at the same time. The effect of the court's ruling is that when you have a nonindustrial disability that develops at the same time as your industrial disability, the insurance carrier can't use that against you to deny you benefits for your industrial injury.

Area of Law #5

Using the treating doctor's report to establish permanent disability. (See Chapter 13, Section A, for a discussion about permanent disability.)

Peterson v. Wausau, 20 CWCR 250

This case says: For dates of injury between January 1, 1991 and December 31, 1993, the treating doctor's report cannot be relied upon for determining the amount of your permanent disability. The law requires that you obtain a QME evaluation. But for injuries on or after January 1, 1994, you can rely on the treating doctor's report to determine the amount of permanent disability if you want to.

Area of Law #6

Which rating manual applies when calculating permanent disability for your injury.

Baglione v. Hertz Car Sales and AIG Adjusting by Cambridge Integrated Services, 72 CCC 444

The Appeals Board, reversing its own decision in this case, held that in order for the 1997 permanent disability rating schedule to apply to a pre-2005 injury claim under Labor Code § 4660(d), the existence of permanent disability must be indicated in either a pre-2005 comprehensive medical-legal report or a pre-2005 report from a treating physician. This holding involved one of the exceptions under Labor Code § 4660(d) which, if triggered, would result in determining permanent disability in a case under the former schedule, rather than under the new schedule, effective January 1, 2005.

Pendergrass v. Duggan Plumbing and State Compensation Insurance Fund, 72 CCC 456

The Appeals Board, reversing its own decision, held that if the last payment of temporary disability indemnity was made for any period of temporary disability ending before January 1, 2005, then the 1997 permanent disability rating schedule applies when determining the extent of permanent disability, pursuant to § 4660(d).

This is because Labor Code § 4061 requires the employer to provide the injured worker with a notice regarding permanent disability "[t]ogether with the last payment of temporary disability indemnity." This holding involved one of the exceptions under Labor Code § 4660(d) which, if triggered, would result in determining permanent disability in a case under the former schedule, rather than under the new effective January 1, 2005.

Aidi v. Carr, McClellan, Ingersoll, Thompson & Horn; Republic Indemnity Company of America, 71 CCC 783

The Board held that the revised permanent disability rating schedule, adopted by the Administrative Director of the Division of Workers' Compensation, effective January 1, 2005, applies to injuries occurring on or after that date, and that in cases of injury occurring prior to January 1, 2005, the revised permanent disability rating schedule applies, unless one of the exceptions delineated in the third sentence of § 4660(d) is present.

Area of Law #7

Calculating permanent disability ratings where there is apportionment.

Nabors v. Piedmont Lumber & Mill Co., 70 CCC 856

The Board held that when the Workers' Compensation Appeals Board awards permanent disability after apportionment, the amount of indemnity due applicant is calculated by determining the overall percentage of permanent disability and then subtracting the percentage of permanent disability caused by other factors (under Labor Code § 4863(c)) or previously awarded under Labor Code § 4664(b); the remainder is applicant's final percentage of permanent disability for which indemnity is calculated pursuant to Labor Code §§ 4453 and 4858.

Chapter 14—Supplemental Job Displacement Benefit

The cases that follow deal with the vocational rehabilitation benefit. This is a workers' compensation benefit that was available to injured workers prior to 2004. Please refer to Chapter 14 to review this subject matter.

Area of Law

Vocational rehabilitation benefits have been eliminated/terminated.

Lawrence Weiner v. Ralphs Company, Permissibly Self-Insured; and Sedgwick Claims Management Services, Inc. (Adjusting Agent), 74 Cal. Comp. Cases 736

This case says: The Appeals Board held that: (1) the repeal of Labor Code § 139.5 terminated any rights to vocational rehabilitation benefits or services pursuant to order or awards that were not final before January 1, 2009; (2) a saving clause was not adopted to protect vocational rehabilitation rights in cases still pending on or after January 1, 2009; and (3) the vocation rehabilitation statutes that were repealed in 2003 do not continue to function as "ghost statutes" on or after January 1, 2009.

Chapter 15—Death Benefits

The cases that follow deal with benefits payable to the surviving dependents of a deceased worker whose death was the result of his employment. Please refer to Chapter 15 for a review of the benefits for which surviving dependents are eligible.

Area of Law #1

The amount of the death benefit payable to minor children is determined by the date of injury that resulted in death and is payable at the temporary disability rate in effect for that date. (This issue is discussed in Chapter 15, Section C.)

Wright Schuchart-Harbor v. WCAB (Morrow, deceased), 60 CCC 1066 (Writ denied), also ***Foodmaker v. WCAB (Prado-Lopez, deceased)***, 60 CCC 124 (Writ denied)

These cases say: If there is a demonstrated need, the judge has the discretion to award death benefits at a rate higher than was in force at the date the worker was injured, up to the amount payable on the date of the request. In the example given in Chapter 15, Section C, Juanita's children could ask the judge to award their payments at the current temporary disability rate of $490 per week instead of $224 per week in force when her husband was injured, if they can show financial necessity for the increase. The judge's discretion is limited to the maximum temporary disability rate in effect at the time of the request.

TIP

Do a budget to show financial necessity. Financial necessity justifying higher death benefits might be proven if the deceased workers' dependents can show that the lower amount in force at the date of the injury is not sufficient to pay the essential living expenses of the family, such as shelter, clothing, food, and medical care.

Area of Law #2

If a deceased employee was entitled to any unpaid temporary or permanent disability benefits at the time of death, that amount is due and payable to his or her surviving heirs. (This issue is discussed in Chapter 15, Section E.)

Manville Sales Corporation v. WCAB, 59 CCC 1093 (Writ denied)

This case says: A surviving heir is entitled to any unpaid temporary disability payments from the time the deceased worker became physically unable to work (in this case from 1985) to his death (on October 10, 1990). This case confirms that the surviving heirs of a deceased employee are entitled to receive the temporary disability benefits that the decedent would have been entitled to.

Area of Law #3

The rate of death benefits is usually determined by the date of injury.

Sacramento Municipal Utilities District v. WCAB (Phillips, deceased), 63 CCC 1091

This case says: The WCAB affirmed that because death benefits are to be paid in the same manner as temporary disability benefits, an increase in rate is called for after two years under Labor Code § 4661.5. The WCAB has jurisdiction to order payment of death benefits at a rate higher than was in existence at the time of death of the injured worker (after two or more years from the date of injury). This decision applies to injury dates on or after July 30, 1998.

Chapter 16—Extraordinary Workers' Compensation Benefits and Remedies

The case that follows deals with employers who discriminate against employees who file workers' compensation claims. (See Chapter 16, Section C, for a review of this subject.)

Area of Law

Employers who discriminate against an employee who has filed or is about to file a workers' compensation claim are in violation of Labor Code § 132a.

Abratte v. WCAB, 65 CCC 790

This case says: Where an employer terminates an employee's health benefits after a worker is injured on the job, the employer is in violation of Labor Code § 132a, unless the employer can show there was a business necessity for terminating the benefits.

Chapter 18—Rating Your Permanent Disability

The cases that follow deal with how to determine the dollar amount of permanent disability you are entitled to as a result of your injury.

Area of Law #1

Estimating ratings of upper extremities (hands, arms, shoulders) based upon work restrictions such as "no repetitive pushing and pulling with both upper extremities" or "no repetitive forceful gripping with both hands" is allowed. (See Chapter 18, Section E, for details concerning this situation.)

***Capistrano Unified School District v. WCAB*, 61 CCC 844**

This case says: A permanent disability rating for upper extremity disability based upon a description of lost ability to use the upper extremities is proper. This is a very important concept. Some disability raters had been taking the position that if a work restriction given by a doctor for an upper extremity was not specifically listed in the rating manual, they would not assign any amount of permanent disability to it. This case says that they are wrong! It is now clear that even if there is no scheduled rating for a given work restriction in the manual, the court or rater may arrive at a permanent disability by interpolation and analogy. In this case, the doctor used the term "loss of use" of an arm—a term not listed in the manual. But instead of saying there was no disability because of use of incorrect terminology, the court looked at the fact that the doctor found that the applicant had lost 75% of his preinjury capacity to use his right arm and equated this to an amputation (which is a scheduled rating). The result was the court used 75% of the disability rating for an amputated right arm.

Area of Law #2

Apportionment of a disability. Apportionment is a concept that an insurance company uses to claim it is not responsible for paying permanent disability because the disability is not fully attributable to the work injury. (See Chapter 18, Section D, for a review of this subject.)

***Bakersfield City School District v. WCAB (Robertson)*, 61 CCC 260 (Writ denied)**

This case says: Apportionment of a disability to outside factors (factors other than the work injury) is not proper where no evidence is presented to establish that the disability would have existed absent applicant's industrial injury. In the example in Chapter 18, Section D1, this means the unsupported conclusion by the doctor that Kathleen's disability is 50% due to the prior sports injury is not valid apportionment. The doctor would have had to find that Kathleen had an actual disability immediately prior to the industrial injury as a result of the prior sports injury. For example, an apportionment would be proper if the doctor said that, based upon his review of medical records, it is clear that Kathleen had treatment for her prior high school injury all the way up to a few weeks before her industrial injury, indicating she still had a disability from the prior injury.

***Monterey County v. WCAB (Moses)*, 61 CCC 273 (Writ denied)**

This case says: Apportionment to the natural progression of a preexisting condition is not valid where the doctor does not specifically state that the natural progression would have occurred absent the industrial injury or exposure. In the example in Section D1, the doctor would have to find that as a result of the natural progression of Kathleen's sports injury, she would have 50% of her current disability absent her industrial injury (for valid apportionment to the natural progression of a pre-existing injury).

***Ashley v. WCAB*, 43 Cal.Rptr.2d 589, 60 CCC 683**

Labor Code § 4750.5 says: "An employee who has sustained a compensable injury covered by workers' compensation and who subsequently sustains an unrelated condition, shall not receive permanent disability indemnity for any permanent disability caused solely by the subsequent condition." The key issue here is that Labor Code § 4750.5 requires apportionment only when an injury covered by workers' compensation (a compensable injury) is followed by one not covered by workers' compensation (a noncompensable injury) and does not apply when an applicant becomes pregnant or unemployed, because neither condition constitutes a "noncompensable injury" within the meaning of the statute. In other words, for apportionment of benefits to apply, there must be a real noncompensable injury. Pregnancy and/or periods of unemployment are simply not considered "injuries" within the meaning of Labor Code § 4750.5.

***Pullman Kellogg v. WCAB (Normand)*, 26 Cal.3d 450, 45 CCC 170 (California Supreme Court case)**

This case says: The defendant insurance company always has the burden of proving that there should be apportionment between injuries covered and not covered by workers' compensation, based on their claim that part of your overall disability is due to non-work-related factors. In short, you do not have to prove anything unless the insurance company presents convincing evidence that an apportionment should be made.

Tanenbaum v. IAC (1935), 4 Cal.2d 615

This case says: For workers' compensation purposes, an employer takes the employee as the employee is at the time of employment. This means, when an industrial injury aggravates a previously existing condition with the result that the worker becomes disabled, there should be no apportionment of part of the disability to the previous condition unless the present disability would still have existed in absence of the new industrial injury. The fact that if the employee had been stronger or healthier at the time of the injury (that is, had no previous injury or health problem) there would have been no disability (or a less severe disability) is not a reason to apportion disability benefits, unless the prior condition was so serious that it alone would have led to the current disability. For example: Mary had a history of preexisting asthma. However, when she went to work for Racafrax Chemical Co., it had been dormant and under control for five years. But as a result of exposure to toxic chemicals at Racafrax, Mary's asthma is aggravated and becomes disabling. There should be no apportionment of Mary's benefits to the preexisting asthma condition just because it probably made her more susceptible to the toxic chemicals, causing her to again suffer asthma.

Sanchez v. County of Los Angeles, (2005) and ***Strong v. City & County of San Francisco*** (2005)

These cases say: Apportionment is required for overlapping injuries and must be allocated by percentages. If the injured worker has received a permanent disability award previously for the same area of the body, that disability must be subtracted from any disability found under the current workers' compensation case. For example, if Mary has a current permanent disability to her back of 30%, but had a prior award of 10% to her back, the amount of the 10% award must be subtracted, leaving her with a 20% award. (The prior award is conclusively presumed to apply.)

See Labor Code § 4664. The defendant (insurance carrier) has the burden of proving the existence of any prior permanent disability award(s) relating to the same region of the body.

Escobedo v. Marshalls and CNA Insurance Company, 70 CCC 604

This case says: (1) Labor Code § 4663(a)'s statement that the apportionment of permanent disability shall be based on "causation" refers to the cause of the permanent disability, not the cause of the injury, and the analysis of the causal factors of permanent disability for purposes of apportionment may be different from the analysis of the causal factors of the injury itself.
(2) Both a reporting physician and the WCAB must make determinations of what percentage of the permanent disability was directly caused by the industrial injury and what percentage was caused by other factors.
(3) Under Labor Code § 4663, the applicant has the burden of establishing the percentage of permanent disability directly caused by the industrial injury, and the defendant has the burden of establishing the percentage of disability caused by other factors.
(4) Apportionment of permanent disability caused by "other factors both before and subsequent to the industrial injury, including prior industrial injuries," may include not only disability that could have been apportioned prior to SB 899, but also may include disability that formerly could not have been apportioned (e.g., pathology, asymptomatic prior conditions, arid retroactive prophylactic work preclusions), provided there is substantial medical evidence establishing that these other factors have caused permanent disability.

Area of Law #3

Occupational variant. As discussed in Chapter 18, one of the steps in rating your permanent disability is to determine your "occupational variant." This variant is determined by the type of job duties you did in the occupation in which you were injured, and is based on the concept that a particular injury may be more or less limiting depending on the type of work you do. (Please see Chapter 18, Section E, for a complete discussion of this concept.)

Kochevar v. Fremont Unified School District, 19 CWCR 290

This case says: Lots of jobs have a mix of duties at different rating levels. Where this is true, the question becomes, how should the activities be rated? The answer is, if some degree of higher-rated activities are an integral part of your job, even though most of the duties of that job have a lower rating, then the higher-rating occupational variant should be used. In this case the applicant spent about a hundred minutes of a 40-hour work week engaged in strenuous physical education activities that included demonstrating basketball dribbling and shooting, foot dribbling in soccer, use of a balance beam, and jumping rope. The issue the court considered was whether she should be given a group 59 rate for athlete (which would give her a very high permanent disability rating) or a group 41 rating reflecting her job title of school teacher (which would result in a lower permanent disability rating). The court found that the athlete's duties were an integral part of this applicant's duties, and so use of the higher rating variant was proper.

Area of Law #4

Rebutting the percentage of permanent disability established by the revised permanent disability rating schedule (the new, 2005 manual), adopted by the Administrative Director of the Division of Workers' Compensation effective January 1, 2005.

Mario Almaraz v. Environmental Recovery Services (aka Enviroserve); State Compensation Insurance Fund* and *Joyce Guzman v. Milpitas Unified School District, Permissibly Self-Insured; Keenan & Associates, 74 Cal. Comp. Cases 1084

These cases say: These cases are referred to in the industry as "*Almaraz-Guzman*." (1) The language of Labor Code § 4660(c), which provides that "the schedule ... shall be prima facie evidence of the percentage of permanent disability to be attributed to each injury covered by the schedule," unambiguously means that a permanent disability rating established by the schedule is rebuttable (able to be challenged); and (2) One method of rebutting a scheduled permanent disability rating is to successfully challenge one of the component elements of that rating, such as the injured employee's whole person impairment (WPI) under the AMA Guides. A physician may utilize any chapter, table, or method in the AMA Guides that most accurately reflects the injured employee's impairment.

Wanda Ogilvie v. City and County of San Francisco, Permissibly Self-Insured, 74 Cal. Comp. Cases 1127

This case says: (1) The language of Labor Code § 4660(c), which provides that "the schedule...shall be prima facie evidence of the percentage of permanent disability to be attributed to each injury covered by the schedule," unambiguously means that a permanent disability rating established by the schedule is rebuttable (able to be challenged); (2) the burden of rebutting a scheduled permanent disability rating rests with the party disputing that rating; and (3) one method of rebutting a scheduled permanent disability rating is to successfully challenge one of the component elements of that rating, such as the injured employee's DFEC adjustment factor, which may be accomplished by establishing that an individualized adjustment factor most accurately reflects the injured employee's DFEC. The Appeals Board stated further that the individualized DFEC adjustment factor must be consistent with section 4660(b)(2), the RAND data to which section 4660(b)(2) refers, and the numeric formula adopted by the Administrative Director (AD) in the 2005 Schedule, and it also must constitute substantial evidence that the Worker's Compensation Appeals Board (WCAB) determines is sufficient to overcome the DFEC adjustment factor component of the scheduled permanent disability rating.

Area of Law #5

Old vs. New Rating Manual. For injuries that occur on or after 1/1/05, the "new" rating manual is used, and permanent disability is determined by using the whole person impairment (WPI), as opposed to using the "old rating manual," which determined permanent disability by using work restrictions (see Chapter 18 for an explanation). The new manual usually results in the injured worker (you) getting less money for your injury than you did under the old manual. It is no surprise that issues have arisen as to whether the new manual applies to dates of injury before 1/1/05. That is what these cases deal with.

Elizabeth Aldi v. Carr, McClellan, Ingersoll, Thompson & Horn: Republic Indemnity Company of America, 71 Cal. Comp. Cases 599

This case says: The Appeals Board held that the revised permanent disability rating schedule (the new manual) adopted by the Administrative Director of the Division of Workers' Compensation, effective January 1, 2005, applies to injuries occurring on or after that date, and that in cases of injury occurring prior to January 1, 2005, the revised permanent disability rating schedule applies unless one of the exceptions delineated in the third sentence of section 4660(d) is present.

Joseph Baglione v. Hertz Car Sales and AIG, Adjusting by Cambridge Integrated Services, 72 Cal. Comp. Cases 444

This case says: The Appeals Board held that in order for the 1997 Permanent Disability Rating Schedule (old rating manual) to apply to a pre-2005 injury claim under Labor Code § 4660(d), the existence of permanent disability must be indicated in either a pre-2005 comprehensive medical-legal report or a pre-2005 report from a treating physician.

Josh Pendergrass v. Duggan Plumbing and State Compensation Insurance Fund, 72 Cal. Comp. Cases 456

This case says: The Appeals Board held that if the last payment of temporary disability indemnity was made for any period of temporary disability ending before January 1, 2005, then the 1997 Permanent Disability Rating Schedule (old manual) applies to determine the extent of permanent disability, pursuant to Labor Code § 4660(d) because Section 4061 requires the employer to provide the injured worker with a notice regarding permanent disability "together with the last payment of temporary disability indemnity."

Chapter 19—Figure Out a Starting Settlement Amount

Once you have completed your medical treatment and have obtained medical opinions on how much permanent disability you have, you must figure out how much your case is worth and make a settlement demand upon the insurance company. The cases that follow deal with the elements that you must consider when you figure out your starting settlement proposal. You should consider a number of things, including the dollar value of your permanent disability, the amount of any past-due temporary disability and/or vocational rehabilitation maintenance allowance, past-due mileage, reimbursement for self-procured medical benefits, penalties, and interest. Please refer to Chapter 19 for a review of this subject matter.

Area of Law

Penalties. If the insurance carrier failed to pay you the benefits you were entitled to on time, you should consider the dollar value of any penalties you might be entitled to as a result of their unreasonable delay. (Please see Chapter 19, Section C9, for a review of the types of monetary penalties you can petition the court for if the insurance carrier pays your benefits late.)

Pierce Enterprises, Argonaut Insurance Company, Petitioners v. WCAB and George Colchado, Respondents, 60 CCC 1052

This case says: Because the insurance carrier committed separate and distinct acts of delay or nonpayment of a disability award, the WCAB properly awarded five separate 10% penalties as part of setting a temporary disability. The point here is that the insurance company is liable for a separate 10% penalty (figured as a percentage of the total value of the temporary disability benefit) for each act of late payment or nonpayment, not just one 10% penalty covering all the late payments. Also, see *Christian v. WCAB*, below, which discusses what constitutes a separate and distinct act of delay.

TIP

If your insurance company is refusing to pay you, read this entire case. *Pierce Enterprises, Argonaut Insurance Company, Petitioners v. WCAB and George Colchado, Respondents*, presents a good review of the different types of misconduct by an insurance carrier that can constitute grounds for establishing a penalty.

Christian v. WCAB, 15 Cal.4th 505, 24 CWCR 193, 62 CCC 576 (California Supreme Court case)

In this case, the Supreme Court of California held that for multiple and successive penalties to apply to an insurance carrier's improper failure to pay temporary disability benefits, the acts of delay must be distinct and separate. The failure of the insurance carrier to pay temporary disability is one act. The fact that this occurred every two weeks does not make it a separate and distinct act each time the insurance company failed to pay. However, if some intervening event were to occur—for example, after refusing to pay benefits the insurance company paid them for awhile before once again improperly refusing to pay—this would constitute a separate and distinct act and lead to a second penalty. For example, XYZ Insurance improperly fails to pay temporary disability for six consecutive weeks (this is one act, so one penalty would be allowed—not a penalty for each two-week period). Then XYZ pays temporary disability for four weeks before again delaying payment. A new and separate penalty would arise for this second separate and distinct act of delay.

Rhiner v. WCAB (1993), 4 Cal.4th 1213, 18 Cal.Rptr.2d 129, 58 CCC 172 (California Supreme Court case)

This very important case establishes that when an insurance company is guilty of unreasonable delays in paying benefits, the applicant is entitled to a 10% penalty based on the dollar amount of the entire benefit (in workers' compensation jargon, the "entire species of benefit") and not just on the improperly delayed portion of the benefit. For example, if the carrier unreasonably delays paying you one temporary disability check of, say, $772, the penalty is not just 10% of that amount, or $77.20. It is 10% of your entire temporary disability benefit (past, present, and future). So if your entire benefit totals $25,000, you are entitled to a penalty of $2,500 for the delayed payment of $772!

Ready Home Health Care, Inc. v. WCAB (Sharp), 61 CCC 891 (Writ denied)

This case says: An unreasonable failure to timely pay reimbursement for mileage to and from medical appointments is a basis for an award of a 10% penalty against the entire medical treatment portion (species) of benefits. For example, if an injured worker who needs to drive a considerable distance to the doctor submits a request for mileage reimbursement of $50 and the insurance carrier does not pay within a reasonable time period, the applicant may be able to get a 10% penalty on the value of her medical treatment (past, present, and future). This means if the value of this treatment is $75,000, applicant could obtain a $7,500 penalty for failure to timely receive $50!

TIP

Payments after 30 days of request for reimbursement may be unreasonable. It is up to the court to decide what constitutes a reasonable—or unreasonable—time in which to reimburse an applicant for covered expenses. But I would argue that 30 days is ample time to process such a claim, and anything over that is unreasonable.

Avalon Bay Foods v. WCAB (Moore), 63 CCC 902 (California Supreme Court)

This case says: When an insurance company is 60 days or more late in paying medically related transportation expenses (mileage reimbursement), there is a Labor Code § 5814 penalty owed on all medical treatment benefits (of which mileage is a part).

Moulton v. WCAB, 28 CWCR 293

This case says: A worker may be entitled to multiple penalties under Labor Code § 5814 if the insurance company has failed to pay permanent disability in a timely fashion. If you received a portion of your permanent disability payments late, the insurance company must include an automatic 10% penalty on the portion that was late. (Labor Code § 4650(d); see Chapter 19, Section C9.) If it does not automatically pay you this penalty, you are entitled to a 10% penalty on the entire amount awarded for permanent disability (Labor Code § 5814).

Chapter 20—Negotiating a Settlement

Area of Law #1

If you sign a form declining rehabilitation services when you sign the Compromise and Release, you may be waiving your rights.

Cisneros v. WCAB, 60 CCC 1144, 48 Cal.Rptr.2d 655

This case says: If you sign a document declining your rights to vocational rehabilitation services as part of an agreement to settle your workers' compensation claim, you may be forever barred from requesting vocational rehabilitation services again unless you can show a change of circumstances. A mere change of mind will not be sufficient to allow you to obtain additional benefits.

Area of Law #2

When you have agreed on a settlement of your claim by compromise and release (see Chapter 20), the insurance company will prepare the settlement document and send it to you for signature. You will then have to review it and make sure it is correct and does not contain objectionable language.

Jefferson v. California Department of Youth Authority, 66 CCC 343

In this case, the insurance company included an attachment to the compromise and release that contained a general release under Civil Code § 1542. This attachment barred a claim under the California Fair Employment and Housing Act (FEHA) and any other third-party claims the worker may have had, such as a wrongful termination lawsuit or a civil complaint against any party involving the same date of injury.
Note: All compromise and release documents contain this general release under Civil Code § 1542. You should add the following additional language to the end of the clause: "This clause applies to this claim only."

Kohler v. Interstate Brands Corporation, 67 CCC 1447

This case says: A clause common in standard compromise and release settlements can bar a pending Fair Employment and Housing Act (FEHA) action. A compromise and release action that states in Paragraph 3, "said employee ... releases and forever discharges said employer ... from all claims and causes of action, whether now known or ascertained, or which may hereafter arise or develop as a result of said injury," may bar such an action.

Note: Always add the following language to Paragraph 3 of a compromise and release document: "This release applies only to this workers' compensation claim and only to this date of injury."

Chapter 21—Preparing Your Case

The cases that follow deal with issues you should consider when preparing your case for trial. These include identifying possible issues in dispute, how to prove or disprove disputed issues, taking depositions of witnesses, subpoenaing witnesses and documents, preparing for a mandatory settlement conference, and preparing for trial. Please refer to Chapter 21 for a detailed review of this subject matter.

Area of Law #1

Presumption of compensable injury. If you filed a workers' compensation claim and more than 90 days pass with no rejection of the claim by your employer or its insurance carrier, there is a rebuttable presumption that the claim is valid and benefits should be paid. (Please refer to Chapter 21, Section B3b.)

SCIF v. WCAB (Welcher), 60 CCC 717, 32 CWCR 213, 43 Cal.Rptr.2d 660

This case says: Defendant's failure to reject applicant's claim for workers' compensation within 90 days created a presumption that benefits should be paid ("compensability" exists) under Labor Code § 5402. It further held that evidence contained in defendant's later-submitted medical reports was inadmissible to rebut the presumption of compensability because such evidence could have reasonably been obtained and submitted by the carrier within the 90-day period.

TIP

Argue that an insurance carrier must show that new evidence came to light, to reject applicant's claim after 90 days from submission. After 90 days from the submission of a worker's claim, the insurance carrier should only be able to rebut the presumption that benefits should be paid (compensability exists) with new evidence that could not have been reasonably obtained within the first 90 days after the injury was reported. (But see the Rodriguez case, below, which casts doubt on this argument in some circumstances.)

Rodriguez v. WCAB**,** 35 Cal.Rptr.2d 713; 59 CCC 857

This is a bad case for injured workers! Nevertheless, you need to be aware of it and hope your opposition isn't. In this case, the insurance carrier failed to deny the claim until 96 days following completion of the DWC-1. The worker asserted that after 90 days from his application for benefits, the rebuttable presumption under Labor Code § 5402 (discussed in the previous case) meant that his claim could only be rejected if the insurance company based the rejection on evidence not available earlier. In my view this argument should have been strong enough to result in the worker being deemed eligible for benefits. But the court held that all that is required of the defendant is that it made a *determination* to deny the claim within the 90 days, even though the applicant was not told that the claim was denied until after the 90 days. In this case, the insurance carrier was allowed to use oral testimony from a claims examiner who said that she had decided to deny the claim within the 90 days. Probably one factor contributing to the carrier's victory here was the fact that benefits were denied just six days after the end of the 90-day period. A longer delay by the insurance company might have produced a different result.

Area of Law #2

The insurance company may take your statement or set a deposition (a formal legal interview) for you. At the deposition it will ask you many questions. (See Chapter 21, Section C.) The following case addresses the issue of which medical questions are relevant and which are not.

Carol Allison v. WCAB**,** 64 CCC 624

This case says: The court stated that, at a deposition, the worker is not required to answer questions about her medical history that are not relevant to the workers' compensation matter. The court said that questions about medical history should be limited to the past ten years and should deal only with the parts of body injured. Questions that are overly broad are not proper and are a violation of worker's doctor/patient privilege and right to privacy.

Chapter 22—Arranging for a Hearing or Trial

The following cases involve the various types of hearings that you can request before the Workers' Compensation Appeals Board, including a mandatory settlement conference.

Area of Law #1

When you file a Declaration of Readiness to Proceed requesting that your matter be set for a mandatory settlement conference, you should be prepared to go forward to trial if you can't settle your case. (See Chapter 22.)

County of Sacramento v. WCAB (Estrada)**,** 64 CCC 26

This case says: You must never file a Declaration of Readiness to Proceed requesting a mandatory settlement conference unless you are certain you have all the evidence you will need at trial. If you don't have the proper evidence, the judge at a mandatory settlement conference does not have the authority to order a continuance or leave the record open for further discovery unless you can show good cause as to why the evidence was not obtainable prior to the conference. If the insurance company files a Declaration of Readiness to Proceed and you are not ready to go to trial, be sure you immediately object to the conference. (See Chapter 22.)

Area of Law #2

At the mandatory settlement conference, both sides should be prepared to discuss settlement of the case and should have the authority to enter into a settlement.

Rochin v. State of California, Department of Corrections, 26 CWCR 290

This case says: The workers' compensation insurance company must have someone available, either in person at the mandatory settlement conference or reachable by the representative at the hearing by telephone, who has the authority to approve a settlement of the claim. If the attorney or representative for the insurance company tells you that there's no one who can give him settlement authority, then the insurance company is subject to sanctions for failure to have proper settlement authority as required by WCAB Rule 10563.

Chapter 24—Going to a Hearing or Trial

The cases that follow deal with issues that may arise at a hearing or trial before a judge at the Workers' Compensation Appeals Board. Please refer to Chapter 24 for a detailed review of this subject matter.

Area of Law #1

The amount the injured worker earns—the average weekly wage—determines how much the worker is entitled to for temporary or permanent disability payments. (Please see Chapter 12, Section B, for a discussion of how to compute your average weekly wage.) The case below discusses when a defendant can raise a dispute over the amount of the applicant's earnings. This issue can be important, because an insurance carrier will often try to argue you earned less than you really did in an effort to reduce the amount it has to pay you.

Early California Foods v. WCAB (Ellis), 56 CCC 137

This case says: A two-year delay in raising the issue of earnings will justify the workers' compensation judge's denial of the defendant's request to dispute the applicants' average weekly wage. In this case, the defendant waited until the time of trial to dispute how much the applicant earned for purposes of determining the applicant's temporary disability and permanent disability rate, even though the company had been paying the applicant's temporary disability benefits at the maximum allowable rate for more than a year, and had made three appearances at the WCAB without raising the issue. The judge held that waiting for two years from the date of injury to try to raise the issue meant that the defendant forever waived their right to do so. (The judge relied on Administrative Rule 10484, which gives him the discretion to allow or disallow evidence upon matters not previously pleaded.)

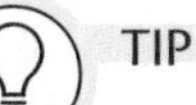

TIP

Cite this case whenever a defendant waits until trial to raise a new issue. New issues should rarely be raised for the first time at trial. If the defendant tries to do so, refer to the *Early California Foods* case as part of your argument that the issue in question has been waived by not having been raised earlier.

Area of Law #2

Admissibility of a medical report where the exam was set up before the mandatory settlement conference (MSC) (see Chapter 24, Section B) but was not actually held until after the MSC.

Henley v. I.I., 20 CWCR 188

This case is important if the defendants have filed a Declaration of Readiness to Proceed (see Chapter 22, Section D) and have gotten a date for an MSC in a situation where the applicant has requested a medical examination by a qualified medical evaluator (QME). The case says if you have requested a medical-legal evaluation (see Chapter 10, Section A) prior to the date of the MSC, the report should be allowed into evidence even if the actual date of the appointment is not until sometime after the date of the MSC. So even if you are caught "off guard" by the carrier's request to proceed to trial, you can still request your QME appointment and have the results considered.

CHAPTER

29

Online Appendixes

FIND IT ONLINE

Appendixes online. All appendixes can be found on the companion page for this book on Nolo's website at **www.nolo.com/back-of-book/WORK9.html.**

Appendix 1: Workers' Compensation Office Addresses and Code Lists

Appendix 2: Temporary Disability Benefits Compensation Chart

Appendix 3: Permanent Disability Indemnity Chart

Appendix 4: Maximum Life Pension Weekly Payments

Appendix 5: Workers' Compensation Forms

Instructions for the forms in Appendix 5 can be found in the following chapters:

DWC-1: Workers' Compensation Claim Form	Claim.pdf	Chapter 5
Application for Adjudication of Claim	Adjudication.pdf	Chapter 5
Application for Adjudication of Claim (Death Case)	Adjudication_Death.pdf	Chapter 5
Declaration in Compliance With Labor Code Section 4906(G)	Compliance.pdf	Chapter 5
Record of Income and Benefits Received	IncomeBenefits.pdf	Chapter 6
Record of Time Off Work	TimeOff.pdf	Chapter 6
Letter to Employer Requesting Copies of Documents and Evidence	RequestCopies.pdf	Chapter 6
Notice of Change of Address	AddressChange.pdf	Chapter 6
Employee's Designation of Personal Physician	PhysicianDesignation.pdf	Chapter 9
Objection to Treating Physician's Recommendation for Spinal Surgery	Objection.pdf	Chapter 10
Record of Medical Expenses and Request for Reimbursement	Reimbursement.pdf	Chapter 11
Medical Mileage Expense Form	MedicalMileage.pdf	Chapter 11
Request for Consultative Rating	RequestRating.pdf	Chapter 18
Settlement Worksheet: Value of Workers' Compensation Claim	SettlementWorksheet.pdf	Chapter 19

Stipulations with Request for Award	Stipulations.pdf	Chapter 20
Compromise and Release	Compromise.pdf	Chapter 20
Subpoena Duces Tecum	SubpoenaDucesTecum.pdf	Chapter 21
Subpoena	Subpoena.pdf	Chapter 21
Declaration of Readiness to Proceed	Declaration.pdf	Chapter 22
Declaration of Readiness to Proceed to Expedited Hearing (Trial)	Declaration_Expedited.pdf	Chapter 22
Proof of Service	ProofService.pdf	Chapter 23
Document Cover Sheet	CoverSheet.pdf	Chapter 23
Document Separator Sheet	Separator.pdf	Chapter 23
Cover Letter to Workers' Compensation Appeals Board	AppealLetter.pdf	Chapter 23
Pre-Trial Conference Statement	Pretrial.pdf	Chapter 24
Minutes of Hearing	Minutes.pdf	Chapter 24

Index

A

B

C

E

F

J

L

P

Q

R

S

T

U

V

W

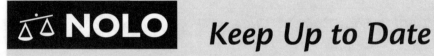

Keep Up to Date

Go to Nolo.com/newsletters to sign up for free newsletters and discounts on Nolo products.

- **Nolo's Special Offer.** A monthly newsletter with the biggest Nolo discounts around.
- **Landlord's Quarterly.** Deals and free tips for landlords and property managers.

Don't forget to check for updates. Find this book at Nolo.com and click "Legal Updates."

Let Us Hear From You

Register your Nolo product and give us your feedback at Nolo.com/book-registration.

- Once you've registered, you qualify for technical support if you have any trouble with a download (though most folks don't).
- We'll send you a coupon for 15% off your next Nolo.com order!

WORK9

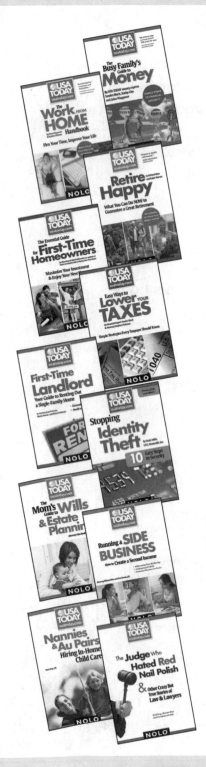